KB087712

CEDU쎄듀는 A **C**omprehensive **E**nglish e**DU**cation(종합적 영어교육)의 약자입니다.

저자

김기훈　現 ㈜ 쎄듀 대표이사
　　　　現 메가스터디 영어영역 대표강사
　　　　前 서울특별시 교육청 외국어 교육정책자문위원회 위원
　　저서　천일문 / 천일문 Training Book / 천일문 GRAMMAR
　　　　어법끝 / 어휘끝 / 첫단추 / 쎈쓰업 / 파워업 / 빈칸백서 / 오답백서 / 독해비
　　　　쎄듀 본영어 / 문법의 골든룰 101 / Grammar Q
　　　　거침없이 Writing / ALL씀 서술형 / 수능실감 등

쎄듀 영어교육연구센터

쎄듀 영어교육센터는 영어 콘텐츠에 대한 전문지식과 경험을 바탕으로
최고의 교육 콘텐츠를 만들고자 최선의 노력을 다하는 전문가 집단입니다.

이혜경 전임연구원 · **구민지** 전임연구원 · **이민영** 연구원 · **심승아** 연구원

마케팅　　　콘텐츠 마케팅 사업본부
영업　　　　문병구
제작　　　　정승호
인디자인 편집　올댓에디팅
디자인　　　윤혜영 · 정지은
영문교열　　James Clayton Sharp

펴낸이　　김기훈 I 김진희
펴낸곳　　(주)쎄듀 I 서울특별시 강남구 논현로 305 (역삼동)
발행일　　2024년 2월 10일 제2개정판 1쇄
내용문의　www.cedubook.com
구입문의　콘텐츠 마케팅 사업본부
　　　　　Tel. 02-6241-2007
　　　　　Fax. 02-2058-0209
등록번호　제 22-2472호
ISBN　　978-89-6806-310-7

Second Edition Copyright © 2025 by CEDU Inc.

All rights reserved. No part of this publication may be reproduced, stored in a retrieval system, or transmitted in any form or by any means, electronic, mechanical, photocopying, recording, or otherwise, without the prior permission of the copyright owner.
본 교재의 독창적인 내용에 대한 일체의 무단 전재 · 모방은 법률로 금지되어 있습니다. 파본은 교환해드립니다.

수능실감 感

STRUCTURE & FEATURES

이 책의 구성과 특징

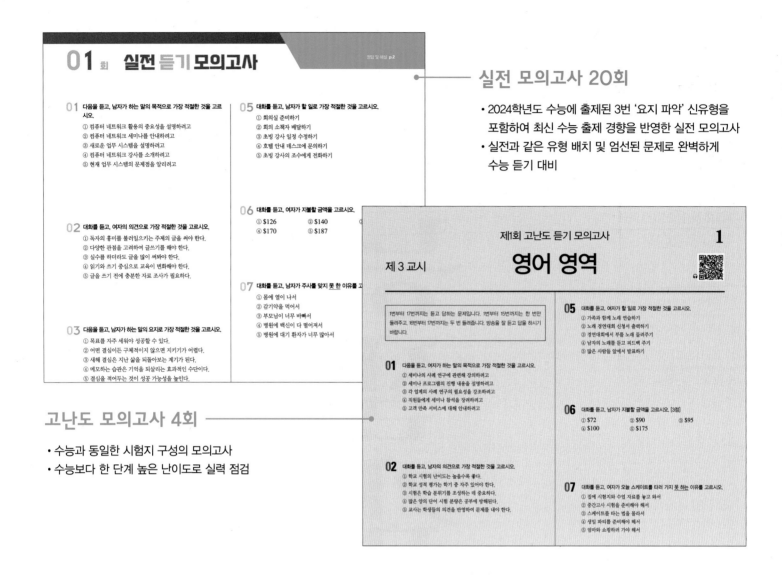

실전 모의고사 20회

- 2024학년도 수능에 출제된 3번 '요지 파악' 신유형을 포함하여 최신 수능 출제 경향을 반영한 실전 모의고사
- 실전과 같은 유형 배치 및 엄선된 문제로 완벽하게 수능 듣기 대비

고난도 모의고사 4회

- 수능과 동일한 시험지 구성의 모의고사
- 수능보다 한 단계 높은 난이도로 실력 점검

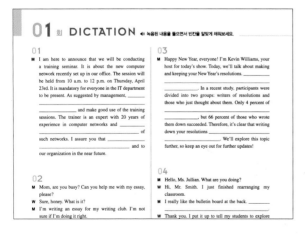

Dictation

- 핵심 내용, 주요 표현, 연음 위주로 받아쓰기 연습이 가능한 Dictation 전 회 수록

  (고난도 Dictation은 www.cedubook.com에서 다운로드 가능합니다.)

정답 및 해설

- 혼자서도 충분한 학습이 가능하도록 스크립트 및 해석과 상세한 해설을 제공

CONTENTS 목차

CEDU MP3 PLAYER

수능실감 듣기 모의고사 24회는 효율적인 듣기 학습을 위해
MP3 PLAYER 기능이 적용되어 있습니다.

1 배속 선택 기능

1.0배속   1.2배속

*1배속은 실제 수능과 동일한 속도

2 전체 듣기

모의고사 전체 음원 듣기

3 문항별 재생

각 문항별 음원을 개별 선택하여
바로 재생

다양한 성우와 살아있는 표현

다양한 원어민들의 목소리와 억양에 익숙해질 수 있도록 총 4명의 남/여
성우가 녹음했습니다.

Rio   Katherine

Janet   Jack

무료 부가서비스

- 회별, 문항별, 배속별 MP3 파일을 무료로 제공합니다.
- 교재에 등장하는 어휘를 학습할 수 있도록 어휘리스트, 어휘테스트도
  무료로 이용 가능합니다.
- 학습을 돕는 부가서비스 자료들은 www.cedubook.com에서
  다운로드 가능합니다.

01 회 실전 듣기 모의고사

01 다음을 듣고, 남자가 하는 말의 목적으로 가장 적절한 것을 고르시오.

① 컴퓨터 네트워크 활용의 중요성을 설명하려고
② 컴퓨터 네트워크 세미나를 안내하려고
③ 새로운 업무 시스템을 설명하려고
④ 컴퓨터 네트워크 강사를 소개하려고
⑤ 현재 업무 시스템의 문제점을 알리려고

02 대화를 듣고, 여자의 의견으로 가장 적절한 것을 고르시오.

① 독자의 흥미를 불러일으키는 주제의 글을 써야 한다.
② 다양한 관점을 고려하여 글쓰기를 해야 한다.
③ 실수를 하더라도 글을 많이 써봐야 한다.
④ 읽기와 쓰기 중심으로 교육이 변화해야 한다.
⑤ 글을 쓰기 전에 충분한 자료 조사가 필요하다.

03 다음을 듣고, 남자가 하는 말의 요지로 가장 적절한 것을 고르시오.

① 목표를 자주 세워야 성공할 수 있다.
② 어떤 결심이든 구체적이지 않으면 지키기가 어렵다.
③ 새해 결심은 지난 삶을 되돌아보는 계기가 된다.
④ 메모하는 습관은 기억을 되살리는 효과적인 수단이다.
⑤ 결심을 적어두는 것이 성공 가능성을 높인다.

04 대화를 듣고, 그림에서 대화의 내용과 일치하지 <u>않는</u> 것을 고르시오.

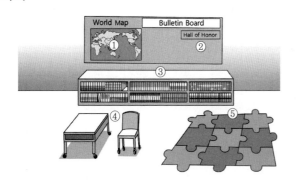

05 대화를 듣고, 남자가 할 일로 가장 적절한 것을 고르시오.

① 회의실 준비하기
② 회의 소책자 배달하기
③ 초빙 강사 일정 수정하기
④ 호텔 안내 데스크에 문의하기
⑤ 초빙 강사의 조수에게 전화하기

06 대화를 듣고, 여자가 지불할 금액을 고르시오.

① $126   ② $140   ③ $153
④ $170   ⑤ $187

07 대화를 듣고, 남자가 주사를 맞지 <u>못</u> 한 이유를 고르시오.

① 몸에 열이 나서
② 감기약을 먹어서
③ 부모님이 너무 바빠서
④ 병원에 백신이 다 떨어져서
⑤ 병원에 대기 환자가 너무 많아서

08 대화를 듣고, 아르바이트에 관해 언급되지 <u>않은</u> 것을 고르시오.

① 근무지   ② 근무 시간   ③ 담당 업무
④ 급여   ⑤ 자격 요건

09 Club Promotion Project에 관한 다음 내용을 듣고, 일치하지 <u>않는</u> 것을 고르시오.

① 올해 교육부가 계획하고 있는 주요 사업이다.
② 100개의 동아리에 자금이 지원된다.
③ 총 5개 분야 중 하나에 지원할 수 있다.
④ 학기 말에 동아리 활동 내용을 발표한다.
⑤ 최종 선정된 10개 동아리에 장학금이 지급된다.

10 다음 표를 보면서 대화를 듣고, 여자가 구매할 태블릿 PC를 고르시오.

Best-Selling Tablet PCs

Model	Price	Capacity	Display	Keyboard
① A	$450	128GB	10-inch	○
② B	$600	256GB	9-inch	×
③ C	$650	256GB	9-inch	○
④ D	$700	256GB	11-inch	×
⑤ E	$800	512GB	11-inch	○

11 대화를 듣고, 여자의 마지막 말에 대한 남자의 응답으로 가장 적절한 것을 고르시오.

① Sorry. I don't have any change on me.
② No, thanks. I will pay it by credit card.
③ Of course. There are not enough $20 bills.
④ Let me see. I'd like four 20s and a 5, please.
⑤ I don't know. This one looks a little bit larger to me.

12 대화를 듣고, 남자의 마지막 말에 대한 여자의 응답으로 가장 적절한 것을 고르시오.

① All right. Let's go to the movies next weekend.
② Let me see. My favorite genre would be horror.
③ Yes. To me, they are a little disturbing to watch.
④ Definitely. Romance movies are my least favorite.
⑤ No, thanks. I enjoy neither action movies nor comedies.

13 대화를 듣고, 여자의 마지막 말에 대한 남자의 응답으로 가장 적절한 것을 고르시오. [3점]

Man: _____

① Nothing changed even though I was injured.
② Injuries are the worst thing for a sports player.
③ I lost interest in everything and just stayed home.
④ I wish you the best with the national soccer game.
⑤ I fell on the ground really hard and hurt my back.

14 대화를 듣고, 남자의 마지막 말에 대한 여자의 응답으로 가장 적절한 것을 고르시오. [3점]

Woman: _____

① Of course. What other choice do I have?
② No worries. I can handle the problem myself.
③ Please tell him to update the system on his PC.
④ No, thanks. I have already updated the system.
⑤ That's okay. I postponed my presentation.

15 다음 상황 설명을 듣고, Mike가 Kelly에게 할 말로 가장 적절한 것을 고르시오. [3점]

Mike: _____

① You have to learn how to say no.
② Do not leave work earlier than required.
③ I think you should be a little bit more devoted.
④ You must balance work and your personal life.
⑤ Could you help the new employee with his work?

[16~17] 다음을 듣고, 물음에 답하시오.

16 여자가 하는 말의 주제로 가장 적절한 것은?

① unique creatures that live underwater
② exotic fish that threaten the native fish
③ endangered marine species around the world
④ controversy over the existence of aliens
⑤ the origin of sea animals' names

17 언급된 동물이 <u>아닌</u> 것은?

① feather star
② mantis shrimp
③ dumbo octopus
④ sea horse
⑤ leafy sea dragon

01

M I am here to announce that we will be conducting a training seminar. It is about the new computer network recently set up in our office. The session will be held from 10 a.m. to 12 p.m. on Thursday, April 23rd. It is mandatory for everyone in the IT department to be present. As suggested by management, _____ _____ _____ and make good use of the training sessions. The trainer is an expert with 20 years of experience in computer networks and _____ _____ of such networks. I assure you that _____ _____ and to our organization in the near future.

02

M Mom, are you busy? Can you help me with my essay, please?

W Sure, honey. What is it?

M I'm writing an essay for my writing club. I'm not sure if I'm doing it right.

W What is your topic sentence?

M It's "Climate change is the greatest threat that we face." But my essay doesn't sound convincing.

W Do you have enough evidence to back up your statement?

M _____. Are they not enough?

W They should be enough, but they also need explanations to support them.

M What do you mean?

W You need to show that _____ _____. That's why you have to do a lot of research before writing.

M Now that I think about it, I don't think _____ _____.

W After you finish with the body, I can read it over for you.

M Thanks, Mom.

03

M Happy New Year, everyone! I'm Kevin Williams, your host for today's show. Today, we'll talk about making and keeping your New Year's resolutions. _____ _____ _____. In a recent study, participants were divided into two groups: writers of resolutions and those who just thought about them. Only 4 percent of _____ _____, but 66 percent of those who wrote them down succeeded. Therefore, it's clear that writing down your resolutions _____ _____. We'll explore this topic further, so keep an eye out for further updates!

04

M Hello, Ms. Jullian. What are you doing?

W Hi, Mr. Smith. I just finished rearranging my classroom.

M I really like the bulletin board at the back. _____ _____.

W Thank you. I put it up to tell my students to explore the world. What do you think about the Hall of Honor?

M You mean the sign _____ _____? What is it for?

W Oh, I hold special events during class, and I give a prize to the winning students. I will put up pictures of those students under "Hall of Honor."

M That's such a good idea. And what's the bookshelf for in front of the bulletin board?

W I am going to get different types of books for my students. Right now, it is empty, but by the end of this month, _____.

M I see. And I really like the desks and chairs with wheels on them. They will be easy to move around.

W Yes. They're the best for having students gather in groups. What do you think about _____ _____?

M Oh, they are so cute. It will be great to have a space where students can sit down on the floor.

W Yes. I always look forward to teaching in this classroom.

05

M Sophie, can I talk to you about the workshop next week for a minute?

W Sure. I thought we had everything prepared.

M I feel like we missed something, but _____ _____.

W All right. Then let's go over everything. Did you call the hotel to confirm the reservation?

M I did that yesterday. The meeting room will _____ _____, and the banquet service will be ready before noon.

W Okay. What about the booklets?

M They will be delivered directly to the hotel. We just need to pick them up at the front desk.

W That's great. What else is there? *[Pause]* Oh, did you _____, Victoria Manu?

M I did that last week. Do I have to check that again?

W Yes, you have to remind her of the date one week before the event. _____ _____.

M Okay. Is there anything else?

W I think that's all. It seems like everything is prepared.

06

W Excuse me, I'm looking for a chair for my son.

M Come this way, ma'am. Do you have something in mind?

W He spends a lot of time studying. So I'd like _____ _____.

M This one is one of our best-selling items. It can help _____.

W That's exactly the one I was thinking about. How much is it?

M It's $110. It comes in three colors, black, gray, and red.

W I'll take a black one, please.

M Is there anything else you need? We also have cushions.

W Okay, how much are they?

M They are $30 each. _____ _____, you can get a 10% discount off the total.

W That sounds like a good deal. Then can I get two, please?

M Of course. _____, correct?

W Yes. I'll pay with my credit card.

M Certainly.

07

W I think flu season has begun. It seems like everyone has caught a cold.

M I know. It's about that time. Did you get your flu shot?

W I did. I got it with my parents at the clinic. What about you?

M I went there to get one too, but I couldn't.

W Really? _____?

M No, they didn't. There weren't many people.

W How come you didn't get it at the clinic?

M Before I went in to get it, the nurse checked my temperature. _____.

W Really? Are you not allowed _____ _____?

M No, it could make your fever worse. So the nurse told me _____ when I'm feeling better.

W Then when are you planning to go back?

M Maybe next week. I'm taking some cold medicine now.

08

M Welcome to District Job Center. How can I help you?

W I'm looking for a part-time job I can do after school.

M Let me see. This one here seems to suit your situation the best. It's a gift shop downtown.

W That sounds interesting. _____ _____?

M They are from 6 p.m. to 10 p.m. on weekdays only.

W That suits my schedule. _____ _____?

M You will mostly be helping customers to choose the right gift. And when needed, _____ _____.

W That sounds fun. How much will I get paid an hour?

M You will be paid $9 an hour.

W That's great. _____?

M Leave your résumé here. Then we can set up a job interview with the employer.

09

W Hello, students. I'd like to inform you of the "Club Promotion Project." This is one of the major projects that the Ministry of Education is planning to do this year. In order _____ _____, the Ministry of Education will recruit 100 clubs within our district and _____. Each club can apply for one of the five areas, including liberal arts and science. Clubs that get selected will work on a specific topic within their area for a semester. At the end of the semester, all 100 clubs will present their activities in front of students, teachers, and parents. A team of judges will assess the presentations, and the top ten clubs will be granted _____ _____. I hope many clubs will apply for this project.

10

W Excuse me, I'm looking for a tablet PC for my daughter.

M Okay. Here are our five best-selling models.

W They all look great. Can you help me choose one? _____.

M Okay. Then what about the capacity?

W The larger, the better. She will _____ _____ on it.

M I see. Next, you have to choose the size of the display. We have either an 11-inch display or a 9-inch display.

W Hmm... The 11-inch one looks too big for her. And it's a little heavy.

M Actually, you're right. I would recommend a 9-inch one. _____ _____.

W Okay. And do I have to choose whether to include a keyboard?

M Yes, you do. Would you like to include one?

W No, thanks. _____ _____.

M Okay, sure. You can pay over there.

11

W The total is $15. How would you like to pay the bill?

M _____. I only have a $100 bill. Can you break it for me?

W Sure. _____?

12

M Hey, Brenda. Have you watched this movie?

W No, I haven't. At first I was interested in it, but I heard _____.

M It does have some violent scenes. _____ _____ too much violence?

13

M Hi, Barbara. Are you any better?

W Hi, Will. Thanks for asking. I need to wear this cast for another two weeks, but _____ _____.

M That's good news. Did you say you broke your arm during soccer practice?

W Yes, I broke my arm when it hit the goal post. But I'm recovering well, so that's what's important.

M But you must be upset since you can't play at the national girls' soccer tournament.

W At first, I was, but now I'm _____ _____ instead.

M Is that why you still go to practices?

W Yes. _____ when I watch my friends train and play.

M Wow, you're such an optimistic person. I was _____
_____.

W Why? What were you like when you got hurt?

14

W Mark, would you mind looking at my presentation?

M Sure, are you finished?

W Nearly, but I'm worried it's so long.

M Okay, just _____!

W Oh, no!

M What's wrong, Leena?

W Everything _____.
I don't know what to do!

M That's terrible. Can I have a look?

W Of course. Do you think you could bring back my files?

M I'll try. *[Pause]* It looks like the update program automatically closes all other programs when it starts.

W So _____?
I am so worried that I won't be able to get them back. I have to do the presentation tomorrow.

M I'm sorry, but I don't think I can solve your problem. But I know someone who can. I can call him and
_____.

15

M Kelly is an associate manager at R&C Company. She is known within the company for her enthusiasm and her devotion to her work. Due to her kind personality, sometimes she helps with her colleagues' work. Kelly
_____
_____, even when she needs to, and ends up doing all of her colleagues' work. One day, her superior, Mike, notices that her personality often _____
_____. Mike knows that Kelly is a capable employee and that she is very helpful and cooperative with others. But he wants to tell her that _____
_____ in her own work. In this situation, what would Mike most likely say to Kelly?

16~17

W Hello, everyone. We are going to continue talking about sea animals today. We are going to see ocean creatures which are so alien-like that _____
_____! But believe it or not, all of the animals can be found right here on planet Earth. Let's check them out. First are feather stars. Look at the picture on the screen. These crazy-looking marine animals wave their "feather legs" to get around underwater. _____
_____. Next is a type of shrimp called mantis shrimp. See how colorful they look? These exotic looking creatures have glowing green backs. Next up is the dumbo octopus. What animal do they resemble? Yes, elephants. They get their name from the elephant cartoon character "Dumbo" due to their flapping ear-fins _____
_____. Our last creature of the day is the leafy sea dragon. I know they look like sea plants,
_____.

02회 실전 듣기 모의고사

01 다음을 듣고, 여자가 하는 말의 목적으로 가장 적절한 것을 고르시오.

① 변경된 학교 행사 일정을 공지하려고
② 장기 자랑에 학생들의 참석을 요청하려고
③ 연간 봉사활동을 할 수 있는 장소를 알리려고
④ 학교 행사를 위한 자원봉사 단원을 모집하려고
⑤ 노숙자 쉼터 설치에 대한 기부금 모금을 홍보하려고

02 대화를 듣고, 남자의 의견으로 가장 적절한 것을 고르시오.

① 에너지 소비효율 등급이 높은 전자제품을 사용해야 한다.
② 쇼핑 목록을 작성하면 불필요한 지출을 줄일 수 있다.
③ 소량의 세제를 사용하여 환경오염을 줄여야 한다.
④ 과일과 채소로 균형 잡힌 식사는 건강에 좋다.
⑤ 메모하는 습관은 기억력 향상에 도움을 준다.

03 다음을 듣고, 여자가 하는 말의 요지로 가장 적절한 것을 고르시오.

① 연말 선물은 진심이 담긴 편지와 함께 전달하는 게 좋다.
② 분수에 지나친 선물은 받는 사람에게 부담이 될 수 있다.
③ 선물할 때는 상대방이 무엇을 좋아하는지 고민해야 한다.
④ 아이들은 그림을 그리면서 미적 감각을 기를 수 있다.
⑤ 아이에게 줄 선물은 함께 고르는 것이 교육적으로 좋다.

04 대화를 듣고, 그림에서 대화의 내용과 일치하지 않는 것을 고르시오.

05 대화를 듣고, 여자가 할 일로 가장 적절한 것을 고르시오.

① 연극에 참여하기
② 학생증 가지고 오기
③ 배우 학원에 등록하기
④ 친구와 저녁 약속하기
⑤ 인터넷으로 표 예약하기

06 대화를 듣고, 남자가 지불할 금액을 고르시오. [3점]

① $77   ② $110   ③ $130
④ $135   ⑤ $140

07 대화를 듣고, 여자가 대학 입학 박람회에 참여할 수 없는 이유를 고르시오.

① 도서관에 책을 반납해야 해서
② 시내에 있는 병원에 가야 해서
③ 가족 모임이 같은 날에 있어서
④ 기말고사 시험 준비를 해야 해서
⑤ 박람회가 시 외곽에서 개최되어서

08 대화를 듣고, Dolphin Cruise Tour에 관해 언급되지 않은 것을 고르시오.

① 준비물   ② 버스 시간   ③ 소요 시간
④ 유람할 장소   ⑤ 가격

09 Dronepia에 관한 다음 내용을 듣고, 일치하지 않는 것을 고르시오.

① 전 학년 학생을 위한 강좌이다.
② 10주간 금요일마다 수업이 진행된다.
③ 수업에 모두 참석해야 수료증을 받는다.
④ 드론에 대한 이론 수업 후에 실전 연습을 할 수 있다.
⑤ 학생들은 한 달 전에 등록하는 것을 권장한다.

10 다음 표를 보면서 대화를 듣고, 두 사람이 구매할 소파를 고르시오.

Sofas on Sale

Model	Material	Arms	Color	Price
① A	fabric	×	black	$300
② B	leather	○	brown	$400
③ C	leather	○	cream	$500
④ D	velvet	×	red	$600
⑤ E	velvet	○	cream	$700

11 대화를 듣고, 남자의 마지막 말에 대한 여자의 응답으로 가장 적절한 것을 고르시오.

① Good. Can I have the rest to go?
② No, thanks. I'm really full right now.
③ Sure. I'd like to have chocolate ice cream.
④ I recommend a slice of cake with coffee.
⑤ Yes, please. I'd like to take a look at it.

12 대화를 듣고, 여자의 마지막 말에 대한 남자의 응답으로 가장 적절한 것을 고르시오.

① Sure. It's been a long time, Susan.
② No, I don't. We're in the same class.
③ Of course. I've heard a lot about you.
④ I'm sorry. You've got the wrong number.
⑤ I'm afraid you taught me American history.

13 대화를 듣고, 남자의 마지막 말에 대한 여자의 응답으로 가장 적절한 것을 고르시오. [3점]

Woman: _____

① All right. It could just be a shower.
② I'm sorry. I don't think I can change the story.
③ I disagree. The actors should wait in their cars.
④ Yes. The weather is supposed to be clear tonight.
⑤ Of course. I'll get my laptop and write the new script.

14 대화를 듣고, 여자의 마지막 말에 대한 남자의 응답으로 가장 적절한 것을 고르시오. [3점]

Man: _____

① All right. I'd love to plant trees in a garden.
② No way. You're just making that garden up.
③ Wow! Let's do some research and plant one soon!
④ No worries. I'll buy the seeds for our indoor garden.
⑤ Now I understand. That's why roof gardens are so expensive.

15 다음 상황 설명을 듣고, Ben이 Rebecca에게 할 말로 가장 적절한 것을 고르시오.

Ben: _____

① How do you like my pasta? I hope you like it.
② I'm sorry, but I don't think I can help you out.
③ This pasta is amazing. You've done a great job.
④ This is too salty. How about adding more water?
⑤ I think the pasta would be better with some salt.

[16~17] 다음을 듣고, 물음에 답하시오.

16 남자가 하는 말의 주제로 가장 적절한 것은?

① ways to protect your skin from fine dust
② various health problems caused by fine dust
③ food that makes our immune systems stronger
④ reasons why healthy blood flow is important
⑤ how to detoxify your body with water

17 언급된 음식이 <u>아닌</u> 것은?

① apples   ② carrots   ③ blueberries
④ broccoli   ⑤ garlic

01

W Good morning, everyone. On behalf of the student council, _____ our annual talent show at Lincoln Senior High School. Join us for a night of entertainment and help our community. Our talent show will be held on Tuesday, May 19th, at 6 p.m. in the school gymnasium. The talent show will be composed of two sessions, one for solo performances and the other for group performances. Admission is $2 and _____ _____. You can also buy raffle tickets for $1 each and win prizes throughout the show! We have over 50 prizes to give away. All proceeds will be donated to our local homeless shelter. _____ at the talent show. Thank you.

02

W Honey, can you help me out with the groceries?

M Sure. *[Pause]* This bag is so heavy. What did you buy?

W Oh, I bought some fruits and vegetables, and meat. I also got some laundry detergent.

M We have enough laundry detergent. Why did you get more?

W Oh, _____.

M Did you make a shopping list before you went?

W No, I didn't. I just decide what to get when I'm shopping.

M You should. You _____ _____.

W I know. I feel like I spend too much on things we don't need. _____.

M Making a list is easy. We could put a piece of paper on the refrigerator. Then we just write down the items we need.

W That sounds like a great idea.

03

W Hello, listeners! My name is Kelly Tuner, and you're tuned in to *Sunlight Digest*. As the year-end season approaches, many people are wondering what gifts to give to their friends and family. When giving gifts, _____ _____. When I was young, _____ _____, and my father bought me an art kit. It ignited my passion for art. Now, years later, I'm a fine arts school teacher. So, _____ _____, select what appeals to their preferences, like a camera or sports equipment. To help you out, I will show you some gift samples for each occasion. Stay tuned!

04

W Honey, I've arranged your study at last.

M You've done a wonderful job. I love it.

W It's good to hear that. What do you think of the blinds on the windows?

M They're perfect. I can close the blinds _____ _____. It was hard to work at my desk in front of the window before.

W I know. I also took the laptop out of the case and _____.

M That's good. Oh, you bought a new chair, too.

W I remembered that you wanted a chair with wheels. Just be careful with it. I don't want any scratches on the floor.

M I will. Did you move the bookcase to the left wall by yourself?

W No, Tom helped me move it. _____ _____. Is it okay on the shelf like that?

M That's fine. There are not _____ _____ anyway.

W Are you satisfied with the present arrangement?

M Yes, definitely.

05

W　What are you doing later today?

M　I'm planning to go to a theater to see a play at Daehakno.

W　A play? I didn't know you enjoyed plays.

M　Really? ＿＿＿＿＿＿＿＿＿＿＿＿＿＿＿＿＿＿＿＿＿.

W　I have never seen a play before. What are you watching then?

M　It's called "Bballae", which means "Doing the Laundry."

W　Oh, I think I read about it once. It was described as ＿＿＿＿＿＿＿＿＿＿＿＿＿＿＿＿＿＿＿＿＿＿＿＿＿＿.

M　That's right. You can come with me if you want.

W　I would love to. ＿＿＿＿＿＿＿＿＿＿＿＿＿＿＿＿＿ ＿＿＿＿＿＿＿＿＿＿＿?

M　Oh, you can go and buy a ticket at the box office.

W　How much is a ticket?

M　It's $30 per ticket and students get a 15% discount with a student ID card.

W　I don't have mine on me right now. ＿＿＿＿＿＿＿＿＿ ＿＿＿＿＿＿＿＿＿＿＿＿＿. What time is the showing?

M　It's at 8 p.m. So I think we should meet 30 minutes before it starts.

W　Okay. See you then.

06

W　Welcome to the Men's Wear department. Have you been helped?

M　Not yet. I am looking for some pants for my son.

W　They're right over here, sir. Is there a particular style he prefers?

M　He needs pants that are not too casual. They are for his graduation.

W　All right. How about these dark gray suit trousers with checks?

M　They are ＿＿＿＿＿＿＿＿＿＿＿＿＿＿＿＿＿＿＿＿＿. How much are they?

W　They are $70. What size does your son wear?

M　Medium, please. Do you also ＿＿＿＿＿＿＿＿＿＿＿＿ ＿＿＿＿＿＿＿＿＿＿＿＿＿＿ with those?

W　Yes. The color dark gray can go with anything. If your son has fair skin, I recommend a plain shirt in light blue.

M　I like it. How much is the shirt?

W　It's $40, but if you buy two, ＿＿＿＿＿＿＿＿＿＿＿＿ ＿＿＿＿＿＿＿＿＿＿＿＿＿＿＿＿＿＿＿＿.

M　Then I will take two. Both in medium, please.

W　Of course, sir. Is there anything else you need?

M　No, that would be all.

W　All right, I will ＿＿＿＿＿＿＿＿＿＿＿＿＿＿＿＿＿＿ ＿＿＿＿＿＿＿＿＿＿＿＿＿ at the counter.

07

M　I can't wait until the finals are over.

W　There are only a few days left. ＿＿＿＿＿＿＿＿＿＿ ＿＿＿＿＿＿＿＿＿＿＿＿＿＿＿＿＿. Do you want to come?

M　Sure. Oh, are you going to attend the college fair next week?

W　I forgot about that. ＿＿＿＿＿＿＿＿＿＿＿＿＿＿＿＿＿?

M　It'll be held from the 25th to the 27th. That's from next Friday to Sunday.

W　Really? Then I don't think I can go.

M　Why not?

W　My family is supposed to ＿＿＿＿＿＿＿＿＿＿＿＿＿＿ ＿＿＿＿＿＿＿＿＿＿＿＿＿＿＿＿＿.

M　Is something the matter with him?

W　He got in a traffic accident. Next weekend is my mother's turn to take care of him at the hospital.

M　I'm sorry to hear that. ＿＿＿＿＿＿＿＿＿＿＿＿＿＿＿ ＿＿＿＿＿＿＿＿＿＿.

W　Thanks.

08

M　Have you heard of the Dolphin Cruise Tour in Guam? Do you want to go on it next month?

W　Sure. I've always wanted to go on a dolphin cruise.

M　This website I'm looking at ＿＿＿＿＿＿＿＿＿＿＿＿ ＿＿＿＿＿＿＿＿＿＿＿＿＿＿＿＿＿.

W　Really? What does it say?

M　The Dolphin Cruise Tour is on a 57-seat boat. It includes fishing and snorkeling activities.

W That sounds interesting. What do we need to bring?

M We just need our own bathing suits and towels. _____, even snacks.

W That's convenient. But how can we get there from our hotel?

M The tour has a pick-up service. Let's see. *[Pause]* The bus comes to Guam Plaza at 10:50.

W That's perfect. _____
_____.

M Exactly. The cruise only takes two hours.

W That couldn't be better. We'll have enough time to look around other places after the cruise.

M A ticket is $48 for one adult. _____
_____?

W Yes, let's go for it.

09

M Good morning, students. As a science teacher, I am very proud to tell you about the special drone program for all students. It is called "Dronepia," which is a combination of the words "Drone" and "Utopia." The program includes 10 classes, starting on April 20th, and _____
_____ You don't have to attend every class, but certificates will be given to those _____
_____. The school will provide enough drone sets for everyone. Throughout the program, you will learn the basics about drones such as the theory, types, and benefits and downsides. In addition, _____
_____ in the last 10 minutes of each class. Since the class is limited to 15 people, it is recommended you _____
_____. If you have any questions, feel free to contact me by email, lewis@sacredheart.ac.ca.

10

M Honey, we really need to change this sofa. It's not firm anymore.

W Let's go over this furniture catalog and decide which one to get.

M Okay. Do you want to get a fabric one like this one? _____
_____.

W I don't like fabric ones. It's hard to get stains and dust out.

M True. Then, we should get either leather or velvet. They are a little more expensive, but if properly cared for, _____.

W All right. Do you want one with or without arms?

M Definitely with arms. I usually leave the remote control on the left arm. What about you?

W Me, too. It seems like there are two colors available.

M How about the one in cream? _____
_____.

W That sounds good. There are two left. _____
_____?

M Yes, $700 is too much for us.

W Okay. I'll make a call to see if the store has that one in stock.

11

M Can I get you anything else, perhaps more potatoes?

W No, thanks. I need to _____
_____. What do you have for dessert?

M We have many different kinds of desserts, including cake and sherbet. _____
if you want.

12

W Pardon me. By any chance, did you attend Harvard Business School?

M Yes, I graduated in the class of '98. _____
_____. Do I know you?

W Yes, I'm Susan Baker. _____
_____ in the first year. Do you remember me?

13

W Don, it just started raining. I don't know if we can film the last scene outside today.

M Really? I didn't hear about rain from the weather forecast.

W It's pouring now. I don't know when it'll stop.

M Let's wait a while. It could get better.

W I have other projects to work on. I don't have much time to waste.

M I know how you feel. _____ _____.

W How about changing the script and shooting the last scene inside?

M I can't. The last scene is very important and it has to be done outside. Otherwise the story won't make sense.

W But the school project is due this Friday. We don't have enough time.

M This is the last scene of the film. _____ _____.

W It may not. But we don't know that.

M _____ _____. I would have to think of a new ending.

W That's true. It could take longer.

M Exactly. _____ to see how things go?

14

W Honey, have you decided where you want to have a garden?

M Oh, yes. How about an indoor garden?

W That's not bad. I've seen several cafes with one.

M We can get those plants that purify the air.

W Well, I was thinking about something else. _____ _____?

M I don't think I have. What's that?

W It's a garden on the roof of a building. _____ _____.

M Really? What are they?

W A roof garden can reduce energy consumption. Because plants absorb heat, we can use less electricity for cooling in summer.

M Oh, that means _____ _____.

W Exactly. Though it might cost a lot to set up, in the long-term we can save a lot.

15

W Rebecca is a high school student whose hobby is cooking. Since this Saturday is her parents' anniversary, she decides to cook a delicious dinner for them. After _____, she thinks she needs to practice the recipes before the anniversary. So, she asks Ben for help because Ben goes to a culinary school and has much more experience in cooking than she does. Rebecca makes pasta and asks Ben to taste it. She thinks her pasta is okay and asks Ben for his opinion. Ben takes a bite, but he doesn't think it's good enough. As he looks around, he notices there is something missing in the kitchen. There is _____ _____. Then he realizes that Rebecca forgot to add salt as she cooked. So, he decides to tell her _____. In this situation, what would Ben most likely say to Rebecca?

16~17

M Hello, everyone. The fine dust issue is getting serious because it causes not only inconvenience in our lives, but also major health problems. Today we are going to talk about foods _____ _____ and help cleanse our bodies. First, apples contain a lot of vitamin C and E, _____ _____. An apple a day is a common phrase that you may have heard before. Blueberries are full of vitamin C, which prevents cells from getting damaged. There are many recipes available for blueberries, but it'd be best to eat them raw instead of cooked. Many of you may not enjoy broccoli, but broccoli is a superfood that _____ _____. It is also proven to reduce the risk of lung cancer. Last but not least is garlic. It is well known for its many health benefits. It can _____ _____ and help prevent cancer. You can wear masks to protect yourselves, but protection really begins at our dinner tables.

03회 실전 듣기 모의고사

01 다음을 듣고, 여자가 하는 말의 목적으로 가장 적절한 것을 고르시오.

① 행사에 참여한 인원을 점검하려고
② 자원봉사자들에게 일을 분배하려고
③ 독거노인들에게 점심을 대접하려고
④ 직원들에게 행사 일정을 설명하려고
⑤ 센터에 필요한 자원봉사자를 모집하려고

02 대화를 듣고, 남자의 의견으로 가장 적절한 것을 고르시오.

① 여행 전에 계획을 잘 세워야 한다.
② 혼자 기차 여행하는 것은 위험하다.
③ 여행을 하는 데 가장 중요한 것은 안전이다.
④ 버스 여행은 목적지에 가는 더 효율적인 방법이다.
⑤ 경비를 줄이기 위해 한 가지 교통수단만 이용해야 한다.

03 다음을 듣고, 여자가 하는 말의 요지로 가장 적절한 것을 고르시오.

① 국가 간의 운동 경기는 개회식을 하는 것을 원칙으로 한다.
② 운동 경기 개회식은 관중과 선수에게 일치감을 준다.
③ 스포츠 경기는 군중을 모으기 위해 다양한 방법을 써야 한다.
④ 경기 중에 노래를 부르는 것은 전통적인 응원 방식이다.
⑤ 개회식은 소모적인 시간으로 여겨질 수 있다.

04 대화를 듣고, 그림에서 대화의 내용과 일치하지 않는 것을 고르시오.

05 대화를 듣고, 여자가 할 일로 가장 적절한 것을 고르시오.

① 컴퓨터 매장에 같이 가기
② 고장 난 컴퓨터를 수리하기
③ 컴퓨터의 기본 특징을 알려주기
④ 최신 컴퓨터 모델을 구매하기
⑤ 컴퓨터 부품에 관해 묻기

06 대화를 듣고, 남자가 지불할 금액을 고르시오. [3점]

① $100   ② $135   ③ $150
④ $175   ⑤ $190

07 대화를 듣고, 여자가 전화를 건 이유를 고르시오.

① 영화에 대한 정보를 얻기 위해서
② 라디오 쇼에 출연하기 위해서
③ 함께 영화 보러 가기 위해서
④ 시험에 대한 정보를 얻기 위해서
⑤ 관람 가능한 영화관을 알기 위해서

08 대화를 듣고, Vera's Kitchen에 관해 언급되지 않은 것을 고르시오.

① 위치   ② 메뉴   ③ 주차장
④ 테이블 수   ⑤ 요리사

09 School Exhibition Day에 관한 다음 내용을 듣고, 일치하지 않는 것을 고르시오.

① 학교 전시회는 금요일에 열린다.
② 전시회 참가 신청은 13일까지이다.
③ 학생들은 21일까지 그림을 제출해야 한다.
④ 미술을 전공하는 학생들은 전시회에 작품을 걸 수 있다.
⑤ 전시회의 도우미 학생들은 교복을 입어야 한다.

10 다음 표를 보면서 대화를 듣고, 두 사람이 예약할 웨딩홀을 고르시오.

Wedding Halls in Richmond City

Venue	Available on May 6th	Minimum Number of Guests	Food Price per Person	Time
① A	○	200	$40	5:00 p.m. ~ 8:00 p.m.
② B	○	200	$45	12:00 p.m. ~ 2:30 p.m.
③ C	×	200	$45	12:00 p.m. ~ 2:30 p.m.
④ D	○	300	$55	5:00 p.m. ~ 8:00 p.m.
⑤ E	○	350	$55	12:00 p.m. ~ 2:30 p.m.

11 대화를 듣고, 여자의 마지막 말에 대한 남자의 응답으로 가장 적절한 것을 고르시오.

① No. I only gave it a quick look.
② Sorry, I found three more errors.
③ Yes, I should've finished it on time.
④ Of course. I won't make any mistakes in the future.
⑤ Not really. I didn't know it was due this morning.

12 대화를 듣고, 남자의 마지막 말에 대한 여자의 응답으로 가장 적절한 것을 고르시오.

① I didn't send an application form to that school.
② I don't know how to apply for another school.
③ I'm afraid I didn't answer an important call.
④ No, I really don't care whether they apply or not.
⑤ The acceptance announcement comes out this week, so I'm waiting.

13 대화를 듣고, 여자의 마지막 말에 대한 남자의 응답으로 가장 적절한 것을 고르시오. [3점]

Man: _____

① All right. Let's donate them to a charity, then.
② Don't worry. I don't like shopping these days.
③ I see. I promise I'll start working out next week.
④ Wait a moment. I'll bring some clothes to donate.
⑤ I agree. They don't accept secondhand clothes anymore.

14 대화를 듣고, 남자의 마지막 말에 대한 여자의 응답으로 가장 적절한 것을 고르시오. [3점]

Woman: _____

① Great. Then let's go and have a look at it first.
② I see. First birthdays are very special to parents.
③ No worries. I already made a reservation for that day.
④ Right. There are many party packages available online.
⑤ No way. I'm still going to call for a buffet catering service.

15 다음 상황 설명을 듣고, Harry가 Kelly에게 할 말로 가장 적절한 것을 고르시오.

Harry: _____

① You should have worked harder to pass the test.
② I also have a ticket for the concert myself.
③ If I were you, I'd accept the suggestion.
④ I'd love to, but I have to study for the big test.
⑤ Sure, I've always wanted to see that singer's concert.

[16~17] 다음을 듣고, 물음에 답하시오.

16 남자가 하는 말의 주제로 가장 적절한 것은?

① how traditional clothes disappeared
② how traditional clothing has changed
③ differences between Europe and Asia
④ traditional garments of Asian countries
⑤ similarities of garments in different countries

17 언급된 나라가 <u>아닌</u> 것은?

① India   ② Vietnam   ③ China
④ Japan   ⑤ South Korea

🔊 녹음된 내용을 들으면서 빈칸을 알맞게 채워보세요. _____

01

W Welcome to the Senior Community Center. I am Julia Kim, in charge of today's special event. First of all, I truly appreciate that _____ _____ at our center. I can feel that you are very energetic. I'm sure we can enjoy today's work together. As you all know, we are going to prepare dinner for the elderly at the center. I _____ _____. You can see which group you belong to on the worksheet which I've just handed out. Group 1 will set the tables and Group 2 will cook some side dishes. Then, Group 3 _____. If you have any questions as you work, please call me any time. My phone number _____ _____. Thank you for your cooperation.

02

W Did I tell you that I'm going on a solo trip next month? I am so excited!

M Wow, you are really doing it. So, do you have everything planned out?

W Well, sort of. I decided to take the train this time.

M Really? _____ _____ than taking trains. How about taking bus trips?

W It's true that bus trips are more affordable, but train journeys seem safer and more romantic.

M Still, _____ _____ because trains can only travel where there are tracks.

W You mean _____ _____, right?

M Right. Trains only get you to a train station. But buses can _____ _____.

03

W Welcome, everyone! I'm Amanda, your favorite sportscaster. Have you ever wondered _____ _____? Opening ceremonies play a crucial role in unifying the crowd and the athletes. For example, _____ _____, everyone, including the crowd and the players, feels like one big team. Even though some argue that ceremonies are a waste of time, in reality, they serve a much deeper purpose. In essence, _____ _____ and athletes together. I will be back next time with more exciting sports facts!

04

M Carla, did you pack everything you need for your trip?

W I'm packing right now, Dad. Can you help me out a little bit?

M Sure. Your mom put a water bottle on your bed. You could get really thirsty_____ _____.

W Oh, that's right. I'll pack that last after I get everything I need. What else should I take?

M You might need sunglasses and a hat to protect your eyes. I heard it could be really sunny tomorrow.

W Really? _____ _____ next to the bed. Can you pass me those, please?

M All right. [Pause] Here you are. You need to take insect repellent. Where do you keep the first-aid kit?

W It's _____.

M Okay, and don't forget to wear a watch. Do you remember where you put it?

W Yes, it's on my desk. I'll put it on tomorrow morning before I leave.

M So, do you have everything you need?

W Yes, I just need to put my towel in the bag. Oh, where did it go?

M You mean _____? It's right under the bag.

05

M This laptop isn't working again. This is the second time this week.

W I think _____ _____ out on the market.

M I don't know. Actually, I'm not really sure _____ _____.

W It's pretty simple. You just need something with a fast processor, a lot of RAM, and a good display, just like a desktop computer.

M But I have no idea what those things are.

W Well, they may all sound confusing at first. How about if I give you more details this weekend?

M I already have other plans for this weekend. _____ _____ after class today? I don't want to look clueless.

W Of course. _____ a good one.

M That sounds good to me!

06

W Hello. How can I help you?

M Hi. It's my sister's birthday next week and I can't decide what to get her.

W Well, since winter is coming, how about getting her a winter coat?

M That sounds great, but _____ _____, I'm afraid.

W Then take a look at this wool sweater. It's on sale. It was originally $80, but it's 50% off now.

M That sounds like a good deal. Should I get two? Just one sweater doesn't seem like enough.

W _____ in cashmere instead? Because they are softer and warmer, they are steady sellers.

M Okay. What colors do you have?

W They come in ivory, pink and black. Right now, black ones are really popular and _____ _____.

M Really? The price tag says they are $110. That's a bit expensive.

W We have a special sale going on until this weekend. So, if you spend more than $100, you can get 10% off the total.

M Cool. _____ and this black cashmere sweater, too.

W Okay. Would you like them gift-wrapped?

M Absolutely, thanks.

07

M Hello, Naomi.

W Ian! Where were you last night? I tried to reach you several times, but your phone was off.

M Sorry about that. I have a big test today, so I turned it off. Anyway, why did you call?

W Do you remember my favorite radio show? Yesterday, _____.

M Really? Did they pick yours?

W Yes, they aired my story and played the song I requested. They also _____.

M Wow, that's awesome!

W Since I have an extra ticket, would you be interested in _____?

M Of course. Which movie do you want to watch? Do you have anything in mind?

W Not really. Luckily, I can use the tickets anywhere and anytime I want.

M Perfect! _____ _____ that just came out?

W I like action movies, too. Let's go this Friday night.

M Cool! I can't wait.

08

W Honey, I don't feel like cooking today. Can we eat out for dinner tonight?

M That's an option. What kind of food do you want?

W Why don't we try something new? I heard that _____ _____ on Park Avenue.

M Are you talking about Vera's Kitchen? Actually, I went there last week.

W Oh, really? How was the food?

M It was okay, but _____
_____ and two kinds of pizza.

W Well, that's fine with me as long as they are delicious.

M Then, let's go there before the traffic is too heavy.

W Is there a parking area?

M Yes, but _____,
so we'd better hurry.

W Then why don't we call and make a reservation?

M That's a good idea. I'll call to see if there is a table available.

09

M Attention, please. Our school's Exhibition Day has been set for Friday, September 25th. I hope _____
_____ in the school auditorium. Those who are interested should apply to participate by Monday, September 14th. And _____
_____, September 21st. Every art student will be allowed to show their paintings in the exhibition. So don't miss out on this great opportunity. Last but not least, I'd like to remind you that all the volunteering student staff members _____
_____ during the exhibition. Thank you for your cooperation.

10

W Since our wedding date is set to May 6th, we need to decide on the wedding hall.

M We visited five places in Richmond City, and I made a list to compare them.

W This place was at the top of my list, but it's _____
_____.

M Oh, right. I'll cross that one out. Most wedding halls ask for the minimum number of guests. How many are you thinking?

W Well, I was thinking about 150 from my side. What about you?

M Me, too. _____
_____.

W How about the price?

M They charge us for the food only. Let's set a price on food per person.

W To me, $55 seems too much for one person. _____
_____?

M Sure. Now, we only have two options left.

W Oh, our flight for the honeymoon leaves at 8 p.m. So we should _____.

M Okay. I'll call this wedding hall to make a reservation.

11

W Did you finish the history report you've been working on?

M Yes, _____.
I handed it in this morning.

W Hmm... Did you _____
in your report?

12

M Did you get accepted into the school you applied to?

W I don't know. _____
yet.

M It's been more than a month. _____
_____ to find out?

13

M What are you doing, honey?

W I'm sorting out our clothes. We have too many of them that _____.

M I know. I'm often surprised to find old clothes that I didn't even know I had.

W Exactly. I think we just buy more and more clothes, just because they are new.

M That's because you don't know what you already have. So, what are you going to do with the old clothes?

W I'm going to _____.
Look, are these yours?

M Oh, those are my old jeans. I forgot I had them. I don't think _____ since I have put on some weight.

W I'll just give them away, then.

M Don't! I think I might need them when I lose weight.

W Honey, _____ even after you lose weight.

14

M Honey, what are we going to do for our daughter's first birthday?

W Well, I was thinking about having a party at home.

M At home? Do you want us to prepare everything?

W That's right. Don't you want to make it special, too?

M I do. But I don't know how having the party at home can make it special.

W You're right. There _____ _____.

M Exactly. It'll be hard to prepare on our own with a baby, too.

W I see your point. Then _____ _____?

M I found a buffet restaurant that has great reviews.

W Really? What did they say?

M _____, and the servers are very nice. Oh, the parking lot is huge, too.

W A large parking lot is really important since most of our guests will drive there.

M The restaurant has special offers that _____ _____, too.

W Okay. I guess we have to call and check if we can still make a reservation.

M I already did. It's not fully booked yet on the date we want.

15

W Harry is majoring in English literature. Last semester he failed one of his courses and had to take it again this semester. Since this is his second try, _____ _____ next week so that he can at least pass the course. Today,

he is having lunch with Kelly, one of his classmates. While having lunch, _____ _____, saying that she has two free tickets. He really wants to go since his favorite singer is performing. However, _____ _____ if he doesn't study hard for it this weekend. So, he wants to tell Kelly that he can't make it. In this situation, what would Harry most likely say to Kelly?

16~17

M Hello, students. Previously, we discussed traditional garments in some European countries. Today, we'll talk about _____ _____. First, a sari is the traditional female garment in India and Sri Lanka. It is a very long strip of unstitched cloth, _____ _____. Second, hanfu is the characteristic clothing for the Han ethnic group in China. It features a loose upper garment with sleeves and a skirt-like lower garment. The belt was often decorated with jade. Third, a kimono is a traditional Japanese garment and _____ _____ by the hanfu. It is a T-shaped robe, which has very long sleeves. Finally, hanbok is the traditional clothing in South Korea. People used to wear hanbok daily up until just 100 years ago, _____ _____. It was originally designed to facilitate ease of movement. Traditional women's hanbok consists of a short blouse shirt, and a wrap-around skirt. Men's hanbok consists of a shirt and loose-fitting trousers.

04 회 실전 듣기 모의고사

01 다음을 듣고, 남자가 하는 말의 목적으로 가장 적절한 것을 고르시오.

① 회의 안건을 모집하려고
② 위원회 가입을 촉구하려고
③ 셔틀버스 운행을 안내하려고
④ 회의 날짜의 변경을 알리려고
⑤ 위원회 폐지에 양해를 구하려고

02 대화를 듣고, 여자의 의견으로 가장 적절한 것을 고르시오.

① 친구와 싸운 후에 험담을 하지 말아야 한다.
② 지나친 휴대전화 사용은 학업에 영향을 준다.
③ 친구 사이 갈등은 만나서 대화로 해결해야 한다.
④ 모둠 과제는 학생들의 자발적인 참여를 유도한다.
⑤ 학교 내 따돌림 문제는 심리상담센터를 통해 해결해야 한다.

03 다음을 듣고, 남자가 하는 말의 요지로 가장 적절한 것을 고르시오.

① 적당한 스트레스는 오히려 일의 능률을 높일 수 있다.
② 큰 과제를 작은 부분으로 나누어 처리하는 게 좋다.
③ 정기적인 휴식을 취하는 것이 작업 효율을 높인다.
④ 청소는 미루지 않고 제때 하는 것이 좋다.
⑤ 큰 목표를 세우고 일하는 것이 더 좋은 결과를 낸다.

04 대화를 듣고, 그림에서 대화의 내용과 일치하지 않는 것을 고르시오.

05 대화를 듣고, 여자가 남자를 위해 할 일로 가장 적절한 것을 고르시오.

① 사진 찍어주기
② 자리 맡아 주기
③ 휴대폰 찾아 주기
④ 유니폼 가져다주기
⑤ 간식거리 사다 주기

06 대화를 듣고, 남자가 지불할 금액을 고르시오. [3점]

① $37   ② $64.50   ③ $65
④ $67   ⑤ $69.50

07 대화를 듣고, 여자가 동창회에 가지 못 한 이유를 고르시오.

① 친구의 결혼식에 가야 해서
② 프랑스에서 공부해야 해서
③ 업무차 출장을 가야 해서
④ 초대장을 받지 못 해서
⑤ 신혼여행을 가서

08 대화를 듣고, 뮤지컬 Under the Sky에 관해 언급되지 않은 것을 고르시오.

① 입장료   ② 공연 시간   ③ 주연 배우
④ 쉬는 시간   ⑤ 공연 기간

09 Good Morning, 7 O'Clock에 관한 다음 내용을 듣고, 일치하지 않는 것을 고르시오.

① 아침 방송이며 진행자는 Paul Farrell이다.
② 직장인과 학생 등 아침 청취자를 위한 프로그램이다.
③ 뉴스, 생활, 교육 등의 분야를 다룰 예정이다.
④ 특별 게스트는 첫 방송 당일 웹사이트에 공개된다.
⑤ 첫 방송일은 방송국 설립기념일인 5월 15일이다.

10 다음 표를 보면서 대화를 듣고, 여자가 구매할 공기청정기를 고르시오.

Air Purifiers

Model	Price	Filter	Warranty	Shape
① A	$200	2-layer	6 months	round
② B	$250	3-layer	6 months	square
③ C	$280	3-layer	1 year	square
④ D	$300	3-layer	1 year	round
⑤ E	$400	3-layer	2 years	round

11 대화를 듣고, 여자의 마지막 말에 대한 남자의 응답으로 가장 적절한 것을 고르시오.

① You can purchase refreshments on the train.
② I am sorry. But the train has already departed.
③ Please stand behind the yellow line for your safety.
④ I don't know. This is my first time at this train station.
⑤ Yes. The screen above also says which platform to go to.

12 대화를 듣고, 남자의 마지막 말에 대한 여자의 응답으로 가장 적절한 것을 고르시오.

① Really? You must be excited to visit the hotel again.
② Good for you. From my experience, the hotel is great.
③ What a coincidence! My conference is also on Saturday.
④ I have a wedding I'm invited to. I guess I'll see you there.
⑤ I really liked it. The hotel has been renovated very nicely.

13 대화를 듣고, 여자의 마지막 말에 대한 남자의 응답으로 가장 적절한 것을 고르시오. [3점]

Man: _____

① I'm terribly sorry. I'd better get off right away.
② Please take this seat. I can wait for another one.
③ You were right about the change in the schedule.
④ I will buy tickets for both of us, please do not worry.
⑤ Let's wait for someone to come and identify the tickets.

14 대화를 듣고, 남자의 마지막 말에 대한 여자의 응답으로 가장 적절한 것을 고르시오. [3점]

Woman: _____

① I brought new people to this park last time.
② Yes. I had a dog as a pet when I was young.
③ Of course. Let's meet back here in 20 minutes.
④ I prefer dogs over cats due to their personalities.
⑤ No problem. I will walk your dog while you travel.

15 다음 상황 설명을 듣고, Emma가 Adam에게 할 말로 가장 적절한 것을 고르시오.

Emma: _____

① Congratulations. You are qualified for the position.
② We are certain that you are the best person for us.
③ Could you come in tomorrow for an interview?
④ I am sorry, but we've selected another candidate.
⑤ Could you speak a little louder and with more confidence?

[16~17] 다음을 듣고, 물음에 답하시오.

16 남자가 하는 말의 주제로 가장 적절한 것은?

① importance of orchestras in classical music
② difference between an orchestra and a band
③ reason why classical music has lost popularity
④ origin and history of classical music in Europe
⑤ different families of instruments in an orchestra

17 언급된 악기가 <u>아닌</u> 것은?

① violin   ② flute   ③ trumpet
④ horn   ⑤ drum

🔊 녹음된 내용을 들으면서 빈칸을 알맞게 채워보세요. _____

01

M Hello, members of the Education Committee. This is the secretary, Bob Wyatt. I have some important notifications regarding our next meeting. I recently sent you _____ via e-mail. While trying to look for a good meeting room that can accommodate all our members, I had no choice but to choose a venue that is far from our usual location. I thought this might cause inconvenience to our members, and looked for ways to deal with the problem. So, _____ that will take you from the train station to the new venue. Please take the shuttle bus from the train station. I will send you _____ _____.

I hope to see everyone at the meeting. Thank you.

02

W John, you've been staring at your phone for an hour. Are you waiting for an important call?

M Well, I'm waiting for Jason to call me back. But I don't know if he is ever going to call me.

W What do you mean? _____ _____?

M I was upset about the history project, but he kept asking me how I did. So I yelled at him in front of other people.

W Did you apologize to him?

M I sent him a text message, but he hasn't replied or called.

W I think _____.

M I don't know how to face him. I don't think he ever wants to talk to me again.

W You should explain how you felt and how much you regret it. He might think a text message is _____ _____.

M Do you really think so?

W Yes, talking is a better way to communicate your feelings.

M You're right. I should _____ _____.

03

M Hi everyone, I'm Jeff Colvin, and it's a pleasure to be with you on *Morning Insight*. _____ _____ of being overwhelmed with a lot of tasks? Well, fear not! I have a solution for you — _____ _____. For example, if cleaning your entire backyard feels like too much to handle, try focusing on one section at a time. This way, you can make progress and achieve great results. Any big thing can be solved _____ _____. In our session today, I'll be sharing more simple tips and tricks to help you handle challenging workloads.

04

W Hello, Mr. Johnson.

M Hi, Ms. Powell. I brought my design plan for your living room. Here it is.

W Wow! It looks great. It's just how I imagined it. I like that _____.

M It's always nice to have some green in the living room. And it should be by the window so it gets a lot of sunlight.

W And I really like _____ _____. It looks very modern and stylish.

M You said you'd like your living room to look neat and modern, and this tall lamp is in style lately.

W It suits the living room very well. And _____ _____. I can read books on the sofa under the lamp.

M That was my idea. How do you like the painting on the wall?

W Yes, you mean the one above the sofa? I always wanted to hang a painting on that wall.

M I'm glad you like it. And please have a look at the table in front of the sofa.

W Oh, _____. I like it.

M Yes. In this style of living room, _____ _____, so I chose the round one.

W That looks perfect. Thank you.

05

W Wow, look how big the crowd is!

M It's one of the most popular games of the year.

W Our seats are right here. We can see the soccer field very well from here.

M _____. I am so excited! It's been a long time since I watched a soccer game at a stadium.

W Yes. I'm looking forward to today's game, too. My favorite player is going to be on the field.

M That's great. Oh, _____ _____. Could you take photos of the game for me?

W I'm not good at taking pictures, so you can just use my cell phone.

M Thanks. Look what I brought! These are jerseys for the team we are cheering for.

W Wow! They look really nice. Can I wear one of them?

M Sure. I brought two so we could wear the same jerseys. _____.

W You can say that again. By the way, I think I should use the bathroom before the game starts. Would you like me to get anything for you on my way back?

M Hmm... Could you _____ _____ while we watch the game?

W Sure. What kind of snack would you like?

M Anything is fine with me. Thanks!

06

W Hello, sir. Can I help you?

M I would like to buy some cookies.

W We have this special Christmas edition for $30. The package of 20 cookies is cheaper than getting 20 individual cookies.

M That sounds like a good deal. _____ _____?

W There are four types, raisin, peanut butter, ginger, and cinnamon.

M Can I change the ginger cookies to chocolate chip cookies?

W Of course, but _____ _____. Is that all right?

M That's fine. _____?

W The chocolate chip cookies are ¢50 more expensive than the ginger cookies. Since there are five ginger cookies in the package, it will cost $2.50 more to change all of them.

M That's fine. I'll take two Christmas packages, and please change all the ginger cookies to chocolate chip cookies.

W Do you want both to be wrapped? _____ _____.

M Yes, please. Here is my credit card.

07

M Barbara? Is that you?

W Oh, hi, Gilbert. It's been a long time. How have you been?

M Great! I heard you are working as an accountant. How is that working out for you?

W The first two years were tough, but it's all right now. _____.

M I was there for about five years and came back last year.

W That's nice. I didn't expect to see you at this wedding.

M Well, Mary and I have been _____ _____. Now that I think about it, you weren't there, were you?

W No, I missed it. I went to _____ _____, except the last one.

M Were you busy at work?

W Not really. It was slow season at the time of the reunion.

M How come you had to miss it, then?

W _____.

M Wow, I didn't know you got married. It's a little late, but congratulations!

08

[Telephone rings.]

M Hello, Grey's Theater. How may I help you?

W Hello, I'd like to ask you about the musical you are playing.

M Oh, "Under the Sky," right?

W Yes. _____?

M The musical starts at 7 p.m. every evening.

W I see. _____
_____? Is it Don Kennedy?

M Yes. He is one of the most popular musical actors.

W I see. And is there an intermission?

M There will be _____.

W Okay. One last thing. _____
_____?

M It's playing for three more weeks. We extended it due to its rising popularity.

W Wow, that's great. I will recommend the musical to people I know if I like it.

M That will be great. I hope to see you at the musical.

09

W Good afternoon. As the head producer at our broadcasting station, I'd like to introduce a new program. It is a morning radio show called "Good Morning, 7 O'Clock," and it will be hosted by Paul Farrell. The show is targeted at _____
_____, including office workers on their way to work, students on their way to school, and many others. It will _____
_____ including news, lifestyle, and education. To celebrate the launch of the program, there will be a special guest on the very first day. We will reveal who this is on our website _____
_____. Our first broadcast is on May 15th, _____
_____, so please do not forget to turn on the radio on that day. Thank you.

10

M Hello, ma'am. Are you looking for an air purifier?

W Yes, I didn't know there would be so many different types to choose from.

M I can help you pick the right one. Is there a certain budget you have in mind?

W Yes. I want to _____.

M All right. Do you prefer the latest models? We also have some models from last year.

W Well, what is the difference?

M The latest models come with 3 layers of filters. That's why they are a bit more expensive.

W I see. _____.

M Good choice. How about the warranty?

W Well, the longer the warranty is, the better, right?

M That's right. Then we only have two options left. Which shape would you like, round or square?

W _____. I think it will go better with my house.

M All right. Come this way. I need you to fill out the delivery form.

11

W Excuse me, sir. I am leaving for Seoul. _____
_____?

M No, ma'am. You are just in time. The train is leaving in 10 minutes.

W That's a relief. And just to confirm, _____
_____?

12

M Have you been to the hotel that was recently built in downtown?

W No, I haven't yet. But I have a conference _____
_____.

M Oh, really? _____
_____, too. It will be my first time.

13

M Excuse me. I think you are sitting in my seat.

W That can't be true. Can I have a look at your ticket, please?

M Of course. It says car number 8 and seat number 7C.

W Hmm... Let me check my ticket, too. [Pause] _____
_____.

M Where are you heading? _____
_____.

W I'm going to Boston. This is very strange. I reserved the ticket online.

M Same here. Could it be that our seats are double-booked?

W Yes, _____.
Can I see your ticket again?

M Sure. The train is about to leave. We have to find a conductor quickly.

W Wait. You are not supposed to be on this train. Your ticket is for _____

_____.

14

W Excuse me. Is something wrong?

M I've been looking for my dog, but _____

_____.

W Oh, no. Where did you lose him?

M I tied him around that tree while I used the bathroom. But when I came out, he was gone.

W That's terrible. I will help you find him.

M That is very kind of you. _____

_____?

W Calm down and try to think. When you came out, was the chain still there?

M Yes. It was still tied to the tree. He must have broken the chain and run away.

W And what does he look like?

M He is a big husky and _____

_____. Oh, and his name is Buddy.

W Okay. I'll look this way and you start looking that way.

M All right. If you find Buddy, _____

_____?

15

W Emma works at the recruitment office. She posted a job hiring notice online, and two candidates applied. One of the applicants was Adam Kindle, but _____

_____. The position he applied for was in the domestic sales department. This job involves dealing with different clients, so the company requires that the candidates be comfortable speaking in public. But when Adam answered the questions at the interview, _____

_____. Eventually, the company chose the other candidate over Adam. As the person in charge of recruitment, Emma has to call Adam and _____.
In this situation, what would Emma most likely say to Adam?

16~17

M Welcome to the world of classical music! Today, I will give you a brief overview about each of the main types of instruments used in an orchestra. There are four families of instruments: strings, woodwinds, brass, and percussion. Let's start with the most notable instrument in the string family, the violin. _____

_____ in an orchestra as its high-pitched sound carries easily over other instruments. Next, the flute is one of the instruments from the woodwind family. Like the violin, the flute may often carry the melody line as it is _____

_____. The third family of instruments is brass, and the one most familiar to us would be the trumpet. But did you know that this instrument has been around since 1500 B.C.? It was often _____

_____ in the old days. The last instrument is the drum, which belongs to the percussion family. Along with other percussion instruments, the drum _____

_____ to orchestra music. Now, let's watch a video of an actual orchestra.

01 다음을 듣고, 여자가 하는 말의 목적으로 가장 적절한 것을 고르시오.

① 다양한 조리법을 제공하는 앱을 홍보하려고
② 유명한 셰프의 음식 조리법을 안내하려고
③ 건강한 저녁 식사 메뉴를 소개하려고
④ 저녁 식사 메뉴의 변경을 통보하려고
⑤ 요리 대회 참가를 장려하려고

02 대화를 듣고, 남자의 의견으로 가장 적절한 것을 고르시오.

① 충분한 휴식을 취하는 것은 정신 건강에 좋다.
② 자료를 효과적으로 사용하여 발표해야 한다.
③ 운동은 스트레스 해소에 효과적이다.
④ 좋은 습관으로 여러 질병들을 예방할 수 있다.
⑤ 한강을 오염시키는 사업을 정부가 규제해야 한다.

03 다음을 듣고, 여자가 하는 말의 요지로 가장 적절한 것을 고르시오.

① 지나치게 샤워를 자주 하면 피부 건조를 유발한다.
② 아침보다는 저녁에 하는 샤워가 건강상 더 바람직하다.
③ 샤워헤드는 정기적으로 세척하고 소독하는 게 필요하다.
④ 샤워기에서 처음 나오는 물로는 샤워하지 않는 것이 좋다.
⑤ 박테리아를 제거하기 위해 집 청소를 하는 것이 중요하다.

04 대화를 듣고, 그림에서 대화의 내용과 일치하지 <u>않는</u> 것을 고르시오.

05 대화를 듣고, 남자가 할 일로 가장 적절한 것을 고르시오.

① 해변 공원 산책하기
② 엄마와 장 보러 가기
③ 방으로 간식 가져다주기
④ 과학박물관 사이트 방문하기
⑤ 지하철역에서 자전거 빌리기

06 대화를 듣고, 여자가 지불할 금액을 고르시오.

① $80 ② $100 ③ $120
④ $160 ⑤ $200

07 대화를 듣고, 남자가 오늘 모임에 참석할 수 <u>없는</u> 이유를 고르시오.

① 치통이 너무 심해서
② 밴드 연습을 해야 해서
③ 과제 준비를 해야 해서
④ 아르바이트를 해야 해서
⑤ 치아 교정을 받아야 해서

08 대화를 듣고, Helping Hands 프로그램에 관해 언급되지 <u>않은</u> 것을 고르시오.

① 참가 조건 ② 참가 비용 ③ 활동 국가
④ 활동 내용 ⑤ 지원 마감일

09 World Youth Forum에 관한 다음 내용을 듣고, 일치하지 <u>않는</u> 것을 고르시오.

① 전체 지원자 40명 중 5명이 선정되었다.
② 세계적인 문제에 대해 논의한다.
③ 파리에서 매년 8월에 열린다.
④ 참가자들은 자신의 나라를 대표한다.
⑤ 참가 전에 준비 워크숍에 참여해야 한다.

10 다음 표를 보면서 대화를 듣고, 두 사람이 예약할 호텔을 고르시오.

Hotels on Price Comparison Site

	Hotel	Rate (per night)	Shuttle Bus Service	Water Park	Hotel Buffet Included
①	A	$75	○	×	×
②	B	$85	○	○	×
③	C	$90	×	○	○
④	D	$95	○	○	○
⑤	E	$110	×	×	○

11 대화를 듣고, 여자의 마지막 말에 대한 남자의 응답으로 가장 적절한 것을 고르시오.

① Sorry, I'll check our number again.
② Right, but it's none of your business.
③ Yes, it is, but there's no Tom Brown here.
④ Well, I think Tom is out of town at the moment.
⑤ Hold on, please. I'm sure he'll wait for your call.

12 대화를 듣고, 남자의 마지막 말에 대한 여자의 응답으로 가장 적절한 것을 고르시오.

① Never mind. I'm sure I can do that well.
② Yes, I will. I have some relatives there, too.
③ I didn't expect that. That was much more than I expected.
④ Of course I won't! I'll try to keep in touch with you online.
⑤ I hope not. There would be mountains of work waiting for me.

13 대화를 듣고, 여자의 마지막 말에 대한 남자의 응답으로 가장 적절한 것을 고르시오. [3점]

Man: _____

① Don't worry. She can find a way to the library.
② I understand. The baby will have a lot of books.
③ Great. I will go to the mall and get her some baby clothes.
④ That sounds perfect. I hope it's not too much trouble for her.
⑤ Of course. We will be in the waiting room in case of an emergency.

14 대화를 듣고, 남자의 마지막 말에 대한 여자의 응답으로 가장 적절한 것을 고르시오. [3점]

Woman: _____

① No. I'll call the restaurant and ask them.
② I think older pictures are in the basement.
③ I'm afraid not. We are not allowed to take pictures.
④ No way. We can't make a video with the pictures.
⑤ I'm sorry. I don't know when our parents' anniversary is.

15 다음 상황 설명을 듣고, Diana의 아버지가 Diana에게 할 말로 가장 적절한 것을 고르시오. [3점]

Diana's father: _____

① I'm afraid you should think about it again.
② Can't you understand why your family cares?
③ You should do whatever you feel comfortable doing.
④ You don't have much in common with other sportswomen.
⑤ What about meeting your counselor to change your decision?

[16~17] 다음을 듣고, 물음에 답하시오.

16 남자가 하는 말의 주제로 가장 적절한 것은?

① potential harmful effects of microplastics
② effects of endangered species on marine life
③ studies on the causes of environmental pollution
④ ideas for producing an alternative material to plastic
⑤ characteristics of microplastics and ways to remove them

17 언급된 미세 플라스틱의 흡입 경로가 아닌 것은?

① seafood   ② fresh air
③ bottled water   ④ vegetables
⑤ tea bags

01

W Hello, everybody! Have you decided what to cook for dinner tonight? It is hard to choose dinner every day. Let Cook's Haven help you with this daily challenge. This is a very unique cooking app you can download on your phone. You will have easy access to _____ _____ by just tapping a button. Just choose one and cook it. The recipes will be updated every two weeks. You can download and save the recipes on your phone, too! Cook's Haven _____ to find your perfect meal with a one-time payment of $30. For a limited time only, with the purchase of Cook's Haven, you might win the opportunity to cook with the world-famous chef Tony Chung. _____ _____.

02

W I feel stressed out from working on the presentation all afternoon. I can't wait to go home and rest.

M _____ to relieve stress. That's why I changed into gym clothes.

W Are you off to the gym?

M Well, I'm going to the Han River for a jog instead.

W That sounds interesting. Maybe _____ _____ instead of relaxing at home.

M You should. It's a healthy way to manage your stress. Exercise such as running can help you relax better, too.

W What do you mean?

M Exercising can improve your sleep. _____ _____ and stay asleep longer.

W I didn't know that. I thought just sleeping longer hours would relieve your stress.

M That could make you more tired. Besides, _____ _____ such as cancer.

W I guess the hardest part is to get started.

M Getting started is always hard. Once you get used to it, it will be a lot easier.

03

W Good to have you here! My name is Becky Blanz, and welcome to *One Minute Health Show*. These days, _____ _____. Here's an easy health tip for you: try to avoid showering with the first splash of water. Recently, a study looking into 50 different showerheads revealed that harmful bacteria can accumulate in showerheads, and _____ _____. Avoiding stepping into the shower during the initial surge of water _____ _____. I'll be back with more health tips next time. Goodbye.

04

M Hey, Jessi. Take a look. Here's the design for your new album cover.

W It's done already? *[Pause]* Wow, I like the decoration on the left side. It makes it look like a notebook.

M Yes. It _____ _____.

W And the phrase "thinking of you" is coming out of my mouth. It looks like I'm singing my song.

M Yes, and people will recognize the song title easily, too.

W I also like this picture of myself. I am _____ _____ on the right side. And you didn't forget to add my shadow, either.

M I think _____ _____.

W You're right. Oh, I see you put my name at the bottom. Those letters really stand out.

M That's because I used bold letters since "Jessi Conner" is the most important part of the cover.

05

M Mom, I'm so excited that my cousins are visiting tomorrow.

W I know. I'll make you guys a delicious seafood meal tomorrow.

M Do you need any help with that?

W Don't worry about me. You go out and have fun with them.

M _____.
Can you make any suggestions?

W What about going for a bike ride? You can rent bicycles near the subway station and ride out to the beach.

M I'm not sure if they'd like it. It is a bit chilly to ride a bike outside, too.

W Okay. Then how about taking them to the science museum near City Hall? I heard that _____
_____
for students under 15.

M That sounds like fun. We should go there instead. Do you know how much the admission fee is?

W I'm not sure. _____
_____ to find out more?

M All right. I'll look for more information on the internet.

W Do you want me to bring some snacks to your room?

M Yes, please. Thanks, Mom.

06

M Pool and Spa Town, how may I help you?

W Hello, _____
for two adults and two kids.

M Okay. Would you like to enter the spa right now? Admission is cheaper after 4 p.m.

W I see. There is only half an hour until then. We will come after 4 p.m. Can I still buy the tickets now?

M Yes, you can. _____
_____ until then.
Are the kids under 12?

W That's right. They are 11 and 9.

M All right. The ticket price for one adult is $60, and for children, it's $40 each.

W Are there any special deals for hotel guests?

M You can _____
_____ here at the hotel.

W Wonderful. I'm staying at the hotel, and my room number is 1205.

M If you want, _____.
Would you like that?

W No, thanks. I'll just pay for it now. Here's my credit card.

07

W We need to talk about our group project. Have you thought of anything?

M Well, there are a few topics in my mind. What about you?

W I thought of some things, too. So I was thinking about _____.
Is that all right with you?

M Oh, I'm afraid I can't.

W Is it _____?

M No, band practice is every Tuesday.

W Then why is it that you can't come?

M I have _____,
so my mom is coming to pick me up.

W I see. Do you have a toothache?

M No, _____.
I am so scared.

W Don't worry. It won't hurt so much.

M Okay. Thanks. Oh, I will text you the list of the topics I thought of. Sorry I can't come today.

08

[Telephone rings.]

W Thank you for calling Helping Hands. This is Janet speaking.

M Hello, Janet. My name is Chris. May I talk to the person _____?

W This is she. How may I help you?

M Is it all right to ask you a few questions over the phone?

W Of course.

M I'd like to apply for a volunteer position abroad. What are the requirements?

W We have an age limit of 30. _____
_____.

M I see. Are there any expenses I have to pay for?

W No, since our volunteer program _____ _____, everything will be free.

M That's good to hear. What kind of volunteer work will I be doing?

W Well, it depends on the area you're applying for. You could build houses or _____ _____.

M Great! When is the deadline to apply?

W It's Thursday, June 15th.

M I see. Thank you so much for your time.

09

M Hello, everyone. Congratulations on being selected to attend the World Youth Forum this year. Selecting 5 excellent students from among the 40 applicants was not easy. All the applicants _____ _____ and deserved to be selected. Well, as you know, the World Youth Forum is an international gathering to talk about _____ _____ to tackle global issues such as climate change. It is _____ _____. You are going to attend as representatives of our country. To prepare for the Forum, you will need to participate in a workshop before you go. I hope you have a great time at the Forum and the workshop as well. I will keep my fingers crossed for a successful trip to Paris.

10

M I found this website that compares hotel rates to one another. Would you come here and take a look at it?

W Wow, they all look great. It is hard to choose just one.

M Then let's start with the price. I _____ _____ from $80 to $120, so we have five choices.

W I see. I think we should spend no more than $100 a night. _____ _____ than accommodation.

M I agree. Oh, are we going to rent a car there?

W Well, it'd be a lot more convenient, but do you think you can drive there?

M I don't think I can. I'm not familiar with the area. Besides, we would have to buy driver's insurance, too.

W Let's forget about rental cars and _____ _____.

M All right. How about a water park? I think our kids would love to visit one.

W Definitely. Remind me to pack swimsuits, okay?

M Sure. Do you think we should eat at the hotel buffet?

W Yes, I think so. Let's _____ _____.

M All right, then. I guess this is it. I'll make a reservation.

11

[Telephone rings.]

W Hello, _____ Tom Brown in the marketing department? This is Mary Smith.

M I'm sorry, but I think you must have the wrong number. _____.

W I was calling 727-2565. Isn't this your number?

12

M Goodbye, Sandy. You are special to us.

W _____ for me, Bill.

M I just want you to know that _____ _____. You shouldn't forget us and your great memories here.

13

M Mary, my sister is having a baby.

W Wow, you are going to be an uncle! Congratulations!

M Thanks. The baby is due next May. I _____ _____.

W How's your sister doing now?

M She's having a hard time with morning sickness, so she spends most of the day in bed.

W Well, it must be really tough on her, but she has to get through it.

M I know. I feel like there is something I could do to help her, but I don't know what.

W Well, _____ _____. She'd love that.

M You think so?

W When my aunt was having a baby, she read a lot of books on pregnancy, _____ _____, and so on.

M There are so many books to choose from. Do you know any good ones?

W I will call my aunt and _____ _____.

14

M Hey, Rose. Mom and Dad's _____ _____.

W I know. I think we should do something special for them.

M Do you have anything in mind?

W How about getting them musical tickets? They've never seen a musical before.

M Hmm... That's not a bad idea but _____ _____.

W What do you mean?

M Well, how about making a video with pictures of Mom and Dad?

W That sounds fantastic. I will get and scan pictures from their photo album. Could you make the video?

M Sure. I'll make the video clip on my laptop. I'm going to add their favorite song to it, too.

W Oh, maybe we should put _____ _____.

M That sounds great. But I'm not sure where they are.

15

W Diana has to choose her career path now. She thinks she is not like any other girl. She hates dressing up and wearing makeup. She likes to play ice hockey and she wants to pursue being a hockey player as a career in

the future. However, there is some conflict between what she wants and _____ _____. Her family tells her to choose figure skating instead if she wants to be an athlete. Although she's won first prize in national figure skating contests, _____ _____. After watching Diana get depressed, her father decides to tell her that _____.

In this situation, what would Diana's father most likely say to Diana?

16~17

M Hello, I am David Clarkson. Today, I'd like to talk about one of the world's major concerns, microplastics. _____ which have broken down over time. They can be harmful to our oceans and aquatic life. They threaten the lives of millions of marine animals and fish. Marine animals and fish eat bits of plastic that float in the ocean. They are dangerous to us, human beings, in much the same way. When we enjoy our favorite seafood dish, we unknowingly eat microplastics. And that is not all. We are also _____ _____ of microplastics in our everyday lives. When we breathe, even when we breathe fresh air, microplastics come into our body and stay somewhere inside it. They can be hidden _____ _____, or even in the tea bags we use. According to one study, we can swallow thousands of microplastic particles from a single cup of breakfast tea. We are almost certainly _____ in one way or another.

06회 실전 듣기 모의고사

01 다음을 듣고, 남자가 하는 말의 목적으로 가장 적절한 것을 고르시오.

① 보안 업체의 변경을 공지하려고
② 외부인 출입에 대해 사과하려고
③ 새로운 제품의 출시를 안내하려고
④ 회사 내 정보 보안 강화를 당부하려고
⑤ 프로젝트 마감 기한의 변경을 알리려고

02 대화를 듣고, 여자의 의견으로 가장 적절한 것을 고르시오.

① 학교의 전통을 존중할 줄 알아야 한다.
② 학교 축제에 유명 인사를 초청해야 한다.
③ 학생회장 선거에 공정한 절차가 필요하다.
④ 학생회 임원들 간에 적극적인 소통이 필요하다.
⑤ 음악과 춤 공연 중심의 학교 축제에 변화가 필요하다.

03 다음을 듣고, 남자가 하는 말의 요지로 가장 적절한 것을 고르시오.

① 건강에 대한 과도한 걱정은 건강을 악화시킬 수 있다.
② 정기적인 건강 검진은 질병 예방에 매우 중요하다.
③ 연령대별로 필요한 건강 검진 항목을 알아두어야 한다.
④ 의료 정책은 치료보다 예방 중심으로 이루어져야 한다.
⑤ 질병 발생률과 건강 검진의 상관관계는 밝혀진 바가 없다.

04 대화를 듣고, 그림에서 대화의 내용과 일치하지 않는 것을 고르시오.

05 대화를 듣고, 여자가 할 일로 가장 적절한 것을 고르시오.

① 회원들에게 주말 연습 가능한지 묻기
② 공연 관람 후 설문조사 하기
③ 공연 음악 목록 정하기
④ 새로운 연습 일정 공지하기
⑤ 주말에 연습실 사용할 수 있는지 알아보기

06 대화를 듣고, 남자가 지불할 금액을 고르시오. [3점]

① $72   ② $90   ③ $108
④ $160   ⑤ $180

07 대화를 듣고, 여자가 학교에 일찍 온 이유를 고르시오.

① 과제물을 끝내야 해서
② 친구 엄마에게 차를 얻어 타서
③ 학교 버스를 평상시보다 일찍 타서
④ 지하철역이 집에서 가까워서
⑤ 엄마가 데려다주셔서

08 대화를 듣고, 특별 강연회에 관해 언급되지 않은 것을 고르시오.

① 작가 이름   ② 주제   ③ 장소
④ 날짜   ⑤ 입장료

09 De Von Gallery에 관한 다음 내용을 듣고, 일치하지 않는 것을 고르시오.

① 10월 11일부터 한 달간 진행된다.
② 연간 가장 특별한 행사 중 하나다.
③ 30명 이상의 인상파 화가의 작품을 전시한다.
④ 전시 예정인 작품은 총 300점 이상이다.
⑤ 다양한 후원금 때문에 입장료는 무료이다.

10 다음 표를 보면서 대화를 듣고, 여자가 빌릴 자동차를 고르시오.

Rental Cars at Rent-A-Car

	Model	Vehicle Type	Car Seat	Door	Insurance Coverage
①	A	van	○	automatic	third-person
②	B	van	×	manual	third-person
③	C	van	○	automatic	fully covered
④	D	van	○	manual	fully covered
⑤	E	SUV	×	manual	fully covered

11 대화를 듣고, 남자의 마지막 말에 대한 여자의 응답으로 가장 적절한 것을 고르시오.

① No, you don't need to take pills.
② Okay. I will follow the instructions carefully.
③ I will call my doctor and get a new prescription.
④ That's okay. Please add the last one to each pack.
⑤ Please take the pills thirty minutes after each meal.

12 대화를 듣고, 여자의 마지막 말에 대한 남자의 응답으로 가장 적절한 것을 고르시오.

① Yes. I am staying at the hotel next to the river.
② No, thanks. I will be there for only one night.
③ I usually have cereal for breakfast.
④ Please give me a room with an ocean view.
⑤ I'd like to include it for the second day only.

13 대화를 듣고, 남자의 마지막 말에 대한 여자의 응답으로 가장 적절한 것을 고르시오.

Woman: _____

① Yes. I'd like to join the debate club next year.
② I disagree. You should stick to voting for Chris.
③ No. Chris has to get perfect grades to get elected.
④ Of course. We should support Chris no matter what.
⑤ Exactly. You know one vote can make a big difference.

14 대화를 듣고, 여자의 마지막 말에 대한 남자의 응답으로 가장 적절한 것을 고르시오. [3점]

Man: _____

① I'm not sure. I'm allergic to tomatoes.
② Not really. I would rather plant roses than daisies.
③ Great. Let's plant some seeds when the weather gets nice.
④ Sorry. Our yard isn't big enough for planting anything.
⑤ We should hurry. The flower market downtown closes soon.

15 다음 상황 설명을 듣고, William이 Sarah에게 할 말로 가장 적절한 것을 고르시오. [3점]

William: _____

① How about playing the guitar instead?
② Don't worry. I'll take you there by car.
③ Thank you for taking me there. You are a lifesaver.
④ We don't have enough time. We have to do something else.
⑤ I don't think I can drive you there. Why don't you ask your father?

[16~17] 다음을 듣고, 물음에 답하시오.

16 남자가 하는 말의 주제로 가장 적절한 것은?

① the traditional clothes in Vietnam
② what each of the body parts means
③ the most interesting recipe in China
④ the symbol of a dog in Asian countries
⑤ the cultural differences that will shock you

17 언급된 나라가 아닌 것은?

① Thailand　　② Vietnam　　③ Indonesia
④ Taiwan　　⑤ China

🔊 녹음된 내용을 들으면서 빈칸을 알맞게 채워보세요. _____

01

M   Good evening. Thank you all for gathering here despite your busy schedules. Our company has just started a new project and we are launching a new product line next month. I know how hard you have been working and I appreciate your time and effort. In such circumstances, the most important thing for us to consider is security. So I ask all employees _____ _____ the company's data from any leaks or theft. You can change your passwords regularly, _____ _____ at night, and back up all of your data on a regular basis. Next month, the maintenance department will start to upgrade the security system, and all of you will be given _____ _____ and even to unlock certain doors. You will be notified with further information by e-mail this week. Thank you for your cooperation.

02

W   Hello, Jake. How are you?

M   I'm good, thanks, Lisa. How was your weekend?

W   I spent the whole weekend thinking about _____ _____.

M   Yes. I talked about it with other members of the student council, too.

W   What did they say? Do they think we should _____ _____?

M   Yes, they do. They think we should keep focusing on music and dance performances just like last year.

W   Well, don't you think our festival is overly focused on music and dance?

M   I agree. But isn't that what school festivals are all about?

W   I don't think so. I want to give a chance to students who have talents _____ _____.

M   You mean we should show different talents at our school festival?

W   Exactly. I think we need a change in our school festival.

03

M   Hello, everyone! I'm Dr. Jude Kohl, the host of your *Five-minute Health Show*. _____ _____, thinking that they are fine. However, there are many silent threats that can go unnoticed. That's why _____ _____. During an annual physical exam, screenings can reveal hidden health issues. For example, these evaluations can detect high blood pressure or cholesterol levels _____ _____. Now, let's take a look at some statistics about medical checkups in our country. Please focus on the chart.

04

M   Mia, I'm Jack, your new manager, and this is your desk.

W   Wow, everything is already set up.

M   There is _____ _____, so you can put your stuff in them.

W   Oh, three drawers are enough to organize my things.

M   And on the drawers, _____ _____ only for documents.

W   Thanks. I see there is _____ _____.

M   It's a welcoming gift from our department.

W   Thank you. And is the laptop on the desk my office computer?

M   Yes. That's your laptop. And I should apologize for _____ for you.

W   Oh, that's why there is a stool without wheels in front of the desk.

M   Yes, we will have a nice chair ready for you tomorrow.

05

W   I'm worried about our performance next month.

M   Me, too. I don't think we are ready to perform in front of an audience.

W It has been hard to get everyone together to practice at one time. But we still have a few more weeks to get ready.

M Yes, it's _____.
So, what should we do first?

W We need to make sure that all the members participate in each practice session.

M Sure. _____
_____?

W When? We were scheduled to practice every Tuesday and Thursday.

M Can we make it on Saturdays, too?

W _____.
They are eager to practice, but some of them may be busy on the weekend.

M You're right. I'll call each of them to make sure they are okay with the new schedule.

W Okay. I'll check _____
_____.

06

W Welcome to Wonderland Amusement Park. How may I help you?

M Hello, I would like to buy tickets for two adults and two children.

W Okay, how old are your children?

M They are 10 and 8.

W _____ for the whole day?

M Yes, please. How much are the tickets?

W For a day pass, one adult is $50, and one child under 13 is $40.

M Well, _____
on the price?

W Of course. It depends on what credit card you are paying with. I can check the discount rate for you.

M Okay, here you go. It's a Visa card.

W Just a moment, sir. *[Pause]* If you pay with this card, you will _____.

M That's great. I'll use that card.

W All right. *[Pause]* Here are your tickets. Have a great day.

07

M Hi, Grace. How did you get to school so fast?

W Hey, Josh. I didn't expect to be so early, either.

M I thought something happened because _____
_____.

W Oh, everything's fine. I left my homework at home, so I had to go back and get it.

M _____.
But that doesn't explain how you got here before me.

W Well, I got pretty lucky.

M Oh, did your parents drive you here?

W Well, not exactly. _____
_____, and my mom doesn't drive.

M Then why did you say you got lucky?

W When I was walking to the subway station, a car pulled over. It was Jane.

M You mean Jane from Spanish class, right?

W Right. She slept in and her mom was driving her to school. They _____, so that's why I got here fast.

08

W Henry, would you like to go to a special lecture with me?

M A special lecture? That sounds interesting. Who is the lecturer?

W It's Jim Scout. He is a famous writer.

M Oh, isn't he the one who _____
_____ on TV?

W Exactly. That writer is coming to our town for the lecture.

M Cool. Where is the event going to be held?

W You know _____?
It's going to be on the 3rd floor of the bookstore.

M I see. When is it? I hope it's not this weekend because I have other plans.

W Oh, it's February 22nd, _____
_____.

M Great. I'll add it to my schedule. By the way, is the lecture free?

W Yes. There is no admission fee, and I heard it was the writer's idea to _____.

M That's very nice of him. I look forward to it.

09

W Welcome, ladies and gentlemen. Thank you for visiting De Von Gallery. I am the executive director, Susanne Lee. I'd like to introduce a special exhibition which will be _____ _____. It is one of the most exciting events of the year, and we have prepared only the best for our visitors. We _____ _____ by more than 30 impressionist artists, including Monet, Renoir, and Pissarro. The total number of art pieces we plan to display is over 300. And the good news is, due to the funding from various donations, the admission fee charged to customers _____.
As this is an extremely rare opportunity, please do not miss out on it. I hope to see every one of you at the upcoming exhibition. Thank you.

10

M Hello, ma'am. Are you here to rent a car?

W Yes. I need to rent a car for my family for three days.

M What kind of vehicle would you like to rent?

W _____ since there will be six people.

M Okay. And, if you need a car seat, there are three models you can choose.

W I need one with a car seat.

M Certainly. Now, would you like a car that has automatic doors? You can choose between automatic and manual.

W _____. I think they will be more convenient for people sitting in the back seat.

M Okay. Now you only have to choose what kind of car insurance you want to sign up for.

W What's the difference between fully covered and third-party coverage?

M Third-party coverage only covers _____ _____ while fully covered also provides damage coverage and theft coverage.

W I think _____ _____.

M All right. Now I will show you to the car. Please follow me.

11

M Your medicine is ready. Have you taken this before?

W No. My doctor gave me a new medication because _____.

M I see. Take two tablets two times a day. _____ _____.

12

[Telephone rings.]

W Tahoma Hotel. How may I help you?

M Hello, _____ for a business room for two nights.

W Okay, sir. _____ breakfast during your stay?

13

M Clara, have you decided whom to vote for for the student council president?

W Not yet. There are three candidates, right?

M Yes. There are not many to choose from but it will be a little tough to pick one. Do you _____ _____?

W Not really. What about you?

M I know the second candidate, Chris. I'm voting for him because _____.

W _____ Chris because he's your friend, are you?

M Well, I think he is kind and trustworthy. He gets fairly good grades in class, too.

W I think someone _____ _____ should be elected. I'm trying to see what those candidates are capable of and who has the best qualities to be a leader.

M You're right. I'll think carefully and decide whom to vote for.

14

W Honey, I still can't believe we are moving into that beautiful house next week.

M I know! I really like the front yard. That's the best part of the house.

W I think we should make it into our little garden.

M How about planting some flowers? The yard will look more beautiful when the flowers bloom.

W I'm not so sure about that. I was thinking about something that _____ _____.

M Oh, okay. Then, how about trees?

W Trees are okay. But _____ _____. You have to cut off branches, sweep after all the leaves fall down, and there are other tasks to do, too. Do you really want to do all that?

M I don't think so. Hmm... If you want to start off with something easy, _____ _____?

W That's a great idea. I'm not an expert at farming, but I can always learn.

M I heard vegetables like lettuce and tomatoes are easy to grow.

W It could be a great experience for kids, too. They could _____ _____.

15

W Sarah is at her grandmother's 80th birthday party. As many as 30 of her family members gather together to celebrate the special day. Sarah _____ _____ music piece with her violin. She's been practicing for weeks. Her cousin William comes and tells her to play it after the dinner, so that everyone at the party can enjoy the performance. Sarah thinks this will give her more time to practice, so she finds a quiet place to practice. As soon as she places her violin bow on one of the strings, _____. She opens her case to see if there is _____ _____, but there aren't any left. So, she goes to William and tells him about the violin. Fortunately, William says that _____ _____. Since there is still one hour left, he _____ _____. In this situation, what would William most likely say to Sarah?

16~17

M Hello, students. Have you ever communicated with someone from another country? _____ _____? Today, we'll learn about the cultural practices of various countries, which will help you understand them more. First, in Thailand, the head is considered to be the most sacred part of the body. So you must be careful never to touch a Thai person on their head. _____ _____?

Is your palm facing up or down? In Vietnam it matters. When you call a person, you signal with your palm facing down, brushing your fingers towards you. In North America and Europe, _____ _____. If you did that in Vietnam you would be in trouble because it means you are calling them over like a dog. Burping in most cultures is considered to be rude. However in Taiwan and China, _____. When you burp loudly you are actually complimenting the chef.

07회 실전 듣기 모의고사

01 다음을 듣고, 남자가 하는 말의 목적으로 가장 적절한 것을 고르시오.

① 서비스 품질의 개선을 요구하려고
② 학생들의 협조에 감사를 표하려고
③ 세탁실 이용 금액의 인상을 알리려고
④ 기숙사 유지 관리에 문제를 제기하려고
⑤ 세탁실 수리의 지연에 대해 양해를 구하려고

02 대화를 듣고, 여자의 의견으로 가장 적절한 것을 고르시오.

① 어릴 때부터 진로를 설정해야 한다.
② 직업의 안정성보다 수입이 더 중요하다.
③ 다양한 분야를 탐구하는 경험이 중요하다.
④ 미래에 전망이 밝은 대학에 지원해야 한다.
⑤ 자신의 관심사에 따라 전공을 선택해야 한다.

03 다음을 듣고, 남자가 하는 말의 요지로 가장 적절한 것을 고르시오.

① 자원봉사는 공동체를 건강하게 해주는 역할을 한다.
② 자원봉사는 숨은 능력을 발견하는 계기가 될 수 있다.
③ 청소년은 단체 활동을 통해 사회성을 개발할 수 있다.
④ 자원봉사는 집이 없는 사람을 도와주는 기회가 된다.
⑤ 다양한 경험을 통해 자신에게 맞는 직업을 찾아야 한다.

04 대화를 듣고, 그림에서 대화의 내용과 일치하지 <u>않는</u> 것을 고르시오.

05 대화를 듣고, 여자가 남자를 위해 할 일로 가장 적절한 것을 고르시오.

① 쿠키 만들어 주기
② 선생님께 전화하기
③ 학교 과제 도와주기
④ 음악 수업 등록하기
⑤ 친구의 어머니 만나기

06 대화를 듣고, 남자가 지불할 금액을 고르시오. [3점]

① $280   ② $320   ③ $340
④ $360   ⑤ $400

07 대화를 듣고, 여자가 은행 면접에 가지 <u>못 한</u> 이유를 고르시오.

① 감기에 걸려서
② 준비가 덜 되어서
③ 신문사에 합격해서
④ 면접 날짜를 착각해서
⑤ 다른 면접 일정과 겹쳐서

08 대화를 듣고, 남자가 다녀온 여행에 관해 언급되지 <u>않은</u> 것을 고르시오.

① 여행 기간   ② 여행사   ③ 여행지
④ 여행 경비   ⑤ 동행 여부

09 특강에 관한 다음 내용을 듣고, 일치하지 <u>않는</u> 것을 고르시오.

① 강연자는 청소년 도서를 여럿 쓴 작가이다.
② 강연 시간은 질의응답을 포함해 약 90분이다.
③ 운동장 옆 새로 지은 건물에서 진행된다.
④ 주제는 시각을 넓히는 법에 관한 것이다.
⑤ 진로상담실 앞에 있는 신청서를 작성하여 신청하면 된다.

10 다음 표를 보면서 대화를 듣고, 여자가 구매할 자외선 차단제를 고르시오.

Types of Sunscreen

	Purpose	Volume	Duration	Waterproof
①	daily use	100ml	3 hours	○
②	outdoor	100ml	3 hours	×
③	outdoor	200ml	3 hours	○
④	outdoor	200ml	5 hours	×
⑤	outdoor	200ml	5 hours	○

11 대화를 듣고, 여자의 마지막 말에 대한 남자의 응답으로 가장 적절한 것을 고르시오.

① It's going to be next Wednesday night at 7:00.
② I have been playing the flute for five years now.
③ The concert is being held in the school auditorium.
④ Sure. I'd love to go to a classical concert with you.
⑤ Yes, I will. I'm going to perform a piece by Mozart.

12 대화를 듣고, 남자의 마지막 말에 대한 여자의 응답으로 가장 적절한 것을 고르시오.

① It takes 20 minutes by bus to the train station.
② Please do not stop until the traffic light turns red.
③ You have already passed the train station a minute ago.
④ I'm sorry, I am a visitor so I don't know the bus system here.
⑤ You should pass five stops and then transfer to another bus from there.

13 대화를 듣고, 여자의 마지막 말에 대한 남자의 응답으로 가장 적절한 것을 고르시오. [3점]

Man: _____

① Cheer up. Not everyone can enjoy such a privilege.
② I am sorry to hear that. I hope you get a new job, soon.
③ I see. Then you should keep working part-time there.
④ Maybe I should reconsider it, too. Thanks for the advice.
⑤ That's really good news. Congratulations on your success.

14 대화를 듣고, 남자의 마지막 말에 대한 여자의 응답으로 가장 적절한 것을 고르시오. [3점]

Woman: _____

① Sorry, I don't like flavored popcorn.
② Let me treat you this time. I'll get the bill.
③ All the tickets are sold out. We should just head home.
④ I don't think so. We only have a few minutes until the movie starts.
⑤ All right. Then I'll print the tickets and get some change for the games.

15 다음 상황 설명을 듣고, Jill이 Timmy에게 할 말로 가장 적절한 것을 고르시오.

Jill: _____

① Can I make a copy of your math handouts?
② Could you help me solve this math problem?
③ Would you like to study together after school?
④ When are you planning to return my notebook?
⑤ Please don't tell anyone I lent you my notebook.

[16~17] 다음을 듣고, 물음에 답하시오.

16 남자가 하는 말의 주제로 가장 적절한 것은?

① choosing a suitable breed of dog for your family
② dog breeds that are most preferred by trainers
③ growing popularity of unique animals as pets
④ benefits of pet ownership for mental health
⑤ difference between wild dogs and pet dogs

17 언급된 견종이 아닌 것은?

① poodle　　　② border collie
③ greyhound　　④ pug
⑤ beagle

01

M Good evening, students. This is the dormitory supervisor speaking. For the past two weeks, there have been some issues with the building maintenance, and again _____ _____ it may have caused you. Recently, a sewage problem has been reported in the laundry room in the basement. We have arranged for a company that specializes in such problems to repair it. Unfortunately, _____ until the maintenance team from the company can start their work. Once they do, the problem will be fixed within only a couple of days. Therefore, I _____ _____ _____ in the repairing of the laundry room. Thank you.

02

W Hello, John. How have you been lately?

M I've been busy searching for universities I can apply to.

W Me, too. For me, _____ is the hardest thing to do.

M In my case, I consider my options based on the outlook of the major.

W You mean, if you can get a job after graduating?

M Exactly. In the long run, you should _____ _____.

W Really? I think you _____ _____.

M But what if the major you choose based on your interests does not guarantee a stable job?

W To me, pursuing what you love is _____ _____.

M I see what you mean.

W I'm going to choose a literature major. I believe that there will be a way in the end if I study what I am passionate about.

03

M Good day, everyone! My name is Mr. Eliot, and I'm here to share benefits of volunteering _____ _____. Volunteering is more than just lending a helping hand. Volunteering reveals hidden abilities, aiding self-discovery. For example, _____ _____, you might find out that you're good at building things, _____ _____.

There are many good things volunteering, and discovering your abilities is one of them. Now, let's explore some more reasons why volunteering is an incredible opportunity! Please listen carefully!

04

M Eve, I can't believe the band concert is tomorrow.

W I know. We have practiced so hard for this. Should we go over the stage setting for the last time?

M Great idea. The curtains are open on both sides.

W Yes, that's done properly. I think it gives the feeling that you're watching a show.

M I agree. And _____ _____ that says "2023 Band Concert."

W Yes, it's just the way we asked for. It comes down from the ceiling. Oh, _____ _____?

M Our drummer says he feels more confident when he plays there.

W I see. There is the microphone stand in the middle for you.

M Yes, I already feel thrilled and nervous at the same time. Oh, where is the screen for our music video?

W _____. I asked the stage team to place the screen on the right so that you don't block the screen.

05

M Hi, Mom. I'm back from school.

W Oh, Kyle. You look a little upset.

M Well, I don't want to talk about it. Talking about it will make me feel worse.

W Okay, but sometimes letting your emotions out really helps.

M You know my friend Jim in music class? I am supposed to sing a duet with him for the music test.

W Is that what you're upset about?

M _____. I am worried that I will get a bad grade because of him.

W _____. Did you talk to him about it?

M I did, but he doesn't care. He said he was okay with failing the test. I don't understand how he could be so selfish!

W _____? We go to the same flower arrangement class.

M No, thanks. I think it's my own problem to solve.

W I understand. _____ _____? How about some chocolate chip cookies? I can make them for you.

M Yes, please. I'll feel better if I have something sweet.

W Okay. I'll start soon.

06

[Telephone rings.]

W Hello, Contemporary Art Center. How may I help you?

M Hi, I'd like to reserve seats for "Notre Dame de Paris." Are there any seats left for this Friday?

W Let me check. We don't have any seats left in the orchestra, but _____ _____. It's $100 per seat.

M That's fine. _____, please.

W Okay. The show is rated over 15. Are there any children under 15 in your group?

M No. I'm going with my wife and my parents.

W We offer a 20% discount for seniors. By any chance, are your parents over 65?

M Yes, they are.

W _____ when you come to pick up your tickets. May I have your name and phone number?

M It's John Smith. My number is 905-476-9162.

W All right, Mr. Smith. You will receive a text message shortly. Please click on the link in the message to pay.

M Okay, thanks.

07

M Cindy, I just got a call from a newspaper publisher yesterday, and they asked me to start working next week.

W I am so happy for you. You must be excited.

M I am. Oh, you said _____ _____, didn't you?

W Right, but I didn't go to that interview.

M Really? Oh, were you sick on the day of the interview?

W No, that's not it. I got _____ _____.

M And? What news did you hear from them?

W They liked my résumé and cover letter and asked me to come for an interview. But it was on the same day as the interview at the bank.

M I see. That's why _____ _____. How did it go?

W I think it went well. I sent a thank-you letter the day after, but haven't got any reply from them.

M Don't worry. You'll hear from them soon.

08

W Danny, long time no see. What have you been up to lately?

M Hey, Yuna. I just came back from a month-long trip.

W That's why I haven't seen you around on campus!

M Yes, _____. I think it was worth it, though I might get behind.

W That must have been a big decision. So, where did you go?

M I traveled around South America. I visited Peru, Colombia, Chile and Brazil.

W Your travel expenses must have been high. How much did it cost you?

M I had to spend everything _____ _____. But I think every single penny was well spent.

W If you learned some important lessons there, that's what matters, isn't it?

M That's right. And it felt even more special to me because _____.

W Why did you go with him?

M I wanted to spend more time with him before he goes off to high school abroad.

W I wish I had an older brother like you.

09

W Hello, students. This is your career counselor speaking. Since the beginning of the school year, numerous students have consulted with me about different issues. Listening to students' concerns, I thought it would be _____ _____, which will give you new inspiration. The speaker for the lecture is Jonathan Perry, who is the author of a number of books that are targeted at teenagers. The lecture will be about 90 minutes long, _____. It will take place in the special lecture hall in the new building _____. The topic of the lecture will be about how to broaden your perspectives. If you would like to sign up for the special lecture, you have to _____ _____ the career counseling office. I hope this special lecture can be a stepping stone for you to think deeply about your future. Thank you.

10

M Hello, ma'am. Are you looking for something?

W Yes. I want to buy sunscreen for myself.

M We have a wide range of selection, but these are the best-selling ones.

W There are so many. Could you recommend one that would best suit me? _____ _____.

M Then that crosses this one out. Sunscreens for outdoor activities provide stronger protection. How about the volume?

W The more, the better. I will be using it a lot.

M Okay. Now, how long would you like it to last?

W Since I stay in the sun a lot, I think _____ _____.

M All right. Now, we have two options left. Would you like one that is waterproof?

W I don't go in the water that often, but I sweat a lot when I do outdoor activities.

M The waterproof function prevents the sunscreen ____ _____.

W Good. I will take that one.

11

W Chris, _____?

M I am going to my orchestra practice for our upcoming school concert.

W That's right, you play the flute in the school orchestra. _____?

12

M Excuse me, which bus should I _____ _____?

W You have to take bus number 511 first and then get on another bus.

M Then, _____ before I get off?

13

M Hey, Amy. Did you have a bad day at work?

W It was okay, but _____ _____ at the same time is not easy.

M Really? I was actually considering getting a part-time job.

W Well, I don't recommend it. _____ _____.

M Hmm... I thought you were holding in there quite well. You seemed okay at school, too.

W Yes, but to tell you the truth, _____ _____ after I started working part-time.

M Are you sure that was caused by the part-time job?

W Yes, because I don't have enough time to study these days. I also _____ _____, so I can't focus properly.

M That's not good. Then why don't you quit?

W My contract says I should work until the end of this month, so I'm waiting for that.

14

M Honey, look at the lines at the ticket office.

W I know. Today is the last day of the holiday. I'm guessing that's why.

M _____?

W No, we don't have to. Do you see the ticket machines over there? We can use one of them to print the tickets we reserved.

M Great, and there are few people using them. It's only going to take a few seconds.

W So, I will go and print the tickets. Meanwhile, _____ _____?

M Sure, I'll buy some popcorn and drinks. Is there anything else you need?

W No, thanks. After that, I'll meet you by the escalators.

M Are we just going to _____ _____ until the movie starts? There is more than half an hour left.

W Then, what do you suggest we do?

M Well, I was thinking about going to the arcade. There are _____, just for fun.

15

W Jill is a new student at Emerson High School. She transferred just three weeks before the final exams, so she has a lot to catch up on. One day, Timmy, one of her classmates, says that Jill's notes look very organized. He asks her if he can borrow Jill's notebook, so Jill lends it to him. When Timmy returns the notebook, he says thanks to Jill and says _____ _____.

A few days later, Jill discovers that she doesn't have a couple of handouts from math class. _____ _____ before she transferred to this school. She wishes _____ _____, but she's not sure whom to ask. Then, she remembers Timmy telling her to ask him for anything she needs. In this situation, what would Jill most likely say to Timmy?

16~17

M Hello, everyone. If you are looking for a pet dog for your family, you can get useful tips from today's lesson. There are three important aspects to consider. The first thing to consider is the dog's personality. For example, poodles have very gentle and obedient personalities, and _____. Secondly, you must choose a suitable size of dog. For example, even if border collies are friendly and smart, they wouldn't suit a family that has never had a dog as a pet before. Larger dogs require special attention and are _____ _____. I would recommend a breed of a smaller size, such as a pug, to new owners. The last important thing to think about is the energy level. Let's say you would like a beagle as your pet. But if you can't deal with _____ _____, your relationship with your pet will be very bad.

08회 실전 듣기 모의고사

01 다음을 듣고, 여자가 하는 말의 목적으로 가장 적절한 것을 고르시오.

① 도서관의 이용 절차를 소개하려고
② 도서관 화재 시 대피 요령을 알리려고
③ 새로 변경된 도서 반납시스템을 공지하려고
④ 도서관 모금 기부에 직원들의 협조를 당부하려고
⑤ 도서관 리모델링으로 인한 임시 폐쇄를 공지하려고

02 대화를 듣고, 남자의 의견으로 가장 적절한 것을 고르시오.

① 도매로 구매해야 단가를 낮출 수 있다.
② 개업 전 철저한 고객 분석이 필요하다.
③ 친절한 서비스는 식당 매출에 영향을 준다.
④ 해충 방제 서비스를 이용하는 것이 안전하다.
⑤ 식당 운영에서 청결이 필수이며 매우 중요하다.

03 다음을 듣고, 여자가 하는 말의 요지로 가장 적절한 것을 고르시오.

① 학생들에게 정확한 정보를 가르치는 것이 중요하다.
② 책보다는 방송을 통해서 더 많은 정보를 얻을 수 있다.
③ 학생들의 사고를 키우는 다양한 정보를 제공하는 것이 좋다.
④ 교육 전문가가 되려면 다방면으로 뇌를 훈련해야 한다.
⑤ 시각적 자료를 사용하여 학생을 가르치는 것이 필요하다.

04 대화를 듣고, 그림에서 대화의 내용과 일치하지 않는 것을 고르시오.

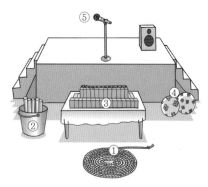

05 대화를 듣고, 남자가 여자에게 부탁한 일로 가장 적절한 것을 고르시오.

① 여행사 가서 여행 예약하기
② 프랑스 어학원에 대신 전화하기
③ 프랑스에서 시간제 일 알아봐 주기
④ 에펠탑의 역사에 대해 조사하기
⑤ 프랑스어 공부 도와주기

06 대화를 듣고, 여자가 지불할 금액을 고르시오.

① $99　　　　② $107　　　　③ $115
④ $123　　　　⑤ $131

07 대화를 듣고, 남자가 치과에 가는 것을 주저하는 이유를 고르시오.

① 선약이 있어서
② 치아 보험이 없어서
③ 드릴 소리가 무서워서
④ 스케일링하기가 싫어서
⑤ 치료비용이 많이 들어가서

08 대화를 듣고, La Tomatina Festival에 관해 언급되지 않은 것을 고르시오.

① 참여 인원　　　　② 숙박 시설
③ 사용되는 토마토 양　　　　④ 날짜
⑤ 참가 비용

09 Techrest Computers Limited에 관한 다음 내용을 듣고, 일치하지 않는 것을 고르시오.

① 컴퓨터와 관련 용품 임대 업체이다.
② 주문한 지 몇 시간 안에 제품을 받아볼 수 있다.
③ 추가 사용 기간에 대한 사용료가 발생한다.
④ 기술 지원 센터는 현재 공사 중이다.
⑤ 현재 전화로만 상담이 가능하다.

10 다음 표를 보면서 대화를 듣고, 두 사람이 선택할 이삿짐 패키지를 고르시오.

Moving Service Packages at Let's Move Express

Package	Moving Truck	Ladder Truck	Packing Service	Price
① A	4-ton	×	×	$900
② B	8-ton	×	○	$1,100
③ C	8-ton	○	×	$1,200
④ D	10-ton	○	○	$1,400
⑤ E	10-ton	○	○	$1,500

11 대화를 듣고, 여자의 마지막 말에 대한 남자의 응답으로 가장 적절한 것을 고르시오.

① Okay. I need you to sign here on the contract.
② No thanks. I think I can walk there from here.
③ Sure. It's an easier access to the subway station.
④ Certainly. Make sure to talk to the landlord about that.
⑤ I'm afraid not. But there are lots of buses to the station.

12 대화를 듣고, 남자의 마지막 말에 대한 여자의 응답으로 가장 적절한 것을 고르시오.

① Okay. I'll pick you up in the parking lot.
② No thanks. I'll just stay home and watch TV.
③ Of course. It'll be so convenient to take the subway.
④ Yes, please. My friends will be here any minute now.
⑤ It's all right. We are going to get something to eat first.

13 대화를 듣고, 여자의 마지막 말에 대한 남자의 응답으로 가장 적절한 것을 고르시오. [3점]

Man: _____

① Certainly. I'll write a book report on that topic.
② Okay. You should be careful of choosing an iPad.
③ That's a great idea. I'll ask my friend how to do it.
④ You're right. I would do the same as you if I read less.
⑤ Don't worry. I can finish reading it by the end of the day.

14 대화를 듣고, 남자의 마지막 말에 대한 여자의 응답으로 가장 적절한 것을 고르시오. [3점]

Woman: _____

① I agree. I think I'd better follow your advice.
② All right. Can you take it to the donation area?
③ Really? If you don't want to, please take them.
④ Are you serious? We do not take any dangerous items.
⑤ Sure. I'll check them out and decide if I want to get them.

15 다음 상황 설명을 듣고, Janet이 Peter에게 할 말로 가장 적절한 것을 고르시오. [3점]

Janet: _____

① Water yoga will be very hard to learn.
② Water yoga will let you be active and relax.
③ Surfing is my surprise for our wedding anniversary.
④ How about celebrating our anniversary in a cold area?
⑤ Why don't you try out an active sport like snorkeling?

[16~17] 다음을 듣고, 물음에 답하시오.

16 남자가 하는 말의 주제로 가장 적절한 것은?

① unique birthday customs
② the origin of birthday celebrations
③ various meanings of birthday gifts
④ Birthday Symbols: Cake and Cards
⑤ the wrong way to wish for good luck

17 언급된 나라가 <u>아닌</u> 것은?

① Canada ② Italy ③ Ireland
④ China ⑤ Vietnam

01

W Thank you for visiting Hansei Public Library. I have an announcement to make _____ _____. Since our library has received funding to renovate the building, we have decided to put in new carpeting. _____ _____, we have no choice but to close the library during the installation. So we will be closed from Monday, November 7th through Friday, November 18th. Any due dates that fall during this time will be extended to Monday, November 21st. We prefer that you return items before or after these closed days. However, if you need to use the outside book return drops, we understand. _____ _____. Proceed to the Lending Services Desk on Level 4 for issues related to the remodeling. We thank you for your support and understanding.

02

W Wow. Your restaurant looks great. I'm so happy for you.

M Thanks. I'm so excited to finally have my own restaurant. Come this way. I'll show you around.

W All right. The kitchen is so big.

M The kitchen is the most important part of the restaurant. _____ _____.

W What are those boxes?

M Oh, I forgot to put them away. Those are the boxes of sanitary gloves and masks.

W You are really well prepared.

M I will have _____ _____ all the time. Sanitation is not a choice. It is a requirement.

W I agree with you. Some restaurants are ignorant about _____.

M I know. Just to make sure, I have a pest control agent coming tomorrow.

W It sounds like your restaurant will be extremely clean!

03

W Good morning, instructors. My name is Marcella Meadow, and I am an education expert. A teacher expressed her concerns about students _____ _____ _____. Utilizing visual aids is crucial. A recent study on teaching methods might provide some insight. The study found that _____ _____ and remember information better. Therefore, when teaching your students, _____ _____. In the next session, I will explain how our brains receive information.

04

W Mr. Green, is everything ready for the afternoon games?

M Yes, I've set up the schoolyard. Would you like to see it?

W Sure, I want to make sure everything is ready to go before lunchtime is over. Why is _____ _____?

M It's for the tug-of-war game. It's the first game scheduled right after lunch.

W I see. Make sure the rope is put away after the game. What's in the bucket over there?

M _____ _____? There are five batons for the relay.

W Okay. Are those _____ _____?

M Yes, they are. There are more in the teachers' room.

W All right. Why are those two rubber balls _____ _____?

M We're going to inflate them before the game starts because it's windy.

W I hope the rest of the games go well in the afternoon. *[Pause]* It's almost time to start.

M I'll make an announcement with the microphone on the podium.

05

M Wow, there is only one month left until summer break.

W I know. Time flies, right? Do you have any plans for this summer?

M Yes. I'm going to visit France for two weeks.

W I wish I could go to France! _____ _____.

M You should go, too. Since you speak French, it would be _____.

W Well, this summer I don't have any plans to travel. I have to get a part-time job to save up some money.

M Oh, I was going to _____ _____. Do you think you can find time for me?

W Of course I can. I won't start looking for a job until the summer break anyway.

M That sounds great. When should we start?

W If you want, we can start next week. _____ _____.

M Fantastic! Thank you so much.

06

M Welcome to Five-Nine Pizza. How may I help you?

W Hi. I'd like to order pizza and chicken for ten people. What would you recommend?

M I recommend the Rose set. The set includes a sweet potato pizza and a fried chicken.

W How much is it?

M It's $30 a set. But if you order two Rose sets, _____ _____.

W That sounds like a good deal. I'll take three then.

M Would you like something to drink?

W Oh, doesn't the set come with a drink?

M Sorry, _____ _____.

W I see. How much is a drink?

M A regular size is $3 and a large one is $5. There is a soda fountain machine over there next to the door. Refills are free.

W Then I'll get _____, please.

M Let me check your order. 3 Rose sets, 9 large drinks, and one regular drink. Is that correct?

W Yes, it is. Here is my credit card.

07

W I have some extra movie tickets for today. Do you want to come?

M Sorry, I wish I could. I have a dentist's appointment this afternoon.

W Really? Do you have a toothache?

M No, I'm just going to _____. It's been a long time since the last time I had them cleaned.

W People say that we should visit a dentist regularly, but it's really hard to do.

M I know. _____ _____ when I hear the drill sound.

W Same here. I will never get used to that sound. Do you have dental insurance?

M I do. Some dental _____ _____.

W That's true. My mom used to be scared to see a dentist because she was worried about the cost. But luckily it's covered by her insurance now.

M I'm glad she doesn't have to worry any more.

08

W Peter, have you ever heard about the La Tomatina Festival?

M No, I haven't. What's that?

W It is one of the world's biggest food fight festivals. It's held in a small town in Spain.

M _____?

W Since 2013, official ticketing has been in place, limiting the number of participants to just 20,000 people.

M _____ _____ who go to La Tomatina?

W No, there aren't. Many people take the easier option of staying in nearby Valencia, which is 38 kilometers away.

M That's amazing. I can't imagine the amount of tomatoes used during the event.

W I know. The report says usually about 40,000 kilograms of over-ripe tomatoes are thrown in the streets. _____ _____.

M Wow, that's a lot! When is the festival held?

W _____ of August every year since 1945. The food fighting event only lasts an hour, but there are many other festivities to enjoy.

09

M Allow us to introduce to you our company, Techrest Computers Limited. Techrest Computers Limited _____ _____, laptops, printers and related equipment for short periods. Our rental system is so advanced that we can have equipment ready for you or delivered to you within hours of your order. We appreciate that sometimes things just _____ _____. That's why we make it so simple for you to rent from us. If you decide you want to keep the equipment for longer than your agreement, you will only _____ that you keep it, with no other fees. We promise to provide quality services with the highest standards of technical support. Have you got a short-term rental need now? _____. You'll be able to reach us by phone only. Get a consult today by contacting us at 070-885-4213.

10

W We need to decide which moving service we'll use.

M I was looking at this moving company on the Internet. It has great reviews from their clients.

W Really? Then let's take a look at moving packages they offer.

M Sure. Here is the list of packages. *[Pause]* Do you think _____?

W No, I don't think so. We have so many things to pack.

M All right. We need _____, too, right?

W Definitely. Do we have enough boxes to pack our things in?

M No, we don't. So we should _____ _____.

W You're right. Since it's our first time moving, it'd be better to get some help from professionals.

M Exactly. Besides, it comes with insurance. Finally, we have two options left.

W How come there is a price difference?

M Let me check. *[Pause]* Oh, it says the price depends on the number of movers.

W _____, then. With more movers, we can finish faster.

M I agree. Then let's go with this one.

11

W This apartment complex is not so bad. How much is the rent?

M It's $1,100, including all utilities except gas. This is _____.

W That's pretty good. _____?

12

M Are you running late? I thought you had a lot of time until the concert.

W _____. But my friends are already downstairs waiting for me.

M Already? _____ if you want.

13

W Wow, did you get a new iPad? Can I see it?

M Sure. I'm so glad that I finally got it.

W I know how much you've wanted to get one. So, what are you planning to do with it?

M Well, mainly I want to read books with it.

W Oh, e-books, right? I thought _____ _____.

M I still do. I like the feel of a book. I can hold it, turn the pages, and feel the paper.

W That's why most readers _____ _____. Also, they don't cause the eye strain that comes with an electronic device.

M Exactly. But since I can't carry multiple books with me, the iPad is very convenient.

W I see what you mean. In one device, _____ _____.

M Yes. Besides, e-books are also cheaper in the long run.

W That's true. But for me printed books are more economical since I don't read much.

14

W You've brought so many things here. Thank you so much for your donations.

M No problem. I'm glad to be a part of a good cause. Where do you want them?

W First, I need to check the things you have here. _____ _____.

M Oh, okay. What are they?

W _____, like liquid cleaners and paints. Did you bring anything like that?

M I don't think so. I have toilet paper, toothpaste, blankets, and some used clothes.

W That sounds perfect. Those things are what our shelter really needs.

M Great. Is there anything else?

W I need you to go through the things again and make sure _____. Some people ask for their things back.

M I went through my stuff many times before I came here. I don't think _____ _____.

15

W Peter and Janet have been married for five years. To celebrate their upcoming anniversary, they have decided to take a trip. They both agree on going to a country with a tropical climate since they love summer. Since Janet is really active, she wants to do activities such as snorkeling and surfing. However, Peter _____ because he's not good at water sports. Janet thinks that _____ _____, they should do something together that they both can enjoy. So she looks for what to do and discovers water yoga. She thinks water yoga is good for both of them because it accommodates people who aren't used to water activities. She wants to suggest that Peter _____ by explaining its benefits. In this situation, what would Janet most likely say to Peter?

16~17

M How do you celebrate your birthday every year? I'm sure many of you get presents and have a birthday cake with candles lit on it. However, there are some birthday customs that we aren't familiar with. In Canada, for example, people _____ _____. Bad luck cannot catch the child because the child is too slippery. In Italy, people _____. How many times do they pull the child's ears? It's one pull for each year. In Ireland, people lift the birthday child upside down and _____ _____. They bump the child as many times as their age plus one. The last bump is for extra good luck. Surprisingly, there is a country where you don't celebrate your birthday at all. In Vietnam, people usually _____. Instead, everyone celebrates together on "Tet", which is the most important celebration in Vietnamese culture. It is the Vietnamese New Year and everyone turns a year older on that day.

09회 실전 듣기 모의고사

01 다음을 듣고, 여자가 하는 말의 목적으로 가장 적절한 것을 고르시오.

① 신속한 대피를 촉구하려고
② 빠른 기름 충전을 요구하려고
③ 인근 공항에 착륙함을 알리려고
④ 관제탑의 신속한 행동을 요구하려고
⑤ 날씨 관계로 안전벨트 착용을 요청하려고

02 대화를 듣고, 남자의 의견으로 가장 적절한 것을 고르시오.

① 경험 많은 노인들의 말씀에 귀를 기울이자.
② 노인 공경에 관한 지속적인 예절 교육이 필요하다.
③ 맞벌이 부부들은 도우미를 고용하도록 권장해야 한다.
④ 정부는 다양한 일자리 창출로 취업률을 높여야 한다.
⑤ 정부는 기업이 노인들을 채용하도록 장려해야 한다.

03 다음을 듣고, 여자가 하는 말의 요지로 가장 적절한 것을 고르시오.

① 자신에게 적절한 학습량을 공부하는 것이 효과적이다.
② 인내심을 가지고 공부하는 것이 중요하다.
③ 복습과 예습을 통해 개념을 정리하는 습관이 필요하다.
④ 학교 수업을 중심으로 공부 계획을 세워야 한다.
⑤ 배운 지식을 실생활에서 적용하는 연습이 필요하다.

04 대화를 듣고, 그림에서 대화의 내용과 일치하지 않는 것을 고르시오.

05 대화를 듣고, 여자가 할 일로 가장 적절한 것을 고르시오.

① 재택 근무하기
② 진단서 신청하기
③ 의사에게 진찰받기
④ 집에서 휴식 취하기
⑤ 동료의 일을 대신하기

06 대화를 듣고, 남자가 지불할 금액을 고르시오. [3점]

① $100 　　② $108 　　③ $120
④ $126 　　⑤ $128

07 대화를 듣고, 여자가 시간제 강사를 할 수 없는 이유를 고르시오.

① 시급이 너무 낮아서
② 지원서가 누락되어서
③ 다른 회사에 취업해서
④ 듣고 있는 수업과 시간이 겹쳐서
⑤ 한 반에 20명의 학생이 너무 많아서

08 대화를 듣고, 기린에 관해 언급되지 않은 것을 고르시오.

① 키 　　② 서식지 　　③ 시력
④ 주요 먹이 　　⑤ 혀의 길이

09 The village gift shop에 관한 다음 내용을 듣고, 일치하지 않는 것을 고르시오.

① 휴일에 일할 봉사자를 찾고 있다.
② 최소 근무 교대 시간은 두 시간이다.
③ 기초 교육 후에, 다른 봉사자와 같이 일해도 된다.
④ 지원자는 18세가 넘어야 하며 혼자 일할 수 있어야 한다.
⑤ 이메일로만 접수가 가능하다.

10 다음 표를 보면서 대화를 듣고, 두 사람이 주문할 케이크를 고르시오.

Cakes at Chung's Bakery

	Type	Price	Shape	Picture	Flavor
①	A	$50	round	×	mocha
②	B	$60	round	○	vanilla
③	C	$70	round	○	mocha
④	D	$80	heart	×	vanilla
⑤	E	$100	heart	○	mocha

11 대화를 듣고, 남자의 마지막 말에 대한 여자의 응답으로 가장 적절한 것을 고르시오.

① I'm not sure. It hasn't arrived yet.
② I don't like it. It was too expensive.
③ It's great. I love everything about it.
④ I'm sorry. This machine is not refundable if used.
⑤ It's unhealthy. You shouldn't drink too much caffeine.

12 대화를 듣고, 여자의 마지막 말에 대한 남자의 응답으로 가장 적절한 것을 고르시오.

① Great. I didn't want to go on the trip anyway.
② Never mind. I'm leaving for school now.
③ All right. I hope it doesn't get canceled.
④ No thanks. I can clean the window myself.
⑤ Of course. I'll get the umbrella from the back.

13 대화를 듣고, 남자의 마지막 말에 대한 여자의 응답으로 가장 적절한 것을 고르시오.

Woman: _____

① I'm so grateful for your help.
② All right. Wish me good luck!
③ Okay. I'll keep my fingers crossed for you!
④ Sure. You need to learn how to write well first.
⑤ As for me, I'd put an emphasis upon the grade.

14 대화를 듣고, 여자의 마지막 말에 대한 남자의 응답으로 가장 적절한 것을 고르시오. [3점]

Man: _____

① I'm sorry, but it sounds a little boring.
② I agree with you. It can be very educational.
③ Of course. I will text you the details of the class.
④ That's nonsense! TV sometimes allows me to reduce stress.
⑤ I agree. After all, TV can help you relax at the end of the day.

15 다음 상황 설명을 듣고, Sam이 Evelyn에게 할 말로 가장 적절한 것을 고르시오. [3점]

Sam: _____

① You should consider buying a house instead.
② How about talking to the landlord and making a deal?
③ I'll make some phone calls to see if anything is available.
④ Why don't we find a place to stay together? Let's be roommates.
⑤ It'd be very difficult to find one within your budget in Newmarket.

[16~17] 다음을 듣고, 물음에 답하시오.

16 여자가 하는 말의 주제로 가장 적절한 것은?

① how to attract tourists with ease
② how to organize a festival effectively
③ cautions when enjoying local festivals
④ special tips for enjoying a local festival
⑤ things to keep in mind when planning a trip

17 언급된 행사가 아닌 것은?

① K-pop concert   ② street parade
③ fireworks   ④ flea market
⑤ light shows

01

W Ladies and gentlemen, this is the captain speaking. We have flown for more than thirteen hours from Seoul. We are about to land at Chicago O'Hare International Airport. We have been circling above the airport for twenty minutes, _____ _____ from the runways long enough to permit a safe landing. However, we have just received news from the ground that the mist is getting thicker and it is not _____ _____. We do not have enough fuel to stay in the air for that long and therefore we will have to make a detour to the nearest airport. A limousine bus will _____ _____. We apologize for any inconvenience that this might cause you.

02

W Greg, the other day, I saw your grandmother walking with a little boy.

M You must be talking about Daniel. My grandmother babysits him for her part-time job.

W Really? That's nice.

M Though it's not a full-time job, she is _____ _____. She said she felt a bit depressed being at home alone.

W I see. It's good to hear that she's happy.

M She got lucky. I heard many _____ _____. But it's very hard to find one.

W Yes, looking for a new job over the age of 60 isn't easy, either.

M Most employers have this wrong idea that the elderly are not capable of working.

W I know. Just because they are old doesn't mean they are useless. _____ _____.

M Exactly. That is why I think the government should encourage more companies to hire the elderly.

W That's right. With their experience and knowledge, _____.

M Yes, I couldn't agree more.

03

W Good day, first-year students! Welcome to our school community! I'm Ms. Brown, your principal. Today, _____. If you aim for a higher score, _____ _____. Think of studying as building a structure. The lectures and reading materials you receive are like the bricks that organize your knowledge. Each brick builds on the previous one, _____ _____, the structure could collapse. Therefore, studying with patience is absolutely vital. Now, your teachers will come out for each subject to guide you through how to study. It's going to be a great experience!

04

M Wow, this park looks amazing. This is the perfect place for our dog, Jason.

W It was so hard to choose which dog park we should go to. But this park seemed perfect.

M I know. On the left, _____ _____.

W Ah, but the pool is empty now because it's April.

M Right. The playground in the center looks so big. Jason can run around there. What's that in the back?

W That's a shower booth _____ _____ after swimming.

M That sounds convenient. Is there any place where we can eat?

W Of course. Do you _____?

M Yes. What's that for?

W That's for the barbecue and picnic areas. There is a barbecue grill you can use. But dogs are not allowed behind the fence for safety.

M I see. [Pause] Oh, where did Jason go?

W _____ _____. It looks like he already made some friends.

M Let's go over there and play with him.

05

[Telephone rings.]

M Hello, this is Brad speaking.

W Hi, Brad. It's Joanna. I don't think I'll be able to _____.

M Is everything all right?

W I'm not feeling well today. I think _____ _____.

M That doesn't sound good. Did you go to see a doctor?

W No, I didn't. I think I'll feel much better after a good rest.

M _____ these days. Besides, you'll get better faster if you get the right medicine.

W You're right. Once again, _____ _____. I feel really bad not coming in today.

M Don't worry about it. I'll have Rebecca cover for you.

W Would you do that for me? Thank you so much.

M Like I said, _____. You won't be of any good to us if you're sick.

W Okay. I will.

06

M Hi. I'm looking for hiking shoes. What types of shoes are available for hiking?

W There is a large collection of hiking shoes on this shelf.

M I'm going to Mt. Jiri this weekend. What do you recommend?

W What about these ones? They're $80. _____ _____.

M They are not bad. But do you have them in black?

W I'm sorry, but the black ones in this design are sold out. How about these black ones with high ankle support?

M Those are nice. How much are they?

W They are $100.

M That's great. I'll get a pair in size 260.

W Of course. Is there anything else you need? You can get 10% off _____.

M I need some socks, too.

W How about these long socks? _____ _____.

M Okay. I'll take those in medium, please.

W All right. Would that be all?

M Yes, please. Here is my credit card.

07

[Telephone rings.]

W Hello.

M Hi. I'm calling from Jefferson Library. I've reviewed your application for the storytelling instructor position. I'd like to see you in person for an interview.

W Jefferson Library? Oh, I remember. But I applied for the job months ago.

M Yes, but the position just opened up. _____ _____.

W I see. What are the hours and the pay?

M It's a two-hour class with 20 people from 3 to 5 p.m. on weekdays. You will get paid $25 per hour.

W 3 to 5? I'm sorry, but I have to turn it down.

M Oh, _____?

W I'm not. I've been unemployed since last May.

M Then how come you have to turn down the offer?

W I've been taking a few classes to prepare for a test. _____

M I see. That's too bad. You seem like the most qualified candidate.

W Thanks. _____, I will definitely apply again.

08

W As we are driving in, we can see the giraffes greeting us.

M They are really tall. _____?

W As the tallest land animals, giraffes stand 4.3 to 5.7 meters tall. Interestingly, baby giraffes are already about 2 meters tall when born.

M That's amazing. Where do they usually live?

W They _____ _____. They don't live in thick forests because it is difficult to see their predators there.

M I thought they could see anything because they are tall.

W They have great eyesight, but trees and leaves can block their view in thick forests. Would you like to give him some food?

M Sure. How do I do that?

W Just reach your arm out the window. _____ _____.

M Wow. Its tongue is really long. How long is it?

W It is about 50 centimeters long. Do you have any more questions about giraffes?

M No, I don't.

W All right. Let's move on to see the buffalos, then.

09

M Our village cannot be more proud to have our own village gift shop. But unfortunately, the shop is short-handed and we need your help. Currently, _____ _____. Although this is not a busy shop, it's essential that we have enough volunteers to provide reliable services and open at regular times. _____ _____. There may not be much to learn, but full training will be provided. If you would prefer to work with another volunteer for a short period after your initial training, this can be arranged. After this period you will _____ _____. Volunteers with good interpersonal skills are preferred. To apply, you must be over 18 and be able to work independently. If you're interested, _____ _____, or email kmsvillageshop@kingston.com. Thank you for your attention.

10

W There are so many cakes here. I don't know what to get.

M Since it's for Dad's retirement, why not customize the cake?

W That's a great idea. But I hope it's not too expensive.

M _____. We need to buy him some presents, too.

W All right. Should we get a heart-shaped one?

M I don't like the heart-shaped one. _____ _____.

W I know what you mean. Oh, we are going to _____ _____, right?

M Definitely. There are only two choices left. What flavor would you like?

W _____. That's his favorite.

M All right. I'll go to the cash register and hand in the form.

11

M Jane, you have _____. Where did you buy it?

W I bought it through the home shopping channel. It's $250.

M Wow, that sounds like a bargain. _____ ?

12

W David, did you look out the window? It's raining heavily.

M Really? _____ _____? I was really looking forward to it.

W _____. I'll make some phone calls to find out about your trip.

13

W Hi, Jinsu. Have you applied for the student exchange program yet?

M Not yet. I'm still _____ _____. Could you help me?

W Sorry, I don't know much about it. Why don't you ask Mr. Butler? He should be able to help you out.

M I already did. He read it through and said that it didn't clearly deliver my study plan.

W Well, keep working on it. _____ _____?

M I need to send out my portfolio and a recommendation letter.

W How about your grades? Are they okay?

M They're not very good. _____ _____?

W Maybe. But I think your essay and study plan are the most important parts of the application.

M Well, it's a little late to change my grades. I'll just focus on those two things.

14

M How long do you watch TV every day?

W I spend about four hours watching TV after coming home.

M Don't you think that's a little too much?

W Well, I may sound like I am addicted to TV, but I think it's okay.

M I used to watch more than five hours a day. But I stopped watching TV when I started to exercise.

W _____, but I usually enjoy watching educational programs, including the news.

M I admit that you can _____ _____, but you cannot control what you get.

W I know. Maybe I'll try to find something else to do.

M How about taking swimming lessons in the evening?

W Oh, I've always wanted to learn how to swim.

M The community center in downtown _____ _____.

W That's great. Can you tell me how to register for it?

15

M Evelyn, a high school teacher, is transferring to a new school in Newmarket this March. Since Newmarket is quite far from where she lives now, she decides to look for a new place to stay close to her school. She wants to find a house _____ _____ and within walking distance to school. Since she doesn't know much about the area, she calls one of her friends, Sam, who lives in Newmarket, and asks for advice. When Sam hears about Evelyn's situation, he thinks it would be best for Evelyn _____.
He thinks that if Evelyn lives too close to school, she won't have any privacy from her students and their parents. Besides, _____ around the school, and it'd be hard to find a place under $600 like Evelyn wants. So Sam decides to explain why Evelyn _____ _____. In this situation, what would Sam most likely say to Evelyn?

16~17

W Good morning, everyone! Welcome to Jinhae Gunhangje Festival. There are many local festivals in Korea, but this is _____ _____. This festival will be held from March 27th to April 6th and is expected to gather much tourist attention thanks to the K-pop stars' performances. In addition to K-pop concerts, performances by the navy military band and street parades will take place. In order to enjoy the festival properly, there are _____ _____. First, you have to set aside at least two days to fully enjoy it. And you should _____ _____ because they get booked up very quickly. Next, try to _____ _____ so that you can avoid the crowds and enjoy the beautiful cherry blossoms in the moonlight. One more thing, special events such as fireworks and light shows will be held every night during the festival. Thank you.

10 회 실전 듣기 모의고사

01 다음을 듣고, 남자가 하는 말의 목적으로 가장 적절한 것을 고르시오.

① 다양한 재활용 기술을 설명하려고
② 자원 재활용의 중요성을 강조하려고
③ 올바른 재활용 방법에 대하여 안내하려고
④ 새로운 재활용 용기의 사용법을 설명하려고
⑤ 시행될 재활용 프로그램에 참여를 권장하려고

02 대화를 듣고, 여자의 의견으로 가장 적절한 것을 고르시오.

① 악성 댓글은 분명한 책임이 따라야 한다.
② 인터넷 실명제는 사생활 침해를 가져올 수 있다.
③ 인터넷신문은 실명 구독자들에게만 배부해야 한다.
④ 사람들의 다양한 생각과 의견을 존중해야 한다.
⑤ 웹사이트의 댓글 쓰는 공간을 없애야 한다.

03 다음을 듣고, 남자가 하는 말의 요지로 가장 적절한 것을 고르시오.

① 칭찬은 적절한 상황에 해야 긍정적 결과를 얻는다.
② 회의에서 제시하는 아이디어는 실용적이어야 한다.
③ 피드백은 개별적으로 하는 것이 업무 의욕을 높인다.
④ 업무 피드백에서는 칭찬과 비판이 동시에 있어야 한다.
⑤ 직장에서의 칭찬이나 피드백은 구체적이어야 한다.

04 대화를 듣고, 그림에서 대화의 내용과 일치하지 **않는** 것을 고르시오.

05 대화를 듣고, 남자가 할 일로 가장 적절한 것을 고르시오.

① 초대장 가져가기
② 세탁소에서 옷 찾아오기
③ 휴대폰 보조 배터리 챙기기
④ 휴대폰 충전기 사기
⑤ 거실 전등 끄기

06 대화를 듣고, 두 사람이 지출할 금액을 고르시오.

① $330　　　② $360　　　③ $420
④ $480　　　⑤ $520

07 대화를 듣고, 여자가 집에 가야 하는 이유를 고르시오.

① 봐야 할 TV 프로그램이 있어서
② 30분 안에 공항에 가야 해서
③ 배가 고프지 않아서
④ 샌드위치를 좋아하지 않아서
⑤ 뉴욕에서 오는 전화를 받아야 해서

08 대화를 듣고, Haenyeo Festival에 관해 언급되지 **않은** 것을 고르시오.

① 행사 목적　　　② 주최 기관　　　③ 개최 장소
④ 개최 기간　　　⑤ 행사 내용

09 Liberal Arts Lectures program에 관한 다음 내용을 듣고, 일치하지 **않는** 것을 고르시오.

① 한 달에 한 번씩 개최된다.
② 모든 강연은 무료이다.
③ 강연은 최소한 일주일 전에 등록해야 한다.
④ 수강 후 설문지를 제출해야 한다.
⑤ 강연 목록은 이미 홈페이지에 올려져 있다.

10 다음 표를 보면서 대화를 듣고, 남자가 구매할 배낭을 고르시오.

Backpacks at Leisure and Sports

Model	Size	Material	Water proof	Promotional gift
① A	small	canvas	×	water bottle
② B	medium	polyester	○	water bottle
③ C	medium	canvas	×	power bank
④ D	large	polyester	○	power bank
⑤ E	large	nylon	×	power bank

11 대화를 듣고, 남자의 마지막 말에 대한 여자의 응답으로 가장 적절한 것을 고르시오.

① No. You should finish your chores first.
② I don't. I live too far away from my parents.
③ You should ask your landlord about the rent.
④ It depends. Living by yourself is not as easy as it sounds.
⑤ Yes. There are more benefits to living with your parents.

12 대화를 듣고, 여자의 마지막 말에 대한 남자의 응답으로 가장 적절한 것을 고르시오.

① Sure. I'll check if the exhibition is still on.
② Of course. This weekend sounds good to me, too.
③ I'm afraid I can't. I have to go to church on Sundays.
④ Friday would be better. I have something else the next day.
⑤ The tickets are not refundable on the day of exhibition.

13 대화를 듣고, 남자의 마지막 말에 대한 여자의 응답으로 가장 적절한 것을 고르시오. [3점]

Woman: _____

① No, Dad. I'll give it another try.
② Absolutely. I never thought I needed a tutor.
③ I'm afraid not. This problem is not for us to solve.
④ All right. I will go to school on my own from now on.
⑤ I agree. You have the ability to solve difficult math questions.

14 대화를 듣고, 여자의 마지막 말에 대한 남자의 응답으로 가장 적절한 것을 고르시오. [3점]

Man: _____

① Of course. I would be happy to do that.
② Sure. I will send you the résumé by e-mail.
③ That's too bad. But you will do better next time.
④ I am sorry. I'm afraid you are not qualified to apply.
⑤ Yes. I recommend not applying for graduate school.

15 다음 상황 설명을 듣고, Scott의 엄마가 Scott에게 할 말로 가장 적절한 것을 고르시오. [3점]

Scott's mother: _____

① Don't worry. I'm sure you'll do great.
② Cheer up. Your speech was not that bad.
③ Congratulations, I knew you could do it.
④ You need to relax. You deserve this award.
⑤ If you prepared more, you wouldn't feel like this.

[16~17] 다음을 듣고, 물음에 답하시오.

16 남자가 하는 말의 주제로 가장 적절한 것은?

① history of African American music culture
② origin and examples of American soul food
③ typical foods enjoyed on American holidays
④ newly arising food culture in southern USA
⑤ influence of slavery on nutrition of Africans

17 언급된 음식이 <u>아닌</u> 것은?

① fried chicken
② fried fish
③ cornbread
④ hushpuppies
⑤ meatloaf

01

M About 70% of the trash from our office is paper that can be recycled. Since businesses produce over 50% of the city's waste, it is critical that _____ _____. Recycling has an additional benefit of reducing our waste disposal expenses. It helps lower the building's operating costs. With this in mind, we are _____ _____. A flyer which describes what can be recycled will be given out in the afternoon. You can call Bob Geller from the maintenance department to obtain desk-side containers. These containers _____ _____ paper at your desks. With everyone's participation, I am confident that we can do our part to help the city's recycling efforts. If you have any questions, please call me at my extension number, 324. Thank you for your assistance and participation.

02

W Tim, did you read this article about the singer?

M I did. Did you also look at the comment section on that article?

W Yes, it was horrible. _____ _____.

M I know. I was really shocked to read them all.

W I understand that we have the freedom of speech. But _____ _____.

M What do you mean by going too far?

W Leaving comments is a way of expressing opinions. But some people spread false rumors or leave abusive comments.

M I agree with you. I don't like those online haters. They don't have to be so mean.

W Exactly. People should _____ _____.

M You're right. We all should be more careful.

W Yes, we should not underestimate the power of our words.

03

M Glad you could join us! I am Martin Lawrence, your business advisor. Today, let's discuss a way of giving praise and feedback in the workplace. It is essential _____ _____. For instance, saying, "I was impressed with _____ _____ in the team meeting," is more effective than saying, "You're really good at leading meetings." _____ and does not offer specific details. When giving feedback or praise, it is crucial to be specific. I will provide you with another example. Let's shift our focus toward the screen.

04

M Honey, here is the birthday cake that you requested this morning.

W Excellent! Please put it on the rectangular table. The flowers should be _____ _____.

M Oh, you almost finished decorating the dining room for her birthday party. It's like a fancy restaurant!

W We don't have to go to a restaurant for this party. _____ _____ at home because we have enough chairs.

M You put up a banner that says "Happy Birthday to You, Jane!" with her photo on the wall!

W Yes, it will be a photo zone for them. Please put _____ _____.

M A low square table? Why do we need one more table?

W I want her friends to put their gifts for her there.

05

W Jason, what time is it?

M Don't worry. We have enough time. The charity concert will start at 7 p.m.

W Okay. Do you have the invitation? _____

_____.

M Yes, I know. I remember we had a problem because we forgot it last year.

W We did. It was terrible. _____

_____.

M That's right. Oh, and it's pretty cold today. Do you have your scarf and gloves?

W Yes, I do.

M Also, we should not forget to take our phones, too.

W Of course not. _____

_____.

M Okay, I will. Are they in the living room?

W Yes, and I already checked. _____

_____.

M Oh, did you? Good. Thank you, Sarah.

06

M Honey, did you finish the budget plan for our trip this weekend?

W Yes, I'm almost done.

M So, _____

_____ on our trip?

W First, $200 for the accommodations.

M Oh, that's cheaper than I expected.

W Yes, it is. The original rate was $300. _____

_____ because we have a membership card.

M Don't worry too much about trying to save money. What about the food?

W Well, I haven't looked for places to eat yet. But I'm thinking about spending $10 per meal. Since it's a three-day trip, _____

_____?

M I think 6 meals per person in 3 days should be enough.

W That's 12 meals in total, then. We also have to consider the highway tolls. It will be around $40 in order to go and return.

M _____

_____. Let's start packing, then.

07

W It was so hectic today at work, wasn't it?

M There were too many meetings. I barely had time for lunch.

W Same here. I only had a salad for lunch because I had to stay at the office.

M Well, I'm just glad today is over. _____

_____ before I go home. Do you want to join?

W I'd love to, but I can't.

M But you only had a salad for lunch. Aren't you hungry?

W I am, but I have to get home before 8 o'clock.

M _____

_____?

W No, I don't like watching TV that much.

M How come you are in such a hurry?

W _____

_____ in New York. He said he'd call me at 8 p.m. in our time zone.

M I see. I was going to take you to the new sandwich place across the street.

W I'll join you next time. I'd better hurry. There's only half an hour left.

08

W John, do you want to go to the Haenyeo Festival?

M The Haenyeo Festival? I've never heard of it before. What is it?

W Haenyeo refers to the female divers in Jeju-do. They are known for their independent spirit and for being the heads of their households.

M So, what is the Haenyeo Festival about?

W _____

_____. The number of divers is declining since they are all over the age of 50.

M I see. Where is it held?

W It is at the Haenyeo Museum, _____

_____.

M When is the festival?

W It runs from September 20th to the 22nd.

M That's the weekend we are in Jeju-do. We should go!

W Yes, we should. When we go, we can also enjoy _____ _____. There will be fresh seafood dishes to try, too.

M Wow, I'm looking forward to it.

09

W Hello, everyone. I'm Jane Owens from the School of Liberal Arts. I'm pleased to announce our Liberal Arts Lectures program to you. Our program is 6 months long _____. Those lectures will be given by renowned lecturers including *2023 Korea Trend* writer Paul Kim. There will also be other guest speakers who will talk about their areas of expertise. All guest lectures are free, and you are welcome to attend, but you should sign up online for each lecture _____ _____. You must also answer a questionnaire after each lecture. Our first guest lecturer is James Miller from Newcastle University. He will talk about AI and its prospects. _____ _____, and I'll be sure to post the list on our homepage soon. To sign up for the program, check the Guest Lectures link. Thank you.

10

W Ricky, Leisure and Sports is having their big annual sale now.

M Oh, I need to buy a backpack. I was thinking about getting a light backpack for my trip next week.

W Have a look at the leaflet here.

M Okay, _____ _____ I have to carry.

W Then I think it should be at least a medium size.

M Yes, I think so, too. What materials are available?

W You can choose nylon, polyester, or canvas. When it comes to its material, I think polyester is the best.

M Well, anything will be okay except canvas. _____ _____.

W All right. Now, there are only two options left to choose from.

M That one is more expensive, but _____

_____, so it seems like a better choice.

W Okay. It's settled then.

11

M I heard you moved out of your parents' house. How do you like living on your own?

W It's not bad. Do you have _____ _____?

M I'm thinking about doing it next year. I'm in no hurry, but do you think _____ _____?

12

W John, _____ the new exhibition about dinosaurs this weekend. Are you interested?

M Of course. You are talking about the one at the Modern Museum, right?

W Right. _____. So I was thinking about going this Friday or Saturday.

13

M Anna, you look upset. What's wrong?

W Hi, Dad. Do you think I need private tutoring?

M What do you mean? I thought you were doing fine in school.

W I feel like _____, especially in math.

M Are your math grades bad?

W I think so. There are weekly assignments, but sometimes I get lost when solving questions.

M Having a private tutor is not a bad idea, but _____ _____ too much.

W That's what I'm worried about, too.

M It's more important that _____ _____ on your own. Do you still think you need a tutor?

14

W Hello, Dr. Quinn. Do you have a moment?

M Yes, Susie. What can I do for you?

W Well, I've been thinking about what to do after graduating. After talking to my parents, I've decided to go to a graduate school instead of getting a job.

M That's a good choice. _____ _____ to become a scholar.

W Thank you so much. But I need a scholarship because I cannot afford the tuition by myself.

M I see. _____ to apply for a scholarship?

W Yes. I have everything ready to apply for it, _____ _____.

M And what is that?

W _____ _____. Do you think you could write one for me?

15

W Scott is a high school student. He has participated in a relief program run by an international volunteering organization. This month the organization recognizes his contributions by awarding him a prize. In addition, _____ the International Volunteer Conference, which will be held in New York in two months. At first, Scott gets very excited about going to New York since he's never been abroad. However, when he finds out about the conference, he gets worried and nervous. He has to participate in a debate with foreign students and _____. He tells his mom about the conference and how nervous he gets giving public speeches. When his mother hears this, _____ _____. In this situation, what would Scott's mother most likely say to Scott?

16~17

M Hello, everyone. I am Joe Robinson on *Are You Hungry?* _____ _____ "soul food?" Many of you would think of fried chicken when you hear "American soul food." But did you know that soul food originated from mid-1960's African American culture in the Southern United States? It uses a variety of ingredients and cooking styles, _____ and were brought over by African slaves. We call it "soul" food because "soul" was a common word used to describe African American culture. Another typical American soul food is fried fish, adapted from the method of frying chicken. Other types of soul food

_____.

An example of this would be cornbread, commonly made with buttermilk. Also, hushpuppies are made with corn, salt and diced onions. Now let's look at a video of how each dish is made, and then have a discussion.

11 회 실전 듣기 모의고사

01 다음을 듣고, 남자가 하는 말의 목적으로 가장 적절한 것을 고르시오.

① 새로 부임한 선생님을 소개하려고
② 축제 날짜가 변경되었음을 안내하려고
③ 지역 특산품과 관련된 행사를 홍보하려고
④ 적극적으로 축제에 참여할 것을 당부하려고
⑤ 축제를 성공적으로 개최한 것에 대해 감사하려고

02 대화를 듣고, 여자의 의견으로 가장 적절한 것을 고르시오.

① 청소년 추천 도서를 읽는 것이 중요하다.
② 독서를 통해 다양한 관점을 접해야 한다.
③ 다른 사람의 말을 경청할 줄 알아야 한다.
④ 자신이 즐기며 읽을 수 있는 책을 골라야 한다.
⑤ 독서의 양보다 질을 더 중요하게 생각해야 한다.

03 다음을 듣고, 남자가 하는 말의 요지로 가장 적절한 것을 고르시오.

① 운동할 때는 빠른 박자의 음악을 선택해야 한다.
② 운동은 강도보다는 지속성이 더 중요하다.
③ 음악은 업무의 집중력을 해치고 생산성을 저하시킨다.
④ 생활 속 가벼운 운동을 지속하는 게 좋다.
⑤ 음악을 들으며 운동하면 운동 시간을 늘릴 수 있다.

04 대화를 듣고, 그림에서 대화의 내용과 일치하지 않는 것을 고르시오.

05 대화를 듣고, 남자가 여자에게 부탁한 일로 가장 적절한 것을 고르시오.

① 회의실 청소 도와주기
② 회의 결과 발표하기
③ 회의 자료 인쇄하기
④ 프린터 잉크 채우기
⑤ 팸플릿 가져오기

06 대화를 듣고, 여자가 지불할 금액을 고르시오. [3점]

① $66 　　② $68 　　③ $72
④ $76 　　⑤ $80

07 대화를 듣고, 남자가 쪽지 시험을 치르지 못한 이유를 고르시오.

① 학교에 결석해서
② 심한 감기로 조퇴해서
③ 시험 날짜를 잘못 알아서
④ 시험 교실을 잘못 알아서
⑤ 버스를 놓쳐 지각을 해서

08 대화를 듣고, Annual Charity Concert에 관해 언급되지 않은 것을 고르시오.

① 공연 시기 　　② 공연 인원 　　③ 공연 장소
④ 티켓 구매 방법 　　⑤ 기념품

09 테니스 수업에 관한 다음 내용을 듣고, 일치하지 않는 것을 고르시오.

① 지역센터 회원에게만 제공되는 무료 프로그램이다.
② 3월 20일까지 신청서를 관리사무소에 제출해야 한다.
③ 강사들은 전직 프로 테니스 선수로 전국대회 수상자이다.
④ 어린이 놀이터 맞은편 테니스코트에서 진행된다.
⑤ 테니스 라켓과 신발은 프로그램에서 제공한다.

10 다음 표를 보면서 대화를 듣고, 여자가 구매할 세탁기를 고르시오.

Best-Selling Washing Machines

Model	Price	Capacity	Wi-Fi	Color
① A	$600	14kg	×	white
② B	$700	16kg	×	white
③ C	$800	16kg	○	silver
④ D	$900	20kg	○	white
⑤ E	$1100	20kg	○	silver

11 대화를 듣고, 여자의 마지막 말에 대한 남자의 응답으로 가장 적절한 것을 고르시오.

① Yes. Music is my favorite subject.
② Sure. I will walk you to the music room.
③ No, the music room is in a different building.
④ No, thanks. I think I can find it on my own.
⑤ Yes. I just moved to this city yesterday.

12 대화를 듣고, 남자의 마지막 말에 대한 여자의 응답으로 가장 적절한 것을 고르시오.

① The class is about an hour long.
② I will tell you the shortcut instead.
③ It's been three weeks now, and I love it.
④ It takes about ten minutes by bus from here.
⑤ I do not like to take too many classes at once.

13 대화를 듣고, 여자의 마지막 말에 대한 남자의 응답으로 가장 적절한 것을 고르시오.

Man: _____

① I think we should stick with last year's plan.
② We should ask the club teacher for new ideas.
③ I will not participate in the club promotion event.
④ Let's give out leaflets to students who visit our table.
⑤ Don't worry. Many students are interested in science.

14 대화를 듣고, 남자의 마지막 말에 대한 여자의 응답으로 가장 적절한 것을 고르시오. [3점]

Woman: _____

① I don't think so. We will be better off on our own.
② Please call back later. I am currently in a meeting.
③ No. They do not provide package tours for Europe.
④ Of course. I enjoyed my trip to Europe last summer.
⑤ Okay. Let's ask for more information and choose the best one.

15 다음 상황 설명을 듣고, Lucy가 Jenny에게 할 말로 가장 적절한 것을 고르시오. [3점]

Lucy: _____

① I don't want to do a solo dance.
② It would be a good idea to change the music.
③ Why don't you join the high school ballet group?
④ Could you please shorten your solo dance a little bit?
⑤ I think you should practice more for the performance.

[16~17] 다음을 듣고, 물음에 답하시오.

16 남자가 하는 말의 주제로 가장 적절한 것은?

① history of tourism at Yellowstone National Park
② how wolves changed the entire ecosystem of an area
③ endangered species in national parks around the world
④ difference between predator species and prey species
⑤ impact of natural disasters on the health of an ecosystem

17 언급된 동물이 아닌 것은?

① wolves ② deer ③ birds
④ beavers ⑤ fish

01

M Good morning, everyone. This is your principal speaking. I hope all of you _____ _____ yesterday. It was great to see your different talents, not to mention the results of various club activities. I heard complimentary words from your parents and other guests who came to the festival. I know that everyone at school and from the local community has put a lot of effort into the festival. _____, the students and teachers at Jefferson High School, that we could _____ _____. You have made everyone proud. Again, _____ and enthusiasm for the school festival, and I hope you enjoy the rest of the year. Thank you.

02

W Jason, what are you reading?

M I'm reading a book called *How Positive Thinking Changes Your Life*.

W Oh, isn't that a bestseller? How do you like it so far?

M To be honest, I'm not really enjoying it.

W Really? Why not?

M Some of the things that the writer talks about _____ _____.

W Isn't that the purpose of reading? You can _____ _____ people have through reading.

M You have a point. But I still believe you should read books that you actually like and enjoy reading.

W Okay, but don't you think that will only _____ _____?

M When you put it that way, I'd have to agree with you. I guess I'll go ahead and finish the book, then.

W Good idea. Tell me what you think after you finish reading it.

03

M Good evening! Welcome to *Health Horizons*. It's Peterson, your on-air exercise coach. Are you ready to increase your exercise time? Music can help you do just that! Recent studies have shown that _____ _____ _____. This is because _____ _____, it can help your body move more efficiently. So, if you want to make your exercise time last longer, try working out with music. It's not just about burning calories, _____ _____. Give it a try from today onwards and see the difference it makes!

04

M Jamie, is this a picture from your summer vacation?

W Yes, it is. I had so much fun at the beach with my relatives.

M I love _____. When I see palm trees, I feel like I am traveling abroad.

W I know what you mean. The scenery was beautiful and the weather was perfect.

M That sounds lovely! Who is the boy flying a kite?

W That's my cousin Jim. He made a beautiful kite himself just for the vacation.

M Wow. That must have been a lot of work. I see _____ _____ next to your cousin.

W That's his younger brother, Matt. He was wearing a hat because he doesn't like sunlight.

M And look at the girl next to him! Is that you?

W Yes, it's me.

M Your hair is tied back in a ponytail! You look cute. It seems like you're making something with the sand. What is it?

W A sandcastle. _____ because no one helped me, but I had a lot of fun. And when I finished, it felt very rewarding.

M I'm glad you had fun. You needed that rest.

W I know. I wish I could go there again next year.

05

W Jack, we should check if we have everything for the meeting this afternoon.

M Oh, right, the meeting. I need _____ _____. It's a little messy from last night's seminar.

W Would you like me to give you a hand?

M It's okay. I can do it by myself.

W All right. What else do we need to do?

M Oh, we _____ from the design company.

W Actually, they sent the pamphlets to our office this morning, so we don't have to worry about them.

M That's great. I should _____ _____ for the meeting.

W Oh, but we need new ink. We just ran out of it this morning.

M Could you _____ while I go upstairs and get the meeting room ready?

W Of course. I can do that.

06

M Welcome to Olive Cosmetics. How may I help you?

W Hello, I'm looking for perfume for my mother.

M Do you have any particular perfume in your mind?

W I brought a sample she wears. _____ _____?

M All right. *[Pause]* It seems like she likes floral scents. How about this one by Marc Kors?

W *[Inhale]* Wow, it's _____ _____. How much is it?

M This 50-milliliter bottle is $60. But _____ _____ for $20 more.

W What's in the gift set?

M It includes another 5-milliliter bottle, hand cream, and a scented candle.

W That sounds like a good deal. I'll take the gift set.

M Of course. _____?

W No, thanks. Oh, can I use this 10% coupon?

M Certainly. How would you like to pay?

W I'll pay by credit card, please.

07

W Peter, you look upset. What's the matter?

M I am worried about my physics grades.

W Why? You have always worked hard in physics. It's your favorite subject.

M I know. That's why I am even more upset. It feels like all the hard work I've put in was wasted.

W Why do you say that?

M Well, there was a really important quiz last week, which is worth 15% of the grade.

W I heard it was difficult. Did you _____ _____?

M No, that's not it. I missed the quiz.

W That's not good. How come you couldn't take it?

M To start with, _____ the night before.

W Did you miss school on the day of the quiz because you were sick with a cold?

M No. I went to school because I really studied hard for the quiz and wanted to take it.

W Then why didn't you take it?

M The cold got a lot worse and I _____ _____ the physics class started.

W That's too bad. I am sure there is a way to make up the quiz.

08

W Ben, are you performing at the Annual Charity Concert?

M Of course. I can't believe it's already September. _____.

W I know. How is your preparation going?

M I have been practicing for my performance for the last two months. I hope people like it.

W I can't wait to see it.

M I'm already nervous.

W I'm sure you'll do great. Is the event happening at the same place as last year?

M No. We decided to _____ _____. It's going to be at the community concert hall.

W That's great. It's closer to my place than last year's venue.

M That's good. Oh, I almost forgot to tell you _____ _____ on your phone.

W What's the app for?

M This year, you can get a souvenir if you buy your ticket through the app.

W That's great. I will do that right now. What's the souvenir?

M I heard they will _____ with your name on it.

09

W Good morning. This is the manager of the Eden Community Center. I would like to introduce our new tennis lessons starting next month. It's a complimentary program offered only to the members of our community center, _____ _____. Since a lot of members wish to sign up for the program, you have to submit a registration form _____. Please understand that registrations after that date will not be accepted. All the instructors are _____ _____, all of whom have won awards in national tournaments. The lessons will take place at the tennis court right across from the children's playground. Please bring your own tennis rackets and shoes, as _____ _____. We wish to offer you the best opportunities, and we hope you enjoy the program. Thank you.

10

M Hello, madam. May I help you?

W I'm looking for a washing machine.

M Okay. _____ _____. How much are you willing to spend?

W I do not want to spend over $1,000.

M All right. That crosses one model out. The next important thing would be the capacity.

W There are five people in my family, so we have a lot of laundry.

M Then I recommend one that can _____ _____.

W Okay. And I would like it to have Wi-Fi so that I can control it when I'm not home.

M I see. That leaves us with two options. Is there a specific color you'd like?

W _____, so I'll take that one.

M That's a good choice. It's one of our best models.

11

W Excuse me, _____. Can I help you?

M Thank you so much. _____ _____.

W It's just around the corner. Are you a new student?

12

M Hi, Susan. Where are you going?

W Oh, Tom. _____. I'm going to my yoga class.

M Really? I didn't know you practiced yoga. _____ _____ the class?

13

W Hello, Ryan. You're earlier than usual.

M Yes. I was waiting for you so we could discuss the club promotion event.

W Right. We need to recruit more members for our science club.

M How about _____ _____ about our science club?

W Last year, that did not work well. I think we should change our plan.

M Hmm... Many students think a science club is difficult and boring.

W How can we make it look fun and interesting?

M How about _____ at our table?

W That sounds like a good idea. That way, _____ _____.

M Right. And we won't have to walk up to anyone.

W Then we need to decide on _____ _____.

14

W Honey, we have to plan our trip for this winter.

M You're right. I am so excited to go to Europe for the first time.

W Me, too. But I can't decide whether we should _____ _____.

M Well, I think going on a package tour is a good idea.

W What do you think is good about a package tour?

M We don't have to _____ _____ to visit. The travel agency does everything for us.

W But we can't choose where to eat or what activities to do.

M I wish we could, but honey, do you think we _____ _____?

W You have a point.

M By going on a package tour, _____ _____, too.

W You're right. I think I will go with your decision.

M Good. Should we call the travel agency?

15

W Lucy is in a high school ballet group. She and her teammate Jenny are preparing for a classical ballet performance at a community event. They have discussed everything together from the beginning, including the music and their costumes. Apart from the dance duet, they have to _____ _____. Lucy's solo dance is right after Jenny's. On the day that they combined all the dances together, Lucy could not _____, because Jenny's solo was longer than expected. Lucy was a little upset because she had prepared very hard for her dance, too. She wants _____ _____. In this situation, what would Lucy most likely say to Jenny?

16~17

M Hello, students. Today, we are going to talk about _____ an ecosystem. The classic example is what happened in Yellowstone National Park. Wolves in the park had been absent for 70 years due to excessive hunting. During that period, the number of deer, wolves' favorite prey, increased tremendously. _____ _____ and this destroyed the vegetation. So people decided to re-introduce wolves into the park. _____, they caused the most remarkable effects. Deer started avoiding certain parts of the park, and this _____ _____. Because the trees were growing back, the number of birds started to increase greatly. Beavers _____ _____ because beavers like to eat tree bark. They also built dams in the river, and this made habitats for many other species. All of this led to the revival of the ecosystem of Yellowstone National Park.

12회 실전 듣기 모의고사

01 다음을 듣고, 남자가 하는 말의 목적으로 가장 적절한 것을 고르시오.

① 새로 도입한 멘토 프로그램에 대해 소개하려고
② 지역 노숙자 쉼터에서 봉사활동을 권유하려고
③ 서비스 센터의 조직 개편에 대해 공지하려고
④ 다양한 여가 생활을 즐기도록 권장하려고
⑤ 새로 입사한 직원에 대해 알리려고

02 대화를 듣고, 여자의 의견으로 가장 적절한 것을 고르시오.

① 전공을 결정하기 전에 주변 어른들에게 조언을 구해야 한다.
② 다양한 직업 선택이 가능한 전공을 선택하는 것이 좋다.
③ 복수 전공을 하면 다양한 분야에서 일할 수 있다.
④ 좋아하는 전공을 쉽게 포기하지 말아야 한다.
⑤ 여러 경험을 통해 견문을 넓혀야 한다.

03 다음을 듣고, 남자가 하는 말의 요지로 가장 적절한 것을 고르시오.

① 적당한 긴장과 불안은 삶의 활기가 되기도 한다.
② 긴장과 불안을 해소하려면 그 원인을 알아야 한다.
③ 심호흡은 긴장과 불안 해소에 도움이 될 수 있다.
④ 제대로 된 숨쉬기 운동은 혈액 순환을 돕는다.
⑤ 명상은 불안한 심리 안정에 도움이 된다.

04 대화를 듣고, 그림에서 대화의 내용과 일치하지 않는 것을 고르시오.

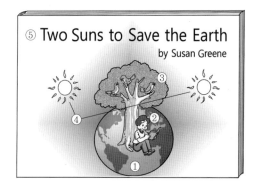

⑤ Two Suns to Save the Earth
by Susan Greene

05 대화를 듣고, 여자가 할 일로 가장 적절한 것을 고르시오.

① 벼룩시장 구경하기
② 문화센터 방문하기
③ 벼룩시장을 홍보하기
④ 문자로 이메일 주소 보내기
⑤ 부모님과 함께 행사 참여하기

06 대화를 듣고, 남자가 지불할 금액을 고르시오.

① $120   ② $200   ③ $260
④ $280   ⑤ $400

07 대화를 듣고, 여자가 일을 그만두려는 이유를 고르시오.

① 자기 개발을 위해 유학 가고 싶어서
② 다른 곳에서 일자리 제의를 받아서
③ 새로운 것을 배우기 위해서
④ 2주 동안 여행을 가고 싶어서
⑤ 적성에 맞는 새 일을 찾기 위해서

08 대화를 듣고, contemporary art exhibition에 관해 언급되지 않은 것을 고르시오.

① 입장료   ② 주차장   ③ 마지막 날짜
④ 예술가 이름   ⑤ 전시 내용

09 Toddler Trek에 관한 다음 내용을 듣고, 일치하지 않는 것을 고르시오.

① 참여 대상은 16개월에서 24개월의 아이들이다.
② 대조를 통해 소통하는 방법을 배우도록 도와준다.
③ 어른과 같이 참여해야 한다.
④ 참여 인원수는 20명으로 제한한다.
⑤ 이번 달에 등록하면 할인을 받을 수 있다.

10 다음 표를 보면서 대화를 듣고, 남자가 구매할 와인을 고르시오.

Wine at Wine Yard

Brand	Type	Price	Country	Sweetness
① A	white	$40	France	semi-sweet
② B	red	$40	France	bitter
③ C	red	$45	Chile	sweet
④ D	red	$50	Italy	semi-sweet
⑤ E	red	$70	France	bitter

11 대화를 듣고, 여자의 마지막 말에 대한 남자의 응답으로 가장 적절한 것을 고르시오.

① Yeah. Dancing is my favorite hobby.
② Cool! I can take whatever lesson I want.
③ Really? Then I'll go and sign up right now.
④ No, thanks. I've already had enough information.
⑤ Don't worry. Dance costumes aren't very expensive.

12 대화를 듣고, 남자의 마지막 말에 대한 여자의 응답으로 가장 적절한 것을 고르시오.

① Certainly. You can test drive mine.
② Not me. I never had the chance to meet him.
③ I think so. Electric cars are cheap in long term.
④ Of course. I can give you his business card if you want.
⑤ I'm afraid not. You need to have your driver's license with you.

13 대화를 듣고, 여자의 마지막 말에 대한 남자의 응답으로 가장 적절한 것을 고르시오. [3점]

Man: _____

① I agree. I prefer taking a bus to driving.
② Okay. I hope he doesn't get too disappointed.
③ Sorry. Let me see what I can do for the bus tour.
④ I don't know. Taking a bus costs less but takes longer.
⑤ That's a relief. We can cancel the trip anytime we want.

14 대화를 듣고, 남자의 마지막 말에 대한 여자의 응답으로 가장 적절한 것을 고르시오. [3점]

Woman: _____

① That's true. I don't like reading news articles.
② Maybe. But I don't want to major in politics.
③ Too bad. I don't use most of the apps.
④ No, thanks. You don't have to tell me bad news.
⑤ I hope so. I won't give up on reading about politics, then.

15 다음 상황 설명을 듣고, Jackson이 Deborah에게 할 말로 가장 적절한 것을 고르시오. [3점]

Jackson: _____

① I am not sure about what to put in my profile.
② You need to be more specific about your hobbies.
③ You have achieved a lot. How about adding that?
④ Why don't you try something else? Teaching is boring.
⑤ There is nothing wrong with it. Let's post it online today.

[16~17] 다음을 듣고, 물음에 답하시오.

16 여자가 하는 말의 주제로 가장 적절한 것은?

① how Greek myths describes octopuses
② places in the ocean octopuses should inhabit
③ the different shapes octopuses can change into
④ the features which make octopuses stand out
⑤ the ink sac that makes octopuses powerful

17 언급된 문어의 부위가 아닌 것은?

① eyes ② skin ③ arms
④ suckers ⑤ ink sac

01

M Good morning, everyone. Ann Thompson is joining our company to _____ customer service. Her first day is Tuesday, April 8th. Ann has worked in customer service for many years and we are happy to welcome her to our team. _____ for her first week on the job. Ann's new employee mentor is Sam Banks, so if you have questions, you can talk with Sam. Take a moment to _____ _____. She says that some of her hobbies include raising cats, dancing, and volunteering at a local homeless shelter. Thanks for joining me in welcoming Ann to the team.

02

W Kevin, is something troubling you? You look so worried.

M Well, I've been thinking about my major for a while.

W What about your major?

M I'm _____ computer engineering. There are more career options related to it.

W Is that the only reason _____ _____?

M I love chemistry and really enjoy learning it. But I'm not sure what I can do with it.

W You are only a sophomore in college. _____ _____? You shouldn't be so quick to give up what you love.

M Are you saying I should stick with it?

W You may not have learned enough chemistry. As you know, students build up basic knowledge during their first two years in college.

M Okay.

W As you learn chemistry in depth, it will broaden your perspective on possible careers.

M You're right. Besides, another year wouldn't do me any harm.

W Exactly. This year might _____ _____.

03

M Hello, dear viewers! I'm Dr. Winfield, your on-air doctor. We all experience tension or anxiety in our busy lives, and it's important _____ _____. Here's _____ _____: take a deep breath when you feel tense or anxious. Inhale through your nose, then exhale slowly while making a "whoo" sound. This practice only takes a few minutes, but _____ _____.

In moments of tension or anxiety, remember to breathe deeply. Give it a try today! I'll be back soon with more health tips.

04

M Ms. Greene, I made a few changes on your book cover.

W Okay. The release date is getting near. We'd better hurry up and finalize it.

M Let's go over the changes one by one.

W All right. _____ _____.

M Since your book is about making the earth clean, I made the globe clean.

W I see. I like the boy under the tree. He's leaning with his back against the trunk.

M He looks calm and peaceful _____ _____.

W You added branches to the tree like I suggested.

M I liked your suggestion. You can see the birds more clearly on the branches.

W I know. I didn't want _____ _____.

M Right. How do you like the title, *Two Suns to Save the Earth*, written under the globe?

W Perfect. _____ _____.

M I also put your name under the title.

W That's fine. Overall, this design suits the title.

05

W Kyle, did you know about a flea market opening near Mirae Tower?

M Sure. My mom is one of the organizers preparing the event.

W Really? I found out about it this morning. I don't think _____ _____.

M I know. That's because there are not enough volunteers.

W If necessary, I can help out. I'd like to take part in it.

M Thanks. I'll talk to my mom when I go to the community center after school.

W I don't _____ after school today. I can go with you if you want.

M Actually, there is something else you should do.

W What is it?

M _____ by text message? I'll send you a form to fill out.

W I'll do that right now. My phone is in my jacket over there.

M Okay. Oh, make sure you _____ _____, too.

06

W How may I help you, sir?

M I'm looking for a gift for my wife.

W _____?

M Yes, it's for our 20th anniversary. Could you recommend something?

W Of course. We have a wide range of selections. How about this gold necklace? It's one of the most popular designs this season.

M It looks beautiful. How much is it?

W It's $200.

M That's a little expensive for a single necklace, isn't it?

W Well, it might seem so. But if you _____ _____, we offer a special discount.

M How much are they together, the necklace and the earrings?

W They were _____ _____, but we are offering a 30% discount off the original price.

M That sounds like a good deal. I'll take them. And can I use this $20 coupon?

W I'm afraid you can't because they are already _____ _____.

M Okay. Here's my credit card.

07

W Sir, may I talk to you for a minute?

M Mary, come on in. Is there something wrong?

W I'd like to give you my two-week notice.

M This is so sudden. _____ _____?

W Yes, I have. It wasn't easy for me to quit like this. I'm sorry.

M You are one of the best workers here. I didn't expect you'd leave.

W Me neither, sir. But _____ since I've been here for so long.

M Oh, did you get a job offer from somewhere else?

W No, I'm not moving on to another job.

M Then, can you tell me why you're leaving? Maybe we can work this out.

W I feel like _____. I'd like to take some time off to learn something new.

M I understand. I'll _____ _____.

W Thank you for understanding.

M I wish you only the best.

08

W Fred, are you planning to go and see the contemporary art exhibition?

M I haven't decided yet. How about you?

W I'm visiting this weekend. _____ _____ like us. Why hesitate?

M True. Since it is a must-see exhibit, there will be a lot of people.

W Exactly. That's why I'm going to take the subway. The traffic there is just unbelievable.

M You really should because _____ _____.

W I know. Besides, the City Hall subway station is nearby.

M That's right. When is the last day of the exhibition?

W I believe _____ _____.

M Maybe I should go before it's over.

W You shouldn't miss this opportunity. There are many sculptures and paintings by promising contemporary artists.

M Don't worry. I won't.

09

W Hello, listeners. I'm pleased to introduce a fun and interactive program called "Toddler Trek." This interactive indoor program is designed for toddlers from 16 to 24 months. At this age, _____ _____. They are running, communicating, and showing interest in friends. The program uses contrast themes to _____ _____. Your child will learn loud and quiet, high and low, and in and out. Through our program, toddlers can build skills like jumping and balancing. As they feel safe with a familiar adult by their side, _____ _____ an adult to participate. The program goes from March 28th to May 20th. Register in advance since _____ 20 people. The registration price is $120, but we offer a 10% discount to those who register this week. For more information, please visit our website, www. toddlertrek.com.

10

W Welcome to Wine Yard. Can I help you find anything?

M Yes, please. Would you recommend wine for beginners like me?

W Of course. There are two types of wine, white and red.

M Which wine is good with a steak?

W I strongly recommend a red one. _____ _____.

M Okay. Can you show me the ones under $60?

W Of course. There are also countries to choose from.

M _____ _____?

W In general French wines have a bitter taste. The ones from Chile and Italy are sweet with a fruity taste.

M Since it's my first time, I'll try French wines later.

W All right. Which one do you prefer, a sweet one or a semi-sweet one?

M I'd go with a semi-sweet one _____ _____.

W That's the perfect choice.

11

W Richard, look at this flyer. It's about dance lessons at the community center.

M Oh, _____ because of the K-pop boom.

W I heard that the instructor there used to _____ _____.

12

M Wow, you finally bought a new electric car. _____ _____?

W I have no complaints. _____ _____. You should consider buying one.

M Maybe I should. Do you think you can introduce me to the dealer?

13

W Honey, what did the doctor say about your back?

M He said that it'll take some time to heal. I really hate having trouble moving around.

W Don't forget to _____ and get enough rest. You'll recover before you know it.

M I will. Oh, could you do me a favor?

W What is it?

M The doctor said I shouldn't drive long distances until I get better. _____.

W Oh, no. What about Jimmy? We are supposed to give him a ride to the airport.

M Do you think you could give him a ride instead? Otherwise, I have to ask him to take the bus.

W I think we should just ask him to take the bus. I'm not sure _____.

M I feel bad. I wanted to take him because of his luggage.

W I know, honey. But there is no other choice. He'll understand.

14

M Cathy, you look so focused. What are you reading?

W I'm reading news articles on my phone.

M I see. Did you find anything interesting?

W Not really. I've been reading some articles in the politics section. But there are so many terms I don't understand.

M In every field, _____ _____ getting used to new information.

W You are right. I guess I have to get familiar with the terms before reading.

M It may take a while at first, but _____ _____.

W Do you think so?

M Absolutely. If you get interested in something, _____ _____.

15

M Deborah is graduating from high school next month. Since she has been accepted into college, she wants to work part-time before school starts. Since she is a straight-A student, she has decided to get into private tutoring. Since this is her first time, she has to create a profile and post it on a tutoring website. She adds information about herself _____ _____. But she isn't sure if her profile shows enough about herself. So she asks her neighbor Jackson for help. He is _____ _____ as a tutor. She asks Jackson what else she needs on her profile. Jackson looks at it and thinks _____ _____. Many students want to know what she's achieved because it clearly proves her skills and abilities. So he wants to tell her to add her achievements. In this situation, what would Jackson most likely say to Deborah?

16~17

W Good morning. People use the word "protean" to describe some species of octopus. _____ _____ "Proteus", the god of the sea in Greek mythology. Proteus had the ability to take on any form he wanted, just like octopuses. Octopuses are very intelligent sea creatures with unique abilities. Surprisingly, _____ _____ is better than that of chameleons. Octopuses are capable of changing their color and size. They can even alter the texture of their skin and blend in with surroundings. It's their way of hiding from their predators and catching their prey. To catch food, octopuses _____ _____. Those suckers restrain and trap their prey. Moreover, they have the amazing ability to shoot ink. There is an ink sac buried under their liver. They eject ink from there to escape from predators. _____, which is used as a distraction. You can take a closer look at how they do it in the video. The video will also explain more about these protean creatures.

13회 실전 듣기 모의고사

01 다음을 듣고, 남자가 하는 말의 목적으로 가장 적절한 것을 고르시오.

① 주거 환경의 개선을 홍보하려고
② 청소에 대한 협조를 부탁하려고
③ 건물의 물청소 필요성을 알리려고
④ 아파트의 유지보수에 관해 설명하려고
⑤ 청소 용역업체 선정투표를 독려하려고

02 대화를 듣고, 여자의 의견으로 가장 적절한 것을 고르시오.

① 아파트에서는 동물을 키워서는 안 된다.
② 동물을 키우려면 청소를 자주 해야 한다.
③ 집의 인테리어를 좌우하는 것은 식물이다.
④ 스투키는 실내에서 기르기 완벽한 공기정화식물이다.
⑤ 반려동물처럼 식물을 키우는 데는 많은 주의가 필요하다.

03 다음을 듣고, 남자가 하는 말의 요지로 가장 적절한 것을 고르시오.

① 오랜 시간 주의 깊게 관찰해야 예술 작품을 이해할 수 있다.
② 예술 작품에 대한 평가는 사람마다 달라진다.
③ 예술 작품은 미술관에서 진품으로 감상하는 것이 좋다.
④ 올바른 작품 이해를 위해서 박물관 안내인의 역할이 중요하다.
⑤ 예술 작품을 제대로 감상하려면 역사적 배경을 알아야 한다.

04 대화를 듣고, 그림에서 대화의 내용과 일치하지 않는 것을 고르시오.

05 대화를 듣고, 여자가 남자를 위해 할 일로 가장 적절한 것을 고르시오.

① 셔츠 다림질하기
② 다리미를 찾아주기
③ 음료수 가져다주기
④ 수선점에서 구두 찾아오기
⑤ 연설 대본을 소리 내어 읽기

06 대화를 듣고, 남자가 지불할 금액을 고르시오.

① $600 ② $610 ③ $660
④ $1,210 ⑤ $1,260

07 대화를 듣고, 여자가 Sally의 가족을 초대하지 못 하는 이유를 고르시오.

① 귀 염증이 낫지 않아서
② 수영대회에 나가야 해서
③ 해외로 출장을 가야 해서
④ 집 청소를 하지 못 해서
⑤ 병원에 가봐야 해서

08 대화를 듣고, World Healthcare Forum에 관해 언급되지 않은 것을 고르시오.

① 개최 도시 ② 참가국 ③ 강연 주제
④ 개최 기간 ⑤ 폐회식

09 YSU Dance Camp에 관한 다음 내용을 듣고, 일치하지 않는 것을 고르시오.

① 6월 21일부터 3일간 진행된다.
② 10명 이상 단체로 참가하면 10%의 할인을 받는다.
③ 모든 캠프 참여자들은 티셔츠와 수건을 받는다.
④ 초보자를 위한 특별 강습도 있다.
⑤ 100명까지 수용 가능하다.

10 다음 표를 보면서 대화를 듣고, 여자가 구매할 댄스화를 고르시오.

Dancing Boots

Model	Price	Weight	Type	Color
① A	$75	light	long	black
② B	$80	light	short	brown
③ C	$90	heavy	ankle	black
④ D	$95	light	long	brown
⑤ E	$120	heavy	short	pink

11 대화를 듣고, 여자의 마지막 말에 대한 남자의 응답으로 가장 적절한 것을 고르시오.

① I didn't. The weather is perfect for a trip.
② Never. I thought it would be raining all day.
③ Sure. I packed my bag for that type of weather.
④ I did. But it doesn't seem quite reliable these days.
⑤ Don't worry. I've finished packing my bag for tomorrow.

12 대화를 듣고, 남자의 마지막 말에 대한 여자의 응답으로 가장 적절한 것을 고르시오.

① Sorry. I have no time to talk to you anymore.
② You are right. It's time to take care of yourself.
③ Okay. Let me see if I can rearrange my schedule.
④ Don't worry. I have a business meeting tomorrow.
⑤ I understand. I have to start my own business soon.

13 대화를 듣고, 여자의 마지막 말에 대한 남자의 응답으로 가장 적절한 것을 고르시오. [3점]

Man: _____

① Don't worry. I will do more research someday.
② Not me. I spent too much time studying the topic.
③ That's okay. I was not going to do the presentation, either.
④ I don't agree. We seem to have enough time for practice.
⑤ All right. Then let's get together and see if we can do that.

14 대화를 듣고, 남자의 마지막 말에 대한 여자의 응답으로 가장 적절한 것을 고르시오. [3점]

Woman: _____

① Who cares? I don't think it is a big deal at all.
② No, thanks. I don't know who the candidates are.
③ Why not? I should consider other candidates, too.
④ Sorry. I have to prepare my campaign speech myself.
⑤ Sure. I might have to take that course this semester.

15 다음 상황 설명을 듣고, Sam이 Rose에게 할 말로 가장 적절한 것을 고르시오. [3점]

Sam: _____

① Would you mind if I borrowed your camera?
② Can you tell me how to take a good picture?
③ Let me tell you about the basic functions of a camera.
④ What are the features of a good camera for beginners?
⑤ I'm wondering if you are interested in joining the photography club.

[16~17] 다음을 듣고, 물음에 답하시오.

16 여자가 하는 말의 주제로 가장 적절한 것은?

① how a species becomes extinct
② the responsibility of the government
③ how Canada categorizes endangered animals
④ the definition of an endangered species
⑤ why we have to protect wildlife

17 언급된 멸종 단계가 <u>아닌</u> 것은?

① special concern ② threatened
③ endangered ④ locally extinct
⑤ totally destroyed

🔊 녹음된 내용을 들으면서 빈칸을 알맞게 채워보세요. _____

01

M Hello, residents. Now, spring is just around the corner, and it's time to clean our building. _____ _____, we are going to clean the exterior windows and the stairs inside of the apartment buildings. The cleaning staff _____ _____ from next Monday through Wednesday. On Monday, Building 201 and 202 will be washed. On Tuesday, they will wash the stairs in Building 203 and 204. Finally, on Wednesday, the stairs of Building 205 and 206 will be done. In order to make their job easier, _____ _____, such as flower pots or bicycles. The exact time of cleaning is from 11 a.m. to 3 p.m., just the same as the last time. Thank you for your cooperation.

02

W Jim, where are you going?

M I'm going to buy something to decorate my living room.

W Oh, what are you going to buy?

M Actually, I'm thinking of buying some plants.

W Are you sure you can take care of them? _____ _____.

M Do you think so? Well, I used to grow stookie plants in my room. Once, I didn't water them for weeks but they were okay.

W Yes, but stookies are the easiest houseplants to grow. Most plants aren't like that. Besides, _____ _____.

M You're right. I'll search for more information before buying them.

W Remember, they need _____ _____.

M Okay, I'll keep that in mind.

03

M Welcome, art lovers! I am Mr. Rivera, and I will be your guide for today's art museum tour. But before we explore the artwork, _____ _____. Understanding the historical context is crucial for a genuine appreciation of art. As time goes by, art changes, and _____ _____ from what was produced 300 or even 20 years ago. Therefore, to truly appreciate a work of art, _____ _____. Now, I will lead you around the museum and explain the artwork. Let's explore together!

04

W What do you have in your hand?

M They are pictures of the concert that I went to last week.

W Wow, the stage looks awesome.

M Yes, the four spotlights _____ _____.

W Oh, the guitarist on the left side is a man, right?

M Yes, his name is John. He always keeps his hair long and wavy.

W I love his hair. Is that _____ _____?

M Yes, it is. The cross necklace is his lucky charm.

W I see. _____?

M That's his signature look. No matter how hot it is, he always wears a leather jacket.

W Really? He must be uncomfortable.

M I know. Oh, do you see the person on the keyboard?

W _____?

M Actually, it is a woman. She is the new member of the band.

05

M Honey, do you know where my leather shoes are?

W You don't remember? You took them to the shoe repair shop to get the heels replaced.

M Oh, right, I wanted to wear them to the staff dinner at my company tonight.

W Would you like _____
_____?

M That's okay. I will do that on my way to the dinner.

W I don't think you have enough time. You'll have to leave in 20 minutes to _____
_____.

M Don't worry. I'll leave as soon as my shirt is ready. Where is the iron?

W It's in the drawer in the closet. Is your speech ready?

M I finished writing it, but nobody has read it yet. Can you _____ so I can check it?

W I was going to get you something to drink. I'm sure it's fine. You are such a good speaker.

M Well, I'm not sure. I didn't really spend enough time working on it.

W All right. I'll read it and _____
_____, okay?

M Thanks.

06

W Hello. Can I help you?

M I saw the promotion advertisement for your gym online. Is the promotion still available?

W Yes, it will be going on until the end of this month.

M Great. _____
_____.

W Okay. Our half-year membership is $1,200, but now it is 50% off. Would you fill out this application form, please?

M Sure, but I have a few questions. Does the membership _____?

W Of course. You can use the fitness center, spa, and even the swimming pool.

M Can I use a locker for free?

W I'm sorry, but _____
_____. Lockers are $10 a month.

M Do I need to pay for towels, too?

W No, _____.
Also, you get a free 7-day yoga pass if you get a membership.

M All right. Let me fill this out. And I need a locker for 6 months, too.

07

M Honey, are you doing anything tomorrow?

W Not really. How about you?

M I think I'm going to invite Sally's family over to our place.

W Oh, what is the occasion?

M _____
_____ when her husband got promoted.

W Right. I couldn't make it because I was on a business trip.

M Yes. So, if it's okay with you, I want to invite them tomorrow.

W Sorry, but can we do that next weekend?

M Why? Is there something wrong?

W Actually, _____
because of an ear infection.

M Oh, you have an ear infection again? I told you to quit swimming.

W Yes, I have to. _____
_____, too. So, I think I'll just rest tomorrow.

M You'll be all right soon. I'll invite Sally's family over next weekend.

08

W Jack, how was the conference?

M It was wonderful. Some famous doctors spoke about how to stay healthy.

W I wish I could have gone, too.

M _____
that kind of conference.

W I'm interested in health-related issues. _____
_____?

M It was held in Budapest. _____
_____ cholesterol in our body.

W That sounds like a good topic.

M Yes, it helped me understand the cholesterol figures from my medical check-up results.

W So, when did the conference start?

M It started on the 19th of November, _____
_____.

W Did you stay there for 5 days then?

M Yes, I participated in both the opening reception and the closing ceremony, and left for the airport at around 9 p.m. on the last day.

09

W Today, I'd like to inform you of one of the greatest opportunities to combine dancing with camping. This year's YSU Dance Camp _____ _____ from June 21st to 24th on the YSU campus. You can participate in this camp if you are interested in any type of dancing. The admission fee is $300, but if you register at least one month in advance, you will get a 10% discount. Also, _____ _____ 10 or more, you will get 10% off. All campers will receive a camp T-shirt and a camp towel. And don't be worried if you are a beginner. We have a special curriculum _____ _____. Moreover, Simon White, a world-famous choreographer, will join us to provide dance lessons for everyone. The program _____ _____, so you'd better hurry up.

10

M Nancy, Topaz Dancing Shoes is having a big sale starting next week.

W Really? They haven't had a sale recently. I need a pair of shoes for the dancing contest next month.

M Here. Have a look at their online catalog.

W They all look nice. I don't know what to choose.

M _____. All of them are pretty expensive, though.

W I don't want to spend more than $100.

M Then you should choose from these four pairs. You _____, right?

W Yes, I don't wear heavy shoes.

M Do you prefer long boots or short ones? They also have ankle boots, if you'd like.

W _____. They'd look great when I dance in a short skirt.

M Then you have to _____ _____.

W I like these brown ones. The shoes I have are almost all black, so I'll buy these ones.

M I think you've made a good choice.

11

W Bob, _____ our school trip next week.

M Me neither. _____.

W Didn't you check the weather forecast yet?

12

M Honey, _____?

W Well, I'm not sure. Why? Do you have any special plans that day?

M Jamie's _____. It's about his behavior at school.

13

W Peter, can I ask you something about our presentation?

M Okay. What do you want to ask?

W I was wondering if we could split up the presentation.

M We did. We did research, gathered information, and made files, so that you can present more easily.

W I meant that _____ _____. Our main topic is mental disorders, but you researched the types of mental disorders, and Gary dug into the cures, and I studied the side effects of medicine.

M Yes. And you wanted to do the presentation.

W I know, but it would be much better if you and Gary _____ _____.

M But we only have 20 minutes for the team presentation. Do you think _____ _____?

W If we practice within the assigned time limit, it won't be a big problem.

14

M Jessica, did you know Tammy is running for class president?

W Actually, I recommended her for that position.

M Wow, I didn't know that.

W Tammy is a responsible student. She _____ _____, and her grades are good.

M She is a good student, but being a class president is different.

W What do you mean?

M First of all, we need somebody who is ready to serve their classmates. Second, _____ _____.

W Still, Tammy is the best candidate for me. She helps her friends a lot, and she is pretty popular in class.

M I think we need to pay attention to other candidates as well.

W You're right. Since it is the beginning of the campaign, let's find out who is _____ _____.

M Sure. I'm going to listen to Samuel's campaign speech now. Do you want to come?

15

M Sam and Rose are high school students. Sam joins the photography club, but he doesn't have a camera. So, now _____ _____. But since he just started taking an interest in photography, _____ _____. So, he decides to ask Rose for help. Her hobby is taking pictures. Sam tells Rose that he joined the photography club, and that he needs to buy a good camera. Now he is about to ask Rose about _____ when he buys a good camera. In this situation, what would Sam most likely say to Rose?

16~17

W Good morning, everyone. Last time we talked about endangered species around the world. Today, let's talk about the ones in Canada. _____ _____, and the number of endangered species in Canada is growing. Seven additional animal species _____ in November. Scientists meet once a year and review species that are at risk of becoming endangered. If they think a species is in trouble, they put it on the list. There are _____. The lowest level is "special concern," followed by "threatened," the second lowest level. The middle level is "endangered." Then if a species _____ _____ in a certain area, it is called "locally extinct," which usually happens when one of its habitat is totally destroyed. Finally, if a species _____ _____, it is called "extinct", which is the highest level. Once a species is listed, it is against the law for people to harm or kill them. It is also illegal to destroy the species' critical habitat.

01 다음을 듣고, 여자가 하는 말의 목적으로 가장 적절한 것을 고르시오.

① 참석자에게 감사하려고
② 오후 일정을 안내하려고
③ 참석 대상자를 확인하려고
④ 회의 주제를 변경하려고
⑤ 점심 메뉴를 정하려고

02 대화를 듣고, 남자의 의견으로 가장 적절한 것을 고르시오.

① 숙제는 여유 있게 미리 해두어야 한다.
② 수업 시간에 조는 학생을 처벌해야 한다.
③ 충분한 수면을 통해 면역력을 강화해야 한다.
④ 시험 기간에는 건강관리가 가장 중요하다.
⑤ 수학 공부 방법에 대한 상담이 필요하다.

03 다음을 듣고, 여자가 하는 말의 요지로 가장 적절한 것을 고르시오.

① 가이드를 동반한 해외여행은 지역 정보를 얻는 데 편리하다.
② 방문하는 나라의 자연을 훼손하지 않도록 유의해야 한다.
③ 새로운 지역을 방문하는 것은 인생을 바꿀 경험을 제공한다.
④ 현지 언어를 배워야 문화적 격차를 해소할 수 있다.
⑤ 해외여행 중에는 지역 문화를 존중하는 태도를 가져야 한다.

04 대화를 듣고, 그림에서 대화의 내용과 일치하지 <u>않는</u> 것을 고르시오.

05 대화를 듣고, 남자가 여자에게 부탁한 일로 가장 적절한 것을 고르시오.

① 과제 검토해 주기
② 수강 신청 도와주기
③ 소설책 추천해 주기
④ 필기 노트 빌려주기
⑤ 전화번호 알려 주기

06 대화를 듣고, 여자가 지불할 금액을 고르시오. [3점]

① $56   ② $80   ③ $86
④ $96   ⑤ $100

07 대화를 듣고, 남자가 슈퍼마켓에 가지 <u>못 한</u> 이유를 고르시오.

① 은행에 대신 다녀와서
② 신용카드를 두고 와서
③ 지하에서 청소하고 있어서
④ 수리공이 집에 오기로 해서
⑤ 슈퍼마켓에 사람이 너무 많아서

08 대화를 듣고, Nuremberg International Toy Fair에 관해 언급되지 <u>않은</u> 것을 고르시오.

① 개최 장소   ② 개최 규모   ③ 참가 회비
④ 행사 연혁   ⑤ 행사 내용

09 Anne Frank Museum에 관한 다음 내용을 듣고, 일치하지 <u>않는</u> 것을 고르시오.

① 이 박물관은 1960년에 설립되었다.
② 언제나 매일 오후 5시까지 관람할 수 있다.
③ 관람 안내인 없이 관람해야 한다.
④ 14명 이상일 경우에는 예약을 해야 한다.
⑤ 시내에 있어서 교통이 편리하다.

10 다음 표를 보면서 대화를 듣고, 두 사람이 구매할 선풍기를 고르시오.

Fans for Sale

	Price	Type	Energy Rating	Noise
①	$100	standing	4-star	55 dB
②	$120	tower	4-star	50 dB
③	$150	tower	5-star	35 dB
④	$170	tower	5-star	40 dB
⑤	$250	bladeless	5-star	30 dB

11 대화를 듣고, 남자의 마지막 말에 대한 여자의 응답으로 가장 적절한 것을 고르시오.

① Can you imagine? I will do whatever I can do.
② Let's see. Who has the authority to do that?
③ The heroine, of course. It's the best part.
④ Well, wait a minute. Let's go back to the topic.
⑤ How can you say that? That's none of your business.

12 대화를 듣고, 여자의 마지막 말에 대한 남자의 응답으로 가장 적절한 것을 고르시오.

① Don't worry. We will do fine without your help.
② That's true, but I did not record our presentation.
③ Forget about it. I have practiced that many times.
④ Never mind. You can lend me your laptop next time.
⑤ No problem. I can go home and get it in 10 minutes.

13 대화를 듣고, 남자의 마지막 말에 대한 여자의 응답으로 가장 적절한 것을 고르시오. [3점]

Woman: _____

① Okay, let's wait and see what will happen.
② No way. What if all of them feel so bored?
③ You're right. Student interest is a top priority.
④ Thanks, I'm definitely going to follow your advice.
⑤ I agree. The topic of the debate class is most important.

14 대화를 듣고, 여자의 마지막 말에 대한 남자의 응답으로 가장 적절한 것을 고르시오.

Man: _____

① Fine. I'll call Andrew and cancel.
② No, I hate it. Why should I stay at home?
③ Don't worry. I won't take a walk with Andrew.
④ Don't say that, Mom. Easier said than done.
⑤ I'm afraid not. The road is so slippery.

15 다음 상황 설명을 듣고, Chris가 John에게 할 말로 가장 적절한 것을 고르시오. [3점]

Chris: _____

① I don't think I can join you.
② I like the old one better than the new one.
③ There are strict rules for the national competition.
④ Why don't we use the old dance to make a new one?
⑤ I love the new dance. Let's practice it after school.

[16~17] 다음을 듣고, 물음에 답하시오.

16 남자가 하는 말의 주제로 가장 적절한 것은?

① using the Internet to find a job
② how to find the most ideal career
③ why your job preferences matter
④ why lectures on career paths are popular
⑤ the advantages and disadvantages of online job hunting

17 언급된 활동이 <u>아닌</u> 것은?

① 관심사 목록 만들기
② 직업의 장단점 나열하기
③ 직업에 종사하는 사람들 만나기
④ 직업이 적성에 맞는지 알아보기
⑤ 직업과 관련된 동아리 활동하기

01

W Hello, participants of the World Youth Organization. We have almost come to the end of the morning session. We have had a wonderful time this morning. I am very _____ _____ and active participation. Your creative ideas on our global cooperation were also amazing. Now, let's take a break and _____ _____. The afternoon session _____. Be sure to be punctual so our session can go smoothly. Please enjoy your lunch. Also, during lunch, try to start a conversation with your fellow participants from all over the world and share new ideas like the ones we talked about during the morning session. _____ _____. Thank you.

02

M Jane, you look really tired.

W Yes, I stayed up all night studying for the math test today.

M What? Why did you stay up?

W I had no choice. _____ _____.

M Maintaining your focus throughout tests is important, too. _____ _____.

W But I think it's more important to cover everything even if you have to cram.

M Well, I'd have to disagree. I think you need enough sleep to keep yourself focused during the exam period. If you are too tired, _____ _____.

W You have a point. _____ _____.

M Yes, I hope you get a good grade.

W Thanks.

03

W Good day, everyone! My name is Ms. Pottenger, and I will be your tour guide for today. As you prepare for your upcoming travels abroad, _____ _____. Visiting a new country can be challenging, but it is very important to maintain a respectful attitude towards the local culture. One way to do this is _____ _____. You can also learn basic phrases in the local language such as greetings, or "please" and "thank you." Remember that _____ _____.

With these considerations in mind, I wish you all a fantastic journey.

04

W Thanks for inviting me to your new place.

M You are welcome. _____ _____.

W Here is your housewarming gift. It's just a bottle of wine.

M Thanks. Come, I'll show you around. [Pause] This is the living room.

W Wow, your new place is much bigger than the last one.

M Oh, please don't mind the drying rack on the left.

W Don't worry. Your TV is huge. Is it new?

M It is. I wanted to hang it on the wall, but it'd cost extra. So I just _____.

W I see. What is in those boxes next to the TV?

M There are some cables and parts for the TV, but I haven't put them away yet.

W Okay. Is the mirror new as well?

M Yes. I wanted to put it in my bedroom, but there is not enough space. So, I placed it _____ _____.

W Oh, what happened to all the plants you had?

M I put them on the balcony.

05

W Nathan, is something troubling you?

M I'm worried that I'll fail Mr. Johnson's literature class. I'm _____ _____.

W Well, his assignments are usually complicated and difficult.

M I heard you took the same class last year. Do you have any tips for me?

W Mr. Johnson expects you to take a lot of notes. I ____ _____ if you want.

M That's okay. I already have my own notes. But I don't know how to use them for the assignment.

W Why don't you ask Chris for advice? I think he got an A in the same class.

M Chris? Wow, that's impressive.

W I have two classes with him this semester. _____ _____.

M Can you _____? I'll text him some questions.

W All right. I left my phone in my locker. Is it okay if I give you his number after lunch?

M That's fine. Thank you.

06

W Excuse me, I'm looking for a sweater for my son.

M Sweaters are over here. We have a wide selection of sweaters and some of them are on sale.

W That's good. How much is _____ _____? The pattern looks very unique.

M That one is $50, but it's not on sale.

W What about the striped sweaters on the shelf?

M They are part of the special sale. They were originally $40, but they are 10% off for this week only.

W All right. Then, _____ _____.

M Okay. Is there anything else you need?

W Actually, I think I need pants that will go well with it.

M Sure, how about those ones in the display window? They are _____ _____.

W They look nice. I will take two large pairs.

M Okay. Would that be all?

W Yes. I have this $10 gift card _____ _____. Can I use it now?

M Of course, ma'am.

W Great. Here is my credit card.

07

W What are you doing in the basement?

M Oh, hi, Mom. I was just looking for my soccer ball. How did it go at the bank?

W Well, not bad. There weren't many people so I didn't have to wait long. Did you go to the supermarket and get the things I asked for?

M Not yet. I was waiting until you got home.

W Why? I left the credit card in the kitchen.

M _____, the repairman called.

W The cable repairman? _____ _____.

M I know. But he said he got an opening between 3 and 4 p.m. today and asked if he could come today instead.

W I see. It's almost 3:30. _____ _____.

M Yes. Now that you are home, I can go to the supermarket.

W Oh, yes. Don't forget the card.

M I won't.

08

W Chris, I heard you are going to Germany soon.

M Yes, I'm going to Germany to visit the Nuremberg International Toy Fair.

W I heard it's one of the largest trade fairs for toys and games in the world.

M That's right. This year, about 2,800 exhibitors from over 60 countries _____ _____.

W Wow, that's a huge event!

M Yes, it is. They say more than 80,000 trade visitors and purchasers are expected to attend the fair.

W That's great. The fair surely has a long history, right?

M Yes, it started in 1949 and since then, _____ _____.

W I guess you can meet _____ _____ there.

M That's right. Also, _____ _____.

W I hope you have a wonderful time.

M Thanks. It will be exciting!

09

M Hi, everyone. I'm going to introduce the recently renovated Anne Frank Museum. It was established in 1960. You can learn about Anne Frank's life, from birth to death. The museum is open daily from 9 a.m. to 5 p.m., _____ _____ In July and August, the museum is open until 6 p.m. every day. _____ _____, and no tour guides are available. When there are 14 or more people in a group, you should make a reservation. Since the museum is located in downtown, _____ _____. If you're interested in Anne Frank, please take the time to visit the museum.

10

W The electric fan doesn't work any more. We need to buy a new one, honey.

M Yes, I agree. Let's take a look at this flyer about electrical appliances.

W Let's see. This bladeless fan seems like the most cutting-edge product.

M Well, we should consider our budget. $250 is too expensive. _____ _____.

W Then my choice is a tower fan. _____ _____.

M What about the energy rating?

W A higher rating is always better.

M _____. How about getting the one with lower decibels?

W Sure. A quiet fan would be better. _____ _____. Let's get it!

11

M Did you hear there will be an audition for our school play next week?

W Yes, I'm going to apply for one of the roles. I have been _____.

M What role do you _____?

12

W John, _____ _____?

M I forgot about that. I only brought my notebook with me.

W You said you wanted to _____ _____. What should we do now?

13

M Michelle, I heard you are going to visit a school in a rural town.

W Yes, I'm planning to show a movie on the topic of justice.

M A movie about justice?

W Do you think it'll be too boring?

M It could be. The topic seems too heavy for students. You _____ _____.

W But I've already found the perfect movie for them.

M Well, then how about adding another activity?

W _____?

M Let the students watch one scene from the movie. Then have an open discussion about it.

W Oh, then I guess I have to provide them with a few questions before the movie. That way they will know what they have to discuss.

M Exactly. That way the students _____ _____.

14

W Jack, why did you get dressed? Are you going out?

M Did you look out the window, Mom? It's snowing outside!

W I understand why you are excited. But you can't go outside. _____ _____ from your flu yet.

M But it's the first snowfall of the year. I already told Andrew to meet me _____ _____.

W You shouldn't have done that. Your top priority should be your health, Jack.

M I know, Mom, but I am really tired of staying inside. You know I was in the hospital for about a week.

W I understand how you feel, Jack. However, _____ _____. Why don't we take a short walk together around the block instead?

15

W Chris and John are members of the school dance club. One day, they are selected as the best dancers in the regional dancing contest. So, they have the opportunity to participate in the National Dancing Festival. Chris thinks that _____ _____, they should do the same dance as they did in the regional. However, John thinks since it's for the national festival, they should make new choreography. John says to win the contest they have to do _____. Chris is not sure if they can come up with a new dance. Besides, even if they do, _____ _____. Since he understands how ambitious John is, he wants to suggest making a new dance by changing the old

one. In this situation, what would Chris most likely say to John?

16~17

M Good morning, everyone. Did you have a wonderful discussion with your family regarding the topic I told you about? Today, let's continue to talk about the same topic. In choosing a career, first, make a list of _____ _____. To help you, there are many sites on the Internet, plus books at your local library, that can tell you what occupations other people find enjoyable. Next, write a short profile on each job, _____ _____. If you find one or more that might be especially interesting, try to _____ _____. Ask them what they like and dislike about their job, and find out why they stay and why some people leave. _____ _____, including whether it fits your abilities or not. If possible, volunteer to work alongside someone in the occupation to get a better understanding of it. If you are still happy, maybe you have found your place. Good luck.

15 회 실전 듣기 모의고사

01 다음을 듣고, 남자가 하는 말의 목적으로 가장 적절한 것을 고르시오.

① 분리수거의 중요성을 강조하려고
② 쓰레기 규격 봉투의 사용을 홍보하려고
③ 쓰레기 투기꾼에 대한 신고를 권장하려고
④ 반려견 산책에 대한 중요성을 강조하려고
⑤ 환경오염을 막는 방법에 대해 소개하려고

02 대화를 듣고, 여자의 의견으로 가장 적절한 것을 고르시오.

① 동물 보호를 위한 엄격한 법이 필요하다.
② 유기견들에게 사랑과 관심을 주어야 한다.
③ 동물 보호소에서 유기견을 입양해야 한다.
④ 반려견을 더 쉽게 입양할 수 있도록 해야 한다.
⑤ 자원봉사 활동에 적극 참여하도록 홍보해야 한다.

03 다음을 듣고, 남자가 하는 말의 요지로 가장 적절한 것을 고르시오.

① 직업을 고를 때는 전문가의 충고를 듣는 것이 유익하다.
② 성공하기 위해서는 큰 꿈을 갖는 것부터 시작해야 한다.
③ 미디어에서 권장하는 내용을 바탕으로 직업을 고르는 게 좋다.
④ 미디어에 현혹되지 말고 현실에 맞는 직업을 찾아야 한다.
⑤ 인기 있는 직업을 가지려면 꿈을 가지고 계속 노력해야 한다.

04 대화를 듣고, 그림에서 대화의 내용과 일치하지 <u>않는</u> 것을 고르시오.

05 대화를 듣고, 남자가 할 일로 가장 적절한 것을 고르시오.

① 블로그 운영하기
② 출판사에 전화하기
③ 포토 에세이집 출간하기
④ 자신의 명함 제작하기
⑤ 포트폴리오 준비하기

06 대화를 듣고, 여자가 지불할 금액을 고르시오. [3점]

① $15 　　　② $20 　　　③ $21
④ $22 　　　⑤ $27

07 대화를 듣고, 남자가 전화를 건 이유를 고르시오.

① 가장 가까운 병원을 문의하려고
② 열을 내리는 방법을 물어보려고
③ 예약 없이 진료를 부탁하려고
④ 병원 예약을 변경하려고
⑤ 아들과 전화 통화하려고

08 대화를 듣고, 학자금 대출 신청에 관해 언급되지 <u>않은</u> 것을 고르시오.

① 현재 학년　　　② 전공과목
③ 현재 거주지　　　④ 서류 제출 여부
⑤ 타 은행 대출 여부

09 Boldt Castle에 관한 다음 내용을 듣고, 일치하지 <u>않는</u> 것을 고르시오.

① Thousand Islands에 있는 관광 명소이다.
② 5월 중순에서 10월 중순까지 개방한다.
③ 1900년에 완성된 석조 건축물이다.
④ 아내에게 주는 선물로 지어진 건물이다.
⑤ Thousand Islands Bridge Authority가 관리한다.

10 다음 표를 보면서 대화를 듣고, 두 사람이 선택할 우주 캠프를 고르시오.

Space Camps

Program	Target Age	Cost	Dates	No. of Teachers
① A	10~13	$400	Jul. 27 ~ Jul. 30	12
② B	10~13	$500	Aug. 01 ~ Aug. 04	15
③ C	10~13	$600	Aug. 06 ~ Aug. 10	12
④ D	10~13	$650	Aug. 12 ~ Aug. 16	15
⑤ E	12~14	$700	Aug. 18 ~ Aug. 22	15

11 대화를 듣고, 여자의 마지막 말에 대한 남자의 응답으로 가장 적절한 것을 고르시오.

① I think we will start a new unit in art class today.

② I heard that the new art teacher is a professional painter.

③ Well, I guess there will be a substitute teacher for a while.

④ We'd better get back to class. Mr. Miller will be there soon.

⑤ Since class is canceled, we are going to take a music lesson instead.

12 대화를 듣고, 남자의 마지막 말에 대한 여자의 응답으로 가장 적절한 것을 고르시오.

① Okay. It's time to recruit the new members.

② Of course not. I wish we had won first prize.

③ Yes. It'll probably take a whole month to practice.

④ Sorry. The other team was just way better than us.

⑤ You're right. We'd better cherish our time spent together.

13 대화를 듣고, 여자의 마지막 말에 대한 남자의 응답으로 가장 적절한 것을 고르시오.

Man: _____

① Why don't we get a refund to get better seats?

② It's too bad that we don't get to see the concert.

③ I can't give up the convenience of being seated.

④ Let's hurry and book seats before they get sold out.

⑤ Don't worry about it. We already booked two tickets.

14 대화를 듣고, 남자의 마지막 말에 대한 여자의 응답으로 가장 적절한 것을 고르시오. [3점]

Woman: _____

① Why don't we make a film instead?

② Sure. I'll help you with your assignment.

③ That's unnecessary. I'll book the tickets tonight.

④ What a great idea! I wanted to see a Korean film.

⑤ I'm sorry, but I need to focus on my paper this weekend.

15 다음 상황 설명을 듣고, Amanda가 Mr. Smith에게 할 말로 가장 적절한 것을 고르시오. [3점]

Amanda: _____

① Why don't you come over to my place?

② No, thanks. My daughter is allergic to cats.

③ Would you like to join us? It will be so much fun.

④ I'd appreciate it if you could do that. You're the best.

⑤ It's all right. The cats will stay at the pet hotel for a week.

[16~17] 다음을 듣고, 물음에 답하시오.

16 여자가 하는 말의 주제로 가장 적절한 것은?

① how stress affects us

② the nutrients that reduce anxiety

③ how to manage stress effectively

④ food that helps you have a healthy lifestyle

⑤ how to differentiate positive stress from negative stress

17 언급된 음식이 아닌 것은?

① Brazil nuts ② salmon

③ almonds ④ pumpkin seeds

⑤ dark chocolate

01

M Have you ever dropped a candy wrapper or soda can on the ground? Have you ever failed to clean up after your dog? If you answered yes, then you are a litterbug. A litterbug is a person _____ _____. Doing this contributes to pollution, which contaminates our oceans and waterways. To become a part of the solution, there are simple steps you can follow. _____ _____. In case there are no trash cans nearby, just hold off until you see a trash can. You can also use reusable plates and utensils when you eat somewhere outdoors. Instead of plastic bottles, thermal bottles are a great alternative. When you are out on a walk with your dog, it's very important to clean up after your dog and _____ _____. Last but not least, _____. Your change in behavior can make a difference.

02

W Ron, do you still volunteer at an animal shelter?

M I do. I help out with cleaning and feeding animals.

W I'm looking for some volunteer work. I was just wondering if the shelter needed more people.

M Definitely. The shelter welcomes _____ _____. Would you be interested?

W Of course. I love playing and interacting with animals.

M Okay. Oh, you have to understand that the work can be difficult since some of them can get a little aggressive. They are brought in after they were abandoned or abused by their owners.

W I can't believe _____ _____. Once they adopt a pet, they should take good care of it for life.

M I know. People have to be more careful and responsible.

W Yes, we need to _____ _____, too. Sometimes it makes me angry when people get away with doing horrible things to their pets.

M That's how I feel, too.

03

M Hi there, folks! I'm Kelvin, your job consultant for today. _____ _____, you will have a lot of thoughts about which job to choose. In this situation, it is important to find a job that fits your own reality. _____ like pop stars as the path to success, making people think that big dreams lead to success. However, in reality, _____ _____. Don't be fooled by the fancy image presented in the media. Discover a job that aligns with the present circumstances. Let's move on to practical advice for your career decisions. Stay with me!

04

W Mr. Kim, is this a photo from your last vacation?

M Yes, it is. This was taken at a beach we went to last summer.

W Oh, I see the beautiful beach on the left. It seems like your family had a great time.

M We sure did. There was a carriage running along the beach for visitors. So we gave it a try.

W I've never seen a carriage on a beach before, _____ _____.

M I know. You didn't expect to see that, right? This was my first time to see one on a beach.

W Who is the man holding the rope? It must've been really _____.

M Oh, he drove the carriage with the horse. It was not really safe for us to drive the carriage on our own.

W I see. Oh, is this _____ _____?

M It is. She was a bit scared, so I had to _____.

W I almost didn't recognize you because of the hat and sunglasses. Who is the woman standing behind the carriage?

M That's my wife. _____ _____. She was too scared to go for a ride.

05

W I really like your photos and posts on your blog. Some of your pictures blew my mind.

M Thanks. I take pictures and just write what comes to mind.

W It's amazing that you have over 500,000 subscribers, too.

M I guess I got pretty lucky. I didn't expect it to get this popular.

W You're so talented. You should _____ _____.

M Do you think publishers would like my work?

W Why don't you give it a try?

M But I don't know where to start.

W I know someone at a publishing company. If you are interested, I could give you a business card.

M Should I call him now? I haven't prepared anything yet.

W _____? You should include at least 10 photos of your work.

M I don't have one yet.

W Okay, then _____ _____. I'll call him and see if you can get a meeting with him.

M That sounds great. Thanks.

06

M Good evening. Are you ready to order now?

W Hi, there. Is a bulgogi burger still $5?

M Oh, _____. But french fries are still $3.

W I see. Then I'd like to buy three bulgogi burgers and french fries.

M Did you mean three bulgogi burgers and three french fries?

W No, _____, please.

M Okay. But for an extra $4, you can change one burger to a combination set. _____.

W What kind of drinks do you have?

M We have soft drinks, orange juice and milkshakes.

W Can I get a milkshake with that?

M Sure. We have vanilla and strawberry flavors. Which one would you like?

W I'll take a vanilla.

M _____. One bulgogi burger combination set with a vanilla milkshake and two additional bulgogi burgers, right?

W That's right. Here's my credit card.

07

[Telephone rings.]

W Dr. Kevin's office. How may I help you?

M Good morning. This is David Kerr. I was wondering if your clinic takes walk-in patients.

W Hello, Mr. Kerr. Appointments are usually required but _____.

M Well, it's my son. He's been throwing up since last night, and he also has a high fever.

W We have a lot of patients today, so you may _____ without an appointment.

M We've been seeing Dr. Kevin for a long time, and your clinic is the closest one I can find. _____ since it's an emergency?

W Let me see. How fast can you get here?

M We could get there in 20 minutes.

W Okay, after you get here, you might have to wait 10 minutes or so. Is that okay with you?

M That's fine with me. Thank you so much. I'll be there soon.

08

M Hello. I'd like to apply for a student loan.

W Sure. _____.

M Here you are.

W I'm going to ask you a few questions to check if you wrote down the information correctly.

M That's all right.

W Your name is Chanwook Kim, and you go to Yonsei University, correct?

M That's right. I'm a junior now.

W Oh, _____
_____ here. What do you study in school?

M I major in chemistry.

W Chemistry. *[Pause]* Okay. Do you reside at the address you wrote down here?

M No. I wrote down my parents' address instead because currently I live in the school dormitory.

W I see. Then can you tell me the phone number for that address? _____.

M Okay. It's 032-012-5570.

W All right. Just one more left. _____
_____ at any other bank?

M No, I don't. _____.

09

W Hello, students! My name is Tina Robbins, and I'll be your guide today. I'm briefly going to talk about Boldt Castle, which we are going to visit soon. Boldt Castle is _____
_____ in the Thousand Islands region of the U.S. state of New York. _____
_____, it is located on Heart Island in the Saint Lawrence River. In 1900, George Boldt launched an ambitious construction campaign _____,
one of the largest private homes in the United States. He engaged hundreds of workers for a six-story "castle" as a present to his wife. Boldt Castle is maintained today by the Thousand Islands Bridge Authority as a tourist attraction. Any questions? Okay. Let's get going!

10

M Honey, you've been on the computer for so long. What have you been looking at?

W Oh, I found a list of space camps for our son.

M That's great. Adam's been really interested in outer space and planets recently.

W I know. It will be a great experience for him. There are five different ones we can choose from.

M All right. Let's take a look. *[Pause]* Oh, this one is not suitable for our son. _____
_____.

W Okay. How about this one? Everything is included in the price, but it seems too expensive, doesn't it?

M Then _____.

W $600 or under seems reasonable. _____
_____.

M I have the last week of July off for the summer holiday. We should go on a family trip that week.

W That's a good idea. Then there are only two options left. _____
in the camp?

M More teachers, definitely. It'll be safer, too.

W All right. This is it, then. I'll make the payment.

11

W Did you hear that Mr. Miller _____
_____?

M Yes, I heard he is _____
_____. I hope it's not something serious.

W Same here. So, what do you think is going to happen to our art class?

12

M I feel so bad that our choir didn't win the contest.
_____.

W I know. I feel like all our efforts went to waste.

M Well, I believe it was a valuable experience. _____
_____.

13

W John, we only have 5 minutes until the tickets are available for sale.

M Already? I've always wanted to go to the band's concert. I'm so excited!

W Oh, have you thought about the type of seats you want?

M Yes, _____.
Since it's heavy metal, I think it'd be more fun in the standing area.

W Well, you can stand and dance to music, but sometimes _____
_____.

M True, but that's the fun part of a concert. You listen to music and just enjoy yourself.

W I know. But I won't be able to move when there are so many people around me.

M You're right. _____
_____.

W _____.
With seated tickets, we could also get a better view of the screens. *[Pause]* Oh, it's almost time to book.

14

M What are you doing this weekend?

W I have to finish a history assignment. I need to write 20 pages by Monday, so _____
_____.

M Even Saturday night? That's a shame.

W Why do you ask?

M I heard that the Film Club will be showing three award-winning films at the student center, and the entry price will be quite cheap.

W How much will it be?

M $8 for three movies.

W Wow, that's so cheap! What are they showing?

M I can't remember the exact names, but I heard that they will be playing movies from France, Mexico, and Russia.

W Really? I haven't seen many foreign films. _____
_____.

M If you work hard, you could finish your assignment before the film night begins. _____.

15

M Amanda is a math teacher at a high school. The school will be closed for renovation for a week, so she gets a week off from classes and other school duties. Amanda thinks this will be a great chance to take a vacation abroad. So, she decides to go to Bali during this break. Since Amanda has been raising two kittens, she has to _____
_____ while she's gone. She looks for pet hotels near her house, _____
_____ she's on the trip. One day, she is talking with Mr. Smith in the teacher's lounge. When Mr. Smith hears about Amanda's problem, he asks her if he can watch the cats for her since his kids love cats. He also says he wants to see _____
_____. Amanda thinks it would be good if Mr. Smith took care of her cats because _____
_____. In this situation, what would Amanda most likely say to Mr. Smith?

16~17

W While stress helps us concentrate and focus, its negative influences also make us overalert and unable to relax. Therefore _____
_____. First, know your stressors. Determine what distresses you and recognize what you can change. Second, shorten your exposure to stress by taking a break. Leave a stressful environment for a while. Third, lead a healthy lifestyle. _____
_____.
Try to avoid smoking and drinking too much caffeine. There are also foods that help you relieve stress. Brazil nuts are a great source of vitamin E, which lowers anxiety. Fatty fish such as salmon can also improve your mood. Try pumpkin seeds, too. They help _____
_____
and anxiety. Dark chocolate may help, too. You can also try breathing control exercises, which only take a minute or two. I'll demonstrate the exercises after playing this video clip about how stress affects us.

16 회 실전 듣기 모의고사

01 다음을 듣고, 남자가 하는 말의 목적으로 가장 적절한 것을 고르시오.

① 대학 입학 성적을 알리려고
② 현장 학습에 대해 안내하려고
③ 현장 학습 취소를 공지하려고
④ 대학 설명회의 연기를 알리려고
⑤ 대학 입학 지원 절차를 설명하려고

02 대화를 듣고, 여자의 의견으로 가장 적절한 것을 고르시오.

① TV 시청은 스트레스 해소에 도움을 준다.
② 일부 프로그램들은 어린이 교육에 도움을 준다.
③ 방송국은 프로그램의 시간대에 신경을 써야 한다.
④ 방송국의 자체 검열을 이제는 완화할 필요가 있다.
⑤ 탄원서와 서명을 받는 것이 문제 해결의 지름길은 아니다.

03 다음을 듣고, 남자가 하는 말의 요지로 가장 적절한 것을 고르시오.

① 반복해서 책을 읽는 것이 독서의 이해도를 높여준다.
② 저자의 서문을 꼼꼼히 읽는 게 책의 이해에 도움이 된다.
③ 노트 필기는 기억력을 높이는 데 효과가 있다.
④ 책에 메모를 하며 읽는 것이 효과적인 독서 방법이다.
⑤ 책을 많이 읽는 것보다 제대로 이해하는 것이 더 중요하다.

04 대화를 듣고, 그림에서 대화의 내용과 일치하지 않는 것을 고르시오.

05 대화를 듣고, 남자가 할 일로 가장 적절한 것을 고르시오.

① 마이크 점검하기
② 행사장을 청소하기
③ 프로젝터 점검하기
④ 포인터의 배터리 교체하기
⑤ 프로젝터 담당 기사에게 전화하기

06 대화를 듣고, 두 사람이 지불할 금액을 고르시오. [3점]

① $405
② $450
③ $480
④ $505
⑤ $510

07 대화를 듣고, 여자가 영화를 보러 갈 수 없는 이유를 고르시오.

① 식중독에 걸려서
② 집을 수리해야 해서
③ 영화표를 잃어버려서
④ 좋아하는 가수가 아니라서
⑤ 여동생과 콘서트에 가야 해서

08 대화를 듣고, Great Pyramid에 관해 언급되지 않은 것을 고르시오.

① 공사 기간
② 위치
③ 높이
④ 건설 목적
⑤ 방의 개수

09 Saturday Art School에 관한 다음 내용을 듣고, 일치하지 않는 것을 고르시오.

① 5세부터 14세 아이들이 참여할 수 있다.
② 그림을 그리고 칠할 기회를 얻는다.
③ 새로 지어진 Raum 아트센터에서 수업이 있다.
④ 수업이 끝날 때, 부모와 형제들이 미술실에 초대된다.
⑤ 온라인 신청보다는 직접 와서 등록하는 것을 선호한다.

10 다음 표를 보면서 대화를 듣고, 남자가 수강할 강좌를 고르시오.

Golf Lessons

	Level	Days	Price	Coach
①	basic	Mon. ~ Fri.	$1,000	female
②	basic	Wed. ~ Sun.	$1,000	female
③	basic	Wed. ~ Sun.	$1,200	male
④	intermediate	Mon. ~ Fri.	$2,000	female
⑤	intermediate	Wed. ~ Sun.	$2,200	male

11 대화를 듣고, 여자의 마지막 말에 대한 남자의 응답으로 가장 적절한 것을 고르시오.

① Yes. I realized my decision was right.
② I disagree. It's within walking distance.
③ I think so. That's a long commute to work.
④ Exactly. I feel happy whenever I'm working.
⑤ Not really. I don't want to change my decision.

12 대화를 듣고, 남자의 마지막 말에 대한 여자의 응답으로 가장 적절한 것을 고르시오.

① Sorry. I'm not really into reading.
② Be careful. There is a lot of fake news.
③ Turn to the next page. You will find the sports section.
④ Don't worry. You don't have to subscribe to any newspaper.
⑤ Try it for 10 minutes a day. Then gradually increase the time.

13 대화를 듣고, 여자의 마지막 말에 대한 남자의 응답으로 가장 적절한 것을 고르시오.

Man: _____

① Absolutely! I can help you catch up.
② Certainly. Ballroom dancing is not easy.
③ That sounds great. Let's choose that one.
④ Really? Why don't we sign up for it?
⑤ Yes, I do. You already look like a pro.

14 대화를 듣고, 남자의 마지막 말에 대한 여자의 응답으로 가장 적절한 것을 고르시오. [3점]

Woman: _____

① Don't worry about it. I'll give you a hand.
② Yes. I should have worked more diligently.
③ I should have applied for the travel agency earlier.
④ No. Is there any chance to study more history?
⑤ No, that's all. I hope to hear from you soon.

15 다음 상황 설명을 듣고, Mike가 Susan에게 할 말로 가장 적절한 것을 고르시오. [3점]

Mike: _____

① I'm so sorry. I can't find my paper anywhere.
② Can I hand in the paper before finishing today's class?
③ Would you give me a little more time to finish the paper?
④ If your mother is home, why don't you ask her for help?
⑤ How about if I take you to your house by bike? It'll be faster.

[16~17] 다음을 듣고, 물음에 답하시오.

16 남자가 하는 말의 주제로 가장 적절한 것은?

① how to bring up children wisely
② how to make tasty food at home
③ how to do the chores at home effectively
④ how to encourage children to save money
⑤ how to motivate children to do housework

17 언급된 격려 방법이 <u>아닌</u> 것은?

① 디저트 제공　　　② 성취감 주기
③ 선물 주기　　　　④ 용돈 주기
⑤ 놀이공원 가기

01

M Attention, students. I have an important announcement to make. For those who are graduating next year, the school has planned a field trip _____ _____. The fair will be held in a convention center downtown, and more than 130 colleges will be there to help you make your important decision. This will be _____ _____ from schools you've been thinking about applying to. But before you attend the fair, it is best to visit the fair's site to see _____ so that you can select which booths to spend the most time at. You should also make a list of the questions you need to ask so that you do not forget while you are there. For further information about the fair, please visit the school website, where you will find a direct link to the fair's site. Thank you.

02

W Chris, do you know the TV program "Die Horribly IV"?

M I've never heard of it. I don't really enjoy TV programs. What's the show about?

W It's about a man taking revenge on bad people who killed his parents. But as the title indicates, _____ _____.

M Well, I think as long as it is aired late at night, it shouldn't be a problem.

W You're right. But the problem with the program is that even though it has age-15 rating, it is too violent. Besides, _____ _____.

M The show is originally scheduled late at night, but the reruns are in the afternoon? That doesn't sound right.

W I know. I feel like _____ _____.

M What do you mean?

W I'm thinking about filing a complaint with the broadcasting station about the program time.

M Is there anything I can help you with?

W Yes. Let's write the complaint together.

03

M Good morning, everyone! This is Eric Thompson, your book instructor. Do you ever have trouble understanding the author's ideas while reading? _____ _____? Also, if you agree or disagree with the author, make note of it by using "yes" or "no" _____ _____. It allows for a dialogue between the reader and the text, _____ _____. This active note-taking can be an effective reading method. Now, I'll show you a real example, so pay close attention.

04

W Hi, John. I heard that you're opening your own coffee shop soon.

M That's right. It'll be ready for business next week. If you have time, feel free to come by.

W Of course I will.

M _____, so I took a picture of it. Do you want to see it?

W Sure. [Pause] Wow, I like how you arranged the counter here. _____ _____.

M I placed it behind the cashier so that customers can see it well.

W That's good. After I order, where do I pick up the coffee?

M Oh, you order and _____ _____. Then you move to the right end of the counter to pick up the coffee.

W I see. That's why you put the coffee machine in the middle.

M That's right. Check out _____ _____.

W You put it on the right side of the cashier for convenience. Oh, what is that on the wall behind the counter?

M I _____ and placed some coffee mugs on it.

W Wow, it seems like you have everything ready.

05

W Hi, Mr. Lee. Why don't we check if everything's ready for the graduation ceremony?

M Sure. Did the janitors clean up the event hall?

W Yes, the hall was clean and ready to be set up.

M Oh, how far are you on the pamphlets?

W I was just preparing them. But don't worry about them. They'll be ready before the event starts. What about the projector?

M I'm not sure. I'll check it now.

W Okay. I'll check the microphone, then.

M *[Pause]* Oh, no. _____ _____. It won't turn on.

W That's not good.

M Why don't we ask someone from the maintenance department to have a look?

W All right. I'll make a call at once.

M How's the microphone? I think the amplifier should be on to see if it's working properly.

W Oh, _____. Can you test it for me instead?

M No problem.

06

W Mike, have you made a choice about the tile for our bathroom?

M Well, I was looking at this glossy brown tile. What do you think?

W It's nice. It looks like wood. How much is it?

M One unit is 300mm by 300mm and costs $15.

W That's not bad. Then how many tiles do we need for our bathroom?

M _____? We can come back and buy more if 30 is not enough.

W All right. Oh, we need a new bathroom sink, too.

M Right, I almost forgot. _____ _____?

W Not really. Let's get the same type we have now. How about that one in the corner?

M Okay. It's $60. I think that's reasonable.

W I think so, too. _____?

M It says it's in aisle 27, on shelf 5.

W All right. Let's go and pick up a sink first, and then tiles.

07

M Hi, Brittany. How was your weekend?

W Hi, Tim. I just stayed home.

M Why? Don't you usually go out on weekends?

W I had food poisoning, so _____ _____.

M That must have been terrible. Do you feel better now?

W Yes, I'm okay. What about you? Did you do anything special?

M On Sunday, I went to see the movie Julie recommended.

W Oh, I heard she got you movie tickets for your birthday. How did you like the movie?

M It was amazing. Why don't we _____ _____? I don't mind seeing it twice.

W I wish I could go with you, but I can't.

M Why not?

W I'm going to _____ _____.

M I thought you didn't like noisy places.

W I have no choice. _____.

M You're such a nice sister.

08

W We're going to see the pyramids and the Sphinx. If you have any questions, feel free to ask me. Okay?

M Sure.

W As you may know, no one really knows _____ _____. There are many theories and new discoveries, but it still remains a mystery.

M How long did it take to build a pyramid?

W _____ the tallest and oldest one, the Great Pyramid, which is one of three pyramids in Giza.

M It must be huge since it took 20 years to complete.

W It's about 139 meters tall. _____
_____ until the Eiffel Tower was built.

M That's amazing! _____
_____ in the Great Pyramid?

W I believe there are three.

09

W Good morning, everyone. My name is Susan Thompson, a manager from Raum Art Center. I'm here to introduce you to a fun way to experience and learn art. Starting this year, we are providing a Saturday Art School _____
_____. It is an amazing opportunity for them to explore the wonderful world of art. _____
_____.
Saturday Art School will also help kids learn about artists from around the world _____
_____. At the end of every session, we _____
into the art room to see all the beautiful artworks, and the kids are encouraged to speak positively about each other's work. To register, walk-ins are welcome, _____
_____.
For more information, please visit our website, www. raum-art.com. Thank you.

10

W How may I help you?

M Hello. I'd like to sign up for golf lessons here.

W Okay. What level are you interested in taking?

M I've never played golf before, so _____
_____.

W Okay. At the basic level, you will learn to hold a golf club and the basic pose.

M That sounds perfect. _____
_____.

W Oh, then you have to choose a coach who is available from Wednesday to Sunday.

M All right. Oh, why is there a price difference between these two coaches here?

W The price depends on their experience as a pro. The male coach played as a professional golfer longer than the female coach.

M Well, _____,
so I will go with the female coach.

11

W Chris, I hear that you got another job offer. Have you decided where to go?

M Not yet. The new offer includes _____
_____. But it's _____
_____.

W Does that mean you have to move if you accept the offer?

12

M Jenny, you seem to spend a lot of time reading the newspaper lately.

W _____
_____. There are so many benefits. You should try it, too.

M I was thinking about it, but _____
_____.

13

W Kevin, what's that poster over there?

M Oh, _____
_____. It's a class at the community center. Actually, I've been taking it for about two years.

W Wow, I didn't know you liked ballroom dancing.

M It's great exercise. Besides, I get to meet new people. What do you do when you're free?

W Well, I usually read, go shopping and hang out with friends.

M _____,
how about ballroom dancing? There is a free sample lesson this Friday at 7 p.m.

W Actually, _____. How did you get involved with the dance in the first place?

M Well, one of my friends dragged me into it, but now it's become a big part of my life. Watch this video.

W Wow, it looks so complicated. Do you think _____ _____?

14

M Hello, Miss Kelly. Have a seat and take it easy. *[Pause]* How did you get here?

W I took the subway. It only took half an hour from my house.

M I see. So, your résumé says _____ _____.

W That's right. I majored in Korean history. I've been interested in history since I was a little girl.

M I wonder _____, since you have various career options.

W Every place I visited had interesting stories and they always intrigued me. But some people don't bother to learn history. So, growing up, I've always wanted to make history seem easier to understand.

M Interesting. _____ you think it is. It can be very difficult and hard unless you are really passionate about it.

W I understand the hard parts of the job, but I think _____.

M I see. Is there anything you'd like to add?

15

W Susan and Mike are high school students. They worked on a science group assignment together, which is due today. Susan is supposed to finish the last part and bring it to school today. However, when she arrives at school, _____ _____. She calls her mother, but she isn't answering her phone. Then she checks the timetable and finds out science class is after lunch in fifth period today. She tells Mike that she'll _____ _____.

But Mike thinks that Susan won't have enough time to come back before the science class. He realizes if he _____,

they will make it before the class. So _____ _____ Susan and get the assignment together. In this situation, what does Mike most likely say to Susan?

16~17

M Hello, ladies and gentlemen! There are many household chores to do, but sometimes your children _____ _____. How can we encourage our children to participate in the housework willingly? Here are some ideas. First, you can _____ whenever he or she helps to clean up. Second, you can also give your child a sense of achievement. Just draw a bar graph for each child, and then every time they do chores, _____.

Third, keep a record on a calendar. If you think your child is doing chores very well, you should give them a small present at the end of the month. If your child is big enough to do things like lawn-mowing and gardening, _____ instead of rewarding them with treats? This will also teach children about earning money.

17회 실전 듣기 모의고사

01 다음을 듣고, 여자가 하는 말의 목적으로 가장 적절한 것을 고르시오.

① 직원 채용 계획을 알리려고
② 구독자 수 조사 참여를 권장하려고
③ 신문 배달 방법 변경 사항을 안내하려고
④ 광고주에게 광고료 인상을 안내하려고
⑤ 독자들에게 후원금을 요청하려고

02 대화를 듣고, 남자의 의견으로 가장 적절한 것을 고르시오.

① 전공 관련 인턴 경험은 취업할 때 도움이 된다.
② 다양한 아르바이트 경험은 취업 준비에 밑거름이 된다.
③ 전문 인력을 양성하기 위한 다양한 프로그램을 기획해야 한다.
④ 취업 센터를 통해 다양한 정보를 얻는 것이 중요하다.
⑤ 여러 자격증을 취득하는 것은 채용 가산점이 된다.

03 다음을 듣고, 여자가 하는 말의 요지로 가장 적절한 것을 고르시오.

① 암기보다는 이미지 연상을 통한 학습이 집중력을 높인다.
② 매일 하는 꾸준한 학습이 실력 향상으로 이어진다.
③ 신체 리듬에 따라 각자 효과적인 공부 시간대가 있다.
④ 깨끗이 정돈된 책상은 학습 능률을 높이는 효과를 준다.
⑤ 애착 있는 물품을 가지고 공부하면 집중력을 높일 수 있다.

04 대화를 듣고, 그림에서 대화의 내용과 일치하지 않는 것을 고르시오.

05 대화를 듣고, 여자가 할 일로 가장 적절한 것을 고르시오.

① 근무 시간 확인하기
② 서류 가방 정리하기
③ 함께 분실물 찾으러 가기
④ 신분 증빙 서류 대신 발급받기
⑤ 분실물 보관소 위치를 문자로 보내기

06 대화를 듣고, 남자가 지불할 금액을 고르시오. [3점]

① $144 ② $160 ③ $180
④ $240 ⑤ $280

07 대화를 듣고, 여자가 강의 수강을 취소하려는 이유를 고르시오.

① 취업을 하게 되어서
② 이번 학기에 수강 신청을 많이 해서
③ Kelly 교수님의 강의 방식이 맞지 않아서
④ 친구가 대신 수업을 듣고 싶다고 해서
⑤ 강의 진도를 따라가기가 힘들어서

08 대화를 듣고, SNT Concert에 관해 언급되지 않은 것을 고르시오.

① 공연 일자 ② 관객 수 ③ 가격
④ 다음 공연 정보 ⑤ 할인 정보

09 Blue Star Airlines에 관한 다음 내용을 듣고, 일치하지 않는 것을 고르시오.

① 현재 시속 400마일로 날고 있다.
② 난기류 때문에 도착이 지연되고 있다.
③ 원래 런던 도착시간은 9시 15분경이었다.
④ 20분쯤 후에 간단한 간식과 음료가 제공될 것이다.
⑤ 간식 제공 후에 기내 영화가 상영될 것이다.

10 다음 표를 보면서 대화를 듣고, 여자가 구매할 치약을 고르시오.

Toothpaste at Bason Drugstore

	Type	Special Feature	Price	Capacity	Flavor
①	A	daily repair	$13	120g (mini)	lemon
②	B	sensitive teeth	$20	150g (small)	lemon
③	C	sensitive teeth	$20	150g (small)	fresh mint
④	D	sensitive teeth	$25	200g (medium)	fresh mint
⑤	E	gum strengthening	$30	300g (large)	strawberry

11 대화를 듣고, 여자의 마지막 말에 대한 남자의 응답으로 가장 적절한 것을 고르시오.

① Okay. You'll have to come in before noon.
② Great. Then I'd like to schedule it for 10:30.
③ No, thanks. I will just find another clinic to go to.
④ All right. There is an overdue charge for this book.
⑤ Sorry. I need to cancel the appointment for this Friday.

12 대화를 듣고, 남자의 마지막 말에 대한 여자의 응답으로 가장 적절한 것을 고르시오.

① No problem. I have another ID in my car.
② Sorry. The ID must include your photo and date of birth.
③ Of course. Please come this way and I'll show your car.
④ Yes. We take any form of ID issued by the government.
⑤ I'm afraid not. You can only exchange the euro into U.S. dollars.

13 대화를 듣고, 여자의 마지막 말에 대한 남자의 응답으로 가장 적절한 것을 고르시오.

Man: _____

① Certainly. Don't forget to train harder.
② I'm sorry to disappoint you. It's my fault.
③ Okay, I'll try my best to finish it next time.
④ Thank you. I'm so glad to have your support.
⑤ That's right. The next marathon will be different.

14 대화를 듣고, 남자의 마지막 말에 대한 여자의 응답으로 가장 적절한 것을 고르시오. [3점]

Woman: _____

① Good idea. She will be disappointed by it, though.
② Okay. Once the dates are set, I'll look for hotels.
③ It makes sense, but how can we persuade her?
④ Sure, but we should think about what to eat.
⑤ Yes, let's talk to Mom about the destination.

15 다음 상황 설명을 듣고, Robert가 Carol에게 할 말로 가장 적절한 것을 고르시오. [3점]

Robert: _____

① Cheer up. Santa is coming soon.
② Why don't we start wrapping our gifts?
③ How about a cheeseburger? It's your favorite.
④ Shall we ask Santa to come home on Christmas?
⑤ Christmas is about helping others and giving generously.

[16~17] 다음을 듣고, 물음에 답하시오.

16 여자가 하는 말의 주제로 가장 적절한 것은?

① how to cooperate with robots when learning
② strengths and weaknesses of robotic teachers
③ reasons teachers will never be replaced by robots
④ the development of AI-powered systems in the classroom
⑤ differences in education level between AI and a human teacher

17 언급된 인성이나 능력이 **아닌** 것은?

① 공감 능력　　② 이해심　　③ 창의력
④ 희생정신　　⑤ 지식 전달력

◀» 녹음된 내용을 들으면서 빈칸을 알맞게 채워보세요. _____

01

W Hello, I'm Ella Brown from the Globe. We feel happy and proud that more people are reading and supporting our newspaper. Recently we made the choice to provide our readers with less advertising for their convenience, _____. For that reason, we have a small favor to ask of you. _____ to keep delivering quality journalism. Every reader contribution, however big or small, is so valuable. Support the Globe with as little as $1. It only takes a minute. At a time when factual information is a necessity, we believe that people _____ and useful information. Your support will allow the Globe to keep up its quality journalism. We will make a continued effort to report the most critical issues of our time for you. Thank you.

02

M Mina, do you have any plans for this summer?

W I think I'll get a part-time job at a restaurant. It'll be a great chance to save up money before graduation.

M That's true. We only have one year left until graduation. Why don't you try something _____?

W What do you mean?

M Since your major is accounting, _____ is a good way to spend your summer.

W Actually, that doesn't sound too bad. I could _____ _____ at the same time.

M Exactly. You may not make much but you can use that experience after you graduate to get a job.

W Do you think I stand a chance? I'm only in my third year in college.

M You've learned all the basics. Now, you need to _____ _____.

W You're right. I should head to the job center on campus.

M That's a good place to start. It has lots of useful information.

03

W Hi everyone, welcome to *Melanie's Learning Lounge*! Today, I have an effective trick _____ _____. Before you study, try to neatly organize your desk. This will create a conducive environment for focus and concentration. _____, enhances productivity, and psychologically prepares you for a more effective and efficient study. Believe me, and tidy up your desk. _____! I will give you an example from my experience. So stick around!

04

M Hello, Judy. How was your family trip?

W It was good. I went to the Namhan River. Would you like to see a picture?

M Sure. *[Pause]* Oh, there are _____ _____.

W Yes, there are. At night, the light from the lampposts makes the river more beautiful.

M And _____?

W They're my cousins. They really enjoyed riding the two-person bike standing next to them.

M That must have been great. Oh, the bicycle lane goes along the river.

W Yes, you can see the entire river while riding.

M Wonderful. And there's _____ _____.

W Yes, it's the area's mascot.

M I'll try to visit next fall. Oh, I think I see you! Is that you under the pine tree?

W Yes, that's me. I was really tired from riding my bike.

05

[Telephone rings.]

W Lost and Found. What can I do for you?

M Hello, I lost my briefcase this morning. Do you have a black leather briefcase by any chance?

W We have a few black leather briefcases here. _____ _____?

M Certainly. It has a long strap. Oh, there should be a blue tumbler inside.

W All right. Let me check first. *[Pause]* Oh, yes. It's here. May I have your name, please?

M It's Mike West.

W Okay, Mr. West. We are open until 6 p.m. today. Please come in 30 minutes before then. It could take a while to _____.

M I don't think I can find the time to visit today. I'll come and pick it up tomorrow morning.

W That's fine. Please bring your ID with you when you visit. You know where our office is located, right?

M No, I don't. Could you _____ _____ to this number?

W Okay, _____ by text message after this call.

M Thank you so much. I'll see you tomorrow.

06

M Hello, I'd like to check out, please. Here is my room key.

W Certainly, sir. How did you enjoy your stay at our hotel?

M It was lovely. I really loved the pool and spa here.

W I'm glad to hear that. Before we proceed with the payment, I need to confirm a few things.

M All right.

W Our record shows that you stayed for 2 nights, _____ _____. Is that correct?

M Yes, that was the price when I made the reservation.

W In addition, you ordered room service yesterday, which was $30. Is that right, sir?

M That's right. Oh, I also had a massage the day before. _____.

W Yes, sir. The massage was $50. Please check the screen for the total price.

M Okay. I have a membership with this hotel chain. Is there any discount available?

W Of course. We provide a 20% discount, _____ _____.

M Oh, that's fine. Here's my credit card.

07

M Hey, Cindy. Where are you going now?

W Hey, John. I'm going to the registration building to see _____.

M What class is that?

W It's a law class, LAW 321. That's the one with Professor Kelly.

M He is one of the most popular professors here on this campus. Some of my friends _____ _____ because it was already full.

W I know. But I have no choice.

M Oh, did you get a job?

W No, I really want to _____.

M Then why are you dropping the law class?

W I'm not sure _____ _____. Besides, the law class is an optional class, not a requirement.

M That makes sense. Can one of my friends take your place?

W Sure.

08

M Lucy, what are you reading? Anything interesting?

W I was just reading an article about my favorite K-pop group, SNT.

M I heard they performed at London Stadium last week.

W Yes, they _____.

M The concert must have been so exciting.

W Yes. I _____ who went to the concert.

M That's incredible!

W I know. And it only took 10 minutes for all 60,000 tickets for the concert to sell out.

M That's so fast. How much were the tickets?

W It depended on how close to the stage you were. I heard the prices ranged from $100 to $300.

M Wow, I didn't know SNT was that popular in the UK.

W Yes, 140,000 fans _____ _____.

M When is their next concert?

W It'll be in August in Paris. I wish I could go!

09

M Good afternoon passengers. This is your captain speaking. I'd like to welcome everyone on Blue Star Airlines. We are currently cruising at an altitude of 33,000 feet at an airspeed of 400 miles per hour. The time is 1:25 p.m. The weather looks good and we have the wind on our side. _____ _____ at 9 p.m., approximately fifteen minutes ahead of schedule. The cabin crew will be coming around in about twenty minutes to _____. The in-flight _____ _____. I'll talk to you again before we reach our destination. Until then, sit back, relax and enjoy the rest of the flight.

10

M Good morning. How may I help you?

W Hello. There are so many types of toothpaste. I don't know which one to choose.

M Okay. Let me help you with that. _____ _____ you are looking for?

W Well, I want something that can improve my dental health. _____.

M I see. For sensitive teeth and gums, these are very popular ones. They are also highly recommended by dentists.

W Really? They sound perfect. How much are they?

M Since they repair and strengthen teeth and gums, they are more expensive than other ones.

W Well, I don't want to _____ _____. It seems a bit too much.

M All right, then. They also come in different sizes.

W _____ since I might not like it.

M Okay. This brand has two different flavors.

W I'll take the fresh mint one because I'm used to it.

M Sure. Here you are.

11

[Telephone rings.]

W Jun's Hair. How may I help you?

M Hello. I'd like to make an appointment for a haircut. _____ this Saturday?

W _____.

[Pause] The only time we have on Saturday is before 11 in the morning.

12

M Hello. I'd like to change 500 U.S. dollars into euros, please.

W Okay. _____?
One dollar is worth 1.2 euros today.

M That's fine. Oh, and _____ _____. Is that all right?

13

W You made it! I am proud of you, David. How do you feel?

M I'm so excited. I can't believe I finished the race!

W You did so well. I was so worried that _____ _____ during the marathon.

M Mom, you didn't need to worry. It was only a 10 km race.

W Don't be so modest. You have prepared for this race for the past two months. I know _____ _____.

M I didn't do well enough. I didn't even get close to the goal I had in mind.

W It's good to set high goals, but you shouldn't _____ _____.

M Right. I'll do my best to complete the half marathon next time.

W You shouldn't _____.
But I'm sure you can do it.

14

M Jane, we decided to send Mom on a trip for her 50th birthday, correct?

W Yes, but I think we have to cancel.

M Why? She said _____ _____ like Tom's mom did.

W I know what she said. But Tom's mom took the trip with her entire family. I think that's what Mom really wants.

M You think so? But I don't think I can afford for all of us to go to Europe.

W I think the destination doesn't matter. _____ _____.

M Then how about taking a trip to somewhere nearby? A place within a two-hour drive should be okay.

W That's a great idea. Since Mom loves hiking, we should head to Mt. Taebaek.

M That sounds like a good plan. Besides, this time of the year is _____ _____.

W I know. She'll enjoy the autumn leaves.

M I can't wait! First, let's discuss the dates with Dad.

15

M Every Christmas, Robert would buy Christmas gifts for his children and hide them in the closet. On the night of Christmas Eve, Robert would tell his children a story about Santa Claus. However, this Christmas season, Robert _____ _____ Carol. She doesn't talk about what she wants to get from Santa. Even when she sees Santa on TV, _____ _____. Then Robert realizes Carol may have found out Santa doesn't exist. So, he starts to look for tips on how to tell kids about Santa. He finds a comment by another parent. It says that _____ _____.

After reading the comment, Robert takes Carol out to lunch. When they finish their meal, he decides to talk about Christmas. In this situation, what would Robert most likely say to Carol?

16~17

W According to a recent report, about half of today's jobs could be automated by 2055. Does this mean teachers can be replaced by Artificial Intelligence? _____ _____ that robots don't have. It's empathy. Human teachers can empathize with students and encourage them to pursue their goals. While robotic guidance would be limited because they have no feelings, teachers help _____.

Also, teachers have the ability to understand young people with diverse backgrounds and values. They have the experience and understanding to support students as they grow through childhood. And, human teachers _____, which robots don't have. For example, teachers improvise and add their own stories, which makes the classes more interesting. Lastly, teachers have a spirit of sacrifice with respect to their students. Only human beings can _____.

Because human teachers are capable of providing greater support than AIs, I believe they will always be superior. Knowledge alone is not enough to become a good teacher.

18 회 실전 듣기 모의고사

01 다음을 듣고, 남자가 하는 말의 목적으로 가장 적절한 것을 고르시오.

① 가게의 폐업을 알리려고
② 할인 행사를 홍보하려고
③ 가게 이전을 공지하려고
④ 회원권 가입을 안내하려고
⑤ 할인 기간 변경을 알리려고

02 대화를 듣고, 여자의 의견으로 가장 적절한 것을 고르시오.

① 학생에게 과목 선택권을 주어야 한다.
② 현장 학습에도 교육적 목적이 있어야 한다.
③ 학생들에게 놀 수 있는 기회를 주어야 한다.
④ 현장 학습 장소는 학생 투표로 결정해야 한다.
⑤ 학급별로 다른 장소로 현장 학습을 가야 한다.

03 다음을 듣고, 남자가 하는 말의 요지로 가장 적절한 것을 고르시오.

① 중요한 일일수록 더 많은 시간을 투자해야 한다.
② 일의 능률이 오르는 시간은 사람마다 다르다.
③ 적절한 시간 배분이 일의 처리 능력을 향상시킨다.
④ 중요한 일은 아침에 처리하는 것이 더 효과적이다.
⑤ 자기 전에 다음날 계획을 세우는 것을 습관화해야 한다.

04 대화를 듣고, 그림에서 대화의 내용과 일치하지 <u>않는</u> 것을 고르시오.

① LISA JAMES
② DISAPPEARANCE
③
④ "Thrilling and enchanting, it will take your breath away."
⑤ ★ ★ ★ ★ ★

05 대화를 듣고, 남자가 여자에게 부탁한 일로 가장 적절한 것을 고르시오.

① 세탁소에서 재킷 찾아오기
② 감기약 사다 주기
③ 사진 찍어주기
④ 누나에게 전화 걸기
⑤ 카메라 충전기 가져오기

06 대화를 듣고, 여자가 지불할 금액을 고르시오.

① $39   ② $60   ③ $70
④ $74   ⑤ $79

07 대화를 듣고, 남자가 퇴임식에 가지 <u>못 하는</u> 이유를 고르시오.

① 미용실에 가야 해서
② 누나의 결혼식과 겹쳐서
③ 선물을 준비하지 못 해서
④ 취업 면접을 준비해야 해서
⑤ 이미 교수님을 만나 뵈어서

08 대화를 듣고, 헬스클럽에 관해 언급되지 <u>않은</u> 것을 고르시오.

① 이름   ② 위치
③ 운동 기구 종류   ④ 무료 수업
⑤ 회원권 가격

09 Scuba Diving Camp에 관한 다음 내용을 듣고, 일치하지 <u>않는</u> 것을 고르시오.

① 모든 비용은 수영센터에서 지불한다.
② 6개월 이상 등록한 회원만 참여할 수 있다.
③ 다양한 물고기를 볼 수 있는 Fish Eye에서 진행된다.
④ 스쿠버다이빙에 필요한 모든 장비가 제공된다.
⑤ 프로그램에 식사비용이 포함되어 있다.

10 다음 표를 보면서 대화를 듣고, 여자가 수강할 크로스핏 프로그램을 고르시오.

CrossFit Programs at Always Stay Fit

Class	Period	Special Diet	Days
① A	1 month	×	Mon. ~ Fri.
② B	1 month	○	Mon. ~ Fri.
③ C	3 months	×	Mon. Wed. Fri.
④ D	3 months	○	Mon. Wed. Fri.
⑤ E	6 months	○	Tue. Thurs. Sat.

11 대화를 듣고, 여자의 마지막 말에 대한 남자의 응답으로 가장 적절한 것을 고르시오.

① It looks like it's going to rain for another week.
② Don't worry! You look just the way you wish to.
③ I'm sorry, but I have no idea of what it looks like.
④ It doesn't cost that much to make a photo album.
⑤ Look at these. I saved pictures of each page on my phone.

12 대화를 듣고, 남자의 마지막 말에 대한 여자의 응답으로 가장 적절한 것을 고르시오.

① You should go to a new doctor. It could help.
② Of course. I'll give you a list of good clinics for children.
③ I recommend going to the doctor before it gets any worse.
④ There is a new clinic downtown that specializes in neck pain.
⑤ I am sorry, but I don't know anything about relieving back pain.

13 대화를 듣고, 여자의 마지막 말에 대한 남자의 응답으로 가장 적절한 것을 고르시오. [3점]

Man: _____

① Of course. I have solved the problem on my own.
② Thanks. I will consider the options you gave me.
③ Okay. I'll get the receipt and call the manager.
④ I would like a full refund. Here is my credit card.
⑤ The only option is to turn it off and turn it on again.

14 대화를 듣고, 남자의 마지막 말에 대한 여자의 응답으로 가장 적절한 것을 고르시오. [3점]

Woman: _____

① I am staying in this city for two nights.
② Let's ask the hotel to store our luggage.
③ I don't think so. Let's just cancel the concert.
④ I think we can. We'll just have to plan our trip well.
⑤ The mall is way too far from the hotel. Let's just stay home.

15 다음 상황 설명을 듣고, Johnny가 Ben에게 할 말로 가장 적절한 것을 고르시오. [3점]

Johnny: _____

① Unfortunately I have to resign from this position.
② Would you like to go to the welcoming event with me?
③ Let's prepare a performance to welcome the freshmen.
④ I don't want to do a performance for the upper-classmen.
⑤ What kind of performance do you expect from the freshmen?

[16~17] 다음을 듣고, 물음에 답하시오.

16 남자가 하는 말의 주제로 가장 적절한 것은?

① life of Michelangelo and his artwork
② most influential popes in Roman history
③ characteristics of the tourism industry in Rome
④ construction and collapse of the Sistine Chapel
⑤ history of the Sistine Chapel and its famous ceiling

17 언급된 인물이 <u>아닌</u> 것은?

① Pope Sixtus IV   ② Michelangelo
③ Botticelli   ④ Leonardo Da Vinci
⑤ Pope Julius II

18 회 DICTATION

01

M Hello, dear customers of G-mart. Thank you for using G-mart and being a loyal customer of our store. We would like to _____. The sale starts on September 13th and lasts until the last day of the month, so _____ to enjoy our biggest sale of the year. For those who have a membership with us, there will be flyers sent out by mail. You can check the items on sale and the prices. Most of our merchandise will have up to a 70% discount, including groceries, household goods, car parts, and so on. Thank you again and we _____ _____.

02

M Good morning, Ms. Schneider.

W Hello, Mr. Long. Did you think of places _____ _____?

M Well, I have a few ideas. I think a field trip should be a day to have fun.

W Sure. We should make it fun. Through a school field trip, students can relieve stress.

M Exactly. So I think an amusement park will be the perfect place to go.

W An amusement park is not the only way to relieve stress. Students will _____ _____. Besides, some students might not like going on rides at all.

M Oh, I didn't think about that. Do you have any better ideas?

W I thought of a museum tour or a cultural heritage spot in our town. The field trip is part of the curriculum so _____ _____.

M You are right. But I'm worried that students could get bored.

W Well, _____. That's our responsibility.

M You're right. Let's discuss it with the other teachers at the meeting.

03

M Hello, I'm Ian Baldwin, your productivity advisor. One key to maximizing productivity is having a solid strategy. So, let me ask: _____ _____? Completing important tasks in the morning is more effective. By starting your day with crucial tasks, you can ensure you have the energy and focus needed to accomplish them efficiently. The morning is the most productive time _____ _____. To make things more visual, _____ that breaks down our productivity by time of day. Would you like to take a look at it?

04

[Telephone rings.]

M Hello, London Publishers. How can I help you?

W Hello, this is Lisa James calling. Is this Mr. Jennings?

M Oh, hello, Ms. James. I was about to call you so we could talk about your book cover.

W Yes, you sent the design to my e-mail address. I am looking at it right now.

M Good. I am, too. _____ _____? I put it in capital letters to make it stand out.

W Yes. And I also like the title under my name in tall, thin letters.

M How do you like the drawing under the title?

W _____. I see the cat's shadow, but not the man's shadow.

M Oh, my mistake. I am terribly sorry. I will _____ _____.

W Okay. Everything else is great. I really like that you added a review from a critic in quotation marks.

M That was my colleague's idea. I'm glad you like it. Also, I _____ to show that your book got a great response in the review.

W That's a great idea. Thank you for your hard work.

M My pleasure. I will send you the revised design as soon as I have it.

05

W Jerry, have you packed everything for the school trip?

M I am doing it right now, Mom. Do you know where my light jacket is?

W It's at the dry cleaner's now, but I asked your father _____.

M Oh, good. I really need that jacket to wear at night.

W I know. It can get cold at night.

M That's right. What else do I need? Oh, I almost forgot to _____.

W Don't put your camera in your bag. Carry it with you all the time to prevent damage or theft.

M I will. Don't worry.

W And don't forget _____. The charger is in your sister's room.

M Are you sure? I looked in her room a while ago and I didn't see it there.

W Really? She took the camera and the charger into her room yesterday to move the photos to her computer.

M Then could you call her and _____? I have to continue packing for tomorrow.

W Of course, honey. I'll do that right now.

06

M Welcome to Everything Eco-Friendly. How can I help you?

W Hello. I'm looking for eco-friendly paint. Could you recommend one for me?

M Sure. This type right here is _____.

W How much is it for one container?

M They are $20 each. Would you like to see some color samples, too?

W Sure. *[Pause]* Wow, this one is great. _____, please.

M Certainly. Is there anything else you need?

W Oh, yes. _____.

M I strongly recommend using both a brush and a roller. Rollers are better for painting a large area, and brushes are better when finishing the corners.

W How much are they?

M Brushes are $5 each while rollers are $7 each.

W _____.

M Certainly. I'll have them ready for you at the counter.

07

W You need to go to a barbershop. Your hair is so long that it covers your eyes.

M I know. I was going to get it trimmed a bit later today. I want to look good for my job interview next week.

W I see. I hope you get the position you're applying for.

M Thank you. Where are you going?

W I am going to the store _____ Professor Robertson's retirement.

M Oh, right. _____. He was one of my favorite professors.

W I know. He is so enthusiastic in class. So are you going to his retirement ceremony?

M I really wish I could, but unfortunately I can't.

W Why not? Is it because of your job interview?

M No. My sister is getting married, and _____.

W That's too bad. But everyone will understand.

M But I am going _____ and give him my congratulations.

W Good idea. He will be very pleased.

08

W I'm looking for a gym to join. Do you know any good ones?

M Oh, you should join the gym I go to. _____. It's really nice.

W Okay, what's its name?

M It's called Cal-Burn Gym. _____. Do you get it?

W Oh, that's a good name for a gym. What about the machines?

M There are many treadmills. The gym also _____. The staff is always there to help you out with the tricky machines.

W There are people who can help on-site? That's nice. In some gyms you have to pay extra for that.

M I know. Cal-Burn also offers free classes. But you might have to reserve a spot since classes like yoga are really popular.

W I see. I'll think about that. So _____ _____?

M It's $100 for a three-month membership. Before you decide on anything, get a free trial workout.

09

W How many of you have gone scuba diving before? It's not a common experience, and our swimming center is offering you _____ _____. Even though the camp normally costs over $500, all the expenses for the camp will be covered by our center. But this camp is only available to members who have signed up for a membership of six months or more. The camp will be at an area known as "Fish Eye" and _____ _____ you have never seen in person before. The camp provides all the equipment needed for scuba diving, including aqua shoes and an oxygen tank. However, _____ _____, so please make note of this point.

10

M Welcome to Always Stay Fit. How may I help you?

W Hello. I'd like to sign up for a CrossFit program at your gym.

M Okay. As you can see, there are five different beginner programs offered.

W All right. How long should I take the class to see changes?

M It depends on how hard you work. I recommend to _____. That's how long it takes to get your body used to an intense workout.

W I see. I will follow your advice. What is this special diet?

M Many people don't know _____ _____ while you are working out. So, we make a personalized meal plan for each client.

W Wow, that's amazing. _____ _____ the special diet.

M Okay, the three remaining classes are every two days, three times a week. You just have to choose the time you'll be most likely to come.

W I don't think _____.

M All right. Then, this is the class for you. Please fill out this form. After you're done, I'll show you around.

11

W My father's birthday is coming up, and I don't know what to get him.

M How about _____? That's what I gave my father, and he loved it.

W That's a great idea. _____?

12

M Ouch! My neck hurts so much.

W _____. Haven't you been getting treatment for a while?

M Well, maybe I should go to a different clinic. _____ _____?

13

W Whoa!

M What's wrong?

W The microwave suddenly stopped working.

M Really? We just bought it last week.

W I know. I think we should _____ _____.

M Hmm... Can I have a look? Let's see what went wrong. What did you put in it?

W I just wanted to warm up some food. It's a glass container. I didn't put in _____ _____.

M Well, we have used it for a week already. I don't think they will give us a new one.

W We could try. _____

_____.

M It could be. Let's go over the manual here. *[Pause]* It doesn't say anything about what to do when it won't turn on.

W See? Let's just _____

_____. They will help us.

14

M Honey, I can't believe the concert is only a week away!

W I know. I've been waiting for it for so long.

M Yes. Since the concert is in the evening, why don't we do some sightseeing in the city before the concert?

W Good idea. Oh, _____

_____?

M Of course. I even double-checked that we will get an ocean-facing room.

W Great. _____.
It will definitely be a good time for us.

M I agree. By the way, what do you plan to bring since we are spending a night there?

W I think I'll have to bring a small suitcase. Oh, I heard _____.

Do you want to go shopping?

M Sure. But do you think _____

_____? We are only staying in the city for two days.

15

W Johnny is a member of the student body. He is in charge of organizing the welcoming event for new freshmen at the beginning of the school year. Traditionally, they have _____

_____ for the upper-classmen and the teachers. The purpose is to give freshmen a chance to get to know each other and learn how to cooperate. However, when Johnny was a freshman the year before, he felt like he was _____

_____. He felt embarrassed on stage because he did not have any singing or dancing talent.

So this year, as the student in charge of this event, he wants to try something new and have _____

_____ instead.
But in order to do so, he knows he has to convince Ben first, as he is the student body president. In this situation, what would Johnny most likely say to Ben?

16~17

M Welcome to the lesson, everyone. Today, we will continue talking about the historical places in Rome, Italy. Look at this picture. Can anyone tell me what you are looking at? Yes, that's right. It's the Sistine Chapel, which is located in the Vatican City, _____

_____. The chapel takes its name from Pope Sixtus IV, who restored it between 1477 and 1480. _____

the fresco interior, particularly the Sistine Chapel ceiling painted by Michelangelo. During the reign of the same pope, Renaissance painters including the famous artist Botticelli created a series of frescos on the left and right walls. Between 1508 and 1512, under the order of Pope Julius II, Michelangelo _____

_____, a project which changed the course of Western art. This painting is _____

_____ of human history.

19회 실전 듣기 모의고사

01 다음을 듣고, 여자가 하는 말의 목적으로 가장 적절한 것을 고르시오.

① 강당 사용 규칙을 안내하려고
② 강당 개관식 행사를 공지하려고
③ 강당 보수 공사 계획을 발표하려고
④ 학교 위원회의 재정 적자를 알리려고
⑤ 학교 기부 행사에 참여를 독려하려고

02 대화를 듣고, 남자의 의견으로 가장 적절한 것을 고르시오.

① 과도한 휴대폰 사용은 아이들의 집중력을 저하시킨다.
② 휴대폰에서 유용한 앱을 찾아 활용해야 한다.
③ 식사 시간에는 TV를 보지 말아야 한다.
④ 부모들은 아이들의 휴대폰 사용 시간을 제한해야 한다.
⑤ 부모들은 휴대폰 사용을 자제하여 아이들에게 본보기가 되어야 한다.

03 다음을 듣고, 여자가 하는 말의 요지로 가장 적절한 것을 고르시오.

① 자세를 바르게 하고 걷는 것이 건강을 향상시킨다.
② 의자에 앉은 시간을 줄이는 것이 허리 통증을 줄인다.
③ 허리 통증을 막으려면 의자에 등을 대고 똑바로 앉아야 한다.
④ 허리 통증은 약물치료의 시기를 놓치지 않는 게 중요하다.
⑤ 허리 통증을 완화하려면 체형에 맞는 의자를 사용해야 한다.

04 대화를 듣고, 그림에서 대화의 내용과 일치하지 않는 것을 고르시오.

05 대화를 듣고, 여자가 남자에게 부탁한 일로 가장 적절한 것을 고르시오.

① 포스터의 틀린 철자 고치기
② 선생님에게 최종본 보내기
③ 교장 선생님에게 전화하기
④ 자원봉사자 찾아보기
⑤ 포스터 인쇄하기

06 대화를 듣고, 남자가 지불할 금액을 고르시오. [3점]

① $25   ② $28   ③ $30
④ $34   ⑤ $40

07 대화를 듣고, 여자가 쿠키를 환불하는 이유를 고르시오.

① 포장이 손상되어서
② 유통 기한이 짧아서
③ 엄마가 쿠키를 싫어해서
④ 쿠키에 견과류가 들어 있어서
⑤ 유기농 재료로 만들어지지 않아서

08 대화를 듣고, canopy walkway에 관해 언급되지 않은 것을 고르시오.

① 중량   ② 소재   ③ 초기 목적
④ 높이   ⑤ 길이

09 Eco-Car에 관한 다음 내용을 듣고, 일치하지 않는 것을 고르시오.

① 미래지향적인 디자인을 가졌다.
② 중량이 가벼워 바람의 저항을 적게 받는다.
③ 배터리로 운행되어 충전식이다.
④ 지붕에 태양에너지 판이 설치되어 있다.
⑤ 좌석에 쓰인 플라스틱은 신소재로 만들어졌다.

10 다음 표를 보면서 대화를 듣고, 두 사람이 예약할 항공편을 고르시오.

Schedule for Flights to Spain

Flight	Carrier Type	Departure Time	Arrival Airport	Stops
① A	low cost	morning	Madrid	connecting flight
② B	low cost	morning	Barcelona	non-stop flight
③ C	low cost	afternoon	Madrid	connecting flight
④ D	low cost	morning	Barcelona	connecting flight
⑤ E	full service	afternoon	Madrid	non-stop flight

11 대화를 듣고, 여자의 마지막 말에 대한 남자의 응답으로 가장 적절한 것을 고르시오.

① No. I don't want to work out at night.
② Good. You should go on a diet right away.
③ Sure. I heard swimming is good for burning calories.
④ Yes. My dream is to become a swimming coach.
⑤ Of course. I don't need to lose any more weight.

12 대화를 듣고, 남자의 마지막 말에 대한 여자의 응답으로 가장 적절한 것을 고르시오.

① Good idea. I'll treat you to dinner then.
② No, thanks. I already have plans for that day.
③ Okay. I will see you at the movie theater in one hour.
④ That's amazing. I wish I could go there to see them in person.
⑤ Oh, no! I can't believe they canceled the show because of the storm.

13 대화를 듣고, 여자의 마지막 말에 대한 남자의 응답으로 가장 적절한 것을 고르시오. [3점]

Man: _____

① You're right. I think I'll do exactly what you said.
② You should finish writing the script by tomorrow.
③ Thanks for introducing such an experienced MC to me.
④ If you don't mind, I want you to be the MC at my wedding.
⑤ On second thought, I think it would give me more confidence.

14 대화를 듣고, 남자의 마지막 말에 대한 여자의 응답으로 가장 적절한 것을 고르시오.

Woman: _____

① Yes, please. We're planning to leave early.
② No worries. The photo album is already done.
③ Of course. She will be happy to see you there.
④ Not really. I don't want to make an album any more.
⑤ Definitely. I need someone to get a few photos enlarged.

15 다음 상황 설명을 듣고, Carol이 Lydia에게 할 말로 가장 적절한 것을 고르시오. [3점]

Carol: _____

① I'm terribly sorry. I will quiet him down.
② You look tired. Why don't you take a nap?
③ Thank you. It was very kind of you to drop by.
④ He is such a sweet boy. I brought him some candy.
⑤ I'm from downstairs. Could you please make your boy be quiet?

[16~17] 다음을 듣고, 물음에 답하시오.

16 여자가 하는 말의 주제로 가장 적절한 것은?

① how to characterize the butterfly
② how moths and butterflies are different
③ things moths and butterflies have in common
④ why butterflies sleep with their wings open
⑤ how moths and butterflies find food

17 언급된 특징이 <u>아닌</u> 것은?

① 활동 시간   ② 더듬이의 모양
③ 날개 색상   ④ 알 부화 시기
⑤ 몸과 날개에 난 털

01

W Good morning, everyone. Today, I'm very glad to say that _____
_____.
Many of you and your families have donated a lot of money for the renovation, so I'd like to express my deep gratitude for your generosity. To show our appreciation for your support, the school committee
_____
next Monday. The new auditorium will be open to the public for the first time. There will be great food from local restaurants and music by the school orchestra.
_____
your families and friends to celebrate this special event. Once again, on behalf of the committee, I appreciate your support.

02

M It seems like many parents let their kids watch videos on their phones during mealtimes.
W I know. I've seen my sister do it a couple of times.
M Cell phones may be helpful sometimes, _____
_____. Don't you think so?
W I agree, but at the same time I understand why parents let their kids use their phones.
M I know how hard and difficult parenting can be. But
_____
_____.
W I'm sure most parents are trying hard and doing their best in their own ways.
M That's right. I'm just saying that _____
_____ or let their kids use them under parental control.
W I'm with you on that.

03

W Welcome to the Pain Clinic. I'm Dr. Olivia Williams, and today I'd like to share some tips on maintaining good posture for those who experience back pain. _____, make sure to sit up straight

with your back against the chair. This will help your body feel better _____.
Sitting makes up most of our waking hours. This means that poor sitting posture can cause back pain. So, sit straight in the chair with your back well-supported to prevent recurring back pain. _____
_____, I'll be using a visual aid. Please direct your attention to the screen.

04

M Miss Kim, we just finished decorating the classroom for Hannah.
W Wow, it's amazing! Well done, Chris. I'm sure Hannah will love this. How did you do it?
M First, _____
_____.
W Okay. Who wrote "Welcome Back!" on the board?
M Joanna did it because she has such good handwriting.
W Did she also _____
_____?
M Yes, she did. She said Hannah loves flowers, so she added a few.
W They are so pretty. Oh, all the presents and the stuffed bunny are on my desk!
M Yes. _____
_____. Is that all right?
W Of course. The cake is on the student's desk in the center of the room. What's that on the other desk?
M Oh, it's a card. We wrote a card for Hannah.
W Is there any space left on the card? I want to write something, too.
M Sure. Here is a pen.

05

M Hey, Annie. Have you checked the final version of the poster I sent you?
W Of course. It's perfect.
M Are you sure you corrected all those typos that I marked?
W Don't worry. _____,
and I had Sarah double-check it, too.

M I'm glad to hear that. Then you can send it to Mr. Williams now.

W I already did and he really liked the design. He said he would talk to the principal about it, and she would make the final decision.

M Great. When the principal says yes, _____ _____.

W All right. Oh, one more thing. _____ _____ who can put up posters. Can you ask some of our classmates if they will be available?

M Okay. I'll ask them and let you know.

06

W Hello. Can I help you?

M Yes, I'm looking for a cake for my daughter's birthday.

W Okay. We have a variety of cakes over here.

M She likes chocolate very much.

W Oh, in that case, we have this white chocolate cake which is popular with girls.

M It looks delicious. How much is it?

W It is $25, and _____ _____ if you buy our milk.

M Cool. Wait a minute. I think it's too small. Do you have anything a little bigger?

W Sure, this cake is made of dark chocolate. So this one is less sweet than the white chocolate one.

M _____, is it?

W No, it's not. It has sweet cream inside, so the sweetness is well-balanced.

M Oh, really? Is it also $25?

W No, sir. This one is $5 more expensive than the other one.

M All right. I'll take the dark chocolate one. Oh, I need to buy milk to get 20% off the cake, right?

W That's right. A carton of milk is $5. _____ _____?

M Yes, please. I'll take two cartons. Here is my credit card.

W Okay, I will help you with the payment over there.

07

M Cindy, where are you heading to?

W Hey, Tom. I'm going to Lee's Bakery.

M Oh, I know that place. It's one of the few places in town that use only organic ingredients. What are you getting?

W Actually, I'm going there _____ _____.

M Is there something wrong with them?

W No, there is nothing wrong. I didn't even open the package.

M Then why are you returning them?

W I bought them for my mom but _____ _____.

M Is it because she doesn't like cookies?

W No, not that. It turns out _____ _____, and she is allergic to them.

M Oh, I'm sorry to hear that. She didn't have any contact with them, did she?

W No, she didn't. _____.

08

W Eric, what are you up to this weekend?

M I've been busy this whole week, so I might stay home and get some rest. How about you?

W I'm thinking about going tree hiking.

M Tree hiking? What's that?

W It is hiking in the treetops with help from canopy walkways.

M That sounds interesting. Tell me more about it.

W You climb on bridgelike trails that are suspended high in the forest. They are _____ _____.

M Isn't it dangerous?

W The trails were _____ _____ studying wildlife in the treetops. But now people hike them to get a great view of the forest.

M How high are those trails?

W _____ _____, and stretch about 400 meters long.

M That sounds like a huge adventure. Can I join you this weekend?

09

M Thank you for your time today. My name is Chris and I am from Solar Motors. Today, I am presenting one of the coolest green inventions, the Eco-Car. This car looks like something from the future, _____

_____. First, its light weight and flat design help minimize wind resistance. This car glides through the wind rather than push against it. Second, it runs on a battery that goes about 160 kilometers before it needs to be recharged. Plus, it has panels on the roof, _____

_____. The radio, air conditioner, and headlights get power from them. Even the plastic used in the seats, dashboard and carpet _____

_____.

There is no doubt that this car is green inside and out.

10

M Laura, we're going on a trip to Spain next month. Do you remember?

W Sure. I am taking three days off so that we can stay for at least five days there.

M Great. Did you book the flight?

W Not yet. Sorry, I've been busy finishing a project at work. Why don't we book it together now?

M Okay. Do you think we should take a low-cost carrier or full-service carrier?

W Actually, I don't care. Unless we fly business class,

_____.

M Okay. If you don't mind low-cost carriers, let's go with that. Do you prefer morning flights or afternoon ones?

W _____. If we take afternoon flights, we will be wasting a whole day.

M I see. Which city do you want to visit first?

W I like Barcelona. I really want to visit the Gaudi Museum first.

M All right. Then we have two options left, _____

_____.

W Well, five days may not be enough to enjoy the trip. So, _____

_____.

M Me, too. I'll make the payment with my credit card now.

11

W Matt, do you have any plans after school?

M Yes, _____

last week because I put on some weight.

W Swimming is great. Do you think _____

_____?

12

M Did you hear that there is going to be a movie premiere in our town?

W Really? I thought movie premieres usually _____

_____. Why our town?

M Maybe it's because _____

_____. The director and actors are coming to promote the movie.

13

W Honey, what time are you heading out for the wedding tomorrow?

M I have to be there by noon, so I was thinking about leaving around 11:30.

W It starts at one in the afternoon. Why are you going there so early?

M Oh, I forgot to tell you. Jason _____

_____ at the wedding.

W Really? Is he not coming to the wedding?

M He is coming, but he said he wasn't sure he could make it on time.

W I see. Then did you have enough time to practice?

M Not really. Jason gave me the script today, but he told me to try to go with the flow.

W Go with the flow? But _____

_____, have you?

M No, it's my first time.

W Honey, the wedding day is very special to the bride and groom. You could ruin it by making mistakes.

M I don't want to do that. Maybe _____ _____ and practice more.

W You should. That way you won't forget what to say and when to say it. Oh, make sure you practice the tone, too.

14

M Cindy, did you know that Jessie is going abroad to study?

W Yes, she told me yesterday. _____ _____.

M Same here. When is she leaving?

W She's leaving next month. The school year starts in September, so she is going there _____ _____.

M I see. Do you know how long she's going away?

W I heard she is planning to stay there until she graduates from high school.

M Wow, that's longer than I thought. It must've been a tough decision for her to move.

W I know. So, I was thinking _____ _____ to remember us by.

M That sounds great. I want to be a part of it. Is there _____ _____?

15

M Carol works at home as a writer. She lives in an apartment that doesn't have good soundproof walls. Her neighbor, Lydia, has a 10-year-old boy who is very active. When he is at school, _____ _____. But when he comes home, he starts making terrible noise and Carol can't concentrate on her work. She wants to be on good terms with Lydia, but _____ _____ because of her son. One day, Carol hears the boy screaming and yelling when she is taking a nap. This time, she makes up _____.

In this situation, what would Carol most likely say to Lydia?

16~17

W Hello, students. Today, we are going to learn about one of the most beautiful insects in nature, the butterfly, and its similar-looking relative, the moth. _____ _____? They may look alike, but they are quite different in some ways. First, _____ _____, while moths are active at night. Butterflies are seen to gather food in the daytime, but moths are seen mostly at nighttime. Second, though butterflies tend to rest with their wings closed, moths do so with their wings open. Third, if you look closely at their antennae, you will see they are very different. Moth antennae _____ _____. However, butterflies have long and thin ones. Lastly, _____. In general, moths are duller and less colorful, whereas butterflies have brightly colored wings. Now let's take a look at some photos, and then we'll go meet these amazing insects in person.

20_회 실전 듣기 모의고사

01 다음을 듣고, 남자가 하는 말의 목적으로 가장 적절한 것을 고르시오.

① 도로공사 계획을 발표하려고
② 비가 예상되는 지역을 알리려고
③ 도로공사 관련 인력을 모집하려고
④ 현재 도로 교통상황을 안내하려고
⑤ 교통체증 원인 조사를 의뢰하려고

02 대화를 듣고, 여자의 의견으로 가장 적절한 것을 고르시오.

① 하이브리드 차와 전기차를 구입해야 한다.
② 미세먼지가 심한 날에는 외출을 자제해야 한다.
③ 미세먼지가 심한 날에는 차량 5부제를 적용해야 한다.
④ 대기오염을 줄이기 위해서는 모두가 노력해야 한다.
⑤ 대기오염을 없애려면 공장 가동을 중단해야 한다.

03 다음을 듣고, 남자가 하는 말의 요지로 가장 적절한 것을 고르시오.

① 운동을 할 때 무리하게 하지 않는 것이 좋다.
② 운동의 효과를 높이기 위해서는 매일 운동해야 한다.
③ 운동 지도자가 되기 위해서는 중용의 자세가 요구된다.
④ 의사의 진단에 따라 알맞은 운동을 선택하는 것이 좋다.
⑤ 자신의 흥미에 맞는 운동을 골라서 집중하는 것이 효과적이다.

04 대화를 듣고, 그림에서 대화의 내용과 일치하지 <u>않는</u> 것을 고르시오.

05 대화를 듣고, 남자가 할 일로 가장 적절한 것을 고르시오.

① 식당 예약하기
② 공항 주차장에 주차하기
③ 예약 확인 이메일 출력하기
④ 여행자 보험 구매하기
⑤ 트렁크에 짐 싣기

06 대화를 듣고, 여자가 지불할 금액을 고르시오. [3점]

① $90 ② $100 ③ $170
④ $180 ⑤ $200

07 대화를 듣고, 남자가 오디션에 참가할 수 <u>없는</u> 이유를 고르시오.

① 출장을 가야 해서
② 치과에 가야 해서
③ 오전에 일이 있어서
④ 봉사활동에 가야 해서
⑤ 아버지를 마중해야 해서

08 대화를 듣고, 송별회에 관해 언급되지 <u>않은</u> 것을 고르시오.

① 날짜　　　　　② 예약 여부
③ 참석 예정 인원　④ 만나는 장소
⑤ 참가 회비

09 Amazon rainforest에 관한 다음 내용을 듣고, 일치하지 <u>않는</u> 것을 고르시오.

① 아마존은 지구 전체 산소의 20%를 만들어 낸다.
② 오늘 현재 아마존에서 1,750건의 산불을 진화했다.
③ 아마존 화재 건수는 지난해보다 80% 늘었다.
④ 아마존 화재는 온실가스 배출의 원인이 된다.
⑤ 이번 주말에 아마존 보호 집회가 열릴 것이다.

10 다음 표를 보면서 대화를 듣고, 여자가 구매할 믹싱 볼을 고르시오.

Mixing Bowls at Kay's Kitchen

Model	Material	Size	Lid	Price
① A	plastic	small	×	$20
② B	plastic	medium	○	$30
③ C	stainless steel	medium	×	$30
④ D	stainless steel	medium	○	$40
⑤ E	stainless steel	large	×	$40

11 대화를 듣고, 남자의 마지막 말에 대한 여자의 응답으로 가장 적절한 것을 고르시오.

① Yes, please. That is really kind of you.
② Yes, it is, but I feel relieved sometimes.
③ You can say that again. It's a piece of cake.
④ Just a minute. Do you know the math teacher?
⑤ Why? You already took the same online course.

12 대화를 듣고, 여자의 마지막 말에 대한 남자의 응답으로 가장 적절한 것을 고르시오.

① Well, where did you buy the socks?
② So sorry. You should go and see a doctor.
③ I'm sure you can get a refund with no problem.
④ I'll never be late for the meeting again.
⑤ Don't worry. Nobody noticed.

13 대화를 듣고, 남자의 마지막 말에 대한 여자의 응답으로 가장 적절한 것을 고르시오. [3점]

Woman: _____

① Don't worry about it. I can solve it myself.
② Okay. Hotels cost too much money, anyway.
③ I don't understand. What do you mean by that?
④ What's the rush? We should talk more about it.
⑤ Please don't do that. You will understand me.

14 대화를 듣고, 여자의 마지막 말에 대한 남자의 응답으로 가장 적절한 것을 고르시오.

Man: _____

① Well, the instructor said to do it that way.
② I think so. We have no means to do that.
③ Yes, you're right. Let's do that.
④ You can add some water to make it less salty.
⑤ We should sign up for an online cooking class.

15 다음 상황 설명을 듣고, Jason이 Lisa에게 할 말로 가장 적절한 것을 고르시오. [3점]

Jason: _____

① I'm so full. I don't think I can go to lunch.
② I am so glad that the meeting is finally over.
③ I'm heading out for coffee. Do you want one?
④ What do you want for lunch today? It's my treat.
⑤ The deadline is getting nearer. Let's get back to work.

[16~17] 다음을 듣고, 물음에 답하시오.

16 여자가 하는 말의 주제로 가장 적절한 것은?

① the true image of an extrovert
② how to change our personality
③ the misconceptions about introverts
④ how to overcome negative character traits
⑤ the difference between an introvert and an extrovert

17 언급된 성격이 <u>아닌</u> 것은?

① outgoing　　② careful　　③ social
④ quiet　　⑤ shy

01

M This is Bob from Channel 11 News, reporting to you live. For those of you heading south on your commute home from work, expect some delays around the 200 Interchange. The snowfall this morning _____ _____ at that interchange. However, the snow melted away and some reports have come in on patches of black ice on roads in that area. Forecasters predict freezing rain later into the night, so _____ _____ if you are traveling around that area. The northbound highway looks good until you reach the 17 Interchange, but from there you _____.

02

M Judy, did you hear the news about the fine dust? The concentration level is so high that outdoor activities should be limited.

W Yes. These days, I don't see any children playing outside anymore.

M I know. I can't believe _____ _____.

W Me neither. The surprising part is that people don't even bother to improve the air quality.

M What do you mean?

W Well, I believe if we just gave up a little convenience, _____ _____. For example, we can take public transportation instead of driving.

M You are right. Driving a hybrid or electric vehicle is another option.

W Exactly. But other than driving, we should _____ _____.

M I agree with you. I can't remember the last day I went outside without a mask.

W Maybe we should _____ _____ about the air pollution.

M How about discussing it with the student council to get more ideas?

W That sounds great. I'll think of something, too.

03

M Greetings, listeners! I'm Noah, your broadcasting sports coach. As we all know, exercising is an excellent way to maintain good health. However, if not done carefully, _____. It's advisable to exercise _____ _____. Some people tend to go beyond what is expected, wanting immediate results. This excessive approach can put unnecessary pressure on the body and lead to injuries. _____ _____, and moderation is key. This is especially important if you're new to exercise. Next time, we'll talk about common exercise injuries. See you then!

04

W Hey, Gary. I heard you won first prize in an art contest. Congratulations!

M Thanks. I think I got pretty lucky.

W I'm sure you deserved it. Too bad I didn't get to see your painting.

M Oh, I have a picture of it. Would you like to see it?

W Of course. *[Pause]* Wow, it's amazing. The people in the center are supposed to be a couple, right?

M Right. That's why I drew them _____ _____ under an umbrella.

W The two lampposts on the left side seem to be guiding them.

M Yes, that's what I intended. I also put trees behind those lamp posts.

W Nice. I guess they are heading home because it's raining.

M Yes, and that's their house in front of them.

W Oh, _____?

M You mean the guy on the right side of the painting?

W Yes, _____ _____.

M I wanted the couple to show a striking contrast with the lonely man.

05

M Honey, _____
tomorrow's trip?

W I think so. We booked all the tickets we needed, reserved a room for two, and packed our luggage.

M I just want to make sure since we are leaving for the airport really early in the morning.

W I know. Don't worry. _____
_____ just in case.

M Great. I was just checking where to park at the airport. That way we don't have to walk far to the terminal we check in at.

W I see. *[Pause]* Did you purchase traveler's insurance?

M Actually, no. I was going to do that at the airport before we check in.

W I don't know if we will have enough time at the airport. There could be a long waiting line. _____
_____
_____ before departing.

M All right. Then I will do that online right now.

W Okay. Meanwhile, _____
_____, just to make sure we didn't miss anything.

M All right, thanks.

06

W I'd like to buy earphones. Where can I find them?

M They're here in the display case, ma'am. Do you have any particular design in mind?

W _____
_____. They seem to be very convenient.

M They are very popular these days. How about this pair? There are three colors available, white, black, and pink.

W They are nice. How much are they?

M They are $100. But if you buy two pairs, _____
_____.

W That seems like a good deal. I'll take two pairs, then.

M Of course. What colors would you like?

W I'll take one pair in white, and the other in black, please.

M Okay, is there anything else you need? We also sell cases.

W No, thanks. I think _____
_____. Oh, can I use this 5% coupon here, too?

M Let me check. *[Pause]* Yes, you can use it. With this coupon, _____
_____.

W That sounds great. Here's my credit card.

07

W Patrick, the community center will have an audition for a play. You should sign up for it.

M That's great news. I have wanted to act in another play for a while. _____
_____?

W The audition is this Saturday at 4 p.m.

M At 4 p.m.? I don't think I can make it.

W Oh, is it because of your dentist appointment?

M _____, and it won't take long.

W Then how come you have to miss it?

M I'm going to the airport with my mom and sister. My dad is coming home from a business trip, and _____
_____.

W I see. It would've been nice to see you acting again. It's been a while _____
_____.

M Thanks. I hope I have the chance to act again soon.

08

W Jack, would you like to come to a farewell party for Jane this Saturday? She is going back to Switzerland next Monday.

M Of course I will.

W Great. This is a farewell party for our debate club members. I already made a reservation at a restaurant.

M Okay, what are we going to do at the party?

W Well, first, _____
at 9 a.m. to take some photos. And then we will go to _____
last month.

M Ah, that Korean restaurant! Great.

W You _____ in advance. It's for the meal and some special gifts for Jane.

M Okay, how much is it?

W It's $20. Would that be okay?

M Of course. I'll bring the money tomorrow.

09

W Hello, everyone. I'm Sandy Jones, representative of the Youth Amazon Watch. I'm here to tell you about the Amazon rainforest. _____ _____ so it is sometimes called the "lungs of the planet." However, _____ _____ for a few months. The satellite data shows that more than 1,750 fires have been active in the area. There has been an 80% increase from last year. _____ _____ and cause greenhouse gas emissions. _____ _____. Due to this urgent situation, we are planning to hold an Amazon Protection Rally at the City Hall Plaza this weekend. The rally is _____ _____ the Amazon rainforest. I ask for your participation and strong support.

10

M Welcome to Kay's Kitchen. How may I help you?

W Hello. I'm looking for mixing bowls.

M Oh, we have a large variety of mixing bowls. This way, please. _____ _____? We have plastic and stainless bowls.

W _____ because they cannot be cleaned in a dishwasher.

M I see. They usually come in three different sizes. What size are you looking for?

W Well, I was thinking about a medium bowl. _____ _____.

M Okay, then do you prefer to have one with or without a lid?

W I prefer one with a lid.

M The one with a lid is $10 more expensive than the one without. Is that all right?

W I didn't want to spend more than $30, but I guess _____.

M Good choice. The lid is good for keeping food fresh.

11

M What are you going to do during the winter vacation?

W I'm going to take a course in math. _____ _____.

M Really? I thought you were quite good at it. _____ _____?

12

W _____ when I attended the staff meeting this morning.

M Why? What happened?

W _____. I didn't realize until the end of the meeting!

13

M Mary, are you taking a trip overseas this vacation?

W Yes, I'm going to go to France.

M Wow, that sounds like fun. How long are you going for?

W I'm going away for two weeks. _____ _____. I haven't booked my accommodation yet, but I'm thinking about staying at a hotel.

M Why don't you stay at a guesthouse? You like to make friends with people from other countries.

W I know, but _____ than a guesthouse because it'll be a long trip.

M Sure, hotels can be really convenient and _____ _____. I just think it'll be a great chance to meet people and experience different cultures.

W You're right. Traveling abroad is about _____ _____.

M Exactly. You won't regret it.

14

M I'm home, honey. What are you cooking?

W Come on in. Remember the bulgogi we ate at the Seoul Food Festival? It was really delicious, wasn't it?

M Sure, it was. So, is that what you are making?

W Yes, I wanted to make it after _____ _____.
Here, try some.

M All right. *[Pause]* Hmm...

W Well, is it all right? What do you think?

M It's not bad, but I think _____ _____.

W Oh, no. I was afraid you'd say that.

M I think _____ _____.

W Really? There's more bulgogi in the refrigerator. What should I do with it?

M No problem, honey. We can fix it.

W How can we do that?

15

M Jason and Lisa are co-workers. They have worked on several projects together as a team. Today their boss calls them into his office for the first time. He tells them _____ for their hard work, but one of them has to be transferred to a different department. Jason and Lisa get excited at first, but then realize that from now on, they won't be able to work together. As they leave the meeting with their boss, they congratulate each other on their promotions. Jason feels that _____ _____ because of Lisa's support. So, to celebrate, he wants _____ _____ to show his appreciation for her help. In this situation, what would Jason most likely say to Lisa?

16~17

W Would you call yourself an extrovert? Most people believe that extroverts are friendly and outgoing. While that may be true, that is not the full meaning. An extrovert is a person _____ _____. If you enjoy working on a team project or in a study group rather than working alone, the chances are high that you are extroverted. However, while extroverts can be very quick _____ _____, the degree of such behavior varies more within a person than between people. It means that extroverts are strongly social in some circumstances and less in other situations. Surprisingly, _____, too. Once they're around others, they may immediately brighten up. Another thing that many people don't realize is that _____ _____. Though extroverts really do crave company, the shyness can make it difficult to succeed in interactions with people they don't know.

ANSWER

01회
01 ②	02 ⑤	03 ⑤	04 ③	05 ⑤
06 ③	07 ①	08 ⑤	09 ⑤	10 ②
11 ④	12 ⑤	13 ⑤	14 ①	15 ①
16 ①	17 ④			

02회
01 ②	02 ②	03 ③	04 ⑤	05 ②
06 ③	07 ②	08 ④	09 ③	10 ③
11 ⑤	12 ①	13 ①	14 ③	15 ⑤
16 ③	17 ②			

03회
01 ②	02 ④	03 ②	04 ⑤	05 ①
06 ②	07 ③	08 ⑤	09 ②	10 ②
11 ①	12 ⑤	13 ①	14 ①	15 ④
16 ④	17 ②			

04회
01 ③	02 ③	03 ②	04 ⑤	05 ⑤
06 ④	07 ⑤	08 ①	09 ④	10 ④
11 ⑤	12 ③	13 ①	14 ⑤	15 ④
16 ⑤	17 ④			

05회
01 ①	02 ③	03 ④	04 ③	05 ④
06 ④	07 ⑤	08 ③	09 ③	10 ④
11 ③	12 ④	13 ④	14 ②	15 ③
16 ①	17 ④			

06회
01 ④	02 ⑤	03 ②	04 ⑤	05 ⑤
06 ②	07 ②	08 ②	09 ⑤	10 ①
11 ②	12 ⑤	13 ⑤	14 ③	15 ②
16 ⑤	17 ③			

07회
01 ⑤	02 ⑤	03 ②	04 ⑤	05 ①
06 ④	07 ⑤	08 ②	09 ③	10 ⑤
11 ⑤	12 ⑤	13 ④	14 ⑤	15 ①
16 ①	17 ③			

08회
01 ⑤	02 ⑤	03 ⑤	04 ④	05 ⑤
06 ④	07 ③	08 ⑤	09 ④	10 ⑤
11 ⑤	12 ⑤	13 ④	14 ②	15 ②
16 ①	17 ④			

09회
01 ③	02 ⑤	03 ②	04 ②	05 ③
06 ②	07 ④	08 ④	09 ⑤	10 ②
11 ③	12 ③	13 ③	14 ③	15 ⑤
16 ④	17 ④			

10회
01 ⑤	02 ①	03 ⑤	04 ⑤	05 ③
06 ②	07 ⑤	08 ②	09 ⑤	10 ④
11 ④	12 ④	13 ①	14 ①	15 ①
16 ②	17 ⑤			

11회
01 ⑤	02 ②	03 ⑤	04 ⑤	05 ④
06 ③	07 ②	08 ②	09 ⑤	10 ④
11 ⑤	12 ③	13 ②	14 ⑤	15 ④
16 ②	17 ⑤			

12회
01 ⑤	02 ④	03 ③	04 ⑤	05 ④
06 ④	07 ③	08 ④	09 ⑤	10 ④
11 ③	12 ④	13 ②	14 ⑤	15 ③
16 ④	17 ①			

13회
01 ②	02 ⑤	03 ⑤	04 ④	05 ⑤
06 ③	07 ①	08 ②	09 ①	10 ④
11 ④	12 ③	13 ⑤	14 ③	15 ④
16 ③	17 ⑤			

14회
01 ④	02 ④	03 ⑤	04 ⑤	05 ⑤
06 ③	07 ④	08 ③	09 ②	10 ③
11 ③	12 ⑤	13 ④	14 ①	15 ④
16 ②	17 ⑤			

15회
01 ⑤	02 ①	03 ④	04 ⑤	05 ⑤
06 ④	07 ③	08 ④	09 ③	10 ②
11 ⑤	12 ⑤	13 ④	14 ⑤	15 ④
16 ③	17 ③			

16회
01 ⑤	02 ③	03 ④	04 ⑤	05 ①
06 ⑤	07 ⑤	08 ④	09 ⑤	10 ②
11 ③	12 ⑤	13 ①	14 ⑤	15 ⑤
16 ⑤	17 ⑤			

17회
01 ⑤	02 ①	03 ④	04 ④	05 ⑤
06 ④	07 ②	08 ⑤	09 ②	10 ⑤
11 ②	12 ④	13 ④	14 ②	15 ⑤
16 ③	17 ⑤			

18회
01 ②	02 ②	03 ④	04 ③	05 ④
06 ⑤	07 ②	08 ②	09 ⑤	10 ④
11 ⑤	12 ⑤	13 ③	14 ④	15 ③
16 ⑤	17 ④			

19회
01 ②	02 ④	03 ③	04 ⑤	05 ④
06 ④	07 ④	08 ①	09 ⑤	10 ②
11 ④	12 ④	13 ①	14 ④	15 ⑤
16 ②	17 ④			

20회
01 ④	02 ④	03 ①	04 ⑤	05 ④
06 ③	07 ⑤	08 ③	09 ②	10 ④
11 ①	12 ⑤	13 ②	14 ④	15 ④
16 ①	17 ②			

고난도 1회
01 ②	02 ④	03 ①	04 ①	05 ②
06 ②	07 ⑤	08 ②	09 ⑤	10 ④
11 ④	12 ②	13 ②	14 ④	15 ④
16 ⑤	17 ③			

고난도 2회
01 ⑤	02 ④	03 ②	04 ⑤	05 ③
06 ②	07 ④	08 ③	09 ⑤	10 ③
11 ④	12 ⑤	13 ③	14 ②	15 ④
16 ④	17 ②			

고난도 3회
01 ⑤	02 ⑤	03 ④	04 ④	05 ②
06 ③	07 ②	08 ④	09 ②	10 ③
11 ②	12 ①	13 ③	14 ⑤	15 ③
16 ③	17 ②			

고난도 4회
01 ⑤	02 ③	03 ⑤	04 ②	05 ②
06 ④	07 ④	08 ②	09 ②	10 ①
11 ④	12 ④	13 ④	14 ②	15 ⑤
16 ④	17 ③			

New Edition
천일문 개정판

길고 복잡한
영어 문장도
오역없이 정확하게!

수능 영어 고득점을 위한 **고난도 구문 집중 학습**

천일문 완성

1 고난도 구문과 오역 포인트 수록

2 길고 복잡한 문장에 대처하는 전략적 해결법

3 500개의 예문으로 독해 시간을 줄이는 연습

4 문장 구조 분석과 자세한 해설이 담긴 천일비급

길고 복잡한 고난도 구문!
독해 연습 및 점검을 하고 싶다면?

천일문 완성 문제집 별매

· 본책과 다른 예문 수록, 구문 이해 점검

· 구문 이해 적용, 어법, 문장 핵심 파악, 해석 등
다양한 유형의 문제

쎄듀북닷컴(www.cedubook.com)에서 부가 자료를 무료로 다운로드할 수 있습니다.

더 빨리, 더 많이, 더 오래 남는 어휘

쎄듀런 프리미엄 VOCA

학생용 COUPON

**프리미엄 VOCA
한 달 무료 체험**

LF6JED6LRBV5

쿠폰 이용 방법 *PC에서만 신청 가능

1. 메뉴 - 쿠폰 등록하기
2. 프리미엄 보카 신청하기→구매하기
3. '30일' 구매하기 →보유 쿠폰 사용 결제

나만의 자동 어휘 단어장!

학생의 학습 최적화!

내게 맞춰 암기하니까, 외워질 수밖에!

미암기 단어 70%

미암기 단어 30%

LEVEL UP

미암기 단어 0%

 쎄듀런

📞 02-2088-0132
🏠 www.cedulearn.com
💬 cafe.naver.com/cedulearnteacher
✉ cedulearn@ceduenglish.com

프리미엄 VOCA 바로가기

'나'에게 딱! 맞는 암기&문제모드만 골라서 학습!

5가지 암기모드

8가지 문제모드

 암기모드를 선택하면, 최적의 문제 모드를 자동 추천!

2 **미암기 단어는 단어장에! 외워질 때까지 반복 학습 GO!**

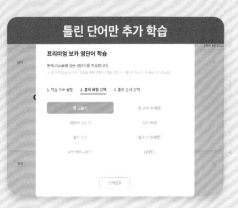

어법의 시작과 끝은 쎄듀다!

파워업 어법어휘 모의고사의
최신 개정판

어법끝
실전 모의고사

수능 어법의 실전감 향상

1 완벽한 기출 분석 및 대처법 소개
2 TOP 5 빈출 어법 및 24개 기출 어법 정리
3 최신 경향에 꼭 맞춘 총 288문항
4 [파워업 어법어휘 모의고사]의 어휘 부분을 제외하고
  어법을 보강하여 개정!

기출편 ➡ **실전편**

| 기출의 맥 | 기출 꿰뚫기 | 핵심 예상문제 20회 | 실전 모의고사 33회 | 고난도 모의고사 5회 |

고등 어법 입문 (예비고1~고1)   고등 내신 서술형 입문 (고1~고2)   고등 어법 실전 적용 (고2)   수능 어법 실전 마무리 (고3~고등 심화)

어법끝 START · 실력다지기   **어법끝 서술형**   **어법끝 ESSENTIAL**   **어법끝 실전 모의고사**

| 수능·내신 어법 기본기 | | 서술형 빈출 유형·기준 학습 | | 고등 실전 어법의 완성 | | 수능 어법의 실전 감각 향상 |

· 수능, 모의고사 최신 경향 반영   · 출제 포인트별 서술형 빈출 유형 수록   · 역대 기출의 출제 의도와 해결전략 제시   · 완벽한 기출 분석 및 대처법 소개
· 부담 없는 단계적 어법 학습   · 단계별 영작 문항 작성 가이드 제공   · 출제진의 함정 및 해결책 정리   · TOP 5 빈출 어법 및 24개 기출 어법 정리
· 적용, 복습용 다양한 문제 유형 수록   · 출제자 시각에서 출제 문장 예상하기 훈련   · 누적 테스트, 실전모의고사로   · 최신 경향에 꼭 맞춘 총 288문항
· 실전 모의 15회분 제공   · 현직 교사 공동 저술로 내신 채점 기준 수록   실전 적용력 강화

쎄듀북닷컴(www.cedubook.com)에서 부가 자료를 무료로 다운로드할 수 있습니다.

쎄듀

안정적인 수능영어 상위권을 위한

수능영어 절대유형

약점을 강점으로 바꾸는 절대 공략으로

Level Up!

대의 파악 유형
집중 대비

3점 문항 유형
집중 대비

총 25회

총 12회

절대유형 2024

20~24번 대의 파악 유형 집중 공략

· 대의파악의 Key point '주제문'의 공통적 특징 학습

· 수능·모의 기출 분석을 통한 유형별 해결전략

· 실전대비를 위한 25회의 고품질 2024 모의고사

· 지문마다 배치된 변형문제로 독해력 강화

절대유형 3142

31~42번 고난도 3점 문항 완벽 대비

· 내용의 추상성 등 높은 오답률의 원인 요소 완벽 반영

· 철저한 수능·모의 기출 분석을 통한 유형별 최신 전략

· 12회의 고품질 모의고사로 충분한 전략 적용 연습

· 대의파악 유형의 변형 문제로 본질적인 독해력 Up!

한 지문으로 학습 효과를 두 배로 끌어올리는 추가 문제

요약문 완성 유형의 20·22·23·24번 변형 문제	**20** PLUS+ 변형문제	윗글의 내용을 한 문장으로 요약하고자 (A), (B)에 들 Since our ___(A)___ attitude toward social pheno critical eye to ___(B)___ those who are trying to ta (A) (B) ① unconditional ...... choose ② ind
제목 찾기 유형의 21번 변형 문제	**21** PLUS+ 변형문제	윗글의 제목으로 가장 적절한 것은? ① Love Yourself, You Deserve It ② Conflict: Our Greatest Fear to Overcome ③ Be Strong! Learn How to Handle Conflict ④ The Disconnect Between Fear and Strength ⑤ Why Aggression Matters: Winning in a Conflic

제목·요지· 주제·주장을 묻는 대의파악 유형 변형 문제를 31번~39번까지 배치	**PLUS+** 변형문제 윗글의 제목으로 가장 적절한 것은? ① Does Arts Education Boost Young Brains? ② Good at Math Means Good at Playing Piano ③ Advantages of Teaching Piano and Computer
	PLUS+ 변형문제 윗글의 요지로 가장 적절한 것은? ① 목적에 맞는 최적의 전략을 선택해야 한다. ② 성공을 위해 전략적 사고는 필수 불가결하다. ③ 지나친 전문화는 전략적 사고에 오히려 해가 된다.
	PLUS+ 변형문제 윗글의 주제로 가장 적절한 것은? ① reasons alternates are seldom made in science ② constant efforts to prove capability of retooling ③ various ways to demonstrate a paradigm's validity
	PLUS+ 변형문제 윗글에서 필자가 주장하는 바로 가장 적절한 것은? ① 역사는 결정론의 관점에서 바라볼 필요가 있다. ② 역사에 과학 법칙을 적용하는 것은 삼가야 한다. ③ 과학 교육에 있어서 역사 교육이 선행되어야 한다.

쎄듀북닷컴(www.cedubook.com)에서 부가 자료를 무료로 다운로드할 수 있습니다.

쎄듀

쎄듀 초·중등 커리큘럼

	예비초	초1	초2	초3	초4	초5	초6
구문		천일문 365 일력 |초1-3| 교육부 지정 초등 필수 영어 문장		초등코치 천일문 SENTENCE 1001개 통문장 암기로 완성하는 초등 영어의 기초			
문법				초등코치 천일문 GRAMMAR 1001개 예문으로 배우는 초등 영문법			
			왓츠 Grammar		Start (초등 기초 영문법) / Plus (초등 영문법 마무리)		
독해			왓츠 리딩 30|40 / 50 / 60 / 70 / 80 / 90 / 100		쉽고 재미있게 완성되는 영어 독해력		
어휘				초등코치 천일문 VOCA&STORY 1001개의 초등 필수 어휘와 짧은 스토리			
		패턴으로 말하는 초등 필수 영단어 1 / 2		문장 패턴으로 완성하는 초등 필수 영단어			
ELT	Oh! My PHONICS 1 / 2 / 3 / 4		유·초등학생을 위한 첫 영어 파닉스				
	Oh! My SPEAKING 1 / 2 / 3 / 4 / 5 / 6			핵심 문장 패턴으로 더욱 쉬운 영어 말하기			
	Oh! My GRAMMAR 1 / 2 / 3			쓰기로 완성하는 첫 초등 영문법			

	예비중	중1	중2	중3
구문		천일문 STARTER 1 / 2		중등 필수 구문 & 문법 총정리
문법		개정 천일문 중등 GRAMMAR LEVEL 1 / 2 / 3		예문 중심 문법 기본서
		GRAMMAR Q Starter 1, 2 / Intermediate 1, 2 / Advanced 1, 2		학기별 문법 기본서
		잘 풀리는 영문법 1 / 2 / 3		문제 중심 문법 적용서
		GRAMMAR PIC 1 / 2 / 3 / 4		이해가 쉬운 도식화된 문법서
			1센치 영문법	1권으로 핵심 문법 정리
문법+어법			첫단추 BASIC 문법·어법편 1 / 2	문법·어법의 기초
문법+쓰기		EGU 영단어&품사 / 문장 형식 / 동사 써먹기 / 문법 써먹기 / 구문 써먹기		서술형 기초 세우기와 문법 다지기
				올씀 1 기본 문장 PATTERN 내신 서술형 기본 문장 학습
쓰기		개정 천일문 중등 WRITING LEVEL 1 / 2 / 3 *거침없이 Writing 개정		중등 교과서 내신 기출 서술형
		중학 영어 쓰작 1 / 2 / 3		중등 교과서 패턴 드릴 서술형
어휘		천일문 VOCA 중등 스타트/필수/마스터		2800개 중등 3개년 필수 어휘
		어휘끝 중학 필수편	중학 필수어휘 1000개	어휘끝 중학 마스터편 고난도 중학어휘 +고등기초 어휘 1000개
독해		ReadingGraphy LEVEL 1 / 2 / 3 / 4		중등 필수 구문까지 잡는 흥미로운 소재 독해
		Reading Relay Starter 1, 2 / Challenger 1, 2 / Master 1, 2		타교과 연계 배경 지식 독해
		READING Q Starter 1, 2 / Intermediate 1, 2 / Advanced 1, 2		예측/추론/요약 사고력 독해
독해전략			리딩 플랫폼 1 / 2 / 3	논픽션 지문 독해
독해유형			Reading 16 LEVEL 1 / 2 / 3	수능 유형 맛보기 + 내신 대비
			첫단추 BASIC 독해편 1 / 2	수능 유형 독해 입문
듣기		Listening Q 유형편 / 1 / 2 / 3		유형별 듣기 전략 및 실전 대비
		쎄듀 빠르게 중학영어듣기 모의고사 1 / 2 / 3		교육청 듣기평가 대비

수능실감

感

듣기 모의고사 **24**회

정답 및 해설

01 | 정답 | ②

남자는 컴퓨터 네트워크에 대한 연수 세미나를 안내하고 있으므로 남자가 하는 말의 목적으로 가장 적절한 것은 ②이다.

- announce 안내하다
- conduct 실시하다
- training 연수, 교육
- session (특정 활동을 위한) 시간, 기간
- mandatory 의무적인
- participate 참여하다
- operation 작동
- organization 조직

M I am here to announce that we will be conducting a training seminar. It is about the new computer network recently set up in our office. The session will be held from 10 a.m. to 12 p.m. on Thursday, April 23rd. It is mandatory for everyone in the IT department to be present. As suggested by management, **everyone should actively participate in this program** and make good use of the training sessions. The trainer is an expert with 20 years of experience in computer networks and **will train you to fully understand the operation** of such networks. I assure you that **this training will be very helpful to you** and to our organization in the near future.

남 저는 연수 세미나 실시를 안내하기 위해 이 자리에 섰습니다. 세미나는 저희 사무실에서 최근에 설치한 새 컴퓨터 네트워크에 대한 것입니다. 세미나 시간은 4월 23일 목요일 오전 10시부터 오후 12시까지 진행될 예정입니다. IT 부서 모든 직원은 의무적으로 참석해야 합니다. 관리부서에서 권장하는 바에 따라 모든 분은 프로그램에 적극적으로 참여해야 하며 연수 시간을 잘 활용해야 합니다. 강사는 컴퓨터 네트워크에서 20년의 경력을 갖고 있는 전문가이며, 여러분이 그러한 네트워크의 작동을 충분히 이해할 수 있도록 교육시킬 겁니다. 이 연수가 곧 다가올 미래에 여러분과 우리 조직에 아주 유용할 것이라고 확신합니다.

02 | 정답 | ⑤

여자는 주제문을 뒷받침할 근거가 타당하려면 글을 쓰기 전 충분한 연구가 필요하다고 말하고 있으므로 여자의 의견으로 가장 적절한 것은 ⑤이다.

- essay (학교 제출용의 짧은 논문식) 에세이, 과제물
- convincing 설득력 있는
- back up 뒷받침하다
- support 지지하다, 받치다
- valid 타당한
- reasonable 합리적인
- body (글의) 본문, 본론

M Mom, are you busy? Can you help me with my essay, please?
W Sure, honey. What is it?
M I'm writing an essay for my writing club. I'm not sure if I'm doing it right.
W What is your topic sentence?
M It's "Climate change is the greatest threat that we face." But my essay doesn't sound convincing.
W Do you have enough evidence to back up your statement?
M **There are three key points to support it**. Are they not enough?
W They should be enough, but they also need explanations to support them.
M What do you mean?
W You need to show that **your points are valid and reasonable with examples**. That's why you have to do a lot of research before writing.
M Now that I think about it, I don't think **I've done enough research on the topic**.
W After you finish with the body, I can read it over for you.
M Thanks, Mom.

남 엄마, 바쁘세요? 제 에세이 관련해서 좀 도와주실 수 있어요?
여 물론이지, 얘야. 뭔데 그러니?
남 글쓰기 동아리 때문에 에세이를 쓰고 있어요. 잘하고 있는지 모르겠어요.
여 주제문이 무엇인데?
남 '기후 변화는 우리가 직면한 가장 큰 위험이다.'예요. 하지만 제 에세이가 설득력 있게 보이질 않아요.
여 네 진술을 뒷받침할 충분한 근거가 있니?
남 뒷받침하는 세 개의 주요 논점이 있어요. 그걸로 충분하지 않을까요?
여 충분한 것 같은데, 뒷받침하려면 각각 설명이 필요해.
남 무슨 뜻이세요?
여 예시를 통해서 네 논점들이 타당하고 합리적이라는 것을 보여줘야 해. 그것이 글을 쓰기 전 많은 연구를 해야 하는 이유지.
남 지금 생각해 보니, 제가 주제에 대해 연구를 충분히 한 것 같지 않네요.
여 본론을 다 쓰면 내가 읽어봐 줄게.
남 고마워요, 엄마.

03 | 정답 | ⑤

결심을 적어둔 사람이 그렇지 않은 사람보다 더 많이 성공했다는 연구 결과를 인용하면서 결심을 적어두는 것이 성공의 가능성을 높인다고 말하고 있으므로 남자가 하는 말의 요지로 가장 적절한 것은 ⑤이다.

- host 진행자, 사회자; 주인; 주최하다
- resolution 결심, 다짐
- likelihood 가능성
- explore 탐구하다, 조사하다
- keep an eye out 지켜보다, 살펴보다

M Happy New Year, everyone! I'm Kevin Williams, your host for today's show. Today, we'll talk about making and keeping your New Year's resolutions. **Writing down your goals increases the likelihood of success**. In a recent study, participants were divided into two groups: writers of resolutions and those who just thought about them. Only 4 percent of **those who didn't write their resolutions succeeded**, but 66 percent of those who wrote them down succeeded. Therefore, it's clear that writing down your resolutions **can help you get closer to achieving them**. We'll explore this topic further, so keep an eye out for further updates!

남 여러분, 새해 복 많이 받으세요! 오늘 방송의 진행자인 Kevin Williams입니다. 오늘은 새해 결심을 세우고 지키는 것에 대해 이야기해 보겠습니다. 여러분의 목표를 적어두는 것이 성공의 가능성을 높입니다. 최근 한 연구에서, 참가자들은 결심을 적은 사람들과 그저 생각만 한 사람들 두 그룹으로 나뉘었습니다. 결심을 적지 않았던 사람들은 4%만이 성공했지만, 그것을 적었던 사람들은 66%가 성공했습니다. 그러므로 여러분의 결심을 적는 것이 여러분이 그것을 성취하는 데에 더 가까워지는 데 도움을 줄 수 있다는 것은 분명합니다. 앞으로 이 주제를 더 자세히 살펴볼 것이므로, 앞으로의 업데이트를 지켜봐 주세요!

04 | 정답 | ③

게시판 앞에 책꽂이가 있는 것은 옳지만 여자가 현재 책꽂이는 비어 있다고 말하고 있으므로 대화 내용과 일치하지 않는 것은 ③이다.

* rearrange 다시 정리하다
* bulletin board 게시판
* hall of honor 명예의 전당

M Hello, Ms. Jullian. What are you doing?
W Hi, Mr. Smith. I just finished rearranging my classroom.
M I really like the bulletin board at the back. **The world map on the left is a good idea**.
W Thank you. I put it up to tell my students to explore the world. What do you think about the Hall of Honor?
M You mean the sign **on the right side of the bulletin board**? What is it for?
W Oh, I hold special events during class, and I give a prize to the winning students. I will put up pictures of those students under "Hall of Honor."
M That's such a good idea. And what's the bookshelf for in front of the bulletin board?
W I am going to get different types of books for my students. Right now, it is empty, but by the end of this month, **it will be filled with books**.
M I see. And I really like the desks and chairs with wheels on them. They will be easy to move around.
W Yes. They're the best for having students gather in groups. What do you think about **the puzzle mats on the floor**?
M Oh, they are so cute. It will be great to have a space where students can sit down on the floor.
W Yes. I always look forward to teaching in this classroom.

남 안녕하세요, Jullian 선생님. 뭐 하세요?
여 안녕하세요, Smith 선생님. 지금 막 제 교실을 다시 정리해 봤어요.
남 뒤편에 게시판이 참 마음에 들어요. 왼쪽에 세계지도가 정말 좋은 생각이네요.
여 감사합니다. 학생들에게 세계를 탐험하라고 말하려고 붙여 놨어요. 명예의 전당은 어떻게 생각하세요?
남 게시판의 오른편에 있는 표시 말씀하시는 거죠? 저건 어떤 용도인가요?
여 아. 제가 수업 중에 특별 이벤트를 많이 하는데, 우승하는 학생들에게 상을 주거든요. 그 학생들의 사진을 '명예의 전당' 아래에 붙일 거예요.
남 너무나도 좋은 생각이네요. 게시판 앞의 책꽂이는 무슨 용도인가요?
여 학생들을 위해 다양한 종류의 책을 살 예정이에요. 지금은 비어 있지만 이번 달 말에는 책으로 꽉 찰 거예요.
남 그렇군요. 그리고 바퀴 달린 책상과 의자도 정말 마음에 드네요. 여기저기 움직이기에 쉽겠어요.
여 네. 학생들을 모둠별로 모을 때 최고랍니다. 바닥에 있는 퍼즐 매트는 어떤가요?
남 아. 너무 귀엽네요. 학생들이 바닥에 앉을 수 있는 공간이 있으면 참 좋겠습니다.
여 네. 이 교실에서 가르칠 게 항상 기대돼요.

05 | 정답 | ⑤

워크숍을 위한 모든 것이 준비되었는지 남자와 여자가 확인하는 상황이다. 여자가 초빙 강사의 조수에게 전화를 하여 최종 일정을 다시 한번 상기시켜야 한다고 하였으므로 남자가 할 일로 가장 적절한 것은 ⑤이다.

* workshop 워크숍, 연수회
* go over 점검하다, 검토하다
* confirm 확인하다
* set up 준비하다
* banquet 연회, 축하연
* booklet 팸플릿, 소책자
* remind A of B A에게 B를 생각나게 하다
* assistant 조수, 보조자

M Sophie, can I talk to you about the workshop next week for a minute?
W Sure. I thought we had everything prepared.
M I feel like we missed something, but **I don't know what it is**.
W All right. Then let's go over everything. Did you call the hotel to confirm the reservation?
M I did that yesterday. The meeting room will **be set up in the morning**, and the banquet service will be ready before noon.
W Okay. What about the booklets?
M They will be delivered directly to the hotel. We just need to pick them up at the front desk.
W That's great. What else is there? *[Pause]* Oh, did you **check the schedule with the guest speaker**, Victoria Manu?
M I did that last week. Do I have to check that again?
W Yes, you have to remind her of the date one week before the event. **You should call her assistant**.
M Okay. Is there anything else?
W I think that's all. It seems like everything is prepared.

남 Sophie, 다음 주에 있을 워크숍에 대해서 잠시 이야기할 수 있을까요?
여 물론이죠. 저는 우리가 모든 준비를 다 했다고 생각했어요.
남 뭔가 빠뜨린 것이 있는 것 같은데, 그게 뭔지 모르겠어요.
여 좋아요. 그러면 전부 점검해 보죠. 호텔에 전화해서 예약 확인했나요?
남 네, 어제 확인했어요. 회의실은 오전에 준비될 예정이고, 연회 서비스는 정오 전에 준비될 겁니다.
여 좋아요. 팸플릿은요?
남 팸플릿은 호텔로 바로 배달될 겁니다. 저희가 호텔 프런트에서 받으면 됩니다.
여 잘됐군요. 또 뭐가 있지요? [잠시 후] 아. 초빙강사 Victoria Manu와 스케줄 확인했나요?
남 네, 지난주에 확인했어요. 다시 확인해야 할까요?
여 그래요, 행사 일주일 전에 날짜를 다시 확인해 드려야 합니다. 조수에게 전화하셔야 해요.
남 알겠습니다. 그 외 또 다른 게 있나요?
여 제 생각엔 이게 전부예요. 모두 준비가 된 것 같아요.

06 | 정답 | ③

여자는 110달러짜리 의자 하나와 30달러짜리 쿠션 두 개를 구입하고자 한다. 여기서 10% 특별 할인을 받을 수 있으므로 여자가 지불할 총금액은 ③이다.

* comfortable 편안한
* total 총액, 합계

W Excuse me, I'm looking for a chair for my son.
M Come this way, ma'am. Do you have something in mind?
W He spends a lot of time studying. So I'd like **something comfortable for his back**.
M This one is one of our best-selling items. It can help **you sit up straight and it supports your back**.
W That's exactly the one I was thinking about. How much is it?
M It's $110. It comes in three colors, black, gray, and red.
W I'll take a black one, please.

여 실례합니다. 제 아들을 위한 의자를 찾고 있는데요.
남 이쪽으로 오시죠, 손님. 생각하고 계신 게 있나요?
여 아들이 공부하는 데 오랜 시간을 보내거든요. 그래서 허리에 편안한 게 좋겠어요.
남 이 의자는 가장 인기 있는 품목 중 하나입니다. 곧게 앉도록 도와줄 수 있고 허리를 받쳐 주지요.
여 그게 정확히 제가 생각하고 있던 거네요. 얼마인가요?
남 110달러입니다. 세 가지 색상으로 나오는데요, 검정색, 회색, 그리고 빨간색이 있습니다.
여 검정색으로 부탁드립니다.

M	Is there anything else you need? We also have cushions.	남 다른 필요한 것은 없으신가요? 쿠션도 있습니다.
W	Okay, how much are they?	여 네, 쿠션은 얼마인가요?
M	They are $30 each. **If you add this cushion to your chair**, you can get a 10% discount off the total.	남 하나에 30달러입니다. 이 쿠션을 의자에 추가하실 경우 총금액에서 10% 할인을 받으실 수 있습니다.
W	That sounds like a good deal. Then can I get two, please?	여 좋은 가격이네요. 그러면 쿠션 두 개 주실 수 있나요?
M	Of course. **One chair and two cushions**, correct?	남 물론입니다. 의자 하나에 쿠션 두 개, 맞죠?
W	Yes. I'll pay with my credit card.	여 네, 신용카드로 결제하겠습니다.
M	Certainly.	남 물론이죠.

07 | 정답 | ①

남자는 독감 예방 접종을 위해 병원에 갔지만 열이 약간 있어서 접종하지 못했고 몸이 낫고 나면 다시 병원에 가야 한다고 말하고 있으므로 주사를 맞지 못 한 이유로 가장 적절한 것은 ①이다.

- flu 독감
- shot 주사
- clinic 개인 병원, 클리닉
- run out 떨어지다, 소진되다
- vaccine (예방) 백신
- temperature 온도
- slight 약간의

W	I think flu season has begun. It seems like everyone has caught a cold.	여 독감 시즌이 시작된 것 같아. 모든 사람들이 감기에 걸린 것 같아.
M	I know. It's about that time. Did you get your flu shot?	남 맞아. 벌써 그런 때이지. 독감 예방 주사 접종했니?
W	I did. I got it with my parents at the clinic. What about you?	여 응. 병원에서 부모님이랑 했어. 너는?
M	I went there to get one too, but I couldn't.	남 나도 접종하러 병원에 갔는데 접종 못 했어.
W	Really? **Did the clinic run out of vaccines**?	여 정말? 병원에서 백신이 다 떨어졌데?
M	No, they didn't. There weren't many people.	남 아니. 그렇지는 않았어. 사람은 별로 많지 않았어.
W	How come you didn't get it at the clinic?	여 그러면 병원에서 왜 접종을 하지 않았니?
M	Before I went in to get it, the nurse checked my temperature. **It turned out I had a slight fever**.	남 접종하러 들어가기 전에 간호사가 내 체온을 쟀거든. 내가 약간의 열이 있었던 거야.
W	Really? Are you not allowed **to get a flu shot when you have a fever**?	여 정말? 열이 있을 때 독감 주사를 맞으면 안 돼?
M	No, it could make your fever worse. So the nurse told me **I'd better come back** when I'm feeling better.	남 그래. 열을 더 심하게 만들 수 있대. 그래서 간호사는 내가 상태가 나아지면 다시 오는 게 낫다고 말했어.
W	Then when are you planning to go back?	여 그러면 언제 다시 방문할 거야?
M	Maybe next week. I'm taking some cold medicine now.	남 아마 다음 주에. 지금은 감기약을 좀 먹고 있거든.

08 | 정답 | ⑤

취업센터에서 소개받은 아르바이트는 시내에 있는 선물 가게이며 근무시간은 주중 오후 6시부터 10시까지라고 하였다. 주로 손님 응대와 선물을 포장하는 일이며 시급은 9달러라고 했지만, 자격 요건에 대한 언급은 없었으므로 정답은 ⑤이다.

- part-time job 아르바이트
- downtown 시내
- working hours 근무 시간
- duty 업무, 의무
- apply for ~에 지원하다
- employer 고용주

M	Welcome to District Job Center. How can I help you?	남 지역 취업센터에 오신 것을 환영합니다. 어떻게 도와드릴까요?
W	I'm looking for a part-time job I can do after school.	여 학교 끝나고 할 수 있는 아르바이트를 구하려고 합니다.
M	Let me see. This one here seems to suit your situation the best. It's a gift shop downtown.	남 한 번 봅시다. 여기 이곳이 학생의 상황에 가장 잘 맞을 것 같네요. 시내에 있는 선물 가게예요.
W	That sounds interesting. **What are the working hours**?	여 흥미롭네요. 근무 시간은 어떻게 되나요?
M	They are from 6 p.m. to 10 p.m. on weekdays only.	남 평일 오후 6시부터 10시입니다.
W	That suits my schedule. **So what would be my duties at the gift shop**?	여 제 일정에 맞네요. 그러면 선물 가게에서 제가 해야 할 업무는 무엇인가요?
M	You will mostly be helping customers to choose the right gift. And when needed, **you'll have to do some gift wrapping**.	남 대부분 손님들이 적절한 선물을 고르는 일을 도와드릴 겁니다. 그리고 필요한 경우 선물 포장을 좀 해야 합니다.
W	That sounds fun. How much will I get paid an hour?	여 재있겠네요. 시간당 얼마를 지급받게 되나요?
M	You will be paid $9 an hour.	남 시간당 9달러를 받게 됩니다.
W	That's great. **How do I apply for the job**?	여 좋네요. 어떻게 지원하면 되나요?
M	Leave your résumé here. Then we can set up a job interview with the employer.	남 이력서를 여기 남겨 주세요. 그러면 저희가 고용주와 취업 면접을 잡아 놓겠습니다.

09 | 정답 | ⑤

동아리 활성화 프로젝트에 관해 설명하는 내용이다. 올해 교육부가 주관하여 100개의 동아리를 선정하여 자금을 지급할 예정이며, 5개 분야 중 하나를 골라 신청 가능하며, 학기 말에는 활동 내용에 대해 발표를 해야 한다고 했다. 상위 10개 동아리를 선정하여 특별 캠프에 참여할 기회를 줄 것이라고 하였으므로 일치하지 않는 것은 ⑤이다.

- inform 알리다, 통지하다
- Ministry of Education 교육부
- promote 촉진시키다, 증진시키다
- recruit 선발하다

W	Hello, students. I'd like to inform you of the "Club Promotion Project." This is one of the major projects that the Ministry of Education is planning to do this year. In order **to promote and support students' club activities**, the Ministry of Education will recruit 100 clubs within our district and **provide funds to them**. Each club can apply for one of the five areas, including liberal arts and science. Clubs that get selected will work on a specific topic within their area for a semester. At the end of the semester, all 100 clubs will present their activities in front of students, teachers, and parents. A team of judges will assess the presentations, and the top ten clubs	여 학생 여러분, 안녕하십니까. '동아리 활성화 프로젝트'에 대해 알려드리고자 합니다. 이것은 교육부에서 올해 계획하고 있는 주요 프로젝트 중 하나입니다. 학생들의 동아리 활동을 촉진하고 지원하기 위해 교육부는 우리 지역 내에서 100개의 동아리를 선정해 자금을 제공하려고 합니다. 각 동아리는 문과와 이과를 포함한 5개의 분야 중 하나에 지원할 수 있습니다. 선정된 동아리들은 한 학기 간 그들의 분야 내의 특정 주제에 대해 활동할 것입니다. 학기 말에는 100개 모두의 동아리가 학생, 교사, 그리고 부모님들 앞에서 활동에 대해 발표하게 될 것입니다. 심사위원단이 발표를 평가할 것이고 상위 10개 동아리는 특별 캠프에 참가할 기회가 주어지게 될 것입니다. 많은 동아리가 이 프로젝트에 지원하길 바랍니다.

* **district** 지역, 구역
* **fund** 자금, 기금
* **liberal arts** 문과, 인문학
* **judge** 심사위원, 심판
* **assess** 평가하다
* **grant** 주다, 수여하다

will be granted **an opportunity to participate in a special camp**. I hope many clubs will apply for this project.

---

10 | 정답 | ②

여자는 750달러 이내의 예산에서 용량이 더 큰 9인치 크기 화면의 태블릿 PC를 구매하기로 했고 키보드는 포함시키지 않겠다고 말하고 있으므로 여자가 선택할 태블릿 PC로 가장 적절한 것은 ②이다.

* **up to** (특정한 수) 까지
* **capacity** 용량
* **display** 화면

W Excuse me, I'm looking for a tablet PC for my daughter.
M Okay. Here are our five best-selling models.
W They all look great. Can you help me choose one? **I can pay up to $750**.
M Okay. Then what about the capacity?
W The larger, the better. She will **need to save a lot of files** on it.
M I see. Next, you have to choose the size of the display. We have either an 11-inch display or a 9-inch display.
W Hmm... The 11-inch one looks too big for her. And it's a little heavy.
M Actually, you're right. I would recommend a 9-inch one. **It's more popular among students**.
W Okay. And do I have to choose whether to include a keyboard?
M Yes, you do. Would you like to include one?
W No, thanks. **We already have a keyboard at home**.
M Okay, sure. You can pay over there.

여 실례합니다. 제 딸을 위한 태블릿 PC를 찾고 있습니다.
남 네. 여기 가장 인기 있는 종류 5가지가 있습니다.
여 모두 멋져 보이네요. 하나 고르는 것을 도와주시겠어요? 750달러까지 지불할 수 있습니다.
남 알겠습니다. 그러면 용량은요?
여 클수록 좋습니다. 제 딸이 파일을 많이 저장해야 할 겁니다.
남 그렇군요. 다음으로 화면 크기를 결정하셔야 합니다. 저희는 11인치짜리 화면과 9인치짜리 화면이 있습니다.
여 음… 11인치짜리는 딸에겐 너무 커 보이네요. 그리고 약간 무겁네요.
남 사실, 고객님 말씀이 맞아요. 9인치짜리를 추천합니다. 학생들 사이에서 더 인기가 좋기도 하고요.
여 알겠습니다. 그리고 키보드를 포함할지를 선택해야 하나요?
남 네, 선택하셔야 합니다. 같이 포함할까요?
여 괜찮습니다. 집에 이미 키보드가 있어서요.
남 네, 좋아요. 계산은 저쪽에서 하실 수 있습니다.

---

11 | 정답 | ④

100달러짜리 지폐를 어떻게 잔돈으로 바꿀지 물어보는 여자의 말에 가장 적절한 남자의 응답은 ④ '잠시만요. 20달러짜리 네 장에 5달러짜리 한 장으로 부탁드립니다.'이다.

* **pay a bill** 돈을 치르다[계산하다]
* **change** 잔돈

W The total is $15. How would you like to pay the bill?
M **I'd like to pay in cash**. I only have a $100 bill. Can you break it for me?
W Sure. **How would you like your change**?
M Let me see. I'd like four 20s and a 5, please.

여 총 15달러입니다. 지불은 어떻게 하시겠습니까?
남 현금으로 지불하겠습니다. 100달러 지폐뿐이네요. 좀 작은 단위로 바꿔주시겠어요?
여 물론입니다. 잔돈을 어떻게 나눠드릴까요?
남 잠시만요. 20달러짜리 네 장에 5달러짜리 한 장으로 부탁드립니다.

① 죄송합니다. 제가 잔돈이 없네요.
② 괜찮습니다. 신용카드로 지불하겠습니다.
③ 물론입니다. 20달러짜리 지폐가 충분하지 않습니다.
⑤ 모르겠습니다. 저한테는 이게 좀 더 커 보이네요.

---

12 | 정답 | ③

폭력성을 담고 있는 영화를 싫어하는지 묻는 남자의 말에 가장 적절한 여자의 응답은 ③ '응. 난 그런 영화가 보기에 좀 거북해.'이다.

* **contain** 담다, 포함하다
* **violence** 폭력

[선택지]
* **disturbing** 불편한, 불안감을 주는

M Hey, Brenda. Have you watched this movie?
W No, I haven't. At first I was interested in it, but I heard it **contains a lot of violence**.
M It does have some violent scenes. **Do you dislike movies with** too much violence?
W Yes. To me, they are a little disturbing to watch.

남 안녕, Brenda. 이 영화 봤니?
여 아니, 안 봤어. 처음엔 재밌을 것 같았는데 폭력적인 내용을 많이 담고 있다는 말을 들었어.
남 폭력적인 장면이 좀 있어. 너무 폭력성이 짙은 영화는 안 좋아하니?
여 응. 난 그런 영화가 보기에 좀 거북해.

① 알았어. 다음 주말에 영화 보러 가자.
② 어디 보자. 내가 가장 좋아하는 장르는 공포일 거야.
④ 물론이지. 로맨스 영화는 내가 가장 싫어하는 영화야.
⑤ 아니. 나는 액션 영화나 코미디를 좋아하지 않아.

---

13 | 정답 | ③

남자가 다친 여자에게 위로의 말을 하면서 자신과 너무 다르게 낙천적이라고 말하는 상황이다. 따라서 다쳤을 때 어땠는지 물어보는 여자의 말에 가장 적절한 남자의 응답은 ③ '난 모든 것에 흥미를 잃고 집에서만 지냈어.'이다.

* **goal post** 골대
* **recover** 회복하다

M Hi, Barbara. Are you any better?
W Hi, Will. Thanks for asking. I need to wear this cast for another two weeks, but **I don't feel any pain in my arm any more**.
M That's good news. Did you say you broke your arm during soccer practice?
W Yes, I broke my arm when it hit the goal post. But I'm recovering well, so that's what's important.

남 안녕, Barbara. 아픈 건 좀 나았니?
여 안녕, Will. 물어봐 줘서 고마워. 이 깁스를 2주 더 착용해야 하지만 팔에 통증은 더 이상 없어.
남 그거 좋은 소식이네. 축구 연습 중에 팔이 부러졌다고 했었나?
여 맞아. 골대에 부딪쳤을 때 팔이 부러졌어. 그래도 잘 회복하고 있어서 그게 중요한 거지.

- national 전국적인, 국가의
- optimistic 낙천적인
- injure 부상을 입히다

M But you must be upset since you can't play at the national girls' soccer tournament.

W At first, I was, but now I'm **excited to cheer for my teammates** instead.

M Is that why you still go to practices?

W Yes. **It makes me feel a lot better** when I watch my friends train and play.

M Wow, you're such an optimistic person. I was **so different from you when I got injured**.

W Why? What were you like when you got hurt?

M I lost interest in everything and just stayed home.

남 하지만 전국 여학생 축구 토너먼트에 못 뛰게 되어서 아쉽겠다.

여 처음엔 그랬는데 지금은 대신 팀원들을 응원하게 되어 기뻐.

남 그래서 아직도 연습에 나가는 거야?

여 응. 친구들이 훈련하고 경기를 하는 모습을 보면 기분이 훨씬 나아져.

남 와, 너 정말 낙천적인 사람이다. 내가 다쳤을 때와 너무 달라.

여 왜? 너는 다쳤을 때 어땠는데?

남 난 모든 것에 흥미를 잃고 집에서만 지냈어.

① 내가 부상을 당했지만 아무것도 변하지 않았어.
② 운동선수에게 부상은 최악의 일이지.
④ 전국 축구 경기에서 잘하길 바랄게.
⑤ 아주 심하게 넘어져서 허리를 다쳤어.

---

14 | 정답 | ①

작업 중이던 파일이 사라져 여자가 남자에게 도움을 요청하는 상황이다. 고칠 수 있는 사람을 불러줄 수 있다는 남자의 말에 가장 적절한 여자의 응답은 ① '물론이지. 나한테 무슨 다른 선택권이 있겠어?'이다.

- bring back 돌려놓다
- automatically 자동으로
- restore 복구하다

W Mark, would you mind looking at my presentation?

M Sure, are you finished?

W Nearly, but I'm worried it's so long.

M Okay, just **show it to me**!

W Oh, no!

M What's wrong, Leena?

W Everything **I was working on just disappeared**. I don't know what to do!

M That's terrible. Can I have a look?

W Of course. Do you think you could bring back my files?

M I'll try. *[Pause]* It looks like the update program automatically closes all other programs when it starts.

W So **is there any way to restore my lost files**? I am so worried that I won't be able to get them back. I have to do the presentation tomorrow.

M I'm sorry, but I don't think I can solve your problem. But I know someone who can. I can call him and **ask if he can come over**.

W Of course. What other choice do I have?

여 Mark, 내 발표를 한번 봐줄 수 있을까?

남 물론이지, 다 했니?

여 거의. 그런데 너무 길까 봐 걱정이야.

남 알겠어. 그냥 나한테 보여줘!

여 아, 안 돼!

남 무슨 일이야, Leena?

여 내가 작업하고 있던 게 그냥 사라졌어. 뭘 해야 할지 모르겠어!

남 끔찍한데. 내가 잠깐 봐도 될까?

여 물론이지. 내 파일을 돌려놓을 수 있을 것 같아?

남 시도해 볼게. *[잠시 후]* 내가 보기엔 업데이트 프로그램이 시작될 때 자동으로 다른 모든 프로그램들을 닫아 버리는 것 같아.

여 그러면 내 사라진 파일들을 복구할 방법이 없을까? 다시 못 찾을까 봐 너무도 걱정돼. 내일 발표를 해야 하거든.

남 미안하지만 내가 문제를 해결할 수 없을 것 같아. 하지만 할 수 있는 사람을 알고 있어. 그에게 전화해서 이쪽으로 올 수 있는지 물어볼 수 있어.

여 물론이지. 나한테 무슨 다른 선택권이 있겠어?

② 걱정 마. 내가 스스로 문제를 처리할 수 있어.
③ 그에게 PC 시스템을 업데이트하라고 말해 줘.
④ 괜찮아. 난 벌써 시스템을 업데이트했어.
⑤ 괜찮아. 내 발표를 연기했어.

---

15 | 정답 | ①

다른 사람들을 도와주는 것을 거절하지 못하는 Kelly에게 업무에 문제가 생기지 않도록 때때로 거절해야 한다는 조언의 말이 가장 자연스럽다. 따라서 Mike가 Kelly에게 할 말로 가장 적절한 것은 ① '당신은 거절하는 법을 알아야 해요.' 이다.

- associate (직함 앞에 붙여) 부-, 준-
- enthusiasm 열정
- devotion 헌신
- colleague 동료
- refuse 거절하다
- end up v-ing 결국 ~하게 되다
- superior 상사
- delay 지연
- cooperative 협조적인
- generous 너그러운
- attitude 태도

M Kelly is an associate manager at R&C Company. She is known within the company for her enthusiasm and her devotion to her work. Due to her kind personality, sometimes she helps with her colleagues' work. Kelly **does not know how to refuse to help someone**, even when she needs to, and ends up doing all of her colleagues' work. One day, her superior, Mike, notices that her personality often **causes delays in important tasks**. Mike knows that Kelly is a capable employee and that she is very helpful and cooperative with others. But he wants to tell her that **her generous attitude may result in problems** in her own work. In this situation, what would Mike most likely say to Kelly?

Mike You have to learn how to say no.

남 Kelly는 R&C사의 부매니저이다. 그녀는 회사 내에서 그녀의 일에 대한 열정과 헌신으로 잘 알려져 있다. 그녀의 친절한 성격 때문에 가끔 동료들의 일을 도와준다. Kelly는 필요한 경우에도 누군가를 도와주는 걸 거절하는 법을 몰라서 결국 동료들의 일까지 모두 하게 된다. 하루는 그녀의 상사인 Mike가 그녀의 성격이 중요한 일을 지연시킨다는 것을 알아챈다. Mike는 Kelly가 유능한 직원이고 다른 사람들을 아주 잘 도와주며 협조적인 사람인 것을 알고 있다. 하지만 그는 그녀의 너그러운 태도가 그녀 자신의 업무에 문제를 일으킬 수 있다는 것을 그녀에게 말해 주고 싶다. 이러한 상황에서 Mike가 Kelly에게 할 말로 가장 적절한 것은 무엇인가?

Mike 당신은 거절하는 법을 알아야 해요.

② 회사에서 정해진 시간보다 일찍 퇴근하지 마세요.
③ 제 생각에 당신은 조금 더 헌신할 필요가 있어요.
④ 당신은 일과 개인적인 삶의 균형을 잡을 줄 알아야 해요.
⑤ 신입사원의 일을 좀 도와줄 수 있나요?

16 | 정답 | ①

지구에서 사는 생물이 아닌 것 같은 특이한 외모를 가진 해양 생물들을 예시로 들어 여자가 설명하고 있다. 따라서 정답은 ① '해저에 사는 독특한 생물체들'이다.

17 | 정답 | ④

특이한 외모를 가진 해양 생물 중에 '해마'에 대한 언급은 없었으므로 정답은 ④이다.

- **creature** 생물(체)
- **marine** 해양의
- **underwater** 해저
- **shallow** 얕은
- **exotic** 이국적인
- **flap** 펄럭이다
- **fin** 지느러미

W Hello, everyone. We are going to continue talking about sea animals today. We are going to see ocean creatures which are so alien-like that **you will not believe they aren't from outer space**! But believe it or not, all of the animals can be found right here on planet Earth. Let's check them out. First are feather stars. Look at the picture on the screen. These crazy-looking marine animals wave their "feather legs" to get around underwater. **They are mostly found in shallow water**. Next is a type of shrimp called mantis shrimp. See how colorful they look? These exotic looking creatures have glowing green backs. Next up is the dumbo octopus. What animal do they resemble? Yes, elephants. They get their name from the elephant cartoon character "Dumbo" due to their flapping ear-fins **that look like the ears of elephants**. Our last creature of the day is the leafy sea dragon. I know they look like sea plants, **but they are actually a type of fish**.

여 안녕하세요, 여러분. 오늘은 이어서 해양 생물에 대해 이야기할 거예요. 우리는 너무도 외계 생물체처럼 생겨서 우주에서 온 동물이 아니라는 것을 믿지 못할 만한 해양 생물을 볼 것입니다! 하지만 믿거나 말거나 모든 동물들은 바로 이 지구상에서 볼 수 있는 동물들이랍니다. 이제 그들에 대해 알아봅시다. 첫 번째는 바다나리입니다. 화면의 사진을 보십시오. 이 독특하게 생긴 해양 생물은 그들의 '깃털 모양 다리'를 움직여 해저를 돌아다닙니다. 그들은 보통 얕은 물에서 발견됩니다. 다음은 갯가재라고 불리는 새우의 한 종류입니다. 얼마나 형형색색인지 보이죠? 이 이국적인 생김새의 생물체들은 빛나는 초록색 등을 갖고 있습니다. 다음 차례는 덤보 문어입니다. 어떤 동물과 닮았나요? 네, 코끼리입니다. 그들은 코끼리 귀처럼 생긴 펄럭이는 귀 같은 지느러미 때문에 코끼리 만화 캐릭터인 '덤보'에서 이름이 지어졌습니다. 오늘의 마지막 생물체는 나뭇잎 해룡입니다. 해초처럼 생겼지만 이들은 사실 물고기의 한 종류랍니다.

16 ① 해저에 사는 독특한 생물체들
② 토종 물고기를 위협하는 외래 물고기
③ 멸종 위기에 처한 세계의 해양 생물들
④ 외계인의 존재에 대한 논란
⑤ 해양 생물의 이름의 유래

17 ① 바다나리 ② 갯가재 ③ 덤보 문어
④ 해마 ⑤ 나뭇잎 해룡

02회 실전 듣기 모의고사

| 01 ② | 02 ② | 03 ③ | 04 ⑤ | 05 ② | | 06 ③ | 07 ② | 08 ④ | 09 ③ | 10 ③ |
| 11 ⑤ | 12 ① | 13 ① | 14 ③ | 15 ⑤ | | 16 ③ | 17 ② | | | |

본문 p.10

01 | 정답 | ②

학생회에서 장기 자랑에 대해 소개하는 내용이다. 일정, 행사 내용 등을 소개하며, 마지막에 모두 장기 자랑에서 만나기를 바란다고 하는 내용으로 보아 여자가 하는 말의 목적으로 가장 적절한 것은 ②이다.

- **on behalf of** ~을 대표하여
- **gymnasium** 체육관
- **available** 이용 가능한
- **purchase** 구매하다
- **raffle ticket** 경품 응모권, 추첨 티켓
- **give away** 나눠주다
- **proceeds** 수익금

W Good morning, everyone. On behalf of the student council, **I am pleased to invite you to** our annual talent show at Lincoln Senior High School. Join us for a night of entertainment and help our community. Our talent show will be held on Tuesday, May 19th, at 6 p.m. in the school gymnasium. The talent show will be composed of two sessions, one for solo performances and the other for group performances. Admission is $2 and **snacks will be available to purchase.** You can also buy raffle tickets for $1 each and win prizes throughout the show! We have over 50 prizes to give away. All proceeds will be donated to our local homeless shelter. **We are looking forward to seeing all of you** at the talent show. Thank you.

여 안녕하세요. 학생회를 대표하여, 여러분을 Lincoln 고등학교의 연례행사인 장기 자랑에 초대하게 되어 기쁩니다. 오락의 밤에 참석하셔서 지역 사회에 도움을 주시기 바랍니다. 장기 자랑은 학교 체육관에서 5월 19일 화요일 오후 6시에 열릴 예정입니다. 장기 자랑은 두 세션으로 구성이 되는데, 하나는 솔로 공연 다른 하나는 그룹 공연으로 이루어집니다. 입장료는 2달러이며 간식은 구매 가능합니다. 한 장당 1달러에 경품 응모권을 구매할 수도 있으며 장기 자랑이 진행되는 동안 경품을 받을 수 있습니다! 나눠드릴 경품이 50개 이상 있습니다. 모든 수익금은 지역 노숙자 쉼터에 기부될 것입니다. 장기 자랑에서 여러분 모두를 뵙기를 바랍니다. 감사합니다.

02 | 정답 | ②

남자가 여자에게 필요 없는 물건들을 구매하지 않기 위해 미리 쇼핑 목록을 작성하는 것을 제안하는 상황이다. 쇼핑할 때 쇼핑 목록을 적는 것이 잘못된 물건을 사지 않게 한다는 남자의 말로 보아 남자의 의견으로는 ②가 가장 적절하다.

- **grocery** 식료품
- **laundry detergent** 세탁용 세제
- **run out** 다 떨어지다
- **refrigerator** 냉장고

W Honey, can you help me out with the groceries?
M Sure. *[Pause]* This bag is so heavy. What did you buy?
W Oh, I bought some fruits and vegetables, and meat. I also got some laundry detergent.
M We have enough laundry detergent. Why did you get more?
W Oh, **I thought we were running out**.
M Did you make a shopping list before you went?
W No, I didn't. I just decide what to get when I'm shopping.
M You should. You **won't buy the wrong thing if you have a list**.
W I know. I feel like I spend too much on things we don't need. **Maybe from now on I should make a list**.
M Making a list is easy. We could put a piece of paper on the refrigerator. Then we just write down the items we need.
W That sounds like a great idea.

여 여보, 식료품 산 것 좀 도와주실래요?
남 물론이요. *[잠시 후]* 가방이 무겁네요. 뭘 샀어요?
여 아, 과일과 채소와 고기를 샀어요. 그리고 세탁용 세제도 좀 샀어요.
남 세제는 충분히 있는데요. 왜 더 샀어요?
여 아, 다 떨어졌다고 생각했어요.
남 가기 전에 쇼핑 목록을 작성했나요?
여 아니요. 난 그냥 무엇을 살지 쇼핑할 때 결정해요.
남 목록을 작성해야 해요. 목록을 가지고 쇼핑하면 잘못된 것을 사지 않을 거예요.
여 알아요. 필요 없는 것을 사는 데 돈을 너무 많이 쓰는 것 같아요. 지금부터라도 목록을 작성해야겠네요.
남 작성하는 것은 쉬워요. 종이 하나를 냉장고에 붙여 놓으면 돼요. 그리고 우리가 필요한 물건들을 적는 거예요.
여 아주 좋은 생각인 것 같네요.

03 | 정답 | ③

그림 그리기에 흥미가 있어 미술 도구 세트를 받았고, 그로 인해 미술 학교 교사가 되었다는 자신의 경험을 예로 들면서 선물을 줄 때는 받는 사람이 좋아하는 것을 고려해야 한다고 말하고 있다. 따라서 여자가 하는 말의 요지로 가장 적절한 것은 ③이다.

- **tune** (라디오·텔레비전 채널을) 맞추다
- **year-end** 연말
- **kit** 도구 한 벌, 용구 한 벌
- **ignite** 불을 붙이다
- **fine art** ((복수형)) 미술
- **appeal** 관심을 끌다; 호소하다; 매력
- **preference** 선호(도)
- **equipment** 장비, 용품; 설비

W Hello, listeners! My name is Kelly Tuner, and you're tuned in to *Sunlight Digest*. As the year-end season approaches, many people are wondering what gifts to give to their friends and family. When giving gifts, **take some time to deeply consider what they like and enjoy**. When I was young, **I was interested in drawing**, and my father bought me an art kit. It ignited my passion for art. Now, years later, I'm a fine arts school teacher. So, **when selecting a gift for your loved ones**, select what appeals to their preferences, like a camera or sports equipment. To help you out, I will show you some gift samples for each occasion. Stay tuned!

여 안녕하세요, 청취자 여러분! 제 이름은 Kelly Tuner이고, 여러분은 Sunlight Digest에 채널을 맞추고 계십니다. 연말 시즌이 다가오면서, 많은 사람들이 친구들과 가족들에게 어떤 선물을 줘야 할지 궁금해하고 있습니다. 선물을 줄 때, 그들이 무엇을 좋아하고 즐기는지 깊게 생각하는 시간을 가져보세요. 제가 어렸을 때, 저는 그림 그리는 것에 흥미가 있었고, 아버지는 저에게 미술 도구 세트를 사 주셨어요. 그것이 미술에 대한 제 열정에 불을 붙였죠. 몇 년이 지난 지금, 저는 미술 학교 교사입니다. 그래서 사랑하는 사람들을 위한 선물을 고를 때는 카메라나 스포츠 장비처럼 그들의 취향을 저격하는 것을 선택하세요. 여러분을 돕기 위해, 여러분께 각각의 경우에 맞는 몇 가지 선물 예시를 보여드리겠습니다. 채널을 고정하세요!

04 | 정답 | ⑤

책장 선반 위에 지구본이 있다고 하였으므로 일치하지 않는 것은 ⑤이다.

* arrange 배열하다
* study (특히 개인 가정의) 서재
* at last 드디어, 마침내
* laptop 노트북
* scratch 긁힘, 스크래치
* globe 지구본
* fill 채우다

W Honey, I've arranged your study at last.
M You've done a wonderful job. I love it.
W It's good to hear that. What do you think of the blinds on the windows?
M They're perfect. I can close the blinds **if there is too much light**. It was hard to work at my desk in front of the window before.
W I know. I also took the laptop out of the case and **placed it in the middle of the desk**.
M That's good. Oh, you bought a new chair, too.
W I remembered that you wanted a chair with wheels. Just be careful with it. I don't want any scratches on the floor.
M I will. Did you move the bookcase to the left wall by yourself?
W No, Tom helped me move it. **I didn't know where to put the globe**. Is it okay on the shelf like that?
M That's fine. There are not **enough books to fill all the shelves** anyway.
W Are you satisfied with the present arrangement?
M Yes, definitely.

여 여보, 당신 서재 배치를 드디어 끝냈어요.
남 정말 잘했어요. 맘에 드네요.
여 다행이네요. 창문에 있는 블라인드 어때요?
남 완벽해요. 빛이 지나치게 많이 들어올 땐 블라인드를 치면 되네요. 전엔 창문 앞에서 일하는 것이 힘들었거든요.
여 알아요. 가방에서 노트북을 꺼내어 책상 가운데에다 놓았어요.
남 좋아요. 아, 의자도 새로 샀네요.
여 당신이 바퀴 달린 의자를 원했던 것이 기억났어요. 조심히 다루어야 해요. 바닥에 흠집 나는 거 싫어요.
남 그럴게요. 책장을 혼자서 좌측 벽에다 옮겼어요?
여 아뇨, Tom이 옮기는 것을 도와줬어요. 지구본을 어디에 놓을지 몰랐는데요. 저렇게 책장 선반 위에 놓은 거 괜찮아요?
남 좋아요. 어차피 책장을 채울 책도 충분하지 않은데요, 뭐.
여 지금 이 배치에 만족해요?
남 네, 그럼요.

05 | 정답 | ②

여자에게 연극을 보러 가자고 제안하는 상황이다. 티켓 할인을 받기 위해서는 학생증이 필요하다는 남자의 말에 집에 가서 가져오겠다고 여자가 말했으므로 정답은 ②이다.

* visit a theater 연극을 보러 가다
* do the laundry 빨래를 하다
* be described as ~라고 평하다

W What are you doing later today?
M I'm planning to go to a theater to see a play at Daehakno.
W A play? I didn't know you enjoyed plays.
M Really? **I sometimes visit theaters by myself**.
W I have never seen a play before. What are you watching then?
M It's called "Bballae," which means "Doing the Laundry."
W Oh, I think I read about it once. It was described as **one of the best and longest running shows**.
M That's right. You can come with me if you want.
W I would love to. **Do you have an extra ticket for me**?
M Oh, you can go and buy a ticket at the box office.
W How much is a ticket?
M It's $30 per ticket and students get a 15% discount with a student ID card.
W I don't have mine on me right now. **I have to go home to pick it up**. What time is the showing?
M It's at 8 p.m. So I think we should meet 30 minutes before it starts.
W Okay. See you then.

여 오늘 이따가 뭐 할 거야?
남 대학로로 연극 보러 극장에 갈 계획이야.
여 연극? 연극을 즐기는 줄 몰랐네.
남 정말? 난 가끔 혼자서 연극을 보러 가.
여 난 연극을 본 적이 없어. 그러면 뭘 보려는데?
남 '빨래'라는 연극인데, 그건 '세탁하다'라는 의미야.
여 아, 그것에 대한 기사를 한 번 읽은 것 같아. 가장 훌륭하고 장기 공연한 작품 중 하나로 평하던데.
남 맞아. 원하면 같이 가도 돼.
여 그럴게. 남는 티켓이 있는 거니?
남 아, 매표소에서 하나 살 수 있어.
여 티켓 한 장에 얼마야?
남 한 장에 30달러이고 학생들은 학생증이 있으면 15% 할인받을 수 있어.
여 지금 나한테 학생증이 없어. 집에 가서 가져와야겠다. 몇 시에 공연하니?
남 오후 8시야. 연극 시작 30분 전까지는 만나는 게 좋을 것 같아.
여 알았어. 그때 보자.

06 | 정답 | ③

바지는 70달러이며 셔츠는 40달러이고, 셔츠 두 개를 사면 두 번째 셔츠는 50% 할인된다고 하였다. 따라서 남자는 바지와 셔츠 2개를 구매하여, 총금액은 130달러($70 + $40 + $40 × 50%)로 정답은 ③이다.

* particular 특정한
* graduation 졸업(식)
* trousers 바지
* go well with ~와 잘 어울리다
* fair skin 하얀 피부

W Welcome to the Men's Wear department. Have you been helped?
M Not yet. I am looking for some pants for my son.
W They're right over here, sir. Is there a particular style he prefers?
M He needs pants that are not too casual. They are for his graduation.
W All right. How about these dark gray suit trousers with checks?
M They are **exactly the ones I was looking for**. How much are they?
W They are $70. What size does your son wear?
M Medium, please. Do you also **have a shirt that can go well** with those?

여 남성복 매장에 오신 것을 환영합니다. 직원 도움을 받으셨습니까?
남 아직이요. 아들이 입을 바지를 찾고 있어요.
여 그것들은 바로 이쪽에 있습니다. 아드님이 선호하는 특정한 스타일이 있나요?
남 너무 캐주얼하지 않은 게 필요해요. 졸업식에서 입으려고 합니다.
여 좋아요. 체크무늬가 들어간 이 짙은 회색 양복바지는 어떨까요?
남 딱 제가 찾고 있던 제품이네요. 얼마예요?
여 70달러입니다. 아드님이 어떤 사이즈를 입으시나요?
남 미디엄으로 주세요. 그 바지와 어울릴 셔츠도 있나요?

	W Yes. The color dark gray can go with anything. If your son has fair skin, I recommend a plain shirt in light blue. M I like it. How much is the shirt? W It's $40, but if you buy two, **you can get your second one 50% off**. M Then I will take two. Both in medium, please. W Of course, sir. Is there anything else you need? M No, that would be all. W All right, I will **get the pants and the two shirts ready** at the counter.	여 네. 짙은 회색은 어느 것이나 다 어울려요. 아드님의 피부가 하얗다면, 엷은 하늘색의 무늬 없는 셔츠를 추천합니다. 남 마음에 드네요. 셔츠는 얼마예요? 여 40달러입니다. 하지만 두 장을 사시면 두 번째 제품은 50% 할인해 드릴게요. 남 그러면 두 장 구입할게요. 두 장 모두 미디엄으로 주세요. 여 물론입니다. 손님. 그밖에 필요한 것이 있나요? 남 아니요, 그게 전부입니다. 여 좋습니다. 바지와 셔츠 두 장을 계산대에 준비해 놓겠습니다.

---

07 | 정답 | ②

금요일부터 일요일까지 열리는 대학 박람회에 가는지 묻는 남자에게 여자는 주말 동안 시내에 있는 병원으로 할아버지를 뵈러 간다고 하면서 못 가는 이유를 설명하고 있다. 따라서 정답은 ② 이다.

- head to ~로 가다
- college fair 대학 (입학) 박람회
- be held 열리다
- be supposed to-v ~하기로 되어 있다
- turn 차례

M I can't wait until the finals are over.
W There are only a few days left. **I'm heading to the library to study**. Do you want to come?
M Sure. Oh, are you going to attend the college fair next week?
W I forgot about that. **When will it be held**?
M It'll be held from the 25th to the 27th. That's from next Friday to Sunday.
W Really? Then I don't think I can go.
M Why not?
W My family is supposed to **go downtown and visit my grandfather**.
M Is something the matter with him?
W He got in a traffic accident. Next weekend is my mother's turn to take care of him at the hospital.
M I'm sorry to hear that. **I hope he gets better soon**.
W Thanks.

남 기말고사가 얼른 끝났으면 좋겠다.
여 이제 며칠만 고생하면 돼. 공부하러 도서관에 가고 있어. 같이 갈래?
남 좋아. 아, 다음 주에 대학 박람회에 참석할 거니?
여 잊고 있었네. 언제 열리지?
남 25일부터 27일까지 열려. 다음 주 금요일에서 일요일까지야.
여 정말? 그럼 난 못 가겠는데.
남 왜 못 가는데?
여 우리 가족이 시내로 가서 할아버지를 찾아뵈려고 하거든.
남 할아버지에게 무슨 일 있니?
여 교통사고를 당하셨어. 다음 주는 엄마가 병원에서 할아버지를 돌볼 차례거든.
남 안됐구나. 빨리 회복하시길 바랄게.
여 고마워.

---

08 | 정답 | ④

괌의 Dolphin Cruise 투어에 수영복과 수건을 가져가야 하며, Guam Plaza에서 10시 50분에 버스를 탈 수 있다고 하였다. 유람선 여행은 2시간이 소요되며 성인 한 명당 48달러라고 하였지만, 유람선이 어디로 유람할 것인지에 대한 내용은 언급되지 않았으므로 정답은 ④ 이다.

- cruise 유람선 여행
- describe 설명하다
- in detail 자세히, 상세히
- bathing suit 수영복
- convenient 편리한
- look around 둘러보다
- book 예약하다
- Let's go for it. 실행합시다.

M Have you heard of the Dolphin Cruise Tour in Guam? Do you want to go on it next month?
W Sure. I've always wanted to go on a dolphin cruise.
M This website I'm looking at **describes the tour in detail**.
W Really? What does it say?
M The Dolphin Cruise Tour is on a 57-seat boat. It includes fishing and snorkeling activities.
W That sounds interesting. What do we need to bring?
M We just need our own bathing suits and towels. **Everything else is included**, even snacks.
W That's convenient. But how can we get there from our hotel?
M The tour has a pick-up service. Let's see. [Pause] The bus comes to Guam Plaza at 10:50.
W That's perfect. **We will have enough time to get ready**.
M Exactly. The cruise only takes two hours.
W That couldn't be better. We'll have enough time to look around other places after the cruise.
M A ticket is $48 for one adult. **Should I book two tickets now**?
W Yes, let's go for it.

남 괌의 Dolphin Cruise 투어에 대해 들어본 적 있어요? 다음 달에 그걸 가볼래요?
여 물론이죠. 항상 돌고래 유람선 여행을 가고 싶었거든요.
남 제가 보고 있는 이 웹사이트가 그 투어에 대해 자세히 설명하고 있어요.
여 정말요? 뭐라고 하는데요?
남 Dolphin Cruise 투어는 57석의 배로 한대요. 낚시와 스노클링 활동도 포함되어 있고요.
여 재밌겠는데요. 무엇을 가져가야 하나요?
남 수영복하고 수건만 있으면 돼요. 그 밖의 모든 것이 포함되어 있는데 심지어는 간식도 포함되어 있대요.
여 편리하네요. 하지만 호텔에서 그곳에 어떻게 가나요?
남 그 투어에는 픽업서비스가 있어요. 한번 봅시다. [잠시 후] 버스가 Guam Plaza에 10시 50분에 오네요.
여 완벽하네요. 준비할 시간도 충분히 있고요.
남 맞아요. 유람선 여행은 2시간 정도 걸린대요.
여 최고네요. 유람선 여행을 하고 나서 또 다른 곳을 둘러볼 시간도 충분히 있네요.
남 성인 한 명당 48달러네요. 지금 두 장 예약할까요?
여 네, 그럽시다.

---

09 | 정답 | ③

전 학년이 참여 가능하며 10주간 금요일마다 수업이 진행된다고 하였다. 이론 수업 이후 10분 동안 드론을 직접 날릴 수 있으며 자리가 한정되어 있기 때문에 한 달 전에 미리 신청해야 한다고 하

M Good morning, students. As a science teacher, I am very proud to tell you about the special drone program for all students. It is called "Dronepia," which is a combination of the words "Drone" and "Utopia." The program includes 10 classes, starting on April 20th, and **each class is**

남 안녕하세요, 학생 여러분. 과학 교사로서, 모든 학생을 위한 특별 드론 프로그램에 대해 설명하게 되어 매우 자랑스럽습니다. 프로그램은 'Dronepia'라고 불리는데, 그것은 '드론'과 '유토피아'라는 단어의 합성어입니다. 그 프로그램은 10번의 수업으로 이루어지는데 4월 20일에 시작되며 각 수업은 금요일 오후 4시로 예정되어

였다. 모든 수업에 참석할 필요는 없지만, 출석률 80% 이상일 경우에만 수료증을 준다고 하였으므로 일치하지 않는 것은 ③이다.

* combination 합성어
* be scheduled 예정되어 있다
* certificate 수료증
* participation 참석
* provide B for A A에게 B를 제공하다
* benefit 이로움, 이익
* downside 단점, 덜 긍정적인 것
* in advance 미리
* feel free to do 부담 없이 ~하다

scheduled for Fridays at 4 p.m. You don't have to attend every class, but certificates will be given to those **who have above 80% participation**. The school will provide enough drone sets for everyone. Throughout the program, you will learn the basics about drones such as the theory, types, and benefits and downsides. In addition, **you will get to fly a drone** in the last 10 minutes of each class. Since the class is limited to 15 people, it is recommended you **sign up one month in advance**. If you have any questions, feel free to contact me by email, lewis@sacredheart.ac.ca.

있습니다. 모든 수업에 참석할 필요는 없지만 수료증은 80% 이상 참석한 학생들에게 주어집니다. 학교에서는 모두에게 드론 세트를 충분히 제공할 것입니다. 그 프로그램을 통해, 여러분은 드론에 대한 기본 즉 이론, 유형 그리고 이점과 단점에 대해 배울 것입니다. 게다가, 여러분은 각 수업의 마지막 10분 동안 드론을 날리게 됩니다. 수업이 15명으로 제한되기 때문에, 한 달 전에 미리 등록할 것을 추천드립니다. 질문이 있으면 저에게 이메일(lewis@sacredheart.ac.ca)로 부담없이 연락 주세요.

---

10 | 정답 | ③

두 사람이 구매할 소파는 가죽으로 된, 팔걸이가 있는 크림색 소파이며 700달러보다 저렴하다고 했으므로 정답은 ③이다.

* firm 단단한, 딱딱한
* furniture 가구
* catalog 카탈로그, 목록
* fabric 천, 직물
* leather 가죽
* velvet 벨벳
* stain 얼룩, 때
* definitely 분명히, 틀림없이, 절대로

M Honey, we really need to change this sofa. It's not firm anymore.
W Let's go over this furniture catalog and decide which one to get.
M Okay. Do you want to get a fabric one like this one? **Fabric ones are cheaper than leather or velvet ones**.
W I don't like fabric ones. It's hard to get stains and dust out.
M True. Then, we should get either leather or velvet. They are a little more expensive, but if properly cared for, **they last longer**.
W All right. Do you want one with or without arms?
M Definitely with arms. I usually leave the remote control on the left arm. What about you?
W Me, too. It seems like there are two colors available.
M How about the one in cream? **It'll make our living room look brighter**.
W That sounds good. There are two left. **Should we get the cheaper one**?
M Yes, $700 is too much for us.
W Okay. I'll make a call to see if the store has that one in stock.

남 여보, 우리 이 소파를 정말 바꿔야겠어요. 더 이상 단단하지 않아요.
여 먼저 이 가구 카탈로그를 보고 어느 것을 살 건지 결정합시다.
남 좋아요. 이것처럼 천으로 된 것이 좋나요? 천으로 된 것이 가죽이나 벨벳으로 된 것보다 값이 저렴해요.
여 천으로 된 것은 마음에 안 들어요. 얼룩이나 먼지를 없애기가 어렵거든요.
남 맞아요. 그럼, 가죽이나 벨벳으로 사야겠네요. 조금 더 비싸지만 잘 관리하면 더 오래 쓸 수 있어요.
여 알겠어요. 당신은 팔걸이가 있는 것과 없는 것 중에 어느 것이 좋아요?
남 당연히 팔걸이가 있는 것이 좋지요. 내가 보통 왼쪽 팔걸이에 리모컨을 놓아두잖아요. 당신은요?
여 저도 그게 좋아요. 색깔은 두 가지가 있는 것 같아요.
남 크림색 어때요? 그 색깔이 거실을 더 환하게 할 것 같은데요.
여 좋아요. 2개가 남네요. 가격이 더 저렴한 걸로 할까요?
남 네. 700달러는 우리에겐 너무 과해요.
여 알겠어요. 제가 가구점에 그것이 재고가 남아 있는지 전화해 볼게요.

---

11 | 정답 | ⑤

남자가 여자에게 디저트를 권유하는 상황이다. 남자가 여러 종류의 디저트를 언급하며 메뉴를 가져다주겠다고 한 말에 대한 응답으로 가장 적절한 여자의 응답은 ⑤ '네, 그래 주세요. 한번 볼게요.'이다.

* perhaps 아마, 어쩌면
* room 공간
* sherbet 셔벗 (과즙 아이스크림)

M Can I get you anything else, perhaps more potatoes?
W No, thanks. I need to **leave room for dessert**. What do you have for dessert?
M We have many different kinds of desserts, including cake and sherbet. **I can bring you the menu** if you want.
W Yes, please. I'd like to take a look at it.

남 더 필요한 거 있으신가요, 어쩌면 감자가 더 필요하신가요?
여 아니요, 됐습니다. 디저트도 먹어야 하니까요. 디저트로는 어떤 것들이 있나요?
남 케이크와 셔벗을 포함해 다양한 종류의 디저트가 있습니다. 원하시면 메뉴판 가져다드릴까요?
여 네, 그래 주세요. 한번 볼게요.

① 좋아요. 남은 음식은 싸주시겠어요?
② 아뇨, 괜찮아요. 전 지금 정말 배불러요.
③ 물론이죠. 초콜릿 아이스크림 먹고 싶어요.
④ 커피와 케이크 한 조각을 추천드립니다.

---

12 | 정답 | ①

남자도 여자 얼굴이 익숙하다고 하자 여자는 이름을 말하며 같이 수업을 들었다고 설명한다. 이에 대한 남자의 응답으로 가장 적절한 것은 ① '물론이죠. 오랜만이에요, Susan.'이다.

* by any chance 혹시
* graduate 졸업하다
* the class of '98 98년 졸업반
* familiar 익숙한; 잘 알고 있는

W Pardon me. By any chance, did you attend Harvard Business School?
M Yes, I graduated in the class of '98. **You look familiar**. Do I know you?
W Yes, I'm Susan Baker. **We had a few classes together** in the first year. Do you remember me?
M Sure. It's been a long time, Susan.

여 실례합니다. 혹시, 하버드 경영 대학원 다니셨나요?
남 네, 1998년에 졸업했습니다. 낯이 익은데, 저를 아시나요?
여 네, 저 Susan Baker예요. 1학년 때 수업 몇 개 같이 들었잖아요. 기억나나요?
남 물론이죠. 오랜만이에요, Susan.

② 아니요, 우리 같은 반이에요.
③ 물론이죠. 말씀 많이 들었어요.
④ 죄송합니다만, 전화 잘못 거셨어요.
⑤ 당신이 저에게 미국사를 가르쳐 주신 것 같은데요.

13 | 정답 | ①

야외 촬영을 앞두고 갑자기 비가 오는 상황이다. 남자는 이 장면이 중요하며, 대본을 수정해서 실내에서 촬영하는 것이 더 어렵다고 설명하고 있다. 따라서 한 시간만 더 기다려보자는 남자의 말에 대한 여자의 응답으로 가장 적절한 것은 ① '알았어. 소나기일 수도 있으니까.'이다.

- film 찍다, 촬영하다
- weather forecast 일기예보
- pour 퍼붓다
- script 대본

W Don, it just started raining. I don't know if we can film the last scene outside today.
M Really? I didn't hear about rain from the weather forecast.
W It's pouring now. I don't know when it'll stop.
M Let's wait a while. It could get better.
W I have other projects to work on. I don't have much time to waste.
M I know how you feel. **But there is only one scene left**.
W How about changing the script and shooting the last scene inside?
M I can't. The last scene is very important and it has to be done outside. Otherwise the story won't make sense.
W But the school project is due this Friday. We don't have enough time.
M This is the last scene of the film. **It won't take long to finish it**.
W It may not. But we don't know that.
M **But changing the script is not easy either**. I would have to think of a new ending.
W That's true. It could take longer.
M Exactly. **Why don't we wait another hour** to see how things go?
W All right. It could just be a shower.

여 Don, 막 비가 내리기 시작했어. 오늘 밖에서 마지막 장면을 찍을 수 있을지 모르겠네.
남 정말? 난 일기예보에서 비 온다는 말을 못 들었는데.
여 지금 막 퍼붓고 있어. 언제 그칠지 몰라.
남 조금만 기다리자. 괜찮아지겠지.
여 난 해야 할 다른 프로젝트가 있어. 낭비할 시간이 없어.
남 네 기분 알아. 하지만 한 장면만 남았잖아.
여 대본을 고쳐서 마지막 장면을 실내에서 찍는 게 어떨까?
남 안 돼. 마지막 장면은 매우 중요하고, 밖에서 찍어야만 해. 그렇지 않으면 그 이야기가 말이 안 되거든.
여 하지만 학교 프로젝트는 이번 주 금요일이 마감이야. 시간이 충분하지 않아.
남 이게 영화의 마지막 장면이야. 끝내는 데 오래 걸리지는 않을 거야.
여 그렇지 않을 수도 있어. 하지만 그건 알 수 없지.
남 하지만 대본을 고치는 것 또한 쉽지 않아. 새로운 결말을 생각해야 하거든.
여 맞아. 더 오래 걸릴 수 있고.
남 맞아. 상황이 어떻게 될지 한 시간만 더 기다려보는 게 어때?
여 알았어. 소나기일 수도 있으니까.

② 미안해. 이야기를 바꿀 수 없을 것 같아.
③ 나는 동의하지 않아. 배우들은 차에서 기다려야 해.
④ 그래. 오늘 밤은 날씨가 맑을 거야.
⑤ 물론이야. 노트북을 가져와서 새 대본을 쓸게.

14 | 정답 | ③

여자가 옥상 정원을 만들자고 제안하는 상황이다. 옥상 정원은 에너지 소비를 줄이고 장기적으로 많은 것을 절감하는 효과가 있다고 하였으므로 남자의 응답으로 가장 적절한 것은 ③ '와! 조사를 해서 곧 하나 만들어 봅시다!'이다.

- purify 정화시키다
- roof garden 옥상 정원
- consumption 소비
- absorb 흡수하다
- power bill 전기세
- in the long-term 장기적인 관점에서

W Honey, have you decided where you want to have a garden?
M Oh, yes. How about an indoor garden?
W That's not bad. I've seen several cafes with one.
M We can get those plants that purify the air.
W Well, I was thinking about something else. **Have you heard of a roof garden**?
M I don't think I have. What's that?
W It's a garden on the roof of a building. **They have many benefits**.
M Really? What are they?
W A roof garden can reduce energy consumption. Because plants absorb heat, we can use less electricity for cooling in summer.
M Oh, that means **we could have a lower power bill**.
W Exactly. Though it might cost a lot to set up, in the long-term we can save a lot.
M Wow! Let's do some research and plant one soon!

여 여보, 어디에 정원을 만들지 결정했어요?
남 아, 네. 실내 정원 어때요?
여 나쁘지 않네요. 실내 정원을 갖고 있는 카페를 몇 군데 본 적 있거든요.
남 공기 정화용 식물을 마련할 수도 있어요.
여 음, 전 다른 것을 생각하고 있었어요. 옥상 정원에 대해 들어봤어요?
남 들어본 적 없는 것 같네요. 그게 뭔데요?
여 건물 옥상에 있는 정원이에요. 그것들은 많은 장점을 가지고 있어요.
남 정말요? 그게 뭔데요?
여 옥상 정원은 에너지 소비를 줄일 수 있어요. 식물이 열을 흡수하기 때문에 여름에 선선하게 하는 데 전기를 적게 써도 되죠.
남 아, 그건 전기세를 적게 낸다는 말이네요.
여 맞아요, 비록 설치하는 데 비용이 많이 들기는 하지만 장기적으로 볼 때 많은 것을 절약할 수 있어요.
남 와! 조사를 해서 곧 하나 만들어 봅시다!

① 알겠어요. 정원에 나무를 심고 싶어요.
② 말도 안 돼요. 정원 얘기는 지어낸 거죠.
④ 걱정 말아요. 제가 우리의 실내 정원을 위해 씨앗들을 사 올게요.
⑤ 이제 알겠어요. 그래서 옥상 정원이 그렇게 비용이 많이 드는군요.

15 | 정답 | ⑤

Rebecca가 요리 학교에 다니는 Ben에게 자신이 만든 음식을 맛보게 하고 의견을 물어보는 상황이다. Rebecca가 만든 요리가 싱겁다고 생각하는 Ben이 할 말로 가장 적절한 것은 ⑤ '파스타에 소금이 좀 들어가면 더 맛있을 것 같아.'이다.

W Rebecca is a high school student whose hobby is cooking. Since this Saturday is her parents' anniversary, she decides to cook a delicious dinner for them. After **she selects what recipes to use**, she thinks she needs to practice the recipes before the anniversary. So, she asks Ben for help because Ben goes to a culinary school and has much more experience in cooking than she does. Rebecca makes pasta and asks Ben to taste it. She

여 Rebecca는 고등학교 학생이며 그녀의 취미는 요리하는 것이다. 이번 주 토요일은 부모님의 결혼기념일이므로 부모님을 위해 맛있는 저녁을 요리하기로 결심한다. 어떤 조리법을 사용할지 고른 후에, 그녀는 기념일 전에 그 조리법을 연습해 봐야 한다고 생각한다. 그래서 그녀는 Ben이 요리 학교에 다니고 있고 그녀보다 훨씬 더 많은 요리 경험이 있기 때문에 그에게 도와달라고 부탁을 한다. Rebecca는 파스타를 만들고 나서 Ben에게 맛을 보라고 한다. 자신의 파스타가 괜찮은

- anniversary 기념일
- recipe 조리법
- practice 실습하다. 실행하다
- culinary 요리의
- take a bite 한 입 먹다
- good enough 충분히 좋은
- missing 빠져 있는
- seasoning 양념

thinks her pasta is okay and asks Ben for his opinion. Ben takes a bite, but he doesn't think it's good enough. As he looks around, he notices there is something missing in the kitchen. There is **no salt or any seasoning in sight**. Then he realizes that Rebecca forgot to add salt as she cooked. So, he decides to tell her **to add salt to make food taste better**. In this situation, what would Ben most likely say to Rebecca?

Ben I think the pasta would be better with some salt.

것 같아 Ben에게 그의 의견을 묻는다. Ben은 한 입 먹지만 그것이 부족하다고 생각한다. 그는 주변을 둘러보면서 부엌에 뭔가가 없다는 걸 알아챈다. 소금도 없고 어떠한 양념도 보이지 않는 것이었다. 그러고 나서 그는 Rebecca가 요리할 때 소금 넣는 것을 잊었음을 깨닫는다. 그래서 그는 그녀에게 음식의 맛을 더 잘 내기 위해서는 소금을 넣으라고 말해 주기로 한다. 이러한 상황에서 Ben이 Rebecca에게 할 말로 가장 적절한 것은 무엇인가?

Ben 파스타에 소금이 좀 들어가면 더 맛있을 것 같아.

① 내 파스타 어때? 좋아하길 바라.
② 미안한데, 도와줄 수 없을 것 같아.
③ 이 파스타 놀라운 맛인걸. 잘했어.
④ 이거 너무 짠데. 물 좀 넣는 게 어때?

---

16 | 정답 | ③
미세먼지로부터 건강을 지킬 수 있도록 면역력을 높이는 음식을 소개하는 내용이므로, 남자가 하는 말의 주제로 가장 적절한 것은 ③ '면역 체계를 더 강하게 해 주는 음식'이다.

17 | 정답 | ②
면역력을 높여주는 음식으로 '당근'은 언급되지 않았으므로 정답은 ②이다.

- fine dust 미세먼지
- inconvenience 불편
- strengthen 강화하다
- immune system 면역 체계
- cleanse 깨끗이 하다
- contain 함유하다
- common phrase 상투적인 문구
- prevent A from B A가 B하지 못하게 하다
- raw 날것의
- reduce 줄이다
- last but not least 마지막으로

M Hello, everyone. The fine dust issue is getting serious because it causes not only inconvenience in our lives, but also major health problems. Today we are going to talk about foods **that strengthen our immune systems** and help cleanse our bodies. First, apples contain a lot of vitamin C and E, **which keep your lungs healthy**. An apple a day is a common phrase that you may have heard before. Blueberries are full of vitamin C, which prevents cells from getting damaged. There are many recipes available for blueberries, but it'd be best to eat them raw instead of cooked. Many of you may not enjoy broccoli, but broccoli is a superfood that **cleanses your blood and protects your skin and eyes**. It is also proven to reduce the risk of lung cancer. Last but not least is garlic. It is well known for its many health benefits. It can **decrease the chance of heart disease** and help prevent cancer. You can wear masks to protect yourselves, but protection really begins at our dinner tables.

남 여러분, 안녕하세요. 미세먼지 문제는 우리 삶에 불편을 유발할 뿐만 아니라 주요 건강 문제를 일으키기 때문에 점점 심각해지고 있습니다. 오늘은 우리의 면역 체계를 강화해 주고 몸을 깨끗하게 해주는 음식에 대해 이야기하고자 합니다. 먼저 사과는 비타민 C와 E를 많이 함유하고 있는데, 그것들은 우리의 폐를 건강하게 해 줍니다. 하루에 사과 하나 전에도 흔히 들어본 말일 겁니다. 블루베리는 비타민 C가 많은데, 이것은 우리의 세포가 해를 입는 것을 막아 줍니다. 블루베리를 이용한 많은 요리법이 있지만 조리하지 않고 생으로 먹는 것이 가장 좋습니다. 여러분 중 많은 분이 브로콜리를 좋아하지 않을 수도 있을 텐데요. 브로콜리는 피를 맑게 해주고 피부와 눈을 보호하는 슈퍼푸드입니다. 폐암의 위험을 줄여 준다는 것 또한 증명된 사실입니다. 마지막으로 마늘입니다. 이것이 주는 건강상 이익은 잘 알려져 있죠. 심장병의 가능성을 줄여 주고 암을 예방해 주죠. 자신을 보호하기 위해 마스크를 쓰는 방법도 있지만 보호라는 것은 사실 밥상에서부터 시작합니다.

16 ① 미세먼지로부터 피부를 보호하는 법
② 미세먼지가 유발하는 다양한 건강 문제
③ 면역 체계를 더 강하게 해 주는 음식
④ 건강한 혈액 순환이 중요한 이유
⑤ 물로 신체를 해독하는 방법

17 ① 사과 ② 당근 ③ 블루베리
④ 브로콜리 ⑤ 마늘

03. 실전 듣기 모의고사

| 01 ② | 02 ④ | 03 ② | 04 ⑤ | 05 ① | | 06 ② | 07 ③ | 08 ⑤ | 09 ② | 10 ② |
| 11 ① | 12 ⑤ | 13 ① | 14 ① | 15 ④ | | 16 ④ | 17 ② | | | |

본문 **p.16**

01 | 정답 | ②

자원봉사자들에게 모인 목적과 함께 분담되는 일이 무엇인지 설명하고 있으므로 여자가 하는 말의 목적으로 ②가 가장 적절하다.

- in charge of ~을 담당하는
- energetic 활기찬
- the elderly 노인들
- belong to ~에 속하다
- worksheet 작업 계획표[진행표]
- hand out 나눠 주다
- set the table 상을 차리다
- side dish 반찬
- cooperation 협조

W Welcome to the Senior Community Center. I am Julia Kim, in charge of today's special event. First of all, I truly appreciate that **you have come to volunteer** at our center. I can feel that you are very energetic. I'm sure we can enjoy today's work together. As you all know, we are going to prepare dinner for the elderly at the center. **I divided all the volunteers into three groups**. You can see which group you belong to on the worksheet which I've just handed out. Group 1 will set the tables and Group 2 will cook some side dishes. Then, Group 3 **will wash the dishes**. If you have any questions as you work, please call me any time. My phone number **is written on the worksheet**. Thank you for your cooperation.

여 Senior Community Center에 오신 걸 환영합니다. 저는 오늘의 특별 행사를 담당하고 있는 Julia Kim입니다. 먼저, 여러분이 우리 센터에서 자원봉사를 위해 와 주신 것에 대해 진심으로 감사드립니다. 여러분이 아주 활기찬 것이 느껴지네요. 우리가 오늘의 작업을 함께 즐길 수 있을 것이라는 확신이 듭니다. 여러분 모두 알다시피, 우리는 센터의 노인 분들을 위한 저녁을 준비하려고 합니다. 모든 자원봉사자들을 세 개의 조로 나눴습니다. 여러분이 어느 조에 속하는지는 제가 방금 나눠 드린 작업 계획표에서 알 수 있습니다. 1조는 상을 차릴 것이고, 2조는 일부 반찬을 만들 거예요. 그리고 나서 3조는 설거지를 할 거예요. 일하면서 질문이 있으면 언제든 제게 연락해 주시기 바랍니다. 제 전화번호는 작업 계획표에 적혀 있습니다. 여러분의 협조에 감사드립니다.

02 | 정답 | ④

버스를 타는 것이 기차보다 저렴하고, 바로 최종목적지까지 갈 수 있다고 말하는 것으로 보아 남자의 의견으로 가장 적절한 것은 ④이다.

- solo trip 혼자 하는 여행
- sort of 어느 정도
- affordable (가격이) 알맞은, 적당한
- restricted to ~에 제한된
- route 경로, 노선
- track 철로, 선로
- efficient 효율적인
- destination 목적지

W Did I tell you that I'm going on a solo trip next month? I am so excited!
M Wow, you are really doing it. So, do you have everything planned out?
W Well, sort of. I decided to take the train this time.
M Really? **Taking buses is usually cheaper** than taking trains. How about taking bus trips?
W It's true that bus trips are more affordable, but train journeys seem safer and more romantic.
M Still, **train travel is restricted to a certain route** because trains can only travel where there are tracks.
W You mean **bus trips can be faster and more efficient**, right?
M Right. Trains only get you to a train station. But buses can **take you directly to your final destination**.

여 내가 다음 달에 혼자 여행 간다고 말했나? 정말 신나!
남 와, 정말 가는구나. 그럼 계획은 다 세운 거야?
여 음, 어느 정도는. 이번에는 기차를 타기로 결정했어.
남 정말? 버스를 타는 게 기차 타는 것보다 보통 더 싸. 버스 여행을 하는 게 어때?
여 버스 여행이 더 저렴한 건 맞지만 기차 여행이 더 안전하고 낭만적인 것 같아.
남 그래도 기차는 철로가 있는 곳에만 다닐 수 있으니까 기차 여행은 특정 경로에 제한되어 있잖아.
여 버스 여행이 더 빠르고 효율적이라는 뜻이지, 그렇지?
남 맞아. 기차는 단지 기차역에만 데려다주잖아. 하지만 버스는 너를 최종목적지에 바로 데려다 줄 수 있어.

03 | 정답 | ②

운동 경기의 개회식 행사가 관중과 선수들을 하나로 모으는 데 중요한 역할을 한다고 말하고 있으므로 여자가 하는 말의 요지로 가장 적절한 것은 ②이다.

- sportscaster 스포츠 방송 진행자
- opening ceremony 개회식, 입장식
- crucial 중대한
- unify 통합하다
- national anthem 국가
- vital 지극히 중요한

W Welcome, everyone! I'm Amanda, your favorite sportscaster. Have you ever wondered **why sports teams have opening ceremonies**? Opening ceremonies play a crucial role in unifying the crowd and the athletes. For example, **when the national anthem is played before a big soccer game**, everyone, including the crowd and the players, feels like one big team. Even though some argue that ceremonies are a waste of time, in reality, they serve a much deeper purpose. In essence, **these starting events are vital for bringing the crowd** and athletes together. I will be back next time with more exciting sports facts!

여 모두 환영합니다! 저는 여러분이 가장 좋아하는 스포츠 캐스터인 Amanda입니다. 스포츠 팀들이 왜 개회식을 하는지 궁금한 적이 있나요? 개회식은 관중과 선수들을 하나로 묶는 데 중요한 역할을 합니다. 예를 들어, 큰 축구 경기 전에 국가가 연주되면 관중과 선수들을 포함한 모든 사람들은 하나의 큰 팀처럼 느낍니다. 일부는 개회식이 시간 낭비라고 주장하지만, 실제로는 훨씬 더 깊은 목적에 기여합니다. 본질적으로, 이러한 시작 행사들은 관중과 선수들을 하나로 모으는데 매우 중요합니다. 다음 시간에는 더 신나는 스포츠 상식으로 돌아오겠습니다!

04 | 정답 | ⑤

줄무늬 수건이 가방 밑에 있다고 했으므로 일치하지 않는 것은 ⑤이다.

- pack 짐을 싸다
- bedside 침대 옆
- insect repellent 해충 퇴치제

M Carla, did you pack everything you need for your trip?
W I'm packing right now, Dad. Can you help me out a little bit?
M Sure. Your mom put a water bottle on your bed. You could get really thirsty **when you go mountain climbing**.
W Oh, that's right. I'll pack that last after I get everything

남 Carla, 네 여행에 필요한 모든 짐을 쌌니?
여 지금 싸고 있어요, 아빠. 저 좀 도와주실 수 있어요?
남 물론이지. 엄마가 침대 위에 물병을 놓아뒀단다. 등산을 가면 아주 목이 마를 수 있어.
여 아, 맞아요. 필요한 걸 다 챙기고 난 다음에 마지막으로 넣을게요. 다른 건 뭘 챙겨야 하죠?

- **first-aid kit** 구급상자
- **stripe** 줄무늬

I need. What else should I take?

M You might need sunglasses and a hat to protect your eyes. I heard it could be really sunny tomorrow.

W Really? **My sunglasses are on the bedside table** next to the bed. Can you pass me those, please?

M All right. *[Pause]* Here you are. You need to take insect repellent. Where do you keep the first-aid kit?

W It's **on top of the bookcase**.

M Okay, and don't forget to wear a watch. Do you remember where you put it?

W Yes, it's on my desk. I'll put it on tomorrow morning before I leave.

M So, do you have everything you need?

W Yes, I just need to put my towel in the bag. Oh, where did it go?

M You mean **the one with stripes**? It's right under the bag.

남 눈을 보호하려면 아마 선글라스와 모자가 필요할 거야. 내일 아주 화창할 거라고 들었어.

여 정말요? 제 선글라스는 침대 옆 탁자 위에 있어요. 그것 좀 건네주실래요?

남 그래. *[잠시 후]* 여기 있다. 해충 퇴치제도 가져가야 해. 구급상자는 어디에 두니?

여 책장 맨 위에 있어요.

남 좋아, 그리고 시계 차는 것도 잊지 마. 어디에 두었는지 기억나니?

여 네, 책상 위에 있어요. 내일 아침 떠나기 전에 찰게요.

남 그럼, 필요한 것들 다 챙긴 거니?

여 네, 제 수건만 가방에 넣으면 돼요. 아, 어디 갔지?

남 줄무늬 수건 말이니? 가방 바로 밑에 있어.

---

05 | 정답 | ①

남자가 자신의 노트북이 자주 고장 난다고 하자, 여자는 새것을 사라고 조언하지만 남자는 어떻게 좋은 컴퓨터를 고르는지 모른다고 한다. 여자는 그에 대해 자신이 함께 매장에 가서 도와주겠다고 말하고 있으므로 정답은 ①이다.

- **latest** 최신의
- **pretty** 꽤
- **processor** (컴퓨터) 프로세서, 처리장치
- **RAM** (컴퓨터) 램, 기억장치
- **confusing** 혼란스러운
- **clueless** 아무것도 모르는

M This laptop isn't working again. This is the second time this week.

W I think **you should buy one of the latest models** out on the market.

M I don't know. Actually, I'm not really sure **what to look for in a laptop**.

W It's pretty simple. You just need something with a fast processor, a lot of RAM, and a good display, just like a desktop computer.

M But I have no idea what those things are.

W Well, they may all sound confusing at first. How about if I give you more details this weekend?

M I already have other plans for this weekend. **Could you come with me to the store** after class today? I don't want to look clueless.

W Of course. **I'll help you pick out** a good one.

M That sounds good to me!

남 이 노트북이 또 작동을 안 하네. 이번이 이번 주에 두 번째야.

여 네가 시장에 나와 있는 최신모델 중 하나를 사는 게 좋을 것 같아.

남 모르겠어. 사실. 난 노트북에서 무얼 알아봐야 하는지 잘 몰라.

여 꽤 간단해. 보통 데스크톱 컴퓨터처럼 빠른 프로세서, 많은 RAM, 그리고 좋은 디스플레이를 가진 게 필요해.

남 하지만 난 그런 것들이 뭔지 전혀 몰라.

여 음, 처음에는 모든 게 혼란스럽게 들릴지도 몰라. 이번 주말에 더 자세히 알려줄까?

남 이번 주말은 이미 다른 계획이 있어. 오늘 방과 후에 매장에 같이 가줄 수 있어? 아무것도 모르는 것처럼 보이고 싶지 않아서 말이야.

여 물론이야. 내가 좋은 것 고르는 걸 도와줄게.

남 그거 좋은데!

---

06 | 정답 | ②

울 스웨터는 80달러에서 50% 할인된다고 하였다. 캐시미어 스웨터는 110달러이며 총금액은 150달러인데, 100달러 이상 구매 시 10% 할인 적용된다고 하였으므로 남자가 지불할 금액은 135달러로 정답은 ②이다.

- **price range** 가격대
- **originally** 원래
- **deal** 거래
- **cashmere** 캐시미어
- **steady seller** 꾸준히 판매되는 제품
- **stock** 재고
- **price tag** 가격표
- **gift-wrap** 선물용으로 포장하다

W Hello. How can I help you?

M Hi. It's my sister's birthday next week and I can't decide what to get her.

W Well, since winter is coming, how about getting her a winter coat?

M That sounds great, but **it is out of my price range**, I'm afraid.

W Then take a look at this wool sweater. It's on sale. It was originally $80, but it's 50% off now.

M That sounds like a good deal. Should I get two? Just one sweater doesn't seem like enough.

W **How about adding another sweater** in cashmere instead? Because they are softer and warmer, they are steady sellers.

M Okay. What colors do you have?

W They come in ivory, pink and black. Right now, black ones are really popular and **we don't have many left in stock**.

M Really? The price tag says they are $110. That's a bit expensive.

W We have a special sale going on until this weekend. So, if you spend more than $100, you can get 10% off the total.

여 안녕하세요. 어떻게 도와드릴까요?

남 안녕하세요. 다음 주에 누나 생일인데, 무엇을 사 줘야 할지 결정을 못 하겠어요.

여 겨울이 다가오니 겨울 코트 선물이 어떠세요?

남 좋긴 한데. 그건 제가 생각하고 있는 가격대에서 벗어나는 것 같아요.

여 그럼 이 울 스웨터를 보세요. 세일 중이거든요. 원래 80달러였는데, 지금 50% 할인해요.

남 그거 좋은 것 같네요. 제가 두 개를 사야 할까요? 한 개는 충분하지 않은 것 같아서요.

여 대신 캐시미어로 된 다른 스웨터를 추가하시는 건 어때요? 더 부드럽고 따뜻해서 꾸준히 판매되는 제품이에요.

남 좋아요. 무슨 색이 있죠?

여 아이보리, 분홍, 검은색으로 나와요. 지금은 검은색이 정말 인기가 있어서 재고가 많이 남아 있지 않아요.

남 정말요? 가격표에는 110달러라고 쓰여 있네요. 조금 비싸군요.

여 이번 주말까지 진행되는 특별세일이 있어요. 그래서, 100달러 이상을 구매하시면 총액에서 10% 할인을 받을 수 있어요.

M Cool. **I'll take this wool sweater** and this black cashmere sweater, too.
W Okay. Would you like them gift-wrapped?
M Absolutely, thanks.

남 좋네요. 이 울 스웨터와 이 검은색 캐시미어 스웨터도 주세요.
여 네. 선물용으로 포장해 드릴까요?
남 물론이죠, 고마워요.

---

07 | 정답 | ③

여자는 남자에게 라디오 쇼에서 자신의 사연이 뽑혀 영화표를 탔으니 함께 영화 보러 가자는 말을 하려고 전화했다. 따라서 정답은 ③이다.

* reach 연락하다
* request 신청; 신청하다
* air 방송하다
* awesome 멋진
* extra 여분의

M Hello, Naomi.
W Ian! Where were you last night? I tried to reach you several times, but your phone was off.
M Sorry about that. I have a big test today, so I turned it off. Anyway, why did you call?
W Do you remember my favorite radio show? Yesterday, **I sent in my story and song request**.
M Really? Did they pick yours?
W Yes, they aired my story and played the song I requested. They also **sent me two movie tickets**.
M Wow, that's awesome!
W Since I have an extra ticket, would you be interested in **going to the movies with me**?
M Of course. Which movie do you want to watch? Do you have anything in mind?
W Not really. Luckily, I can use the tickets anywhere and anytime I want.
M Perfect! **Why don't we watch the new action movie** that just came out?
W I like action movies, too. Let's go this Friday night.
M Cool! I can't wait.

남 안녕, Naomi.
여 Ian! 어젯밤에 어디 갔었어? 여러 번 연락했는데 전화기가 꺼져 있더라.
남 미안해. 오늘 큰 시험이 있어서 꺼놨어. 아무튼, 왜 전화했어?
여 내가 가장 좋아하는 라디오 쇼 기억나? 어제 사연과 신청곡을 보냈거든.
남 정말? 그들이 네 걸 뽑았어?
여 응. 내 사연을 방송해 주고 내가 신청한 곡을 틀어 줬어. 영화표 두 장도 보내줬어.
남 와, 멋지다!
여 내게 여분의 표가 있어서, 나랑 같이 영화 보러 갈 생각 있어?
남 물론이지. 어떤 영화 볼래? 보고 싶은 게 있어?
여 딱히 없어. 다행히도 영화표는 내가 원하는 아무 데서나 언제든지 사용할 수 있어.
남 완벽하다! 이제 막 개봉한 새로운 액션영화 보는 게 어때?
여 나도 액션영화 좋아해. 이번 주 금요일 밤에 가자.
남 좋아! 너무 기다려진다.

---

08 | 정답 | ⑤

이탈리아 레스토랑 Vera's Kitchen은 Park 거리에 있고 파스타 세 가지와 피자 두 가지가 메뉴이며, 주차장이 있고, 테이블 수가 10개 정도이다. 그러나 요리사에 대한 언급은 없으므로 정답은 ⑤이다.

* feel like v-ing ~하고 싶다
* eat out 외식하다
* serve (음식을) 제공하다
* as long as ~하는 한
* make a reservation 예약하다
* available 이용할 수 있는

W Honey, I don't feel like cooking today. Can we eat out for dinner tonight?
M That's an option. What kind of food do you want?
W Why don't we try something new? I heard that **there is a new Italian restaurant** on Park Avenue.
M Are you talking about Vera's Kitchen? Actually, I went there last week.
W Oh, really? How was the food?
M It was okay, but **they only serve three kinds of pasta** and two kinds of pizza.
W Well, that's fine with me as long as they are delicious.
M Then, let's go there before the traffic is too heavy.
W Is there a parking area?
M Yes, but **there are only about ten tables**, so we'd better hurry.
W Then why don't we call and make a reservation?
M That's a good idea. I'll call to see if there is a table available.

여 여보, 나 오늘 요리하고 싶지 않네요. 오늘 저녁은 외식할까요?
남 그것도 좋죠. 어떤 종류의 음식을 원해요?
여 새로운 거 먹어 보는 게 어때요? Park 거리에 새로운 이탈리아 레스토랑이 문을 열었다는 얘길 들었어요.
남 Vera's Kitchen에 대해 말하는 거예요? 사실, 나 지난주에 거기 갔었어요.
여 아, 정말요? 음식은 어땠어요?
남 괜찮았는데, 파스타는 세 가지 종류, 피자는 두 가지 종류밖에 없어요.
여 음식이 맛있기만 하면 그건 괜찮아요.
남 그럼 길이 너무 막히기 전에 그곳으로 가요.
여 주차장이 있나요?
남 있어요. 하지만 테이블이 10개 정도밖에 없어서 서둘러야 해요.
여 그럼 전화해서 예약을 하는 게 어때요?
남 좋은 생각이에요. 내가 전화해서 이용 가능한 테이블이 있는지 알아볼게요.

---

09 | 정답 | ②

학교 전시회 날은 9월 25일 금요일이며, 그림을 제출하는 마감은 21일이다. 미술을 전공하는 학생들은 전시 공간이 마련되며, 자원봉사 학생들은 교복을 입어야 한다. 그러나 전시회 참가 신청은 14일까지이므로 일치하지 않는 것은 ②이다.

* exhibition 전시회, 전시
  cf. exhibit 전시하다
* auditorium 강당
* miss out on ~을 놓치다

M Attention, please. Our school's Exhibition Day has been set for Friday, September 25th. I hope **every student can have their paintings exhibited** in the school auditorium. Those who are interested should apply to participate by Monday, September 14th. And **you can hand in your paintings by the following Monday**, September 21st. Every art student will be allowed to show their paintings in the exhibition. So don't miss out on this great opportunity. Last but not least, I'd like to remind you that all the volunteering student staff members **are supposed to wear school uniforms** during the exhibition. Thank you for your cooperation.

남 주목해 주세요. 교내 전시회 날이 9월 25일 금요일로 정해졌습니다. 저는 모든 학생들이 학교 강당에 자신의 그림을 전시할 수 있기를 바랍니다. 관심 있으신 분들은 9월 14일 월요일까지 참가 신청을 해야 합니다. 그리고 그 다음 주 월요일인 9월 21일까지 그림을 제출하면 됩니다. 미술을 전공하는 모든 학생들은 전시회에 그림을 전시하도록 허가될 것입니다. 그러니 이 좋은 기회를 놓치지 마세요. 마지막으로, 모든 자원봉사 학생 스태프들은 전시회 동안 교복을 입어야 한다는 것을 다시 공지합니다. 협조해 주셔서 감사합니다.

* last but not least 마지막이긴 하나
  중요한 것은
* remind 상기시키다
* be supposed to-v ~하기로 되어 있다

10 | 정답 | ②

결혼 날짜인 5월 6일에 예약이 가능해
야 하며, 최소 하객 수는 300명 이하이
고 일 인당 식비는 50달러 미만이어야
한다. 또한 신혼여행 항공편이 오후 8시
에 출발하므로 결혼식은 12시에 진행되
어야 한다고 했다. 따라서 두 사람이 선
택할 웨딩홀로 가장 적절한 것은 ②이다.

* compare 비교하다
* cross A out A를 선을 그어 지우다
* minimum 최소한의, 최저의
* charge 청구하다
* budget 예산
* flight 항공편
* honeymoon 신혼여행

W Since our wedding date is set to May 6th, we need to decide on the wedding hall.
M We visited five places in Richmond City, and I made a list to compare them.
W This place was at the top of my list, but it's **not available on our wedding date**.
M Oh, right. I'll cross that one out. Most wedding halls ask for the minimum number of guests. How many are you thinking?
W Well, I was thinking about 150 from my side. What about you?
M Me, too. **Then we can't choose this one since it's 350**.
W How about the price?
M They charge us for the food only. Let's set a price on food per person.
W To me, $55 seems too much for one person. **How about keeping the budget under $50**?
M Sure. Now, we only have two options left.
W Oh, our flight for the honeymoon leaves at 8 p.m. So we should **have the wedding at noon**.
M Okay. I'll call this wedding hall to make a reservation.

여 우리 결혼식이 5월 6일로 정해졌으니 웨딩홀을 정해
   야 해요.
남 우리는 Richmond시에 있는 다섯 군데를 다녀왔는데,
   비교해보기 위해 제가 목록을 만들었어요.
여 이 장소가 제 관심 1순위였는데 여긴 우리 결혼 날짜에
   이용할 수 없어요.
남 아, 맞네요. 그걸 지울게요. 대부분의 웨딩홀이 최소 하
   객 수를 물어보더라고요. 몇 명 생각하고 있어요?
여 음, 제 쪽에서는 150명 정도 생각하고 있었어요. 당신
   은요?
남 저도요. 그러면 여긴 350명이니 고를 수 없겠네요.
여 가격은요?
남 웨딩홀은 저희한테 음식 비용만 청구해요. 인당 식비를
   정해봐요.
여 저한텐 일 인당 55달러는 너무 과한 것 같아요. 50달
   러 미만으로 예산을 유지하는 게 어때요?
남 물론이죠. 이제 두 가지 선택 사항만 남았어요.
여 아, 우리 신혼여행 비행기가 오후 8시에 출발하잖아요.
   그럼 우리 결혼식은 정오에 하는 게 좋겠네요.
남 알겠어요. 제가 이 웨딩홀에 전화해서 예약할게요.

11 | 정답 | ①

완성한 보고서에 있을지도 모르는 실수
를 다시 한번 점검했는지 물어보는 여자
의 말에 대한 남자의 응답으로 ① '아니.
빨리 한 번만 훑어봤어.'가 가장 적절
하다.

* work on 작성하다, 작업하다
* hand in 제출하다, 내다
* double-check 다시 확인하다

W Did you finish the history report you've been working on?
M Yes, **I completed it just in time**. I handed it in this morning.
W Hmm... Did you **double-check for any errors** in your report?
M No. I only gave it a quick look.

여 네가 작성하던 역사학 보고서 끝냈니?
남 응. 시간에 딱 맞게 끝냈어. 오늘 아침에 제출했어.
여 음... 보고서에서 실수를 다시 확인했니?
남 아니. 빨리 한 번만 훑어봤어.

② 미안하지만, 나는 실수를 3개 더 찾았어.
③ 응. 난 제시간에 끝냈어야 했어.
④ 물론이지. 난 앞으로 어떤 실수도 하지 않을 거야.
⑤ 아니. 난 오늘 아침까지 내야 하는 줄 몰랐어.

12 | 정답 | ⑤

학교 입학 허가 여부를 확인하기 위해
입학처에 전화해 보라는 남자의 말에
대한 여자의 응답으로 가장 적절한 것
은 ⑤ '이번 주에 합격 발표를 한다고
해서 기다리는 중이야.'이다.

* apply to ~에 지원하다
* admission 입학
  [선택지]
* application form 지원서
* acceptance 승인; 수락
* announcement 발표

M Did you get accepted into the school you applied to?
W I don't know. **I haven't heard anything** yet.
M It's been more than a month. **Why don't you call the admissions office** to find out?
W The acceptance announcement comes out this week, so I'm waiting.

남 네가 지원한 학교에 입학 허가받았니?
여 모르겠어. 아직 아무런 소식도 못 들었어.
남 한 달도 더 되었잖아. 입학처에 전화해서 알아보지 그
   래?
여 이번 주에 합격 발표를 한다고 해서 기다리는 중이야.

① 나는 그 학교에는 지원서를 보내지 않았어.
② 나는 다른 학교에 어떻게 지원하는지 몰라.
③ 나는 중요한 전화를 받지 못한 것 같아.
④ 아니, 나는 그들이 지원을 하는지 안 하는지 별로 신경
   쓰지 않아.

13 | 정답 | ①

자선단체에 기부할 오래된 옷을 정리하
는 상황이다. 작아진 청바지를 두고 남
자가 살이 빠져도 입지 않을 것이라고
말하는 여자의 말에 가장 적절한 응답
은 ① '알겠어요. 그럼 자선단체에 기부
해요.'이다.

M What are you doing, honey?
W I'm sorting out our clothes. We have too many of them that **we don't wear anymore**.
M I know. I'm often surprised to find old clothes that I didn't even know I had.
W Exactly. I think we just buy more and more clothes, just because they are new.
M That's because you don't know what you already have.

남 뭐 하고 있어요, 여보?
여 옷을 분류하고 있어요. 우리는 더 이상 입지 않는 옷이
   너무 많아요.
남 맞아요. 나는 내가 가지고 있었는지도 몰랐던 오래된
   옷을 발견하고 자주 놀라요.
여 그러니까요. 우리는 그저 새것이라는 이유로 계속 옷
   을 사들이고 있어요.
남 그건 무엇을 이미 가지고 있는지 몰라서 그렇죠. 그래
   서 그 오래된 옷으로 무얼 하려고요?

- sort out 분류하다
- donate 기부하다
- charity 자선단체
- fit 맞다
- put on weight 살이 찌다
- give away 기부하다
- lose weight 살이 빠지다

[선택지]
- secondhand 중고의

So, what are you going to do with the old clothes?

W I'm going to **donate them to a charity**. Look, are these yours?

M Oh, those are my old jeans. I forgot I had them. I don't think **they will fit me anymore** since I have put on some weight.

W I'll just give them away, then.

M Don't! I think I might need them when I lose weight.

W Honey, **you are not going to wear them** even after you lose weight.

M All right. Let's donate them to a charity, then.

여 자선단체에 기부하려고요. 이것 봐요, 이거 당신 거예요?

남 아, 그거 내 오래된 청바지예요. 내가 가지고 있었는지도 잊어버렸어요. 내가 살이 좀 쪄서 더 이상 맞지 않을 거예요.

여 그럼 그냥 기부할게요.

남 안 돼요! 살이 빠지면 필요할지도 몰라요.

여 여보, 당신이 살이 빠져도 그걸 입지는 않을 거예요.

남 알겠어요. 그럼 자선단체에 기부해요.

② 걱정 마세요. 난 요즘에는 쇼핑하는 것을 좋아하지 않아요.

③ 알겠어요. 다음 주에 운동 시작하겠다고 약속할게요.

④ 잠깐만요. 내가 기부할 옷을 좀 가져올게요.

⑤ 맞아요. 그들은 더 이상 중고 의류는 받지 않아요.

---

14 | 정답 | ①

집에서 생일 파티를 하자는 여자의 말에 남자가 아기를 데리고서 준비하기에는 어려울 것 같다며 뷔페 음식점을 제안한다. 이미 원하는 날짜에 예약이 가능한 것을 확인했다는 남자의 말에 대한 여자의 응답으로 ① '좋아요. 그럼 가서 먼저 한 번 봐요.'가 적절하다.

- prepare 준비하다
- on one's own 혼자 힘으로
- huge 거대한, 큰
- special offer 특가품, 특가 판매
- book 예약하다

[선택지]
- package 일괄 상품, 패키지 상품
- call for ~을 요청하다
- catering service 출장 요리 서비스

M Honey, what are we going to do for our daughter's first birthday?

W Well, I was thinking about having a party at home.

M At home? Do you want us to prepare everything?

W That's right. Don't you want to make it special, too?

M I do. But I don't know how having the party at home can make it special.

W You're right. There **might be a lot of work to do**.

M Exactly. It'll be hard to prepare on our own with a baby, too.

W I see your point. Then **are you suggesting we do it elsewhere**?

M I found a buffet restaurant that has great reviews.

W Really? What did they say?

M **There is a variety of great food**, and the servers are very nice. Oh, the parking lot is huge, too.

W A large parking lot is really important since most of our guests will drive there.

M The restaurant has special offers that **include a photographer and decorations**, too.

W Okay. I guess we have to call and check if we can still make a reservation.

M I already did. It's not fully booked yet on the date we want.

W Great. Then let's go and have a look at it first.

남 여보, 우리 딸 첫 번째 생일에 뭘 할까요?

여 음, 나는 집에서 파티를 할 생각을 하고 있었어요.

남 집에서요? 모든 것을 우리가 준비하는 건가요?

여 그래요. 당신도 아이 생일을 특별하게 만들고 싶지 않나요?

남 그러고 싶죠. 그렇지만 집에서 파티를 하는 게 생일을 어떻게 특별하게 만드는 건지 모르겠어요.

여 당신 말이 맞아요. 할 일이 아주 많겠죠.

남 맞아요. 아기를 데리고 우리끼리 준비하기도 어려울 거예요.

여 무슨 말인지 알겠어요. 그러면 다른 데서 하는 건가요?

남 평가가 아주 좋은 뷔페 음식점을 찾았어요.

여 정말요? 뭐라고 했는데요?

남 맛있는 음식 종류가 다양하고 직원들이 아주 친절하다고요. 아, 주차장도 아주 넓다고 해요.

여 대부분의 손님이 운전해서 올 테니 주차장이 넓은 것이 아주 중요해요.

남 이 식당에는 사진사와 장식을 포함한 특별한 상품들이 준비되었다고 하네요.

여 알겠어요. 그럼 전화해서 아직 예약할 수 있는지 확인해야겠네요.

남 내가 이미 했어요. 우리가 원하는 날짜에 아직 예약이 꽉 차지 않았는데요.

여 좋아요. 그럼 가서 먼저 한 번 봐요.

② 알겠어요. 첫 번째 생일은 부모에게 아주 특별한 날이지요.

③ 걱정 마세요. 내가 이미 그날로 예약을 했어요.

④ 맞아요. 온라인으로 이용할 수 있는 파티 패키지 상품이 많아요.

⑤ 절대 안 돼요. 나는 그래도 뷔페 음식 출장 요리 서비스를 요청할 거예요.

---

15 | 정답 | ④

Harry는 다음 주에 중요한 시험을 봐야 하는데 친구인 Kelly가 그가 좋아하는 가수의 콘서트 티켓이 있다고 말하며 토요일에 같이 가자고 제안한다. 그는 공부해야 하기 때문에 안 된다고 말해야 하므로 ④ '정말 가고 싶은데, 중요한 시험이 있어서 공부해야 해.'가 가장 적절하다.

- major in ~을 전공하다
- literature 문학
- semester 학기
- fail (학과·시험에) 떨어지다, 낙제하다
- pass (시험에) 합격통과하다

W Harry is majoring in English literature. Last semester he failed one of his courses and had to take it again this semester. Since this is his second try, **he really needs to pass an important test** next week so that he can at least pass the course. Today, he is having lunch with Kelly, one of his classmates. While having lunch, **she suggests going to a concert this Saturday**, saying that she has two free tickets. He really wants to go since his favorite singer is performing. However, **he is worried that he will fail the test** if he doesn't study hard for it this weekend. So, he wants to tell Kelly that he can't make it. In this situation, what would Harry most likely say to Kelly?

Harry I'd love to, but I have to study for the big test.

여 Harry는 영문학을 전공하고 있다. 그는 지난 학기에 그의 수강 강의 중 하나를 통과하지 못해서 이번 학기에 다시 들어야 했다. 이번이 두 번째이기 때문에, 그는 적어도 이번 강의를 통과할 수 있도록 다음 주에 있는 중요한 시험을 통과해야 한다. 오늘 그는 동기 중 하나인 Kelly와 점심을 먹고 있다. 점심을 먹는 중에, 그녀는 자신에게 무료 티켓 두 장이 있다고 말하며 이번 토요일에 콘서트에 같이 가자고 제안한다. 그는 자신이 가장 좋아하는 가수가 공연하기 때문에 정말 가고 싶다. 하지만 이번 주말에 열심히 공부하지 않으면 그 시험에 통과하지 못할 것 같아서 걱정된다. 그래서 그는 Kelly에게 자신이 갈 수 없다고 말하고 싶다. 이러한 상황에서 Harry가 Kelly에게 할 말로 가장 적절한 것은 무엇인가?

Harry 정말 가고 싶은데, 중요한 시험이 있어서 공부해야 해.

① 너는 그 시험을 통과하려면 더 열심히 공부했었어야지.
② 나도 그 콘서트 티켓이 있어.
③ 내가 너라면, 그 제안을 받아들일 텐데.
⑤ 물론, 난 그 가수의 콘서트를 항상 보고 싶었어.

---

* perform 공연하다
* make it (모임 등에) 가다, 참석하다

---

16 | 정답 | ④

남자는 여러 아시아 국가들의 전통 의상과 그 특징에 대해 설명하고 있으므로 정답은 ④ '아시아 국가들의 전통 의상'이다.

17 | 정답 | ②

아시아의 인도, 스리랑카, 중국, 일본, 대한민국의 전통 의상이 언급되었지만, '베트남'에 대한 언급은 없었으므로 정답은 ②이다.

* previously 전에
* garment 의상
* strip 가느다란 조각
* unstitched 바느질하지 않은
* cloth 천, 옷감
* range from A to B (범위가) A에서 B까지 이르다
* characteristic 독특한, 특징적인
* ethnic group 민족 집단, 인종 집단
* feature ~을 특징으로 하다
* loose 헐렁한
* sleeve 소매
* jade 옥(玉)
* T-shaped T자형의
* robe 길고 헐거운 겉옷
* festive 축하하는, 축제의
* occasion 때, 경우; 행사
* facilitate 가능하게 하다
* consist of ~로 구성되다
* wrap-around (몸에) 두르게 되어 있는
* trousers 바지

M Hello, students. Previously, we discussed traditional garments in some European countries. Today, we'll talk about **traditional clothing in several Asian countries**. First, a sari is the traditional female garment in India and Sri Lanka. It is a very long strip of unstitched cloth, **ranging from 4 to 9 meters in length**. Second, hanfu is the characteristic clothing for the Han ethnic group in China. It features a loose upper garment with sleeves and a skirt-like lower garment. The belt was often decorated with jade. Third, a kimono is a traditional Japanese garment and **it is thought to have been directly influenced** by the hanfu. It is a T-shaped robe, which has very long sleeves. Finally, hanbok is the traditional clothing in South Korea. People used to wear hanbok daily up until just 100 years ago, **but now it is only worn on festive occasions**. It was originally designed to facilitate ease of movement. Traditional women's hanbok consists of a short blouse shirt, and a wrap-around skirt. Men's hanbok consists of a shirt and loose-fitting trousers.

남 안녕하세요, 여러분. 전에 우리는 일부 유럽 국가의 전통 의상에 대해 논의했습니다. 오늘은 여러 아시아 국가들의 전통 의상에 대해 말해 볼게요. 먼저, 사리는 인도와 스리랑카의 전통 여자 의상입니다. 바느질을 하지 않은 아주 긴 천 조각으로 길이가 4에서 9미터 정도입니다. 두 번째로 한푸는 중국의 한족을 위한 독특한 복장입니다. 그것은 소매가 있는 헐렁한 상의와 치마 같은 하의가 특징입니다. 벨트는 보통 옥으로 장식되었죠. 세 번째로 기모노는 일본의 전통 의상으로 한푸에 의해 직접적으로 영향을 받았다고 생각됩니다. T자형의 긴 의상으로, 아주 긴 소매가 있습니다. 마지막으로 한복은 대한민국의 전통 의상입니다. 사람들은 100년 전까지만 해도 한복을 일상적으로 입었었지만 지금은 축하하는 때에만 입습니다. 그것은 원래 움직임의 수월함을 가능하게 하기 위해 디자인되었어요. 여자 전통 한복은 짧은 블라우스 셔츠와 두르게 되어 있는 치마로 구성됩니다. 남자의 한복은 셔츠와 헐렁한 바지로 구성되지요.

16 ① 전통 의상이 어떻게 사라졌는가
② 전통 의상이 어떻게 변했는가
③ 유럽과 아시아의 차이
④ 아시아 국가들의 전통 의상
⑤ 여러 나라들의 의상의 유사점

17 ① 인도 ② 베트남 ③ 중국
④ 일본 ⑤ 대한민국

04회 실전 듣기 모의고사

01 ③ 02 ③ 03 ② 04 ⑤ 05 ⑤ 06 ④ 07 ⑤ 08 ① 09 ④ 10 ④
11 ⑤ 12 ③ 13 ① 14 ③ 15 ④ 16 ⑤ 17 ④

01 | 정답 | ③

남자는 평소보다 먼 곳으로 회의 장소가 정해진 점을 감안하여 회원들을 위해 셔틀버스를 마련했다고 말하며 첨부된 정류장과 시간표를 참고해 달라고 말하고 있으므로 정답은 ③이다.

* committee 위원회
* secretary 총무, 서기관; 비서
* notification 알림, 안내
* regarding ~에 관하여
* via ~을 통하여
* accommodate 수용하다
* venue (회담 등의) 장소

M Hello, members of the Education Committee. This is the secretary, Bob Wyatt. I have some important notifications regarding our next meeting. I recently sent you **where and when the meeting is going to be held** via e-mail. While trying to look for a good meeting room that can accommodate all our members, I had no choice but to choose a venue that is far from our usual location. I thought this might cause inconvenience to our members, and looked for ways to deal with the problem. So, **I arranged a shuttle bus** that will take you from the train station to the new venue. Please take the shuttle bus from the train station. I will send you **information about the bus stop and the bus schedule**. I hope to see everyone at the meeting. Thank you.

남 안녕하십니까, 교육 위원회 회원 여러분. 저는 총무 Bob Wyatt입니다. 다음 회의에 관해 중요한 안내 사항이 있습니다. 최근에 제가 이메일로 회의가 언제 어디서 열릴지를 보내드렸습니다. 모든 회원을 수용할 적당한 회의실을 찾아보다가 어쩔 수 없이 우리의 평소 위치에서 멀리 떨어진 곳을 선정해야 했습니다. 이것이 저희 회원들에게 불편을 끼칠 수 있을 것 같다고 생각해서 문제를 해결할 만한 방법을 찾아보았습니다. 그래서 기차역에서 새 회의 장소까지 여러분을 모시고 올 셔틀버스를 마련했습니다. 부디 기차역에서 셔틀버스를 타시기 바랍니다. 버스 정류장과 버스 시간표에 대한 정보를 보내드리겠습니다. 회의에서 모두 뵙길 바랍니다. 감사합니다.

02 | 정답 | ③

여자는 Jason에게 문자 메시지로 사과했다는 남자의 말에 문자 메시지보다는 직접 만나서 대화할 것을 권하고 있으므로 여자의 의견으로 가장 적절한 것은 ③이다.

* stare 쳐다보다, 응시하다
* call back 다시 전화해 주다
* yell 소리 지르다
* apologize 사과하다
* in person 직접
* sincere 진심어린

W John, you've been staring at your phone for an hour. Are you waiting for an important call?
M Well, I'm waiting for Jason to call me back. But I don't know if he is ever going to call me.
W What do you mean? **Did you guys have a fight**?
M I was upset about the history project, but he kept asking me how I did. So I yelled at him in front of other people.
W Did you apologize to him?
M I sent him a text message, but he hasn't replied or called.
W I think **you should talk to him in person**.
M I don't know how to face him. I don't think he ever wants to talk to me again.
W You should explain how you felt and how much you regret it. He might think a text message is **not sincere enough**.
M Do you really think so?
W Yes, talking is a better way to communicate your feelings.
M You're right. I should **go up to him and apologize in person**.

여 John, 너 한 시간 동안 전화기만 쳐다보고 있어. 중요한 전화를 기다리니?
남 음, Jason이 다시 전화해 주길 기다리고 있어. 근데 걔가 나한테 전화할지 모르겠다.
여 무슨 말이야? 둘이 싸웠어?
남 역사 과제 때문에 화가 좀 나 있었는데 그가 계속 과제를 어떻게 했는지 묻는 거야. 그래서 다른 사람들 앞에서 그에게 소리를 질렀어.
여 걔한테 사과했어?
남 문자 메시지를 보냈는데 답장도 없고 전화하지도 않았어.
여 네가 걔랑 직접 만나서 얘기해야 할 것 같아.
남 어떻게 대해야 할지 모르겠어. 나와 다시는 말하고 싶지 않은 것 같아.
여 네가 어떤 감정이 들었고 얼마나 후회하고 있는지 설명해야 해. 어쩌면 그는 문자 메시지로는 진심이 아니라고 생각할지도 몰라.
남 정말 그렇게 생각해?
여 응, 대화를 나누는 게 너의 감정을 전달하는 더 좋은 방법이야.
남 네 말이 맞아. 내가 그에게 가서 직접 사과해야겠어.

03 | 정답 | ②

큰 프로젝트에 압도감을 느낄 때는 작은 일로 나누어서 하라고 해결책을 제시하고 있으므로 남자가 하는 말의 요지로 가장 적절한 것은 ②이다.

* sensation 마음, 기분
* overwhelm 압도하다
* break down 나누다, 나누어지다
* proceed 계속하여 행하다
* one by one 하나씩, 차례차례
* trick 비결, 요령
* workload 작업부하

M Hi everyone, I'm Jeff Colvin, and it's a pleasure to be with you on *Morning Insight*. **Have you ever experienced the sensation** of being overwhelmed with a lot of tasks? Well, fear not! I have a solution for you — **break down a large project into smaller tasks**. For example, if cleaning your entire backyard feels like too much to handle, try focusing on one section at a time. This way, you can make progress and achieve great results. Any big thing can be solved **if you proceed slowly from the little things**. In our session today, I'll be sharing more simple tips and tricks to help you handle challenging workloads.

남 여러분, 안녕하세요. 저는 Jeff Colvin이고 Morning Insight에서 여러분과 함께 하게 되어 기쁩니다. 많은 업무로 압도당하는 느낌을 경험해 본 적이 있나요? 자, 걱정하지 마세요! 제게 여러분을 위한 해결책이 있는데, 큰 프로젝트를 작은 작업으로 나누세요. 예를 들어, 뒷마당 전체를 청소하는 것이 너무 감당하기 어려울 것 같이 느껴진다면 한 번에 한 구역에 집중해 보세요. 이런 식으로 여러분은 진전을 이루고 훌륭한 결과를 달성할 수 있습니다. 어떤 큰일도 작은 일부터 천천히 진행하다 보면 해결될 수 있습니다. 오늘 우리 활동에서는 여러분이 힘이 드는 작업을 처리하는 데 도움이 되는 간단한 비결과 요령을 더 공유해드리겠습니다.

04 | 정답 | ⑤

남자는 이러한 스타일의 거실에는 사각 테이블보다 원형 테이블이 더 잘 어울리기 때문에 원형을 골랐다고 말하고 있으므로 대화 내용과 일치하지 않는 부분은 ⑤이다.

* modern 모던한, 현대적인
* in style 유행인
* cozy 아늑한

W Hello, Mr. Johnson.

M Hi, Ms. Powell. I brought my design plan for your living room. Here it is.

W Wow! It looks great. It's just how I imagined it. I like that **you put a tall plant by the window**.

M It's always nice to have some green in the living room. And it should be by the window so it gets a lot of sunlight.

W And I really like **the tall lamp by the wall**. It looks very modern and stylish.

M You said you'd like your living room to look neat and modern, and this tall lamp is in style lately.

W It suits the living room very well. And **the sofa next to the lamp looks very cozy**. I can read books on the sofa under the lamp.

M That was my idea. How do you like the painting on the wall?

W Yes, you mean the one above the sofa? I always wanted to hang a painting on that wall.

M I'm glad you like it. And please have a look at the table in front of the sofa.

W Oh, **it's a round wooden table**. I like it.

M Yes. In this style of living room, **a round table is more suitable than a square one**, so I chose the round one.

W That looks perfect. Thank you.

여 안녕하세요, Johnson 씨.

남 안녕하세요, Powell 씨. 고객님의 거실에 대한 디자인 계획안을 가져왔습니다. 여기 있습니다.

여 우와! 멋져 보이네요. 제가 상상했던 그대로입니다. 창문 옆에 키 큰 식물을 배치한 것이 마음에 드네요.

남 거실에 초록색이 있으면 항상 좋죠. 그리고 꼭 창문 옆에 두어서 햇빛을 많이 받을 수 있도록 해주세요.

여 그리고 벽 옆에 긴 조명이 정말 마음에 드네요. 아주 모던하고 세련되었어요.

남 거실이 깔끔하고 모던하게 보였으면 좋겠다고 하셨어요. 이 긴 조명이 최근에 유행이거든요.

여 거실에 참 잘 어울리네요. 그리고 조명 옆의 소파도 아주 아늑해 보여요. 조명 아래 소파에 앉아서 책을 읽을 수 있어요.

남 그게 제 생각이었습니다. 벽에 걸린 그림은 마음에 드시나요?

여 네, 소파 위에 있는 것 말씀이시죠? 저는 항상 저 벽에 그림을 걸어두고 싶었어요.

남 마음에 드신다니 다행입니다. 그리고 소파 앞 테이블을 좀 봐 주세요.

여 아, 둥근 원목 테이블이네요. 좋습니다.

남 네. 이런 스타일의 거실에는 각진 것보다 둥근 테이블이 더 잘 어울려서 둥근 테이블로 선택했습니다.

여 완벽하네요. 감사합니다.

05 | 정답 | ⑤

여자가 화장실에 다녀오는 길에 무언가 사다 줄까 묻자 남자가 간식거리를 사다 달라고 했으므로 정답은 ⑤이다.

* reserve 예약하다, 예매하다
* jersey (운동 경기용) (저지) 셔츠

W Wow, look how big the crowd is!

M It's one of the most popular games of the year.

W Our seats are right here. We can see the soccer field very well from here.

M **That's why I reserved these seats**. I am so excited! It's been a long time since I watched a soccer game at a stadium.

W Yes. I'm looking forward to today's game, too. My favorite player is going to be on the field.

M That's great. Oh, **I think I left my phone in the car**. Could you take photos of the game for me?

W I'm not good at taking pictures, so you can just use my cell phone.

M Thanks. Look what I brought! These are jerseys for the team we are cheering for.

W Wow! They look really nice. Can I wear one of them?

M Sure. I brought two so we could wear the same jerseys. **We'll look so cool cheering in these jerseys**.

W You can say that again. By the way, I think I should use the bathroom before the game starts. Would you like me to get anything for you on my way back?

M Hmm... Could you **get some snacks we can enjoy** while we watch the game?

W Sure. What kind of snack would you like?

M Anything is fine with me. Thanks!

여 우와, 관중이 얼마나 많은지 봐봐!

남 올해 가장 인기 있는 경기 중 하나잖아.

여 우리 자리는 바로 여기야. 여기서 축구장이 아주 잘 보여.

남 그래서 이 좌석을 예매했어. 너무 흥분돼! 경기장에 와서 축구 경기를 본 지 정말 오래됐어.

여 그래, 나도 오늘 경기 기대돼. 내가 가장 좋아하는 선수가 출전하거든.

남 잘됐다. 아, 내가 차에 휴대폰을 놓고 온 것 같아. 나 대신 경기 사진 좀 찍어줄 수 있어?

여 나는 사진을 잘 못 찍어서 내 휴대폰을 써도 돼.

남 고마워. 내가 뭘 갖고 왔는지 봐! 우리가 응원하는 축구팀 저지 셔츠야.

여 우와! 정말 멋져 보인다. 내가 하나 입어도 돼?

남 물론이지. 같은 저지 셔츠를 입었으면 해서 두 벌을 가져 왔어. 이 저지 셔츠를 입고 응원하면 우리 정말 멋져 보일 거야.

여 맞아. 근데 경기 시작 전에 화장실에 다녀와야 할 것 같아. 돌아오는 길에 뭘 좀 사다 줄까?

남 음… 우리가 경기를 보면서 먹을 만한 간식 좀 사다 줄래?

여 물론이지. 어떤 간식을 먹고 싶어?

남 난 아무거나 좋아. 고마워!

06 | 정답 | ④

남자는 초콜릿 칩 쿠키로 변경된 크리스마스 상품 2개를 구매 후 선물 포장하고자 한다. 초콜릿 칩 쿠키로 변경할 경우 원래 가격에 2달러 50센트의 추가

W Hello, sir. Can I help you?

M I would like to buy some cookies.

W We have this special Christmas edition for $30. The package of 20 cookies is cheaper than getting 20 individual cookies.

여 안녕하세요, 손님. 무엇을 도와드릴까요?

남 쿠키를 좀 사고 싶습니다.

여 여기 크리스마스 특별 상품이 30달러입니다. 20개의 쿠키 묶음 상품은 개별 쿠키 20개를 사는 것보다 저렴합니다.

비용이 들며 선물 포장도 하나당 1달러가 추가되므로 총금액은 67달러($30 × 2 + $2.50 × 2 + $1 × 2)로 정답은 ④이다.

* package 묶음 상품
* individual 개별적인, 각각의
* raisin 건포도
* ginger 생강
* cinnamon 계피
* gift-wrap 선물용으로 포장하다

M That sounds like a good deal. **What kind of cookies are included in the package**?
W There are four types, raisin, peanut butter, ginger, and cinnamon.
M Can I change the ginger cookies to chocolate chip cookies?
W Of course, but **you will have to pay the difference**. Is that all right?
M That's fine. **How much is the difference**?
W The chocolate chip cookies are ¢50 more expensive than the ginger cookies. Since there are five ginger cookies in the package, it will cost $2.50 more to change all of them.
M That's fine. I'll take two Christmas packages, and please change all the ginger cookies to chocolate chip cookies.
W Do you want both to be wrapped? **Gift-wrapping is $1 for each package**.
M Yes, please. Here is my credit card.

남 괜찮은 것 같네요. 그 묶음 상품에 어떤 종류의 쿠키가 포함되어 있나요?
여 네 가지 종류가 있는데, 건포도, 땅콩버터, 생강, 그리고 계피 쿠키입니다.
남 생강 쿠키를 초콜릿 칩 쿠키로 바꿀 수 있나요?
여 물론 교체할 수 있지만 차액을 지불하셔야 합니다. 그래도 괜찮으십니까?
남 괜찮습니다. 차액이 얼마입니까?
여 초콜릿 칩 쿠키가 생강 쿠키보다 50센트 더 비쌉니다. 묶음 상품에는 다섯 개의 생강 쿠키가 있으니 그것들 모두를 바꾸려면 2달러 50센트가 추가로 듭니다.
남 괜찮습니다. 크리스마스 묶음 상품 두 개 주시고, 생강 쿠키는 모두 초콜릿 칩 쿠키로 바꿔주세요.
여 두 개 모두 선물 포장해 드릴까요? 선물 포장은 하나에 1달러입니다.
남 네, 부탁드립니다. 여기 제 신용카드입니다.

---

07 | 정답 | ⑤

여자는 세부로 신혼여행에 가 있어서 동창회에 가지 못 했다고 말하고 있으므로 정답은 ⑤이다.

* accountant 회계사
* be[keep] in touch 연락하며 지내다
* school reunion 동창회
* slow season 비수기
* honeymoon 신혼여행

M Barbara? Is that you?
W Oh, hi, Gilbert. It's been a long time. How have you been?
M Great! I heard you are working as an accountant. How is that working out for you?
W The first two years were tough, but it's all right now. **I thought you were living in France**.
M I was there for about five years and came back last year.
W That's nice. I didn't expect to see you at this wedding.
M Well, Mary and I have been **in touch since the last school reunion**. Now that I think about it, you weren't there, were you?
W No, I missed it. I went to **every single one since graduation**, except the last one.
M Were you busy at work?
W Not really. It was slow season at the time of the reunion.
M How come you had to miss it, then?
W **I was in Cebu on my honeymoon**.
M Wow, I didn't know you got married. It's a little late, but congratulations!

남 Barbara? Barbara 맞니?
여 아, 안녕, Gilbert. 정말 오랜만이다. 어떻게 지냈니?
남 잘 지냈어! 네가 회계사로 일하고 있다고 들었어. 일은 어떻게 돼가고 있니?
여 처음 2년은 힘들었지만 지금은 괜찮아. 난 네가 프랑스에서 살고 있는 줄 알았는데.
남 그곳에 5년 정도 있다가 작년에 돌아왔어.
여 잘됐다. 이 결혼식에서 널 보게 될 줄 몰랐어.
남 그러니까 Mary와 나는 지난번 학교 동창회 이후로 연락을 이어오고 있어. 이제 생각해 보니 그때 넌 없었지, 그렇지?
여 응. 난 못 갔어. 졸업 후에 지난번만 빼고 매번 나갔었는데.
남 일 때문에 바빴어?
여 아니. 동창회 때는 바쁘지 않은 시기였어.
남 그러면 왜 빠진 거야?
여 세부로 신혼여행에 갔었어.
남 와, 네가 결혼했는지 몰랐어. 좀 늦었지만, 축하해!

---

08 | 정답 | ①

공연 시간은 매일 저녁 7시이며 주연 배우는 Don Kennedy이다. 15분의 쉬는 시간이 있으며 공연은 3주 동안 더 진행된다. 입장료에 대한 언급은 없으므로 정답은 ①이다.

* intermission 쉬는 시간
* extend 연장하다
* popularity 인기

[Telephone rings.]
M Hello, Grey's Theater. How may I help you?
W Hello, I'd like to ask you about the musical you are playing.
M Oh, "Under the Sky," right?
W Yes. **When does the musical start**?
M The musical starts at 7 p.m. every evening.
W I see. **Who is the actor playing the main character**? Is it Don Kennedy?
M Yes. He is one of the most popular musical actors.
W I see. And is there an intermission?
M There will be **an intermission of 15 minutes**.
W Okay. One last thing. **How long will it be playing**?
M It's playing for three more weeks. We extended it due to its rising popularity.
W Wow, that's great. I will recommend the musical to people I know if I like it.
M That will be great. I hope to see you at the musical.

[전화벨이 울린다.]
남 여보세요, Grey's 극장입니다. 무엇을 도와드릴까요?
여 안녕하세요. 현재 공연 중인 뮤지컬에 대해 문의 좀 드리고 싶습니다.
남 아, 'Under the Sky' 말씀이세요?
여 네. 뮤지컬이 몇 시에 시작하나요?
남 뮤지컬은 매일 저녁 7시에 시작합니다.
여 그렇군요. 주인공을 연기하는 배우가 누구인가요? Don Kennedy인가요?
남 네. 그는 가장 인기 있는 뮤지컬 배우 중 한 명이죠.
여 그렇군요. 그리고 쉬는 시간이 있나요?
남 15분의 쉬는 시간이 있습니다.
여 알겠습니다. 마지막으로 한 가지만요. 얼마나 더 공연할 예정인가요?
남 3주간 더 공연합니다. 인기가 높아져서 저희가 연장했습니다.
여 와, 잘됐네요. 뮤지컬이 마음에 들면 제가 아는 사람들에게 추천할게요.
남 그러면 정말 좋죠. 뮤지컬에서 뵙길 바랍니다.

09 | 정답 | ④

여자는 새로운 라디오 프로그램의 특별 게스트를 첫 방송일 전날 웹사이트에 공개한다고 말하고 있으므로 내용과 일치하지 않는 것은 ④이다.

- **head** 제일(위)의, 최상위의
- **producer** 프로듀서, 감독
- **broadcasting station** 방송국
- **host** 진행하다: 진행자
- **target** 대상으로 삼다
- **deal with** (주제로) 다루다
- **launch** 개시, 출시
- **reveal** 밝히다
- **anniversary** 설립기념일

W Good afternoon. As the head producer at our broadcasting station, I'd like to introduce a new program. It is a morning radio show called "Good Morning, 7 O'Clock," and it will be hosted by Paul Farrell. The show is targeted at **people who listen to the radio in the morning**, including office workers on their way to work, students on their way to school, and many others. It will **deal with various areas** including news, lifestyle, and education. To celebrate the launch of the program, there will be a special guest on the very first day. We will reveal who this is on our website **the day before the first broadcast**. Our first broadcast is on May 15th, **which is our station's anniversary**, so please do not forget to turn on the radio on that day. Thank you.

여 안녕하십니까. 저희 방송국의 책임 프로듀서로서 저는 새로운 프로그램을 소개하려고 합니다. 이 프로그램은 '좋은 아침입니다. 7시'라고 하는 아침 라디오 프로그램이며 Paul Farrell 에 의해 진행될 것입니다. 이 프로그램 대상은 출근길의 직장인들, 등굣길의 학생들, 그리고 많은 다른 사람들을 포함하여 아침에 라디오를 듣는 사람들입니다. 이것은 뉴스, 생활, 교육을 포함해 다양한 분야를 다룰 예정입니다. 프로그램의 시작을 축하하기 위해 첫날 특별 게스트가 있을 예정입니다. 이분이 누구인지는 첫 방송 하루 전날 저희 웹사이트에 공개하겠습니다. 저희의 첫 방송은 저희 방송국 설립기념일인 5월 15일이니 그날 라디오를 켜는 걸 잊지 마세요. 감사합니다.

---

10 | 정답 | ④

여자는 350달러 미만의 예산 범위에서 필터가 세 겹이고 보증기간이 긴 둥근 모양의 공기청정기를 사기로 했으므로 정답은 ④이다.

- **air purifier** 공기 청정기
- **certain** 특정한
- **budget** 예산
- **layer** 겹, 층
- **filter** 필터, 여과 장치
- **warranty** 보증기간

M Hello, ma'am. Are you looking for an air purifier?
W Yes, I didn't know there would be so many different types to choose from.
M I can help you pick the right one. Is there a certain budget you have in mind?
W Yes. I want to **spend less than $350**.
M All right. Do you prefer the latest models? We also have some models from last year.
W Well, what is the difference?
M The latest models come with 3 layers of filters. That's why they are a bit more expensive.
W I see. **Then I'll go with a new model**.
M Good choice. How about the warranty?
W Well, the longer the warranty is, the better, right?
M That's right. Then we only have two options left. Which shape would you like, round or square?
W **I will take the round one**. I think it will go better with my house.
M All right. Come this way. I need you to fill out the delivery form.

남 안녕하세요. 공기 청정기를 찾고 계신가요?
여 네. 선택할 수 있는 종류가 이렇게 많은 줄 몰랐네요.
남 고르는 것을 도와드리겠습니다. 생각하고 계신 특정한 예산이 있으신가요?
여 네. 350달러 미만으로 지출하고 싶습니다.
남 알겠습니다. 최신 모델을 선호하십니까? 작년 모델도 몇 개 있습니다.
여 글쎄요. 차이점이 무엇인가요?
남 최신 모델은 필터가 세 겹입니다. 그래서 조금 더 비싼 겁니다.
여 그렇군요. 그러면 새로운 모델로 하겠습니다.
남 좋은 선택이십니다. 그러면 보증기간은요?
여 글쎄요. 보증기간은 길수록 좋은 거죠, 맞죠?
남 맞습니다. 그러면 이제 두 개의 선택사항이 남았습니다. 둥근 모양과 각진 모양 중 어느 모양이 좋으세요?
여 둥근 모양으로 하겠습니다. 그게 저의 집에 더 잘 어울릴 것 같습니다.
남 알겠습니다. 이쪽으로 오세요. 배달 신청서를 작성해 주셔야 합니다.

---

11 | 정답 | ⑤

여자는 자신이 기차를 타기 위해 어느 플랫폼으로 가야 하는지 묻고 있으므로 이에 대한 적절한 응답은 ⑤ '네. 위 화면에서 어느 승강장으로 가야 할지도 알려줍니다.'이다.

- **depart** 떠나다, 출발하다
- **confirm** 확인하다
- **platform** (역의) 승강장, 플랫폼
  [선택지]
- **refreshment** 《복수형》 음식물, 다과

W Excuse me, sir. I am leaving for Seoul. **Has the train departed yet**?
M No, ma'am. You are just in time. The train is leaving in 10 minutes.
W That's a relief. And just to confirm, **does my train leave from platform six**?
M Yes. The screen above also says which platform to go to.

여 실례합니다. 저는 서울로 가려고 하는데요. 기차가 벌써 떠났나요?
남 아뇨. 시간을 딱 맞춰서 오셨습니다. 기차는 10분 뒤에 출발합니다.
여 다행이네요. 그리고 그냥 확인하는 건데, 제 기차가 6번 승강장에서 출발하나요?
남 네. 위 화면에서 어느 승강장으로 가야 할지도 알려줍니다.

① 기차에서 음식물을 구입하실 수 있습니다.
② 죄송합니다. 기차는 이미 출발했습니다.
③ 안전을 위해 노란 선 뒤에 서 주십시오.
④ 잘 모르겠습니다. 이 기차역에 저도 처음이라서요.

---

12 | 정답 | ③

남자는 이번 주 토요일에 시내에 새로 지은 호텔에 처음으로 방문할 예정이라고 말하고 있으므로 이에 대한 여자의 응답으로 적절한 것은 ③ '우연의 일치네! 내 회의도 토요일에 있어.'이다.

M Have you been to the hotel that was recently built in downtown?
W No, I haven't yet. But I have a conference **to attend at that hotel this weekend**.
M Oh, really? **I'm going to that hotel this Saturday**, too. It will be my first time.
W What a coincidence! My conference is also on Saturday.

남 시내에 최근에 지은 호텔에 가봤니?
여 아니, 아직 못 가봤어. 하지만 이번 주말에 그 호텔에서 참석해야 할 회의가 있어.
남 아, 정말? 나도 이번 주 토요일에 그 호텔에 가. 난 그 호텔이 처음이야.
여 우연의 일치네! 내 회의도 토요일에 있어.

① 정말? 그 호텔에 다시 방문하게 되어서 기쁘겠다.
② 잘됐네. 내 경험상 그 호텔은 정말 멋져.
④ 난 결혼식에 초대받았어. 거기서 널 만나겠구나.
⑤ 난 정말 좋았어. 호텔이 정말 멋지게 수리되었어.

---

13 | 정답 | ①

기차에서 한 자리를 두고 남자와 여자 모두 자신의 자리라고 말하고 있는 상황이다. 남자가 이 기차 다음에 출발하는 기차를 예매했다고 알려주는 여자의 말에 대한 남자의 응답으로 가장 적절한 것은 ① '정말 죄송합니다. 바로 내려야겠네요.'이다.

* bound for ~로 가는
* double-booked 중복 예약된
* conductor 안내원, 승무원

M Excuse me. I think you are sitting in my seat.
W That can't be true. Can I have a look at your ticket, please?
M Of course. It says car number 8 and seat number 7C.
W Hmm... Let me check my ticket, too. *[Pause]* **Mine also says the same thing**.
M Where are you heading? **This train is bound for Boston**.
W I'm going to Boston. This is very strange. I reserved the ticket online.
M Same here. Could it be that our seats are double-booked?
W Yes, there must have been a technical error. Can I see your ticket again?
M Sure. The train is about to leave. We have to find a conductor quickly.
W Wait. You are not supposed to be on this train. Your ticket is for **the train that departs right after this one**.
M I'm terribly sorry. I'd better get off right away.

남 실례합니다. 제 자리에 앉아 계신 것 같은데요.
여 그럴 리가 없어요. 당신의 티켓을 좀 볼 수 있을까요?
남 물론이죠. 티켓에는 객차 번호는 8번, 좌석 번호는 7C 복도 좌석이라고 쓰여 있네요.
여 음… 저도 제 티켓을 확인해 볼게요. *[잠시 후]* 제 것도 똑같이 쓰여 있어요.
남 목적지가 어디신가요? 이 기차는 보스턴으로 갑니다.
여 보스턴으로 갑니다. 정말 이상하네요. 저는 온라인으로 티켓을 예약했어요.
남 저도 그래요. 저희 좌석이 중복 예약된 걸까요?
여 네, 기술적인 문제가 있었나 봐요. 제가 티켓을 다시 한번 볼 수 있을까요?
남 물론입니다. 기차가 막 떠나려고 하네요. 안내원을 빨리 찾아야겠어요.
여 잠시요. 당신은 이 기차에 타면 안 돼요. 당신의 티켓은 이 기차 바로 다음에 출발하는 기차의 티켓이에요.
남 정말 죄송합니다. 바로 내려야겠네요.

② 이 자리에 앉으세요. 저는 다음 차를 기다리면 됩니다.
③ 일정에 변경이 있었다는 당신 말이 옳았어요.
④ 저희 둘 모두의 표를 제가 사겠습니다. 걱정하지 마세요.
⑤ 누군가 와서 티켓을 확인해 주기를 기다립시다.

---

14 | 정답 | ③

공원에서 개를 잃어버린 남자를 여자가 도와주려고 하는 상황에서 남자는 여자에게 개를 찾게 되는 경우 원래 만난 자리로 돌아오자고 제안하고 있으므로 이에 대한 여자의 적절한 응답은 ③ '물론이죠. 20분 후에 여기서 다시 만나요.'이다.

* nowhere 아무 데도 (~없다)
* possibly 과연
* collar (개 등의 목에 거는) 목걸이

W Excuse me. Is something wrong?
M I've been looking for my dog, but **he is nowhere in sight**.
W Oh, no. Where did you lose him?
M I tied him around that tree while I used the bathroom. But when I came out, he was gone.
W That's terrible. I will help you find him.
M That is very kind of you. **Where could he possibly be off to**?
W Calm down and try to think. When you came out, was the chain still there?
M Yes. It was still tied to the tree. He must have broken the chain and run away.
W And what does he look like?
M He is a big husky and **he's wearing a leather collar around his neck**. Oh, and his name is Buddy.
W Okay. I'll look this way and you start looking that way.
M All right. If you find Buddy, **could you bring him back here**?
W Of course. Let's meet back here in 20 minutes.

여 실례합니다. 무슨 문제가 있나요?
남 제 개를 계속 찾고 있는데 아무 데도 보이질 않아요.
여 아, 이런. 어디서 잃어버렸어요?
남 제가 화장실을 사용하는 동안 저쪽 나무에 묶어 두었거든요. 그런데 제가 나와 보니 개가 사라졌어요.
여 큰일이네요. 그를 찾는 걸 도와드릴게요.
남 정말 친절하시네요. 과연 어디로 갔을까요?
여 진정하시고 생각해 보세요. 당신이 밖으로 나왔을 때 목줄이 그대로 거기에 있었나요?
남 네. 여전히 나무에 묶여 있었어요. 목줄을 끊고 달아난 게 틀림없어요.
여 그리고 어떻게 생겼나요?
남 덩치가 큰 허스키인데 목에 가죽 목걸이를 하고 있어요. 아, 그리고 개 이름은 Buddy예요.
여 알겠어요. 저는 이쪽을 찾아볼 테니 당신은 저쪽을 찾아봐요.
남 그럴게요. Buddy를 찾게 된다면 여기로 데려와 주실 수 있나요?
여 물론이죠. 20분 후에 여기서 다시 만나요.

① 지난번에 새로운 사람들을 이 공원에 데려왔어요.
② 네. 어렸을 때 개를 반려동물로 키웠어요.
④ 성격 때문에 고양이보다 개가 더 좋아요.
⑤ 물론이죠. 당신이 여행 간 동안 당신의 개를 산책시켜 줄게요.

---

15 | 정답 | ④

두 명의 취업 지원자 중 한 명인 Adam Kindle은 면접에서 불확실하고 자신감이 없어 보여서 결국 다른 지원자를 채용했다는 내용이다. 따라서 채용 담당자인 Emma가 Adam에게 전화로 할 말은 ④ '유감스럽지만, 다른 후보자를 선택

W Emma works at the recruitment office. She posted a job hiring notice online, and two candidates applied. One of the applicants was Adam Kindle, but **at the interview he was a little weak**. The position he applied for was in the domestic sales department. This job involves dealing with different clients, so the company requires that the candidates be comfortable speaking in public. But when

여 Emma는 채용 사무실에서 일한다. 그녀는 온라인으로 채용 공고를 냈고 두 명의 후보자가 지원했다. 지원자 중 한 명은 Adam Kindle인데 면접에서 그는 좀 약했다. 그가 지원한 부서는 국내 영업부였다. 이 일은 다양한 고객을 상대하는 일을 수반하기 때문에 회사는 후보들이 대중 앞에서 편하게 말할 것을 바란다. 하지만 Adam이 면접에서 질문에 답했을 때 그는 약간 불안정하고 자신감이 없어 보였다. 결국 회사는 Adam

하게 되었습니다.'이다.

- **recruitment** 채용, 신규 모집, 보충
- **hire** 고용하다
- **candidate** 후보자, 지원자
- **applicant** 지원자
- **domestic** 국내의, 가정의
- **uncertainty** 불안정, 불확실
[선택지]
- **qualify** 자격을 주다[얻다]

Adam answered the questions at the interview, **he showed some uncertainty and lacked confidence**. Eventually, the company chose the other candidate over Adam. As the person in charge of recruitment, Emma has to call Adam and **inform him of the results**. In this situation, what would Emma most likely say to Adam?

Emma I am sorry, but we've selected another candidate.

대신 다른 후보를 선택했다. 채용을 담당하는 사람으로서 Emma는 Adam에게 전화를 걸어 결과를 알려야 한다. 이러한 상황에서 Emma가 Adam에게 할 말로 가장 적절한 것은 무엇인가?

Emma 유감스럽지만, 다른 후보자를 선택하게 되었습니다.

① 축하합니다. 당신은 이 자리에 합격하셨습니다.
② 당신이 우리에게 최고의 사람이라는 것을 확신합니다.
③ 내일 면접을 보러 방문할 수 있습니까?
⑤ 더 자신감을 갖고 좀 더 크게 말씀해 주시겠어요?

---

16 | 정답 | ⑤

오케스트라에서 사용되는 주요 악기를 현악기, 목관악기, 금관악기, 그리고 타악기의 4가지 계열로 분류해서 각 악기군의 특성과 용도에 대해서 설명하고 있으므로 남자가 하는 말의 주제로 가장 적절한 것은 ⑤ '오케스트라의 다양한 악기군'이다.

17 | 정답 | ④

오케스트라에 사용되는 주요 악기 중 '호른'에 대한 언급은 없었으므로 정답은 ④이다.

- **brief** 간략한
- **overview** 개관, 개요
- **instrument** 악기
- **strings** 현악기
- **woodwinds** 목관 악기
- **brass** 금관악기
- **percussion** 타악기
- **notable** 눈에 띄는
- **high-pitched** (음이) 아주 높은
- **religious** 종교적인
- **texture** (음악에서 여러 요소의) 조화[어우러짐]
[선택지]
- **popularity** 인기
- **origin** 유래

M Welcome to the world of classical music! Today, I will give you a brief overview about each of the main types of instruments used in an orchestra. There are four families of instruments: strings, woodwinds, brass, and percussion. Let's start with the most notable instrument in the string family, the violin. **The violin often carries the melody** in an orchestra as its high-pitched sound carries easily over other instruments. Next, the flute is one of the instruments from the woodwind family. Like the violin, the flute may often carry the melody line as it is **easy to hear above the others**. The third family of instruments is brass, and the one most familiar to us would be the trumpet. But did you know that this instrument has been around since 1500 B.C.? It was often **used for sending messages and for religious purposes** in the old days. The last instrument is the drum, which belongs to the percussion family. Along with other percussion instruments, the drum **provides a variety of rhythms and textures** to orchestra music. Now, let's watch a video of an actual orchestra.

남 클래식 음악의 세계에 오신 것을 환영합니다! 오늘은 오케스트라에서 쓰이는 각각의 주요 악기에 대해 간략하게 설명하겠습니다. 악기에는 현악기, 목관악기, 금관악기, 그리고 타악기 4가지 계열이 있습니다. 현악기 중 가장 눈에 띄는 악기인 바이올린부터 시작합시다. 바이올린은 높은 음조의 소리가 다른 악기에 쉽게 전달되기 때문에 종종 오케스트라에서 멜로디를 전달합니다. 다음으로 플루트는 목관 악기 중 하나입니다. 바이올린처럼 플루트는 다른 것들보다 듣기 쉽기 때문에 종종 멜로디 라인을 전달합니다. 세 번째 악기군은 금관악기인데, 우리에게 가장 친숙한 것은 트럼펫일 것입니다. 하지만 이 악기가 기원전 1500년부터 있었다는 사실을 알고 계셨나요? 트럼펫은 옛날에 메시지를 전달하는 일이나 종교적인 목적으로 자주 쓰였습니다. 마지막으로 타악기 계열에 속하는 드럼입니다. 타악기군의 다른 악기와 같이 드럼은 오케스트라 음악에 다양한 리듬과 조화를 제공합니다. 이제 실제 오케스트라 영상을 봅시다.

16 ① 클래식 음악에서 오케스트라의 중요성
② 오케스트라와 밴드의 차이
③ 클래식 음악이 인기를 잃은 이유
④ 유럽의 클래식 음악의 유래와 역사
⑤ 오케스트라의 다양한 악기군

17 ① 바이올린 ② 플루트 ③ 트럼펫
④ 호른 ⑤ 드럼

05회 실전 듣기 모의고사

| 01 ① | 02 ③ | 03 ④ | 04 ③ | 05 ④ | 06 ④ | 07 ⑤ | 08 ③ | 09 ③ | 10 ④ |
| 11 ③ | 12 ④ | 13 ④ | 14 ② | 15 ③ | 16 ① | 17 ④ |

본문 p.28

01 | 정답 | ①

다양한 메뉴와 유명 셰프의 조리법을 쉽게 활용할 수 있는 앱을 설명하는 내용이다. 앱의 기능 및 가격을 언급하는 것으로 보아 여자가 하는 말의 목적은 ①이다.

- **haven** 피난처, 안식처
- **challenge** 도전
- **access** 접속, 접근; 이용, 입수
- **celebrity** 유명인
- **tap** 가볍게 두드리다
- **provide** 제공하다
- **purchase** 구입, 구매
- **opportunity** 기회
- **miss out** 놓치다

W Hello, everybody! Have you decided what to cook for dinner tonight? It is hard to choose dinner every day. Let Cook's Haven help you with this daily challenge. This is a very unique cooking app you can download on your phone. You will have easy access to **a variety of dishes and celebrity chefs' recipes** by just tapping a button. Just choose one and cook it. The recipes will be updated every two weeks. You can download and save the recipes on your phone, too! Cook's Haven **will provide you with easy ways** to find your perfect meal with a one-time payment of $30. For a limited time only, with the purchase of Cook's Haven, you might win the opportunity to cook with the world-famous chef Tony Chung. **Don't miss out on this great opportunity**.

여 여러분, 안녕하세요! 오늘 저녁은 무엇을 요리할지 정하셨나요? 매일 저녁 식사 메뉴를 고르는 일은 어렵지요. Cook's Haven이 여러분이 매일 겪는 이 도전 과제에 도움을 드리겠습니다. 이것은 여러분의 휴대폰에 다운로드 받을 수 있는 독특한 요리 앱입니다. 단지 단추 하나를 누르기만 하면 다양한 요리와 유명 셰프의 요리법을 쉽게 활용할 수 있습니다. 그냥 하나를 골라 요리해 보세요. 요리법은 2주마다 새로 올라올 것입니다. 여러분의 휴대폰에 요리법을 다운로드 받고 저장하실 수도 있습니다! Cook's Haven이 일시불 30달러로 완벽한 식사를 찾을 수 있는 쉬운 방법을 알려줄 겁니다. 한정된 기간 동안 Cook's Haven을 구입하시면 세계적으로 유명한 셰프 Tony Chung과 함께 요리할 수 있는 기회를 얻을 수도 있습니다. 이 멋진 기회를 놓치지 마세요.

02 | 정답 | ③

집에 가서 쉬고 싶다고 말하는 여자에게 남자는 운동을 하는 것이 스트레스를 관리하는 데 효과적이라고 말하고 있다. 이어서 운동의 이점들을 언급하는 것으로 보아 남자의 의견으로 가장 적절한 것은 ③이다.

- **stressed out** 스트레스가 쌓인
- **break a sweat** 땀을 빼다
- **relieve** (고통 등을) 덜어 주다, 없애 주다
- **relax** 편히 쉬다
- **manage** 관리하다
- **reduce** 감소시키다
- **risk** 위험
- **cancer** 암
- **once** 일단 ~하면

W I feel stressed out from working on the presentation all afternoon. I can't wait to go home and rest.
M **I'd rather break a sweat** to relieve stress. That's why I changed into gym clothes.
W Are you off to the gym?
M Well, I'm going to the Han River for a jog instead.
W That sounds interesting. Maybe **I should be more active** instead of relaxing at home.
M You should. It's a healthy way to manage your stress. Exercise such as running can help you relax better, too.
W What do you mean?
M Exercising can improve your sleep. **It helps you to fall asleep faster** and stay asleep longer.
W I didn't know that. I thought just sleeping longer hours would relieve your stress.
M That could make you more tired. Besides, **exercising can reduce the risk of diseases** such as cancer.
W I guess the hardest part is to get started.
M Getting started is always hard. Once you get used to it, it will be a lot easier.

여 오후 내내 발표 준비하고 나니까 스트레스가 너무 쌓여. 얼른 집에 가서 쉬고 싶어.
남 나는 차라리 땀을 빼서 스트레스를 풀고 싶어. 그래서 운동복으로 갈아입은 거야.
여 헬스장으로 갈 거니?
남 아, 그것보다는 한강으로 가서 조깅을 하려고 해.
여 재밌을 것 같네. 나도 집에서 쉬는 것보다 좀 더 움직여야 할 것 같아.
남 그렇게 해. 그게 스트레스를 관리하는 건강한 방법이야. 달리기 같은 운동이 긴장을 더 잘 풀도록 도와줄 거야.
여 무슨 뜻이니?
남 운동이 수면을 도와줄 수 있어. 그건 더 빨리 잠들게 하고 더 오래 잠을 수 있게 해 주거든.
여 그건 몰랐어. 나는 그저 더 오래 자는 것이 스트레스를 덜어줄 거라고 생각했어.
남 그건 오히려 너를 더 피곤하게 할 수 있어. 뿐만 아니라, 운동은 암 같은 질병의 위험을 감소시키기도 하지.
여 가장 어려운 건 시작하는 거 같아.
남 시작하는 건 언제나 어려워. 일단 익숙해지면, 훨씬 더 쉬워질 거야.

03 | 정답 | ④

샤워헤드를 조사한 연구 결과를 언급하며 해로운 박테리아가 샤워헤드에 축적될 수 있으므로 처음 나오는 물로 샤워하는 것을 피하라고 말하고 있다. 따라서 여자가 하는 말의 요지로 가장 적절한 것은 ④이다.

- **splash** 물, 방류된 물
- **look into** 조사하다
- **accumulate** 축적되다, 축적하다
- **burst** 폭발, 연속발사
- **surge** 밀려듦; 급증
- **overall** 전반적인, 종합적인

W Good to have you here! My name is Becky Blanz, and welcome to *One Minute Health Show*. These days, **more and more people are worried about the water quality**. Here's an easy health tip for you: try to avoid showering with the first splash of water. Recently, a study looking into 50 different showerheads revealed that harmful bacteria can accumulate in showerheads, and **the first burst of water is the most dangerous**. Avoiding stepping into the shower during the initial surge of water **can have a significant impact on your overall health**. I'll be back with more health tips next time. Goodbye.

여 반갑습니다! 제 이름은 Becky Blanz이고 "One minute Health Show"에 오신 것을 환영합니다. 요즘 점점 더 많은 사람들이 수질에 대해 걱정하고 있습니다. 여기 여러분을 위한 간단한 건강 정보가 있는데, 처음에 나오는 물로 샤워하는 것을 피하세요. 최근 50개의 다른 샤워헤드를 조사한 연구는 해로운 박테리아가 샤워헤드에 축적될 수 있다는 것을 밝혀냈고, 처음에 나오는 물 발사가 가장 위험하다고 합니다. 처음 물이 밀려드는 동안 샤워기에 들어가는 걸 피하는 것이 여러분의 전반적인 건강에 중대한 영향을 미칠 수 있습니다. 다음에 더 많은 건강 정보로 다시 찾아뵐게요. 안녕히 계세요.

04 | 정답 | ③

대화 내용에서 여자가 오른쪽 가로등에 등을 기대고 서 있다고 했으나 그림에서는 벤치 앞에 서 있으므로 ③이 대화의 내용과 일치하지 않는다.

* suit ~와 어울리다
* theme 주제
* phrase 어구
* recognize 알아보다, 인식하다
* lean (against) (~에) 기대다
* shadow 그림자
* loneliness 외로움
* stand out 눈에 띄다, 두드러지다
* bold 굵은 글씨체의, 볼드체(의)

M Hey, Jessi. Take a look. Here's the design for your new album cover.

W It's done already? *[Pause]* Wow, I like the decoration on the left side. It makes it look like a notebook.

M Yes. It **suits the theme of the whole album**.

W And the phrase "thinking of you" is coming out of my mouth. It looks like I'm singing my song.

M Yes, and people will recognize the song title easily, too.

W I also like this picture of myself. I am **leaning against the streetlight** on the right side. And you didn't forget to add my shadow, either.

M I think **the shadow gives a sense of loneliness**.

W You're right. Oh, I see you put my name at the bottom. Those letters really stand out.

M That's because I used bold letters since "Jessi Conner" is the most important part of the cover.

남 Jessi, 이것 좀 봐. 네 새 앨범 표지 디자인이야.

여 벌써 다 되었어? *[잠시 후]* 와. 왼쪽 디자인이 마음에 든다. 앨범을 공책처럼 보이게 하네.

남 맞아. 그 디자인이 전체 앨범 주제와 잘 어울려.

여 그리고 'thinking of you'라는 문구가 내 입에서 나오고 있네. 마치 내가 내 노래를 부르고 있는 것처럼 보여.

남 그래. 그리고 사람들이 그 노래 제목을 쉽게 알아볼 수도 있을 거야.

여 내 사진도 마음에 든다. 내가 오른쪽에 있는 가로등에 등을 기대고 있네. 거기다가 내 그림자를 그려 넣는 것도 잊지 않았구나.

남 내 생각에 그림자가 외로운 느낌을 주는 것 같아.

여 맞아. 아, 내 이름도 밑에 넣었구나. 글자가 정말 눈에 잘 띄네.

남 'Jessi Conner'가 이 앨범 표지에서 가장 중요한 부분이니까 굵은 글씨체를 썼거든.

05 | 정답 | ④

과학박물관의 우주 체험 프로그램 입장료를 확인하기 위해 홈페이지에 접속하라는 여자의 말을 듣고 남자는 인터넷에서 정보를 더 찾아보겠다고 말하는 것으로 보아 정답은 ④이다.

* suggestion 의견, 제안
* rent 빌리다
* chilly 쌀쌀한
* admission fee 입장료
* find out (~에 대해) 알아내다

M Mom, I'm so excited that my cousins are visiting tomorrow.

W I know. I'll make you guys a delicious seafood meal tomorrow.

M Do you need any help with that?

W Don't worry about me. You go out and have fun with them.

M **I haven't really thought of what to do**. Can you make any suggestions?

W What about going for a bike ride? You can rent bicycles near the subway station and ride out to the beach.

M I'm not sure if they'd like it. It is a bit chilly to ride a bike outside, too.

W Okay. Then how about taking them to the science museum near City Hall? I heard that **the museum started a space program** for students under 15.

M That sounds like fun. We should go there instead. Do you know how much the admission fee is?

W I'm not sure. **How about visiting the website** to find out more?

M All right. I'll look for more information on the internet.

W Do you want me to bring some snacks to your room?

M Yes, please. Thanks, Mom.

남 엄마. 내일 사촌들이 온다고 해서 정말 신나요.

여 그래. 내가 내일 맛있는 해물 요리를 해 줄게.

남 그 일 좀 도와드릴까요?

여 내 걱정은 하지 마. 사촌들하고 나가서 재미있게 놀아.

남 무엇을 할지 별로 생각해 보지 않았어요. 의견 좀 주실 수 있나요?

여 자전거 타러 나가는 건 어떠니? 지하철역 근처에서 자전거 빌려서 해변으로 타고 가면 될 것 같은데.

남 사촌들이 그걸 좋아할지 모르겠어요. 밖에서 자전거를 타기에는 좀 쌀쌀하기도 하고요.

여 그래. 그러면 시청 근처에 있는 과학박물관에 데리고 가는 건 어때? 박물관에서 15세 미만 학생들을 위한 우주 체험 프로그램을 시작했다고 들었거든.

남 그거 재미있을 것 같아요. 대신 거길 가는 게 좋겠어요. 입장료가 얼마인지 아세요?

여 잘 모르겠구나. 웹사이트에 들어가서 더 알아보지 그러니?

남 알았어요. 인터넷에서 정보를 더 찾아볼게요.

여 방에 간식 좀 갖다줄까?

남 네. 주세요. 고마워요, 엄마.

06 | 정답 | ④

입장료는 어른 1인당 60달러, 아이는 1인당 40달러 기준으로, 어른 둘, 아이 둘의 입장료는 총 200달러이다. 여기서 호텔 투숙객이면 20% 할인을 받을 수 있으므로 20%인 40달러를 뺀 160달러가 여자가 지불할 금액이다. 따라서 정답은 ④이다.

* admission 입장(료)
* entrance 입구
* deal 거래
* charge 요금을 청구하다

M Pool and Spa Town, how may I help you?

W Hello, **I'd like to buy admission tickets** for two adults and two kids.

M Okay. Would you like to enter the spa right now? Admission is cheaper after 4 p.m.

W I see. There is only half an hour until then. We will come after 4 p.m. Can I still buy the tickets now?

M Yes, you can. **You just have to wait by the entrance** until then. Are the kids under 12?

W That's right. They are 11 and 9.

M All right. The ticket price for one adult is $60, and for children, it's $40 each.

W Are there any special deals for hotel guests?

M You can **get a 20% discount if you are staying** here at the hotel.

W Wonderful. I'm staying at the hotel, and my room number is 1205.

남 Pool and Spa Town입니다. 어떻게 도와드릴까요?

여 안녕하세요. 어른 두 명과 아이 두 명의 입장권을 사려고 합니다.

남 알겠습니다. 지금 바로 스파에 들어가려고 하시나요? 오후 4시 이후에는 입장료가 더 저렴합니다.

여 그렇군요. 그때까지 30분 남았네요. 4시 이후에 올게요. 그래도 입장권은 지금 살 수 있나요?

남 네. 구입하실 수 있습니다. 그때까지 입구 옆에서 기다리셔야 합니다. 아이들이 12세 미만인가요?

여 맞아요. 11살과 9살입니다.

남 알겠습니다. 입장료는 어른 1인당 60달러이고 아이들은 각각 40달러입니다.

여 호텔 투숙객에 대한 특별 혜택이 있나요?

남 이 호텔에 묵고 계시면 20% 할인을 받으실 수 있습니다.

여 좋아요. 호텔에 묵고 있는데요, 방 번호는 1205호입니다.

	M If you want, **it can be charged to your room**. Would you like that?	남 원하시면 호텔 객실로 요금을 청구할 수도 있습니다. 그렇게 해 드릴까요?
	W No, thanks. I'll just pay for it now. Here's my credit card.	여 아니요. 괜찮습니다. 그냥 지금 지불할게요. 여기 제 신용 카드 받으세요.

---

07 | 정답 | ⑤

그룹 프로젝트를 위해 모이자는 여자의 제안을 거절하며 남자는 치아 교정기를 하러 치과에 간다고 설명하고 있다. 따라서 정답은 ⑤이다.

* in one's mind ~의 마음속에
* brace 《복수형》 치아 교정기

W We need to talk about our group project. Have you thought of anything?

M Well, there are a few topics in my mind. What about you?

W I thought of some things, too. So I was thinking about **having a group meeting later today**. Is that all right with you?

M Oh, I'm afraid I can't.

W Is it **because of the band practice**?

M No, band practice is every Tuesday.

W Then why is it that you can't come?

M I have **a dentist's appointment after school**, so my mom is coming to pick me up.

W I see. Do you have a toothache?

M No, **I'm getting braces today**. I am so scared.

W Don't worry. It won't hurt so much.

M Okay. Thanks. Oh, I will text you the list of the topics I thought of. Sorry I can't come today.

여 우리 그룹 프로젝트에 대해 이야기를 해야 해. 뭐 좀 생각해 봤어?

남 음, 몇 가지 주제를 생각하고 있는데. 너는?

여 나도 몇 가지 정도 생각했어. 그래서 오늘 오후 모임을 가지려고 해. 넌 괜찮니?

남 아, 난 안 될 것 같아.

여 밴드 연습 때문에 그래?

남 아니. 밴드 연습은 매주 화요일이야.

여 그럼 왜 안 된다는 거야?

남 방과 후에 치과 예약이 있어서 엄마가 날 데리러 오실 거야.

여 그렇구나. 이가 아프니?

남 아니. 치아 교정기를 오늘 해야 되거든. 너무 무서워.

여 걱정하지 마. 그렇게 아프진 않을 거야.

남 알았어. 고마워. 아, 내가 생각했던 주제 목록은 문자로 보내 줄게. 오늘 못 가서 미안해.

---

08 | 정답 | ③

해외 자원봉사자 모집 담당자에게 참가 조건, 참가 비용, 활동 내용, 지원 마감일에 대해서는 문의하였지만 활동 국가에 대해서는 언급하지 않았으므로 정답은 ③이다.

* in charge of ~을 담당하는
* recruit 모집하다
* over the phone 전화로
* apply for ~에 지원하다
* volunteer 자원봉사자
* requirement (필요)조건, 요건
* expense 비용, 경비
* fund 자금을 제공하다
* entirely 전적으로
* depend on ~에 따라 다르다
* supply 보급품, 물자
* in need 어려움에 처한, 궁핍한

[Telephone rings.]

W Thank you for calling Helping Hands. This is Janet speaking.

M Hello, Janet. My name is Chris. May I talk to the person **in charge of recruiting**?

W This is she. How may I help you?

M Is it all right to ask you a few questions over the phone?

W Of course.

M I'd like to apply for a volunteer position abroad. What are the requirements?

W We have an age limit of 30. **Someone with great communication skills is preferred**.

M I see. Are there any expenses I have to pay for?

W No, since our volunteer program **is funded entirely by the government**, everything will be free.

M That's good to hear. What kind of volunteer work will I be doing?

W Well, it depends on the area you're applying for. You could build houses or **deliver supplies to those in need**.

M Great! When is the deadline to apply?

W It's Thursday, June 15th.

M I see. Thank you so much for your time.

[전화벨이 울린다.]

여 Helping Hands에 전화 주셔서 감사합니다. Janet입니다.

남 Janet, 안녕하세요. 제 이름은 Chris입니다. 모집을 담당하시는 분과 통화할 수 있을까요?

여 접니다. 어떻게 도와드릴까요?

남 전화로 몇 가지 질문을 드려도 될까요?

여 물론 됩니다.

남 해외 자원봉사자 자리에 지원하고 싶습니다. 갖추어야 할 조건이 뭔가요?

여 저희는 30세 연령 제한이 있습니다. 뛰어난 의사소통 능력을 갖춘 분을 우대합니다.

남 알겠습니다. 제가 지불해야 할 비용이 있나요?

여 아니요. 우리 자원봉사 프로그램은 전적으로 정부에서 자금을 지원받기 때문에 모든 것이 무료입니다.

남 좋네요. 어떤 자원봉사 일을 하게 되나요?

여 지원하시는 지역에 따라 다릅니다. 집을 짓거나 어려움에 처한 분들에게 보급품을 배달하기도 할 겁니다.

남 좋네요. 지원 마감은 언제인가요?

여 6월 15일 목요일입니다.

남 알겠습니다. 시간 내주셔서 감사합니다.

---

09 | 정답 | ③

담화에서는 포럼이 파리에서 2년에 한 번씩 8월 중에 열린다고 했으므로 일치하지 않는 내용은 ③이다.

* select 선정하다, 선택하다
* attend 참가하다
* applicant 지원자
* turn out to-v ~임이 판명되다
* competent 유능한
* deserve to-v ~할 만하다
* gathering 모임, 회합

M Hello, everyone. Congratulations on being selected to attend the World Youth Forum this year. Selecting 5 excellent students from among the 40 applicants was not easy. All the applicants **turned out to be very competent** and deserved to be selected. Well, as you know, the World Youth Forum is an international gathering to talk about **what the youth of the world should do** to tackle global issues such as climate change. It is **held every two years in Paris during the month of August**. You are going to attend as representatives of our country. To prepare for the Forum, you will need to participate in

남 안녕하세요, 여러분. 올해 세계 청소년 포럼에 참가자로 선정된 것을 축하합니다. 40명 지원자 중에서 우수한 학생 5명을 선정하는 일은 쉽지 않았습니다. 모든 지원자들이 매우 유능하고 선정될 만했기 때문입니다. 알다시피, 세계 청소년 포럼은 세계의 젊은이들이 기후 변화와 같은 세계적인 문제를 해결하기 위해서 무엇을 해야 하는지에 대하여 논의하는 국제적인 모임입니다. 포럼은 파리에서 2년에 한 번씩 8월 중에 열립니다. 여러분은 우리나라 대표로 참가하게 됩니다. 포럼을 준비하기 위해서 여러분은 출발하기 전에 워크숍에 참가해야 합니다. 포럼과 워크숍에서도 즐거운 시간을 갖기를 바랍니다. 성공적인 파리 여행이 되도록 행운을 빕니다.

* **tackle** (문제 등을) 다루다, 해결하다
* **global issue** 세계적인 문제
* **representative** 대표(자)
* **keep A's fingers crossed** 행운을 빌다

a workshop before you go. I hope you have a great time at the Forum and the workshop as well. I will keep my fingers crossed for a successful trip to Paris.

---

10 | 정답 | ④

1박에 100달러 넘게 쓰지 말아야 한다고 했고, 렌터카 대신에 셔틀버스를 이용하자고 언급했다. 또한 아이들을 위한 워터 파크가 있어야 하고, 호텔 뷔페를 이용하기로 했으므로 두 사람이 예약할 호텔은 ④이다.

* **compare** 비교하다
* **rate** 요금, 가격
* **range** 범위
* **accommodation** 숙박(시설)
* **insurance** 보험
* **rental car** 렌터카, 임대 자동차
* **definitely** 물론, 분명히
* **remind** 상기시키다, 생각나게 하다
* **pack** (짐 등을) 챙기다, 싸다
* **swimsuit** 수영복

M I found this website that compares hotel rates to one another. Would you come here and take a look at it?
W Wow, they all look great. It is hard to choose just one.
M Then let's start with the price. I **set the price range** from $80 to $120, so we have five choices.
W I see. I think we should spend no more than $100 a night. **I'd rather spend money on food** than accommodation.
M I agree. Oh, are we going to rent a car there?
W Well, it'd be a lot more convenient, but do you think you can drive there?
M I don't think I can. I'm not familiar with the area. Besides, we would have to buy driver's insurance, too.
W Let's forget about rental cars and **use the shuttle bus service instead**.
M All right. How about a water park? I think our kids would love to visit one.
W Definitely. Remind me to pack swimsuits, okay?
M Sure. Do you think we should eat at the hotel buffet?
W Yes, I think so. Let's **choose one that offers a free buffet**.
M All right, then. I guess this is it. I'll make a reservation.

남 호텔 요금을 서로 비교해 주는 웹사이트를 찾았어요. 이리 와서 한번 볼래요?
여 와, 모두 다 좋아 보이네요. 하나만 선택하기가 어려워요.
남 그럼, 요금부터 봅시다. 제가 80달러에서 120달러로 가격 범위를 정했는데, 그러면 다섯 군데가 있군요.
여 알겠어요. 1박에 100달러 넘게 쓰면 안 될 것 같아요. 숙박보다는 음식에 돈을 쓰고 싶거든요.
남 나도 그렇게 생각해요. 아, 우리 거기서 자동차를 빌릴 건가요?
여 음, 그게 훨씬 더 편리하겠지만, 거기서 운전할 수 있겠어요?
남 못 할 것 같아요. 그 지역이 익숙하지 않아요. 게다가, 운전자 보험도 들어야 해요.
여 렌터카는 없던 일로 하고 대신에 셔틀버스를 이용하기로 해요.
남 좋아요. 워터 파크는 어때요? 아이들이 거기 가는 걸 무척 좋아할 것 같은데요.
여 분명히 그럴 거예요. 제게 수영복 챙기라고 얘기 좀 해 주세요. 알겠죠?
남 알았어요. 우리가 호텔 뷔페에서 식사해야 한다고 생각하나요?
여 네, 그럴 것 같아요. 무료 뷔페를 제공하는 걸 골라요.
남 좋아요. 결정된 것 같네요. 제가 예약할게요.

---

11 | 정답 | ③

Tom Brown이라는 이름을 가진 사람이 없다고 했으므로 번호를 확인하는 여자의 말에 대한 남자의 응답은 ③ '네, 번호는 맞는데 Tom Brown이라는 분은 여기 없습니다.'가 가장 적절하다.

* **marketing department** 마케팅 부서
[선택지]
* **be out of town** 출장 중이다

[Telephone rings.]
W Hello, **may I speak to** Tom Brown in the marketing department? This is Mary Smith.
M I'm sorry, but I think you must have the wrong number. **There's no one here by that name**.
W I was calling 727-2565. Isn't this your number?
M Yes, it is, but there's no Tom Brown here.

[전화벨이 울린다.]
여 안녕하세요. 마케팅 부서에 있는 Tom Brown 씨와 통화할 수 있을까요? 저는 Mary Smith라고 합니다.
남 죄송합니다만, 전화를 잘못 거신 것 같습니다. 여기 그런 이름을 가진 분은 없는데요.
여 제가 727-2565로 전화를 걸었는데요, 맞는 번호 아닌가요?
남 네, 번호는 맞는데 Tom Brown이라는 분은 여기 없습니다.

① 죄송한데, 저희 전화번호를 다시 확인하겠습니다.
② 맞습니다만, 우리 일에 신경 쓰지 마세요.
④ 음, Tom은 지금 출장 중인 것 같습니다.
⑤ 잠깐만 기다리세요. 그 사람도 분명 당신 전화를 기다리고 있을 겁니다.

---

12 | 정답 | ④

두 사람이 헤어지는 상황에서 이곳에서의 멋진 추억을 잊지 말라고 부탁하는 남자의 말에 대한 가장 적절한 여자의 응답은 ④ '물론 잊지 않을 거야! 온라인으로 계속 연락하도록 할게.'이다.

* **memory** 추억, 기억
[선택지]
* **relative** 친척
* **mountains of** 산더미 같은

M Goodbye, Sandy. You are special to us.
W **Thanks for having this wonderful party** for me, Bill.
M I just want you to know that **we will miss you a lot**. You shouldn't forget us and your great memories here.
W Of course I won't! I'll try to keep in touch with you online.

남 잘 가, Sandy. 너는 우리에게 특별한 사람이야.
여 나를 위해서 이렇게 멋진 파티를 열어 주어서 고마워, Bill.
남 단지 우리가 너를 무척 보고 싶어 할 것이라는 걸 알아주면 좋겠어. 우리와 여기서 가졌던 멋진 추억을 잊어서는 안 돼.
여 물론 잊지 않을 거야! 온라인으로 계속 연락하도록 할게.

① 신경 쓰지 마. 나는 분명 그것을 잘할 수 있어.
② 그래, 그렇게. 나는 거기 친척들도 좀 있어.
③ 나는 그걸 예상하지 못했어. 그건 내가 예상한 것보다 훨씬 대단했어.
⑤ 나도 그런 일이 없으면 좋겠어. 산더미 같은 일이 나를 기다리고 있을 거야.

13 | 정답 | ④

여자가 남자에게 이모가 추천하는 도서 목록을 물어봐 준다고 말하고 있으므로 남자의 응답으로 가장 적절한 것은 ④ '아주 좋을 것 같아. 이모에게 너무 많은 부담이 아니길 바라.'이다.

- **due** ~하기로 되어 있는[예정된]
- **morning sickness** 입덧
- **tough** 힘든
- **get through** 견뎌내다
- **pregnancy** 임신
- **newborn** 《복수형》 신생아
  [선택지]
- **in case of emergency** 비상시에

M Mary, my sister is having a baby.
W Wow, you are going to be an uncle! Congratulations!
M Thanks. The baby is due next May. I **can't wait to meet the little one**.
W How's your sister doing now?
M She's having a hard time with morning sickness, so she spends most of the day in bed.
W Well, it must be really tough on her, but she has to get through it.
M I know. I feel like there is something I could do to help her, but I don't know what.
W Well, **you could get her some books to read**. She'd love that.
M You think so?
W When my aunt was having a baby, she read a lot of books on pregnancy, **how to take care of newborns**, and so on.
M There are so many books to choose from. Do you know any good ones?
W I will call my aunt and **ask for a list of the books she recommends**.
M That sounds perfect. I hope it's not too much trouble for her.

남 Mary, 내 여동생이 아기 엄마가 된대.
여 와, 네가 삼촌이 되네! 축하해!
남 고마워. 출산 예정일은 내년 5월이래. 작은 아기를 빨리 만나고 싶어.
여 네 여동생은 지금 어떻게 지내?
남 입덧으로 고생하고 있어서 하루의 대부분을 침대에서 보내고 있어.
여 정말 힘들겠다. 하지만 견뎌야지.
남 맞아. 내가 동생을 도울 수 있는 뭔가가 있을 것 같은데 무엇을 해야 할지 모르겠어.
여 음, 읽을 책을 좀 사다 줄 수도 있잖아. 그걸 좋아할 거야.
남 그렇게 생각해?
여 우리 이모가 아기를 가졌을 때, 임신과 신생아 육아 등에 대한 책을 많이 읽으셨거든.
남 고를 수 있는 책이 너무 많네. 좋은 책을 좀 알고 있니?
여 내가 이모에게 전화해서 추천하는 책의 목록을 물어볼게.
남 아주 좋을 것 같아. 이모에게 너무 많은 부담이 아니길 바라.

① 걱정 마. 그녀는 도서관에 가는 길을 찾을 수 있어.
② 이해해. 아기가 많은 책을 가지게 될 거야.
③ 잘됐어. 쇼핑몰에 가서 그녀에게 아기 옷을 사다 줄 거야.
⑤ 물론. 우리는 비상시에 대비해서 대기실에 있을 거야.

14 | 정답 | ②

결혼기념일을 위해 부모님의 사진이 들어 있는 비디오를 만들자고 남자가 제안했고, 이어서 부모님의 어린 시절 사진이 어디에 있는지 모르겠다는 남자의 말에 대한 여자의 응답으로는 ② '옛날 사진은 지하실에 있는 것 같아.'가 가장 적절하다.

- **anniversary** 기념일
- **meaningful** 의미 있는
- **scan** (스캐너로) 스캔하다
- **laptop** 노트북(휴대용) 컴퓨터
  [선택지]
- **basement** 지하실

M Hey, Rose. Mom and Dad's **20th anniversary is coming up**.
W I know. I think we should do something special for them.
M Do you have anything in mind?
W How about getting them musical tickets? They've never seen a musical before.
M Hmm... That's not a bad idea but **I'd rather do something more meaningful**.
W What do you mean?
M Well, how about making a video with pictures of Mom and Dad?
W That sounds fantastic. I will get and scan pictures from their photo album. Could you make the video?
M Sure. I'll make the video clip on my laptop. I'm going to add their favorite song to it, too.
W Oh, maybe we should put **pictures of them when they were little kids**.
M That sounds great. But I'm not sure where they are.
W I think older pictures are in the basement.

남 이봐, Rose. 곧 엄마와 아빠의 결혼 20주년이야.
여 맞아. 우리가 두 분께 특별한 걸 해 드려야 한다는 생각이 들어.
남 생각해 둔 거 있니?
여 뮤지컬 입장권을 사 드리면 어떨까? 두 분은 뮤지컬을 보신 적이 없잖아.
남 음… 그것도 나쁘지 않은 생각이지만 뭔가 더 의미 있는 것을 해 드리는 것이 나을 것 같아.
여 무슨 의미야?
남 음, 엄마와 아빠의 사진이 들어 있는 비디오를 만들어 드리면 어떨까?
여 아주 좋을 것 같은데. 내가 두 분의 앨범에서 사진을 찾아 스캔할게. 네가 비디오를 만들어줄래?
남 그럼. 내가 노트북 컴퓨터로 동영상을 만들게. 거기에다가 두 분이 가장 좋아하는 노래도 넣을 거야.
여 아, 두 분이 아주 어렸을 적 사진도 넣는 게 좋을 것 같아.
남 좋은 생각이야. 근데 그런 사진이 어디 있는지 잘 모르겠어.
여 옛날 사진은 지하실에 있는 것 같아.

① 아니. 음식점에 전화해서 물어볼게.
③ 안 될 것 같아. 우리는 사진을 못 찍게 되어 있어.
④ 절대 안 돼. 우리는 그 사진을 가지고 비디오를 만들 수 없어.
⑤ 미안해. 부모님의 기념일이 언제인지 모르겠어.

15 | 정답 | ③

원하는 진로와 가족들이 추천하는 진로 사이에서 갈등을 겪고 우울해하고 있는 Diana에게 아버지가 위로하면서 할 말은 ③ '네가 가장 편안한 마음으로 할 수 있는 것은 무슨 일이든 해야 한다.'이다.

- **career path** 진로
- **dress up** (옷을) 잘 차려입다
- **wear makeup** 화장하다

W Diana has to choose her career path now. She thinks she is not like any other girl. She hates dressing up and wearing makeup. She likes to play ice hockey and she wants to pursue being a hockey player as a career in the future. However, there is some conflict between what she wants and **what her family recommends she should do**. Her family tells her to choose figure skating instead if she wants to be an athlete. Although she's won first prize in national figure skating contests, **she still doesn't want to give up ice hockey**. After watching Diana get

여 Diana는 이제 자신의 진로를 결정해야 한다. 그녀는 자신이 다른 여자아이들과 같지 않다고 생각한다. 그녀는 옷을 잘 차려입는다든지 화장하는 것을 싫어한다. 그녀는 아이스하키를 하는 것을 좋아하고 장래 직업으로 아이스하키 선수가 되고 싶어 한다. 그러나 그녀가 원하는 것과 가족들이 그녀에게 하라고 권하는 것 사이에 갈등이 좀 있다. 그녀의 가족들은 운동선수가 되고자 한다면 피겨 스케이팅을 선택하라고 말한다. 그녀는 여러 번 전국 피겨 스케이팅 대회에서 1등상을 받았지만 아직 아이스하키를 포기하길 원치 않는다. Diana가 우울해하는 것을 본 후에 그녀의 아버지는 Diana에게 그녀의 결정을 이해하고 존중한다고 말

- pursue 추구하다
- conflict 갈등
- recommend 추천하다
- athlete 운동선수
- depressed 우울한, 의기소침한
[선택지]
- have in common with ~와 공통점이 있다
- counselor (학교의) 상담 교사

depressed, her father decides to tell her that **he understands and respects her decision**. In this situation, what would Diana's father most likely say to Diana?

Diana's father You should do whatever you feel comfortable doing.

하기로 결심한다. 이러한 상황에서 Diana의 아버지가 Diana에게 할 말로 가장 적절한 것은 무엇인가?

Diana의 아버지 네가 가장 편안한 마음으로 할 수 있는 것은 무슨 일이든 해야 한단다.

① 네가 그걸 다시 한번 생각해야 할 것 같구나.
② 가족들이 왜 걱정하는지 모르겠니?
④ 너는 다른 운동선수들과 공통점이 별로 없어.
⑤ 상담 교사를 만나서 네 결정을 바꿔 보는 것이 어떠니?

---

16 | 정답 | ①

미세 플라스틱이 해양 동물과 인간에게 해롭다고 이야기하면서 우리가 모르는 사이에 미세 플라스틱 조각을 먹게 되는 경우를 예시로 들고 있다. 그러므로 남자가 하는 말의 주제로 ① '미세 플라스틱의 잠재적인 해로운 영향'이 적절하다.

17 | 정답 | ④

미세 플라스틱을 먹게 되는 경로로 '채소'는 언급되지 않았으므로 정답은 ④이다.

- break down 부서지다
- harmful 해로운
- aquatic life 수생 생물
- threaten 위협하다
- millions of 수백만의
- marine 해양의
- bit 조각
- unknowingly 모르는 사이에
- be exposed to ~에 노출되다
- tap water 수돗물
- particle (아주 작은) 조각, 입자
- unwitting 자신도 모르는, 무의식적인
- consumer 소비자
- in one way or another 어떻게든
[선택지]
- potential 잠재적인
- endangered 멸종 위기에 처한
- alternative 대체의

M Hello, I am David Clarkson. Today, I'd like to talk about one of the world's major concerns, microplastics. **Microplastics are tiny pieces of plastic** which have broken down over time. They can be harmful to our oceans and aquatic life. They threaten the lives of millions of marine animals and fish. Marine animals and fish eat bits of plastic that float in the ocean. They are dangerous to us, human beings, in much the same way. When we enjoy our favorite seafood dish, we unknowingly eat microplastics. And that is not all. We are also **exposed to other harmful effects** of microplastics in our everyday lives. When we breathe, even when we breathe fresh air, microplastics come into our body and stay somewhere inside it. They can be hidden **in the tap or bottled water we drink**, or even in the tea bags we use. According to one study, we can swallow thousands of microplastic particles from a single cup of breakfast tea. We are almost certainly **an unwitting consumer of microplastics** in one way or another.

남 여러분, 안녕하세요. David Clarkson입니다. 오늘 저는 세계 주요 관심사 중의 하나인 미세 플라스틱에 대해서 이야기하고자 합니다. 미세 플라스틱은 시간이 지나면서 부서진 작은 플라스틱 조각입니다. 미세 플라스틱은 해양과 수생 생물에게 해로울 수 있습니다. 그것들은 수많은 해양 동물들과 물고기의 생명을 위협합니다. 해양 동물과 물고기는 바다에 떠다니는 플라스틱 조각들을 먹습니다. 이 플라스틱 조각은 우리 인간들에게도 마찬가지로 위험합니다. 우리가 좋아하는 해산물을 즐길 때, 우리도 모르는 사이에 미세 플라스틱을 먹고 있는 것입니다. 그리고 그게 전부가 아닙니다. 우리는 또한 일상생활 속에서 미세 플라스틱의 다른 해로운 영향들에 노출되어 있습니다. 우리가 호흡을 할 때, 심지어 신선한 공기를 마실 때조차도, 미세 플라스틱이 우리 몸에 들어와 몸속 어딘가에 남게 됩니다. 이 미세 플라스틱은 우리가 마시는 수돗물이나 병에 든 생수 속, 또는 우리가 사용하는 티백에도 숨어 있습니다. 한 연구에 따르면, 아침 차 단 한 잔으로도 우리는 많은 미세 플라스틱 조각을 삼킬 수 있습니다. 우리는 어떤 식으로든 자신도 모르게 미세 플라스틱을 거의 확실하게 먹고 있다는 것입니다.

16 ① 미세 플라스틱의 잠재적인 해로운 영향
② 멸종 위기 종이 해양생물에 끼치는 영향
③ 환경 오염의 원인에 관한 연구
④ 플라스틱 대체재 생산 아이디어
⑤ 미세 플라스틱의 특징과 제거 방법

17 ① 해산물 ② 신선한 공기 ③ 병에 든 생수
④ 채소 ⑤ 티백

06회 실전 듣기 모의고사

| 01 ④ | 02 ⑤ | 03 ② | 04 ⑤ | 05 ⑤ | 06 ② | 07 ② | 08 ② | 09 ⑤ | 10 ① |
| 11 ② | 12 ⑤ | 13 ⑤ | 14 ③ | 15 ② | 16 ⑤ | 17 ③ | | | |

본문 p.34

01 | 정답 | ④

남자는 회사가 새로운 프로젝트를 준비하느라 바쁜 와중에 가장 중요한 것은 보안임을 직원들에게 강조하고 있다. 따라서 남자가 하는 말의 목적으로 ④가 가장 적절하다.

- despite ~에도 불구하고
- launch 출시하다, 개시하다
- circumstance 상황
- security 보안
- cautious 조심하는
- leak 유출
- theft 도용, 도난
- back up (파일·프로그램 등을) 백업하다
- on a regular basis 정기적으로
- maintenance 유지, 보수 관리
- upgrade (컴퓨터 시스템 등을) 개선하다
- certain 특정한, 어떤
- notify 알리다

M Good evening. Thank you all for gathering here despite your busy schedules. Our company has just started a new project and we are launching a new product line next month. I know how hard you have been working and I appreciate your time and effort. In such circumstances, the most important thing for us to consider is security. So I ask all employees **to be more cautious about protecting** the company's data from any leaks or theft. You can change your passwords regularly, **lock up your computers** at night, and back up all of your data on a regular basis. Next month, the maintenance department will start to upgrade the security system, and all of you will be given **a key card to enter the building** and even to unlock certain doors. You will be notified with further information by e-mail this week. Thank you for your cooperation.

남 안녕하십니까. 바쁜 일정에도 불구하고 여기에 모두 모여 주셔서 감사합니다. 우리 회사는 새로운 프로젝트를 막 시작했고 다음 달에 새로운 제품이 출시됩니다. 여러분이 얼마나 열심히 일해 왔는지 알고 있고 여러분의 시간과 노력에 감사드립니다. 이러한 상황에서 고려해야 할 가장 중요한 것은 보안입니다. 따라서 모든 직원들에게 유출이나 도용으로부터 회사의 정보를 보호하는 일에 유의하시길 부탁드립니다. 비밀번호를 정기적으로 바꾸고 밤에는 컴퓨터를 잠그고 규칙적으로 여러분의 데이터를 백업해 놓으십시오. 다음 달에, 관리부서에서 보안 시스템을 개선하기 시작할 것이고 여러분 모두에게 건물을 출입하고 심지어는 특정 출입구도 열 수 있는 출입 카드를 드릴 것입니다. 이번 주에 추가 정보를 이메일로 안내해 드리겠습니다. 협조해 주셔서 감사합니다.

02 | 정답 | ⑤

여자는 학교 축제가 지나치게 노래와 춤 공연 중심인 점을 지적하며 다른 재능이 있는 학생들에게도 기회를 주어야 한다고 말하고 있다. 따라서 여자의 의견으로 가장 적절한 것은 ⑤이다.

- student council 학생회
- stick to ~을 고수하다

W Hello, Jake. How are you?
M I'm good, thanks, Lisa. How was your weekend?
W I spent the whole weekend thinking about **how we should design our school festival this year**.
M Yes. I talked about it with other members of the student council, too.
W What did they say? Do they think we should **stick to our traditional way**?
M Yes, they do. They think we should keep focusing on music and dance performances just like last year.
W Well, don't you think our festival is overly focused on music and dance?
M I agree. But isn't that what school festivals are all about?
W I don't think so. I want to give a chance to students who have talents **other than music or dancing**.
M You mean we should show different talents at our school festival?
W Exactly. I think we need a change in our school festival.

여 안녕, Jake. 잘 지냈어?
남 잘 지냈어, Lisa. 주말 잘 보냈어?
여 올해 학교 축제를 어떻게 짜야 할지 주말 내내 생각했어.
남 그래. 나도 학생회 다른 임원들과 그것에 대해 이야기해봤어.
여 애들이 뭐라고 했어? 전통적인 방식을 고수해야 한다고 생각한대?
남 응. 그렇대. 작년처럼 계속 음악과 춤 공연에 집중하는 게 좋을 것 같대.
여 음. 우리 축제가 음악과 춤에 지나치게 집중된 것 같다고 생각하지 않니?
남 그렇긴 해. 하지만 그게 학교 축제의 전부가 아닐까?
여 난 그렇게 생각하지 않아. 나는 음악과 춤 이외의 재능이 있는 학생들에게도 기회를 주고 싶어.
남 우리 학교 축제에 다양한 재능을 선보여야 한다는 말이니?
여 바로 그거야. 우리 학교 축제에 변화가 필요하다고 생각해.

03 | 정답 | ②

눈에 띄는 증상으로 나타나지 않는 질병을 예방하기 위해서는 정기적인 건강 검진을 받아야 한다고 조언하고 있으므로 남자가 하는 말의 요지로 가장 적절한 것은 ②이다.

- unnoticed 눈에 띄지 않는
- checkup 건강 진단
- screening (질병 등을 찾기 위한) 검사
- evaluation (의학상의) 평가, 사정
- detect 발견하다
- noticeable 눈에 띄는, 두드러진

M Hello, everyone! I'm Dr. Jude Kohl, the host of your *Five-minute Health Show*. **Many people avoid going to the doctor**, thinking that they are fine. However, there are many silent threats that can go unnoticed. That's why **regular health checkups are crucial for disease prevention**. During an annual physical exam, screenings can reveal hidden health issues. For example, these evaluations can detect high blood pressure or cholesterol levels **that might not display noticeable symptoms**. Now, let's take a look at some statistics about medical checkups in our country. Please focus on the chart.

남 안녕하세요. 여러분! 저는 "5분 건강 쇼"의 진행자인 Jude Kohl입니다. 많은 사람들이 자신은 괜찮다고 생각하여 병원에 가는 것을 피합니다. 그러나 눈에 띄지 않을 수 있는 조용한 위협들이 많이 있습니다. 그렇기 때문에 정기적인 건강 검진은 질병 예방에 매우 중요합니다. 연례 건강 검진에서 검사는 숨겨진 건강 문제를 드러낼 수 있습니다. 예를 들어, 이러한 (의학적) 평가는 눈에 띄는 증상을 드러내지 않을 수도 있는 고혈압이나 콜레스테롤 수치를 발견할 수 있습니다. 이제, 우리나라의 건강 검진에 대한 몇 가지 통계를 살펴봅시다. 도표에 집중해주세요.

04 | 정답 | ⑤

남자는 여자를 위해 아직 제대로 된 사무용 의자를 준비해 두지 못한 것에 대해 사과하고 있으며, 여자가 책상 앞에 바퀴가 없는 스툴(등받이가 없는 의자)이 있다고 말하고 있으므로 대화 내용과 일치하지 않는 부분은 ⑤이다.

- a chest of drawers (서랍이 여러 개 달린) 서랍장
- organize 정리하다
- document 서류, 문서
- department 부서
- apologize 사과하다
- stool (등받이가 없는) 의자

M Mia, I'm Jack, your new manager, and this is your desk.
W Wow, everything is already set up.
M There is **a chest of drawers at the left of your desk**, so you can put your stuff in them.
W Oh, three drawers are enough to organize my things.
M And on the drawers, **there is another chest of drawers** only for documents.
W Thanks. I see there is **a small plant on the shelf**.
M It's a welcoming gift from our department.
W Thank you. And is the laptop on the desk my office computer?
M Yes. That's your laptop. And I should apologize for **not having a proper office chair** for you.
W Oh, that's why there is a stool without wheels in front of the desk.
M Yes. we will have a nice chair ready for you tomorrow.

남 Mia, 저는 당신의 새로운 매니저인 Jack이고, 이쪽이 당신의 책상이에요.
여 와, 이미 모든 게 준비되어 있네요.
남 책상 왼쪽에 서랍장이 있어서 물건들을 안에 넣으시면 됩니다.
여 아, 세 칸의 서랍이면 물건을 정리하는 데 충분하죠.
남 그리고 서랍장 위에 서류만을 위한 별도의 서랍장이 있습니다.
여 감사합니다. 선반에 작은 식물이 보이네요.
남 우리 부서에서 드리는 환영 선물입니다.
여 감사합니다. 그리고 책상 위의 노트북 컴퓨터가 제 사무용 컴퓨터인가요?
남 네, 당신의 노트북 컴퓨터가 맞습니다. 그리고 당신을 위한 제대로 된 사무용 의자를 준비해 두지 못한 것을 사과드려야겠어요.
여 아, 그래서 책상 앞에 바퀴와 등받이가 없는 의자가 있는 거였군요.
남 네, 내일 멋진 의자를 준비해 두겠습니다.

05 | 정답 | ⑤

남자는 새로운 연습 일정을 제안하며 부원들에게 전화한다고 했고, 여자는 연습실이 주말에도 사용할 수 있는지 확인해 본다고 했으므로 정답은 ⑤이다.

- audience 관객
- give up 포기하다
- participate in ~에 참여하다
- session (특정) 시간
- schedule 일정을 잡다, 예정하다; 일정
- make it (모임 등에) 가다, 참석하다
- eager 열심인, 열렬한
- available 이용할 수 있는

W I'm worried about our performance next month.
M Me, too. I don't think we are ready to perform in front of an audience.
W It has been hard to get everyone together to practice at one time. But we still have a few more weeks to get ready.
M Yes, it's **too early to give up now**. So, what should we do first?
W We need to make sure that all the members participate in each practice session.
M Sure. **Why don't we practice one more day a week?**
W When? We were scheduled to practice every Tuesday and Thursday.
M Can we make it on Saturdays, too?
W **We'd better ask our members first.** They are eager to practice, but some of them may be busy on the weekend.
M You're right. I'll call each of them to make sure they are okay with the new schedule.
W Okay. I'll check **if our practice room is available on the weekend**.

여 다음 달에 있을 우리 공연이 걱정돼.
남 나도 그래. 난 우리가 관객 앞에서 공연할 준비가 되어 있지 않은 것 같아.
여 모두 모여서 동시에 연습하기 힘들었지. 하지만 아직 준비할 시간이 몇 주 더 남아 있잖아.
남 그래, 지금 포기하긴 너무 일러. 그럼 뭐부터 해야 할까?
여 모든 부원들이 각 연습 시간에 참석하도록 해야 해.
남 물론이야. 일주일에 하루 더 연습하는 건 어때?
여 언제? 매주 화요일과 목요일에 연습하기로 되어 있잖아.
남 토요일에도 참석할 수 있을까?
여 부원들에게 먼저 물어봐야 할 거야. 연습하고 싶어 하겠지만 몇 명은 주말에 바쁠지도 몰라.
남 네 말이 맞아. 내가 각자에게 전화해서 새로운 일정이 괜찮은지 확인할게.
여 좋아. 나는 우리 연습실이 주말에도 이용할 수 있는지 확인해 볼게.

06 | 정답 | ②

남자는 50달러인 성인용 티켓 2장과 40달러인 어린이용 티켓 2장을 구매했고, 전체 금액에서 50% 할인되는 신용카드로 결제했으므로 남자가 지불할 금액은 90달러이므로 정답은 ②이다.

- pass 이용권, 탑승권
- special offers 특별 행사
- depend on ~에 달려 있다
- discount rate 할인율

W Welcome to Wonderland Amusement Park. How may I help you?
M Hello, I would like to buy tickets for two adults and two children.
W Okay, how old are your children?
M They are 10 and 8.
W **Would you like a pass** for the whole day?
M Yes, please. How much are the tickets?
W For a day pass, one adult is $50, and one child under 13 is $40.
M Well, **do you have any special offers** on the price?
W Of course. It depends on what credit card you are paying with. I can check the discount rate for you.
M Okay, here you go. It's a Visa card.
W Just a moment, sir. *[Pause]* If you pay with this card, you will **get 50% off the total price**.
M That's great. I'll use that card.
W All right. *[Pause]* Here are your tickets. Have a great day.

여 Wonderland 놀이동산에 오신 것을 환영합니다. 무엇을 도와드릴까요?
남 안녕하세요. 성인 2명과 어린이 2명의 티켓을 구매하려고 합니다.
여 알겠습니다. 아이들이 몇 살인가요?
남 10살과 8살입니다.
여 하루 종일 이용할 수 있는 이용권을 원하십니까?
남 네, 맞아요. 티켓은 얼마인가요?
여 일일 이용권은 성인 한 명은 50달러, 13세 미만 어린이 한 명은 40달러입니다.
남 저, 금액과 관련해서 특별 행사가 있나요?
여 물론입니다. 어떤 신용카드로 결제하시는지에 따라 다릅니다. 고객님의 할인율을 확인해 드리겠습니다.
남 네, 여기 있습니다. Visa 카드입니다.
여 잠시만요, 고객님. *[잠시 후]* 이 카드로 결제하시면 전체 금액에서 50% 할인받으실 수 있습니다.
남 좋습니다. 그 카드로 결제할게요.
여 알겠습니다. *[잠시 후]* 여기 티켓 있습니다. 좋은 하루 보내십시오.

07 | 정답 | ②

여자는 집에 숙제를 두고 와서 버스를 놓쳤고 지하철역으로 가던 중 Jane과 Jane의 어머니를 만나 차를 얻어 탔다고 했으므로 정답은 ②이다.

- **as usual** 평상시처럼
- **pretty** 꽤, 상당히
- **pull over** (길가에) 차를 세우다
- **sleep in** 늦잠을 자다
- **ride** (차량·자전거 등을) 타고 가기

M Hi, Grace. How did you get to school so fast?

W Hey, Josh. I didn't expect to be so early, either.

M I thought something happened because **you weren't on the school bus as usual**.

W Oh, everything's fine. I left my homework at home, so I had to go back and get it.

M **That's why you missed the bus**. But that doesn't explain how you got here before me.

W Well, I got pretty lucky.

M Oh, did your parents drive you here?

W Well, not exactly. **My dad had already left home**, and my mom doesn't drive.

M Then why did you say you got lucky?

W When I was walking to the subway station, a car pulled over. It was Jane.

M You mean Jane from Spanish class, right?

W Right. She slept in and her mom was driving her to school. They **offered me a ride**, so that's why I got here fast.

남 안녕, Grace. 너 학교에 어떻게 이렇게 빨리 왔니?

여 안녕, Josh. 나도 이렇게 일찍 올지 몰랐어.

남 나는 네가 평상시처럼 버스에 타지 않아서 무슨 일이 있나 했어.

여 아, 아무 일 없어. 집에 숙제를 놓고 와서 다시 가서 가지고 와야 했거든.

남 그래서 네가 버스를 놓쳤구나. 그렇지만 그걸로는 네가 어떻게 나보다 먼저 왔는지 설명이 되지 않아.

여 음, 내가 운이 좋았어.

남 아, 부모님이 여기까지 태워다 주셨니?

여 아니, 그런 건 아니야. 아빠는 이미 집에 안 계셨고, 엄마는 운전을 안 하셔.

남 그럼, 운이 좋았다는 건 무슨 말이니?

여 내가 지하철역으로 걸어가고 있었는데, 차가 하나 와서 섰어. Jane이었던 거야.

남 스페인어반 Jane 말하는 거지, 맞아?

여 그래. Jane이 늦잠을 자서 엄마가 학교에 태워다 주고 있었던 거야. 나를 태워다 줘서 빨리 올 수 있었어.

08 | 정답 | ②

특별 강연회의 강연자, 장소, 날짜, 입장료에 대한 언급은 있었지만 주제에 대한 언급은 없었으므로 정답은 ②이다.

- **lecturer** 강연자, 강사
- **admission fee** 입장료

W Henry, would you like to go to a special lecture with me?

M A special lecture? That sounds interesting. Who is the lecturer?

W It's Jim Scout. He is a famous writer.

M Oh, isn't he the one who **got popular after being on a talk show** on TV?

W Exactly. That writer is coming to our town for the lecture.

M Cool. Where is the event going to be held?

W You know **the big bookstore by City Hall**? It's going to be on the 3rd floor of the bookstore.

M I see. When is it? I hope it's not this weekend because I have other plans.

W Oh, it's February 22nd, **which will be the last Saturday of the month**.

M Great. I'll add it to my schedule. By the way, is the lecture free?

W Yes. There is no admission fee, and I heard it was the writer's idea to **make it a free event**.

M That's very nice of him. I look forward to it.

여 Henry, 나랑 특별 강연회 갈래?

남 특별 강연회? 재밌겠는걸. 강연자가 누군데?

여 Jim Scout야. 유명한 작가셔.

남 아, TV 토크쇼에 나온 이후에 인기가 많아진 작가 아니니?

여 맞아. 그 작가가 강연회를 위해 우리 동네로 올 거야.

남 멋지다. 행사가 어디서 열리는데?

여 시청 옆에 큰 서점 알지? 그 서점 3층에서 있을 거야.

남 그렇구나. 행사는 언제야? 다른 일정이 있어서 이번 주말은 아니었으면 좋겠다.

여 아, 2월 22일, 이번 달 마지막 토요일이야.

남 잘됐다. 일정표에 추가해 놓을게. 그건 그렇고 강연회는 무료니?

여 응. 입장료가 없고, 무료 행사로 한 건 작가의 생각이래.

남 정말 좋은 분이다. 기대돼.

09 | 정답 | ⑤

다양한 후원금 덕분에 입장료가 정가의 50%라고 말하고 있으므로 입장료는 무료가 아니다. 따라서 정답은 ⑤이다.

- **executive director** 전무이사
- **exhibition** 전시회
- **feature** 특별히 포함하다, 특징으로 삼다
- **impressionist** 인상파
- **display** 전시하다
- **funding** 자금
- **charge** (요금 등을) 청구하다
- **extremely** 극히, 극도로
- **rare** 드문
- **miss out on** ~을 놓치다
- **upcoming** 다가오는

W Welcome, ladies and gentlemen. Thank you for visiting De Von Gallery. I am the executive director, Susanne Lee. I'd like to introduce a special exhibition which will be **held for a month starting from October 11th**. It is one of the most exciting events of the year, and we have prepared only the best for our visitors. We **will be featuring art pieces** by more than 30 impressionist artists, including Monet, Renoir, and Pissarro. The total number of art pieces we plan to display is over 300. And the good news is, due to the funding from various donations, the admission fee charged to customers **will be half the regular price**. As this is an extremely rare opportunity, please do not miss out on it. I hope to see every one of you at the upcoming exhibition. Thank you.

여 신사 숙녀 여러분, 환영합니다. De Von 갤러리를 방문해 주셔서 감사합니다. 저는 전무이사인 Susanne Lee입니다. 저는 10월 11일부터 시작해서 한 달 동안 열릴 특별 전시회를 소개해 드리고자 합니다. 이 전시회는 한 해의 가장 흥미진진한 행사 중 하나로 방문객을 위해 최고만을 준비했습니다. Monet, Renoir, Pissarro를 포함한 30명 이상의 인상파 화가의 작품을 선보일 예정입니다. 전시될 작품의 총개수는 300점이 넘습니다. 그리고 좋은 소식은 다양한 후원 자금 덕분에 고객들이 지불해야 할 입장가가 정가의 절반 가격이라는 것입니다. 이는 극히 드문 기회이므로 놓치지 마시길 바랍니다. 다가올 전시회에서 여러분 모두를 뵙기를 바랍니다. 감사합니다.

10 | 정답 | ①

여자는 승합차를 빌리려고 한다. 유아용 카시트를 추가했으며 자동문을 원하고 있다. 또 차량 보험으로 제3자 피해 보상만으로 충분하다고 말하고 있으므로 정답은 ①이다.

* vehicle 탈것
* automatic 자동의
* manual 수동의
* insurance 보험
* cover 보상하다; 보상
* third-party 제3자
* coverage 보상 (범위)

M Hello, ma'am. Are you here to rent a car?
W Yes. I need to rent a car for my family for three days.
M What kind of vehicle would you like to rent?
W **I was thinking about a van** since there will be six people.
M Okay. And, if you need a car seat, there are three models you can choose.
W I need one with a car seat.
M Certainly. Now, would you like a car that has automatic doors? You can choose between automatic and manual.
W **I'd like automatic ones.** I think they will be more convenient for people sitting in the back seat.
M Okay. Now you only have to choose what kind of car insurance you want to sign up for.
W What's the difference between fully covered and third-party coverage?
M Third-party coverage only covers **damage done by a third person** while fully covered also provides damage coverage and theft coverage.
W I think **third-party coverage will be enough for me**.
M All right. Now I will show you to the car. Please follow me.

남 안녕하세요. 차를 빌리러 오셨나요?
여 네. 우리 가족을 위해 3일 동안 차를 빌려야 해요.
남 어떤 차종을 빌리고 싶으세요?
여 6명이 탈 예정이라서 승합차를 생각 중이에요.
남 알겠습니다. 그리고 만약 유아용 카시트가 필요하시다면 고르실 수 있는 모델이 세 개가 있습니다.
여 유아용 카시트가 있는 것이 필요합니다.
남 물론이죠. 다음으로 자동문이 달린 차를 원하세요? 자동과 수동 중 하나를 선택할 수 있습니다.
여 자동으로 하겠습니다. 뒷좌석에 앉은 사람들에게 그게 더 편할 것 같아요.
남 네. 이제 어떤 자동차 보험에 가입하고 싶은지만 선택하시면 됩니다.
여 완전 보상과 제3자 보상의 차이점은 무엇인가요?
남 제3자 보상은 제3자에 의한 피해만 보상이 되는 반면 완전 보상은 거기에 추가로 피해 보상과 도난에 대한 보상을 제공합니다.
여 저는 제3자 보상이면 충분할 것 같습니다.
남 알겠습니다. 이제 차로 안내해 드리겠습니다. 저를 따라오세요.

---

11 | 정답 | ②

남자가 약 섭취 방법을 안내하고 있으므로 이에 대한 여자의 적절한 응답은 지시를 잘 따르겠다는 ② '네. 지시를 잘 따르겠습니다.'가 가장 적절하다.

* medication 약, 약물치료
* tablet 알약
* empty stomach 공복
[선택지]
* instruction 지시
* prescription 처방전

M Your medicine is ready. Have you taken this before?
W No. My doctor gave me a new medication because **the pain is just getting worse**.
M I see. Take two tablets two times a day. **Don't take it on an empty stomach**.
W Okay. I will follow the instructions carefully.

남 약이 준비되었습니다. 전에 이 약을 복용하신 적이 있나요?
여 아뇨. 통증이 계속 심해지고 있어서 의사가 새로운 약을 주었습니다.
남 그렇군요. 하루에 두 번 두 알씩 드십시오. 공복에 드시지 마시고요.
여 네. 지시를 잘 따르겠습니다.

① 아뇨, 약을 드실 필요 없습니다.
③ 제 의사에게 전화해서 처방전을 새로 받을게요.
④ 괜찮습니다. 마지막 약을 각각 봉투에 추가해 주세요.
⑤ 식후 30분에 약을 드세요.

---

12 | 정답 | ⑤

여자가 지내는 동안 조식을 포함하기 원하는지 묻고 있으므로 이에 대한 남자의 적절한 응답은 ⑤ '둘째 날에만 포함하고 싶습니다.'이다.

* include 포함하다

[Telephone rings.]
W Tahoma Hotel. How may I help you?
M Hello, **I'd like to make a reservation** for a business room for two nights.
W Okay, sir. **Would you like to include** breakfast during your stay?
M I'd like to include it for the second day only.

[전화벨이 울린다.]
여 Tahoma 호텔입니다. 무엇을 도와드릴까요?
남 안녕하세요. 비즈니스 룸을 2박 동안 예약하고 싶습니다.
여 알겠습니다. 머무시는 동안 조식을 포함하시겠습니까?
남 둘째 날에만 포함하고 싶습니다.

① 네. 저는 강가 옆 호텔에서 지내고 있습니다.
② 아뇨, 괜찮아요. 저는 그곳에서 1박만 지낼 겁니다.
③ 저는 보통 아침 식사로 시리얼을 먹습니다.
④ 바다가 보이는 방으로 주세요.

---

13 | 정답 | ⑤

같은 토론 동아리에 있다는 이유로 Chris를 학생회장으로 뽑겠다는 남자의 말에 대해 여자는 리더의 자질이 있는 사람을 뽑아야 한다고 말하고 있다. 이에 남자도 동의하며 더 고심해 보겠다고 말하고 있으므로 이에 대한 여자의 적절한 응답은 ⑤ '바로 그거야. 한 표가 큰 변화를 가져올 수 있잖아.'이다.

* vote for ~에 투표하다
* student council president 학생회장
* candidate 후보자
* debate 토론
* trustworthy 신뢰할 수 있는

M Clara, have you decided whom to vote for for the student council president?
W Not yet. There are three candidates, right?
M Yes. There are not many to choose from but it will be a little tough to pick one. Do you **know any of them personally**?
W Not really. What about you?
M I know the second candidate, Chris. I'm voting for him because **we are in the same debate club**.
W **You are not just voting for** Chris because he's your friend, are you?
M Well, I think he is kind and trustworthy. He gets fairly good grades in class, too.
W I think someone **who can solve important issues** should

남 Clara. 학생회장으로 누구를 뽑을지 결정했니?
여 아직. 세 명의 후보가 있지, 맞아?
남 응. 선택할 사람이 많지 않지만 한 명을 뽑는다는 게 좀 어려운 것 같아. 그중에 개인적으로 아는 사람 있니?
여 아니. 너는 어때?
남 두 번째 후보인 Chris를 알아. 같은 토론 동아리라서 그를 뽑을 거야.
여 너의 친구라는 이유만으로 그를 뽑는 건 아니지, 그렇지?
남 글쎄. 난 그가 친절하고 믿을 만하다고 생각해. 수업에서 꽤 좋은 성적을 받기도 하고.
여 난 중요한 문제들을 해결할 수 있는 사람이 선출되어야 한다고 생각해. 후보들이 어떤 일을 할 수 있고 누가 리더가 될 최고의 자질을 갖고 있는지를 보려고 해.

- **elect** 선출하다
- **be capable of** ~할 수 있다
- **quality** (사람의) 자질

be elected. I'm trying to see what those candidates are capable of and who has the best qualities to be a leader.

M You're right. I'll think carefully and decide whom to vote for.

W Exactly. You know one vote can make a big difference.

남 네 말이 맞아. 나도 누구를 뽑을지 신중하게 생각하고 결정할게.

여 바로 그거야. 한 표가 큰 변화를 가져올 수 있잖아.

① 응. 내년에 토론 동아리에 가입하고 싶어.
② 난 동의하지 않아. 너는 Chris를 뽑겠다는 생각을 고수해야지.
③ 아니. Chris는 선출되려면 완벽한 성적을 받아야 해.
④ 물론이지. 어떤 일이 있더라도 우린 Chris를 지지해야 해.

---

14 | 정답 | ③

앞마당에 무엇을 심을지 상의하던 중 채소를 심자는 남자의 말에 동의하며 여자가 아이들에게도 배울 기회가 될 것이라고 말하고 있으므로 이에 대한 남자의 응답으로 가장 적절한 것은 ③ '좋아요. 날씨가 좋아지면 씨를 좀 심읍시다.'이다.

- **yard** 마당
- **bloom** (꽃이) 피다
- **branch** 가지
- **sweep** 쓸다

W Honey, I still can't believe we are moving into that beautiful house next week.

M I know! I really like the front yard. That's the best part of the house.

W I think we should make it into our little garden.

M How about planting some flowers? The yard will look more beautiful when the flowers bloom.

W I'm not so sure about that. I was thinking about something that **could last longer than flowers**.

M Oh, okay. Then, how about trees?

W Trees are okay. But **growing trees takes a lot of work**. You have to cut off branches, sweep after all the leaves fall down, and there are other tasks to do, too. Do you really want to do all that?

M I don't think so. Hmm... If you want to start off with something easy, **how about growing some vegetables**?

W That's a great idea. I'm not an expert at farming, but I can always learn.

M I heard vegetables like lettuce and tomatoes are easy to grow.

W It could be a great experience for kids, too. They could **watch and learn how vegetables grow**.

M Great. Let's plant some seeds when the weather gets nice.

여 여보, 다음 주에 그 아름다운 집으로 이사를 간다니 아직도 믿기지 않아요.

남 맞아요! 저는 앞마당이 정말 마음에 들어요. 그 집의 가장 멋진 부분이죠.

여 내 생각엔 그곳을 우리의 작은 정원으로 만들어야 할 것 같아요.

남 꽃을 좀 심는 건 어때요? 꽃이 피면 마당이 더 아름다워 보일 거예요.

여 그 생각이 괜찮은지 잘 모르겠네요. 저는 꽃보다 더 오래 갈 수 있는 걸 생각하고 있었어요.

남 아, 그래요. 그러면 나무는 어때요?

여 나무도 괜찮죠. 하지만 나무를 키우는 데는 많은 일이 필요해요. 가지치기도 해야 하고 나뭇잎이 모두 떨어지면 그걸 쓸어야 하고 그 외에도 다른 해야 할 일들이 있죠. 그 모든 걸 정말 하고 싶어요?

남 아닌 것 같아요. 음… 무언가 쉬운 걸로 시작하고 싶다면 채소를 좀 키워보는 건 어때요?

여 정말 좋은 생각이에요. 농사에 전문가는 아니지만 항상 배우면 되니까요.

남 상추나 토마토 같은 채소는 키우기 쉽다고 들었어요.

여 아이들에게도 멋진 경험이 될 수 있을 거예요. 채소가 어떻게 자라는지 보고 배울 수 있으니까요.

남 좋아요. 날씨가 좋아지면 씨를 좀 심읍시다.

① 저는 잘 모르겠네요. 저는 토마토에 알레르기가 있어요.
② 딱히요. 데이지꽃보다는 장미를 심겠어요.
④ 미안해요. 우리 마당은 무언가를 심기에 충분히 크지 않아요.
⑤ 서둘러야겠어요. 시내 꽃시장은 곧 닫아요.

---

15 | 정답 | ②

Sarah는 할머니의 팔순 잔치 때 바이올린 연주를 하기로 했으나 현이 끊어지는 바람에 William이 근처 악기점에 태워다 주기로 한 상황이므로 정답은 ② '걱정하지 마. 내가 차로 거기에 데려다줄게.'이다.

- **bow** 활
- **string** (악기의) 현

W Sarah is at her grandmother's 80th birthday party. As many as 30 of her family members gather together to celebrate the special day. Sarah **is supposed to perform her grandmother's favorite** music piece with her violin. She's been practicing for weeks. Her cousin William comes and tells her to play it after the dinner, so that everyone at the party can enjoy the performance. Sarah thinks this will give her more time to practice, so she finds a quiet place to practice. As soon as she places her violin bow on one of the strings, **it suddenly breaks**. She opens her case to see if there is **an extra string for the violin**, but there aren't any left. So, she goes to William and tells him about the violin. Fortunately, William says that **there is a small music shop nearby**. Since there is still one hour left, he **decides to drive her to the shop**. In this situation, what would William most likely say to Sarah?

William Don't worry. I'll take you there by car.

여 Sarah는 할머니의 팔순 잔치에 와 있다. 특별한 날을 축하하기 위해 30명 가까이 되는 가족들이 모여 있다. Sarah는 할머니께서 가장 좋아하시는 음악 작품을 바이올린으로 연주하기로 되어 있다. 그녀는 몇 주간 연습을 해 왔다. 그녀의 사촌인 William이 다가와 잔치에 온 모든 사람들이 공연을 즐길 수 있도록 저녁 식사 이후에 연주해 달라고 말한다. Sarah는 연습할 시간이 더 생겼다고 생각해서 연습할 수 있는 조용한 장소를 찾아낸다. 그녀가 바이올린 현에 활을 갖다 대자마자 현이 끊어진다. 그녀가 상자를 열어 여분의 바이올린 현이 있는지 확인하지만 남은 것이 아무것도 없다. 그래서 William에게 가서 바이올린에 대해 말한다. 다행히 William은 근처에 작은 악기점이 있다고 말한다. 아직 한 시간이 남아 있던 터라 그는 그녀를 악기점에 태워다 주기로 결심한다. 이런 상황에서 William이 Sarah에게 할 말로 가장 적절한 것은 무엇인가?

William 걱정하지 마. 내가 차로 거기에 데려다줄게.

① 대신에 기타를 연주하는 게 어때?
③ 그곳에 데려다줘서 고마워. 네 덕분에 살았어.
④ 시간이 충분하지 않아. 다른 걸 해야 할 것 같아.
⑤ 그곳에 널 태워다주지 못할 것 같아. 아버지께 부탁드리는 게 어때?

---

16 | 정답 | ⑤

여러 나라의 다른 문화를 소개하며 문화적 차이점에 대해 설명하는 내용이다. 여러 나라의 문화적 관습에 대해 배워 보자고 하며 이에 대한 여러 예시에 대해 언급하는 것으로 보아 남자가 하는 말의 주제로 가장 적절한 것은 ⑤ '당신을 놀라게 할 문화적 차이'이다.

17 | 정답 | ③

여러 나라의 문화적 차이에 대한 예시를 설명하면서 '인도네시아'는 언급하지 않았으므로 정답은 ③이다.

- **sacred** 성스러운
- **signal** ~에게 신호하다
- **come over** 이리 오다
- **palm** 손바닥
- **face** 향하다, 마주 보다
- **brush** (솔이나 손으로) 쓸다, 털다
- **burp** 트림(하다)
- **politeness** 예의 바름
- **compliment** 칭찬하다

M Hello, students. Have you ever communicated with someone from another country? **Did any of their behavior surprise or shock you**? Today, we'll learn about the cultural practices of various countries, which will help you understand them more. First, in Thailand, the head is considered to be the most sacred part of the body. So you must be careful never to touch a Thai person on their head. **How do you signal someone to come over**? Is your palm facing up or down? In Vietnam it matters. When you call a person, you signal with your palm facing down, brushing your fingers towards you. In North America and Europe, **it is reversed with your palm facing up**. If you did that in Vietnam you would be in trouble because it means you are calling them over like a dog. Burping in most cultures is considered to be rude. However in Taiwan and China, **it is a sign of politeness at the dinner table**. When you burp loudly you are actually complimenting the chef.

남 안녕하세요, 여러분. 다른 나라의 사람들과 소통해 본 적이 있나요? 그들의 행동 중 여러분을 놀라게 하거나 경악하게 한 것이 있었나요? 오늘은 여러 나라의 문화적 관습에 대해 배워볼 텐데, 여러분이 그들에 대해 더 잘 이해할 수 있도록 도울 것입니다. 먼저, 태국에서는 머리가 신체에서 가장 성스러운 부분으로 여겨집니다. 그래서 여러분은 태국 사람의 머리를 만지지 않도록 조심해야 합니다. 여러분은 누군가를 오라고 할 때 어떻게 신호를 보내나요? 손바닥을 위로 또는 아래로 향하게 하나요? 베트남에서 그것은 중요합니다. 여러분이 누군가를 부를 때는, 손바닥을 아래로 향한 채로, 여러분 쪽으로 손가락을 쓸면서 신호를 합니다. 북미와 유럽에서는 반대로 손바닥을 위로 향한 채로 합니다. 만약 여러분이 베트남에서 그렇게 했다면, 그건 사람을 개처럼 부르는 의미이기 때문에 곤란을 겪게 될 것입니다. 대부분의 문화권에서 트림은 무례하다고 여겨집니다. 하지만 대만과 중국에서는 그것이 저녁 식사 자리에서 예의의 표시입니다. 여러분이 트림을 크게 하면 사실상 요리사를 칭찬하고 있는 것입니다.

16 ① 베트남에서의 전통 의상
② 신체의 각 부분이 의미하는 것
③ 중국에서의 가장 흥미로운 조리법
④ 아시아권 나라에서의 개의 상징성
⑤ 당신을 놀라게 할 문화적 차이

17 ① 태국 ② 베트남 ③ 인도네시아
④ 대만 ⑤ 중국

07회 실전 듣기 모의고사

01 ⑤	02 ⑤	03 ②	04 ⑤	05 ①		06 ④	07 ⑤	08 ②	09 ③	10 ⑤
11 ⑤	12 ⑤	13 ④	14 ⑤	15 ①		16 ①	17 ③			

본문 p.40

01 | 정답 | ⑤

남자는 기숙사 건물의 세탁실 수리가 지연되는 문제에 대해 학생들에게 양해를 구하고 있으므로 남자가 하는 말의 목적으로 가장 적절한 것은 ⑤이다.

- dormitory 기숙사
- supervisor 관리자, 감독관
- sewage 하수, 오수
- basement 지하실
- specialize in ~에 특화된
- patience 인내심

M Good evening, students. This is the dormitory supervisor speaking. For the past two weeks, there have been some issues with the building maintenance, and again **we apologize for any inconveniences** it may have caused you. Recently, a sewage problem has been reported in the laundry room in the basement. We have arranged for a company that specializes in such problems to repair it. Unfortunately, **it will take one more week** until the maintenance team from the company can start their work. Once they do, the problem will be fixed within only a couple of days. Therefore, I **ask for your patience and understanding about the delay** in the repairing of the laundry room. Thank you.

남 학생 여러분, 안녕하십니까. 기숙사 관리인입니다. 지난 2주 동안 건물 유지관리에 문제가 있었고, 다시 한번 여러분에게 끼쳤을 불편에 대해 사과드립니다. 최근 지하실에 있는 세탁실에서 하수 문제가 보고된바 있습니다. 그것을 고치기 위해 그러한 문제에 특화된 회사에 연락을 취해 두었습니다. 유감이지만 그 회사의 유지관리팀이 작업을 시작하기까지 일주일이 더 걸릴 겁니다. 그들이 작업을 시작하기만 하면 문제는 단지 이틀 정도면 고쳐질 겁니다. 따라서 세탁실 수리의 지연에 대하여 여러분의 인내와 양해를 구합니다. 감사합니다.

02 | 정답 | ⑤

남자는 안정적인 직업을 보장하는 전공이 중요하다고 생각하는 반면, 여자는 자신이 열정을 느끼는 분야를 전공으로 선택해야 한다고 말하고 있으므로 여자의 의견으로 가장 적절한 것은 ⑤이다.

- apply to (대학, 회사 등에) 지원하다
- major in ~을 전공하다
- outlook 전망
- make a living 생계를 유지하다
- passionate 열정적인
- guarantee 보장하다
- stable 안정된, 안정적인
- pursue 추구하다

W Hello, John. How have you been lately?
M I've been busy searching for universities I can apply to.
W Me, too. For me, **deciding what to major in** is the hardest thing to do.
M In my case, I consider my options based on the outlook of the major.
W You mean, if you can get a job after graduating?
M Exactly. In the long run, you should **be able to make a living for yourself**.
W Really? I think you **should study something you truly feel passionate about**.
M But what if the major you choose based on your interests does not guarantee a stable job?
W To me, pursuing what you love is **as important as having a stable job**.
M I see what you mean.
W I'm going to choose a literature major. I believe that there will be a way in the end if I study what I am passionate about.

여 안녕, John. 최근에 어떻게 지냈니?
남 내가 지원할 수 있는 대학을 찾느라 바빴어.
여 나도. 나한테는 무엇을 전공할지 결정하는 게 가장 어려워.
남 내 경우엔 그 전공의 전망에 근거해서 선택을 고려해.
여 그러니까 졸업한 후에 적당한 직업을 얻을 수 있는지 말이야?
남 그렇지. 장기적으로 봤을 때 스스로 생계를 유지할 수 있어야 하잖아.
여 정말? 나는 네가 정말로 열정을 느끼는 걸 공부해야 한다고 생각해.
남 하지만 관심사를 바탕으로 결정한 전공이 안정적인 직업을 보장하지 못하면 어떡해?
여 나한테는 좋아하는 일을 추구하는 것이 안정적인 직업을 갖는 일만큼이나 중요하거든.
남 네 입장은 이해가 되네.
여 나는 문학 전공을 선택할 거야. 내가 열정을 갖고 있는 것에 관해 공부하다 보면 결국 길이 생길 거라고 믿어.

03 | 정답 | ②

집이 없는 사람들을 위해 집을 지어주는 봉사를 하다 보면 그것에 재능이 있다는 것을 알 수 있는 것을 예로 들어 자원봉사가 봉사자 자신의 숨겨진 능력을 알아낼 수 있는 기회가 될 수 있다고 말하고 있다. 따라서 남자가 하는 말의 요지로 가장 적절한 것은 ②이다.

- unsure 확신이 없는, 의심스러워하는
- incredible 믿을 수 없을 정도의

M Good day, everyone! My name is Mr. Eliot, and I'm here to share benefits of volunteering **for those unsure about getting involved**. Volunteering is more than just lending a helping hand. Volunteering reveals hidden abilities, aiding self-discovery. For example, **if you help build homes for people who don't have one**, you might find out that you're good at building things, **which could lead to new opportunities for you**. There are many good things volunteering, and discovering your abilities is one of them. Now, let's explore some more reasons why volunteering is an incredible opportunity! Please listen carefully!

남 안녕하세요, 여러분! 저는 Eliot이라고 합니다. 참여하는 것에 대해 확신이 서지 않는 분들을 위해 자원봉사의 이점을 나누려고 이 자리에 왔습니다. 자원봉사는 단순히 도움의 손길을 제공하는 것 그 이상입니다. 자원봉사는 숨겨진 능력을 드러내며 자기 발견을 돕습니다. 예를 들어, 집이 없는 사람들을 위해 집을 짓는 것을 돕다 보면, 여러분은 자신이 무언가를 만드는 것에 능숙하다는 것을 알게 될 수 있고, 이것은 여러분에게 새로운 기회로 이어질 수 있습니다. 자원봉사에는 많은 좋은 점들이 있는데, 여러분의 능력을 발견하는 것도 그중 하나입니다. 자, 자원봉사가 왜 놀라운 기회인지 몇 가지 이유를 더 살펴봅시다! 잘 들어주세요!

04 | 정답 | ⑤

여자는 뮤직비디오를 보여줄 화면이 무대 오른편에 위치해 있다고 말하고 있

M Eve, I can't believe the band concert is tomorrow.
W I know. We have practiced so hard for this. Should we go over the stage setting for the last time?

남 Eve, 밴드 공연이 내일이라는 게 믿어지지 않아.
여 그러니까 말이야. 이걸 위해 너무나 열심히 연습했잖아. 마지막으로 무대 구성을 점검해 볼까?

으로 대화의 내용과 일치하지 않는 것은 ⑤이다.

* ceiling 천장
* thrilled 흥분한

M Great idea. The curtains are open on both sides.

W Yes, that's done properly. I think it gives the feeling that you're watching a show.

M I agree. And **I like the large sign in the center** that says "2023 Band Concert."

W Yes, it's just the way we asked for. It comes down from the ceiling. Oh, **why are the drums on the left**?

M Our drummer says he feels more confident when he plays there.

W I see. There is the microphone stand in the middle for you.

M Yes, I already feel thrilled and nervous at the same time. Oh, where is the screen for our music video?

W **It's next to the microphone**. I asked the stage team to place the screen on the right so that you don't block the screen.

남 좋은 생각이야. 커튼을 양쪽으로 모두 걷었네.

여 응, 그건 제대로 됐네. 공연을 보고 있다는 느낌을 주는 거 같아.

남 나도 동의해. 그리고 가운데 '2023 밴드 공연'이라고 쓰여 있는 큰 현수막 맘에 들어.

여 응, 우리가 부탁했던 그대로야. 천장에서 내려오는 방식이래. 어, 왜 드럼이 왼쪽에 있어?

남 드럼 연주자가 저기에서 연주할 때 더 자신감을 느낀다고 했거든.

여 그렇구나. 너를 위한 스탠딩 마이크가 가운데 있네.

남 응, 흥분되는 동시에 긴장되기도 한다. 아, 뮤직비디오를 보여줄 화면은 어딨지?

여 마이크 옆에 있잖아. 네가 화면을 가리지 않도록 무대 전담팀에게 화면을 오른쪽에 놔 달라고 했어.

---

05 | 정답 | ①

학교에서 안 좋은 일이 있었던 남자에게 여자는 쿠키를 만들어주기로 했으므로 정답은 ①이다.

* emotion 감정
* frustrating 짜증스러운
* selfish 이기적인

M Hi, Mom. I'm back from school.

W Oh, Kyle. You look a little upset.

M Well, I don't want to talk about it. Talking about it will make me feel worse.

W Okay, but sometimes letting your emotions out really helps.

M You know my friend Jim in music class? I am supposed to sing a duet with him for the music test.

W Is that what you're upset about?

M **He isn't practicing as much as I am**. I am worried that I will get a bad grade because of him.

W **That must be very frustrating**. Did you talk to him about it?

M I did, but he doesn't care. He said he was okay with failing the test. I don't understand how he could be so selfish!

W **How about if I talk to his mother**? We go to the same flower arrangement class.

M No, thanks. I think it's my own problem to solve.

W I understand. **What can I do to make you feel better**? How about some chocolate chip cookies? I can make them for you.

M Yes, please. I'll feel better if I have something sweet.

W Okay. I'll start soon.

남 엄마, 학교 다녀왔습니다.

여 어, Kyle. 기분이 조금 안 좋아 보이네.

남 글쎄요, 별로 얘기하고 싶지 않아요. 그 얘기를 하면 기분이 더 나빠질 것 같아요.

여 알았어. 하지만 어떨 땐 감정을 표출하는 게 정말 도움이 된단다.

남 음악 수업에 제 친구 Jim 아시죠? 음악 시험으로 Jim이랑 듀엣으로 노래해야 해요.

여 그게 네가 화가 난 이유니?

남 걔가 저만큼 열심히 연습하지 않아요. 걔 때문에 제가 안 좋은 점수를 받을까 봐 걱정돼요.

여 정말 짜증이 났겠구나. 그것에 대해 그 아이에게 말해 봤니?

남 말했는데 신경 쓰지 않아요. 걔는 나쁜 점수를 받아도 괜찮대요. 어떻게 그렇게 이기적일 수 있는지 이해가 안 가요!

여 내가 그 아이 엄마와 이야기해 볼까? 우리는 같은 꽃꽂이 수업에 다니거든.

남 괜찮아요. 제가 직접 해결해야 할 문제인 것 같아요.

여 알겠다. 네 기분이 나아지게 뭐라도 해줄까? 초콜릿 칩 쿠키는 어때? 만들어 줄 수 있어.

남 네, 부탁드려요. 뭔가 단 걸 먹으면 기분이 나아질 거예요.

여 좋아. 금방 만들기 시작할게.

---

06 | 정답 | ④

100달러짜리 좌석 네 자리를 예약했으며, 그중 두 자리는 경로 우대 할인을 20% 받을 수 있다고 하였으므로, 남자가 지불할 금액은 360달러($200 + $200 × 80%)이므로 정답은 ④이다.

* contemporary 현대의, 당대의
* orchestra (무대 앞의) 1등석; 오케스트라, 관현악단
* balcony (극장의) 2층 특별석; 발코니
* rate 등급을 매기다
* senior 노인, 고령자
* by any chance 혹시

[Telephone rings.]

W Hello, Contemporary Art Center. How may I help you?

M Hi, I'd like to reserve seats for "Notre Dame de Paris." Are there any seats left for this Friday?

W Let me check. We don't have any seats left in the orchestra, but **there are some seats available in the balcony**. It's $100 per seat.

M That's fine. **I'd like to get four seats**, please.

W Okay. The show is rated over 15. Are there any children under 15 in your group?

M No. I'm going with my wife and my parents.

W We offer a 20% discount for seniors. By any chance, are your parents over 65?

M Yes, they are.

[전화벨이 울린다.]

여 Contemporary Art Center입니다. 뭘 도와드릴까요?

남 안녕하세요, 'Notre Dame de Paris'의 좌석을 예약하고 싶습니다. 이번 금요일 좌석이 남아 있나요?

여 확인해 볼게요. 1등석에 남은 좌석은 없는데, 2층 특별석에는 좌석이 몇 개 있습니다. 좌석당 100달러입니다.

남 잘됐네요. 좌석 4개 예약할게요.

여 알겠습니다. 이 공연은 15세 이하 입장 불가입니다. 일행 중에 15세 이하 어린이가 있나요?

남 아니요. 저와 아내, 그리고 부모님과 갑니다.

여 저희가 경로 우대로 20% 할인을 해드립니다. 혹시 부모님 연세가 65세가 넘으셨나요?

남 네, 넘으셨어요.

	W **Just make sure they bring their IDs** when you come to pick up your tickets. May I have your name and phone number?	여 매표소에 표 찾으러 오실 때 부모님이 신분증을 꼭 가지고 오셔야 합니다. 성함하고 전화번호 말씀해 주시겠어요?
	M It's John Smith. My number is 905-476-9162.	남 John Smith입니다. 제 번호는 905-476-9162입니다.
	W All right, Mr. Smith. You will receive a text message shortly. Please click on the link in the message to pay.	여 알겠습니다. Smith 씨. 곧 문자 하나를 받게 되실 텐데요. 문자의 링크를 클릭하셔서 결제하시면 됩니다.
	M Okay, thanks.	남 알겠습니다. 감사합니다.

07 | 정답 | ⑤

여자는 더 마음에 드는 회사로부터 면접에 올 것을 제안받아서 원래 예정되어 있던 은행 면접에 가지 못했다고 말하고 있으므로 정답은 ⑤이다.

* publisher 출판사
* cover letter 자기소개서

M Cindy, I just got a call from a newspaper publisher yesterday, and they asked me to start working next week.
W I am so happy for you. You must be excited.
M I am. Oh, you said **you were going for an interview at a bank**, didn't you?
W Right, but I didn't go to that interview.
M Really? Oh, were you sick on the day of the interview?
W No, that's not it. I got **another call from a company I liked better**.
M And? What news did you hear from them?
W They liked my résumé and cover letter and asked me to come for an interview. But it was on the same day as the interview at the bank.
M I see. That's why **you chose that interview over the one at the bank**. How did it go?
W I think it went well. I sent a thank-you letter the day after, but haven't got any reply from them.
M Don't worry. You'll hear from them soon.

남 Cindy, 어제 신문사에서 전화를 받았는데 다음 주부터 일해 줬으면 좋겠대.
여 네가 잘돼서 너무 기뻐. 진짜 기분 좋겠다.
남 응. 정말 좋아. 아, 너 은행에 면접 보러 간다고 했잖아, 그렇지 않아?
여 맞아. 하지만 그 면접에 가지 못 했어.
남 정말? 아, 면접 당일에 몸이 안 좋았어?
여 아니. 그 이유는 아니야. 더 마음에 드는 다른 회사에서도 전화를 받았거든.
남 그래서? 무슨 소식을 들었는데?
여 내 이력서랑 자기소개서가 마음에 든다고 면접에 오라고 했어. 그런데 은행 면접과 같은 날에 있던 거야.
남 그랬구나. 그래서 은행 면접 대신에 그 면접을 선택했구나. 면접은 어땠어?
여 괜찮았던 것 같아. 다음 날 감사 편지를 보냈는데 아직 그쪽에서 답장을 받진 못 했어.
남 걱정 마. 그쪽으로부터 곧 연락을 받을 거야.

08 | 정답 | ②

남자는 한 달 동안 남동생과 남미 여행을 다녀왔고, 아르바이트를 통해 모은 모든 돈을 여행 경비로 썼다고 말하고 있으므로 대화에서 언급되지 않은 것은 ②이다.

* semester 학기
* get behind (일·공부 따위가) 뒤지다
* expense 경비, 비용

W Danny, long time no see. What have you been up to lately?
M Hey, Yuna. I just came back from a month-long trip.
W That's why I haven't seen you around on campus!
M Yes, **I took the whole semester off**. I think it was worth it, though I might get behind.
W That must have been a big decision. So, where did you go?
M I traveled around South America. I visited Peru, Colombia, Chile and Brazil.
W Your travel expenses must have been high. How much did it cost you?
M I had to spend everything **that I had saved from doing a part-time job**. But I think every single penny was well spent.
W If you learned some important lessons there, that's what matters, isn't it?
M That's right. And it felt even more special to me because **I traveled with my younger brother**.
W Why did you go with him?
M I wanted to spend more time with him before he goes off to high school abroad.
W I wish I had an older brother like you.

여 Danny, 오랜만이야. 최근에 뭐 하고 지냈니?
남 안녕, Yuna. 난 한 달짜리 여행에서 막 도착했어.
여 학교에서 못 본 이유가 그거였구나!
남 응, 한 학기 전체를 휴학했어. 좀 뒤처지겠지만 그럴 만한 가치가 있었다고 생각해.
여 큰 결정이었겠다. 그래서 어디 갔었어?
남 남미 여기저기를 여행했어. 페루, 콜롬비아, 칠레, 그리고 브라질에 갔었지.
여 여행 경비가 엄청 많이 들었겠다. 돈이 얼마나 들었니?
남 아르바이트하면서 모은 돈 모두를 써야 했지. 하지만 한 푼 한 푼 다 소중하게 쓰인 것 같아.
여 거기서 중요한 교훈을 얻었다면 그게 중요한 거지. 안 그래?
남 맞아. 그리고 내 남동생과 함께 여행해서 더 특별하게 느껴졌어.
여 남동생이랑 왜 같이 갔어?
남 걔가 해외로 고등학교에 가기 전에 같이 더 많은 시간을 좀 보내고 싶었거든.
여 나도 너 같은 오빠가 있었으면 좋겠다.

09 | 정답 | ③

청소년 도서를 쓴 작가가 강연할 예정이며 시간은 질의응답을 포함하여 90분이라고 하였다. 강연 주제는 시각을 넓히는 방법에 관한 것이며 강연을 신청

W Hello, students. This is your career counselor speaking. Since the beginning of the school year, numerous students have consulted with me about different issues. Listening to students' concerns, I thought it would be **a good idea to hold a special lecture**, which will give you new

여 학생 여러분, 안녕하세요. 진로 상담 선생님입니다. 학기가 시작하고부터 지금까지 수많은 학생들이 여러 가지 문제로 저와 상담을 했습니다. 학생들의 고민에 대해 들으면서 여러분에게 새로운 감명을 줄 특강을 진행하면 좋겠다는 생각을 했습니다. 특강 강연자는 Jonathan Perry이며, 그는 십 대 청소년들을 대상으로

하려면 진로상담실 앞에 있는 신청서를 작성해야 한다고 했다. 강연은 학교 식당 옆에 새로 지은 건물에서 진행한다고 하였으므로 일치하지 않는 것은 ③이다.

* numerous 수많은, 다수의
* stepping stone 발판, 디딤돌

inspiration. The speaker for the lecture is Jonathan Perry, who is the author of a number of books that are targeted at teenagers. The lecture will be about 90 minutes long, **including a question and answer session**. It will take place in the special lecture hall in the new building **next to the school cafeteria**. The topic of the lecture will be about how to broaden your perspectives. If you would like to sign up for the special lecture, you have to **fill out a registration form in front of** the career counseling office. I hope this special lecture can be a stepping stone for you to think deeply about your future. Thank you.

한 여러 도서의 작가입니다. 특강은 질의응답 시간을 포함하여 90분 정도 될 겁니다. 특강은 학교 식당 옆 새로 지은 건물의 특별 강의실에서 진행됩니다. 특강의 주제는 여러분의 시각을 넓히는 법에 대한 것입니다. 특강에 신청하고 싶다면 진로상담실 앞의 신청서를 작성하면 됩니다. 이 특강이 학생 여러분이 미래에 대해 깊게 생각해 보는 발판이 되기를 바랍니다. 감사합니다.

---

10 | 정답 | ⑤

여자는 야외용으로 용량이 크고 오랜 시간 지속되는 방수 기능이 있는 자외선 차단제를 선택했으므로 정답은 ⑤이다.

* a wide range of 광범위한, 다양한
* selection 선택
* protection 차단, 보호
* volume 용량
* last (기능이) 지속되다
* duration 지속 시간
* waterproof 방수 기능의
* dissolve 녹다, 용해되다

M Hello, ma'am. Are you looking for something?
W Yes. I want to buy sunscreen for myself.
M We have a wide range of selection, but these are the best-selling ones.
W There are so many. Could you recommend one that would best suit me? **I need it for outdoor activities**.
M Then that crosses this one out. Sunscreens for outdoor activities provide stronger protection. How about the volume?
W The more, the better. I will be using it a lot.
M Okay. Now, how long would you like it to last?
W Since I stay in the sun a lot, I think **one with a longer duration would fit me better**.
M All right. Now, we have two options left. Would you like one that is waterproof?
W I don't go in the water that often, but I sweat a lot when I do outdoor activities.
M The waterproof function prevents the sunscreen **from being dissolved by sweat or water**.
W Good. I will take that one.

남 안녕하세요. 어떤 걸 찾고 계신가요?
여 네. 저를 위한 자외선 차단제를 사고 싶어요.
남 선택의 폭이 굉장히 넓은데요, 이것들이 가장 잘 팔리는 제품입니다.
여 종류가 너무 많네요. 저에게 가장 잘 맞는 거로 추천해 주실 수 있나요? 야외 활동에 필요한 겁니다.
남 그러면 이 제품은 제외되겠네요. 야외용 자외선 차단제는 더 강한 차단력을 제공합니다. 용량은 어떤 걸 원하십니까?
여 많을수록 좋죠. 저는 많이 사용할 것 같아요.
남 네. 그러면 얼마 동안 지속되는 것을 원하시나요?
여 제가 햇볕 아래 많이 있기 때문에 지속 시간이 더 긴 제품이 저에게 더 적합하겠네요.
남 네, 알겠습니다. 이제 두 종류가 남았네요. 방수 기능이 있는 것을 원하세요?
여 물속에 자주 들어가지는 않지만 야외 활동을 할 때 땀을 많이 흘려요.
남 방수 기능은 땀이나 물로 인해 자외선 차단제가 녹아내리지 않도록 해 줍니다.
여 잘됐네요. 그 제품으로 할게요.

---

11 | 정답 | ⑤

여자가 학교 오케스트라에서 독주도 할 것인지 물어보는 말에 대한 남자의 응답으로 가장 적절한 것은 ⑤ '응. 모차르트의 곡을 연주할 거야.'이다.

* head 가다, 향하다
* upcoming 곧 있을, 다가오는
[선택지]
* auditorium 강당, 대강의실
* piece 작품, 한 편의 악곡[글, 각본]

W Chris, **where are you heading**?
M I am going to my orchestra practice for our upcoming school concert.
W That's right, you play the flute in the school orchestra. **Are you going to do a solo as well**?
M Yes, I will. I'm going to perform a piece by Mozart.

여 Chris, 어디 가니?
남 곧 있을 학교 콘서트를 위한 오케스트라 연습에 가고 있어.
여 아, 맞다. 너 학교 오케스트라에서 플루트 연주하지. 독주도 할 예정이니?
남 응. 모차르트의 곡을 연주할 거야.

① 다음 주 수요일 저녁 7시에 열릴 거야.
② 이제 플루트를 연주한 지 5년이 됐어.
③ 콘서트는 학교 강당에서 열릴 거야.
④ 물론이지. 너와 함께 클래식 공연에 가고 싶어.

---

12 | 정답 | ⑤

다른 버스로 갈아타기 전에 첫 번째 버스에서 몇 정류장을 가야 하는지 묻는 남자의 말에 대한 여자의 응답으로 가장 적절한 것은 ⑤ '정류장 다섯 개를 지난 다음 거기서 다른 버스로 환승하시면 됩니다.'이다.

* stop 정류장, 정거장; 멈추다
[선택지]
* transfer 환승하다; 이동하다; 전학 가다

M Excuse me, which bus should I **take to get to the train station**?
W You have to take bus number 511 first and then get on another bus.
M Then, **how many stops should I pass** before I get off?
W You should pass five stops and then transfer to another bus from there.

남 실례합니다만, 기차역에 가려면 어떤 버스를 타야 하나요?
여 먼저 511번 버스를 탄 다음 다른 버스로 환승하셔야 합니다.
남 그럼 내리기 전에 몇 개의 정류장을 지나야 하나요?
여 정류장 다섯 개를 지난 다음 거기서 다른 버스로 환승하시면 됩니다.

① 기차역까지 버스로 20분 걸립니다.
② 신호등이 빨간불이 될 때까지 멈추지 말아 주십시오.
③ 당신은 조금 전에 기차역을 이미 지나쳤습니다.
④ 죄송하지만, 전 방문객이라 이곳의 버스 체계를 몰라요.

13 | 정답 | ④

학업과 일을 같이 하는 것은 너무 힘들고 심지어 성적도 떨어졌다는 여자의 말에, 아르바이트를 고려하던 남자의 응답으로 가장 적절한 것은 ④ '나도 다시 생각해 봐야겠다. 조언해 줘서 고마워.'이다.

* consider 고려하다
* hold 견디다
* constantly 계속해서, 끊임없이
* rushed 조급한
* contract 계약서
  [선택지]
* reconsider 다시 생각하다; 재고하다

M Hey, Amy. Did you have a bad day at work?
W It was okay, but **going to school and doing a part-time job** at the same time is not easy.
M Really? I was actually considering getting a part-time job.
W Well, I don't recommend it. **It uses up too much energy.**
M Hmm... I thought you were holding in there quite well. You seemed okay at school, too.
W Yes, but to tell you the truth, **my grades have dropped a little bit** after I started working part-time.
M Are you sure that was caused by the part-time job?
W Yes, because I don't have enough time to study these days. I also **constantly feel stressed and rushed**, so I can't focus properly.
M That's not good. Then why don't you quit?
W My contract says I should work until the end of this month, so I'm waiting for that.
M Maybe I should reconsider it, too. Thanks for the advice.

남 이봐, Amy. 직장에서 안 좋은 일 있었니?
여 그냥저냥 괜찮았어. 하지만 학교에 다니면서 동시에 아르바이트를 하는 건 쉽지 않아.
남 정말? 나는 사실 아르바이트를 구할지 생각하던 중이었어.
여 음, 난 추천하지 않아. 너무 많은 에너지를 소모하거든.
남 음… 난 네가 꽤 잘 버티고 있다고 생각했는데. 학교에서도 괜찮아 보였거든.
여 그래. 하지만 솔직히 말하면 아르바이트를 시작하고 나서 성적이 좀 떨어졌어.
남 아르바이트 때문이라고 확신하니?
여 응. 요즘 공부할 시간이 충분하지 않거든. 계속해서 스트레스를 받고 조급하기도 해서, 제대로 집중할 수 없어.
남 그건 좋지 않지. 그러면 그만두는 게 어때?
여 내 계약서에는 이번 달 말까지 일해야 한다고 쓰여 있어서 기다리고 있어.
남 나도 다시 생각해 봐야겠다. 조언해 줘서 고마워.

① 힘내. 모든 사람들이 그런 특권을 누리지는 못하잖아.
② 유감이다. 곧 새로운 직장을 찾길 바랄게.
③ 그렇구나. 그러면 거기서 계속 아르바이트를 해야겠다.
⑤ 정말 좋은 소식이다. 너의 성공을 축하해.

---

14 | 정답 | ⑤

영화가 시작하기 전 남은 시간 동안 오락실에 가자고 제안하는 남자의 말에 가장 적절한 여자의 응답은 ⑤ '알겠어요. 그럼 티켓을 출력하고 게임에 필요한 잔돈을 좀 바꿔 올게요.'이다.

* ticket office 매표소
* meanwhile 그동안에
* escalator 에스컬레이터
* arcade 오락실
* for fun 재미로
  [선택지]
* flavored 맛이 나는, 양념한

M Honey, look at the lines at the ticket office.
W I know. Today is the last day of the holiday. I'm guessing that's why.
M **Should we wait until the lines get shorter?**
W No, we don't have to. Do you see the ticket machines over there? We can use one of them to print the tickets we reserved.
M Great, and there are few people using them. It's only going to take a few seconds.
W So, I will go and print the tickets. Meanwhile, **can you get something to eat?**
M Sure, I'll buy some popcorn and drinks. Is there anything else you need?
W No, thanks. After that, I'll meet you by the escalators.
M Are we just going to **wait in the waiting area** until the movie starts? There is more than half an hour left.
W Then, what do you suggest we do?
M Well, I was thinking about going to the arcade. There are **some games we can play together**, just for fun.
W All right. Then I'll print the tickets and get some change for the games.

남 여보, 매표소에 줄 좀 보세요.
여 그러니까요. 오늘이 휴일 마지막 날이잖아요. 그래서 그런가 봐요.
남 줄이 더 짧아질 때까지 기다려야 할까요?
여 아니요, 그럴 필요 없어요. 저쪽에 티켓 발권기 보이죠? 우리가 예매한 티켓을 출력하기 위해 저 기계 중 하나를 이용할 수 있어요.
남 잘됐네요. 그리고 이용하는 사람도 거의 없어요. 시간이 얼마 안 걸리겠어요.
여 그러면 내가 가서 티켓을 뽑을게요. 그동안 먹을 걸 좀 사 올래요?
남 물론이죠. 팝콘과 음료수를 좀 살게요. 다른 것 필요한 게 있나요?
여 괜찮아요. 그리고 나서 에스컬레이터 옆에서 만나요.
남 영화 시작하기 전에 대기 장소에서 기다리기만 할 건가요? 영화 시작하기 전까지 30분 넘게 남아서요.
여 그러면 뭘 했으면 좋겠어요?
남 글쎄요, 난 오락실에 갈까 생각했죠. 거기 가면 같이 할 수 있는 게임이 좀 있거든요. 그냥 재미로요.
여 알겠어요. 그럼 티켓을 출력하고 게임에 필요한 잔돈을 좀 바꿔 올게요.

① 미안하지만, 나는 양념한 팝콘을 좋아하지 않아요.
② 이번에는 내가 낼게요. 내가 계산할 거예요.
③ 표는 다 팔렸어요. 그냥 집으로 가는 게 좋겠어요.
④ 그렇지 않아요. 영화가 시작되기까지 몇 분 안 남았어요.

---

15 | 정답 | ①

Jill이 중요한 수학 수업 자료를 빌릴 친구를 찾던 중 자신에게 도움받은 적이 있는 Timmy를 떠올리게 된다. 이러한 상황에서 Jill이 Timmy에게 할 말로 가장 적절한 것은 ① '내가 네 수학 수업 자료를 좀 복사해도 될까?'이다.

* catch up on 따라잡다, 따라가다
* organized 정돈된, 정리된
* handout (수업 시간에 나눠주는) 수업 자료, 인쇄물

W Jill is a new student at Emerson High School. She transferred just three weeks before the final exams, so she has a lot to catch up on. One day, Timmy, one of her classmates, says that Jill's notes look very organized. He asks her if he can borrow Jill's notebook, so Jill lends it to him. When Timmy returns the notebook, he says thanks to Jill and says **that she can ask him for help anytime**. A few days later, Jill discovers that she doesn't have a couple of handouts from math class. **Those handouts had been given out** before she transferred to this school. She wishes **she could copy the handouts**, but she's not sure whom to ask. Then, she remembers Timmy telling her to ask him for anything she needs. In

여 Jill은 Emerson 고등학교에 새로 온 학생이다. 그녀는 기말고사 3주 전에 전학을 와서 따라잡을 것이 많다. 하루는 같은 반 친구인 Timmy가 Jill의 필기가 아주 잘 정돈되어 있다고 말한다. 그가 Jill의 노트를 빌려도 되는지 묻자, Jill은 그에게 노트를 빌려준다. Timmy는 노트를 돌려주면서 Jill에게 고맙다고 말하며 언제든지 도움이 필요하면 말하라고 한다. 며칠 후, Jill은 수학 수업 자료가 몇 장이 없다는 것을 알게 된다. 그 수업 자료는 그녀가 이 학교로 전학 오기 전에 나누어 준 것이었다. 그녀는 수업 자료를 빌려서 복사하고 싶지만 누구에게 부탁해야 할지 확신이 서지 않는다. 그러다 Timmy가 필요한 것이 있으면 무엇이든 말하라고 했던 것을 떠올린다. 이러한 상황에서 Jill이 Timmy에게 할 말로 가장 적절한 것은 무엇인가?

Jill Can I make a copy of your math handouts?

Jill 내가 네 수학 수업 자료를 좀 복사해도 될까?

② 이 수학 문제 푸는 것 좀 도와줄래?
③ 방과 후에 같이 공부할래?
④ 언제 내 공책을 돌려줄 계획이니?
⑤ 너한테 공책 빌려준 것을 아무한테도 말하지 말아 줘.

16 | 정답 | ①

가족에게 알맞은 반려견을 고르는 방법을 소개하는 내용이다. 견종의 기질, 크기, 그리고 에너지 수준을 고려하여 가장 적절한 반려견을 고르는 것이 중요하다는 내용이므로 정답은 ① '당신의 가족에게 딱 맞는 견종 찾기'이다.

17 | 정답 | ③

여러 견종의 기질과 크기, 에너지 수준에 대해 설명한 내용 중에서 '그레이하운드'에 대한 언급은 없었으므로 정답은 ③이다.

* aspect 측면
* obedient 순종적인
* experienced 경험 있는, 숙련된
* breed 품종
  [선택지]
* psychological 심리의, 정신의

M Hello, everyone. If you are looking for a pet dog for your family, you can get useful tips from today's lesson. There are three important aspects to consider. The first thing to consider is the dog's personality. For example, poodles have very gentle and obedient personalities, and **they get along well with kids**. Secondly, you must choose a suitable size of dog. For example, even if border collies are friendly and smart, they wouldn't suit a family that has never had a dog as a pet before. Larger dogs require special attention and are **more suitable for an experienced owner**. I would recommend a breed of a smaller size, such as a pug, to new owners. The last important thing to think about is the energy level. Let's say you would like a beagle as your pet. But if you can't deal with **the high energy level that the beagle has**, your relationship with your pet will be very bad.

남 안녕하세요, 여러분. 여러분의 가족에게 딱 맞는 반려견을 찾고 있다면 오늘 수업에서 유용한 팁을 얻을 수 있습니다. 고려할 것으로 세 가지 중요한 측면이 있습니다. 첫 번째 고려 사항은 개의 기질입니다. 예를 들어, 푸들은 아주 부드럽고 순종적인 성격을 갖고 있고 아이들과 잘 지냅니다. 두 번째로 적합한 개의 크기를 골라야 합니다. 예를 들어, 보더 콜리가 친근하고 똑똑하긴 하지만 지금까지 개를 반려동물로 키워 본 적이 없는 가족에게는 맞지 않습니다. 대형견은 특별한 주의를 요하며 경험 있는 주인에게 더 맞습니다. 저는 처음으로 반려견을 키운다면 퍼그와 같이 좀 더 작은 견종을 추천하겠습니다. 마지막으로 중요하게 생각해야 할 부분은 에너지 수준입니다. 여러분이 비글을 반려동물로 키우고 싶다고 해 봅시다. 하지만 비글이 가진 높은 에너지 수준을 감당할 수 없다면 반려동물과의 관계는 매우 나빠질 것입니다.

16 ① 당신의 가족에게 딱 맞는 견종 찾기
② 훈련가들이 가장 선호하는 견종
③ 반려동물로서 독특한 동물의 높아지는 인기
④ 정신 건강에 반려동물이 주는 이점
⑤ 야생견과 반려견의 차이

17 ① 푸들 ② 보더 콜리 ③ 그레이하운드
④ 퍼그 ⑤ 비글

본문 **p.46**

01 | 정답 | ⑤

도서관에서 나오는 안내 방송의 내용이다. 건물을 개조하기 위해서 며칠간 문을 닫을 것이라는 내용으로 보아 여자가 하는 말의 목적으로 가장 적절한 것은 ⑤이다.

- temporary 일시적인
- closure 폐쇄
- renovate 개조하다, 새롭게 하다
- installation 설치
- due date 반납 기한, 만기일
- drop (도서) 반납함
- proceed to ~으로 나아가다
- related to ~와 관련된

W Thank you for visiting Hansei Public Library. I have an announcement to make **about the temporary closure of our library**. Since our library has received funding to renovate the building, we have decided to put in new carpeting. **Because there will be a lot of noise**, we have no choice but to close the library during the installation. So we will be closed from Monday, November 7th through Friday, November 18th. Any due dates that fall during this time will be extended to Monday, November 21st. We prefer that you return items before or after these closed days. However, if you need to use the outside book return drops, we understand. **We will still empty the drops daily**. Proceed to the Lending Services Desk on Level 4 for issues related to the remodeling. We thank you for your support and understanding.

여 Hansei 공공 도서관을 방문해 주셔서 감사합니다. 도서관의 일시적인 폐쇄에 대해 안내 말씀드립니다. 저희 도서관은 건물을 개조하기 위한 자금 지원을 받아서 새 카펫을 깔기로 결정했습니다. 소음이 심할 것이기 때문에 설치 중에 도서관을 닫을 수밖에 없습니다. 그래서 저희는 11월 7일 월요일부터 11월 18일 금요일까지 문을 닫을 예정입니다. 이 기간에 해당하는 반납 기한은 11월 21일 월요일까지 연장됩니다. 폐쇄 기간 전이나 후에 빌려 간 책을 반납해 주시길 바랍니다. 그러나 밖에 있는 반납함을 이용하셔도 괜찮습니다. 저희는 매일 함을 비울 것입니다. 리모델링과 관련된 문제가 있으시면 4층에 있는 대출 서비스 데스크로 가시기 바랍니다. 여러분의 성원과 이해에 감사드립니다.

02 | 정답 | ⑤

레스토랑을 새로 개업한 남자가 위생 장갑과 마스크를 보여주며 위생은 선택이 아니라 필수라고 말하는 내용으로 보아 남자의 의견으로 가장 적절한 것은 ⑤이다.

- show around 둘러보다
- put away 치우다
- sanitary 위생의
- requirement 필요조건
- ignorant 모르는
- pest control agent 해충 방제 관리인

W Wow. Your restaurant looks great. I'm so happy for you.
M Thanks. I'm so excited to finally have my own restaurant. Come this way. I'll show you around.
W All right. The kitchen is so big.
M The kitchen is the most important part of the restaurant. **I wanted a big kitchen to make it easy to clean**.
W What are those boxes?
M Oh, I forgot to put them away. Those are the boxes of sanitary gloves and masks.
W You are really well prepared.
M I will have **my kitchen staff wear the gloves and masks** all the time. Sanitation is not a choice. It is a requirement.
W I agree with you. Some restaurants are ignorant about **keeping the kitchen clean**.
M I know. Just to make sure, I have a pest control agent coming tomorrow.
W It sounds like your restaurant will be extremely clean!

여 와, 네 레스토랑 멋지다. 네가 잘돼서 너무 기뻐.
남 고마워. 드디어 내 식당을 갖게 돼서 너무 좋아. 이쪽으로 와. 내가 구경시켜 줄게.
여 알았어. 주방이 엄청 크다.
남 주방이 레스토랑의 가장 중요한 부분이거든. 난 청소하기 쉽도록 큰 주방을 원했어.
여 저 상자들은 뭐야?
남 아, 치우는 걸 깜빡했어. 저건 위생 장갑과 마스크 상자야.
여 정말로 잘 준비했구나.
남 주방 직원들에게 장갑과 마스크를 항상 착용하도록 할 거야. 위생은 선택이 아냐. 그것은 반드시 필요한 것이거든.
여 네 말이 맞아. 일부 레스토랑은 주방을 깨끗하게 유지하는 데 무지해.
남 그래. 확실히 하기 위해서, 내일 해충 방제 관리인이 올 거야.
여 네 레스토랑은 엄청 깨끗하겠는걸!

03 | 정답 | ⑤

그림과 도표 같은 시각 자료를 수업에 사용하는 것이 학생들이 정보를 더 잘 이해하고 기억하도록 돕는다고 말하고 있으므로 여자가 하는 말의 요지로 가장 적절한 것은 ⑤이다.

- expert 전문가
- aid 보조물, 보조기구; 도움
- insight 통찰력
- diagram 도표, 도식

W Good morning, instructors. My name is Marcella Meadow, and I am an education expert. A teacher expressed her concerns about students **not being able to understand complex concepts presented to them**. Utilizing visual aids is crucial. A recent study on teaching methods might provide some insight. The study found that **using pictures and diagrams in lessons helps students understand** and remember information better. Therefore, when teaching your students, **it's necessary to use effective visual tools**. In the next session, I will explain how our brains receive information.

여 안녕하세요, 강사 여러분. 저는 교육 전문가이고 Marcella Meadow라고 합니다. 한 선생님이 학생들이 그들에게 제시된 모든 정보를 이해하지 못하는 것에 대해 우려를 표명했습니다. 시각적 보조물을 사용하는 것은 매우 중요합니다. 교육 방법에 대한 최근의 연구는 약간의 통찰력을 제공할 수 있습니다. 그 연구는 그림과 도표를 수업에 사용하는 것이 학생들이 정보를 더 잘 이해하고 기억하도록 돕는다는 것을 발견했습니다. 따라서 학생들을 가르칠 때, 효과적인 시각적인 도구를 사용하는 것이 필요합니다. 다음 시간에는 우리의 뇌가 정보를 받아들이는 방식에 대해 설명하겠습니다.

04 | 정답 | ④

책상 옆에 있는 공들은 안에 바람이 빠져 있다고 하였으므로 일치하지 않는 것은 ④이다.

W Mr. Green, is everything ready for the afternoon games?
M Yes, I've set up the schoolyard. Would you like to see it?
W Sure, I want to make sure everything is ready to go before lunchtime is over. Why is **the rope in the middle of**

여 Green 선생님, 오후 게임 준비는 다 되었나요?
남 네, 운동장은 준비가 다 되었어요. 한번 보실래요?
여 물론이죠. 점심시간이 끝나기 전에 모든 것이 준비되었는지 확인하고 싶어요. 밧줄이 왜 운동장 한가운데

* set up 설치하다
* schoolyard 운동장
* tug-of-war 줄다리기
* bucket 양동이
* baton (계주용) 배턴
* relay 계주, 릴레이 경주
* rubber 고무의
* flat 바람이 빠진
* inflate (공기나 가스로) 부풀리다
* podium 지휘대, 연단, 단

the schoolyard?

M It's for the tug-of-war game. It's the first game scheduled right after lunch.

W I see. Make sure the rope is put away after the game. What's in the bucket over there?

M **You mean the one next to the desk**? There are five batons for the relay.

W Okay. Are those **presents on the desk for the winners**?

M Yes, they are. There are more in the teachers' room.

W All right. Why are those two rubber balls **next to the presents still flat**?

M We're going to inflate them before the game starts because it's windy.

W I hope the rest of the games go well in the afternoon. *[Pause]* It's almost time to start.

M I'll make an announcement with the microphone on the podium.

에 있는 거죠?

남 줄다리기 경기용이에요. 점심 식사 직후에 예정된 첫 경기입니다.

여 그렇군요. 경기 후 밧줄은 반드시 치워야 해요. 저기 양동이에는 뭐가 있죠?

남 책상 옆에 있는 것 말씀이죠? 계주용 배턴이 5개 있습니다.

여 좋습니다. 책상 위에 있는 선물들은 우승한 학생들을 위한 것이죠?

남 맞습니다. 교무실에 더 있습니다.

여 좋아요. 선물 옆에 있는 고무공 두 개는 왜 아직 바람이 빠져 있는 거죠?

남 지금은 바람이 불어서 경기 시작 전에 부풀리려고 합니다.

여 오후에도 남은 경기들이 잘 진행될 수 있기를 바랍니다. *[잠시 후]* 시작할 시간이 거의 되었네요.

남 단상 위에 있는 마이크로 알리겠습니다.

---

05 | 정답 | ⑤

남자가 여름방학 때 프랑스로 여행 갈 계획이라고 설명하면서 여자에게 프랑스어 공부를 도와줄 수 있는지 물어보는 상황이므로 남자가 여자에게 부탁한 일로 가장 적절한 것은 ⑤이다.

* summer break 여름방학
* Time flies. 시간이 빠르다.
* practice 연습하다
* not A until B B하고 나서야 비로소 A하다
* anyway 어쨌든

M Wow, there is only one month left until summer break.

W I know. Time flies, right? Do you have any plans for this summer?

M Yes. I'm going to visit France for two weeks.

W I wish I could go to France! **I'd love to see the Eiffel Tower**.

M You should go, too. Since you speak French, it would be **the perfect chance to practice the language**.

W Well, this summer I don't have any plans to travel. I have to get a part-time job to save up some money.

M Oh, I was going to **ask you to help me with my French**. Do you think you can find time for me?

W Of course I can. I won't start looking for a job until the summer break anyway.

M That sounds great. When should we start?

W If you want, we can start next week. **I have to get some books first**.

M Fantastic! Thank you so much.

남 와, 한 달만 있으면 여름방학이네.

여 그러네. 시간 빨리 간다. 그렇지? 이번 여름방학 계획 있어?

남 응. 2주 동안 프랑스를 다녀오려고.

여 나도 프랑스 가고 싶다! 에펠탑을 보고 싶거든.

남 너도 가봐야 해. 프랑스어를 하니까 그 언어를 연습할 수 있는 완벽한 기회가 될 텐데.

여 그런데, 이번 여름엔 여행 계획은 없어. 돈을 모으기 위해 아르바이트를 해야 하거든.

남 아, 너한테 프랑스어 도움을 부탁하려고 했는데. 나를 위해 시간을 낼 수 있겠니?

여 물론이지. 어쨌거나 여름방학을 하고 나서야 일자리를 찾기 시작할 거야.

남 잘됐다. 언제 시작할까?

여 원한다면 다음 주에 시작하자. 나도 먼저 책을 구해야 하니까.

남 아주 좋아! 정말 고마워.

---

06 | 정답 | ④

Rose 세트는 하나에 30달러인데, 3개를 사면 하나를 50% 할인해 준다고 하였으므로 Rose 세트 3개의 가격은 75달러이다. 음료수는 라지 사이즈는 5달러, 레귤러 사이즈는 3달러이므로 라지 9개, 레귤러 1개의 금액은 48달러이다. 그러므로 여자가 지불할 총금액은 123달러로 정답은 ④이다.

* come with ~이 딸려 있다
* exclude 제외하다
* soda fountain 음료수 공급기

M Welcome to Five-Nine Pizza. How may I help you?

W Hi. I'd like to order pizza and chicken for ten people. What would you recommend?

M I recommend the Rose set. The set includes a sweet potato pizza and a fried chicken.

W How much is it?

M It's $30 a set. But if you order two Rose sets, **you can get 50% off a third one**.

W That sounds like a good deal. I'll take three then.

M Would you like something to drink?

W Oh, doesn't the set come with a drink?

M Sorry, **drinks are excluded from special deals**.

W I see. How much is a drink?

M A regular size is $3 and a large one is $5. There is a soda fountain machine over there next to the door. Refills are free.

W Then I'll get **9 large ones and a regular one**, please.

M Let me check your order. 3 Rose sets, 9 large drinks, and one regular drink. Is that correct?

W Yes, it is. Here is my credit card.

남 Five-Nine 피자입니다. 뭘 도와드릴까요?

여 안녕하세요. 피자하고 치킨을 10인분 주문하고 싶은데요. 어떤 것을 추천해 주시겠어요?

남 Rose 세트를 추천합니다. 그 세트는 고구마피자와 프라이드치킨이 들어 있어요.

여 얼마예요?

남 한 세트에 30달러입니다. 하지만 만약 Rose 세트 두 개를 시키면, 세 번째는 50% 할인해 드리죠.

여 좋은 것 같군요. 그럼 세 개 주문할게요.

남 마실 것을 원하시나요?

여 아, 세트 메뉴에는 음료수가 없나요?

남 죄송하지만, 모든 음료는 특가 상품에서는 제외됩니다.

여 그렇군요. 음료수 하나에 얼마예요?

남 레귤러 사이즈는 3달러, 라지 사이즈는 5달러입니다. 문 옆에 음료수 기계가 있습니다. 리필은 무료예요.

여 라지 사이즈로 9개, 레귤러 사이즈는 1개 주세요.

남 주문 확인할게요. 로즈 세트 3개, 라지 사이즈 음료 9개, 레귤러 음료 1개. 맞으시죠?

여 네, 맞습니다. 여기 제 신용 카드입니다.

07 | 정답 | ③

남자가 치과에 가는 것을 주저하는 이유는 드릴 소리가 너무 무섭기 때문이라고 하였으므로 정답은 ③이다.

- get one's teeth cleaned 스케일링을 하다
- regularly 규칙적으로
- hesitant 주저하는, 망설이는
- treatment 치료
- cover (보험으로) 보장하다

W I have some extra movie tickets for today. Do you want to come?

M Sorry, I wish I could. I have a dentist's appointment this afternoon.

W Really? Do you have a toothache?

M No, I'm just going to **get my teeth cleaned**. It's been a long time since the last time I had them cleaned.

W People say that we should visit a dentist regularly, but it's really hard to do.

M I know. **I get hesitant to go because I get so scared** when I hear the drill sound.

W Same here. I will never get used to that sound. Do you have dental insurance?

M I do. Some dental **treatments can be quite expensive**.

W That's true. My mom used to be scared to see a dentist because she was worried about the cost. But luckily it's covered by her insurance now.

M I'm glad she doesn't have to worry any more.

여 나 오늘 여분의 영화표가 몇 장 있는데. 같이 갈래?
남 미안. 갔으면 좋겠는데. 오늘 오후에 치과 예약이 있어.
여 정말? 이가 아프니?
남 아니, 그냥 스케일링하려고. 스케일링한 지 오래돼서 말이야.
여 사람들은 정기적으로 치과에 가야 한다고 하지만 그렇게 하기가 정말 힘들어.
남 맞아. 드릴 소리를 들으면 너무 무서워서 가기가 망설여져.
여 나도 그래. 난 그 소리가 절대 익숙해지지 않을 거야. 너 치과 보험 있니?
남 있어. 일부 치과 치료는 꽤 비싸잖아.
여 맞아. 우리 엄마는 치과 비용이 걱정돼서 치과에 가는 걸 무서워하셨어. 하지만 다행히도 지금은 보험이 처리해 주지.
남 어머니가 더 이상 걱정하지 않아도 되니 다행이다.

08 | 정답 | ⑤

2013년부터는 2만 명으로 참여 인원을 제한하고 대부분의 사람은 근처 Valencia에서 숙박한다고 하였다. 축제에 사용되는 토마토는 약 15만 개라고 하였으며 1945년 이후로 매년 8월 마지막 수요일에 축제가 열린다고 하였지만, 참가 비용에 대한 언급은 없었으므로 정답은 ⑤이다.

- gather 모이다
- accommodation 숙박 시설
- over-ripe 아주 많이 익은
- equal to ~와 동등한
- last 마지막의; 지속하다

W Peter, have you ever heard about the La Tomatina Festival?

M No, I haven't. What's that?

W It is one of the world's biggest food fight festivals. It's held in a small town in Spain.

M **How many people usually gather for the festival**?

W Since 2013, official ticketing has been in place, limiting the number of participants to just 20,000 people.

M **Are there enough accommodations for people** who go to La Tomatina?

W No, there aren't. Many people take the easier option of staying in nearby Valencia, which is 38 kilometers away.

M That's amazing. I can't imagine the amount of tomatoes used during the event.

W I know. The report says usually about 40,000 kilograms of over-ripe tomatoes are thrown in the streets. **That's equal to about 150,000 tomatoes**.

M Wow, that's a lot! When is the festival held?

W **It's been held on the last Wednesday** of August every year since 1945. The food fighting event only lasts an hour, but there are many other festivities to enjoy.

여 Peter, La Tomatina 축제에 대해 들어 본 적 있니?
남 아니. 그게 뭔데?
여 세계에서 가장 큰 음식 싸움 축제 중의 하나야. 그 행사는 스페인에 있는 한 작은 마을에서 열리지.
남 그 축제에 보통 몇 명이나 모이는데?
여 2013년 이래로 공식적인 입장권 발매를 실시해서 2만 명으로 참가 인원을 제한하고 있어.
남 La Tomatina 축제에 오는 사람들을 위한 숙박 시설은 충분하니?
여 아니, 그렇지 않아. 많은 사람들이 근처 Valencia에서 머무는 더 쉬운 방법을 선택하는데, 그곳은 38킬로미터 떨어져 있어.
남 놀랍다. 축제 기간 동안 사용되는 토마토 양은 얼마나 될지 상상이 안 가.
여 그래. 기사에 따르면 보통 약 4만 킬로그램의 아주 많이 익은 토마토가 거리에 뿌려진대. 토마토 약 15만 개와 맞먹는 양이지.
남 와. 엄청난 양이네. 축제는 언제 열리는데?
여 1945년부터 매년 8월의 마지막 수요일에 열려. 이 음식 싸움 행사는 한 시간 정도만 진행되지만, 즐길 수 있는 다른 많은 축제 행사들이 있어.

09 | 정답 | ④

컴퓨터 관련 용품을 임대하는 회사를 소개하는 내용이다. 주문한 지 몇 시간 안으로 제품을 받을 수 있고, 계약 후에도 추가 사용 기간에 대한 비용만 발생하며, 웹사이트가 현재 보수 중이라서 전화로만 상담이 가능하다고 하였다. 따라서 일치하지 않는 것은 ④이다.

- specialize in ~을 전문으로 하다
- appreciate 이해하다, 인지하다
- agreement 협약(서), 동의; 계약
- standard 수준, 기준
- short-term 단기간의
- under construction 수리 중, 공사 중
- reach 연락하다
- consult 상담; 상담하다

M Allow us to introduce to you our company, Techrest Computers Limited. Techrest Computers Limited **specializes in the rental of desktop computers**, laptops, printers and related equipment for short periods. Our rental system is so advanced that we can have equipment ready for you or delivered to you within hours of your order. We appreciate that sometimes things just **need to be done in a hurry**. That's why we make it so simple for you to rent from us. If you decide you want to keep the equipment for longer than your agreement, you will only **be charged for the extra days** that you keep it, with no other fees. We promise to provide quality services with the highest standards of technical support. Have you got a short-term rental need now? **Currently our website is under construction**. You'll be able to reach us by

남 저희 Techrest Computers Limited에 대해 소개합니다. Techrest Computers Limited는 데스크톱 컴퓨터, 노트북, 프린터 및 관련 장비를 단기간 대여해 주는 것을 전문으로 합니다. 저희 임대 시스템은 아주 발달되어 있어서 주문하신 후 몇 시간 안에 장비를 준비하거나 고객님께 배달해 드릴 수 있습니다. 저희는 가끔은 서둘러 일들이 처리되어야 하는 것도 이해합니다. 그런 이유로 해서 임대하는 것을 간단하게 만들었죠. 만약 고객님이 계약 기간보다 더 오래 장비를 쓰고 싶으면 고객님이 장비를 보관하고 있는 추가 기간에 대한 비용만 지불하면 되며 다른 수수료는 없습니다. 최고 수준의 기술 지원을 통해 고품질의 서비스를 제공할 것을 약속합니다. 지금 단기간 임대가 필요한가요? 현재 저희 웹사이트는 수리 중입니다. 전화로만 문의가 가능합니다. 오늘 070-885-4213으로 전화하셔서 상담하시기 바랍니다.

10 | 정답 | ⑤

4톤 트럭이 작기 때문에 그보다 큰 트럭이어야 하며, 사다리가 필요하다고 하였다. 물건을 포장할 상자가 부족하고 처음 이사 가기 때문에 포장 서비스를 이용할 것이며, 가격은 좀 더 비싼 것으로 하자고 하였으므로 정답은 ⑤이다.

* moving 이사용의; 이사
* review 평가, 평론
* pack 짐을 싸다; (수송 목적으로 물건을) 포장하다
* professional 전문가
* depend on ~에 달려 있다
* mover 이삿짐 운송업자

W We need to decide which moving service we'll use.
M I was looking at this moving company on the Internet. It has great reviews from their clients.
W Really? Then let's take a look at moving packages they offer.
M Sure. Here is the list of packages. *[Pause]* Do you think a 4-ton truck is enough for us?
W No, I don't think so. We have so many things to pack.
M All right. We need another truck with a ladder, too, right?
W Definitely. Do we have enough boxes to pack our things in?
M No, we don't. So we should use a packing service.
W You're right. Since it's our first time moving, it'd be better to get some help from professionals.
M Exactly. Besides, it comes with insurance. Finally, we have two options left.
W How come there is a price difference?
M Let me check. *[Pause]* Oh, it says the price depends on the number of movers.
W Let's spend a little more, then. With more movers, we can finish faster.
M I agree. Then let's go with this one.

여 우리는 어떤 이사 서비스를 이용할지 결정해야 해.
남 내가 인터넷에서 이 이사업체를 보고 있었어. 여기는 고객들로부터 좋은 평가를 받았거든.
여 정말? 그럼 제공하고 있는 이삿짐 패키지를 살펴보자.
남 좋아. 여기 패키지 리스트가 있어. *[잠시 후]* 4톤 트럭이면 충분할 것 같아?
여 아니, 모자랄 것 같아. 싸야 할 짐이 너무 많아.
남 알겠어. 사다리 달린 다른 트럭도 필요해. 그렇지?
여 물론이야. 물건을 포장할 상자가 충분히 있나?
남 아니, 없어. 그래서 포장 서비스를 이용해야만 해.
여 맞아. 첫 이사니까 전문가들의 도움을 받는 것이 나을 거야.
남 맞아. 게다가 보험도 들어 있어. 마지막으로 두 개의 선택 사항만 남았네.
여 왜 가격 차이가 있는 거지?
남 확인해 볼게. *[잠시 후]* 아, 가격이 이삿짐을 나르는 사람들의 수에 따라 다르다고 되어 있네.
여 그럼 좀 더 돈을 쓰자. 이삿짐을 나르는 사람이 많으면, 더 빨리 끝낼 수 있잖아.
남 나도 같은 생각이야. 그럼 이것으로 하자.

11 | 정답 | ⑤

근처에 지하철역이 있는지 물어보는 여자의 말에 가장 적절한 남자의 응답은 ⑤ '없습니다. 하지만 역까지 가는 버스는 많습니다.'이다.

* complex 단지
* utilities 공공요금 《전기세, 수도세》
[선택지]
* contract 계약(서)
* access 접근

W This apartment complex is not so bad. How much is the rent?
M It's $1,100, including all utilities except gas. This is a good deal in this neighborhood.
W That's pretty good. Is there a subway station nearby?
M I'm afraid not. But there are lots of buses to the station.

여 이 아파트 단지는 나쁘지 않네요. 집세는 얼마인가요?
남 가스비를 제외한 모든 공공요금을 포함해서 1,100달러예요. 이 동네에서는 좋은 가격입니다.
여 꽤 괜찮은데요. 근처에 지하철역이 있나요?
남 없습니다. 하지만 역까지 가는 버스는 많습니다.

① 알겠습니다. 여기 계약서에 서명해 주세요.
② 사양하겠습니다. 여기서 거기로 걸어갈 수 있을 것 같아요.
③ 물론이죠. 지하철역까지 더 쉽게 갈 수 있어요.
④ 그럼요. 집주인에게 그 얘기를 하세요.

12 | 정답 | ⑤

급하게 서두르는 여자에게 남자가 콘서트장까지 데려다주겠다고 말하는 상황이다. 남자의 제안에 여자의 응답으로 가장 적절한 것은 ⑤ '괜찮아요. 먼저 먹을 것을 사려고요.'이다.

* plenty of 많은
* downstairs 아래층에서

M Are you running late? I thought you had a lot of time until the concert.
W I do have plenty of time. But my friends are already downstairs waiting for me.
M Already? I can give you guys a ride if you want.
W It's all right. We are going to get something to eat first.

남 너 늦었니? 콘서트까지 시간이 많은 줄 알았는데.
여 시간은 충분해요. 하지만 아래층에서 친구들이 이미 저를 기다리고 있어요.
남 벌써? 원한다면 너희들 태워다 줄 수 있어.
여 괜찮아요. 먼저 먹을 것을 사려고요.

① 좋아요. 당신을 주차장에서 태울게요.
② 괜찮아요. 전 그냥 집에서 TV나 볼래요.
③ 당연하죠. 전철 타는 것은 아주 편리할 거예요.
④ 네, 그래 주세요. 친구들이 곧 여기로 올 거예요.

13 | 정답 | ④

전자책과 종이책에 관해 대화를 나누고 있는 상황이다. 남자는 책을 많이 읽기 때문에 자신에게는 전자책이 훨씬 낫다고 말하고 있으며, 여자는 그에 비해 자주 읽지 않기 때문에 자신에게는 종이책이 더 경제적이라고 말하였다. 따라서 이에 대한 남자의 응답으로 가장 적절

W Wow, did you get a new iPad? Can I see it?
M Sure. I'm so glad that I finally got it.
W I know how much you've wanted to get one. So, what are you planning to do with it?
M Well, mainly I want to read books with it.
W Oh, e-books, right? I thought you'd prefer print books since you already have a big book collection.

여 우와, 너 새 아이패드를 산 거야? 좀 봐도 돼?
남 그래. 드디어 갖게 되어 정말 기뻐.
여 네가 얼마나 갖고 싶어 했는지 알지. 그래서 그걸로 뭘 할 거야?
남 글쎄. 난 주로 그걸로 책을 읽고 싶어.
여 아. 전자책 말하는 거야? 난 네가 이미 책을 잔뜩 모았으니까 인쇄된 책을 좋아할 거라고 생각했는데.

한 것은 ④ '맞아. 나도 책을 덜 읽는다면 너처럼 똑같이 했을 거야.'이다.

* prefer 선호하다
* eye strain 눈의 피로
* electronic device 전자 기기
* store 저장하다
* economical 경제적인

M I still do. I like the feel of a book. I can hold it, turn the pages, and feel the paper.
W That's why most readers **can't give up print books**. Also, they don't cause the eye strain that comes with an electronic device.
M Exactly. But since I can't carry multiple books with me, the iPad is very convenient.
W I see what you mean. In one device, **you can store as many books as you'd like**.
M Yes. Besides, e-books are also cheaper in the long run.
W That's true. But for me printed books are more economical since I don't read much.
M You're right. I would do the same as you if I read less.

여 여전히 좋아해. 난 책의 느낌을 좋아하거든. 그것을 들고, 페이지를 넘기고 그리고 종이 촉감을 느낄 수 있지.
여 그런 이유로 대부분의 독서가들이 인쇄된 책을 포기 못하는 거야. 또한 전자 기기가 주는 눈의 피로도 없잖아.
남 맞아. 하지만 내가 많은 책을 들고 다닐 수는 없으니까, 아이패드가 아주 편리해.
여 무슨 말인지 알겠다. 하나의 장치에 네가 원하는 많은 책을 저장할 수 있잖아.
남 맞아. 전자책이 장기적으로는 더 저렴하기도 하고.
여 사실이야. 하지만 내 경우엔 책을 많이 읽지 않아서 인쇄된 책이 더 경제적이야.
남 맞아. 나도 책을 덜 읽는다면 너처럼 똑같이 했을 거야.

① 물론이지. 난 그 주제에 관해 독서 감상문을 쓸 거야.
② 좋아. 넌 아이패드 고르는 데 신중을 기해야 해.
③ 좋은 생각이야. 난 그것을 어떻게 하는지 친구에게 물어볼 거야.
⑤ 걱정하지 마. 난 오늘까지 그것을 다 읽을 수 있어.

14 | 정답 | ②

여자는 남자가 기부한 물건들을 확인하면서 보호소에서 받지 않는 물건들에 대해 설명하는 상황이다. 더 확인하지 않아도 된다는 남자의 말에 대한 여자의 응답으로 가장 적절한 것은 ② '좋아요. 그걸 기부 구역에 가져가 주시겠습니까?'이다.

* donation 기부
* hazardous 위험한
* liquid 액체의
* cleaner 세제
* toilet paper 화장지
* shelter 피난처, 보호소, 쉼터
* go through ~을 살펴보다, 통과하다

W You've brought so many things here. Thank you so much for your donations.
M No problem. I'm glad to be a part of a good cause. Where do you want them?
W First, I need to check the things you have here. **There are some things we can't take**.
M Oh, okay. What are they?
W **We do not accept any hazardous materials**, like liquid cleaners and paints. Did you bring anything like that?
M I don't think so. I have toilet paper, toothpaste, blankets, and some used clothes.
W That sounds perfect. Those things are what our shelter really needs.
M Great. Is there anything else?
W I need you to go through the things again and make sure **you really want to donate them**. Some people ask for their things back.
M I went through my stuff many times before I came here. I don't think **I need to go through the box again**.
W All right. Can you take it to the donation area?

여 물건들을 많이 가져오셨네요. 기부해 주셔서 정말 감사합니다.
남 고맙군요. 좋은 일에 참여하게 되어 기쁩니다. 어디다 둘까요?
여 우선 가져온 물건을 확인해야 합니다. 저희가 받지 않는 물건들이 있거든요.
남 아, 알겠습니다. 그것들이 뭔데요?
여 우리는 액체 세제와 페인트와 같은 위험한 물질은 받지 않습니다. 그런 물건들을 가져왔나요?
남 그런 것 같지 않은데요. 전 화장지, 치약, 담요 그리고 헌 옷 몇 벌을 가져왔어요.
여 좋아요. 그것들은 저희 보호소에 정말 필요한 것들입니다.
남 잘됐네요. 그 밖의 다른 것이 있나요?
여 다시 한번 물건들을 살펴보시고 그것들을 정말 기부할 것인가를 확인하시기 바랍니다. 어떤 사람들은 자기 물건들을 돌려달라고 해요.
남 여기 오기 전에 여러 번 살펴보았어요. 다시 상자를 살펴볼 필요가 없을 것 같아요.
여 좋아요. 그걸 기부 구역에 가져가 주시겠습니까?

① 알겠습니다. 당신의 충고를 따르는 게 좋을 것 같습니다.
③ 정말요? 싫으시면 그것들을 가져가세요.
④ 진심이에요? 저희는 어떤 위험한 물건도 받지 않습니다.
⑤ 알겠습니다. 확인 후 구매 여부를 결정하겠습니다.

15 | 정답 | ②

여행을 가서 쉬고 싶어 하는 Peter에게 Janet이 둘이서 즐길 수 있는 스포츠를 제안하는 상황이다. 모든 사람이 즐기면서 할 수 있는 수상 요가의 이점에 관해 설명하는 내용이 들어가야 자연스럽다. 따라서 Janet이 Peter에게 할 말로 가장 적절한 것은 ② '수상 요가는 활동적이면서 편히 쉴 수 있게 할 거예요.'이다.

* celebrate 축하하다
* anniversary 기념일
* tropical climate 열대성 기후
* accommodate 수용하다
* try out 시도하다
* benefit 이점, 혜택

W Peter and Janet have been married for five years. To celebrate their upcoming anniversary, they have decided to take a trip. They both agree on going to a country with a tropical climate since they love summer. Since Janet is really active, she wants to do activities such as snorkeling and surfing. However, Peter **would rather relax on the beach** because he's not good at water sports. Janet thinks that **since it's their first time traveling abroad**, they should do something together that they both can enjoy. So she looks for what to do and discovers water yoga. She thinks water yoga is good for both of them because it accommodates people who aren't used to water activities. She wants to suggest that Peter **should try out water yoga during the trip** by explaining its benefits. In this situation, what would Janet most likely say to Peter?

여 Peter와 Janet은 결혼한 지 5년 되었다. 다가오는 기념일을 축하하기 위해, 그들은 여행을 가기로 결정했다. 두 사람 모두 여름을 좋아하기 때문에 열대성 기후의 나라로 가기로 한다. Janet은 아주 활동적이어서, 스노클링과 서핑 같은 활동을 하길 원한다. 하지만 Peter는 수상스포츠를 잘하지 못하기 때문에 차라리 해변에서 휴식을 취하려고 한다. Janet은 그들의 첫 해외여행인 만큼 둘이 함께 즐길 수 있는 것을 해야 한다고 생각한다. 그래서 그녀는 무엇을 할지 찾다가 수상 요가에 대해 알게 된다. 그녀는 수상 요가가 수상 활동에 익숙하지 않은 사람들을 수용하기 때문에 두 사람 모두에게 좋다고 생각한다. 그녀는 수상 요가의 이점을 설명해서 여행하는 동안 Peter에게 수상 요가를 해보길 제안하고 싶어 한다. 이러한 상황에서 Janet이 Peter에게 할 말로 가장 적절한 것은 무엇인가?

Janet Water yoga will let you be active and relax.

Janet 수상 요가는 활동적이면서 편히 쉴 수 있게 할 거예요.

① 수상 요가는 배우기에 너무 힘들 거예요.
③ 서핑을 하는 것은 우리 결혼기념일을 위한 제 깜짝 선물이에요.
④ 추운 지역에서 기념일을 축하하는 게 어때요?
⑤ 스노클링처럼 활동적인 스포츠를 해보는 게 어때요?

---

16 | 정답 | ①

각 나라의 독특한 풍습을 예시로 들며 생일을 어떻게 기념하는지에 대해 설명하고 있으므로 남자가 하는 말의 주제로 가장 적절한 것은 ①이다.

17 | 정답 | ④

각 나라의 독특한 생일 풍습에 대한 예시 중 '중국'은 대한 언급은 없었으므로 정답은 ④이다.

• lit 불이 밝혀진
• custom 풍습, 관습
• familiar 친숙한
• slippery 미끄러운
• lift 들어 올리다
• upside down 거꾸로
• bump 부딪히다; 부딪침
• celebration 축하 행사
• turn (어떤 나이 · 시기가) 되다

M How do you celebrate your birthday every year? I'm sure many of you get presents and have a birthday cake with candles lit on it. However, there are some birthday customs that we aren't familiar with. In Canada, for example, people **put butter on the birthday child's nose**. Bad luck cannot catch the child because the child is too slippery. In Italy, people **pull the child's ears for good luck**. How many times do they pull the child's ears? It's one pull for each year. In Ireland, people lift the birthday child upside down and **bump their head on the floor**. They bump the child as many times as their age plus one. The last bump is for extra good luck. Surprisingly, there is a country where you don't celebrate your birthday at all. In Vietnam, people usually **don't celebrate their individual birthdays**. Instead, everyone celebrates together on "Tet," which is the most important celebration in Vietnamese culture. It is the Vietnamese New Year and everyone turns a year older on that day.

남 여러분은 매년 생일을 어떻게 축하하십니까? 많은 사람들이 선물을 받고 촛불이 켜진 케이크를 갖게 되겠죠. 그러나 우리에게 낯선 방식의 생일 풍습이 있습니다. 예를 들어 캐나다에서는 생일을 맞는 아이의 코에 버터를 바릅니다. 아이가 너무 미끄러워서 불운이 아이를 잡지 못하게 하기 위함이죠. 이탈리아에서는 행운을 위해 아이의 귀를 잡아당깁니다. 몇 번이나 잡아당길까요? 나이 한 살에 한 번입니다. 아일랜드에서는 생일을 맞은 아이를 거꾸로 들고 머리를 마루에 부딪칩니다. 그들은 아이의 나이에서 한 살을 더한 숫자만큼 부딪칩니다. 마지막으로 부딪치는 것은 추가 행운을 위한 것이지요. 놀랍게도, 생일을 전혀 축하하지 않는 나라가 하나 있습니다. 베트남에서는 보통 개인의 생일을 축하하지는 않습니다. 대신 모든 사람들은 'Tet'을 함께 축하하는데, 그것은 베트남 문화에서 가장 중요한 축하 행사입니다. 그것은 베트남의 새해이고 모든 사람은 그날 한 살을 더 먹습니다.

16 ① 독특한 생일 풍습
② 생일 축하 행사의 기원
③ 생일 선물의 다양한 의미
④ 생일의 상징: 케이크와 카드
⑤ 행운을 비는 잘못된 방법

17 ① 캐나다 ② 이탈리아 ③ 아일랜드
④ 중국 ⑤ 베트남

01 | 정답 | ③

안개가 너무 짙어서 비행기가 착륙하지 못한다고 안내하는 상황이다. 앞으로 날씨 상태가 더 좋아지지 않을 것이라 예상되므로 근처 가까운 공항으로 우회한다는 내용이므로 여자가 하는 말의 목적으로 가장 적절한 것은 ③이다.

* land 착륙하다
* circle 선회하다, (공중을) 빙빙 돌다
* mist 안개
* runway 활주로
* make a detour 우회하다
* transport 운송하다
* baggage 수하물
* apologize for ~에 대해 사과하다

W Ladies and gentlemen, this is the captain speaking. We have flown for more than thirteen hours from Seoul. We are about to land at Chicago O'Hare International Airport. We have been circling above the airport for twenty minutes, **waiting for the mist to clear** from the runways long enough to permit a safe landing. However, we have just received news from the ground that the mist is getting thicker and it is not **expected to clear for at least another hour**. We do not have enough fuel to stay in the air for that long and therefore we will have to make a detour to the nearest airport. A limousine bus will **transport you and your baggage to O'Hare from that airport**. We apologize for any inconvenience that this might cause you.

여 신사 숙녀 여러분. 저는 기장입니다. 우리는 서울에서부터 13시간 넘게 비행했습니다. 우리는 곧 Chicago O'Hare 국제 공항에 착륙할 것입니다. 안전 착륙 허가를 받을 수 있도록 활주로에서 안개가 걷히길 충분히 오랫동안 기다리면서 20분 동안 공항 상공을 선회하고 있습니다. 하지만 방금 지상으로부터 안개가 점점 짙어지고 있으며 앞으로 적어도 한 시간 동안은 걷히지 않을 것이라는 소식이 들어왔습니다. 우리는 공중에 그렇게 오랫동안 머무를 연료가 충분하지 않기 때문에 가장 가까운 공항으로 우회해야 할 것입니다. 공항 리무진 버스가 여러분과 여러분의 수하물을 그 공항에서 O'Hare 공항까지 운송할 것입니다. 이로 인해 불편을 끼쳐드려 죄송합니다.

02 | 정답 | ⑤

대부분의 고용주는 노인들은 일을 할 수 없다는 잘못된 생각을 하고 있으며, 정부가 더 많은 기업들이 노인들을 고용하도록 장려해야 한다고 말하고 있다. 따라서 남자의 의견으로 가장 적절한 것은 ⑤이다.

* babysit 아기를 봐 주다
* depressed 우울한
* elderly 나이가 드신
* desperately 간절히, 필사적으로
* be capable of ~할 수 있다
* hire 고용하다
* the elderly 노인들
* benefit from ~로부터 이익을 얻다

W Greg, the other day, I saw your grandmother walking with a little boy.
M You must be talking about Daniel. My grandmother babysits him for her part-time job.
W Really? That's nice.
M Though it's not a full-time job, she is **very happy to work again**. She said she felt a bit depressed being at home alone.
W I see. It's good to hear that she's happy.
M She got lucky. I heard many **elderly people are desperately looking for jobs**. But it's very hard to find one.
W Yes, looking for a new job over the age of 60 isn't easy, either.
M Most employers have this wrong idea that the elderly are not capable of working.
W I know. Just because they are old doesn't mean they are useless. **They are usually wiser and have more experience**.
M Exactly. That is why I think the government should encourage more companies to hire the elderly.
W That's right. With their experience and knowledge, **companies could benefit from them**.
M Yes, I couldn't agree more.

여 Greg, 며칠 전에 네 할머니가 어린아이와 함께 걸어가는 걸 봤어.
남 Daniel을 말하는구나. 할머니가 아르바이트로 걜 돌보고 계시거든.
여 정말? 잘됐다.
남 정규직은 아니라도, 다시 일을 하게 되어 매우 행복해하셔. 집에 혼자 계실 때는 좀 우울하다고 하셨거든.
여 그렇구나. 할머니가 행복하시다는 말을 들으니 좋아.
남 운이 좋으셨어. 많은 노인들이 일자리를 간절히 찾고 있다고 들었어. 하지만 일자리 잡기는 정말 어려워.
여 그래. 60세가 넘어 새로운 일자리를 구하는 것은 쉽지 않지.
남 대부분의 고용주들이 노인들은 일을 할 수 없다는 잘못된 생각을 갖고 있어.
여 그래. 단지 나이가 들었다고 해서 그들이 쓸모없는 게 아니잖아. 그들은 보통 더 현명하고 더 많은 경험을 가지고 있어.
남 바로 그거야. 그렇기 때문에 난 정부가 더 많은 기업들이 노인들을 채용하도록 장려해야 한다고 생각해.
여 맞아. 경험과 지식이 있기 때문에, 회사들은 그들로부터 이익을 얻을 수 있어.
남 그래. 전적으로 동감이야.

03 | 정답 | ②

벽돌을 쌓듯 인내심을 가지고 공부하라고 조언하고 있으므로 여자가 하는 말의 요지로 가장 적절한 것은 ②이다.

* principal 교장
* aim 목표하다; 목표
* brick 벽돌
* collapse 무너지다, 붕괴하다

W Good day, first-year students! Welcome to our school community! I'm Ms. Brown, your principal. Today, **I want to provide some helpful study tips**. If you aim for a higher score, **you need to study patiently**. Think of studying as building a structure. The lectures and reading materials you receive are like the bricks that organize your knowledge. Each brick builds on the previous one, **so if you rush without patience**, the structure could collapse. Therefore, studying with patience is absolutely vital. Now,

여 안녕하세요. 1학년 학생 여러분! 우리 학교 커뮤니티에 온 것을 환영합니다! 저는 교장인 Brown 선생님입니다. 오늘은 몇 가지 유용한 학습 팁을 제공하려고 합니다. 여러분이 높은 점수를 목표로 한다면, 인내심을 가지고 공부해야 합니다. 공부를 하나의 구조물을 짓는 것으로 생각하세요. 여러분이 받는 강의와 읽기 자료는 여러분의 지식을 정리해 주는 벽돌과 같습니다. 각각의 벽돌은 이전 벽돌 위에 지어지기 때문에, 여러분이 인내심 없이 서두르면 그 구조물은 무너질 수 있습니다. 그러므로 인내심을 가지고 공부하는 것이 절대적으로 중요합니다. 이제 여러분에게 어떻게 공부해야

your teachers will come out for each subject to guide you through how to study. It's going to be a great experience!

하는지 안내하기 위해 각 과목마다 선생님들이 나오실 것입니다. 그것은 좋은 경험이 될 것입니다!

---

04 | 정답 | ②

뒤쪽에 있는 것은 샤워실이라고 하였으므로 일치하지 않는 것은 ②이다.

* playground 놀이터
* shower booth 샤워실
* convenient 편리한
* fence 울타리
* barbecue 바비큐 파티; 바비큐
* safety 안전

M Wow, this park looks amazing. This is the perfect place for our dog, Jason.
W It was so hard to choose which dog park we should go to. But this park seemed perfect.
M I know. On the left, **there is a swimming pool for dogs**.
W Ah, but the pool is empty now because it's April.
M Right. The playground in the center looks so big. Jason can run around there. What's that in the back?
W That's a shower booth **where people wash their dogs** after swimming.
M That sounds convenient. Is there any place where we can eat?
W Of course. Do you **see the fence on the right**?
M Yes. What's that for?
W That's for the barbecue and picnic areas. There is a barbecue grill you can use. But dogs are not allowed behind the fence for safety.
M I see. *[Pause]* Oh, where did Jason go?
W **He's playing with other dogs on the playground**. It looks like he already made some friends.
M Let's go over there and play with him.

남 와, 이 공원 아주 멋지네요. 우리 개 Jason을 위한 완벽한 장소네요.
여 어느 애견 공원으로 가야 할지 결정하기가 너무 힘들었어요. 하지만 이 공원은 완벽해 보였어요.
남 맞아요. 왼쪽에는 개들을 위한 수영장이 있군요.
여 아, 그렇지만 4월이라 지금은 수영장이 텅 비었어요.
남 그러네요. 중앙에 놀이터가 정말 크네요. Jason이 뛰어 놀 수도 있겠어요. 뒤쪽에 있는 저건 뭐죠?
여 수영 후에 개들을 씻기는 샤워실이에요.
남 아주 편리한 것 같네요. 여기서 식사할 수 있는 곳이 있나요?
여 물론이죠. 오른쪽에 울타리 보여요?
남 네. 저건 뭘 위한 건가요?
여 바비큐 파티와 피크닉을 위한 장소예요. 우리가 사용해도 되는 바비큐용 그릴이 있어요. 하지만 개들은 안전상 울타리 뒤로 갈 수는 없어요.
남 그렇군요. *[잠시 후]* 아, Jason은 어디 갔지?
여 바로 저기 놀이터에서 다른 개들과 놀고 있어요. 벌써 친구들을 사귄 것 같은데요.
남 저쪽으로 가서 같이 놀아요.

---

05 | 정답 | ③

여자가 몸이 좋지 않아서 하루 쉬겠다고 말하자 남자는 독감이 유행이니 병원에 가라고 권유했고 여자가 알겠다고 했으므로 정답은 ③이다.

* make it in to work 출근하다
* come down with (질병) ~에 걸리다
* flu 독감
* call in sick 전화로 병결을 알리다
* cover for (자리를 비운 사람의 일을) 대신 하다

[Telephone rings.]
M Hello, this is Brad speaking.
W Hi, Brad. It's Joanna. I don't think I'll be able to **make it in to work today**.
M Is everything all right?
W I'm not feeling well today. I think **I came down with something over the weekend**.
M That doesn't sound good. Did you go to see a doctor?
W No, I didn't. I think I'll feel much better after a good rest.
M **There is a bad flu going around** these days. Besides, you'll get better faster if you get the right medicine.
W You're right. Once again, **I'm sorry I'm calling in sick like this**. I feel really bad not coming in today.
M Don't worry about it. I'll have Rebecca cover for you.
W Would you do that for me? Thank you so much.
M Like I said, **go and see a doctor**. You won't be of any good to us if you're sick.
W Okay. I will.

[전화벨이 울린다.]
남 안녕하세요, Brad입니다.
여 안녕하세요, Brad. Joanna예요. 오늘 출근하지 못할 것 같아서요.
남 무슨 일 있어요?
여 오늘 몸이 안 좋네요. 주말에 뭔가에 걸린 것 같아요.
남 안됐군요. 의사에게 진찰받으러 갔어요?
여 아니요. 푹 쉬면 나을 것 같아요.
남 요즘 심한 독감이 유행이잖아요. 게다가 제대로 된 약을 먹으면 더 빨리 나을 거예요.
여 맞아요. 이렇게 병가를 내서 다시 한번 죄송해요. 오늘 출근하지 못해 기분이 안 좋네요.
남 걱정 마세요. 당신을 대신해서 Rebecca에게 일을 맡길게요.
여 그래 주실래요? 정말 고마워요.
남 말한 것처럼, 병원을 가봐요. 당신이 아프면 우리에게도 좋지 않으니까요.
여 알겠어요. 그럴게요.

---

06 | 정답 | ②

남자가 구매하는 등산화는 100달러이며, 추가로 20달러 양말을 구매하여 120달러이다. 여자는 총금액이 120달러 이상이면 10% 할인이 된다고 하였으므로 남자가 지불할 금액은 108달러로 정답은 ②이다.

* available 이용 가능한
* a large collection of ~의 종류가 아주 많은
* shelf 선반
* be sold out 다 팔리다; 매진되다

M Hi. I'm looking for hiking shoes. What types of shoes are available for hiking?
W There is a large collection of hiking shoes on this shelf.
M I'm going to Mt. Jiri this weekend. What do you recommend?
W What about these ones? They're $80. **The price just went down by 10% last week**.
M They are not bad. But do you have them in black?
W I'm sorry, but the black ones in this design are sold out. How about these black ones with high ankle support?
M Those are nice. How much are they?

남 안녕하세요. 등산화를 찾고 있는데요. 등산용으로 어떤 종류의 신발이 있을까요?
여 이 선반에 등산화가 많이 있습니다.
남 이번 주말에 지리산에 갈 거예요. 어떤 걸 추천하시나요?
여 이 신발은 어떠신가요? 80달러입니다. 지난주에 가격이 막 10% 내렸어요.
남 나쁘지 않군요. 그런데 검은색도 있나요?
여 죄송합니다만, 같은 디자인으로 검은색은 다 팔렸습니다. 이 발목 받침이 높은 검은색 신발은 어때요?
남 그거 좋은데요. 얼마예요?

- **ankle support** 발목 받침
- **bundle** 묶음

W They are $100.
M That's great. I'll get a pair in size 260.
W Of course. Is there anything else you need? You can get 10% off **if the total bill is $120 or more**.
M I need some socks, too.
W How about these long socks? **This bundle of 10 pairs costs $20**.
M Okay. I'll take those in medium, please.
W All right. Would that be all?
M Yes, please. Here is my credit card.

여 100달러입니다.
남 잘됐네요. 260 사이즈로 한 켤레 주세요.
여 네. 그 밖에 더 필요한 건 없으신가요? 총금액이 120달러 이상이면 10% 할인받을 수 있거든요.
남 양말도 필요해요.
여 이 긴 양말은 어때요? 10개 한 묶음이 20달러입니다.
남 좋아요. 미디엄 사이즈로 주세요.
여 네. 그게 다인가요?
남 네. 그렇게 주세요. 여기 신용카드 드릴게요.

---

07 | 정답 | ④

남자는 오후 3시부터 5시까지의 시간제 강사직을 제안했지만, 여자는 오후 4시부터 7시까지 수업을 듣기 때문에 강사를 할 수 없다고 설명하고 있으므로 정답은 ④이다.

- **in person** 직접, 개인적으로
- **open up** (일자리가) 열려 있다
- **turn down** 거절하다
- **employed** 취직한
- **unemployed** 실직한, 고용되지 않은
- **qualified** 자격을 갖춘
- **candidate** 후보자
- **once** 일단 ~하면
- **be done with** ~을 마치다

[Telephone rings.]
W Hello.
M Hi. I'm calling from Jefferson Library. I've reviewed your application for the storytelling instructor position. I'd like to see you in person for an interview.
W Jefferson Library? Oh, I remember. But I applied for the job months ago.
M Yes, but the position just opened up. **You are the first person I called for an interview**.
W I see. What are the hours and the pay?
M It's a two-hour class with 20 people from 3 to 5 p.m. on weekdays. You will get paid $25 per hour.
W 3 to 5? I'm sorry, but I have to turn it down.
M Oh, **are you currently employed**?
W I'm not. I've been unemployed since last May.
M Then how come you have to turn down the offer?
W I've been taking a few classes to prepare for a test. **The classes are from 4 to 7 p.m.**
M I see. That's too bad. You seem like the most qualified candidate.
W Thanks. **Once I'm done with classes**, I will definitely apply again.

[전화벨이 울린다.]
여 여보세요.
남 안녕하세요. Jefferson 도서관에서 전화 드리는 건데요. 스토리텔링 강사직 지원서를 검토했습니다. 면접을 위해 직접 뵙고 싶습니다.
여 Jefferson 도서관이라고요? 아, 이제 기억이 나네요. 하지만 전 그 일자리에 수개월 전에 지원했는데요.
남 네, 하지만 막 자리가 났어요. 면접을 보도록 전화 드린 분은 당신이 처음이에요.
여 그렇군요. 근무 시간과 급여는 어떻게 되나요?
남 평일 오후 3시에서 5시까지 20명이 참여하는 두 시간짜리 수업이에요. 시간당 25달러를 받으실 거예요.
여 3시에서 5시까지라고요? 죄송하지만 거절해야겠네요.
남 아, 현재 취업이 되셨나요?
여 아니요. 지난 5월부터 미취업 상태였어요.
남 그럼 제안을 왜 거절하시는 거죠?
여 시험 준비를 위해 수업을 몇 개 듣고 있거든요. 수업이 4시부터 7시까지예요.
남 그렇군요. 안됐네요. 당신이 적임자인 것 같았는데요.
여 감사합니다. 수업이 종료되면 반드시 다시 지원하겠습니다.

---

08 | 정답 | ④

기린은 4.3미터에서 5.7미터까지 자란다고 하였으며, 초원이나 옅은 삼림 지대에서 서식한다고 하였다. 시력이 좋으며 혀의 길이는 50센티미터 정도 된다고 하였으므로 언급하지 않은 것은 ④이다.

- **greet** 인사하다, 환영하다
- **grassland** 초원, 풀밭
- **woodland** 삼림지대
- **thick** 울창한, 빽빽한
- **predator** 포식자, 약탈자
- **move on to** ~로 이동하다

W As we are driving in, we can see the giraffes greeting us.
M They are really tall. **How tall are they**?
W As the tallest land animals, giraffes stand 4.3 to 5.7 meters tall. Interestingly, baby giraffes are already about 2 meters tall when born.
M That's amazing. Where do they usually live?
W They **live in grasslands or light woodlands**. They don't live in thick forests because it is difficult to see their predators there.
M I thought they could see anything because they are tall.
W They have great eyesight, but trees and leaves can block their view in thick forests. Would you like to give him some food?
M Sure. How do I do that?
W Just reach your arm out the window. **The giraffe will eat it with its tongue**.
M Wow. Its tongue is really long. How long is it?
W It is about 50 centimeters long. Do you have any more questions about giraffes?
M No, I don't.
W All right. Let's move on to see the buffalos, then.

여 운전해 들어가면서 기린이 우리를 맞이하는 걸 볼 수 있어요.
남 기린은 엄청 키가 크네요. 키가 얼마나 되죠?
여 가장 키가 큰 육지 동물로서 기린은 4.3미터에서 5.7미터 정도입니다. 재있는 것은 아기 기린은 태어날 때부터 이미 약 2미터라는 거예요.
남 정말 대단해요. 주로 어디서 살죠?
여 초원이나 옅은 삼림지대에 살아요. 울창한 숲속에서는 포식자들을 보기 어렵기 때문에 그곳에서는 살지 않습니다.
남 키가 커서 다 볼 수 있다고 생각했어요.
여 그것들은 시력이 좋지만 울창한 숲속에서는 나무와 잎들이 시야를 가릴 수 있어요. 기린에게 먹이를 줘 볼래요?
남 네. 어떻게 하나요?
여 창문 밖으로 팔을 내밀기만 하면 돼요. 기린이 혀로 그걸 먹을 겁니다.
남 와. 혀가 정말 길어요. 얼마나 길죠?
여 50센티미터 정도 됩니다. 기린에 대해 더 궁금한 게 있나요?
남 아니요, 없습니다.
여 알겠습니다. 그럼 물소 있는 데로 이동합시다.

09 | 정답 | ⑤

현재 휴일에 근무가 가능한 사람을 찾고 있으며, 최소 교대 근무 시간은 두 시간이고 기초 교육 후에는 다른 봉사자와 잠시 같이 일해도 된다고 하였다. 지원자의 조건으로 18세가 넘어야 하며 기초 교육 후에는 혼자서 일할 수 있어야 한다고 했지만, 접수는 가게에 직접 오거나 이메일로 가능하다고 하였으므로 일치하지 않는 것은 ⑤이다.

- **short-handed** 일손이 부족한
- **essential** 필수적인
- **reliable** 신뢰할 수 있는
- **minimum** 최소의
- **shift** 교대 근무시간
- **initial** 처음의
- **arrange** 조정하다
- **interpersonal skill** 대인관계 능력
- **leave A with B** A를 B에 남기다
- **details** 상세한 사항
- **attention** 관심, 흥미

M Our village cannot be more proud to have our own village gift shop. But unfortunately, the shop is short-handed and we need your help. Currently, **volunteers who can cover holidays are needed**. Although this is not a busy shop, it's essential that we have enough volunteers to provide reliable services and open at regular times. **The minimum length of one shift is 2 hours**. There may not be much to learn, but full training will be provided. If you would prefer to work with another volunteer for a short period after your initial training, this can be arranged. After this period you will **be expected to work on your own**. Volunteers with good interpersonal skills are preferred. To apply, you must be over 18 and be able to work independently. If you're interested, **please leave your details with the shop**, or email kmsvillageshop@kingston.com. Thank you for your attention.

남 우리 마을은 마을 기념품 가게가 있는 것에 대단한 자부심을 갖고 있습니다. 하지만 안타깝게도, 가게에 일손이 부족해서 여러분의 도움이 필요합니다. 현재, 휴일에 근무할 자원봉사자들이 필요합니다. 비록 바쁜 가게는 아닐지라도 신뢰할 수 있는 서비스를 제공하고 정시에 가게 문을 열 수 있는 충분한 자원봉사자가 있어야 합니다. 최소 교대 근무 시간은 2시간입니다. 배울 것이 별로 없을 수도 있지만, 충분한 교육이 준비되어 있습니다. 기초 교육 후에 짧은 기간 동안 다른 자원봉사자들과 함께 일하고 싶다면, 이것은 조정이 될 수 있습니다. 이 기간이 지나면 여러분은 혼자 일해야 할 것입니다. 대인관계 능력이 뛰어난 자원봉사자를 선호합니다. 지원하려면 18세가 넘어야 하고 독립적으로 일할 수 있어야 합니다. 관심이 있으면 여러분의 신상정보를 가게에 남기시거나, kmsvillageshop@kingston.com으로 이메일을 보내 주세요. 관심을 기울여 주셔서 감사드립니다.

10 | 정답 | ③

가격은 90달러 이하이고, 하트 모양이 아닌 케이크를 찾고 있다. 위에 사진을 추가할 수 있어야 하며, 모카 맛으로 주문한다고 하였으므로 정답은 ③이다.

- **retirement** 은퇴
- **customize** 주문 제작하다
- **heart-shaped** 하트 모양의
- **even** 같은, 동일한
- **flavor** 맛, 향, 풍미
- **mocha** 모카(커피)
- **cash register** 계산대
- **hand in** 제출하다

W There are so many cakes here. I don't know what to get.
M Since it's for Dad's retirement, why not customize the cake?
W That's a great idea. But I hope it's not too expensive.
M **Then let's not spend more than $90**. We need to buy him some presents, too.
W All right. Should we get a heart-shaped one?
M I don't like the heart-shaped one. **It would be hard to cut into even pieces**.
W I know what you mean. Oh, we are going to **put Dad's picture on it**, right?
M Definitely. There are only two choices left. What flavor would you like?
W **We have to get mocha.** That's his favorite.
M All right. I'll go to the cash register and hand in the form.

여 케이크가 너무 많아. 뭘 사야 할지 모르겠어.
남 아빠의 은퇴를 위한 것이니까 아빠만을 위한 케이크를 주문 제작하는 게 어때?
여 좋은 생각이야. 하지만 너무 비싸지 않았으면 좋겠어.
남 그럼 90달러 넘게 쓰지 말자. 아빠께 선물도 사드려야 하니까.
여 좋아. 하트 모양의 케이크를 살까?
남 나는 하트 모양은 좋아하지 않아. 같은 크기로 조각내기가 힘들 거야.
여 무슨 말인지 알겠어. 아, 케이크 위에 아빠 사진을 넣을 거지, 그렇지?
남 물론이지. 그럼 이젠 선택이 두 개만 남았어. 무슨 맛이 좋을까?
여 모카 맛으로 사야 할걸. 아빠가 좋아하시는 맛이잖아.
남 알겠어. 계산대로 가서 주문서를 낼게.

11 | 정답 | ③

홈쇼핑으로 저렴한 가격에 산 커피 기계가 어떤지 물어보는 남자의 말에 대한 여자의 응답으로 가장 적절한 것은 ③ '아주 좋아. 전부 마음에 들어.'이다.

- **bargain** 싸게 산 물건, 특가품
- **so far** 지금까지

[선택지]
- **refundable** 환불 가능한
- **unhealthy** 건강에 좋지 않은

M Jane, you have **a wonderful coffee machine**. Where did you buy it?
W I bought it through the home shopping channel. It's $250.
M Wow, that sounds like a bargain. **How do you like the machine so far?**
W It's great. I love everything about it.

남 Jane, 너 멋진 커피 기계가 있네. 그걸 어디서 샀어?
여 홈쇼핑 채널을 통해서 샀어. 250달러야.
남 와, 정말 싼 것 같구나. 지금까지 그 기계 써 보니 어때?
여 아주 좋아. 전부 마음에 들어.

① 잘 모르겠어. 아직 도착하지 않았어.
② 맘에 안 들어. 너무 비쌌거든.
④ 죄송한데요. 이 기계는 사용했으면 환불이 안 됩니다.
⑤ 그건 건강에 좋지 않아. 카페인을 너무 많이 마시면 안 돼.

12 | 정답 | ③

비가 와서 가기로 한 견학 일정을 확인하기 위해 전화를 하겠다는 여자의 말에 대한 남자의 응답으로 가장 적절한 것은 ③ '알겠어요. 견학이 취소되지 않았으면 좋겠어요.'이다.

- **heavily** 아주 많이, 심하게
- **field trip** 견학, 현장 학습
- **shower** 소나기

W David, did you look out the window? It's raining heavily.
M Really? **What will happen to the field trip today**? I was really looking forward to it.
W **It could just be a shower**. I'll make some phone calls to find out about your trip.
M All right. I hope it doesn't get canceled.

여 David, 창밖을 봤니? 비가 아주 많이 오는구나.
남 정말요? 오늘 견학은 어떻게 될까요? 정말 기대하고 있었거든요.
여 그냥 소나기일 수도 있어. 내가 견학에 대해 알아보기 위해 몇 군데 전화해 볼게.
남 알겠어요. 견학이 취소되지 않았으면 좋겠어요.

① 좋아요. 어쨌든 견학을 가고 싶지 않았어요.
② 신경 쓰지 마세요. 지금 학교로 갈게요.
④ 아니, 괜찮아요. 저 혼자 창문을 닦을게요.
⑤ 물론이죠. 뒤에서 우산을 가져올게요.

13 | 정답 | ③

제출 서류 중에서 가장 중요한 것은 성적보다는 자기소개서와 학업 계획이라고 설명하는 여자의 말에 남자는 그 두 가지에 집중할 것이라고 말하고 있다. 이에 대한 여자의 응답으로 가장 적절한 것은 ③ '알겠어. 행운을 빌게'이다. ②의 경우 행운을 비는 대상이 잘못된 표현이다.

- student exchange program 교환학생 프로그램
- self-introduction 자기소개
- document 서류
- portfolio 포트폴리오, 작품집
- recommendation letter 추천서
- matter 중요하다
- focus on 집중하다

[선택지]
- put an emphasis on A A에 중점을 두다, A를 강조하다

W Hi, Jinsu. Have you applied for the student exchange program yet?

M Not yet. I'm still **working on my self-introduction essay**. Could you help me?

W Sorry, I don't know much about it. Why don't you ask Mr. Butler? He should be able to help you out.

M I already did. He read it through and said that it didn't clearly deliver my study plan.

W Well, keep working on it. **What other documents do you need to send**?

M I need to send out my portfolio and a recommendation letter.

W How about your grades? Are they okay?

M They're not very good. **Do you think it matters very much**?

W Maybe. But I think your essay and study plan are the most important parts of the application.

M Well, it's a little late to change my grades. I'll just focus on those two things.

W Okay. I'll keep my fingers crossed for you!

여 안녕, Jinsu. 너 교환학생 프로그램에 지원했니?

남 아직 안 했어. 나는 아직도 자기소개서를 작성하고 있어. 나 좀 도와줄 수 있어?

여 미안하지만, 난 그것에 대해 잘 몰라. Butler 선생님에게 부탁해 보는 게 어때? 선생님은 널 도와주실 거야.

남 이미 부탁했지. 선생님께선 그것을 끝까지 읽으셨는데, 나의 학업 계획을 분명하게 표현하지 못하고 있다고 말씀하셨어.

여 음. 계속 작성해 봐. 이 외에 어떤 서류를 보내야 하는데?

남 내 포트폴리오랑 추천서를 보내야 해.

여 성적은 어때? 괜찮니?

남 별로 좋지 않아. 그게 많이 중요한 것 같아?

여 아마도. 그래도 지원서에서 가장 중요한 부분은 자기소개서하고 학업 계획인 것 같아.

남 음. 성적을 바꾸기엔 좀 늦었어. 그냥 그 두 가지에 집중해야겠어.

여 알겠어. 행운을 빌게!

① 도와줘서 진심으로 고마워.
② 좋아. 나에게 행운을 빌어줘!
④ 물론이지. 너는 먼저 글을 잘 쓰는 법을 배워야 해.
⑤ 나라면 성적에 중점을 두겠어.

---

14 | 정답 | ③

남자가 TV 보는 시간을 줄이고 대신 수영 강습을 받는 것을 권하면서 주민 센터에서 제공하는 수영 강좌가 있다고 말하자, 여자는 강좌 등록 방법을 알려줄 수 있는지 묻고 있다. 이에 대한 남자의 응답으로 가장 적절한 것은 ③ '그럼요. 강좌의 세부 사항들을 문자로 보내줄게요.'이다.

- addicted 중독된
- admit 인정하다

[선택지]
- nonsense 말도 안 되는

M How long do you watch TV every day?

W I spend about four hours watching TV after coming home.

M Don't you think that's a little too much?

W Well, I may sound like I am addicted to TV, but I think it's okay.

M I used to watch more than five hours a day. But I stopped watching TV when I started to exercise.

W **Watching TV can be a bad habit**, but I usually enjoy watching educational programs, including the news.

M I admit that you can **get some information through TV**, but you cannot control what you get.

W I know. Maybe I'll try to find something else to do.

M How about taking swimming lessons in the evening?

W Oh, I've always wanted to learn how to swim.

M The community center in downtown **provides a class for beginners at a reasonable price**.

W That's great. Can you tell me how to register for it?

M Of course. I will text you the details of the class.

남 매일 TV를 얼마나 시청하시나요?

여 집에 와서 4시간 정도 TV를 봐요.

남 그건 좀 많은 것 같지 않아요?

여 음, 제가 TV에 중독된 것처럼 들리겠지만, 괜찮은 것 같아요.

남 저는 하루에 5시간 넘게 보곤 했어요. 하지만 운동을 시작했을 때 TV를 그만 봤어요.

여 TV 시청은 나쁜 습관이 될 수 있지만, 저는 보통 뉴스를 포함한 교육 프로그램을 즐겨 봐요.

남 TV를 통해 정보를 얻을 수 있다는 건 인정하지만, 어떤 정보를 얻을지 통제할 수는 없잖아요.

여 맞아요. 아마 다른 할 일을 찾아봐야겠네요.

남 저녁에 수영 강습을 받는 건 어때요?

여 아, 저는 항상 수영을 배워보고 싶었어요.

남 시내에 있는 주민 센터에서 합리적인 가격으로 초보자를 위한 강좌를 제공해요.

여 좋은데요. 어떻게 등록하는지 알려줄 수 있나요?

남 그럼요. 강좌의 세부 사항들을 문자로 보내 줄게요.

① 죄송하지만, 좀 지루하게 들리네요.
② 당신의 의견에 동의해요. 그것은 매우 교육적일 수 있습니다.
④ 말도 안 돼요! TV는 때때로 내가 스트레스를 줄이도록 해 줘요.
⑤ 맞아요. 어쨌든 TV가 일과 후 긴장을 푸는 데 도움을 줄 수 있어요.

---

15 | 정답 | ⑤

학교 근처로 이사 갈 계획을 하는 Evelyn이 Sam에게 근처 지역이 어떤지 물어보는 상황이다. Evelyn의 한정된 예산으로 집을 찾기 어렵기 때문에 다른 곳에서 집을 구하는 것을 제안하는 Sam이 할 말로 가장 적절한 것은 ⑤ 'Newmarket에서 너의 예산 안에 있는 집을 찾는 것은 정말 어려울 거야.'이다.

- transfer 전근 가다, 이동하다
- limited 제한된, 한정된
- budget 예산

M Evelyn, a high school teacher, is transferring to a new school in Newmarket this March. Since Newmarket is quite far from where she lives now, she decides to look for a new place to stay close to her school. She wants to find a house **with a limited budget of $600 a month** and within walking distance to school. Since she doesn't know much about the area, she calls one of her friends, Sam, who lives in Newmarket, and asks for advice. When Sam hears about Evelyn's situation, he thinks it would be best for Evelyn **to find a place in a different area**. He thinks that if Evelyn lives too close to school, she won't have any privacy from her students and their parents. Besides,

---

남 고등학교 교사인 Evelyn은 이번 3월에 Newmarket에 있는 새로운 학교로 전근 간다. Newmarket은 지금 그녀가 사는 곳에서 꽤 멀기 때문에 그녀의 학교와 가깝게 새로 머물 곳을 찾기로 한다. 그녀는 제한된 예산인 한 달 600달러 월세에 학교까지 걸을 수 있는 거리 안에 있는 집을 찾고 싶어 한다. 그 지역에 대해 잘 모르기 때문에, 그녀는 자기 친구 중 Newmarket에 사는 Sam에게 전화하여 조언을 구한다. Sam은 Evelyn의 상황을 듣고 그녀가 다른 지역에서 집을 찾는 것이 더 좋을 것이라 생각한다. 그는 Evelyn이 학교에서 너무 가까이 살면, 학생들과 학부모님들로부터 사생활이 없을 것이라고 생각한다. 게다가 학교 주변 월세는 더 높은 경향이 있으며, Evelyn이 원하는 것처럼 월 600달러 이하의 집을 찾는 것은 어려울 것이다. 그래서 Sam은

---

* privacy 사생활, 혼자 있는 상태
* elsewhere (어딘가) 다른 곳에서
[선택지]
* landlord 집주인
* make a deal 협상하다, 흥정하다
* roommate 룸메이트

rents tend to be higher around the school, and it'd be hard to find a place under $600 like Evelyn wants. So Sam decides to explain why Evelyn should look for apartments elsewhere. In this situation, what would Sam most likely say to Evelyn?

Sam It'd be very difficult to find one within your budget in Newmarket.

Evelyn이 왜 다른 곳에서 아파트를 찾아야 하는지 설명하려고 한다. 이러한 상황에서 Sam이 Evelyn에게 할 말로 가장 적절한 것은 무엇인가?

Sam Newmarket에서 너의 예산 안에 있는 집을 찾기는 정말 어려울 거야.

① 대신 집을 사는 것을 고려하는 것이 좋아.
② 집주인이랑 얘기하고 협상하는 것이 어때?
③ 어디든 거주할 수 있는 집이 있는지 몇 군데 전화 좀 해 볼게.
④ 우리 같이 지낼 곳을 찾는 것이 어때? 룸메이트가 되자.

---

16 | 정답 | ④

진해 군항제에 대한 설명이며, 이 축제를 즐기기 위해 알아야 할 사항에 대해 언급하고 있으므로 여자가 하는 말의 주제로 가장 적절한 것은 ④ '지역 축제를 즐기기 위한 특별한 조언'이다.

17 | 정답 | ④

진해 군항제 진행에 있어서 '벼룩시장'은 언급하지 않았으므로 정답은 ④이다.

* tourist attention 관광객들의 관심
* navy 해군
* military band 군악대
* street parade 거리 행진
* take place 일어나다, 개최되다
* properly 적절히
* keep in mind 명심하다
* set aside (돈·시간을) 따로 떼어두다
* book 예약하다(= reserve)
* in advance 미리
* crowd 붐빔
[선택지]
* with ease 쉽게
* organize 조직하다
* caution 주의 (사항)

W Good morning, everyone! Welcome to Jinhae Gunhangje Festival. There are many local festivals in Korea, but this is **one of Korea's largest cherry blossom festivals**. This festival will be held from March 27th to April 6th and is expected to gather much tourist attention thanks to the K-pop stars' performances. In addition to K-pop concerts, performances by the navy military band and street parades will take place. In order to enjoy the festival properly, there are **a few things you should keep in mind**. First, you have to set aside at least two days to fully enjoy it. And you should **book a hotel at least a month in advance** because they get booked up very quickly. Next, try to **get there in the evening** so that you can avoid the crowds and enjoy the beautiful cherry blossoms in the moonlight. One more thing, special events such as fireworks and light shows will be held every night during the festival. Thank you.

여 안녕하세요, 여러분! 진해 군항제에 오신 것을 환영합니다. 한국에 많은 지역 축제가 있지만 진해 군항제는 한국에서 가장 규모가 큰 벚꽃 축제 중 하나입니다. 이 축제는 3월 27일부터 4월 6일까지 개최될 예정이며 K-pop 스타들의 공연 덕분에 관광객들의 많은 관심을 끌 것으로 예상됩니다. K-pop 콘서트 이외에도 해군 군악대 공연과 길거리 행진이 행해질 것입니다. 축제를 제대로 즐기기 위해서는 몇 가지 명심해야 할 점이 있습니다. 우선 충분히 축제를 즐기기 위해서는 적어도 이틀의 여유가 있어야 합니다. 그리고 호텔도 한 달 전에 미리 예약해야 합니다. 왜냐하면 호텔이 매우 빠르게 예약이 끝나기 때문입니다. 다음으로 사람 붐비는 것을 피하고 달빛에 비친 아름다운 벚꽃을 즐길 수 있도록 저녁에 그곳에 도착하도록 하세요. 한 가지 더 있는데요. 불꽃놀이와 불빛 쇼와 같은 특별 행사도 축제 기간 동안 매일 밤 열릴 예정입니다. 감사합니다.

16 ① 관광객들을 쉽게 끌어들이는 방법
② 축제를 효과적으로 조직하는 방법
③ 지역 축제들을 즐길 때의 주의 사항
④ 지역 축제를 즐기기 위한 특별한 조언
⑤ 여행을 계획할 때 유의해야 할 것들

17 ① K-pop 공연 ② 거리 행진 ③ 불꽃놀이
④ 벼룩시장 ⑤ 불빛 쇼

01 | 정답 | ⑤

사무실에서 배출되는 종이를 재활용하고자 새로 시행될 재활용 프로그램에 대해 소개하는 내용이다. 프로그램 관련 안내문을 전달할 예정이며 책상에서도 바로 재활용할 수 있도록 용기를 제공한다고 언급하므로 정답은 ⑤이다.

* recycle 재활용하다
* critical 매우 중요한
* share 몫
* reduce 줄이다
* additional 추가적인
* disposal 처리
* expenses 비용
* lower 낮추다
* operate 운영하다
* implement 시행하다
* flyer 전단지
* maintenance 보수 관리, 유지
* obtain 얻다, 구하다
* container 용기, 그릇
* extension number 내선 번호

M About 70% of the trash from our office is paper that can be recycled. Since businesses produce over 50% of the city's waste, it is critical that **we do our share to reduce waste**. Recycling has an additional benefit of reducing our waste disposal expenses. It helps lower the building's operating costs. With this in mind, we are **implementing a new recycling program in our office**. A flyer which describes what can be recycled will be given out in the afternoon. You can call Bob Geller from the maintenance department to obtain desk-side containers. These containers **will make it very easy for you to recycle** paper at your desks. With everyone's participation, I am confident that we can do our part to help the city's recycling efforts. If you have any questions, please call me at my extension number, 324. Thank you for your assistance and participation.

남 우리 사무실에서 나오는 쓰레기 중 대략 70%가 재활용 가능한 종이입니다. 우리 시의 쓰레기의 50%가 넘는 양이 기업체에서 나오는 것이기 때문에 쓰레기를 줄이는 데 우리 몫을 다하는 것이 매우 중요합니다. 재활용을 하게 되면 쓰레기 처리 비용을 절감하는 추가 혜택을 누릴 수 있습니다. 그것은 건물 운영 비용을 낮추는 데 도움이 됩니다. 이런 것들을 염두에 두고, 우리 사무실에서는 새로운 재활용 프로그램을 시행할 것입니다. 무엇이 재활용이 가능한 것인지 설명하는 홍보지가 오후에 배부될 것입니다. 보수 관리부의 Bob Geller씨에게 전화하시면 책상 근처에 둘 수 있는 용기를 받으실 수 있습니다. 이 용기를 사용하시면 여러분이 책상에서 종이를 재활용하는 일이 훨씬 쉬워질 것입니다. 저는 여러분의 참여로 우리가 해야 할 몫을 이행함으로써 우리 시의 재활용하고자 하는 노력에 도움을 줄 수 있을 것이라고 믿습니다. 질문이 있으시면 제 내선 번호 324번으로 전화해 주십시오. 여러분의 도움과 참여에 감사드립니다.

02 | 정답 | ①

언론의 자유가 있지만 댓글로 거짓 소문을 퍼뜨리거나 악의적인 댓글을 다는 것은 잘못된 행동이라고 하면서 온라인에 남기는 말이나 글에 대한 책임이 따라야 한다고 했으므로 정답은 ①이다.

* article 신문 기사
* comment section 댓글난
* horrible 끔찍한
* freedom of speech 언론의 자유
* go too far 도를 지나치다
* spread 퍼뜨리다
* false rumor 거짓 소문
* abusive 악의적인, 독설적인
* online hater 악플러
* mean 못된, 심술궂은
* responsible for ~에 대한 책임이 있는
* underestimate 과소평가하다

W Tim, did you read this article about the singer?
M I did. Did you also look at the comment section on that article?
W Yes, it was horrible. **There were so many negative comments about him**.
M I know. I was really shocked to read them all.
W I understand that we have the freedom of speech. But **some people have gone too far**.
M What do you mean by going too far?
W Leaving comments is a way of expressing opinions. But some people spread false rumors or leave abusive comments.
M I agree with you. I don't like those online haters. They don't have to be so mean.
W Exactly. People should **be more responsible for what they say online**.
M You're right. We all should be more careful.
W Yes, we should not underestimate the power of our words.

여 Tim, 그 가수에 관한 기사 읽어 봤어?
남 읽어 봤어. 그 기사 댓글란도 봤니?
여 응. 정말 끔찍했어. 그 가수에 대한 부정적인 댓글이 정말 많았어.
남 맞아. 그 댓글을 모두 읽고 정말 놀랐어.
여 우리에게 언론의 자유가 있다는 건 알아. 하지만 일부 사람들은 정말 너무 지나쳐.
남 지나치다는 말은 무슨 뜻이야?
여 댓글을 남기는 건 자기 견해를 표현하는 한 가지 방법이지. 그러나 어떤 사람들은 거짓 소문을 퍼뜨리거나 악의적인 댓글을 달기도 해.
남 나도 같은 생각이야. 나는 그런 악플러들을 좋아하지 않아. 그렇게까지 못되게 굴 필요는 없잖아.
여 그렇고말고. 사람들은 자신이 온라인에서 말하는 것에 대해서 책임을 져야 해.
남 네 말이 맞아. 우리 모두 좀 더 신중해야 해.
여 그래, 우리가 하는 말이 가진 힘을 과소평가해서는 안 돼.

03 | 정답 | ⑤

구체적으로 칭찬이나 피드백을 하는 것의 예시를 들며 이것의 중요성을 말하고 있으므로 남자가 하는 말의 요지로 가장 적절한 것은 ⑤이다.

* advisor 조언자, 고문
* essential 가장 중요한, 본질적인
* specific 구체적인
* latter 후자(의)
* shift 옮기다

M Glad you could join us! I am Martin Lawrence, your business advisor. Today, let's discuss a way of giving praise and feedback in the workplace. It is essential **to provide detailed and specific feedback or praise**. For instance, saying, "I was impressed with **how you encouraged everyone to share ideas** in the team meeting," is more effective than saying, "You're really good at leading meetings." **The latter is too general** and does not offer specific details. When giving feedback or praise,

남 함께 해주셔서 기쁩니다! 저는 여러분의 비즈니스 조언자인 Martin Lawrence입니다. 오늘은 직장에서 칭찬과 피드백을 주는 방법에 대해 이야기해 봅시다. 상세하고 구체적인 피드백이나 칭찬을 제공하는 것이 가장 중요합니다. 예를 들어, "당신이 팀 회의에서 모든 사람이 아이디어를 공유하도록 독려하는 방식에 감명을 받았습니다."라고 말하는 것이 "회의를 정말 잘 이끌어 가시네요."라고 말하는 것보다 더 효과적입니다. 후자는 너무 일반적이고 구체적인 세부 사항을 제시하지 않습니다. 피드백이나 칭찬을 할 때는 구체적으로 말

it is crucial to be specific. I will provide you with another example. Let's shift our focus toward the screen.

하는 것이 중요합니다. 또 다른 한 예를 들어보겠습니다. 화면으로 우리의 초점을 옮겨 보죠.

---

04 | 정답 | ⑤

현수막 앞에 놓은 테이블의 모양은 정사각형이라고 했으므로 일치하지 않는 것은 ⑤이다.

* request 요청하다
* rectangular 직사각형의
* decorate 장식하다
* fancy 화려한, 고급의
* banner 현수막
* square 정사각형의

M Honey, here is the birthday cake that you requested this morning.
W Excellent! Please put it on the rectangular table. The flowers should be **on the right side of the cake**.
M Oh, you almost finished decorating the dining room for her birthday party. It's like a fancy restaurant!
W We don't have to go to a restaurant for this party. **As many as 8 people can be served** at home because we have enough chairs.
M You put up a banner that says "Happy Birthday to You, Jane!" with her photo on the wall!
W Yes, it will be a photo zone for them. Please put **a low square table in front of the banner**.
M A low square table? Why do we need one more table?
W I want her friends to put their gifts for her there.

남 여보, 오늘 아침에 당신이 부탁한 생일 케이크 여기 있어요.
여 좋아요! 직사각형 테이블 위에 놓아 주세요. 꽃은 케이크 오른쪽에 있어야 해요.
남 아, 생일 파티를 위해 식당 방을 거의 다 꾸며 놓았네요. 멋진 레스토랑 같아 보여요!
여 이 파티 때문에 레스토랑에 갈 필요 없어요. 의자도 충분히 있으니 여덟 명까지는 집에서 대접할 수 있어요.
남 우리 아이 사진이 있는 '생일 축하해요, Jane!'이라고 쓴 현수막을 벽에 붙였네요!
여 네, 거기가 아이들의 포토 존이 될 거예요. 현수막 앞에 낮은 정사각형 테이블을 놓아 주세요.
남 낮은 정사각형 테이블? 테이블이 왜 하나 더 필요하지요?
여 그 애 친구들이 가지고 오는 선물을 거기에 두게 하려고요.

---

05 | 정답 | ③

자선 음악회에 가기 전에 챙겨야 하는 것들이 있는지 확인하는 상황이다. 남자가 전화기를 챙겨야 한다고 하자 보조 배터리도 챙기라고 여자가 말하고 있다. 따라서 남자가 할 일로 가장 적절한 것은 ③이다.

* charity 자선
* extra 여분의
* charge 충전하다

W Jason, what time is it?
M Don't worry. We have enough time. The charity concert will start at 7 p.m.
W Okay. Do you have the invitation? **We need it to get in**.
M Yes, I know. I remember we had a problem because we forgot it last year.
W We did. It was terrible. **We should not make the same mistake twice**.
M That's right. Oh, and it's pretty cold today. Do you have your scarf and gloves?
W Yes, I do.
M Also, we should not forget to take our phones, too.
W Of course not. **Please bring the extra phone batteries**.
M Okay, I will. Are they in the living room?
W Yes, and I already checked. **They are fully charged**.
M Oh, did you? Good. Thank you, Sarah.

여 Jason, 지금 몇 시니?
남 걱정 마. 시간 충분해. 자선 음악회는 7시에 시작해.
여 알았어. 초대장 있지? 입장하려면 그게 있어야 해.
남 알아. 작년에 그것을 잊어버려서 문제가 있었잖아.
여 그랬지. 끔찍했어. 같은 실수를 두 번 하면 안 돼.
남 맞아. 아, 오늘 꽤 추워. 스카프하고 장갑 가지고 있지?
여 응, 가지고 있어.
남 또, 우리 전화기 챙기는 것도 잊으면 안 돼.
여 물론이지. 전화기 보조 배터리도 여분으로 더 챙겨.
남 알았어. 그건 거실에 있어?
여 응, 그리고 내가 이미 확인했어. 충전이 다 되었더라.
남 정말? 잘했네. 고마워, Sarah.

---

06 | 정답 | ②

2박 3일 여행 예산을 계산하는 상황이다. 숙소는 200달러이며, 식사는 1인 1식 기준으로 10달러이며 총 열두 번의 식사는 120달러이다. 마지막으로 통행료는 왕복 40달러이므로 두 사람이 지출할 금액은 360달러로 정답은 ②이다.

* budget 예산
* accommodations 숙박 시설
* original 원래의
* rate 요금
* toll 통행료
* pack 짐을 싸다

M Honey, did you finish the budget plan for our trip this weekend?
W Yes, I'm almost done.
M So, **how much money do we expect to spend** on our trip?
W First, $200 for the accommodations.
M Oh, that's cheaper than I expected.
W Yes, it is. The original rate was $300. **We got a discount** because we have a membership card.
M Don't worry too much about trying to save money. What about the food?
W Well, I haven't looked for places to eat yet. But I'm thinking about spending $10 per meal. Since it's a three-day trip, **how many meals do you think we will have**?
M I think 6 meals per person in 3 days should be enough.
W That's 12 meals in total, then. We also have to consider the highway tolls. It will be around $40 in order to go and return.
M **Our budget is much lower than I expected**. Let's start packing, then.

남 여보, 이번 주말여행 예산 계획 다 끝냈어요?
여 네, 거의 다 끝냈어요.
남 그럼, 우리 여행에 돈을 얼마나 쓰게 될 것 같아요?
여 우선, 숙박비는 200달러예요.
남 아, 생각한 것보다 싸네요.
여 그래요. 원래 요금은 300달러였어요. 우리가 회원 카드를 가지고 있어서 할인을 받았어요.
남 돈을 절약하려고 너무 염려하지 말아요. 식비는요?
여 음, 아직 식사할 곳을 찾아보지 않았어요. 그렇지만 한 끼에 10달러 정도 쓸 생각하고 있어요. 3일 여행이니까, 우리가 식사를 몇 번 하게 될까요?
남 내 생각에 3일 동안에 1인당 여섯 끼면 되지 않을까 해요.
여 그러면 총 열두 끼네요. 고속도로 통행료도 생각해야 해요. 오고 가는 데 40달러 정도일 것 같네요.
남 내가 생각한 것보다 예산이 훨씬 더 적네요. 그럼, 짐을 쌉시다.

07 | 정답 | ⑤

집에 가기 전에 간단하게 먹자는 남자의 제안을 거절하고 여자가 서둘러 집에 가야 한다고 말하는 상황이다. 뉴욕에서 사는 친구 전화를 받기 위해 8시 전에 집에 가야 한다고 했으므로 정답은 ⑤이다.

* hectic 몹시 바쁜
* barely 간신히, 가까스로
* grab a bite 간단히 먹다
* how come 왜, 어찌하여
* in a hurry 서둘러서
* time zone 표준시간대

W It was so hectic today at work, wasn't it?
M There were too many meetings. I barely had time for lunch.
W Same here. I only had a salad for lunch because I had to stay at the office.
M Well, I'm just glad today is over. **I'm going to grab a bite** before I go home. Do you want to join?
W I'd love to, but I can't.
M But you only had a salad for lunch. Aren't you hungry?
W I am, but I have to get home before 8 o'clock.
M **Is there a TV show you have to catch on TV**?
W No, I don't like watching TV that much.
M How come you are in such a hurry?
W **I have to answer a phone call from a friend** in New York. He said he'd call me at 8 p.m. in our time zone.
M I see. I was going to take you to the new sandwich place across the street.
W I'll join you next time. I'd better hurry. There's only half an hour left.

여 오늘 직장에서 무척 바빴죠, 그렇지 않나요?
남 회의가 너무 많았어요. 점심도 간신히 먹었어요.
여 저도 그랬어요. 계속 사무실에 있어야 해서 점심으로 샐러드만 먹었네요.
남 아, 아무튼 오늘이 끝나서 좋아요. 집에 가기 전에 뭘 좀 먹어야겠어요. 같이 갈래요?
여 그러고 싶은데 못 갈 것 같아요.
남 점심에 샐러드만 먹었잖아요. 배고프지 않아요?
여 배고프지만, 8시 전에는 집에 가 있어야 해요.
남 꼭 봐야 할 TV 프로그램이 있어요?
여 아니요, 텔레비전 보는 걸 그렇게 좋아하지 않아요.
남 그럼 왜 그렇게 서둘러 가야 해요?
여 뉴욕에 있는 친구 전화를 받아야 해서요. 우리 시간으로 오후 8시에 전화한다고 했거든요.
남 알겠어요. 길 건너에 새로 생긴 샌드위치 가게에 데려가려고 했거든요.
여 다음에 갈게요. 서둘러야겠어요. 이제 30분밖에 안 남았거든요.

08 | 정답 | ②

대화 내용에서 주최 기관에 대한 언급은 없으므로 정답은 ②이다.

* refer to ~을 가리키다
* be known for ~로 (잘) 알려지다
* household 가구, 세대
* aim ~을 목표로 하다
* promote 장려하다
* decline 감소하다

W John, do you want to go to the Haenyeo Festival?
M The Haenyeo Festival? I've never heard of it before. What is it?
W Haenyeo refers to the female divers in Jeju-do. They are known for their independent spirit and for being the heads of their households.
M So, what is the Haenyeo Festival about?
W **It aims to maintain their culture and promote it**. The number of divers is declining since they are all over the age of 50.
M I see. Where is it held?
W It is at the Haenyeo Museum, **where you can learn about their history and lifestyle**.
M When is the festival?
W It runs from September 20th to the 22nd.
M That's the weekend we are in Jeju-do. We should go!
W Yes, we should. When we go, we can also enjoy **fun activities like catching fish with our hands**. There will be fresh seafood dishes to try, too.
M Wow, I'm looking forward to it.

여 John, 너 Haenyeo 축제에 가볼래?
남 Haenyeo 축제? 들어 본 적이 없어. 그게 뭐야?
여 Haenyeo는 제주도의 여자 잠수부를 가리키는 말이야. 그분들은 독립심과 집안의 가장이라는 것으로 잘 알려져 있어.
남 그럼, Haenyeo 축제는 어떤 거야?
여 Haenyeo 축제는 그들의 문화를 지키고 장려하고자 하는 것이 목적이야. 그분들 모두가 50세가 넘는 분들이라서 해녀 수가 줄어들고 있거든.
남 그렇구나. 어디서 열리니?
여 Haenyeo 박물관에서 열리는데 그곳에서 그들의 역사와 생활상을 배울 수 있어.
남 축제는 언제야?
여 9월 20일에서 22일까지 열려.
남 우리가 제주도에 있는 주말이구나. 우리 가보는 게 좋을 것 같아!
여 그래. 그때 가면, 맨손으로 물고기 잡기 같은 재미있는 활동도 할 수 있어. 신선한 해산물도 먹어볼 수 있을 거야.
남 와, 기대된다.

09 | 정답 | ⑤

한 달에 한 번씩 강연이 있고, 모든 강연은 무료이지만 최소 일주일 전에는 신청해야 한다고 하였다. 강연 후에는 설문지를 제출해야 한다고 했으며 강연 목록은 곧 홈페이지에 올리겠다고 했으므로 일치하지 않는 것은 ⑤이다.

* Liberal Arts 교양 과목, 인문학
* lecture 강연, 강의
* renowned 유명한
* expertise 전공 지식
* attend 참석하다
* questionnaire 설문지
* prospect 전망
* line up 준비하다, 마련하다

W Hello, everyone. I'm Jane Owens from the School of Liberal Arts. I'm pleased to announce our Liberal Arts Lectures program to you. Our program is 6 months long **with a special lecture once a month**. Those lectures will be given by renowned lecturers including *2023 Korea Trend* writer Paul Kim. There will also be other guest speakers who will talk about their areas of expertise. All guest lectures are free, and you are welcome to attend, but you should sign up online for each lecture **at least one week in advance**. You must also answer a questionnaire after each lecture. Our first guest lecturer is James Miller from Newcastle University. He will talk about AI and its prospects. **We have additional guest lectures lined up**, and I'll be sure to post the list on our

여 안녕하세요, 여러분. 저는 문과 대학에서 온 Jane Owens입니다. 여러분에게 교양 과목 프로그램을 알려드리게 되어서 기쁩니다. 우리 프로그램은 한 달에 한 번씩 특별한 강연과 함께 6개월간 진행됩니다. 그 강연들은 〈2023년 한국의 트렌드〉를 쓰신 Paul Kim을 비롯한 유명한 강사들이 참여하실 것입니다. 뿐만 아니라 다른 초청 강사들이 오셔서 자신들의 전공 분야에 대한 말씀을 해 주실 것입니다. 모든 초청 강연은 무료이며, 많이 참석해 주시되, 모든 강연은 적어도 일주일 전에 미리 온라인으로 신청하셔야 합니다. 여러분께서는 각 강연이 끝난 후에 설문에도 답해 주셔야 합니다. 첫 번째 강사는 Newcastle 대학교의 James Miller입니다. 그분은 인공지능과 그것의 전망에 대하여 말씀해 주실 것입니다. 다른 초청 강연들도 준비되어 있으며, 곧 우리 홈페이지에 목록을 올리겠습니다. 프로그램을 신청하시려면 초청 강연 링크를 확인해 주세요. 감사합니다.

homepage soon. To sign up for the program, check the Guest Lectures link. Thank you.

---

10 | 정답 | ④

중간 사이즈 이상에 캔버스 천 재질이 아니며 방수가 되는 가방을 원한다고 했다. 행사 선물은 보조 배터리인 것으로 구매한다고 하였으므로 남자가 구매할 가방은 ④이다.

* annual 연례의
* leaflet 전단지
* material 재료
* available 이용 가능한
* nylon 나일론
* polyester 폴리에스터 (섬유)
* canvas 캔버스 천
* waterproof 방수의
* power bank 보조 배터리
* settle 결정하다

W Ricky, Leisure and Sports is having their big annual sale now.
M Oh, I need to buy a backpack. I was thinking about getting a light backpack for my trip next week.
W Have a look at the leaflet here.
M Okay, **it should be big enough for the many things** I have to carry.
W Then I think it should be at least a medium size.
M Yes, I think so, too. What materials are available?
W You can choose nylon, polyester, or canvas. When it comes to its material, I think polyester is the best.
M Well, anything will be okay except canvas. **And I need it to be waterproof**.
W All right. Now, there are only two options left to choose from.
M That one is more expensive, but **it comes with a power bank**, so it seems like a better choice.
W Okay. It's settled then.

여 Ricky, Leisure and Sports에서 연례 세일 행사를 하고 있어.
남 아, 나 배낭 하나 사야 하는데. 다음 주에 갈 여행용으로 가벼운 배낭을 살 생각이었거든.
여 여기 전단지를 좀 봐.
남 알았어. 여러 가지를 넣고 다녀야 해서 충분히 커야 해.
여 그럼 적어도 중간 사이즈는 되어야 하겠네.
남 그래. 나도 그렇게 생각해. 재질은 어떤 것들이 있니?
여 나일론, 폴리에스터, 아니면 캔버스 천을 선택할 수 있어. 재질에 관해서 말하면 나는 폴리에스터가 제일이라고 생각해.
남 음. 캔버스 천만 아니면 괜찮을 것 같네. 그리고 방수가 되는 거여야 해.
여 그래. 그럼. 나머지 두 가지 중에서 선택하면 되겠네.
남 저건 좀 비싸긴 하지만 보조 배터리도 준다니까 더 나은 것 같아.
여 알았어. 그럼 정해졌네.

---

11 | 정답 | ④

혼자 사는 여자에게 남자가 부모님으로부터 더 빨리 독립해야 하는지 의견을 물어보는 상황이다. 따라서 남자의 말에 가장 적절한 여자의 응답은 ④ '상황에 따라 다르지. 혼자 산다는 건 말처럼 쉽지는 않아.'이다.

* in no hurry 급하지 않은
[선택지]
* chore 《복수형》 집안일
* landlord 집주인
* It depends. 상황에 따라 다르다.

M I heard you moved out of your parents' house. How do you like living on your own?
W It's not bad. Do you have **any plans to get a place of your own**?
M I'm thinking about doing it next year. I'm in no hurry, but do you think **I should move out sooner**?
W It depends. Living by yourself is not as easy as it sounds.

남 네가 부모님 집에서 독립했다고 들었어. 혼자 사니까 어떠니?
여 나쁘지 않아. 너도 혼자 지낼 곳을 마련할 계획이니?
남 내년에 그렇게 할 생각이야. 급할 건 없지만 내가 더 빨리 나와야 할 것 같아?
여 상황에 따라 다르지. 혼자 산다는 건 말처럼 쉽지는 않아.

① 안 돼. 너는 먼저 집안일을 끝내야 해.
② 아니. 나는 부모님과 너무 멀리 떨어져 살아.
③ 너는 집주인에게 집세를 물어봐야 해.
⑤ 응. 부모님과 함께 사는 게 이점이 더 많아.

---

12 | 정답 | ④

이번 주 금요일이나 토요일에 새 전시회에 가자고 제안하는 여자의 말에 가장 적절한 남자의 응답은 ④ '금요일이 더 좋을 것 같아. 다음 날은 다른 게 있어.'이다.

* exhibition 전시회
* dinosaur 공룡
[선택지]
* refundable 환불 가능한

W John, **I'm planning to visit** the new exhibition about dinosaurs this weekend. Are you interested?
M Of course. You are talking about the one at the Modern Museum, right?
W Right. **The exhibition is on until this Sunday**. So I was thinking about going this Friday or Saturday.
M Friday would be better. I have something else the next day.

여 John, 이번 주말에 새로 열리는 공룡 전시회에 가려고 해. 너도 관심 있니?
남 물론 가고 싶어. Modern Museum에서 열리는 전시회 말하는 거지?
여 맞아. 전시회가 이번 주 일요일까지야. 그래서 이번 주 금요일이나 토요일에 가려고 하는데.
남 금요일이 더 좋을 것 같아. 다음 날은 다른 게 있어.

① 좋아. 전시회가 아직 열리나 확인할게.
② 물론이지. 나도 이번 주 주말이 좋아.
③ 미안하지만 안 돼. 일요일마다 교회에 가야 해.
⑤ 전시회 당일에 입장권 환불은 안 돼.

---

13 | 정답 | ①

수학 성적 때문에 과외를 고민하는 여자에게 남자는 스스로 문제를 인지하고 해결책을 찾는 것이 중요하다고 조언하고 있다. 따라서 남자의 마지막 말에 여자의 응답으로 가장 적절한 것은 ① '아니요, 아빠. 한 번 더 해볼게요.'이다.

* private tutoring 개인 과외
* assignment 과제
* rely on ~에 의존하다
* recognize 인지하다

M Anna, you look upset. What's wrong?
W Hi, Dad. Do you think I need private tutoring?
M What do you mean? I thought you were doing fine in school.
W I feel like **I am a little bit behind in class**, especially in math.
M Are your math grades bad?
W I think so. There are weekly assignments, but sometimes I get lost when solving questions.
M Having a private tutor is not a bad idea, but **I don't want you to rely on one** too much.

남 Anna, 기분이 안 좋아 보이네. 무슨 일 있니?
여 예, 아빠. 제가 개인 과외를 받을 필요가 있을까요?
남 무슨 뜻이니? 나는 네가 학교에서 공부를 잘하고 있다고 생각했는데.
여 저는 반에서 좀 뒤처지는 것 같아요, 특히 수학에서요.
남 수학 성적이 안 좋니?
여 그런 것 같아요. 주간 과제가 있는데 가끔 문제를 풀다 보면 어떻게 해야 할지 모르겠어요.
남 개인 과외 선생님을 두는 것이 나쁘지는 않지만 네가 거기에 너무 많이 의존하는 것을 바라지 않아.

W That's what I'm worried about, too.
M It's more important that **you recognize your problem and find the solution** on your own. Do you still think you need a tutor?
W No, Dad. I'll give it another try.

여 그게 저도 걱정돼요.
남 네 문제를 인지하고 스스로 해결책을 찾는 것이 더 중요하지. 그래도 개인 과외 선생님이 필요하다고 생각하니?
여 아니요, 아빠. 한 번 더 해 볼게요.

② 당연히 그렇지요. 저는 개인 과외가 필요하다고 생각하지 않았어요.
③ 아니에요. 이 문제는 우리가 해결할 것이 아니네요.
④ 알겠어요. 이제부터는 제가 알아서 학교에 갈게요.
⑤ 저도 같은 생각이에요. 아빠는 어려운 수학 문제를 풀 수 있어요.

---

14 | 정답 | ①

취업 대신에 대학원으로 진학하기로 했다는 여자에게 남자가 격려하는 상황이다. 장학금을 신청하기 위해 교수님의 추천서가 필요하다는 여자의 말에 남자가 기꺼이 써주겠다고 말하는 것이 자연스러우므로 정답은 ① '물론이지. 기쁜 마음으로 써 줄 수 있어.'이다.

* graduate school 대학원
* potential 가능성
* scholar 학자
* scholarship 장학금
* tuition 등록금, 수업료
* qualify 자격을 주다
* recommendation 추천
  [선택지]
* résumé 이력서

W Hello, Dr. Quinn. Do you have a moment?
M Yes, Susie. What can I do for you?
W Well, I've been thinking about what to do after graduating. After talking to my parents, I've decided to go to a graduate school instead of getting a job.
M That's a good choice. **I've always thought you had the potential** to become a scholar.
W Thank you so much. But I need a scholarship because I cannot afford the tuition by myself.
M I see. **Do your grades qualify you** to apply for a scholarship?
W Yes. I have everything ready to apply for it, **except for one thing**.
M And what is that?
W **I need a recommendation letter from a professor**. Do you think you could write one for me?
M Of course. I would be happy to do that.

여 안녕하세요, Quinn 교수님. 잠깐 시간 있으신가요?
남 그럼. Susie. 뭘 도와줄까?
여 졸업한 후에 뭘 할지에 대해서 생각해 왔는데요. 부모님과 얘기를 나누고 나서 취업 대신 대학원에 가기로 했습니다.
남 잘 생각했네. 나는 항상 네가 학자가 될 가능성이 있다고 생각해 왔거든.
여 감사합니다. 그렇지만 제가 혼자 힘으로 등록금을 낼 여유가 없어서 장학금이 필요한데요.
남 그렇구나. 장학금을 신청할 성적은 되니?
여 네. 한 가지만 빼고 신청할 준비가 모두 되었어요.
남 그게 뭔데?
여 교수님의 추천서가 필요해요. 저를 위해서 써 주실 수 있으신가요?
남 물론이지. 기쁜 마음으로 써 줄 수 있어.

② 알았어. 내가 이메일로 이력서를 보낼게.
③ 안됐구나. 그렇지만 다음에는 더 잘할 거야.
④ 미안해. 너는 신청할 자격이 안 되는 것 같아.
⑤ 그래. 나는 대학원을 지원하지 않는 걸 권하겠어.

---

15 | 정답 | ①

해외 토론회에 참가하게 된 Scott이 긴장하여 많은 사람 앞에서 말하는 것에 대해 걱정이 된다고 하자, 그의 엄마가 격려의 말을 건네는 상황이다. 따라서 정답은 ① '걱정하지 마. 너는 잘할 거라 믿어.'이다.

* relief 구호
* contribution 공헌
* conference 회의, 학회
* debate 토론
* in public 사람들 앞에서, 공적으로
* cheer up 기운을 돋우다
* encourage 격려하다

W Scott is a high school student. He has participated in a relief program run by an international volunteering organization. This month the organization recognizes his contributions by awarding him a prize. In addition, **he has been chosen to attend** the International Volunteer Conference, which will be held in New York in two months. At first, Scott gets very excited about going to New York since he's never been abroad. However, when he finds out about the conference, he gets worried and nervous. He has to participate in a debate with foreign students and **prepare a speech to give in public**. He tells his mom about the conference and how nervous he gets giving public speeches. When his mother hears this, **she wants to cheer him up and encourage him**. In this situation, what would Scott's mother most likely say to Scott?

Scott's mother Don't worry. I'm sure you'll do great.

여 Scott은 고등학교 학생이다. 그는 한 국제자원봉사기구가 운영하는 구호 프로그램에 참여해 왔다. 그 기구에서 이번 달에 그의 공헌을 인정해서 그에서 상을 주게 된다. 뿐만 아니라, 그는 국제자원봉사 회의에 참석자로 선정되는데 그것은 두 달 후에 뉴욕에서 열릴 것이다. Scott은 해외에 가 본 적이 없어서 처음에는 뉴욕에 가는 것에 무척 기뻐한다. 그러나 그 회의에 관해 알게 되고는 걱정하며 불안해한다. 그는 외국 학생들과 토론회에 참가해야 하고 대중 연설을 준비해야 한다. 그는 엄마에게 그 회의와 자신이 대중 연설을 할 때 얼마나 긴장하는지에 대해 이야기한다. 그의 엄마는 이 말을 듣고, 그의 기운을 돋워 주고 그를 격려하고자 한다. 이러한 상황에서 Scott의 엄마가 Scott에게 할 말로 가장 적절한 것은 무엇인가?

Scott의 엄마 걱정하지 마, 너는 잘할 거라 믿어.

② 힘내. 네 연설이 그렇게 나쁘지 않았어.
③ 축하해. 나는 네가 해낼 수 있다는 걸 알고 있었어.
④ 마음을 편히 해야 해. 너는 이 상을 받을 자격이 있어.
⑤ 네가 더 준비했다면 이렇게 느끼지 않았겠지.

---

16 | 정답 | ②

soul food가 미국 흑인 문화에서 시작되었다고 하며, 여러 soul food라고 불리는 음식들을 예시로 들어 설명하고 있다. 따라서 남자가 하는 말의 주제로 가장 적절한 것은 ② '미국 soul food의 유래와 예'이다.

M Hello, everyone. I am Joe Robinson on *Are You Hungry?* **Are you familiar with the expression** "soul food?" Many of you would think of fried chicken when you hear "American soul food." But did you know that soul food originated from mid-1960's African American culture in the Southern United States? It uses a variety of ingredients and cooking styles, **some of which came from Africa** and were brought over by African slaves. We call it "soul"

남 안녕하세요, 여러분. 〈Are You Hungry?〉의 Joe Robinson입니다. 여러분은 'soul food'라는 표현 알고 계신가요? '미국의 soul food'라는 말을 들으면 많은 분들은 프라이드치킨을 생각할 겁니다. 그러나 soul food는 원래 1960년대 중반 미국 남부의 흑인 문화에서 유래한 것이라는 것을 알고 계셨나요? 이 soul food는 여러 가지 식재료와 요리 방법을 쓰는데요. 일부는 아프리카에서 온 것으로 아프리카 노예들이 가지고 온 것이었습니다. 'soul'이 미국의 흑인 문화를 설명할 때 쓰이는 일상적인 단어였기 때문에 우리가 그것을

17 | 정답 | ⑤

soul food의 예시로 '미트로프'에 대한 언급은 없었으므로 정답은 ⑤이다.

- originate from ~에서 유래하다
- a variety of 다양한
- ingredient 재료
- common 흔히 쓰이는
  cf. commonly 흔히, 보통
- typical 전형적인
- adapt from ~에서 응용하다
- buttermilk 버터밀크 《버터를 만들고 남은 우유》
- dice 깍둑썰기를 하다
  [선택지]
- origin 유래, 기원
- arising 떠오르는
- slavery 노예제도
- nutrition 영양

food because "soul" was a common word used to describe African American culture. Another typical American soul food is fried fish, adapted from the method of frying chicken. Other types of soul food **use corn as their main ingredient**. An example of this would be cornbread, commonly made with buttermilk. Also, hushpuppies are made with corn, salt and diced onions. Now let's look at a video of how each dish is made, and then have a discussion.

'soul' 푸드라고 부르는 것입니다. 또 한 가지 대표적인 미국의 soul food는 닭을 튀기는 방법을 응용한 생선튀김입니다. 다른 soul food 종류에서는 주재료로 옥수수를 사용하는데요. 이 soul food의 예로 보통 버터밀크로 만드는 옥수수빵이 있겠습니다. 또 허시퍼피(hushpuppy)도 옥수수, 소금, 그리고 다진 양파로 만든 것입니다. 자, 이제 이런 음식을 어떻게 만드는지 비디오를 먼저 보고 이야기를 나눠 봅시다.

16 ① 미국 흑인 음악 문화의 역사
② 미국 soul food의 유래와 예
③ 미국 명절 때 즐겨 먹는 대표 음식
④ 미국 남부에서 새롭게 떠오르는 음식 문화
⑤ 노예제가 아프리카인의 영양에 끼친 영향

17 ① 프라이드치킨 ② 생선튀김 ③ 옥수수빵
④ 허시퍼피 ⑤ 미트로프

01 | 정답 | ⑤

남자는 학교 축제가 성공적으로 개최되었다는 말과 함께 이는 모두 학교의 학생들과 선생님들 덕분이라고 말하고 있으므로 남자가 하는 말의 목적으로 ⑤가 가장 적절하다.

* principal 교장
* annual 연례의, 매년의
* talent 재능, 끼
* complimentary 칭찬하는; 무료의
* local community 지역 사회
* thanks to ~ 덕분에
* appreciate 감사하다
* enthusiasm 열정

M Good morning, everyone. This is your principal speaking. I hope all of you **enjoyed the annual school festival** yesterday. It was great to see your different talents, not to mention the results of various club activities. I heard complimentary words from your parents and other guests who came to the festival. I know that everyone at school and from the local community has put a lot of effort into the festival. **It was all thanks to you**, the students and teachers at Jefferson High School, that we could **hold yesterday's event successfully**. You have made everyone proud. Again, **I appreciate your hard work** and enthusiasm for the school festival, and I hope you enjoy the rest of the year. Thank you.

남 좋은 아침입니다. 여러분. 교장 선생님입니다. 여러분 모두 어제 학교 연례 축제를 즐겁게 보냈길 바랍니다. 다양한 동아리 활동의 결과물은 말할 것도 없고 여러분의 다양한 재능을 볼 수 있어 정말 좋았습니다. 축제에 오신 학부모님들과 내빈들로부터 칭찬의 말씀을 들었습니다. 우리 학교와 지역 사회의 모든 분이 축제에 많은 노력을 기울인 것을 알고 있습니다. 어제의 행사를 성공적으로 개최할 수 있었던 것은 모두 Jefferson 고등학교의 학생들과 선생님들 덕분입니다. 여러분이 모두를 자랑스럽게 만들었습니다. 한 번 더 학교 축제를 위한 여러분의 노고와 열정에 대해 감사를 표합니다. 그리고 남은 한 해를 즐겁게 보내길 바랍니다. 감사합니다.

02 | 정답 | ②

자신이 즐기며 읽을 수 있는 책을 읽어야 한다는 남자와는 반대로 여자는 다양한 관점에 대해 배우는 것이 독서의 목적이라고 말하고 있으므로 여자의 의견으로 가장 적절한 것은 ②이다.

* to be honest 솔직히 말하면
* against ~와 반대되는
* belief 신념, 의견, 확신
* perspective 관점
* have a point 일리 있다
* keep A from B A가 B하지 못하게 하다

W Jason, what are you reading?
M I'm reading a book called How Positive Thinking Changes Your Life.
W Oh, isn't that a bestseller? How do you like it so far?
M To be honest, I'm not really enjoying it.
W Really? Why not?
M Some of the things that the writer talks about **are against my beliefs**.
W Isn't that the purpose of reading? You can **learn about different perspectives** people have through reading.
M You have a point. But I still believe you should read books that you actually like and enjoy reading.
W Okay, but don't you think that will only **keep you from learning about different beliefs**?
M When you put it that way, I'd have to agree with you. I guess I'll go ahead and finish the book, then.
W Good idea. Tell me what you think after you finish reading it.

여 Jason, 무얼 읽고 있니?
남 〈긍정적 사고가 어떻게 당신의 삶을 바꾸는가〉라는 책을 읽고 있어.
여 아, 그 책 베스트셀러 아니야? 지금까지 어때?
남 솔직히 말하면, 별로 재미있지 않아.
여 정말? 왜?
남 작가가 하는 말 중 일부가 나의 신념과는 반대이거든.
여 그게 독서의 목적 아닐까? 독서를 통해 사람들이 갖고 있는 서로 다른 관점에 대해 배울 수 있잖아.
남 너의 말에도 일리가 있어. 하지만 나는 읽는 사람이 정말로 좋아하고 즐기며 읽을 수 있는 책을 읽어야 한다고 생각해.
여 그래, 하지만 그렇게 하면 다양한 신념에 대해 배울 수 없을 것 같지 않아?
남 그렇게 말한다면 동의할 수밖에 없겠다. 그럼, 계속해서 책을 끝까지 읽어 봐야 할 것 같네.
여 좋은 생각이야. 끝까지 읽어 보고 네 생각이 어떤지 얘기해 줘.

03 | 정답 | ⑤

연구 결과를 인용하여 음악이 운동의 리듬과 일치하면 신체를 더 효율적으로 움직이는 데 도움을 주어 운동 시간을 늘릴 수 있다고 말하고 있으므로 남자가 하는 말의 요지로 가장 적절한 것은 ⑤이다.

* on-air 방송(중)의
* duration 지속 기간
* workout 운동
* give it a try 시도하다, 한 번 해보다
* onward 앞으로

M Good evening! Welcome to Health Horizons. It's Peterson, your on-air exercise coach. Are you ready to increase your exercise time? Music can help you do just that! Recent studies have shown that **listening to music while exercising can increase the duration of your workout**. This is because **when music matches the rhythm of your exercise**, it can help your body move more efficiently. So, if you want to make your exercise time last longer, try working out with music. It's not just about burning calories, **but also about enjoying the experience**. Give it a try from today onwards and see the difference it makes!

남 좋은 저녁입니다! Health Horizons에 오신 것을 환영합니다. 여러분의 방송 운동 코치 Peterson입니다. 운동 시간을 늘릴 준비가 되셨나요? 음악이 여러분이 그것을 할 수 있도록 도울 수 있습니다! 최근 연구들은 운동을 하는 동안 음악을 듣는 것이 운동의 지속 시간을 늘릴 수 있다는 것을 보여주었습니다. 이것은 음악이 운동의 리듬과 일치하면 신체가 더 효율적으로 움직이는 데 도움을 줄 수 있기 때문입니다. 그러므로 여러분이 운동 시간을 더 오래 지속시키고 싶다면, 음악과 함께 운동을 해보세요. 그것은 단지 칼로리를 태우는 것뿐만 아니라, 그 경험을 즐기는 것이기도 합니다. 오늘부터 그것을 시도해보고 그것이 어떤 차이를 만드는지 알아보세요!

04 | 정답 | ⑤

아무도 도와주는 사람이 없어 여자 혼자 모래성을 지어야 했다고 말하고 있으므로 대화의 내용과 일치하지 않는

M Jamie, is this a picture from your summer vacation?
W Yes, it is. I had so much fun at the beach with my relatives.
M I love **the tall palm tree on the left**. When I see palm trees, I feel like I am traveling abroad.

남 Jamie, 이거 여름휴가 때 사진이니?
여 응. 맞아. 해변에서 친척들과 너무나 즐거운 시간을 보냈어.
남 왼쪽에 큰 야자수가 맘에 든다. 야자수를 보면 해외여행을 하고 있는 기분이 들어.

것은 ⑤이다.

* relative 친척
* palm tree 야자수
* scenery 경치, 풍경
* rewarding 보람 있는

W I know what you mean. The scenery was beautiful and the weather was perfect.

M That sounds lovely! Who is the boy flying a kite?

W That's my cousin Jim. He made a beautiful kite himself just for the vacation.

M Wow. That must have been a lot of work. I see **another boy pointing at the kite** next to your cousin.

W That's his younger brother, Matt. He was wearing a hat because he doesn't like sunlight.

M And look at the girl next to him! Is that you?

W Yes, it's me.

M Your hair is tied back in a ponytail! You look cute. It seems like you're making something with the sand. What is it?

W A sandcastle. **I had to build it all by myself** because no one helped me, but I had a lot of fun. And when I finished, it felt very rewarding.

M I'm glad you had fun. You needed that rest.

W I know. I wish I could go there again next year.

여 무슨 말인지 알아. 경치가 너무 아름답고 날씨도 완벽했어.

남 정말 좋았겠네! 연을 날리고 있는 남자아이는 누구니?

여 내 사촌 Jim이야. 이번 휴가를 위해서 직접 아름다운 연을 만들었어.

남 우와. 고생 많이 했겠네. 네 사촌 옆에서 연을 가리키고 있는 다른 남자아이도 보이네.

여 Jim의 남동생 Matt야. 햇볕을 안 좋아해서 모자를 쓰고 있었어.

남 옆에 있는 여자아이를 봐! 그게 너니?

여 응, 나야.

남 머리를 포니테일로 묶었구나! 귀엽다. 모래로 뭔가를 만들고 있는 것 같네. 뭘 만들고 있니?

여 모래성이야. 아무도 도와주지 않아서 혼자 지어야 했지만, 그래도 재밌었어. 그리고 다 지었을 때 아주 보람을 느꼈어.

남 재미있었다니 다행이다. 너는 휴식이 좀 필요했어.

여 맞아. 내년에 또 가고 싶어.

---

05 | 정답 | ④

프린터에 잉크가 떨어졌다는 여자의 말에 자신이 회의실을 정리하는 동안 새 잉크를 넣어 줄 수 있냐고 남자가 여자에게 부탁하고 있으므로 정답은 ④이다.

* messy 지저분한, 엉망인
* give A a hand A를 도와주다
* pamphlet 팸플릿, 소책자
* handout 유인물, 인쇄물
* run out of ~을 다 써 버리다, ~을 바닥내다

W Jack, we should check if we have everything for the meeting this afternoon.

M Oh, right, the meeting. I need **to clean up our meeting room**. It's a little messy from last night's seminar.

W Would you like me to give you a hand?

M It's okay. I can do it by myself.

W All right. What else do we need to do?

M Oh, we **have to pick up the pamphlets** from the design company.

W Actually, they sent the pamphlets to our office this morning, so we don't have to worry about them.

M That's great. I should **print out the handouts** for the meeting.

W Oh, but we need new ink. We just ran out of it this morning.

M Could you **get the ink for the printer** while I go upstairs and get the meeting room ready?

W Of course. I can do that.

여 Jack, 오늘 오후 회의를 위해 모든 게 준비됐는지 확인해야 해요.

남 아, 맞네요. 회의. 저는 회의실을 청소해야겠어요. 어젯밤 세미나 때문에 약간 지저분하거든요.

여 제가 도와드릴까요?

남 괜찮아요. 저 혼자 할 수 있어요.

여 알겠어요. 뭘 더 해야 할까요?

남 아, 디자인 회사에서 팸플릿을 찾아와야 하네요.

여 사실 그 회사에서 오늘 아침에 우리 사무실로 팸플릿을 보내줘서 그건 신경 쓰지 않아도 돼요.

남 잘됐네요. 회의에 필요한 유인물을 인쇄해야겠어요.

여 아, 그런데 프린터에 새 잉크가 필요해요. 오늘 아침에 막 떨어졌거든요.

남 제가 위층에 가서 회의실을 정리하는 동안 잉크를 넣어 주시겠어요?

여 물론이죠. 그렇게 할게요.

---

06 | 정답 | ③

향수가 50ml 한 병에 60달러이지만 선물세트는 20달러가 추가되므로 총액은 80달러이고 10% 할인을 적용하면 72달러이다. 따라서 정답은 ③이다.

* cosmetics 화장품
* perfume 향수
* particular 특정한
* recommend 추천하다
* similar 비슷한
* floral 꽃의
* scent 향기; 향기가 나다
* gift set 선물 세트

M Welcome to Olive Cosmetics. How may I help you?

W Hello, I'm looking for perfume for my mother.

M Do you have any particular perfume in your mind?

W I brought a sample she wears. **Can you recommend something similar**?

M All right. [Pause] It seems like she likes floral scents. How about this one by Marc Kors?

W [Inhale] Wow, it's **almost exactly like the one I brought**. How much is it?

M This 50-milliliter bottle is $60. But **you can also make it a gift set** for $20 more.

W What's in the gift set?

M It includes another 5-milliliter bottle, hand cream, and a scented candle.

W That sounds like a good deal. I'll take the gift set.

M Of course. **Is there anything else you need**?

W No, thanks. Oh, can I use this 10% coupon?

M Certainly. How would you like to pay?

W I'll pay by credit card, please.

남 Olive Cosmetics에 오신 걸 환영합니다. 어떻게 도와드릴까요?

여 안녕하세요. 저는 어머니에게 드릴 향수를 찾고 있어요.

남 특별히 생각하고 계신 향수가 있나요?

여 어머니가 뿌리는 샘플을 가져왔어요. 비슷한 걸로 추천해 주시겠어요?

남 좋아요. [잠시 후] 어머니가 꽃향기를 좋아하시는 것 같네요. Marc Kors에서 나온 이건 어때요?

여 [숨을 들이쉬고] 와, 이건 제가 가져온 것과 거의 똑같네요. 얼마예요?

남 이 50ml 병이 60달러입니다. 하지만 20달러만 더 내면 선물 세트로 만들 수 있어요.

여 선물 세트에는 뭐가 들어가요?

남 5ml 병 하나, 핸드크림, 그리고 향초가 포함되어 있어요.

여 좋은 가격인 것 같아요. 선물 세트로 살게요.

남 알겠습니다. 더 필요한 거 있으세요?

여 아니요, 괜찮아요. 아, 이 10% 쿠폰을 쓸 수 있나요?

남 그럼요. 어떻게 지불하시겠어요?

여 신용카드로 할게요.

07 | 정답 | ②

남자는 심한 감기에 걸렸지만 쪽지 시험 당일 출석을 했고, 감기가 심해져서 조퇴하게 되면서 시험을 치르지 못 하게 되었다고 말하고 있으므로 정답은 ②이다.

* physics 물리학
* grade 성적
* quiz 쪽지 시험
* worth ~의 가치가 있는
* suffer (질병 등에) 시달리다
* make up 보충하다

W Peter, you look upset. What's the matter?

M I am worried about my physics grades.

W Why? You have always worked hard in physics. It's your favorite subject.

M I know. That's why I am even more upset. It feels like all the hard work I've put in was wasted.

W Why do you say that?

M Well, there was a really important quiz last week, which is worth 15% of the grade.

W I heard it was difficult. Did you **make a lot of mistakes on the quiz**?

M No, that's not it. I missed the quiz.

W That's not good. How come you couldn't take it?

M To start with, **I suffered a terrible cold** the night before.

W Did you miss school on the day of the quiz because you were sick with a cold?

M No. I went to school because I really studied hard for the quiz and wanted to take it.

W Then why didn't you take it?

M The cold got a lot worse and I **had to leave school early before** the physics class started.

W That's too bad. I am sure there is a way to make up the quiz.

여 Peter, 기분이 안 좋아 보여. 무슨 일이야?

남 물리학 성적 때문에 걱정이 돼.

여 왜? 너는 물리학 공부를 항상 열심히 해왔잖아. 네가 가장 좋아하는 과목이고.

남 맞아. 그래서 더 기분이 안 좋아. 내가 들인 모든 노력이 헛되었던 것처럼 느껴져.

여 왜 그렇게 말하는데?

남 그러니까, 저번 주에 성적의 15%나 차지하는 정말 중요한 쪽지 시험이 있었어.

여 그 시험 어려웠다고 들었어. 그 쪽지 시험에서 실수를 많이 했니?

남 아니, 그것 때문이 아냐. 난 시험을 못 치렀어.

여 정말 안됐다. 왜 못 치르게 됐어?

남 일단, 그 전날 밤에 심한 감기에 걸렸어.

여 감기에 걸려 아파서 밤에 시험 당일에 결석을 했니?

남 아니. 정말 열심히 공부했기 때문에 시험을 보고 싶어서 출석했어.

여 그러면 왜 안 치른 거야?

남 감기가 훨씬 더 심해져서 물리학 수업 시작 전에 학교에서 조퇴해야 했거든.

여 정말 안됐구나. 시험을 치르지 못한 것을 보충할 방법이 있을 거야.

08 | 정답 | ②

공연의 시기는 10월이며 장소는 커뮤니티 콘서트홀이다. 티켓은 휴대폰 앱을 통해 구입이 가능하며 그렇게 할 경우 기념품이 제공된다. 따라서 언급되지 않은 것은 ②이다.

* perform 공연하다
* preparation 준비
* venue (콘서트, 경기 등의) 장소
* souvenir 기념품

W Ben, are you performing at the Annual Charity Concert?

M Of course. I can't believe it's already September. **The concert is next month**.

W I know. How is your preparation going?

M I have been practicing for my performance for the last two months. I hope people like it.

W I can't wait to see it.

M I'm already nervous.

W I'm sure you'll do great. Is the event happening at the same place as last year?

M No. We decided to **move to a larger concert hall**. It's going to be at the community concert hall.

W That's great. It's closer to my place than last year's venue.

M That's good. Oh, I almost forgot to tell you **to download the ticket app** on your phone.

W What's the app for?

M This year, you can get a souvenir if you buy your ticket through the app.

W That's great. I will do that right now. What's the souvenir?

M I heard they will **give out a bracelet** with your name on it.

여 Ben, 연례 자선 콘서트에서 공연할 예정이니?

남 물론이지. 벌써 9월이라니 믿기지 않아. 콘서트가 다음 달이야.

여 맞아. 준비는 어떻게 돼 가고 있니?

남 공연을 위해 지난 두 달간 연습해 왔어. 사람들이 좋아했으면 좋겠어.

여 얼른 보고 싶어.

남 벌써 긴장돼.

여 잘할 거라고 믿어. 행사는 작년과 같은 곳에서 열리니?

남 아니. 더 큰 콘서트장으로 옮기기로 결정했어. 커뮤니티 콘서트홀에서 열릴 거야.

여 잘됐다. 작년 장소보다 우리 집에서 더 가까워.

남 좋겠다. 아, 네 휴대폰에서 티켓 앱을 다운로드 받으라고 말하는 걸 깜빡할 뻔했네.

여 무슨 앱인데?

남 올해엔 앱을 통해 티켓을 구매하면 기념품을 받을 수 있어.

여 정말 좋다. 지금 당장 해야지. 기념품은 뭔데?

남 본인의 이름이 새겨진 팔찌를 준다고 들었어.

09 | 정답 | ⑤

테니스 라켓과 신발은 프로그램에서 제공되지 않으므로 직접 챙겨오라고 말했다. 따라서 일치하지 않는 내용은 ⑤이다.

* sign up 신청하다
* submit 제출하다
* registration form 신청서
* management 관리
* instructor 강사
* professional 전문적인, 프로의

W Good morning. This is the manager of the Eden Community Center. I would like to introduce our new tennis lessons starting next month. It's a complimentary program offered only to the members of our community center, **so you don't need to pay**. Since a lot of members wish to sign up for the program, you have to submit a registration form **to the management office by March 20th**. Please understand that registrations after that date will not be accepted. All the instructors are **former professional tennis players**, all of whom have won awards in national tournaments. The lessons will take

여 좋은 아침입니다. Eden 지역 센터 관리인입니다. 다음 달에 시작될 새로운 테니스 수업에 대해 안내하고자 합니다. 우리 지역 센터 회원에게만 제공되는 무료 프로그램이기 때문에 수업료를 지불하지 않으셔도 됩니다. 많은 회원들이 프로그램 신청을 희망하고 있기 때문에 3월 20일까지 관리사무소로 신청서를 제출하셔야 합니다. 이 날짜 이후에는 등록이 불가능하다는 점을 양해해 주시기 바랍니다. 모든 강사는 전직 프로 테니스 선수들이고 모두 전국대회에서 수상한 경력이 있습니다. 수업은 어린이 놀이터 맞은편 테니스 코트에서 진행됩니다. 테니스 라켓과 신발은 센터에서 제공되지 않으므로 직접 챙겨 오시기 바랍니다. 여러분께 최고의 기회를 제공하길 바라며, 프로그램을 즐겨 주시면 좋겠습니다. 감사합니다.

place at the tennis court right across from the children's playground. Please bring your own tennis rackets and shoes, as **those will not be provided by the center**. We wish to offer you the best opportunities, and we hope you enjoy the program. Thank you.

---

10 | 정답 | ④

여자는 1,000달러 이하의 예산 안에서 용량 16kg 이상이며 와이파이 기능이 있는 흰색 세탁기를 원한다고 말하고 있으므로 정답은 ④이다.

- consider 고려하다
- budget 예산
- cross out (줄을 그어) 지우다
- capacity 용량
- laundry 빨래

M Hello, madam. May I help you?
W I'm looking for a washing machine.
M Okay. **The first thing to consider is your budget.** How much are you willing to spend?
W I do not want to spend over $1,000.
M All right. That crosses one model out. The next important thing would be the capacity.
W There are five people in my family, so we have a lot of laundry.
M Then I recommend one that can **hold up to at least 16 kilograms**.
W Okay. And I would like it to have Wi-Fi so that I can control it when I'm not home.
M I see. That leaves us with two options. Is there a specific color you'd like?
W **I prefer white to silver**, so I'll take that one.
M That's a good choice. It's one of our best models.

남 안녕하세요, 손님. 무엇을 도와드릴까요?
여 세탁기를 좀 보려고요.
남 그렇군요. 가장 먼저 고려해야 할 것은 예산이죠. 최대 얼마까지를 생각하고 계신가요?
여 1,000달러 넘게 쓰고 싶지 않아요.
남 알겠습니다. 그러면 한 모델은 제외되네요. 다음으로 중요한 것은 용량입니다.
여 가족이 5명이라서 빨래 양이 많아요.
남 그렇다면 적어도 16킬로그램까지 수용할 수 있는 제품을 추천합니다.
여 네. 그리고 제가 집에 없을 때도 제어할 수 있게 와이파이 기능이 있는 것이 좋아요.
남 그렇군요. 그러면 두 가지 제품이 남습니다. 원하는 색상이 따로 있으신지요?
여 저것처럼 은색보다는 흰색이 좋으니 그걸 살게요.
남 좋은 선택입니다. 가장 좋은 모델 중 하나이거든요.

---

11 | 정답 | ⑤

여자가 길을 잃은 남자에게 음악실의 위치를 알려준 뒤, 새로 온 학생인지 묻고 있으므로 이에 적절한 응답은 ⑤ '응. 어제 이 도시로 이사 왔어.'이다.

- around the corner 모퉁이를 돌면
[선택지]
- walk (걸어서) 바래다주다

W Excuse me, **you look lost**. Can I help you?
M Thank you so much. **I am looking for the music room**.
W It's just around the corner. Are you a new student?
M Yes. I just moved to this city yesterday.

여 저기, 길을 잃은 것 같아 보이는데. 내가 도와줄까?
남 정말 고마워. 나는 음악실을 찾고 있어.
여 저 모퉁이를 돌면 바로 있어. 새로 온 학생이니?
남 응. 어제 이 도시로 이사 왔어.

① 응. 음악은 내가 가장 좋아하는 과목이야.
② 그래. 내가 음악실까지 데려다줄게.
③ 아니. 음악실은 다른 건물에 있어.
④ 아니. 괜찮아. 나 혼자 찾을 수 있을 것 같아.

---

12 | 정답 | ③

요가 수업에 가고 있다는 여자의 말을 듣고 남자가 수업을 들은 지 얼마나 됐는지 묻고 있으므로, 적절한 여자의 응답은 ③ '이제 3주 됐는데, 너무 좋아.'이다.

[선택지]
- shortcut 지름길
- at once 한 번에, 한꺼번에

M Hi, Susan. Where are you going?
W Oh, Tom. **It's good to see you.** I'm going to my yoga class.
M Really? I didn't know you practiced yoga. **How long have you been taking** the class?
W It's been three weeks now, and I love it.

남 안녕, Susan. 어디 가니?
여 아, Tom. 만나서 반가워. 나는 요가 수업에 가는 중이야.
남 정말? 네가 요가를 하는 줄 몰랐어. 수업을 들은 지 얼마나 됐니?
여 이제 3주 됐는데, 너무 좋아.

① 수업은 한 시간 정도야.
② 내가 대신 지름길을 알려줄게.
④ 여기서 버스로 10분 정도 걸려.
⑤ 나는 한 번에 여러 수업을 듣는 것을 안 좋아해.

---

13 | 정답 | ②

동아리 홍보 행사에서 실험을 선보이기로 결정한 상황이다. 여자가 실험의 종류를 결정해야 한다고 말하고 있으므로 이에 대한 남자의 적절한 응답은 ② '동아리 담당 선생님께 새로운 아이디어를 여쭤보자.'이다.

- discuss 논의하다
- promotion 홍보
- recruit (신입 회원 등을) 모집하다
- leaflet (광고) 전단
- experiment 실험
- attention 주의, 시선
- walk up 다가가다

W Hello, Ryan. You're earlier than usual.
M Yes. I was waiting for you so we could discuss the club promotion event.
W Right. We need to recruit more members for our science club.
M How about **walking around and giving out leaflets** about our science club?
W Last year, that did not work well. I think we should change our plan.
M Hmm... Many students think a science club is difficult and boring.
W How can we make it look fun and interesting?

여 안녕, Ryan. 평소보다 일찍 왔구나.
남 응. 동아리 홍보 행사에 대해서 논의하려고 널 기다리고 있었어.
여 그래. 우리 과학 동아리 회원을 더 모집해야 하잖아.
남 돌아다니면서 우리 과학 동아리에 대한 전단지를 나눠주는 건 어떨까?
여 작년에 그 방법은 효과가 별로 없었어. 계획을 바꾸는 게 좋을 것 같아.
남 음… 많은 학생들이 과학 동아리를 어렵고 지루한 동아리라고 생각해.
여 어떻게 하면 재미있고 흥미롭게 보이도록 만들 수 있을까?

M How about **showing interesting experiments** at our table?	남 테이블에서 재미있는 실험을 보여주는 건 어때?
W That sounds like a good idea. That way, **we can attract students' attention**.	여 좋은 생각인 것 같아. 그렇게 하면 학생들의 시선을 끌 수 있잖아.
M Right. And we won't have to walk up to anyone.	남 맞아. 그리고 우리가 사람들에게 직접 다가가지 않아도 될 거야.
W Then we need to decide on **what kind of experiments to show people**.	여 그럼 사람들에게 어떤 종류의 실험을 보여줄지 결정해야 해.
M We should ask the club teacher for new ideas.	남 동아리 담당 선생님께 새로운 아이디어를 여쭤보자.

① 작년 계획을 유지해야 한다고 생각해.
③ 난 동아리 홍보 행사에 참여하지 않을 거야.
④ 우리 테이블에 방문하는 학생들에게 전단지를 나눠 주자.
⑤ 걱정 마. 많은 학생들이 과학에 관심이 있어.

---

14 | 정답 | ⑤

고민 끝에 패키지여행을 신청하기로 결정한 뒤 남자가 여행사에 전화해야 할지 묻고 있으므로 이에 대한 적절한 여자의 응답은 ⑤ '그래요. 더 자세한 정보를 물어보고 가장 좋은 것을 선택합시다.'이다.

* come up with ~을 생각해 내다
* tourist attraction 관광지
* travel agency 여행사
[선택지]
* be better off (형편이) 더 낫다
* currently 지금, 현재

W Honey, we have to plan our trip for this winter.	여 여보, 이번 겨울에 떠날 여행 계획을 짜야 해요.
M You're right. I am so excited to go to Europe for the first time.	남 맞아요. 처음으로 유럽에 갈 생각을 하니 정말 신나요.
W Me, too. But I can't decide whether we should **sign up for a package tour or not**.	여 저도요. 그런데 패키지여행을 신청해야 할지 말지 결정을 못 하겠어요.
M Well, I think going on a package tour is a good idea.	남 전 패키지여행으로 가는 건 좋은 생각인 것 같아요.
W What do you think is good about a package tour?	여 패키지여행에 관해 무엇이 좋은 것 같아요?
M We don't have to **come up with all the tourist attractions** to visit. The travel agency does everything for us.	남 방문할 관광지를 생각해 내지 않아도 된다는 점이죠. 여행사에서 모든 걸 우리 대신 해 주니까요.
W But we can't choose where to eat or what activities to do.	여 하지만 어디서 먹고 뭘 할지를 선택할 수가 없잖아요.
M I wish we could, but honey, do you think we **have enough time to plan all that**?	남 그러고 싶지만, 여보, 우리가 그걸 전부 계획할 시간이 있을까요?
W You have a point.	여 당신 말도 일리가 있네요.
M By going on a package tour, **we don't have to worry about transportation**, too.	남 패키지여행을 가면 교통수단도 걱정할 필요가 없어요.
W You're right. I think I will go with your decision.	여 당신이 맞아요. 당신의 결정을 따르겠어요.
M Good. Should we call the travel agency?	남 좋아요. 여행사에 전화할까요?
W Okay. Let's ask for more information and choose the best one.	여 그래요. 더 자세한 정보를 물어보고 가장 좋은 것을 선택합시다.

① 저는 그렇게 생각하지 않아요. 우리 스스로 하는 것이 나을 것 같아요.
② 나중에 다시 전화해 주세요. 지금 회의 중입니다.
③ 아뇨, 거기서는 유럽 패키지여행을 제공하지 않습니다.
④ 물론이죠. 작년 여름 유럽 여행은 무척 즐거웠어요.

---

15 | 정답 | ④

Jenny의 솔로 댄스가 예상보다 길어서 Lucy가 자신의 솔로 댄스를 시간 안에 끝내지 못해 언짢은 상황이므로 솔로 댄스 시간을 조정해야 하는 상황이다. 따라서 Lucy가 Jenny에게 할 말로 가장 적절한 것은 ④ '혹시 너의 솔로 댄스를 조금만 줄여줄 수 있겠니?'이다.

* ballet 발레
* performance 공연
* costume 의상
* apart from ~외에
* combine 합치다, 결합하다
[선택지]
* shorten 줄이다, 짧게 하다

| W Lucy is in a high school ballet group. She and her teammate Jenny are preparing for a classical ballet performance at a community event. They have discussed everything together from the beginning, including the music and their costumes. Apart from the dance duet, they have to **prepare for their solo dances by themselves**. Lucy's solo dance is right after Jenny's. On the day that they combined all the dances together, Lucy could not **finish her solo on time**, because Jenny's solo was longer than expected. Lucy was a little upset because she had prepared very hard for her dance, too. She wants **to show everything she prepared**. In this situation, what would Lucy most likely say to Jenny? | 여 Lucy는 고등학생 발레 단체에 소속되어 있다. 그녀와 그녀의 팀원인 Jenny는 지역 행사에서 선보일 고전 발레 공연을 준비하고 있다. 그들은 처음부터 음악과 의상을 포함하여 모든 것을 함께 의논해 왔다. 듀엣 댄스 외에 그들은 각자 솔로 댄스를 준비해야 한다. Lucy의 솔로 댄스는 Jenny의 댄스 순서 바로 다음이다. 모든 댄스를 합쳐서 연습한 날, Jenny의 솔로 댄스가 예상보다 길어서 Lucy는 제시간에 솔로 댄스를 끝내지 못했다. Lucy 또한 그녀의 춤을 굉장히 열심히 준비했기 때문에 기분이 약간 언짢았다. 그녀는 준비한 모든 것을 보여주고 싶어 한다. 이러한 상황에서 Lucy가 Jenny에게 할 말로 가장 적절한 것은 무엇인가? |
| **Lucy** Could you please shorten your solo dance a little bit? | Lucy 혹시 너의 솔로 댄스를 조금만 줄여줄 수 있겠니? |

① 나는 솔로 댄스를 하고 싶지 않아.
② 음악을 바꾸는 게 좋을 것 같아.
③ 고등학교 발레단에 가입하지 않겠니?
⑤ 내 생각에 너는 공연을 위해 더 연습해야 할 것 같아.

---

16 | 정답 | ②

하나의 동물 종이 생태계에 미치는 영향을 옐로우스톤 국립 공원의 늑대를 예시로 들어 설명하는 내용이다. 과도한 사냥으로 사라졌던 늑대가 다시 공원으

| M Hello, students. Today, we are going to talk about **how one animal species can change** an ecosystem. The classic example is what happened in Yellowstone National Park. Wolves in the park had been absent for 70 years due to excessive hunting. During that period, the number | 남 안녕하세요, 학생 여러분. 오늘 우리는 어떻게 하나의 동물 종이 생태계를 바꿀 수 있는지에 대해 이야기를 나누어 보겠습니다. 대표적인 예는 옐로우스톤 국립공원에서 있었던 일입니다. 그곳에서는 늑대가 과도한 사냥으로 인해 70년 동안 없던 적이 있었습니다. 그 기 |

로 돌아오자, 여러 동물들이 다시 국립 공원을 서식지로 삼았다는 내용으로 보아 남자가 하는 말의 주제로 가장 적절한 것은 ② '어떻게 늑대가 한 지역의 생태계 전체를 바꿨는가'이다.

17 | 정답 | ⑤

옐로우스톤 국립 공원에 서식하는 동물 중 '물고기'에 대한 언급은 없었으므로 정답은 ⑤이다.

* species 종
* ecosystem 생태계
* classic 대표적인; 고전적인
* absent 없는, 부재한
* excessive 과도한, 지나친
* prey 먹이, 사냥감
* tremendously 엄청나게
* feed on ~을 먹다[먹고 살다]
* vegetation 초목
* remarkable 놀라운, 주목할 만한
* habitat 서식지
* revival 회복
  [선택지]
* tourism 관광업
* endangered 멸종 위기에 처한
* predator 포식자
* impact 영향, 충격
* natural disaster 자연재해

of deer, wolves' favorite prey, increased tremendously. **The deer fed on grass and trees** and this destroyed the vegetation. So people decided to re-introduce wolves into the park. **As soon as the wolves arrived**, they caused the most remarkable effects. Deer started avoiding certain parts of the park, and this **allowed the trees to grow again**. Because the trees were growing back, the number of birds started to increase greatly. Beavers **also began to appear and settle** because beavers like to eat tree bark. They also built dams in the river, and this made habitats for many other species. All of this led to the revival of the ecosystem of Yellowstone National Park.

간 동안 늑대가 가장 좋아하는 사냥감인 사슴의 수가 엄청나게 증가했습니다. 사슴들은 풀과 나무를 뜯어 먹었고 이것이 초목을 파괴했습니다. 그래서 사람들은 공원에 늑대를 다시 들여오기로 했습니다. 늑대들이 들어오자마자 가장 놀라운 효과를 가져왔습니다. 사슴들이 공원의 특정 지역을 피해 다니기 시작했고, 이를 통해 나무가 다시 자랐습니다. 나무가 다시 자랐기 때문에 새들의 수가 엄청나게 늘기 시작했습니다. 비버들도 나타나서 정착하기 시작했는데, 이는 비버들이 나무껍질을 좋아하기 때문입니다. 그들은 또한 강에 댐을 짓기도 했고, 이는 다른 많은 종에게 서식지를 제공했습니다. 이 모든 것은 옐로우스톤 국립공원의 생태계가 다시 살아나도록 했습니다.

16 ① 옐로우스톤 국립 공원 관광의 역사
② 어떻게 늑대가 한 지역의 생태계 전체를 바꿨는가
③ 세계 각지의 국립 공원의 멸종 위기에 처한 종
④ 포식자 종과 피식자 종의 차이
⑤ 생태계의 건강에 자연재해가 미치는 영향

17 ① 늑대 ② 사슴 ③ 새 ④ 비버 ⑤ 물고기

본문 p.70

---

01 | 정답 | ⑤

남자는 회사에 합류한 새 직원에 대해 소개하고 있으므로 남자가 하는 말의 목적으로 ⑤가 가장 적절하다.

- join 합류하다; 동참하다
- open position 공석, 빈자리
- customer service 고객 서비스
- welcome 맞이하다, 환영하다
- participate in ~에 참여하다
- employee 직원
- mentor 멘토
- stop by 들르다
- raise 기르다
- shelter 쉼터, 피난처

M Good morning, everyone. Ann Thompson is joining our company to **fill our open position in** customer service. Her first day is Tuesday, April 8th. Ann has worked in customer service for many years and we are happy to welcome her to our team. **She'll participate in employee training** for her first week on the job. Ann's new employee mentor is Sam Banks, so if you have questions, you can talk with Sam. Take a moment to **stop by and welcome Ann to the company**. She says that some of her hobbies include raising cats, dancing, and volunteering at a local homeless shelter. Thanks for joining me in welcoming Ann to the team.

남 좋은 아침입니다, 여러분. Ann Thompson이 고객 서비스 부서의 공석을 채우기 위해 우리 회사에 입사합니다. 출근 첫날은 4월 8일 화요일입니다. Ann은 고객 서비스 분야에서 수년간 일을 해 왔고, 우리는 그녀를 팀원으로 맞이하게 되어 기쁩니다. 그녀는 첫 주 동안 직원 교육에 참여할 것입니다. Ann의 새로운 직원 멘토는 Sam Banks이니, 질문이 있으시면 Sam과 논의 하세요. 잠시 시간을 내어 들러 Ann이 입사한 것을 환영해 주세요. 그녀는 취미는 고양이 기르기, 춤추기, 지역 노숙자 쉼터에서 자원봉사 하기라고 합니다. Ann을 팀원으로 맞이하는 것에 동참해 주셔서 감사합니다.

---

02 | 정답 | ④

남자가 미래의 직업을 고려하여 좋아하는 전공을 포기하려고 하자, 여자는 1, 2학년에는 기본 지식을 쌓을 뿐이니 조금 더 기다려보라고 말하고 있으므로 여자의 의견으로는 ④가 가장 적절하다.

- trouble 괴롭히다
- major 전공
- while 동안, 잠깐
- switch 바꾸다
- computer engineering 컴퓨터 공학
- career 직업, 경력
- related 관련된
- chemistry 화학
- sophomore (4년제 대학, 고교의) 2학년
- stick with ~을 고수하다
- build up 쌓다
- in depth 깊이 있게
- broaden 넓히다
- perspective 시야, 관점
- besides 게다가
- wouldn't do A any harm A에게 나쁠 건 없을 것이다

W Kevin, is something troubling you? You look so worried.
M Well, I've been thinking about my major for a while.
W What about your major?
M I'm **thinking about switching it to** computer engineering. There are more career options related to it.
W Is that the only reason **why you want to change your major**?
M I love chemistry and really enjoy learning it. But I'm not sure what I can do with it.
W You are only a sophomore in college. **Why don't you give it another chance**? You shouldn't be so quick to give up what you love.
M Are you saying I should stick with it?
W You may not have learned enough chemistry. As you know, students build up basic knowledge during their first two years in college.
M Okay.
W As you learn chemistry in depth, it will broaden your perspective on possible careers.
M You're right. Besides, another year wouldn't do me any harm.
W Exactly. This year might **lead you to a job in the field you love**.

여 Kevin, 무슨 걱정 있니? 많이 걱정스러워 보인다.
남 음, 한동안 내 전공에 대해 생각해 봤어.
여 네 전공이 왜?
남 컴퓨터 공학으로 바꿀까 생각 중이야. 그것과 관련된 직업 선택의 여지가 더 많거든.
여 그게 전공을 바꾸고 싶은 유일한 이유야?
남 화학을 엄청 좋아하고 배우는 걸 정말로 즐겨. 하지만 내가 그걸로 뭘 할 수 있을지 확신이 없어.
여 넌 겨우 대학교 2학년이잖아. 한 번 더 기회를 주는 건 어때? 좋아하는 것을 너무 빨리 포기하면 안 돼.
남 화학을 계속하라고 말하는 거니?
여 화학을 충분히 배우지 않았을지도 모르잖아. 알다시피 학생들은 대학 첫 2년 동안은 기본 지식을 쌓아.
남 그래.
여 화학을 깊이 있게 배울수록 가능한 진로에 대한 너의 시야가 넓어질 거야.
남 네 말이 맞아. 게다가 한 해 더 공부한다고 나쁠 건 없어.
여 당연하지. 올해는 너를 네가 좋아하는 분야의 직업으로 이끌어 줄지도 몰라.

---

03 | 정답 | ③

긴장이나 불안을 해소하기 위해 심호흡을 해보라고 권유하고 있으므로 남자가 하는 말의 요지로 가장 적절한 것은 ③이다.

- on-air 방송(중)의
- tension 긴장
- anxiety 불안
- inhale (숨을) 들이마시다, 흡입하다
- exhale (숨을) 내쉬다

M Hello, dear viewers! I'm Dr. Winfield, your on-air doctor. We all experience tension or anxiety in our busy lives, and it's important **to know how to deal with them.** Here's **a simple technique to help you relax**: take a deep breath when you feel tense or anxious. Inhale through your nose, then exhale slowly while making a "whoo" sound. This practice only takes a few minutes, but **it can significantly reduce your anxiety levels**. In moments of tension or anxiety, remember to breathe deeply. Give it a try today! I'll be back soon with more health tips.

남 안녕하세요, 사랑하는 시청자 여러분! 저는 여러분의 방송 주치의 Winfield 박사입니다. 우리 모두는 바쁜 일상 속에서 긴장이나 불안을 경험하는데, 그것들을 어떻게 다뤄야 하는지 아는 것이 중요합니다. 여기 여러분이 긴장을 푸는 데 도움이 되는 간단한 방법이 있습니다. 긴장이 되거나 불안할 때 심호흡을 하세요. 코로 숨을 들이마신 다음 "후" 소리를 내면서 천천히 숨을 내쉬세요. 이 실행은 몇 분밖에 안 걸리지만 여러분의 불안 수준을 상당히 낮출 수 있습니다. 긴장과 불안의 순간에 심호흡을 하는 것을 기억하세요. 오늘 한 번 시도해보세요! 저는 더 많은 건강 비결을 가지고 곧 돌아오겠습니다.

---

04 | 정답 | ⑤

책 표지에서 제목이 지구본 아래 쓰여 있다고 했으므로 정답은 ⑤이다.

* release 출간; 놓아주다
* finalize 마무리하다
* go over 검토하다
* one by one 하나씩
* globe 지구본
* stand out 눈에 띄다, 두드러지다
* lean 기대다
* trunk 나무의 몸통
* suggest 제안하다
  cf. suggestion 제안
* save 구하다
* exactly 정확히
* overall 전반적으로
* suit 어울리다

M Ms. Greene, I made a few changes on your book cover.
W Okay. The release date is getting near. We'd better hurry up and finalize it.
M Let's go over the changes one by one.
W All right. **The globe in the center really stands out**.
M Since your book is about making the earth clean, I made the globe clean.
W I see. I like the boy under the tree. He's leaning with his back against the trunk.
M He looks calm and peaceful **because he's reading**.
W You added branches to the tree like I suggested.
M I liked your suggestion. You can see the birds more clearly on the branches.
W I know. I didn't want **the birds close to the two suns**.
M Right. How do you like the title, *Two Suns to Save the Earth*, written under the globe?
W Perfect. **That's exactly where I wanted the title**.
M I also put your name under the title.
W That's fine. Overall, this design suits the title.

남 Greene 씨, 제가 작가님의 책 표지에 몇 가지 수정을 했어요.
여 네. 출간일이 가까워지고 있네요. 서둘러 마무리 짓는 게 좋겠어요.
남 수정 부분을 하나씩 검토해 보죠.
여 좋아요. 가운데 있는 지구본이 정말 눈에 띄어요.
남 지구를 깨끗하게 만드는 것에 대한 책이니까 지구본을 깨끗하게 했어요.
여 그렇군요. 나무 아래 있는 남자아이가 마음에 들어요. 나무 몸통에 등을 기대고 있네요.
남 책을 읽고 있어서 차분하고 평화로워 보여요.
여 제가 제안한 대로 나무에 가지를 추가했군요.
남 제안이 좋았거든요. 가지 위에 있는 새들을 더 명확하게 볼 수 있어요.
여 맞아요. 두 개의 태양에 새들이 가까이 있는 걸 원하지 않았거든요.
남 네. 지구본 아래 쓰인 제목 〈Two Suns to Save the Earth〉는 어때요?
여 완벽해요. 바로 그 자리에 제목이 있었으면 했어요.
남 제목 아래 작가님 이름도 넣었어요.
여 좋아요. 전반적으로 이 디자인이 제목에 어울리네요.

05 | 정답 | ④

남자가 여자에게 자원봉사 신청서 작성을 위해 이메일 주소를 문자로 보내달라고 말하고 있으므로 정답은 ④이다.

* flea market 벼룩시장
* organizer 주최자
* volunteer 자원봉사자
* necessary 필요한
* take part in ~에 참여하다
* text message 문자 메시지
* form 신청서; 문서의 양식
* fill out 작성하다
* make sure 꼭 ~하다

W Kyle, did you know about a flea market opening near Mirae Tower?
M Sure. My mom is one of the organizers preparing the event.
W Really? I found out about it this morning. I don't think **many people in our town know about it**.
M I know. That's because there are not enough volunteers.
W If necessary, I can help out. I'd like to take part in it.
M Thanks. I'll talk to my mom when I go to the community center after school.
W I don't **have anything planned out** after school today. I can go with you if you want.
M Actually, there is something else you should do.
W What is it?
M **Can you send me your e-mail address** by text message? I'll send you a form to fill out.
W I'll do that right now. My phone is in my jacket over there.
M Okay. Oh, make sure you **have a parent sign the form**, too.

여 Kyle, Mirae 타워 근처에서 열리는 벼룩시장에 대해 알고 있었니?
남 물론이지. 엄마가 그 행사를 준비하는 주최자 중 한 명이야.
여 정말? 난 오늘 아침에 알게 되었어. 그것에 대해 아는 사람이 우리 동네에 많지 않은 것 같아.
남 맞아. 그건 자원봉사자가 충분하지 않아서 그래.
여 필요하다면 내가 도와줄 수 있어. 나도 참여하고 싶거든.
남 고마워. 방과 후에 주민 센터에 가면 내가 엄마한테 말해 볼게.
여 나도 오늘 방과 후에 별 계획이 없어. 원하면 같이 갈 수 있는데.
남 사실. 네가 해야 할 일이 따로 있어.
여 그게 뭔데?
남 네 이메일 주소를 문자로 보내줄래? 작성해야 할 신청서를 보내줄게.
여 지금 바로 할게. 내 전화기가 저쪽 재킷 안에 있어.
남 알겠어. 아. 꼭 부모님 서명도 받아야 해.

06 | 정답 | ④

목걸이와 귀걸이 세트는 목걸이 가격인 200달러의 두 배 가격이라고 했으므로, 남자가 지불해야 할 금액은 400달러에서 30% 할인된 ④이다.

* occasion (특별한) 일, 행사
* anniversary 기념일
* recommend 추천하다
* a wide range of 다양한, 광범위한
* selection 선택사항
* originally 원래
* double 두 배의
* offer 제공하다, 제안

W How may I help you, sir?
M I'm looking for a gift for my wife.
W **Is it for a special occasion**?
M Yes, it's for our 20th anniversary. Could you recommend something?
W Of course. We have a wide range of selections. How about this gold necklace? It's one of the most popular designs this season.
M It looks beautiful. How much is it?
W It's $200.
M That's a little expensive for a single necklace, isn't it?
W Well, it might seem so. But if you **add the matching pair of earrings**, we offer a special discount.
M How much are they together, the necklace and the earrings?
W They were **originally double the price of the necklace**, but we are offering a 30% discount off the original price.

여 어떻게 도와드릴까요, 손님?
남 제 아내에게 줄 선물을 찾고 있어요.
여 특별한 날을 위한 건가요?
남 네, 결혼 20주년 선물이에요. 추천 좀 해주실래요?
여 물론입니다. 다양한 제품들이 있습니다. 이 금목걸이는 어떠세요? 이번 시즌의 가장 인기 있는 디자인 중 하나입니다.
남 아름답네요. 얼마예요?
여 200달러입니다.
남 목걸이 하나치고는 좀 비싸네요. 그렇지 않나요?
여 음. 그렇게 보일 수 있죠. 하지만 세트로 나온 귀걸이를 추가할 경우 특별 할인을 제공하고 있습니다.
남 목걸이와 귀걸이를 같이 하면 얼마인가요?
여 원래는 목걸이의 두 배 가격이었지만, 원래 가격에서 30% 할인해 드리고 있습니다.

M That sounds like a good deal. I'll take them. And can I use this $20 coupon? **W** I'm afraid you can't because they are already **on a special discount**. **M** Okay. Here's my credit card.	남 괜찮은 가격이네요. 그걸로 살게요. 그리고 이 20% 쿠폰을 사용할 수 있을까요? 여 죄송하지만 이미 특별 할인이 적용되어 있어서 어렵습니다. 남 알겠습니다. 여기 제 신용카드입니다.

---

07 | 정답 | ③

여자는 남자에게 자신이 충분히 발전하지 못하고 있다고 느껴 쉬면서 새로운 것을 배우기 위해 퇴사하기로 했다고 말하고 있으므로 정답은 ③이다.

* notice 퇴사[해고] 통보
* sudden 갑작스러운
* think through 충분히 생각하다
* quit 그만두다
* work out 해결하다
* improve 향상시키다
* take time off 쉬다, 시간을 내다
* put up 게시하다
* hire 고용하다

W Sir, may I talk to you for a minute?
M Mary, come on in. Is there something wrong?
W I'd like to give you my two-week notice.
M This is so sudden. **Have you thought this through?**
W Yes, I have. It wasn't easy for me to quit like this. I'm sorry.
M You are one of the best workers here. I didn't expect you'd leave.
W Me neither, sir. But **I feel like it's time for a change** since I've been here for so long.
M Oh, did you get a job offer from somewhere else?
W No, I'm not moving on to another job.
M Then, can you tell me why you're leaving? Maybe we can work this out.
W I feel like **I'm not improving myself enough**. I'd like to take some time off to learn something new.
M I understand. I'll **put up an ad to hire somebody else**.
W Thank you for understanding.
M I wish you only the best.

여 잠시 얘기를 나눌 수 있을까요?
남 Mary, 들어와요. 뭐가 잘못된 게 있나요?
여 2주 후 퇴사 통보를 하려고요.
남 너무 갑작스럽군요. 충분히 생각하셨나요?
여 네. 이렇게 그만두는 건 제게도 쉽지 않았어요. 죄송합니다.
남 당신은 여기서 최고의 직원 중 한 명이에요. 나갈 줄 예상하지 못했어요.
여 저도 그래요. 하지만 제가 여기서 아주 오래 있었기 때문에 변화가 필요한 시기라는 생각이 들어요.
남 아, 다른 곳에서 일자리 제안을 받았나요?
여 아니요, 다른 직장으로 옮기지 않습니다.
남 그렇다면 왜 그만두는지 말해 줄 수 있나요? 우리가 해결할 수 있을 것 같아요.
여 제 자신을 충분히 발전시키고 있는 것 같지 않아서요. 좀 쉬면서 새로운 것을 배우고 싶어요.
남 알겠습니다. 다른 사람을 고용하기 위해 광고를 낼게요.
여 이해해 주셔서 감사합니다.
남 모든 게 잘 되길 바라요.

---

08 | 정답 | ④

전시회는 입장료가 무료이고 주차장은 없으며, 마지막 날은 2월 14일이다. 전시 내용은 유망한 예술가들의 조각품과 그림이라 했지만 예술가 이름은 언급되지 않았으므로 정답은 ④이다.

* contemporary 현대의
* exhibition 전시회
* admission 입장료
* hesitate 망설이다
* must-see 꼭 봐야 하는
* unbelievable 믿기 어려운 정도인
* gallery 미술관
* parking lot 주차장
* opportunity 기회
* sculpture 조각
* promising 유망한

W Fred, are you planning to go and see the contemporary art exhibition?
M I haven't decided yet. How about you?
W I'm visiting this weekend. **Admission is free for students** like us. Why hesitate?
M True. Since it is a must-see exhibit, there will be a lot of people.
W Exactly. That's why I'm going to take the subway. The traffic there is just unbelievable.
M You really should because **the gallery doesn't have a parking lot**.
W I know. Besides, the City Hall subway station is nearby.
M That's right. When is the last day of the exhibition?
W I believe **the exhibition will be held until February 14th**.
M Maybe I should go before it's over.
W You shouldn't miss this opportunity. There are many sculptures and paintings by promising contemporary artists.
M Don't worry. I won't.

여 Fred, 현대 미술 전시회 보러 갈 거니?
남 아직 정하지 못했어. 너는?
여 이번 주말에 가려고. 우리와 같은 학생들은 입장료가 무료야. 왜 망설이겠어?
남 맞아. 꼭 봐야 하는 전시회라서 사람들이 많을 거야.
여 그래. 그래서 내가 지하철을 타려고 하는 거야. 그곳의 교통량은 믿을 수 없을 정도로 심하거든.
남 그 미술관에 주차장이 없어서 정말 그래야 해.
여 알아. 게다가 시청역 지하철이 근처에 있잖아.
남 그렇지. 전시회 마지막 날이 언제니?
여 전시회는 2월 14일까지 하는 것으로 알고 있어.
남 끝나기 전에는 가봐야겠네.
여 이번 기회를 놓치지 않는 게 좋아. 유망한 현대 예술가들의 조각품과 그림들이 많이 있어.
남 걱정 마. 놓치지 않을게.

---

09 | 정답 | ⑤

이번 주에 등록하면 할인을 받는다고 말했으므로 정답은 ⑤이다.

* pleased 기쁜
* interactive 쌍방향의, 상호작용을 하는
* toddler (아장아장 걷는) 아기
* design 고안하다
* explore 탐험하다
* communicate 의사소통하다
* interest 관심
* contrast 대조적인
* theme 주제

W Hello, listeners. I'm pleased to introduce a fun and interactive program called "Toddler Trek." This interactive indoor program is designed for toddlers from 16 to 24 months. At this age, **little ones just can't stop exploring**. They are running, communicating, and showing interest in friends. The program uses contrast themes to **help learn better ways to communicate**. Your child will learn loud and quiet, high and low, and in and out. Through our program, toddlers can build skills like jumping and balancing. As they feel safe with a familiar adult by their side, **each child must be paired with** an adult to participate. The program goes from March 28th to May

여 안녕하세요, 청취자 여러분. 'Toddler Trek'이라는 재미있고 쌍방향적인 프로그램을 소개하게 되어 기쁩니다. 이 상호활동적인 실내 프로그램은 16개월에서 24개월 사이의 아기들을 위해 고안되었습니다. 이 나이에는 아기들은 끊임없이 탐험하죠. 뛰고, 의사소통하고 친구들에게 관심을 보입니다. 이 프로그램은 의사소통하는 더 나은 방법을 배우는 데 도움을 줄 대조적인 주제들을 사용합니다. 여러분의 아기들은 시끄러움과 조용함, 높음과 낮음, 그리고 안과 밖을 배우게 될 것입니다. 우리 프로그램을 통해서 아기들은 점프와 균형 잡기와 같은 기술들을 쌓을 수 있습니다. 아기들은 친숙한 어른이 옆에 있으면 안전함을 느끼기 때문에 각각의 아기들이 참여하기 위해선 어른 한 명과 짝을 지어야 합니다. 이 프로그램은 3월 28일부터 5월 20일까

* familiar 친숙한
* pair 짝을 이루다
* in advance 미리
* limit 제한하다
* participant 참여자

20th. Register in advance since **we limit the number of participants to** 20 people. The registration price is $120, but we offer a 10% discount to those who register this week. For more information, please visit our website, www.toddlertrek.com.

지 진행됩니다. 저희가 참여 인원을 20명으로 제한하고 있기 때문에 미리 등록하십시오. 등록비는 120달러이지만 이번 주에 등록하시는 분들에게는 10% 할인을 제공합니다. 더 많은 정보는 저희 웹사이트 www.toddlertrek.com을 방문해 주십시오.

---

10 | 정답 | ④

남자는 스테이크와 먹을 60달러 미만의 쓰거나 너무 달지 않은 레드와인을 원한다고 했으므로 정답은 ④이다.

* strongly 강력하게
* in general 일반적으로
* bitter 쓴
* fruity 과일의
* semi-sweet 너무 달지 않은

W Welcome to Wine Yard. Can I help you find anything?
M Yes, please. Would you recommend wine for beginners like me?
W Of course. There are two types of wine, white and red.
M Which wine is good with a steak?
W I strongly recommend a red one. **Red wines go well with meat dishes**.
M Okay. Can you show me the ones under $60?
W Of course. There are also countries to choose from.
M **Are there any differences between countries**?
W In general French wines have a bitter taste. The ones from Chile and Italy are sweet with a fruity taste.
M Since it's my first time, I'll try French wines later.
W All right. Which one do you prefer, a sweet one or a semi-sweet one?
M I'd go with a semi-sweet one **since I'm having it with meat**.
W That's the perfect choice.

여 Wine Yard에 오신 걸 환영합니다. 찾으시는 걸 도와드릴까요?
남 네. 저와 같은 와인 초보자들에게 와인을 추천해 주시겠어요?
여 물론이죠. 2가지 종류의 와인이 있는데, 화이트 그리고 레드와인이에요.
남 어떤 와인이 스테이크와 어울리나요?
여 저는 레드와인을 강력히 추천드립니다. 레드와인은 고기 요리와 잘 어울려요.
남 좋아요. 60달러 미만의 와인들을 보여주시겠어요?
여 그럼요. 또한 생산국도 선택하실 수 있어요.
남 생산국마다 어떤 차이가 있나요?
여 일반적으로 프랑스 와인이 쓴맛이 있어요. 칠레와 이탈리아 와인은 과일 맛이 나는 단맛이에요.
남 이번이 처음이니까 그럼 프랑스 와인은 나중에 시도해 볼게요.
여 좋아요. 달콤한 것과 너무 달지 않은 것 중에 어느 것을 선호하세요?
남 고기와 먹을 거니까 너무 달지 않은 것으로 할게요.
여 완벽한 선택이에요.

---

11 | 정답 | ③

여자가 가져온 전단지를 보고 남자가 자신이 춤에 관심이 있다고 말하자, 여자는 강사가 유명한 K-pop 그룹을 가르쳤다고 말하고 있으므로 남자의 응답으로는 ③ '정말? 그럼 바로 가서 신청할래.'가 가장 적절하다.

* flyer 전단지
* boom 붐, 갑작스러운 인기
* instructor 강사

[선택지]
* costume 의상, 복장

W Richard, look at this flyer. It's about dance lessons at the community center.
M Oh, **I've been interested in dancing** because of the K-pop boom.
W I heard that the instructor there used to **teach a famous K-pop group**.
M Really? Then I'll go and sign up right now.

여 Richard, 이 전단지 좀 봐. 주민 센터의 춤 강습에 관한 거야.
남 아, K-pop 붐 때문에 춤에 관심이 많았거든.
여 그곳 강사가 전에 유명한 K-pop 그룹을 가르쳤다고 들었어.
남 정말? 그럼 바로 가서 신청할래.

① 응. 춤추는 건 내가 가장 좋아하는 취미야.
② 멋지다! 내가 원하는 레슨은 무엇이든 받을 수 있어.
④ 괜찮아. 난 이미 충분한 정보를 가지고 있어.
⑤ 걱정 마. 무용 의상은 그렇게 비싸지 않아.

---

12 | 정답 | ④

남자는 여자가 구매한 전기차를 보고 그 판매인을 소개해 달라고 했으므로 여자의 응답으로 '④ 물론이야. 원한다면 그의 명함을 줄 수 있어.'가 가장 적절하다.

* complaint 불평
* consider 고려하다
* dealer 자동차 판매인

[선택지]
* business card 명함

M Wow, you finally bought a new electric car. **How do you like driving it**?
W I have no complaints. **It's very quiet while driving**. You should consider buying one.
M Maybe I should. Do you think you can introduce me to the dealer?
W Of course. I can give you his business card if you want.

남 와. 마침내 새 전기차를 샀구나. 그 차를 운전하는 건 어때?
여 불만은 없어. 운전할 때 아주 조용해. 너도 하나 사는 거 생각해 봐.
남 그래야 할 것 같아. 나한테 그 자동차 판매인을 소개해 줄 수 있어?
여 물론이야. 원한다면 그의 명함을 줄 수 있어.

① 물론이야. 내 걸 시험 운전해도 좋아.
② 난 아냐. 그를 만날 기회가 전혀 없었어.
③ 그런 것 같아. 전기차는 장기적으로 저렴해.
⑤ 안 될 것 같아. 너는 네 운전면허증을 가지고 있어야 해.

---

13 | 정답 | ②

남자가 자신이 허리가 아파 장거리 운전을 못 한다고 말하자 여자는 Jimmy가 버스를 타면 되고, 그가 이해할 거라고 말하고 있으므로 남자의 마지막 응답으로 가장 적절한 것은 ② '그래요. 그가 너무 실망하지 않기를 바랄 뿐이에요.'이다.

W Honey, what did the doctor say about your back?
M He said that it'll take some time to heal. I really hate having trouble moving around.
W Don't forget to **take your medicine on time** and get enough rest. You'll recover before you know it.
M I will. Oh, could you do me a favor?
W What is it?

여 여보, 의사가 당신의 허리에 대해 뭐라고 했어요?
남 낫는 데 시간이 좀 걸릴 거라고 말했어요. 움직이기 힘든 건 정말 질색이에요.
여 제시간에 약 먹고 충분히 쉬는 걸 잊지 마세요. 금방 회복될 거예요.
남 그렇게 할게요. 아. 부탁 하나만 들어줄 수 있어요?
여 뭔데요?

- heal 치유되다
- recover 회복하다
- do A a favor A에게 호의를 베풀다
- distance 거리
- worsen 악화시키다
- be supposed to-v ~하기로 되어 있다
- give A a ride A를 태워주다
- otherwise 그렇지 않으면
- luggage 짐
  [선택지]
- disappointed 실망한

M The doctor said I shouldn't drive long distances until I get better. **It may worsen the pain**.
W Oh, no. What about Jimmy? We are supposed to give him a ride to the airport.
M Do you think you could give him a ride instead? Otherwise, I have to ask him to take the bus.
W I think we should just ask him to take the bus. I'm not sure **if I can drive back by myself**.
M I feel bad. I wanted to take him because of his luggage.
W I know, honey. But there is no other choice. He'll understand.
M Okay. I hope he doesn't get too disappointed.

남 의사가 나을 때까지 장거리 운전은 하지 말라고 했거든요. 통증을 더 악화시킬 수 있다고요.
여 아, 이런. Jimmy는 어떡하죠? 우리가 공항까지 데려다 주기로 했잖아요.
남 당신이 대신 데려다 줄 수 있을까요? 그렇지 않으면, 버스를 타라고 해야 해요.
여 그냥 버스를 타라고 해야 할 것 같아요. 제가 혼자 운전해 돌아올 수 있을지 모르겠어요.
남 마음이 편하지 않네요. 짐 때문에 데려다주고 싶었거든요.
여 알아요, 여보. 하지만 선택의 여지가 없잖아요. 이해할 거예요.
남 그래요. 그가 너무 실망하지 않기를 바랄 뿐이에요.

① 동의해요. 전 운전하는 것보다 버스 타는 걸 선호하거든요.
③ 미안해요. 제가 그 버스 여행에 대해서 뭘 할 수 있는지 볼게요.
④ 모르겠어요. 버스 타는 것은 비용은 적게 들지만 시간이 오래 걸려요.
⑤ 다행이네요. 우린 원하면 언제든지 그 여행을 취소할 수 있어요.

---

14 | 정답 | ⑤

남자는 여자에게 어느 분야에나 초보에겐 어려움이 있다고 말하면서 관심을 가지게 되면 금방 그것을 즐기게 될 것이라고 격려하고 있으므로 여자의 마지막 응답으로 가장 적절한 것은 ⑤ '그러길 바라. 나는 정치 기사를 읽는 것을 포기하지 않을게.'이다.

- focused 집중한
- article 기사
- politics 정치
- section 부문, 부분
- term 용어
- field 분야
- get used to ~에 익숙해지다
- absolutely 당연히
  [선택지]
- give up on ~을 포기하다

M Cathy, you look so focused. What are you reading?
W I'm reading news articles on my phone.
M I see. Did you find anything interesting?
W Not really. I've been reading some articles in the politics section. But there are so many terms I don't understand.
M In every field, **beginners have a hard time** getting used to new information.
W You are right. I guess I have to get familiar with the terms before reading.
M It may take a while at first, but **you'll soon get used to it**.
W Do you think so?
M Absolutely. If you get interested in something, **you will start to enjoy it**.
W I hope so. I won't give up on reading about politics, then.

남 Cathy, 아주 집중하는 모습이구나. 뭘 읽고 있니?
여 내 전화기로 뉴스 기사를 읽고 있어.
남 그렇구나. 흥미로운 것을 좀 찾았니?
여 별로. 정치면의 일부 기사들을 읽고 있어. 하지만 내가 이해하지 못하는 용어가 아주 많아.
남 모든 분야에서 초보자들은 새 정보에 익숙해지는 데 어려움을 겪어.
여 맞아. 읽기 전에 용어들과 친숙해져야 할 것 같아.
남 처음에는 시간이 조금 걸리겠지만 곧 익숙해질 거야.
여 그렇게 생각해?
남 당연하지. 네가 관심을 가지게 되면 그걸 즐기기 시작할 거야.
여 그러길 바라. 그러면 나는 정치 기사를 읽는 것을 포기하지 않을게.

① 맞아. 난 뉴스 기사를 읽는 것을 좋아하지 않아.
② 아마도. 하지만 나는 정치학을 전공하고 싶지 않아.
③ 안됐구나. 나는 대부분의 앱을 사용하지 않아.
④ 난 됐어. 내게 나쁜 소식을 전할 필요 없어.

---

15 | 정답 | ③

Deborah는 Jackson에게 프로필에 추가해야 할 것을 묻고 있고, Jackson은 Deborah가 학교에서 성취한 것들을 추가했으면 좋겠다고 생각하고 있으므로 Jackson이 Deborah에게 할 말로는 ③ '너는 많은 걸 이뤘어. 그걸 추가하는 건 어때?'가 가장 적절하다.

- graduate from ~을 졸업하다
- accept (기관 등에서) 받아 주다
- straight-A 전 과목 A를 받은
- private tutoring 개인 과외
- post (정보 등을) 게시하다, 올리다
- tutor 개인 교습을 하다; 개인 교사
- missing 빠진
- achieve (목적 등을) 성취하다, 이루다
  cf. achievement 성취
- prove 증명하다

M Deborah is graduating from high school next month. Since she has been accepted into college, she wants to work part-time before school starts. Since she is a straight-A student, she has decided to get into private tutoring. Since this is her first time, she has to create a profile and post it on a tutoring website. She adds information about herself **such as her school and what she's good at**. But she isn't sure if her profile shows enough about herself. So she asks her neighbor Jackson for help. He is **a college student with a lot of experience** as a tutor. She asks Jackson what else she needs on her profile. Jackson looks at it and thinks **there are a few things missing**. Many students want to know what she's achieved because it clearly proves her skills and abilities. So he wants to tell her to add her achievements. In this situation, what would Jackson most likely say to Deborah?

Jackson You have achieved a lot. How about adding that?

남 Deborah는 다음 달에 고등학교를 졸업한다. 그녀는 대학에 합격했기 때문에 학교가 시작하기 전에 파트타임으로 일하고 싶어 한다. 그녀는 전 과목 A를 받은 학생이어서 개인 과외를 시작하기로 결정했다. 이번이 처음이기 때문에 그녀는 프로필을 만들어 개인 과외 웹사이트에 올려야 한다. 그녀는 학교와 자신이 잘하는 것과 같은 정보를 추가하려고 한다. 하지만 그녀는 자신의 프로필이 자신에 대해 충분히 보여주는지 확신이 없다. 그래서 이웃인 Jackson에게 도움을 요청한다. 그는 개인 교사로서 경험이 많은 대학생이다. 그녀는 자신의 프로필에 어떤 것이 더 필요한지 Jackson에게 묻는다. Jackson은 그것을 보고 몇 가지 빠진 것이 있다고 생각한다. 많은 학생들은 그녀가 그동안 성취해온 것이 그녀의 기술과 능력을 명확히 증명하기 때문에 그것을 알고 싶어 한다. 그래서 그는 그녀에게 성취해온 것들을 추가하라고 말하고 싶어 한다. 이러한 상황에서 Jackson이 Deborah에게 할 말로 가장 적절한 것은 무엇인가?

Jackson 너는 많은 걸 이뤘어. 그걸 추가하는 건 어때?

① 나는 내 프로필에 무엇을 넣어야 할지 모르겠어.
② 너는 취미에 대해 더 구체적일 필요가 있어.

16 | 정답 | ④

여자는 문어가 어떤 특성을 가지고 있는지 하나씩 나열하여 설명하고 있으므로 정답은 ④ '문어를 두드러지게 만드는 특징들'이다.

17 | 정답 | ①

문어는 형태, 색깔, 크기, 그리고 피부 질감을 바꿀 수 있고, 먹이를 잡을 때 8개의 팔과 빨판을 사용하며 포식자로부터 도망칠 때 먹물을 분출한다고 설명한다. 하지만 문어의 '눈'에 대한 언급은 없었으므로 정답은 ①이다.

* protean 변화무쌍한
* species 종
* octopus 문어
* originate from ~에서 유래하다
* mythology 신화
* take on (특정한 모습 등을) 띠다
* intelligent 지적인
* unique 독특한
* appearance 외형, 외모
* alter 바꾸다
* texture 질감
* blend in with ~와 섞이다
* predator 포식자
* prey 먹이
* sucker 빨판
* restrain 억누르다
* trap 가두다
* shoot 쏘다
* ink sac 먹물주머니
* bury 숨기다
* liver 간
* eject 분출하다
* escape 달아나다, 탈출하다
* distraction 방해하는 것
[선택지]
* inhabit 서식하다; 거주하다, 살다
* feature 특징

W Good morning. People use the word "protean" to describe some species of octopus. **The word is known to have originated from** "Proteus", the god of the sea in Greek mythology. Proteus had the ability to take on any form he wanted, just like octopuses. Octopuses are very intelligent sea creatures with unique abilities. Surprisingly, **their ability to change their appearance** is better than that of chameleons. Octopuses are capable of changing their color and size. They can even alter the texture of their skin and blend in with surroundings. It's their way of hiding from their predators and catching their prey. To catch food, octopuses **use their 8 arms and the suckers on them**. Those suckers restrain and trap their prey. Moreover, they have the amazing ability to shoot ink. There is an ink sac buried under their liver. They eject ink from there to escape from predators. **It creates an ink cloud**, which is used as a distraction. You can take a closer look at how they do it in the video. The video will also explain more about these protean creatures.

여 안녕하세요. 사람들은 '변화무쌍한'이라는 단어를 문어의 일부 종을 설명하기 위해 사용합니다. 그 단어는 그리스 신화의 바다의 신 'Proteus'에게서 유래한 것으로 알려져 있습니다. Proteus는 마치 문어들처럼 자신을 원하는 어떤 형태로든 만들 수 있는 능력을 가지고 있었습니다. 문어는 독특한 능력을 가진 매우 지적인 바다생물입니다. 놀랍게도 외형을 변화시키는 그들의 능력은 카멜레온의 능력보다 더 뛰어납니다. 문어는 색깔과 크기를 변화시킬 수 있습니다. 그들은 심지어 피부의 질감을 변화시켜 주변 환경에 섞일 수 있습니다. 그것이 포식자로부터 숨고 먹이를 잡는 그들의 방법입니다. 먹이를 잡기 위해서 문어는 여덟 개의 팔과 그 위에 있는 빨판을 사용합니다. 그 빨판들은 먹이를 억누르고 가둡니다. 게다가, 그들은 먹물을 뿜어낼 수 있는 놀라운 능력이 있습니다. 그들의 간 아래에는 먹물주머니가 숨겨져 있습니다. 그들은 포식자로부터 도망가기 위해 그곳에서 먹물을 분출합니다. 그것은 먹물 구름을 만들고, 방해 요소로 사용됩니다. 그들이 그걸 어떻게 하는지 비디오에서 더 자세히 볼 수 있습니다. 이 비디오는 또한 이런 변화무쌍한 생물에 대해 더 많은 것을 설명해 줄 것입니다.

16 ① 그리스 신화가 어떻게 문어를 묘사하는지
② 바닷속의 문어가 서식해야 하는 장소
③ 문어가 변화될 수 있는 여러 모양들
④ 문어를 두드러지게 만드는 특징들
⑤ 문어를 강력하게 하는 먹물주머니

17 ① 눈 ② 피부 ③ 팔 ④ 빨판 ⑤ 먹물주머니

본문 p.76

01 | 정답 | ②

남자는 주민들에게 다음 주 월요일부터 수요일까지 계단 물청소가 있으니 계단에 보관한 물건들을 치워달라고 설명하고 있으므로 남자가 하는 말의 목적으로 ②가 가장 적절하다.

- resident 주민
- just around the corner 임박한
- announce 공고하다; 발표하다
- exterior 외부의; 외부
- stairs 계단
- remove 제거하다
- item 물품
- exact 정확한
- cooperation 협조

M Hello, residents. Now, spring is just around the corner, and it's time to clean our building. **As we announced last week**, we are going to clean the exterior windows and the stairs inside of the apartment buildings. The cleaning staff **will be washing the stairs in the buildings** from next Monday through Wednesday. On Monday, Building 201 and 202 will be washed. On Tuesday, they will wash the stairs in Building 203 and 204. Finally, on Wednesday, the stairs of Building 205 and 206 will be done. In order to make their job easier, **please remove all the items you keep on the stairs**, such as flower pots or bicycles. The exact time of cleaning is from 11 a.m. to 3 p.m., just the same as the last time. Thank you for your cooperation.

남 안녕하세요, 주민 여러분. 이제 봄이 다가오고 있으니 건물을 청소할 시간입니다. 지난주에 공고한 대로, 우리는 건물 외부 창문과 아파트 건물 내부의 계단을 청소하려고 합니다. 청소 직원들은 다음 주 월요일부터 수요일까지 건물 안의 계단을 물청소할 것입니다. 월요일에는 201동과 202동이 청소될 예정입니다. 화요일에는 203동과 204동 계단을 청소할 것입니다. 마지막으로 수요일에는 205동과 206동의 계단이 작업될 것입니다. 작업을 더 용이하게 하기 위하여 계단에 보관하시는 화분이나 자전거와 같은 물건들을 모두 치워주시기 바랍니다. 정확한 청소 시간은 지난번과 같은 오전 11시부터 오후 3시까지입니다. 여러분의 협조에 감사드립니다.

02 | 정답 | ⑤

남자는 거실을 꾸밀 식물을 사려고 하지만 여자는 식물을 키우는 데 정성이 많이 든다며 반려동물처럼 사랑이 필요하다고 말하고 있으므로, 여자의 의견으로 ⑤가 가장 적절하다.

- decorate 장식하다
- actually 사실
- indoor 실내의
- besides 게다가
- search for 찾아보다
- care 보살핌
- attention 주의

W Jim, where are you going?
M I'm going to buy something to decorate my living room.
W Oh, what are you going to buy?
M Actually, I'm thinking of buying some plants.
W Are you sure you can take care of them? **Growing indoor plants is not an easy job**.
M Do you think so? Well, I used to grow stookie plants in my room. Once, I didn't water them for weeks but they were okay.
W Yes, but stookies are the easiest houseplants to grow. Most plants aren't like that. Besides, **they need our love just like pets**.
M You're right. I'll search for more information before buying them.
W Remember, they need **a lot of care and attention when growing**.
M Okay, I'll keep that in mind.

여 Jim, 어딜 가고 있니?
남 내 거실을 장식할 물건을 좀 사러 가는 중이야.
여 아, 뭘 사려고 하는데?
남 사실, 식물을 좀 살까 생각 중이야.
여 네가 그것들을 돌볼 수 있을 거라고 확신하니? 실내 식물을 키우는 건 쉬운 일이 아니야.
남 그렇게 생각해? 글쎄, 내 방에서 스투키를 키웠거든. 한번은 몇 주 동안 물을 주지 않았는데도 괜찮았어.
여 그래, 하지만 스투키는 키우기 가장 쉬운 실내 식물이야. 대부분은 그렇지 않거든. 게다가 식물들은 반려동물들처럼 우리의 사랑이 필요해.
남 네 말이 맞아. 식물을 사기 전에 더 많은 정보를 찾아볼게.
여 그들이 자라는 동안 많은 보살핌과 주의가 필요하다는 걸 기억해.
남 알겠어, 명심할게.

03 | 정답 | ⑤

예술을 제대로 이해하기 위해서는 역사적인 맥락을 파악하는 것이 필요하다고 말하며 예술 감상법을 설명하고 있으므로 남자가 하는 말의 요지로 가장 적절한 것은 ⑤이다.

- appreciate 감상하다; 고마워하다
- context 배경, 맥락
- crucial 중대한
- genuine 진정의, 진짜의
- vital 절대 필요한, 지극히 중요한
- lead 안내하다

M Welcome, art lovers! I am Mr. Rivera, and I will be your guide for today's art museum tour. But before we explore the artwork, **let's talk about how to appreciate art**. Understanding the historical context is crucial for a genuine appreciation of art. As time goes by, art changes, and **what artists create today is often vastly different** from what was produced 300 or even 20 years ago. Therefore, to truly appreciate a work of art, **it is vital to know its historical background**. Now, I will lead you around the museum and explain the artwork. Let's explore together!

남 환영합니다, 예술 애호가 여러분! 저는 Rivera이고, 오늘 미술관 투어에서 여러분의 가이드가 될 것입니다. 하지만 우리가 작품을 탐구하기 전에, 예술을 감상하는 법에 대해 이야기해 보겠습니다. 예술의 진정한 이해를 위해서는 역사적인 맥락을 이해하는 것이 매우 중요합니다. 시간이 지남에 따라 예술은 변화하며, 오늘날 예술가들이 창조하는 것은 흔히 300년 혹은 심지어 20년 전에 제작된 것과 크게 다릅니다. 따라서 예술 작품을 진정으로 감상하려면 그것의 역사적인 배경을 아는 것이 절대 필요합니다. 이제 제가 여러분에게 미술관을 안내하며 작품을 설명해 드리겠습니다. 함께 탐험해 보죠!

04 | 정답 | ④

밴드의 가수는 항상 가죽 재킷을 입고 있다고 말했으므로 정답은 ④이다.

- spotlight 스포트라이트, 환한 조명

W What do you have in your hand?
M They are pictures of the concert that I went to last week.
W Wow, the stage looks awesome.
M Yes, the four spotlights **light up each one of the**

여 네 손에 든 건 뭐니?
남 지난주에 갔던 콘서트 사진들이야.
여 와, 무대가 굉장해 보인다.
남 그래, 그 네 개의 스포트라이트는 각 멤버를 비추고 있어.

* cross 십자가; 건너다
* lucky charm 부적
* signature 특징; 서명

members.

W Oh, the guitarist on the left side is a man, right?

M Yes, his name is John. He always keeps his hair long and wavy.

W I love his hair. Is that **a cross around the drummer's neck**?

M Yes, it is. The cross necklace is his lucky charm.

W I see. **Why is the singer wearing a jacket**?

M That's his signature look. No matter how hot it is, he always wears a leather jacket.

W Really? He must be uncomfortable.

M I know. Oh, do you see the person on the keyboard?

W **You mean the man with long hair**?

M Actually, it is a woman. She is the new member of the band.

여 아, 왼쪽에 있는 기타리스트는 남자야, 맞지?

남 응, 그의 이름은 John이야. 항상 머리가 길고 웨이브가 있어.

여 머리가 맘에 든다. 드러머의 목 주변에 저건 십자가니?

남 그래, 맞아. 십자가 목걸이는 그의 부적이거든.

여 그렇구나. 가수는 왜 재킷을 입고 있는 거야?

남 그건 그 사람만의 특유한 스타일이야. 아무리 덥더라도, 그는 항상 가죽 재킷을 입어.

여 정말? 불편하겠는데.

남 그러게. 아, 키보드 연주하는 사람 보이지?

여 머리 긴 남자 말하는 거야?

남 사실은, 여자야. 밴드의 새로운 멤버이거든.

---

05 | 정답 | ⑤

구두 수선점에서 구두를 찾는 일과 셔츠 다림질은 남자가 직접 하겠다고 말하고 있다. 대신 자신이 쓴 연설문을 여자에게 소리 내어 읽어달라고 말하고 있으므로 여자가 남자를 위해 할 일로 가장 적절한 것은 ⑤이다.

* replace 교체하다
* stop by (잠시) 들르다
* iron 다리미; 다림질하다
* closet 옷장
* read out loud 소리 내어 읽다

M Honey, do you know where my leather shoes are?

W You don't remember? You took them to the shoe repair shop to get the heels replaced.

M Oh, right, I wanted to wear them to the staff dinner at my company tonight.

W Would you like **me to pick them up for you**?

M That's okay. I will do that on my way to the dinner.

W I don't think you have enough time. You'll have to leave in 20 minutes to **stop by the repair shop**.

M Don't worry. I'll leave as soon as my shirt is ready. Where is the iron?

W It's in the drawer in the closet. Is your speech ready?

M I finished writing it, but nobody has read it yet. Can you **read it out loud for me** so I can check it?

W I was going to get you something to drink. I'm sure it's fine. You are such a good speaker.

M Well, I'm not sure. I didn't really spend enough time working on it.

W All right. I'll read it and **you listen while you are ironing**, okay?

M Thanks.

남 여보, 제 가죽 구두 어디 있는지 알아요?

여 기억 안 나요? 굽을 교체하려고 신발 수선점에 맡겼잖아요.

남 아, 맞네요. 오늘 저녁에 있는 회사 직원 회식 때 신고 싶었거든요.

여 제가 대신 찾아올까요?

남 괜찮아요. 회식에 가는 길에 제가 찾을게요.

여 당신에게 시간이 충분히 있을지 모르겠네요. 수선점에 들르려면 20분 안에 나가야 해요.

남 걱정 말아요. 셔츠만 준비되면 바로 나갈 거예요. 다리미는 어디에 있나요?

여 옷장 서랍 안에 있어요. 연설은 준비됐나요?

남 대본은 다 썼는데 아직 아무도 읽어 보질 않았어요. 그걸 확인할 수 있게 나에게 소리 내서 읽어 주겠어요?

여 당신이 마실 걸 좀 드리려고 했는데. 연설은 분명히 멋질 것이에요. 당신은 능숙한 연설가잖아요.

남 글쎄요. 잘 모르겠어요. 연설을 쓰는 데 그렇게 많은 시간을 할애하지 않았거든요.

여 알겠어요. 제가 읽을 테니 다림질하는 동안 들어 보세요, 알겠죠?

남 고마워요.

---

06 | 정답 | ③

남자는 체육관에 6개월 등록하려고 하는데 이번 달까지 6개월 회비가 50% 할인하고 있으므로 600달러이고 사물함은 한 달에 10달러이므로 60달러를 더 지불해야 한다. 따라서 정답은 ③이다.

* promotion 홍보; 판촉
* advertisement 광고
* go on 계속되다
* fill out 작성하다
* application form 신청서
* facility 시설
* fitness center 헬스장
* locker 사물함
* extra 추가로
* pass 입장권, 통행증

W Hello. Can I help you?

M I saw the promotion advertisement for your gym online. Is the promotion still available?

W Yes, it will be going on until the end of this month.

M Great. **I'd like to join for six months.**

W Okay. Our half-year membership is $1,200, but now it is 50% off. Would you fill out this application form, please?

M Sure, but I have a few questions. Does the membership **include use of all the facilities**?

W Of course. You can use the fitness center, spa, and even the swimming pool.

M Can I use a locker for free?

W I'm sorry, but **you need to pay extra for that**. Lockers are $10 a month.

M Do I need to pay for towels, too?

W No, **they are available for free**. Also, you get a free 7-day yoga pass if you get a membership.

M All right. Let me fill this out. And I need a locker for 6 months, too.

여 어서 오세요. 도와드릴까요?

남 온라인에서 체육관 홍보 광고를 봤어요. 그 홍보 아직도 유효한가요?

여 네, 이번 달 말까지 계속될 거예요.

남 잘됐군요. 6개월 등록하려고요.

여 알겠습니다. 저희 6개월 회원권은 1,200달러이지만 지금은 50% 할인 중이에요. 이 신청서를 작성해 주시겠어요?

남 네, 하지만 몇 가지 질문이 있어요. 회원권에 모든 시설의 사용이 포함되나요?

여 물론이죠. 헬스장, 스파, 심지어 수영장도 사용할 수 있어요.

남 사물함은 무료로 사용할 수 있나요?

여 죄송하지만, 그것은 추가로 돈을 내셔야 합니다. 사물함은 한 달에 10달러입니다.

남 수건도 돈을 내야 하나요?

여 아니요, 수건은 무료로 사용할 수 있어요. 또한 회원권이 있으면 7일 무료 요가 수업 입장권도 받으실 거예요.

남 알겠어요. 이거 작성하죠. 그리고 6개월 동안 사물함도 필요해요.

07 | 정답 | ①

Sally네 가족을 초대하자는 남자의 말에 여자는 귀의 염증 때문에 쉬어야 한다고 했으므로 정답은 ①이다.

* occasion (특정한) 때, 경우
* promote 승진시키다
* business trip 출장
* infection 염증

M Honey, are you doing anything tomorrow?
W Not really. How about you?
M I think I'm going to invite Sally's family over to our place.
W Oh, what is the occasion?
M **I was invited to her house last month** when her husband got promoted.
W Right. I couldn't make it because I was on a business trip.
M Yes. So, if it's okay with you, I want to invite them tomorrow.
W Sorry, but can we do that next weekend?
M Why? Is there something wrong?
W Actually, I went to see a doctor yesterday because of an ear infection.
M Oh, you have an ear infection again? I told you to quit swimming.
W Yes, I have to. **That's what the doctor said**, too. So, I think I'll just rest tomorrow.
M You'll be all right soon. I'll invite Sally's family over next weekend.

남 여보, 내일 할 일 있어요?
여 별로요. 당신은요?
남 Sally네 가족을 우리 집에 초대할 생각이에요.
여 아, 무슨 날이에요?
남 지난달에 그녀의 남편이 승진했을 때 집에 초대받았잖아요.
여 맞아요. 저는 출장 중이어서 못 갔었죠.
남 그래요. 그래서 당신만 괜찮으면 내일 그들을 초대하고 싶어요.
여 미안한데, 다음 주말에 해도 될까요?
남 왜요? 뭔가 안 좋은 일 있어요?
여 사실, 귀에 염증 때문에 어제 병원에 갔었거든요.
남 아, 귀에 또 염증이 생겼어요? 제가 수영을 그만두라고 말했었죠.
여 네, 그래야 해요. 의사도 그렇게 말했거든요. 그래서 내일은 좀 쉬어야 할 것 같아요.
남 금방 괜찮아질 거예요. Sally네 가족은 다음 주에 초대할게요.

08 | 정답 | ②

남자가 다녀온 학회는 부다페스트에서 11월 19일부터 5일간 열렸고, 그 주제는 콜레스테롤의 기능이었으며 폐회식까지 참석하고 공항으로 출발했다고 말했다. 하지만 참가국에 대한 언급은 없었으므로 정답은 ②이다.

* conference 학회, 회의
* hold 개최하다
* function 기능
* figure 수치
* medical check-up 건강검진
* last 지속되다
* reception 축하 연회, 리셉션

W Jack, how was the conference?
M It was wonderful. Some famous doctors spoke about how to stay healthy.
W I wish I could have gone, too.
M **I didn't know you were interested in** that kind of conference.
W I'm interested in health-related issues. **Where was it held**?
M It was held in Budapest. **The main topic was the function of** cholesterol in our body.
W That sounds like a good topic.
M Yes, it helped me understand the cholesterol figures from my medical check-up results.
W So, when did the conference start?
M It started on the 19th of November, **and lasted for 5 days**.
W Did you stay there for 5 days then?
M Yes, I participated in both the opening reception and the closing ceremony, and left for the airport at around 9 p.m. on the last day.

여 Jack, 학회는 어땠니?
남 훌륭했어. 유명한 의사들 몇 명이 건강 관리에 대해 연설했어.
여 나도 가보고 싶었는데.
남 네가 그런 학회에 관심이 있는 줄 몰랐어.
여 난 건강 관련 문제들에 관심이 있어. 학회는 어디서 열렸니?
남 부다페스트에서 열렸어. 주제는 우리 몸에서의 콜레스테롤의 기능이었어.
여 좋은 주제인 것 같아.
남 그래. 내 건강검진 결과에 나온 콜레스테롤 수치를 이해하는 데 도움이 됐어.
여 그래서 학회는 언제 시작했어?
남 11월 19일에 시작해서 5일간 계속됐어.
여 그럼 거기서 5일 동안 머물렀어?
남 응. 개회 행사와 폐회식에 모두 참여했고, 마지막 날 오후 9시쯤에 공항으로 출발했어.

09 | 정답 | ①

YSU 댄스 캠프는 6월 21일부터 시작하는 4일간의 캠프이므로 정답은 ①이다.

* inform A of B A에게 B를 알리다
* opportunity 기회
* combine A with B A와 B를 결합하다
* run 계속되다
* admission fee 참가비
* register 등록하다
* in advance 미리
* curriculum 교육 과정
* moreover 게다가
* choreographer 안무가
* provide A for B B에게 A를 제공하다
* accommodate 수용하다

W Today, I'd like to inform you of one of the greatest opportunities to combine dancing with camping. This year's YSU Dance Camp **will run for four days** from June 21st to 24th on the YSU campus. You can participate in this camp if you are interested in any type of dancing. The admission fee is $300, but if you register at least one month in advance, you will get a 10% discount. Also, **if you register in a group of** 10 or more, you will get 10% off. All campers will receive a camp T-shirt and a camp towel. And don't be worried if you are a beginner. We have a special curriculum **prepared especially for beginners**. Moreover, Simon White, a world-famous choreographer, will join us to provide dance lessons for everyone. The program **can accommodate up to 100 campers**, so you'd better hurry up.

여 오늘 저는 여러분에게 춤과 캠핑을 결합할 최고의 기회 중 하나를 알려드리고자 합니다. 올해의 YSU 댄스 캠프는 6월 21일부터 24일까지 YSU 캠퍼스에서 4일간 열리게 됩니다. 어떤 종류든 춤에 관심이 있으시면 이번 캠프에 참여할 수 있습니다. 참가비는 300달러인데, 최소 한 달 미리 등록하시면 10%의 할인을 받게 됩니다. 또한, 10명 이상의 단체로 등록하시면, 10%의 할인을 받습니다. 모든 캠프 등록자들은 캠프 티셔츠와 캠프 수건을 받게 됩니다. 그리고 초보라도 걱정하지 마세요. 특히 초보자들을 위해 준비된 특별 교육 과정이 있습니다. 게다가 세계적으로 유명한 안무가 Simon White가 모든 분에게 안무 수업을 제공하기 위해 우리와 함께 할 것입니다. 이 프로그램은 100명까지 수용할 수 있으니 서두르셔야 합니다.

10 | 정답 | ④

여자는 가격이 100달러 이하인 가벼운 갈색의 긴 부츠를 사길 원하고 있으므로 정답은 ④이다.

* recently 최근에
* contest 대회
* catalog 카탈로그
* price range 가격대
* though (문장 끝에 와서) 그렇지만, 하지만
* ankle 발목

M Nancy, Topaz Dancing Shoes is having a big sale starting next week.
W Really? They haven't had a sale recently. I need a pair of shoes for the dancing contest next month.
M Here. Have a look at their online catalog.
W They all look nice. I don't know what to choose.
M **Think about your price range first**. All of them are pretty expensive, though.
W I don't want to spend more than $100.
M Then you should choose from these four pairs. You **need light ones rather than heavy ones**, right?
W Yes, I don't wear heavy shoes.
M Do you prefer long boots or short ones? They also have ankle boots, if you'd like.
W **I prefer long boots.** They'd look great when I dance in a short skirt.
M Then you have to **choose from the two colors left**.
W I like these brown ones. The shoes I have are almost all black, so I'll buy these ones.
M I think you've made a good choice.

남 Nancy, Topaz 댄스화가 다음 주부터 대규모 세일을 해.
여 정말? 최근에 세일을 하지 않았는데. 다음 달에 댄스 경연대회에 신을 댄스화가 하나 필요하거든.
남 여기. 온라인 카탈로그를 봐.
여 모두 다 멋져 보인다. 뭘 골라야 할지 모르겠어.
남 먼저 가격대를 생각해 봐. 다 꽤 비싸긴 하지만.
여 100달러 넘게 쓰고 싶진 않아.
남 그럼 이 네 가지 중에 골라야 해. 무거운 것보다 가벼운 게 필요하지, 맞지?
여 응, 무거운 건 안 신어.
남 긴 부츠와 짧은 부츠 중 어느 것이 더 좋아? 원한다면 앵클부츠도 있어.
여 긴 부츠가 더 좋아. 짧은 치마를 입고 춤을 출 때 그게 더 멋져 보일 거야.
남 그럼 남은 두 개의 색깔 중에 골라야 해.
여 이 갈색 부츠가 마음에 들어. 내가 가지고 있는 신발은 거의 다 검은색이어서 이걸로 살래.
남 선택 잘한 것 같아.

---

11 | 정답 | ④

남자가 수학여행에 무엇을 입고 갈지 아직 결정하지 못했다는 말에 여자는 일기예보를 확인했는지 묻고 있는 상황에서 남자의 응답으로는 ④ '확인했어. 하지만 요즘에 그다지 신뢰할 수 있는 것 같지 않아.'가 가장 적절하다.

* can't wait ~가 너무 기다려지다
* weather forecast 일기예보
[선택지]
* reliable 믿을 수 있는

W Bob, **I can't wait to go on** our school trip next week.
M Me neither. **I haven't decided what to wear**.
W Didn't you check the weather forecast yet?
M I did. But it doesn't seem quite reliable these days.

여 Bob, 난 다음 주 수학여행이 너무 기다려져.
남 나도 그래. 난 뭘 입을지 결정 못 했어.
여 아직 일기예보 확인 안 했니?
남 확인했어. 하지만 요즘에 그다지 신뢰할 수 있는 것 같지 않아.

① 안 했어. 여행에 완벽한 날씨야.
② 절대 안 해. 하루 종일 비가 올 거라고 생각했거든.
③ 물론이지. 난 그런 날씨를 위해 가방을 쌌어.
⑤ 걱정 마. 내일을 위해 가방 싸는 걸 끝냈어.

---

12 | 정답 | ③

남자는 아들의 선생님이 만나자고 한다며 여자에게 하루 휴가 내기를 부탁하는 상황에서 여자의 응답으로 가장 적절한 것은 ③ '알겠어요, 제가 일정을 다시 조정할 수 있는지 알아볼게요.'이다.

* take a day off 하루 휴가 내다
* behavior 행동
[선택지]
* rearrange 재조정하다

M Honey, **can you take a day off tomorrow**?
W Well, I'm not sure. Why? Do you have any special plans that day?
M Jamie's **teacher wants to see us**. It's about his behavior at school.
W Okay. Let me see if I can rearrange my schedule.

남 여보, 내일 하루 휴가 낼 수 있어요?
여 음, 잘 모르겠어요. 왜요? 그날 특별한 계획이라도 있어요?
남 Jamie의 선생님이 우리를 만나길 원하세요. 학교에서 그의 행동에 관해서요.
여 알겠어요. 제가 일정을 다시 조정할 수 있는지 알아볼게요.

① 미안해요. 난 더 이상 당신과 얘기할 시간이 없네요.
② 당신이 맞아요. 자신을 돌볼 때예요.
④ 걱정 마요. 내일 업무 회의가 있어요.
⑤ 이해해요. 곧 저만의 사업을 시작해야 해요.

---

13 | 정답 | ⑤

여자는 남자에게 자신이 모든 발표를 하기보다는 팀원들이 조사한 부분을 각자가 발표하는 것을 제안하면서 연습하면 할 수 있다고 설득하고 있으므로 남자의 마지막 응답으로 가장 적절한 것은 ⑤ '알겠어. 그럼 모여서 우리가 할 수 있는지 보자.'이다.

* presentation 발표
* split up 쪼개다
* research 조사(하다), 연구(하다)
* gather 모으다
* look into 조사하다

W Peter, can I ask you something about our presentation?
M Okay. What do you want to ask?
W I was wondering if we could split up the presentation.
M We did. We did research, gathered information, and made files, so that you can present more easily.
W I meant that **each of us should present what we looked into**. Our main topic is mental disorders, but you researched the types of mental disorders, and Gary dug into the cures, and I studied the side effects of medicine.
M Yes. And you wanted to do the presentation.
W I know, but it would be much better if you and Gary **presented what you researched and studied**.

여 Peter, 우리 발표에 관해 뭐 좀 물어봐도 될까?
남 그래. 물어보고 싶은 게 뭐야?
여 우리가 발표를 나눠서 하면 어떨까 생각하고 있었어.
남 그렇게 했잖아. 네가 더 쉽게 발표할 수 있게 우리는 연구를 하고 정보를 모으고, 파일을 만들었어.
여 내 말은 우리가 조사한 것을 각자 발표해야 한다는 뜻이었어. 우리 주된 주제가 정신질환인데, 너는 정신질환의 종류를 조사하고, Gary는 치료책을 자세히 조사하고, 그리고 나는 약의 부작용을 연구했잖아.
남 그래. 그리고 네가 발표를 하고 싶어 했고.
여 맞아, 하지만 너와 Gary가 너희들이 조사하고 연구한 것을 직접 발표하면 훨씬 더 나을 것 같아.

- **mental disorder** 정신질환
- **dig into** 자세히 조사하다
- **cure** 치료책
- **side effect** 부작용
- **divide** 나누다
- **evenly** 똑같이
- **assigned** 할당된

M But we only have 20 minutes for the team presentation. Do you think **it's possible to divide the time evenly**?

W If we practice within the assigned time limit, it won't be a big problem.

M All right. Then let's get together and see if we can do that.

남 하지만 팀 발표 시간은 20분밖에 없어. 그 시간을 똑같이 나누는 게 가능할 것 같아?

여 우리가 할당된 제한 시간 안에서 연습한다면 문제없을 거야.

남 알겠어. 그럼 모여서 우리가 할 수 있는지 보자.

① 걱정 마. 내가 언젠가는 더 많은 조사를 할 거야.
② 난 아냐. 난 그 주제를 연구하는 데 너무 많은 시간을 썼어.
③ 괜찮아. 나도 발표를 하려고 하지 않았어.
④ 동의하지 않아. 우리에겐 연습할 시간이 충분한 것 같아.

---

14 | 정답 | ③

남자는 여자에게 다른 반장 후보들도 보고 선택을 해야 한다고 설득하면서, 지금 Samuel의 선거 연설을 들으러 가는데 같이 갈 것이냐고 묻고 있으므로 여자의 마지막 응답으로 가장 적절한 것은 ③ '당연하지. 나도 다른 후보들을 고려해야겠어.'이다.

- **run for** ~에 출마하다
- **class president** 반장
- **recommend** 추천하다
- **position** 직책, 자리
- **responsible** 책임감 있는
- **relationship** 관계
- **grade** 성적
- **serve** 봉사하다
- **require** 필요로 하다
- **candidate** 후보
- **pay attention to** ~에 주의를 기울이다
- **as well** 또한
- **campaign** 선거 운동
- **qualified** 자격이 있는

M Jessica, did you know Tammy is running for class president?

W Actually, I recommended her for that position.

M Wow, I didn't know that.

W Tammy is a responsible student. She **has a good relationship with her classmates**, and her grades are good.

M She is a good student, but being a class president is different.

W What do you mean?

M First of all, we need somebody who is ready to serve their classmates. Second, **the position requires leadership experience**.

W Still, Tammy is the best candidate for me. She helps her friends a lot, and she is pretty popular in class.

M I think we need to pay attention to other candidates as well.

W You're right. Since it is the beginning of the campaign, let's find out who is **the most qualified for that job**.

M Sure. I'm going to listen to Samuel's campaign speech now. Do you want to come?

W Why not? I should consider other candidates, too.

남 Jessica, Tammy가 반장 선거에 출마한다는 거 알고 있었어?

여 사실 내가 그 자리에 걜 추천했어.

남 와, 몰랐어.

여 Tammy는 책임감 있는 학생이야. 반 친구들과 사이도 좋고 성적도 좋아.

남 좋은 학생이지만 반장이 되는 건 달라.

여 무슨 의미야?

남 먼저, 우리는 반 친구들에게 봉사할 준비가 된 사람이 필요해. 두 번째로, 그 직책은 지도력 경험이 필요해.

여 그래도, Tammy는 내게 최고의 후보야. 그녀는 친구들을 많이 도와주고 반에서 인기도 꽤 있어.

남 난 다른 후보들에게도 주의를 기울여야 한다고 생각해.

여 네 말이 맞아. 선거 운동의 초반이니까 그 일에 누가 가장 자격이 있는지 알아보자.

남 그래. 나는 지금 Samuel의 선거 연설을 들으려고 해. 같이 갈래?

여 당연하지. 나도 다른 후보들을 고려해야겠어.

① 누가 상관해? 그건 별일이 아니라고 생각해.
② 괜찮아. 난 그 후보들이 누구인지 잘 몰라.
④ 미안해. 난 내 선거 연설을 준비해야 해.
⑤ 물론이야. 이번 학기에 그 과목을 들어야 할 것 같아.

---

15 | 정답 | ④

Sam은 사진 찍는 취미를 가진 Rose에게 초보 사진사에게 좋은 카메라 기능을 물어보려고 하고 있으므로 정답은 ④ '초보자들을 위한 좋은 카메라의 특징들이 뭐니?'가 가장 적절하다.

- **photography** 사진
- **in the market for** ~을 사려고 하는
- **select** 선택하다, 고르다
  [선택지]
- **feature** 특징, 특색

M Sam and Rose are high school students. Sam joins the photography club, but he doesn't have a camera. So, now **he is in the market for a good camera**. But since he just started taking an interest in photography, **he doesn't know how to select a camera**. So, he decides to ask Rose for help. Her hobby is taking pictures. Sam tells Rose that he joined the photography club, and that he needs to buy a good camera. Now he is about to ask Rose about **what kind of functions he should look for** when he buys a good camera. In this situation, what would Sam most likely say to Rose?

Sam What are the features of a good camera for beginners?

남 Sam과 Rose는 고등학생이다. Sam은 사진 동아리에 가입하지만, 카메라가 없다. 그래서, 이제 그는 좋은 카메라를 사려고 한다. 그러나 그는 사진에 이제 겨우 관심을 가지기 시작했기 때문에 어떻게 카메라를 선택해야 하는지 모른다. 그래서 그는 Rose에게 도움을 청하기로 결심한다. 그녀의 취미는 사진을 찍는 것이다. Sam은 Rose에게 자신이 사진 동아리에 가입했고 좋은 카메라를 사야 한다고 말한다. 이제 그는 Rose에게 그가 좋은 카메라를 살 때 어떤 종류의 기능을 찾아봐야 하는지에 대해 물어보려고 한다. 이러한 상황에서 Sam이 Rose에게 할 말로 가장 적절한 것은 무엇인가?

Sam 초보자들을 위한 좋은 카메라의 특징들이 뭐니?

① 너의 카메라를 빌려도 될까?
② 어떻게 좋은 사진을 찍을 수 있는지 말해줄래?
③ 내가 카메라의 기본 기능에 대해 너에게 말해줄게.
⑤ 난 네가 사진 동아리 가입에 관심이 있는지 궁금해.

---

16 | 정답 | ③

여자는 캐나다의 멸종위기의 동물들이 어떻게 분류되는지에 대해 주로 설명하고 있으므로 여자가 하는 말의 주제는 ③ '캐나다가 멸종위기의 동물을 어떻게 분류하는가'이다.

W Good morning, everyone. Last time we talked about endangered species around the world. Today, let's talk about the ones in Canada. **Canada is not an exception**, and the number of endangered species in Canada is growing. Seven additional animal species **were declared endangered** in November. Scientists meet once a year

여 여러분, 좋은 아침입니다. 지난 시간에 우리는 세계의 멸종 위기의 종들에 대해 얘기를 했습니다. 오늘은 캐나다에 있는 멸종 위기의 종들에 대해 말해 봅시다. 캐나다도 예외는 아니며, 캐나다의 멸종 위기종의 수는 늘고 있습니다. 추가로 일곱 개의 동물 종들이 11월에 멸종 위기 상태로 발표되었습니다. 과학자들은 일 년에 한 번 모임을 가지고 멸종 위기 상태로 갈 위험에

17 | 정답 | ⑤

'특별 관심', '위협', '위기', '지역적 멸종', '멸종' 순으로 멸종 단계를 설명하고 있으며, '완전한 파괴'는 언급되지 않았으므로 정답은 ⑤이다.

* endangered 멸종 위기의
* species 종
* exception 예외
* additional 추가적인
* declare 발표하다
* review 검토하다
* at risk of ~의 위험에 있는
* concern 관심, 우려
* threatened 위협을 받는
* habitat 서식지
* destroy 파괴하다
* against the law 위법인
* critical 중요한

and review species that are at risk of becoming endangered. If they think a species is in trouble, they put it on the list. There are **five different levels of risk on the list**. The lowest level is "special concern," followed by "threatened," the second lowest level. The middle level is "endangered." Then if a species **can no longer exist** in a certain area, it is called "locally extinct," which usually happens when one of its habitat is totally destroyed. Finally, if a species **disappears from the planet entirely**, it is called "extinct", which is the highest level. Once a species is listed, it is against the law for people to harm or kill them. It is also illegal to destroy the species' critical habitat.

있는 종들을 검토합니다. 만약 그들이 어떤 종이 위험에 처해 있다고 생각하면 그들은 그 종을 목록에 올립니다. 그 목록에는 다섯 개의 다른 위험 수준이 있습니다. 가장 낮은 수준은 '특별 관심'이며 그다음으로 두 번째로 낮은 수준인 '위협'이 있습니다. 중간 수준은 '위기'입니다. 그리고 만약 한 종이 어떤 지역에서 더 이상 존재하지 않으면 그것을 '지역적 멸종'이라고 부르는데, 이는 보통 그것의 서식지 중 하나가 완전히 파괴될 때 발생합니다. 마지막으로 한 종이 지구상에서 완전히 사라지면 그것을 '멸종'이라고 부르고, 가장 높은 수준입니다. 일단 종이 목록에 오르면 사람들이 그것들에게 해를 주거나 죽이는 것이 위법입니다. 또한 그 종의 중요한 서식지를 파괴하는 것도 불법입니다.

16 ① 한 종이 어떻게 멸종되는가
② 정부의 책임
③ 캐나다가 멸종위기의 동물을 어떻게 분류하는가
④ 멸종 위기의 종에 대한 정의
⑤ 우리는 야생동물을 왜 보호해야 하는가

17 ① 특별 관심 ② 위협 ③ 위기
④ 지역적 멸종 ⑤ 완전한 파괴

14회 실전 듣기 모의고사

| 01 ② | 02 ④ | 03 ⑤ | 04 ⑤ | 05 ⑤ | 06 ③ | 07 ④ | 08 ③ | 09 ② | 10 ③ |
| 11 ③ | 12 ⑤ | 13 ④ | 14 ① | 15 ④ | 16 ② | 17 ⑤ | | | |

본문 p.82

01 | 정답 | ②

아침 일정을 끝마치고, 이후 일정에 관해 설명하는 내용이다. 잠깐의 휴식 후 점심시간이며 오후 2시에 다시 이어서 오후 일정을 시작한다고 하였으므로 여자가 하는 말의 목적으로 가장 적절한 것은 ②이다.

- participant 참가자
- come to the end 끝나다
- session (특정한 활동) 시간; 회의
- enthusiasm 열정
- participation 참여
- cooperation 협력, 협동
- recharge 재충전하다
- be sure to-v 반드시 ~하다
- punctual 시간을 잘 지키는

W Hello, participants of the World Youth Organization. We have almost come to the end of the morning session. We have had a wonderful time this morning. I am very **impressed with your enthusiasm** and active participation. Your creative ideas on our global cooperation were also amazing. Now, let's take a break and **have lunch to recharge our energy**. The afternoon session **will start at 2 p.m. in this room**. Be sure to be punctual so our session can go smoothly. Please enjoy your lunch. Also, during lunch, try to start a conversation with your fellow participants from all over the world and share new ideas like the ones we talked about during the morning session. **See you again this afternoon**. Thank you.

여 세계청소년기구 참가자 여러분, 안녕하세요. 오전 시간이 거의 끝났습니다. 오늘 오전 우리는 정말 멋진 시간을 가졌습니다. 저는 여러분의 열정과 적극적인 참여에 깊은 감명을 받았습니다. 국제적 협력에 관한 여러분의 창의적인 아이디어 또한 놀라웠습니다. 잠시 휴식 시간을 갖고 에너지를 재충전하기 위해 점심을 먹읍시다. 오후 회의는 이 방에서 오후 2시에 시작됩니다. 회의가 순조롭게 진행될 수 있도록 반드시 시간을 잘 지켜주시기를 바랍니다. 점심 맛있게 드시고요. 점심 드시면서 전 세계에서 오신 동료 참가자 여러분과 대화를 나누고 오전 회의 동안에 논의하셨던 것과 같이 새로운 아이디어를 공유하시기 바랍니다. 오후에 다시 뵙겠습니다. 감사합니다.

02 | 정답 | ④

시험 전날까지 밤을 새워 복습했다는 여자의 말에 남자는 충분한 수면을 취해야 시험 기간 동안 집중할 수 있으며, 너무 피곤하면 오히려 집중할 수 없을 것이라고 말하고 있으므로 남자의 의견으로 가장 적절한 것은 ④이다.

- stay up 안 자다, 깨어 있다
- review 복습하다
- maintain 유지하다
- a lack of 부족한
- cover 다루다
- cram 벼락치기 공부를 하다
- concentrate 집중하다
- turn out 결과로 ~이 되다, 판명되다

M Jane, you look really tired.
W Yes, I stayed up all night studying for the math test today.
M What? Why did you stay up?
W I had no choice. **I had so much to review**.
M Maintaining your focus throughout tests is important, too. **A lack of sleep makes it difficult to focus**.
W But I think it's more important to cover everything even if you have to cram.
M Well, I'd have to disagree. I think you need enough sleep to keep yourself focused during the exam period. If you are too tired, **you won't be able to concentrate**.
W You have a point. **Let's see how my math score turns out**.
M Yes, I hope you get a good grade.
W Thanks.

남 Jane, 너 정말 피곤해 보인다.
여 응, 오늘 수학 시험 때문에 공부하느라고 밤을 새웠어.
남 뭐라고? 왜 밤을 새웠니?
여 어쩔 수가 없었어. 복습할 게 너무 많았거든.
남 시험 내내 집중력을 유지하는 것도 중요해. 잠이 모자라면 집중하기가 어렵지.
여 그렇지만 벼락치기를 해야 하더라도 모든 걸 다 살펴보는 것이 더 중요하다고 생각해.
남 글쎄, 나는 생각이 다른데. 내 생각에는 시험 기간 동안에 집중하기 위해서는 충분한 수면이 필요하거든. 너무 피곤하면, 집중을 할 수가 없잖아.
여 일리가 있네. 내 수학 점수가 어떻게 나오나 보자.
남 그래, 네가 시험 잘 보면 좋겠어.
여 고마워.

03 | 정답 | ⑤

새로운 나라를 방문했을 때 그 지역 문화를 존중하는 태도가 중요하다고 하고 있으므로 여자가 하는 말의 요지로 가장 적절한 것은 ⑤이다.

- upcoming 다가오는
- valuable 유용한
- challenging 도전적인
- respectful 존중하는
- consideration 고려 사항, 배려

W Good day, everyone! My name is Ms. Pottenger, and I will be your tour guide for today. As you prepare for your upcoming travels abroad, **I would like to offer you some valuable advice**. Visiting a new country can be challenging, but it is very important to maintain a respectful attitude towards the local culture. One way to do this is **by following the customs of the country**. You can also learn basic phrases in the local language such as greetings, or "please" and "thank you." Remember that **respecting the local culture is highly important**. With these considerations in mind, I wish you all a fantastic journey.

여 안녕하세요, 여러분! 저는 오늘 여러분의 여행 가이드가 될 Pottenger라고 합니다. 여러분이 다가오는 해외 여행을 준비하기에, 제가 몇 가지 유용한 조언을 드리고 싶습니다. 새로운 나라를 방문하는 것은 도전적이긴 하지만 그 지역 문화를 존중하는 태도를 유지하는 것은 매우 중요합니다. 이를 위한 한 가지 방법은 그 나라의 관습을 따르는 것입니다. 또한 인사말이나 "부탁합니다"와 "고맙습니다"와 같은 현지 언어로 된 기본 문구를 배울 수도 있습니다. 그 지역의 문화를 존중하는 것은 매우 중요하다는 것을 기억하세요. 이러한 고려 사항을 염두에 두고 여러분 모두의 환상적인 여행을 기원합니다.

04 | 정답 | ⑤

화분들은 발코니에 두었다고 하였으므로 일치하지 않는 것은 ⑤이다.

- make oneself comfortable 마음 편히 하다
- housewarming 집들이

W Thanks for inviting me to your new place.
M You are welcome. **Please make yourself comfortable**.
W Here is your housewarming gift. It's just a bottle of wine.
M Thanks. Come, I'll show you around. [Pause] This is the living room.
W Wow, your new place is much bigger than the last one.

여 새집으로 초대해 주셔서 고마워요.
남 별말씀을요. 편하게 있으세요.
여 집들이 선물입니다. 그냥 와인 한 병이에요.
남 고맙습니다. 이리 와요, 제가 안내해 드릴게요. [잠시 후] 여기가 거실입니다.
여 와, 여기가 지난번 집보다 훨씬 넓군요.

* drying rack 건조대
* huge 큰, 거대한
* extra 추가 요금; 추가의, 여분의
* part 부(속)품

M Oh, please don't mind the drying rack on the left.
W Don't worry. Your TV is huge. Is it new?
M It is. I wanted to hang it on the wall, but it'd cost extra. So I just **put it on the TV stand**.
W I see. What is in those boxes next to the TV?
M There are some cables and parts for the TV, but I haven't put them away yet.
W Okay. Is the mirror new as well?
M Yes. I wanted to put it in my bedroom, but there is not enough space. So, I placed it **on the right side of the living room**.
W Oh, what happened to all the plants you had?
M I put them on the balcony.

남 아, 왼쪽에 있는 빨래 건조대는 신경 쓰지 마세요.
여 걱정 마세요. TV가 크네요. 새로 장만하신 건가요?
남 네. 벽에 걸려고 했는데 그건 추가 비용이 필요하더라고요. 그래서 그냥 여기 TV 스탠드에 두었어요.
여 그렇군요. TV 옆에 있는 저 상자들은 뭐죠?
남 TV 케이블하고 부품인데, 아직 치우지 않았어요.
여 그렇군요. 이 거울도 새로 사신 건가요?
남 네. 그건 제 침실에 놓고 싶었는데, 공간이 부족해요. 그래서 그걸 거실 오른쪽에 놓았어요.
여 아, 원래 있던 화분들은 어떻게 하셨어요?
남 그것들은 발코니에 갖다 놓았어요.

---

05 | 정답 | ⑤

남자는 자신이 어려움을 겪고 있는 문학 과제를 하는 데 조언을 구하기 위해, 같은 수업에서 좋은 성적을 받은 Chris의 전화번호를 알려줄 수 있는지 여자에게 부탁하고 있으므로 정답은 ⑤이다.

* trouble 괴롭히다; 걱정, 곤란
* assignment 과제
* impressive 인상적인

W Nathan, is something troubling you?
M I'm worried that I'll fail Mr. Johnson's literature class. I'm **having trouble with his assignment**.
W Well, his assignments are usually complicated and difficult.
M I heard you took the same class last year. Do you have any tips for me?
W Mr. Johnson expects you to take a lot of notes. I **can lend you my notes** if you want.
M That's okay. I already have my own notes. But I don't know how to use them for the assignment.
W Why don't you ask Chris for advice? I think he got an A in the same class.
M Chris? Wow, that's impressive.
W I have two classes with him this semester. **I could ask him for you**.
M Can you **give me his number instead**? I'll text him some questions.
W All right. I left my phone in my locker. Is it okay if I give you his number after lunch?
M That's fine. Thank you.

여 Nathan, 무슨 고민 있니?
남 Johnson 선생님의 문학 수업에서 낙제를 할까 봐 걱정돼. 선생님이 주신 과제 때문에 애먹고 있거든.
여 그 선생님의 과제는 보통 복잡하고 어렵지.
남 작년에 네가 그 수업을 수강했다고 들었어. 나한테 해줄 조언 좀 없니?
여 Johnson 선생님은 필기를 많이 하길 원하셔. 원한다면 내 노트를 빌려줄 수 있어.
남 괜찮아. 이미 필기는 직접 다 했어. 그런데 과제에 어떻게 활용해야 할지를 모르겠어.
여 Chris에게 조언을 구하는 게 어때? 내 기억에 걔가 같은 수업에서 A를 받은 것 같아.
남 Chris가? 와, 대단하다.
여 이번 학기에 수업을 두 개 같이 듣거든. 그 애한테 물어봐 줄 수 있어.
남 대신 걔 전화번호를 알려줄 수 있어? 문자로 질문을 몇 가지 하고 싶거든.
여 알겠어. 휴대폰을 사물함에 두고 왔어. 점심시간 후에 번호를 알려줘도 괜찮아?
남 괜찮아. 고마워.

---

06 | 정답 | ③

여자는 40달러에서 10% 할인된 스웨터 한 벌과 30달러짜리 바지 두 벌을 구매하려고 한다. 추가로 10달러짜리 기프트 카드를 사용하려고 하므로 상품 금액의 합인 96달러에서 10달러를 뺀 ③이 정답이다.

* display 전시[진열]하다; 전시, 진열
* originally 원래

W Excuse me, I'm looking for a sweater for my son.
M Sweaters are over here. We have a wide selection of sweaters and some of them are on sale.
W That's good. How much is **that one displayed on the wall**? The pattern looks very unique.
M That one is $50, but it's not on sale.
W What about the striped sweaters on the shelf?
M They are part of the special sale. They were originally $40, but they are 10% off for this week only.
W All right. Then, **I'll take that one in a large size**.
M Okay. Is there anything else you need?
W Actually, I think I need pants that will go well with it.
M Sure, how about those ones in the display window? They are **newly arrived and are only $30**.
W They look nice. I will take two large pairs.
M Okay. Would that be all?
W Yes. I have this $10 gift card **I can use as cash at this mall**. Can I use it now?
M Of course, ma'am.
W Great. Here is my credit card.

여 실례합니다. 제 아들을 위한 스웨터를 사러 왔어요.
남 스웨터는 이쪽에 있습니다. 스웨터 종류가 다양하게 있고, 그중 몇몇은 할인 중이에요.
여 잘됐네요. 벽에 전시된 저 상품은 얼마인가요? 무늬가 참 독특하네요.
남 그 옷은 50달러입니다만 할인 대상은 아닙니다.
여 선반 위에 있는 줄무늬 스웨터는요?
남 그것들은 특별 할인 대상 중 하나예요. 원래 40달러인데 이번 주만 10% 할인합니다.
여 알겠습니다. 그러면 라지 사이즈로 하나 살게요.
남 네. 다른 건 필요하신 것 없으세요?
여 사실 스웨터와 잘 어울릴 만한 바지도 있어야 할 것 같아요.
남 물론이죠. 창가에 전시된 바지는 어떠세요? 새로 들어온 상품이고 30달러밖에 하지 않습니다.
여 멋지네요. 라지 사이즈로 두 벌 주세요.
남 알겠습니다. 이렇게 드릴까요?
여 네. 이 쇼핑몰에서 현금처럼 쓸 수 있는 10달러짜리 기프트 카드가 있어요. 지금 사용할 수 있나요?
남 물론이죠.
여 잘됐네요. 여기 제 신용 카드입니다.

07 | 정답 | ④

은행에서 돌아온 여자가 남자에게 슈퍼마켓에 갔다 왔는지 물어보는 상황이다. 남자는 케이블 수리공이 오기로 해서 집을 비울 수 없었다고 설명하고 있으므로 정답은 ④이다.

- **basement** 지하실
- **repairman** 수리공
- **be supposed to-v** ~하기로 되어 있다
- **opening** 빈틈
- **now that** ~이니까, ~이므로

W What are you doing in the basement?
M Oh, hi, Mom. I was just looking for my soccer ball. How did it go at the bank?
W Well, not bad. There weren't many people so I didn't have to wait long. Did you go to the supermarket and get the things I asked for?
M Not yet. I was waiting until you got home.
W Why? I left the credit card in the kitchen.
M **Just before I was leaving home**, the repairman called.
W The cable repairman? **I thought he was supposed to come tomorrow**.
M I know. But he said he got an opening between 3 and 4 p.m. today and asked if he could come today instead.
W I see. It's almost 3:30. **He should be here any minute now**.
M Yes. Now that you are home, I can go to the supermarket.
W Oh, yes. Don't forget the card.
M I won't.

여 지하실에서 뭐 하니?
남 아, 오셨어요, 엄마. 그냥 축구공을 찾고 있었어요. 은행 일은 잘 보셨어요?
여 응, 그럭저럭. 사람들이 그리 많지 않아서 오래 기다릴 필요가 없었어. 슈퍼마켓에 가서 내가 사 오라는 것 사 왔니?
남 아직요. 엄마가 오실 때까지 기다리고 있었어요.
여 왜? 주방에 신용카드 놔뒀는데.
남 제가 막 나가려고 하는데 수리공이 전화했어요.
여 케이블 수리하는 분? 내일 오기로 한 거로 알고 있는데.
남 알아요. 그런데 오늘 오후 3시와 4시 사이에 빈 시간이 있다고 하면서 오늘 와도 되는지 물어보셨어요.
여 알겠어. 거의 3시 반이 다 되었네. 이제 곧 오시겠구나.
남 네, 이제 엄마가 집에 오셨으니까, 슈퍼마켓에 갈 수 있겠네요.
여 아, 그래. 카드 가져가는 것 잊지 말고.
남 잊지 않을게요.

---

08 | 정답 | ③

독일 Nuremberg(뉘른베르크)에서 개최하며, 60개가 넘는 나라에서 2,800개의 출품 회사와 8만 명의 방문객이 있을 것이라고 하였다. 1949년에 개최된 이후로 매년 열리고 있으며, 완구 산업 종사자들을 볼 수 있고, 관광객을 위한 행사도 있다고 하였으므로 언급되지 않은 것은 ③이다.

- **fair** 박람회
- **trade** 무역, 거래
- **exhibitor** 출품 회사, 참가자
- **purchaser** 구매자
- **annually** 매년
- **professional** 전문가
- **involved** 종사하는, 관여하는

W Chris, I heard you are going to Germany soon.
M Yes, I'm going to Germany to visit the Nuremberg International Toy Fair.
W I heard it's one of the largest trade fairs for toys and games in the world.
M That's right. This year, about 2,800 exhibitors from over 60 countries **will present about one million products**.
W Wow, that's a huge event!
M Yes, it is. They say more than 80,000 trade visitors and purchasers are expected to attend the fair.
W That's great. The fair surely has a long history, right?
M Yes, it started in 1949 and since then, **it's been held annually**.
W I guess you can meet **lots of professionals involved in the toy industry** there.
M That's right. Also, **there are many events for tourists like me**.
W I hope you have a wonderful time.
M Thanks. It will be exciting!

여 Chris, 곧 독일에 간다고 들었어.
남 그래, 독일 Nuremberg 국제완구박람회에 갈 거야.
여 그게 완구와 게임 관련해서 세계에서 가장 큰 박람회라고 들었어.
남 맞아. 올해는 60개가 넘는 나라에서 2,800개 정도 출품 회사들이 와서 백만 개 정도 제품을 선보인다고 해.
여 와, 정말 큰 행사네!
남 그래. 사람들이 그러는데 무역 방문객, 구매자가 8만 명 이상이 박람회에 참석할 거래.
여 대단하네. 그 박람회 역사도 분명히 오래되었겠지, 그렇지?
남 응, 1949년에 시작해서 지금까지 매년 열리고 있어.
여 너 거기서 완구 산업에 종사하는 많은 전문가들을 만나겠다.
남 그렇지. 그리고 나 같은 관광객을 위한 행사도 많대.
여 재미있게 보고 와.
남 고마워. 정말 재미있을 거야!

---

09 | 정답 | ②

박물관은 1960년에 설립되었으며 관람 안내인이 없고, 14명 이상 방문할 때는 예약을 해야 한다고 하였으며, 시내에 위치하여 접근이 쉽다고 하였다. 박물관은 평일에는 주로 오후 5시에 폐장을 하고 주말에만 6시까지 한다고 하였다. 또한 7월과 8월에만 오후 6시에 닫는다고 하였으므로 일치하지 않는 것은 ②이다.

- **establish** 설립하다
- **approximately** 대략
- **entire** 전체의
- **make a reservation** 예약하다
- **tram** 전차

M Hi, everyone. I'm going to introduce the recently renovated Anne Frank Museum. It was established in 1960. You can learn about Anne Frank's life, from birth to death. The museum is open daily from 9 a.m. to 5 p.m., **except Saturdays, when it is open from 9 a.m. to 6 p.m.** In July and August, the museum is open until 6 p.m. every day. **It will take approximately an hour to go through the entire museum**, and no tour guides are available. When there are 14 or more people in a group, you should make a reservation. Since the museum is located in downtown, **you can easily get there by tram or bus**. If you're interested in Anne Frank, please take the time to visit the museum.

남 여러분, 안녕하세요. 저는 최근에 수리한 안네 프랑크 박물관을 소개하려고 합니다. 이 박물관은 1960년에 세워졌어요. 여러분은 출생에서 사망까지, 안네 프랑크의 삶에 대해서 배우게 될 겁니다. 이 박물관은 토요일에는 오전 9시부터 오후 6시까지, 그 외에는 매일 오전 9시부터 오후 5시까지 문을 엽니다. 7월과 8월에는 매일 오후 6시까지 문을 엽니다. 박물관 전체를 보는 데 대략 1시간이 소요되며 관람 안내원이 없습니다. 14명 이상 단체 관람의 경우는 예약을 해야 합니다. 이 박물관은 시내에 있어서 전차나 버스로 쉽게 오실 수 있습니다. 안네 프랑크에 관심이 있으시다면 시간을 내셔서 박물관에 방문하세요.

10 | 정답 | ③

두 사람은 200달러 이내의 타워형 선풍기로 에너지 등급이 더 높으며 소음 데시벨이 낮은 것을 구매한다고 하였으므로 정답은 ③이다.

* flyer 전단지
* electrical appliances 전기기구, 전기제품
* bladeless 날개가 없는, 날 없는
* cutting-edge 최첨단의
* budget 예산
* maximum 최대치
* old-fashioned 구식의
* energy rating 에너지 효율 등급
* decibel 데시벨

W The electric fan doesn't work any more. We need to buy a new one, honey.
M Yes, I agree. Let's take a look at this flyer about electrical appliances.
W Let's see. This bladeless fan seems like the most cutting-edge product.
M Well, we should consider our budget. $250 is too expensive. **$200 should be the maximum**.
W Then my choice is a tower fan. **Standing fans are old-fashioned**.
M What about the energy rating?
W A higher rating is always better.
M **I can't stand noisy fans**. How about getting the one with lower decibels?
W Sure. A quiet fan would be better. **This one has the lowest noise level**. Let's get it!

여 선풍기가 작동을 안 하네요. 새것을 사야겠어요, 여보.
남 네, 그래요. 전기제품에 관한 이 전단지를 살펴봅시다.
여 가만있자. 이 날개 없는 선풍기가 가장 최첨단 제품 같네요.
남 그렇긴 한데, 예산 생각을 해야 해요. 250달러면 너무 비싸지요. 200달러 정도가 최대일 것 같아요.
여 그럼 제가 선택할 것은 타워형 선풍기예요. 스탠드형은 구식이고요.
남 에너지 효율 등급은 어때요?
여 더 높은 등급이 언제나 더 좋아요.
남 저는 소음이 있는 선풍기를 견디기 힘들어요. 더 낮은 데시벨로 사는 게 어때요?
여 좋아요. 조용한 선풍기가 더 좋겠어요. 이게 소음 등급이 가장 낮네요. 이걸 삽시다!

11 | 정답 | ③

연극 오디션을 기다렸다는 여자에게 어떤 역할을 하고 싶은지 묻는 남자의 말에 가장 적절한 여자의 응답은 ③ '당연히 여주인공이지. 그게 최고의 배역이거든.'이다.

* audition 심사
* try out for (배역 등을 위한 경쟁에) 지원하다
[선택지]
* authority 권한
* heroine 여주인공
* business (관여되는) 일

M Did you hear there will be an audition for our school play next week?
W Yes, I'm going to apply for one of the roles. I have been **looking forward to it**.
M What role do you **want to try out for**?
W The heroine, of course. It's the best part.

남 다음 주에 우리 학교 연극을 위한 심사가 있을 거라는 소식 들었어?
여 응, 나도 배역 하나를 지원하려고. 기다렸던 일이거든.
남 너는 무슨 역할에 지원해 보고 싶어?
여 당연히 여주인공이지. 그게 최고의 배역이거든.

① 상상이 가니? 나는 내가 할 수 있는 일이면 뭐든지 할 거야.
② 어디 보자. 그럴 권한을 누가 가지고 있니?
④ 어, 잠깐만. 다시 그 주제로 돌아가 보자.
⑤ 어떻게 그런 말을 할 수가 있어? 네가 상관할 일이 아니야.

12 | 정답 | ⑤

노트북 컴퓨터를 두고 와서 이제 어떻게 해야 하는지 물어보는 여자의 말에 대한 남자의 응답으로 가장 적절한 것은 ⑤ '문제없어. 집에 가서 10분이면 가지고 올 수 있어.'이다.

* laptop 휴대용[노트북] 컴퓨터
* discussion 토론, 토의

W John, **did you bring your laptop for the study group**?
M I forgot about that. I only brought my notebook with me.
W You said you wanted to **record our discussion on your laptop**. What should we do now?
M No problem. I can go home and get it in 10 minutes.

여 John, 스터디 그룹에 필요한 노트북 컴퓨터 가져왔어?
남 깜빡했네. 그냥 노트만 가지고 왔어.
여 네가 우리 토론을 노트북 컴퓨터에 기록하고 싶다고 했잖아. 우리 이제 어떻게 해야 하지?
남 문제없어. 집에 가서 10분이면 가지고 올 수 있어.

① 걱정 마. 네 도움 없이도 우리는 잘할 거야.
② 그건 맞지만, 나는 우리 발표를 기록하지 않았어.
③ 잊어버려. 나는 그것을 많이 연습했어.
④ 신경 쓰지 마. 노트북은 다음에 빌려줘도 돼.

13 | 정답 | ④

학생들을 위해 영화를 준비했다는 여자의 말에 영화만 보는 것은 지루할 것이라 하며, 추가로 토론 수업을 하는 것이 어떤지 남자가 제안하는 상황이다. 남자의 마지막 말에 대한 여자의 응답으로 가장 적절한 것은 ④ '고마워요, 선생님의 조언을 반드시 따를게요.'이다.

* rural 지방의, 시골의
* justice 정의
* boring 지루한
* attract 끌다, 유인하다
[선택지]
* what if~? 만약 ~하면 어쩌지?
* top priority 최우선, 급선무
* debate 토론

M Michelle, I heard you are going to visit a school in a rural town.
W Yes, I'm planning to show a movie on the topic of justice.
M A movie about justice?
W Do you think it'll be too boring?
M It could be. The topic seems too heavy for students. You **should find some other way to attract their attention**.
W But I've already found the perfect movie for them.
M Well, then how about adding another activity?
W **What do you suggest I do**?
M Let the students watch one scene from the movie. Then have an open discussion about it.
W Oh, then I guess I have to provide them with a few questions before the movie. That way they will know what they have to discuss.

남 Michelle 선생님, 지방에 있는 학교를 방문한다고 들었어요.
여 네, 정의에 대한 주제로 영화 한 편을 보여줄 계획이에요.
남 정의에 관한 영화요?
여 너무 지루할까요?
남 그럴 수 있죠. 그 주제는 학생들에게 너무 무거운 것 같아요. 그들의 관심을 끌 수 있는 다른 방법을 찾는 것이 좋을 것 같아요.
여 하지만 이미 딱 맞는 영화를 찾은걸요.
남 음, 그럼 다른 활동을 추가하는 게 어떨까요?
여 제가 뭘 하면 좋을까요?
남 학생들이 영화 한 장면을 시청하게 해요. 그러고 나서 그 장면에 대해 열린 토론을 해보세요.
여 아, 그러면 제가 영화 보여주기 전에 몇 가지 질문들을 줘야겠네요. 그렇게 하면 학생들이 무엇에 대해 논의해야 하는지 알 수 있을 거예요.

M Exactly. That way the students **will better understand the topic**.

W Thanks, I'm definitely going to follow your advice.

남 맞아요. 그렇게 하면 학생들이 그 주제를 더 잘 이해할 수 있을 거예요.

여 고마워요. 선생님의 조언을 반드시 따를게요.

① 알겠어요. 우선 어떻게 될지 기다려 봅시다.

② 절대 안 돼요. 만약 모두 지루해하면 어떻게 해요?

③ 당신 말이 맞아요. 학생들의 관심이 최우선입니다.

⑤ 같은 생각이에요. 토론 수업 주제가 가장 중요하죠.

---

14 | 정답 | ①

몸이 완전히 회복되지 않았는데도 친구와 스케이트장에 가기로 했다는 남자에게 여자는 외출은 아직은 무리라고 말하고 있다. 따라서 여자의 마지막 말에 대한 남자의 응답으로 가장 적절한 것은 ① '좋아요. Andrew한테 전화해서 취소할게요.'이다.

- get dressed 옷을 입다
- recover 회복하다
- be tired of ~하는 것이 지겹다
- block (도시의) 블록, 한 구획

[선택지]
- (It's) Easier said than done. 말하기는 쉽지만 행하기는 어렵다.
- slippery 미끄러운

W Jack, why did you get dressed? Are you going out?

M Did you look out the window, Mom? It's snowing outside!

W I understand why you are excited. But you can't go outside. **You have not completely recovered** from your flu yet.

M But it's the first snowfall of the year. I already told Andrew to meet me **at the outdoor skating rink downtown**.

W You shouldn't have done that. Your top priority should be your health, Jack.

M I know, Mom, but I am really tired of staying inside. You know I was in the hospital for about a week.

W I understand how you feel, Jack. However, **you need to think about your health first**. Why don't we take a short walk together around the block instead?

M Fine. I'll call Andrew and cancel.

여 Jack, 옷을 왜 차려입었니? 밖에 나가려고?

남 엄마, 창문 밖을 보셨어요? 밖에 눈이 오고 있어요!

여 네가 왜 그렇게 신나 하는지 이해는 한다만, 밖에 나가면 안 돼. 넌 아직 독감으로부터 완전히 회복되지 않았잖니.

남 하지만 올해 첫눈이에요. 벌써 Andrew에게 시내 실외 스케이트장에서 만나자고 했어요.

여 그렇게 하지 말았어야지. 너에게 제일 중요한 건 건강이야, Jack.

남 엄마, 알지만 실내에서만 있는 건 정말 지겨워요. 일주일이나 병원에 있었던 거 엄마도 알잖아요.

여 기분이 어떤지는 알아, Jack. 그렇지만 먼저 건강을 생각해야지. 그 대신, 나하고 잠깐 근처나 산책하는 게 어떠니?

남 좋아요. Andrew한테 전화해서 취소할게요.

② 아니요, 싫어요. 왜 집에만 있어야 해요?

③ 걱정 마세요. Andrew와 산책하지 않을게요.

④ 그렇게 말하지 말아요, 엄마. 말하기는 쉽지요.

⑤ 안 될 것 같아요. 길이 아주 미끄러워요.

---

15 | 정답 | ④

John은 전국 댄스 축제를 위해 새로운 안무를 짜고 싶어 하지만, Chris는 시간이 충분하지 않다고 생각한다. John이 매우 의욕적인 것을 알기 때문에, Chris는 새로운 춤 대신 예전 춤을 활용하여 새로운 것을 만들기를 제안하는 상황이다. 따라서 정답은 ④ '새로운 춤을 짜기 위해 예전 춤을 활용하는 게 어떨까?'이다.

- regional 지역의
- choreography 안무
- come up with 생각해 내다, 제안하다
- ambitious 열망하는, 의욕적인

[선택지]
- strict 엄격한
- competition 경쟁, 대회

W Chris and John are members of the school dance club. One day, they are selected as the best dancers in the regional dancing contest. So, they have the opportunity to participate in the National Dancing Festival. Chris thinks that **since there is not much time left**, they should do the same dance as they did in the regional. However, John thinks since it's for the national festival, they should make new choreography. John says to win the contest they have to do **what it takes to impress the judges**. Chris is not sure if they can come up with a new dance. Besides, even if they do, **there won't be enough time to practice it**. Since he understands how ambitious John is, he wants to suggest making a new dance by changing the old one. In this situation, what would Chris most likely say to John?

Chris Why don't we use the old dance to make a new one?

여 Chris와 John은 학교 댄스 동아리 회원이다. 어느 날, 그들은 지역 춤 경연대회에서 최우수 선수로 선정되었다. 그래서 그들은 전국 댄스 축제에 참가할 기회를 갖게 된다. Chris는 시간이 많이 남아 있지 않기 때문에 그들이 지역 대회에서 했던 것과 같은 춤을 해야 한다고 생각한다. 그러나 John은 이제 전국 대회에 참가하는 것이니까 새로운 안무를 짜야 한다고 생각한다. John은 심사위원들에게 깊은 인상을 줄 수 있는 것으로 해야 입상할 수 있다고 말한다. Chris는 새로운 춤을 생각해 낼 수 있을지 확신이 서지 않는다. 게다가, 설령 그렇게 하더라도, 그걸 연습할 시간이 충분하지 않을 것 같다. 그는 John이 얼마나 의욕적인지 알고 있기 때문에 예전 것을 변형해서 새 춤을 만들 것을 제안하고 싶어 한다. 이러한 상황에서 Chris가 John에게 할 말로 가장 적절한 것은 무엇인가?

Chris 새로운 춤을 짜기 위해 예전 춤을 활용하는 게 어떨까?

① 나는 너와 함께할 수 있을 것 같지 않아.

② 나는 새로 짠 춤보다 지난번 것이 더 좋아.

③ 전국 대회에는 규칙이 엄격해.

⑤ 새로 짠 춤이 참 좋다. 방과 후에 함께 연습하자.

---

16 | 정답 | ②

자신에게 알맞은 직업을 선택할 때 무엇을 해야 하는지 설명하는 내용으로, 남자가 하는 말의 주제로 가장 적절한 것은 ② '가장 이상적인 직업을 찾는 방법'이다.

17 | 정답 | ⑤

알맞은 직업을 찾는 데 '직업과 관련된 동아리 활동하기'에 대한 언급은 없었으

M Good morning, everyone. Did you have a wonderful discussion with your family regarding the topic I told you about? Today, let's continue to talk about the same topic. In choosing a career, first, make a list of **those you might find enjoyable**. To help you, there are many sites on the Internet, plus books at your local library, that can tell you what occupations other people find enjoyable. Next, write a short profile on each job, **listing its positives and negatives**. If you find one or more that might be especially interesting, try to **meet people involved in the**

남 안녕하세요, 여러분. 제가 말씀드렸던 주제에 관해서 가족과 좋은 토론을 하셨나요? 오늘도 같은 주제로 계속 이야기해 보겠습니다. 직업을 선택할 때, 먼저 자신이 재미있어 할 것들 목록을 만들어 보세요. 여러분을 도와줄 인터넷 사이트가 많이 있고, 그 외에도 지역 도서관에 책도 많아서 다른 사람들은 어떤 직업을 좋아하는지 알 수 있습니다. 다음으로 각 직업에 관해서 짧은 분석 자료를 만들어 긍정적인 면과 부정적인 면을 나열해 보세요. 만약 여러분이 정말 재미있을 것 같은 것을 한두 가지 찾게 되면 그 직업에 종사하는 사람들을 한번 만나 보세요. 그래서 그들이 자기 직업에 대해서 좋아하거나 싫어하는 것은 무엇인지 물어보시고,

므로 정답은 ⑤이다.

- regarding ~에 관하여
- occupation 직업
- profile 분석표, 개요
- positive 긍정적인 (것)
- negative 부정적인 (것)
- alongside 함께
  [선택지]
- ideal 이상적인
- preference 선호도
- career path 직업 진로

occupation. Ask them what they like and dislike about their job, and find out why they stay and why some people leave. **Learn as much as you can about the job**, including whether it fits your abilities or not. If possible, volunteer to work alongside someone in the occupation to get a better understanding of it. If you are still happy, maybe you have found your place. Good luck.

왜 그들이 그 직업을 고수하고 있는지 그리고 떠나는 사람은 왜 떠나는지 확인해 보세요. 그 직업이 여러분의 능력에 부합하는지 여부를 포함해서 여러분이 할 수 있는 한 최대한 많이 그 직업에 관해서 공부해 보세요. 가능하다면, 그 직업을 좀 더 잘 알아보기 위해서 그 직업을 가진 사람 옆에서 함께 직접 그 일을 해 보세요. 만약 여러분이 여전히 그 일을 좋아한다면, 여러분은 아마 본인이 일할 곳을 찾은 겁니다. 행운을 빌어요.

16 ① 직장을 찾기 위해 인터넷 활용하기
② 가장 이상적인 직업을 찾는 방법
③ 직업에 대한 선호도는 왜 중요한가
④ 직업 진로에 대한 강의는 왜 인기가 있는가
⑤ 온라인 구직의 장단점

01 | 정답 | ⑤

길거리에 쓰레기를 버리는 행위는 오염의 원인이라고 하면서 쓰레기를 줄이는 방법과 올바른 쓰레기 처리 방법에 관해 설명하고 있으므로 남자가 하는 말의 목적으로 가장 적절한 것은 ⑤이다.

• clean up after ~의 뒤처리를 하다
• litter (쓰레기 등을) 버리다
• contribute to ~에 기여하다; ~의 원인이 되다
• contaminate 오염시키다
• utensil 식기; 주방용 기구
• thermal bottle 보온병
• dispose of ~을 처리하다
• last but not least 마지막으로
• make a difference 차이를 만들다, 변화를 가져오다

M Have you ever dropped a candy wrapper or soda can on the ground? Have you ever failed to clean up after your dog? If you answered yes, then you are a litterbug. A litterbug is a person **who litters public places with trash**. Doing this contributes to pollution, which contaminates our oceans and waterways. To become a part of the solution, there are simple steps you can follow. **Put your garbage in the trash can**. In case there are no trash cans nearby, just hold off until you see a trash can. You can also use reusable plates and utensils when you eat somewhere outdoors. Instead of plastic bottles, thermal bottles are a great alternative. When you are out on a walk with your dog, it's very important to clean up after your dog and **dispose of the waste properly**. Last but not least, **think twice before you litter**. Your change in behavior can make a difference.

남 사탕 포장지나 음료수 캔을 땅에다가 버린 적이 있습니까? 당신의 반려견의 뒤처리를 하지 않은 적이 있습니까? 만약 그랬다고 한다면 여러분은 쓰레기 투기꾼입니다. 쓰레기 투기꾼이란 공공장소에 쓰레기를 버리는 사람을 말합니다. 이런 일을 하는 것은 오염의 원인이 되며, 그것이 우리의 바다와 수로를 오염시키는 것입니다. 해결책에 일조하기 위해, 여러분이 따를 수 있는 간단한 단계가 있습니다. 쓰레기를 쓰레기통에 넣으세요. 근처에 쓰레기통이 없는 경우에는 쓰레기통이 보일 때까지 들고 있으세요. 또한 야외에서 먹을 때 재사용이 가능한 접시와 식기를 사용할 수 있습니다. 플라스틱 병 대신에, 보온병이 훌륭한 대체용품이 됩니다. 반려견과 산책하러 나갈 땐, 개의 뒤처리를 하고 쓰레기를 적절하게 처리하는 것은 아주 중요합니다. 마지막으로, 쓰레기를 버리기 전에 다시 생각하세요. 여러분의 행동의 변화는 차이를 만들 수 있습니다.

02 | 정답 | ①

보호소의 버려진 동물에 관해 대화를 나누고 있는 상황이다. 대부분 주인이 학대하거나 버려진 동물이라는 말에 여자는 입양 후에는 끝까지 책임져야 하며, 더 엄격한 동물 보호법이 필요하다고 하였다. 따라서 여자의 의견으로 가장 적절한 것은 ①이다.

• animal shelter 동물 보호소
• interact with ~와 상호작용하다
• aggressive 공격적인
• abandon 버리다, 유기하다
• abuse 학대하다
• irresponsible 무책임한
• adopt 입양하다
• get away 빠져나가다
• horrible 끔찍한

W Ron, do you still volunteer at an animal shelter?
M I do. I help out with cleaning and feeding animals.
W I'm looking for some volunteer work. I was just wondering if the shelter needed more people.
M Definitely. The shelter welcomes **people who treat animals with love and care**. Would you be interested?
W Of course. I love playing and interacting with animals.
M Okay. Oh, you have to understand that the work can be difficult since some of them can get a little aggressive. They are brought in after they were abandoned or abused by their owners.
W I can't believe **how irresponsible some people can be**. Once they adopt a pet, they should take good care of it for life.
M I know. People have to be more careful and responsible.
W Yes, we need to **push for stricter animal protection laws**, too. Sometimes it makes me angry when people get away with doing horrible things to their pets.
M That's how I feel, too.

여 Ron, 너 아직 동물 보호소에서 자원봉사 하니?
남 그래. 청소하고 동물들에게 먹이를 주는 걸 도와.
여 내가 자원봉사 일을 찾고 있어. 그 보호소에 더 많은 사람이 필요한지 궁금했거든.
남 물론이지. 보호소는 사랑과 관심을 가지고 동물들을 대하는 사람들을 환영해. 너 관심 있니?
여 당연하지. 난 동물들과 놀고 교감하는 것을 좋아해.
남 알겠어. 아, 동물들 중 일부는 다소 공격적이기 때문에 일이 힘들 수 있다는 것을 알아야 해. 동물들이 주인에게 버려지거나 학대를 받고 난 이후에 오거든.
여 난 일부 사람들이 얼마나 무책임할 수 있는지 믿기지 않아. 일단 반려동물을 입양했다면 평생토록 잘 보살펴야 하잖아.
남 그래. 사람들이 좀 더 신중하고 책임감이 있어야 해.
여 맞아. 또 더 엄격한 동물 보호법을 요구해야 할 필요가 있어. 때때로 사람들이 반려동물들에게 끔찍한 짓을 하고도 빠져나갈 때 화가 나.
남 나도 그래.

03 | 정답 | ④

미디어는 종종 우리에게 팝스타같이 흥미진진한 직업을 성공의 길로 보여주지만 실제로 성공은 현실적인 선택과 계속적인 노력을 바탕으로 이루어진다고 말하고 있다. 따라서 남자가 하는 말의 요지로 가장 적절한 것은 ④이다.

• consultant 컨설턴트, 고문
• expose 접하게 하다
• persistent 끊임없는, 계속적인
• fool 속이다, 헛되이 쓰다
• align (~에 맞춰) ~을 조정[조절]하다

M Hi there, folks! I'm Kelvin, your job consultant for today. **As you are exposed to many jobs in the media**, you will have a lot of thoughts about which job to choose. In this situation, it is important to find a job that fits your own reality. **The media often shows us exciting careers** like pop stars as the path to success, making people think that big dreams lead to success. However, in reality, **success is built on practical choices and persistent effort**. Don't be fooled by the fancy image presented in the media. Discover a job that aligns with the present circumstances. Let's move on to practical advice for your career decisions. Stay with me!

남 안녕하세요, 여러분! 오늘 여러분의 직업 컨설턴트인 Kelvin입니다. 여러분이 미디어에서 많은 직업을 접하다 보니 어떤 직업을 선택해야 할지에 대해 생각이 많으실 텐데요. 이러한 상황에서는 자신의 현실에 맞는 직업을 찾는 것이 중요합니다. 미디어는 종종 우리에게 팝스타같이 흥미진진한 직업을 성공의 길로 보여주며, 사람들이 큰 꿈이 성공으로 이어진다고 생각하게 합니다. 그러나, 실제로는 성공은 현실적인 선택과 계속적인 노력을 바탕으로 이루어집니다. 미디어에서 제시하는 화려한 이미지에 속지 마세요. 현재 상황에 맞는 직업을 찾으세요. 여러분의 직업 결정을 위한 실용적인 조언으로 넘어가 보도록 하겠습니다. 저와 함께하세요!

04 | 정답 | ⑤

마차 뒤에 서 있는 여자는 손뼉을 치고 있다고 하였으므로 일치하지 않는 것은 ⑤이다.

* carriage 마차
* wear 신다, 착용하다
* scared 무서운
* recognize 알아보다, 인식하다
* clap 박수를 치다

W Mr. Kim, is this a photo from your last vacation?
M Yes, it is. This was taken at a beach we went to last summer.
W Oh, I see the beautiful beach on the left. It seems like your family had a great time.
M We sure did. There was a carriage running along the beach for visitors. So we gave it a try.
W I've never seen a carriage on a beach before, **especially one led by a horse**.
M I know. You didn't expect to see that, right? This was my first time to see one on a beach.
W Who is the man holding the rope? It must've been really **hot to wear boots and a cowboy hat**.
M Oh, he drove the carriage with the horse. It was not really safe for us to drive the carriage on our own.
W I see. Oh, is this **your daughter sitting behind the man**?
M It is. She was a bit scared, so I had to **sit with her**.
W I almost didn't recognize you because of the hat and sunglasses. Who is the woman standing behind the carriage?
M That's my wife. **She just watched us and clapped her hands**. She was too scared to go for a ride.

여 김 선생님, 이게 지난 휴가 중에 찍은 사진인가요?
남 네. 지난여름에 갔던 해변에서 찍은 사진이에요.
여 오, 왼쪽에 아름다운 해변이 보이네요. 가족과 좋은 시간을 보낸 것 같네요.
남 정말 그랬어요. 방문객을 위해 해변을 따라 달리는 마차가 있었어요. 그래서 우리는 그것을 탔죠.
여 한 번도 해변에서 마차를 본 적이 없는데, 특히 말이 끄는 마차요.
남 맞아요. 그걸 볼 줄 몰랐죠? 저는 이번에 해변에서 달리는 마차를 처음 보았어요.
여 줄을 잡고 있는 사람은 누구예요? 부츠를 신고 카우보이 모자를 쓰고 있으니 틀림없이 무척 더웠을 텐데.
남 아, 그는 말이 끄는 마차를 몰았어요. 우리가 직접 마차를 끄는 것은 정말 안전하지 않았거든요.
여 그렇군요. 아, 그 남자 뒤에 앉아 있는 사람이 선생님 딸이에요?
남 맞아요. 애가 좀 무서워해서 제가 같이 앉아야 했어요.
여 모자와 선글라스 때문에 선생님을 거의 알아보지 못했어요. 마차 뒤에 서 있는 여자는 누구예요?
남 아내예요. 아내는 그냥 우리를 보고 손뼉을 쳤죠. 너무 무서워서 마차를 못 탔거든요.

---

05 | 정답 | ⑤

여자가 남자에게 블로그에 올린 사진들과 글을 책으로 출판하는 것을 제안하는 상황이다. 여자가 출판사에 제출하기 전에 포트폴리오가 필요하다고 하였으므로 남자가 할 일로 가장 적절한 것은 ⑤이다.

* post 인터넷 블로그에 올려진 글
* blow one's mind 깜짝 놀라게 하다
* subscriber 구독자
* talented 재능 있는
* publish 출판하다
* portfolio 포트폴리오, 작품집

W I really like your photos and posts on your blog. Some of your pictures blew my mind.
M Thanks. I take pictures and just write what comes to mind.
W It's amazing that you have over 500,000 subscribers, too.
M I guess I got pretty lucky. I didn't expect it to get this popular.
W You're so talented. You should **consider publishing it as a book**.
M Do you think publishers would like my work?
W Why don't you give it a try?
M But I don't know where to start.
W I know someone at a publishing company. If you are interested, I could give you a business card.
M Should I call him now? I haven't prepared anything yet.
W **Do you have a portfolio**? You should include at least 10 photos of your work.
M I don't have one yet.
W Okay, then **let me know when your portfolio is ready**. I'll call him and see if you can get a meeting with him.
M That sounds great. Thanks.

여 네 블로그에 올린 사진과 글이 정말 마음에 들어. 몇몇 사진들은 아주 놀라워.
남 고마워. 사진을 찍고 나서 마음속에 떠오르는 것들을 그냥 쓰는 거야.
여 구독자 수가 50만이 넘기도 하다니 정말 멋지다.
남 꽤 운이 좋았던 것 같아. 이렇게 인기 얻게 될 줄 몰랐어.
여 넌 정말 재능이 있는 것 같아. 그것을 책으로 출판하는 것을 생각해 봐.
남 출판업자들이 내 작품을 좋아할 것 같니?
여 한 번 도전해 보는 게 어때?
남 하지만 어디서부터 시작해야 할지 모르겠어.
여 출판사에 아는 사람이 있어. 관심이 있다면, 너에게 명함을 줄게.
남 지금 전화해야 할까? 아직 준비된 게 없는데.
여 포트폴리오 있어? 포트폴리오에는 적어도 사진을 10장은 포함해야 해.
남 난 아직 하나도 없어.
여 알겠어. 그러면 포트폴리오가 준비되면 나한테 알려 줘. 그에게 전화해서 만날 수 있는지 알아볼게.
남 좋은 생각이야. 고마워.

---

06 | 정답 | ④

불고기 버거 가격은 1달러 올라서 6달러이며 감자튀김은 3달러이고, 음료와 같이 세트로 구성할 시 버거 가격에서 4달러가 추가된다고 하였다. 여자는 불고기 버거 한 세트에 추가로 버거 2개를 주문하였으므로 총금액은 22달러($6 + $4 + $6 × 2개)로 정답은 ④이다.

* combination 조합(물), 결합(물)
* soft drink 탄산음료, 청량음료, 음료수

M Good evening. Are you ready to order now?
W Hi, there. Is a bulgogi burger still $5?
M Oh, **the burger price went up by $1**. But french fries are still $3.
W I see. Then I'd like to buy three bulgogi burgers and french fries.
M Did you mean three bulgogi burgers and three french fries?
W No, **just one order of fries**, please.

남 안녕하세요. 주문하시겠어요?
여 안녕하세요. 불고기 버거가 아직도 5달러인가요?
남 오, 버거 가격이 1달러 올랐어요. 하지만 감자튀김은 여전히 3달러입니다.
여 그렇군요. 그러면 불고기 버거 3개와 감자튀김 주세요.
남 불고기 버거 3개와 감자튀김 3개 말씀인가요?
여 아니요. 감자튀김은 하나만 주세요.

- flavor 맛, 풍미, 향미
- additional 추가적인

M Okay. But for an extra $4, you can change one burger to a combination set. **It comes with fries and a drink.**
W What kind of drinks do you have?
M We have soft drinks, orange juice and milkshakes.
W Can I get a milkshake with that?
M Sure. We have vanilla and strawberry flavors. Which one would you like?
W I'll take a vanilla.
M **Let me check your order**. One bulgogi burger combination set with a vanilla milkshake and two additional bulgogi burgers, right?
W That's right. Here's my credit card.

남 네. 하지만 4달러만 추가하시면 버거 하나를 콤비네이션 세트로 바꿀 수 있어요. 감자튀김과 음료가 함께 나옵니다.
여 음료는 어떤 것들이 있나요?
남 탄산음료, 오렌지 주스 그리고 밀크셰이크가 있습니다.
여 밀크셰이크로 주시겠어요?
남 네. 바닐라 맛과 딸기 맛이 있어요. 어떤 것이 좋으시겠어요?
여 바닐라로 할게요.
남 주문 확인할게요. 바닐라 밀크셰이크가 있는 불고기 콤비네이션 세트와 불고기 버거 두 개 추가, 맞으신가요?
여 맞아요. 카드로 계산할게요.

---

07 | 정답 | ③

예약 없이 진료를 받으려면 오래 기다려야 한다는 여자의 말에 남자는 아들이 너무 아파서 응급환자로 좀 더 빨리 진료받을 수 있는지 물어보는 상황이다. 따라서 남자가 전화를 건 목적으로 ③이 가장 적절하다.

- walk-in 예약이 안 된, 예약이 필요 없는
- appointment 예약, 약속
- make an exception 예외로 하다
- emergency 긴급, 응급
- throw up 토하다
- squeeze ~ in ~을 끼워 넣다

[Telephone rings.]
W Dr. Kevin's office. How may I help you?
M Good morning. This is David Kerr. I was wondering if your clinic takes walk-in patients.
W Hello, Mr. Kerr. Appointments are usually required but **we make an exception in case of emergency**.
M Well, it's my son. He's been throwing up since last night, and he also has a high fever.
W We have a lot of patients today, so you may **have to wait for a long time to see the doctor** without an appointment.
M We've been seeing Dr. Kevin for a long time, and your clinic is the closest one I can find. **Is there any way to squeeze him in** since it's an emergency?
W Let me see. How fast can you get here?
M We could get there in 20 minutes.
W Okay, after you get here, you might have to wait 10 minutes or so. Is that okay with you?
M That's fine with me. Thank you so much. I'll be there soon.

[전화벨이 울린다.]
여 Kevin 의원입니다. 뭘 도와드릴까요?
남 안녕하세요. 저는 David Kerr입니다. 당신 병원에서 예약을 안 한 환자를 받는지 궁금해서요.
여 안녕하세요, Kerr 씨. 보통은 예약을 하셔야 하는데 응급인 경우는 예외입니다.
남 네, 제 아들이 아파서요. 밤새도록 토했고 열이 많이 납니다.
여 오늘 환자가 많아서 예약 없이 의사 선생님을 뵈려면 오래 기다리셔야 할지도 모릅니다.
남 저희는 Kevin 선생님께 오랫동안 진찰을 받아왔어요. 그리고 이 병원이 제가 찾을 수 있는 가장 가까운 곳에 있기도 하고요. 위급한 상황이니 아이를 예약에 끼워 넣어주실 수 없을까요?
여 확인해보겠습니다. 얼마나 빠르게 오실 수 있으세요?
남 20분 안에 갈 수 있어요.
여 알겠습니다. 도착하신 후 10분 정도 기다리셔야 할지도 모릅니다. 괜찮으신가요?
남 괜찮습니다. 감사합니다. 곧 가겠습니다.

---

08 | 정답 | ④

학자금 대출 신청을 하는 상황이다. 남자는 현재 대학교 3학년으로 화학을 전공하고 있으며 다른 은행에서 대출을 받은 적이 없다고 하였다. 하지만 남자가 제출해야 하는 서류에 대한 언급은 없었으므로 정답은 ④이다.

- apply for 신청하다
- loan 대출, 융자금
- application 신청, 지원
- junior (4년제 대학의) 3학년
- chemistry 화학
- reside 거주하다
- currently 현재, 지금
- dormitory 기숙사
- valid 확실한, 유효한

M Hello. I'd like to apply for a student loan.
W Sure. **Please hand me the application form and your ID**.
M Here you are.
W I'm going to ask you a few questions to check if you wrote down the information correctly.
M That's all right.
W Your name is Chanwook Kim, and you go to Yonsei University, correct?
M That's right. I'm a junior now.
W Oh, **you forgot to write down your major** here. What do you study in school?
M I major in chemistry.
W Chemistry. *[Pause]* Okay. Do you reside at the address you wrote down here?
M No. I wrote down my parents' address instead because currently I live in the school dormitory.
W I see. Then can you tell me the phone number for that address? **I need to check if the address is valid**.
M Okay. It's 032-012-5570.
W All right. Just one more left. **Do you have any bank loans in your name** at any other bank?
M No, I don't. **This is my first time applying for a loan**.

남 안녕하세요. 학자금 대출 신청 좀 하려고요.
여 네. 신청서하고 신분증 주세요.
남 여기 있습니다.
여 정보를 정확히 작성했는지 확인하기 위해 몇 가지 질문 드릴게요.
남 좋습니다.
여 이름은 김찬욱이고, 연세대학교에 재학 중이죠, 맞나요?
남 맞습니다. 지금 3학년입니다.
여 아. 여기 전공 쓰는 것을 잊으셨네요. 학교에서 무슨 공부를 하시나요?
남 화학을 전공합니다.
여 화학이요. *[잠시 후]* 좋습니다. 여기 적힌 주소지에 거주하시나요?
남 아뇨. 현재 기숙사에서 거주하기 때문에 부모님 집주소를 대신 썼습니다.
여 알겠어요. 그럼 그 주소의 전화번호는 뭔가요? 주소가 확실한지 확인해야 합니다.
남 네. 032-012-5570입니다.
여 좋아요. 한 가지 더 남았어요. 당신의 이름으로 다른 은행에서 대출을 받은 게 있나요?
남 아니요. 대출 신청은 처음입니다.

09 | 정답 | ③

Boldt 성은 뉴욕에 있는 Thousand Islands 지역에 있고 5월 중순부터 10월 중순까지 개방한다고 하였다. 처음엔 아내에게 줄 선물로 지어졌으며 현재는 지역 교량 당국이 관리한다고 하였다. Boldt 성은 1900년에 짓기 시작하였다고 하였으므로 일치하지 않는 것은 ③이다.

* landmark 랜드마크, 주요 지형지물
* tourist attraction 관광 명소
* be located on ~에 위치해 있다
* engage 고용하다, 채용하다
* maintain 관리하다
* bridge authority 교량 당국

W Hello, students! My name is Tina Robbins, and I'll be your guide today. I'm briefly going to talk about Boldt Castle, which we are going to visit soon. Boldt Castle is **a major landmark and tourist attraction** in the Thousand Islands region of the U.S. state of New York. **Open to visitors between mid-May and mid-October**, it is located on Heart Island in the Saint Lawrence River. In 1900, George Boldt launched an ambitious construction campaign **to build a huge stone structure**, one of the largest private homes in the United States. He engaged hundreds of workers for a six-story "castle" as a present to his wife. Boldt Castle is maintained today by the Thousand Islands Bridge Authority as a tourist attraction. Any questions? Okay. Let's get going!

여 안녕하세요, 학생 여러분! 제 이름은 Tina Robbins입니다. 그리고 저는 오늘 여러분의 가이드입니다. 우리가 곧 방문하게 되는 Boldt 성에 대해 짤막하게 말씀드릴게요. Boldt 성은 미국 뉴욕주 Thousand Islands 지역의 주요 랜드마크이자 관광 명소입니다. 5월 중순부터 10월 중순까지 방문객들에게 개방되는 Boldt 성은 Saint Lawrence 강에 있는 Heart 섬 위에 있습니다. 1900년에 George Boldt는 미국에서 가장 큰 개인 주택 중의 하나인 거대한 석조 건축물을 짓기 위한 야망 찬 건축 캠페인에 착수했습니다. 그는 자신의 아내에게 줄 선물로 6층짜리 '성'을 짓는 데 수백 명의 노동자들을 고용했습니다. 오늘날 Boldt 성은 하나의 관광 명소로 Thousand Islands 교량 당국에 의해 관리됩니다. 질문 있나요? 좋습니다. 가시죠!

10 | 정답 | ②

아들이 12세 이상 프로그램에 참여할 수 없으며 600달러 이하이고 7월 마지막 주가 아닌 날짜에 보내야 한다고 설명하고 있다. 마지막에 남자가 더 많은 선생님이 있으면 더 안전할 거라고 하는 내용으로 보아 두 사람이 선택할 우주 캠프는 ②이다.

* outer space 우주 공간
* suitable 적합한
* reasonable 적당한, (가격이) 합리적인
* select 고르다
* prefer ~을 더 선호하다
* involved in ~에 관계된, ~에 관여하는

M Honey, you've been on the computer for so long. What have you been looking at?
W Oh, I found a list of space camps for our son.
M That's great. Adam's been really interested in outer space and planets recently.
W I know. It will be a great experience for him. There are five different ones we can choose from.
M All right. Let's take a look. *[Pause]* Oh, this one is not suitable for our son. **It's for kids over the age of 12**.
W Okay. How about this one? Everything is included in the price, but it seems too expensive, doesn't it?
M Then **let's not spend more than $600**.
W $600 or under seems reasonable. **We also need to select the dates**.
M I have the last week of July off for the summer holiday. We should go on a family trip that week.
W That's a good idea. Then there are only two options left. **Do you prefer more or less teachers involved** in the camp?
M More teachers, definitely. It'll be safer, too.
W All right. This is it, then. I'll make the payment.

남 여보, 컴퓨터를 오랫동안 하고 있네요. 뭘 보고 있는 건데요?
여 아, 우리 아들을 위한 우주 캠프 목록을 찾았어요.
남 좋네요. Adam은 최근에 우주 공간과 행성에 흥미를 갖는 것 같거든요.
여 맞아요. 그에게 좋은 경험이 되겠어요. 우리가 고를 수 있는 다양한 캠프가 5개 있네요.
남 좋아요. 같이 봅시다. [잠시 후] 아, 이건 아들에게 적합하지 않을 것 같아요. 12살이 넘는 아이를 위한 것이네요.
여 네, 이건요? 모든 것이 가격에 포함이 되어 있어요. 하지만 너무 비싼 것 같아요, 그렇지 않나요?
남 그러면 600달러 넘게 쓰지 맙시다.
여 600달러 이하면 적당할 것 같아요. 날짜도 골라야 해요.
남 제 여름휴가가 7월 마지막 주예요. 그 주에는 가족 여행을 가는 게 좋을 것 같아요.
여 좋은 생각이에요. 그럼 두 개의 선택 사항만 남았네요. 캠프에 관여하는 선생님이 많은 것을 선호해요, 적은 것을 선호해요?
남 당연히 선생님이 많으면 좋죠. 더 안전할 거고요.
여 좋아요. 그럼 결정됐네요. 결제할게요.

11 | 정답 | ③

선생님이 병가를 낸 이후에 미술 수업이 어떻게 달라질 것 같은지 물어보는 여자의 말에 가장 적절한 남자의 응답은 ③ '글쎄, 당분간은 대체 선생님이 오실 것이라고 생각해.'이다.

* on sick leave 병가로
[선택지]
* substitute teacher 대체 교사

W Did you hear that Mr. Miller **left yesterday on sick leave**?
M Yes, I heard he is **going away for three months**. I hope it's not something serious.
W Same here. So, what do you think is going to happen to our art class?
M Well, I guess there will be a substitute teacher for a while.

여 어제 Miller 선생님이 병가를 내시고 떠났다는 말 들었니?
남 응, 3개월간 자리를 비우신다고 하던데. 심각한 것이 아니었으면 좋겠다.
여 나도 그래. 그럼, 우리 미술 수업은 어떻게 될 것 같아?
남 글쎄, 당분간은 대체 선생님이 오실 것이라고 생각해.

① 오늘 미술 수업에서 새 단원을 시작할 거 같아.
② 새로운 미술 선생님이 전문 화가라는 말을 들었어.
④ 교실로 돌아가는 게 좋겠어. Miller 선생님이 곧 오실 거야.
⑤ 수업이 취소돼서 우리는 대신 음악 수업을 듣게 될 거야.

12 | 정답 | ⑤

우승을 하지 못했지만 협력하는 법을 배웠다는 남자의 말에 대한 여자의 응답으로 가장 적절한 것은 ⑤ '맞아. 우리가 함께 보낸 시간을 소중히 여겨야겠어.'이다.

* choir 합창단
* go to waste 허사가 되다

M I feel so bad that our choir didn't win the contest. **We practiced so hard for it**.
W I know. I feel like all our efforts went to waste.
M Well, I believe it was a valuable experience. **We learned to work together as a team**.
W You're right. We'd better cherish our time spent together.

남 우리 합창단이 우승하지 못해서 너무 아쉬워. 우리 진짜 열심히 연습했는데.
여 그래. 우리의 모든 노력이 헛수고가 되어 버린 것 같아.
남 근데, 귀중한 경험이었던 것 같아. 우린 한 팀으로 협력하는 법을 배웠잖아.
여 맞아. 우리가 함께 보낸 시간을 소중히 여겨야겠어.

① 좋아. 새로운 단원을 모집할 때야.

* valuable 귀중한
[선택지]
* recruit 모집하다
* cherish 소중히 하다

---

13 | 정답 | ④

표 판매 시간을 5분 남겨둔 상황에서 어떤 종류의 좌석을 예매할지 대화를 나눈 후 여자가 마지막 말로 표를 예매할 시간이 다 됐다고 했다. 이에 대한 남자의 응답으로 가장 적절한 것은 ④ '표가 매진되기 전에 서둘러서 좌석을 예매하자.'이다.

* available 이용 가능한
* dance to music 음악에 맞춰 춤을 추다
* push 밀다
* step on ~의 발을 밟다
* view 시야, 눈앞
* book 예약하다
[선택지]
* refund 환불(금)
* convenience 편의, 편리

W John, we only have 5 minutes until the tickets are available for sale.

M Already? I've always wanted to go to the band's concert. I'm so excited!

W Oh, have you thought about the type of seats you want?

M Yes, **I prefer standing to sitting**. Since it's heavy metal, I think it'd be more fun in the standing area.

W Well, you can stand and dance to music, but sometimes **it is too hard to stand for 2 to 3 hours**.

M True, but that's the fun part of a concert. You listen to music and just enjoy yourself.

W I know. But I won't be able to move when there are so many people around me.

M You're right. **You can get pushed around and even stepped on.**

W **I'd get more stressed in the standing area.** With seated tickets, we could also get a better view of the screens. *[Pause]* Oh, it's almost time to book.

M Let's hurry and book seats before they get sold out.

여 John, 표 판매 시간까지 5분밖에 안 남았어.
남 벌써? 항상 그 밴드 콘서트를 가고 싶었거든. 너무 신이 나!
여 아, 원하는 좌석 유형에 대해 생각해 봤니?
남 응. 난 앉아 있는 것보다는 서 있는 게 좋아. 헤비메탈 음악이라서 내 생각엔 스탠딩석에서 더 재미있을 것 같아.
여 음. 서서 음악에 맞추어 춤을 출 수 있지만 어쩔 땐 두세 시간 동안 서 있기는 너무 힘들어.
남 사실이지만, 그것이 콘서트의 재밌는 부분이잖아. 음악을 듣고 그냥 즐기는 거지.
여 그래. 하지만 주변에 사람들이 너무 많을 때는 움직일 수가 없잖아.
남 맞아. 밀쳐질 수도 있고 발이 밟힐 수도 있어.
여 난 스탠딩석에서는 더 스트레스를 받아. 지정석 표가 있다면 우리는 스크린을 잘 볼 수 있을 거야. *[잠시 후]* 아, 예매할 시간이 다 됐어.
남 표가 매진되기 전에 서둘러서 좌석을 예매하자.

① 더 좋은 좌석을 얻으려면 환불받는 게 어때?
② 콘서트를 못 봐서 아쉬워.
③ 나는 앉는 편리함을 포기할 수 없어.
⑤ 걱정하지 마. 우리는 이미 두 장을 예매했어.

---

14 | 정답 | ⑤

이번 주말에 학생회관에서 상영하는 영화에 관해 설명하는 내용이다. 남자가 같이 가자고 제안하지만 과제를 끝내야 하는 여자는 이를 거절하는 상황이므로 여자의 응답으로 가장 적절한 것은 ⑤ '미안한데, 이번 주말은 보고서에 집중해야 해.'이다.

* assignment 과제
* shame 애석한[아쉬운] 일
* award-winning 상을 받은
* entry 입장
* exact 정확한
* foreign 외국의
[선택지]
* focus on 집중하다

M What are you doing this weekend?

W I have to finish a history assignment. I need to write 20 pages by Monday, so **I will probably be at the library all weekend**.

M Even Saturday night? That's a shame.

W Why do you ask?

M I heard that the Film Club will be showing three award-winning films at the student center, and the entry price will be quite cheap.

W How much will it be?

M $8 for three movies.

W Wow, that's so cheap! What are they showing?

M I can't remember the exact names, but I heard that they will be playing movies from France, Mexico, and Russia.

W Really? I haven't seen many foreign films. **I wish I had the time to go with you**.

M If you work hard, you could finish your assignment before the film night begins. **I'll pay for the tickets**.

W I'm sorry, but I need to focus on my paper this weekend.

남 이번 주말에 뭐 해?
여 역사 과제를 끝내야 해. 월요일까지 20페이지를 써야 해서 주말 내내 도서관에 있을 것 같아.
남 토요일 밤에도? 아쉽다.
여 왜 묻는 거니?
남 영화 동아리에서 세 개의 수상작을 학생회관에서 상영한다고 들었어. 입장료도 꽤 싸대.
여 얼만데?
남 3편에 8달러야.
여 와, 엄청 저렴하다! 어떤 걸 보여주는데?
남 정확한 제목이 기억이 안 나는데, 프랑스, 멕시코, 러시아에서 만든 영화를 상영한다고 들었어.
여 정말? 난 외국 영화를 많이 보지 않았어. 너랑 같이 갈 수 있으면 좋을 텐데.
남 만약 네가 열심히 하면, 영화의 밤이 시작되기 전에 과제를 끝낼 수 있을 거야. 표는 내가 살게.
여 미안한데, 이번 주말은 보고서에 집중해야 해.

① 대신 영화를 한 편 찍어 보는 게 어떨까?
② 물론이지. 내가 과제를 도와줄게.
③ 필요 없어. 오늘 밤 표를 예약할게.
④ 좋은 생각이야! 난 한국 영화를 보고 싶었어.

---

15 | 정답 | ④

고양이들을 맡길 데가 없어서 고민하는 Amanda에게 Smith 선생님이 돌봐주겠다고 먼저 제안하는 상황이다. Amanda는 그에게 맡기기로 하였으므로 감사의 말을 전하는 것이 자연스럽다. 따라서 Amanda가 할 말로 가장 적절한 것은 ④ '그렇게 해주시면 감사하겠습니다. 선생님은 정말 좋은 분이세요.'이다.

M Amanda is a math teacher at a high school. The school will be closed for renovation for a week, so she gets a week off from classes and other school duties. Amanda thinks this will be a great chance to take a vacation abroad. So, she decides to go to Bali during this break. Since Amanda has been raising two kittens, she has to **find someone to take care of them** while she's gone. She looks for pet hotels near her house, **but there are no vacancies during the week** she's on the trip. One day, she is talking with Mr. Smith in the teacher's

남 Amanda는 고등학교 수학 선생님이다. 학교가 일주일 동안 보수로 인해 문을 닫을 것이다. 그래서 그녀는 수업과 기타 학교 업무로부터 일주일간 휴가를 얻는다. Amanda는 이것이 해외로 휴가를 갈 좋은 기회라고 생각한다. 그래서 그녀는 쉬는 기간 동안 발리에 가기로 결정한다. Amanda는 두 마리의 고양이를 키우고 있기 때문에 그녀가 없는 동안 그들을 돌볼 사람을 찾아야 한다. 그녀는 집 주변에 있는 반려동물 호텔을 찾아보지만, 그녀가 여행 가는 그 주에는 빈자리가 하나도 없다. 어느 날 그녀는 교사 휴게실에서 Smith 선생님과 함께 이야기하고 있다. Smith 선생님은 Amanda

---

• renovation 보수, 수리
• vacancy 빈자리, 빈방
• trustworthy 믿음이 가는
• responsible 책임감 있는
[선택지]
• be allergic to ~에 알레르기가 있다

lounge. When Mr. Smith hears about Amanda's problem, he asks her if he can watch the cats for her since his kids love cats. He also says he wants to see **if his kids are ready to adopt a pet of their own**. Amanda thinks it would be good if Mr. Smith took care of her cats because **he is very trustworthy and responsible**. In this situation, what would Amanda most likely say to Mr. Smith?

Amanda I'd appreciate it if you could do that. You're the best.

의 문제에 대해 들었을 때, 그녀에게 그가 그 고양이들을 보살펴도 될지 묻는데 그 이유는 그의 아이들이 고양이를 너무 좋아하기 때문이다. 그는 또한 아이들이 반려동물을 입양할 준비가 되었는지 보고 싶다고 이야기한다. Amanda는 Smith 선생님이 믿음이 가고 책임감 있는 분이기 때문에 자기 고양이를 돌봐 준다면 좋겠다고 생각한다. 이러한 상황에서 Amanda가 Smith 선생님에게 할 말로 가장 적절한 것은 무엇인가?

Amanda 그렇게 해주시면 감사하겠습니다. 선생님은 정말 좋은 분이세요.

① 우리 집에 놀러 오지 않을래요?
② 아니요, 괜찮아요. 제 딸은 고양이 알레르기가 있어요.
③ 우리와 함께하시겠어요? 정말 재미있을 거예요.
⑤ 괜찮아요. 고양이들은 일주일 동안 반려동물 호텔에 머무를 예정입니다.

---

16 | 정답 | ③

스트레스는 긍정적인 면도 있지만, 부정적인 면은 건강을 해칠 수 있다고 말하면서 관리하는 방법에 대해 소개하는 내용이다. 따라서 여자가 하는 말의 주제로 가장 적절한 것은 ③ '스트레스를 효과적으로 관리하는 방법'이다.

17 | 정답 | ③

스트레스를 줄이는 데 도움을 주는 음식으로 '아몬드'는 언급하지 않았으므로 정답은 ③이다.

• overalert 매우 경계하는
• stressor 스트레스 요인
• distress 고통스럽게 하다
• exposure 노출
• relieve 줄이다, 완화하다
• anxiety 불안감
• fatty 지방이 많은
• demonstrate 시연하다

W While stress helps us concentrate and focus, its negative influences also make us overalert and unable to relax. Therefore **it's important that you manage your stress effectively**. First, know your stressors. Determine what distresses you and recognize what you can change. Second, shorten your exposure to stress by taking a break. Leave a stressful environment for a while. Third, lead a healthy lifestyle. **Exercise regularly and eat well-balanced meals**. Try to avoid smoking and drinking too much caffeine. There are also foods that help you relieve stress. Brazil nuts are a great source of vitamin E, which lowers anxiety. Fatty fish such as salmon can also improve your mood. Try pumpkin seeds, too. They help **manage blood pressure and reduce symptoms of stress** and anxiety. Dark chocolate may help, too. You can also try breathing control exercises, which only take a minute or two. I'll demonstrate the exercises after playing this video clip about how stress affects us.

여 스트레스는 우리가 집중하는 데 도움을 주는 반면에, 그것의 부정적 영향은 우리를 매우 경계하게 만들고 쉴 수 없게 만듭니다. 그러므로 스트레스를 효과적으로 관리하는 것이 중요합니다. 첫째로, 스트레스 요인을 알아두세요. 무엇이 당신을 고통스럽게 하는지를 밝혀내고 무엇을 바꿀 수 있을지 알아보세요. 둘째로, 휴식을 취하며 스트레스에 노출되는 것을 줄이세요. 잠시 동안 스트레스를 주는 환경을 떠나보세요. 셋째로, 건강한 생활 방식을 하세요. 규칙적으로 운동하고 균형 잡힌 식사를 하세요. 흡연과 너무 많은 카페인 섭취를 하지 않도록 하세요. 스트레스를 줄여 주는 음식도 있습니다. 브라질너트는 비타민 E의 중요한 원천으로, 불안감을 낮춥니다. 연어와 같은 지방이 풍부한 생선도 기분을 향상시켜 줄 수 있습니다. 호박씨도 드셔보세요. 그것들은 혈압을 관리해 주고 스트레스와 불안 증상을 줄여 줍니다. 다크 초콜릿 또한 도움이 됩니다. 여러분들은 호흡 조절 운동을 해볼 수도 있는데, 그것은 1~2분밖에 안 걸립니다. 스트레스가 우리에게 어떤 영향을 미치는지에 관한 이 비디오를 보고 나서 제가 운동을 시연해 보이도록 하겠습니다.

16 ① 스트레스가 어떻게 우리에게 영향을 줄까
② 불안을 줄이는 영양소들
③ 스트레스를 효과적으로 관리하는 방법
④ 건강한 생활 방식을 유지하는 데 도움을 주는 음식
⑤ 긍정적인 스트레스와 부정적인 스트레스를 구별하는 방법

17 ① 브라질너트 ② 연어 ③ 아몬드
④ 호박씨 ⑤ 다크 초콜릿

01 | 정답 | ②

졸업하는 학생들을 위해 학교 현장 학습을 대학 박람회로 간다고 공지하는 상황이다. 가기 전에 미리 갈 부스 확인 및 질문들을 정리할 것을 권하며, 박람회 관련 정보는 학교 웹사이트에서 찾을 수 있다고 설명하는 내용으로 보아 남자가 하는 말의 목적으로 가장 적절한 것은 ②이다.

* announcement 고지, 공고
* college fair 대학 박람회
* apply to ~에 지원하다
* make a list of ~의 목록을 작성하다

M Attention, students. I have an important announcement to make. For those who are graduating next year, the school has planned a field trip **to visit a college fair next month**. The fair will be held in a convention center downtown, and more than 130 colleges will be there to help you make your important decision. This will be **a great opportunity for you to gather materials** from schools you've been thinking about applying to. But before you attend the fair, it is best to visit the fair's site to see **which colleges will be attending** so that you can select which booths to spend the most time at. You should also make a list of the questions you need to ask so that you do not forget while you are there. For further information about the fair, please visit the school website, where you will find a direct link to the fair's site. Thank you.

남 안녕하세요, 학생 여러분. 전달할 중요 공지 사항이 있습니다. 내년에 졸업하는 학생을 대상으로 학교에서는 다음 달에 있을 대학 박람회에 갈 현장 학습을 계획했습니다. 그 박람회는 도심지에 있는 컨벤션 센터에서 열리며 130개가 넘는 대학들이 그곳에서 여러분들이 중요한 결정을 내릴 수 있도록 도울 것입니다. 이것은 여러분들이 지원하려고 생각해 왔던 학교로부터 자료를 얻을 수 있는 좋은 기회입니다. 하지만 그 박람회에 참석하기 전에, 어느 대학 부스에서 가장 많은 시간을 할애할지 선택할 수 있도록 어떤 대학들이 참여하는지 알고자 박람회 사이트를 방문하는 것이 가장 좋습니다. 여러분들은 또한 그곳에 가서 잊어버리지 않도록 물어볼 질문 목록을 작성해야 합니다. 박람회에 대한 정보를 알고 싶으면 학교 웹사이트를 방문하시면 박람회 사이트로 바로 연결되는 링크를 찾을 수 있습니다. 감사합니다.

02 | 정답 | ③

여자는 폭력성이 강한 프로그램의 재방송도 방영 시간이 조정되어야 한다고 말하면서 방송국에 불만을 제기하려고 한다고 했으므로 여자의 의견으로 가장 적절한 것은 ③이다.

* take revenge on ~에게 복수하다
* indicate 나타내다, 보여주다
* contain 포함하다
* violence 폭력
* air 방영하다, 방송하다
* rating (영화의) 등급
* rerun 재방송
* file a complaint with ~에게 불만을 제기하다
* broadcasting station 방송국

W Chris, do you know the TV program "Die Horribly IV"?
M I've never heard of it. I don't really enjoy TV programs. What's the show about?
W It's about a man taking revenge on bad people who killed his parents. But as the title indicates, **it contains a lot of violence**.
M Well, I think as long as it is aired late at night, it shouldn't be a problem.
W You're right. But the problem with the program is that even though it has age-15 rating, it is too violent. Besides, **the reruns are even aired in the afternoon**.
M The show is originally scheduled late at night, but the reruns are in the afternoon? That doesn't sound right.
W I know. I feel like **I should do something about this**.
M What do you mean?
W I'm thinking about filing a complaint with the broadcasting station about the program time.
M Is there anything I can help you with?
W Yes. Let's write the complaint together.

여 Chris, 'Die Horribly IV'라는 프로그램에 대해 알아?
남 들어본 적 없어. 요새 TV 프로그램을 즐겨보지 않거든. 어떤 내용인데?
여 부모를 죽인 나쁜 사람들에게 복수를 하는 남자에 대한 내용이야. 그런데 제목이 나타내는 것처럼, 폭력 장면을 많이 포함하거든.
남 음. 밤늦게 방영되는 한 문제 될 것이 없는 것 같아.
여 맞아. 근데 그 프로그램의 문제는 15세 이상 관람가 등급이지만 너무 폭력적이라는 거야. 게다가 재방송은 심지어 오후에 방영되거든.
남 그 프로그램이 원래는 밤늦게 방영하는데 재방송은 오후에 방영된다는 거지? 그건 맞지 않는 것 같아.
여 그래. 이것에 대해서 뭔가 해야 할 것 같아.
남 무슨 뜻이야?
여 방송국에 프로그램 시간에 관한 불만을 제기하려고 생각 중이거든.
남 내가 도울 일이 있을까?
여 응. 불만 사항을 같이 써보자.

03 | 정답 | ④

효과적인 독서 방법으로 책을 읽으면서 저자와 대화하듯이 생각을 책에 적어보라고 조언하고 있으므로 남자가 하는 말의 요지로 가장 적절한 것은 ④이다.

* instructor 강사, 지도자
* converse 대화를 나누다, 이야기하다; 정반대
* promote 촉진하다; 홍보하다; 진급하다
* engagement 참여, 관심
* note-taking 노트하기, 필기

M Good morning, everyone! This is Eric Thompson, your book instructor. Do you ever have trouble understanding the author's ideas while reading? **Why not try writing down your thoughts in a book**? Also, if you agree or disagree with the author, make note of it by using "yes" or "no" **as if you were conversing with them**. It allows for a dialogue between the reader and the text, **promoting a deeper engagement with the material**. This active note-taking can be an effective reading method. Now, I'll show you a real example, so pay close attention.

남 여러분, 좋은 아침입니다! 저는 여러분의 독서 강사인 Eric Thompson입니다. 책을 읽다가 저자의 생각을 이해하는 데 어려움을 겪은 적이 있나요? 여러분의 생각을 책에 적어 보는 것은 어떨까요? 또한 저자에게 동의하거나 혹은 동의하지 않는다면, 마치 그들과 대화를 나누듯이 "네" 또는 "아니오"를 사용하여 그것을 메모하세요. 그것은 독자와 텍스트 사이의 대화를 가능하게 하여 자료에 대한 더 깊은 참여를 촉진합니다. 이 적극적인 노트 필기는 효과적인 독서 방법이 될 수 있습니다. 이제 제가 여러분에게 실제 사례를 보여드릴 테니, 주의 깊게 살펴보세요.

04 | 정답 | ⑤

카운터 뒤쪽 벽에 걸린 것은 선반이며 선반 위에는 커피 머그잔이 있다고 하였으므로 일치하지 않는 것은 ⑤이다.

* **final stage** 막바지 단계
* **arrange** 배열[배치]하다
* **place** 놓다, 두다; 장소
* **check out** 살펴보다
* **convenience** 편리, 편의
* **shelf** 선반, 장식장

W Hi, John. I heard that you're opening your own coffee shop soon.
M That's right. It'll be ready for business next week. If you have time, feel free to come by.
W Of course I will.
M **The interior is in its final stage**, so I took a picture of it. Do you want to see it?
W Sure. *[Pause]* Wow, I like how you arranged the counter here. **The menu is behind the counter on the wall.**
M I placed it behind the cashier so that customers can see it well.
W That's good. After I order, where do I pick up the coffee?
M Oh, you order and **pay at the left end of the counter**. Then you move to the right end of the counter to pick up the coffee.
W I see. That's why you put the coffee machine in the middle.
M That's right. Check out **the food case under the counter**.
W You put it on the right side of the cashier for convenience. Oh, what is that on the wall behind the counter?
M I **put up a shelf on the wall** and placed some coffee mugs on it.
W Wow, it seems like you have everything ready.

여 안녕, John. 커피숍을 곧 개업한다고 들었어.
남 맞아. 다음 주면 영업 준비가 될 거야. 시간 나면 언제든지 와.
여 당연히 가야지.
남 인테리어가 마무리 단계라서 사진을 찍었어. 보여 줄까?
여 물론이지. *[잠시 후]* 와, 카운터를 배치한 방식이 맘에 든다. 메뉴판은 카운터 뒤 벽에 붙어 있네.
남 손님이 잘 볼 수 있게 계산대 뒤에 두었어.
여 좋은데. 주문하고 난 후에 어디서 커피를 받아?
남 아, 카운터 왼쪽 끝에서 주문하고 계산도 하지. 그런 다음 커피를 받기 위해 오른쪽 끝으로 이동하면 돼.
여 그렇구나. 그래서 커피 기계를 가운데에 놓았구나.
남 맞아. 카운터 밑의 음식 진열장 좀 봐.
여 편리를 위해 계산대 오른쪽에 넣었네. 아, 카운터 뒤쪽 벽에 걸려 있는 것은 뭐야?
남 벽에 선반을 걸어두고 그 위에 커피 머그잔을 두고 있어.
여 와, 모든 게 준비된 것 같네.

05 | 정답 | ①

졸업식 전에 최종 점검을 하는 상황이다. 여자가 고장 난 프로젝터 때문에 관리부에 전화하는 동안 남자에게 마이크를 대신 점검해달라고 하였으므로 정답은 ①이다.

* **graduation ceremony** 졸업식
* **janitor** (건물의) 관리인
* **pamphlet** 팸플릿
* **projector** 프로젝터, 영사기
* **maintenance department** 관리부
* **at once** 바로, 즉시
* **amplifier** 앰프, 증폭기

W Hi, Mr. Lee. Why don't we check if everything's ready for the graduation ceremony?
M Sure. Did the janitors clean up the event hall?
W Yes, the hall was clean and ready to be set up.
M Oh, how far are you on the pamphlets?
W I was just preparing them. But don't worry about them. They'll be ready before the event starts. What about the projector?
M I'm not sure. I'll check it now.
W Okay. I'll check the microphone, then.
M *[Pause]* Oh, no. **The projector doesn't seem to be working**. It won't turn on.
W That's not good.
M Why don't we ask someone from the maintenance department to have a look?
W All right. I'll make a call at once.
M How's the microphone? I think the amplifier should be on to see if it's working properly.
W Oh, **I was about to call maintenance**. Can you test it for me instead?
M No problem.

여 안녕하세요, Lee 선생님. 졸업식을 위한 모든 준비가 다 되었는지 점검할까요?
남 좋아요. 관리인들이 행사장 청소를 했나요?
여 네, 행사장은 깨끗했고 모두 준비되었어요.
남 아, 팸플릿은 얼마나 진행되었나요?
여 지금 준비 중이었어요. 근데 걱정하지 마세요. 행사 시작 전에는 준비될 겁니다. 프로젝터는요?
남 잘 모르겠어요. 지금 확인할게요.
여 알겠어요. 그럼 전 마이크를 확인할게요.
남 *[잠시 후]* 이런. 프로젝터가 고장 난 것 같아요. 전원이 안 켜지네요.
여 상황이 좋지 않네요.
남 관리부 사람에게 봐달라고 부탁하는 게 어떨까요?
여 알겠어요. 제가 바로 전화할게요.
남 마이크는 어때요? 제대로 작동하는지 알아보기 위해 앰프를 켜봐야 할 것 같아요.
여 아, 저는 관리부에 전화하려던 참이었는데. 저 대신 점검 좀 해줄래요?
남 문제없어요.

06 | 정답 | ⑤

타일 한 개의 가격은 15달러이며, 먼저 30개를 구매한다고 하였으므로 타일의 가격은 총 450달러이다. 추가로 욕실 싱크대는 60달러이므로 두 사람이 지불할 금액은 510달러로 정답은 ⑤이다.

* **glossy** 광택이 나는
* **reasonable** 적당한, (가격이) 합리적인
* **aisle** 통로
* **pick up** ~을 가서 찾다

W Mike, have you made a choice about the tile for our bathroom?
M Well, I was looking at this glossy brown tile. What do you think?
W It's nice. It looks like wood. How much is it?
M One unit is 300mm by 300mm and costs $15.
W That's not bad. Then how many tiles do we need for our bathroom?
M **How about getting 30 first**? We can come back and buy more if 30 is not enough.
W All right. Oh, we need a new bathroom sink, too.

여 Mike, 욕실용 타일 골랐나요?
남 음, 광택이 나는 갈색 타일을 보고 있어요. 어때요?
여 좋아요. 나무 같네요. 얼마예요?
남 타일 한 개가 가로 300밀리미터 세로 300밀리미터이고 15달러예요.
여 나쁘지 않네요. 그럼 우리 욕실에는 얼마나 많은 타일이 필요한 거죠?
남 일단 30개 정도 사는 게 어때요? 30개로 부족하면 다시 와서 더 사죠.
여 좋아요. 아, 욕실 싱크대도 새것으로 사야 해요.

	M Right, I almost forgot. **Is there any particular type you want**?	남 맞아요. 잊을 뻔했네요. 특별히 원하는 종류가 있나요?
	W Not really. Let's get the same type we have now. How about that one in the corner?	여 없어요. 지금 가지고 있는 것과 같은 종류로 하죠. 구석에 있는 저거 어때요?
	M Okay. It's $60. I think that's reasonable.	남 좋아요. 60달러예요. 가격이 적당한 것 같아요.
	W I think so, too. **Which aisle is it in**?	여 저도 그렇게 생각해요. 어느 통로에 있죠?
	M It says it's in aisle 27, on shelf 5.	남 27번 통로에 5번 선반이라고 나와 있네요.
	W All right. Let's go and pick up a sink first, and then tiles.	여 알겠어요. 일단 싱크대를 가져오고 나서 타일을 찾는 것으로 해요.

07 | 정답 | ⑤

남자는 여자에게 영화를 보러 가자고 말하지만, 여자는 여동생과 콘서트에 가야 한다고 말하고 있으므로 정답은 ⑤이다.

• food poisoning 식중독

M Hi, Brittany. How was your weekend?
W Hi, Tim. I just stayed home.
M Why? Don't you usually go out on weekends?
W I had food poisoning, so **I spent most of the weekend sick in bed**.
M That must have been terrible. Do you feel better now?
W Yes, I'm okay. What about you? Did you do anything special?
M On Sunday, I went to see the movie Julie recommended.
W Oh, I heard she got you movie tickets for your birthday. How did you like the movie?
M It was amazing. Why don't we **watch the movie together this Saturday**? I don't mind seeing it twice.
W I wish I could go with you, but I can't.
M Why not?
W I'm going to **go to the Dreamers' concert with my little sister**.
M I thought you didn't like noisy places.
W I have no choice. **She's a big fan**.
M You're such a nice sister.

남 안녕, Brittany. 주말 어떻게 보냈니?
여 안녕, Tim. 그냥 집에 있었어.
남 왜? 보통 주말에 밖에 나가지 않니?
여 식중독에 걸려서 주말의 대부분을 침대에 누워서 보냈어.
남 끔찍했겠다. 이제 좀 괜찮니?
여 괜찮아. 넌 어때? 뭐 특별한 거 했어?
남 일요일에 Julie가 추천한 영화 보러 갔어.
여 아, 그녀가 네 생일에 영화표를 줬다고 들었어. 영화는 어땠어?
남 굉장했어. 이번 토요일에 같이 그 영화 보는 거 어때? 나는 그거 두 번 보는 거 괜찮거든.
여 나도 너랑 같이 가고 싶은데, 갈 수 없을 것 같아.
남 왜 못 가는데?
여 여동생하고 Dreamers 콘서트에 갈 거야.
남 나는 네가 시끄러운 곳을 안 좋아하는 줄 알았는데.
여 선택권이 없어. 동생이 엄청난 팬이거든.
남 넌 정말 좋은 언니구나.

08 | 정답 | ④

Great Pyramid는 짓는 데 20년 걸렸고 Giza 지역에 있다고 하였다. 높이는 139m로 에펠탑이 지어지기 전까지는 가장 큰 건축물이었으며 안에 3개의 방이 있다고 했지만, 건설 목적에 대한 언급은 없으므로 정답은 ④이다.

• theory 이론
• discovery 발견: 발견된 것
• remain 계속[여전히] ~이다
• structure 건축물, 구조물
• chamber 방, 침실

W We're going to see the pyramids and the Sphinx. If you have any questions, feel free to ask me. Okay?
M Sure.
W As you may know, no one really knows **how the Egyptian pyramids were built**. There are many theories and new discoveries, but it still remains a mystery.
M How long did it take to build a pyramid?
W **It took about 20 years to build** the tallest and oldest one, the Great Pyramid, which is one of three pyramids in Giza.
M It must be huge since it took 20 years to complete.
W It's about 139 meters tall. **It was the world's tallest structure** until the Eiffel Tower was built.
M That's amazing! **How many chambers are there** in the Great Pyramid?
W I believe there are three.

여 우리는 피라미드와 스핑크스를 볼 예정입니다. 질문 있으시면 언제든지 물어보세요. 아셨죠?
남 네.
여 아시는 바와 같이, 이집트의 피라미드가 어떻게 만들어졌는지 아무도 모릅니다. 많은 이론이 있으며 새로운 발견들도 많지만 여전히 미스터리입니다.
남 피라미드를 만드는 데 얼마나 오래 걸렸나요?
여 가장 크고 가장 오래된 Great Pyramid를 짓는 데 약 20년 걸렸어요. Great Pyramid는 Giza에 있는 세 개의 피라미드 중 하나랍니다.
남 짓는 데 20년이나 걸렸으니 분명히 거대하겠는데요.
여 대략 139미터입니다. 에펠탑이 지어지기 전까지 가장 높은 건축물이었지요.
남 놀랍군요! Great Pyramid에는 방이 몇 개가 있어요?
여 제가 알기론 세 개입니다.

09 | 정답 | ⑤

5세부터 14세 아이들이 그림을 그리고, 색칠하며 전 세계의 예술가들에 대해 배울 수 있고 새로 지어진 Raum 아트센터에서 수업이 진행되며 수업 후에는 부모님과 형제들을 초대한다고 하였다. 직접 방문해서 등록하는 것보다 온라인 신청을 더 선호한다고 하였으므로 일치하지 않는 것은 ⑤이다.

• sibling 형제자매

W Good morning, everyone. My name is Susan Thompson, a manager from Raum Art Center. I'm here to introduce you to a fun way to experience and learn art. Starting this year, we are providing a Saturday Art School **for kids aged 5 to 14**. It is an amazing opportunity for them to explore the wonderful world of art. **Kids will get a chance to draw, paint, color, and sculpt**. Saturday Art School will also help kids learn about artists from around the world **at the newly built Raum Art Center**. At the end of every session, we **invite parents and siblings** into the art

여 안녕하세요, 학생 여러분! 제 이름은 Susan Thompson이며 Raum 아트센터 매니저입니다. 미술을 배우고 경험할 수 있는 재미있는 방법을 여러분에게 소개하기 위해 이 자리에 왔습니다. 올해를 시작으로 저희는 5살에서 14살까지의 어린이를 대상으로 하는 토요 미술학교를 제공하기로 했습니다. 그들이 경이로운 미술의 세계를 탐험할 수 있는 놀라운 기회가 될 것입니다. 아이들은 스케치하고 그림물감으로 그리고 색칠하고 조각하는 기회를 얻게 될 것입니다. 토요 미술 학교는 또한 새로 건립된 Raum 아트센터에서 아이들이 전 세계 화가들에 대해 배울 수 있도록 도울 것입니다. 매회 수업이 끝날 때마다, 부모와 형제자매를 미술실로 초대하여

<table>
<tr>
<td>

- **encourage** 격려하다, 장려하다
- **positively** 긍정적으로
- **walk-in** (예약이 안 된) 방문

</td>
<td>

room to see all the beautiful artworks, and the kids are encouraged to speak positively about each other's work. To register, walk-ins are welcome, **but online registration is preferred.** For more information, please visit our website, www.raum-art.com. Thank you.

</td>
<td>

아름다운 예술품을 모두 보게 하고, 아이들은 서로의 작품에 대해 긍정적으로 말하도록 격려합니다. 등록을 하기 위해서는, 방문도 좋지만 온라인 등록을 사용하는 것이 더 좋습니다. 더 자세한 정보는 저희 웹사이트 www.raum-art.com을 방문해 주세요. 감사합니다.

</td>
</tr>
<tr>
<td>

10 | 정답 | ②

남자가 수강할 골프 강좌는 기초 과정이어야 하고 주말을 포함한 수업 일정이어야 한다. 비용은 1,200달러 미만인 여자 코치에게 배우는 레슨을 선택하였으므로 정답은 ②이다.

- **sign up for** ~을 신청하다, 가입하다
- **golf club** 골프채
- **pose** 자세
- **available** (이용) 가능한; 시간이 있는

</td>
<td>

W How may I help you?
M Hello. I'd like to sign up for golf lessons here.
W Okay. What level are you interested in taking?
M I've never played golf before, so **I have to start from the beginning.**
W Okay. At the basic level, you will learn to hold a golf club and the basic pose.
M That sounds perfect. **I think I can come mostly on weekends.**
W Oh, then you have to choose a coach who is available from Wednesday to Sunday.
M All right. Oh, why is there a price difference between these two coaches here?
W The price depends on their experience as a pro. The male coach played as a professional golfer longer than the female coach.
M Well, **$1,200 is too much for me**, so I will go with the female coach.

</td>
<td>

여 무엇을 도와드릴까요?
남 안녕하세요. 여기서 골프 레슨을 신청하고 싶어서요.
여 알겠습니다. 어떤 단계에 관심이 있나요?
남 골프는 한 번도 해본 적이 없어서 기초부터 시작해야 해요.
여 알겠습니다. 기본 단계에서는 골프채를 잡는 방법과 기본 자세를 배우게 됩니다.
남 완벽하네요. 주말에는 대부분 올 수 있을 것 같아요.
여 아. 그럼 수요일부터 일요일까지 가능한 코치를 고르셔야 합니다.
남 알겠습니다. 근데 왜 여기 이 두 코치 사이에 가격 차이가 있는 거죠?
여 가격은 프로 선수로서의 경험에 따라 다릅니다. 남자 코치는 여자 코치보다 프로 선수로서 더 오랫동안 경기를 했기 때문이죠.
남 음, 1,200달러는 너무 과해서 전 이 여자 코치로 할게요.

</td>
</tr>
<tr>
<td>

11 | 정답 | ③

남자가 새로 제안받은 일자리는 집에서 두 시간 거리라서 이사를 해야 하는지 물어보는 여자의 말에 대한 남자의 응답으로 가장 적절한 것은 ③ '그래야 할 것 같아. 통근 거리가 멀어서 말이야.'이다.

- **benefit** 혜택, 이득
- **salary** 급여, 월급
[선택지]
- **commute** 통근 (거리)

</td>
<td>

W Chris, I hear that you got another job offer. Have you decided where to go?
M Not yet. The new offer includes **more benefits with a higher salary.** But it's **a two-hour drive from where I live.**
W Does that mean you have to move if you accept the offer?
M I think so. That's a long commute to work.

</td>
<td>

여 Chris, 너 또 다른 일자리 제안을 받았다고 하던데. 어디로 갈지 정했어?
남 아직 못했어. 새로운 일자리가 더 많은 혜택에 급여도 더 많아. 하지만 내가 사는 곳에서부터 2시간 운전을 해야 해.
여 그 일자리를 수락하면 이사해야 한다는 말이니?
남 그래야 할 것 같아. 통근 거리가 멀어서 말이야.

① 응. 내 결정이 옳았다는 것을 깨달았어.
② 동의하지 않아. 거기까지 걸어갈 수 있다고.
④ 맞아. 일할 때마다 난 행복감을 느껴.
⑤ 사실은 아냐. 난 결정을 바꾸고 싶지 않다고.

</td>
</tr>
<tr>
<td>

12 | 정답 | ⑤

신문을 읽을 시간이 없다고 말하는 남자에게 여자가 읽는 습관을 들이는 방법에 대해 설명하는 것이 자연스러우므로 정답은 ⑤ '하루에 10분 동안 읽어봐. 그리고 나서 서서히 (신문 읽는) 시간을 늘려.'이다.

- **make a habit out of** ~의 습관을 들이다
[선택지]
- **be into** ~에 관심을 갖다, 정통하다
- **subscribe to** ~을 구독하다

</td>
<td>

M Jenny, you seem to spend a lot of time reading the newspaper lately.
W **I'm trying to make a habit out of it.** There are so many benefits. You should try it, too.
M I was thinking about it, but **I just couldn't find the time.**
W Try it for 10 minutes a day. Then gradually increase the time.

</td>
<td>

남 Jenny, 너 최근에 신문 읽는 데 많은 시간을 보내는 것 같아.
여 신문 읽는 습관을 들이려고 하고 있어. 좋은 점이 많거든. 너도 해봐.
남 그걸 할까 했었는데 시간을 낼 수가 없었어.
여 하루에 10분 동안 읽어봐. 그러고 나서 서서히 (신문 읽는) 시간을 늘려.

① 미안해. 난 읽는 데는 정말 관심 없어.
② 조심해. 가짜 뉴스가 많으니까.
③ 다음 페이지를 봐. 스포츠 부분이 나올 거야.
④ 걱정 마. 어떠한 신문도 구독할 필요가 없어.

</td>
</tr>
<tr>
<td>

13 | 정답 | ①

남자가 여자에게 새로 생긴 사교춤 수업을 수강할 것을 제안하는 상황이다. 여자가 춤이 복잡하여 자신처럼 솜씨 없는 사람도 할 수 있는지 물어보는 말에 가장 적절한 남자의 응답은 ① '물론이지! 내가 따라잡을 수 있게 도와줄게.'이다.

</td>
<td>

W Kevin, what's that poster over there?
M Oh, **just a notice about registration for ballroom dancing.** It's a class at the community center. Actually, I've been taking it for about two years.
W Wow, I didn't know you liked ballroom dancing.
M It's great exercise. Besides, I get to meet new people. What do you do when you're free?
W Well, I usually read, go shopping and hang out with

</td>
<td>

여 Kevin, 저쪽에 있는 포스터는 뭐야?
남 아, 사교춤 등록에 관한 광고문이야. 주민 센터에서 하는 수업이야. 사실, 나는 거의 2년째 그 수업을 듣고 있어.
여 와, 난 네가 사교춤을 좋아하는 줄은 몰랐네.
남 좋은 운동이지. 게다가 새로운 사람들을 만나기도 해. 넌 시간 날 때 뭐해?
여 글쎄, 난 보통 책을 읽고, 쇼핑을 하고, 친구들과 어울리지.

</td>
</tr>
</table>

* notice 안내문, 광고문
* registration 등록
* ballroom dancing 사교춤
* get involved 관여하다
* drag A into A를 끌어들이다
* clumsy 솜씨 없는, 어설픈
[선택지]
* catch up (on) ~을 따라잡다

friends.
M **If you want to try something new**, how about ballroom dancing? There is a free sample lesson this Friday at 7 p.m.
W Actually, **that sounds pretty fun**. How did you get involved with the dance in the first place?
M Well, one of my friends dragged me into it, but now it's become a big part of my life. Watch this video.
W Wow, it looks so complicated. Do you think **a clumsy person like me stands a chance**?
M Absolutely! I can help you catch up.

남 새로운 것을 해보고 싶다면, 사교춤은 어때? 이번 금요일 오후 7시에 무료 맛보기 수업이 있어.
여 실은 꽤 재밌을 것 같은데. 애초에 어떻게 해서 그 춤과 인연을 맺었니?
남 그게, 친구 한 명이 날 끌어들였는데 이제는 내 인생에 있어 큰 부분을 차지하게 되었지. 이 영상 좀 봐봐.
여 와, 꽤 복잡해 보이는데. 나같이 솜씨 없는 사람도 가능성이 있는 것 같아?
남 물론이지! 내가 따라잡을 수 있게 도와줄게.

② 물론이지. 사교춤은 쉽지 않아.
③ 좋은 것 같아. 그걸로 하자.
④ 정말? 우리 수업을 신청하는 게 어때?
⑤ 그럼. 넌 이미 프로 같아 보여.

14 | 정답 | ⑤

여자가 여행 가이드 면접을 보고 있는 상황이다. 더할 말이 있는지 물어보는 남자의 말에 가장 적절한 여자의 응답은 ⑤ '아니요. 그게 다입니다. 빠른 시일 내에 소식을 듣길 바랍니다.'이다.

* major in 전공하다
* career 직업
* intrigue ~의 호기심을 돋우다
* passionate 열정적인

M Hello, Miss Kelly. Have a seat and take it easy. *[Pause]* How did you get here?
W I took the subway. It only took half an hour from my house.
M I see. So, your résumé says **that you studied history in college**.
W That's right. I majored in Korean history. I've been interested in history since I was a little girl.
M I wonder **why you want to be a tour guide**, since you have various career options.
W Every place I visited had interesting stories and they always intrigued me. But some people don't bother to learn history. So, growing up, I've always wanted to make history seem easier to understand.
M Interesting. **The job may not be as fun as** you think it is. It can be very difficult and hard unless you are really passionate about it.
W I understand the hard parts of the job, but I think **this is the right career for me**.
M I see. Is there anything you'd like to add?
W No, that's all. I hope to hear from you soon.

남 안녕하세요, Kelly 씨. 앉으시고 긴장 푸세요. *[잠시 후]* 여기까지 어떻게 오셨어요?
여 지하철을 타고 왔습니다. 집에서부터 30분밖에 걸리지 않았습니다.
남 그렇군요. 자, 이력서에는 당신이 대학에서 역사를 공부했다고 나와 있네요.
여 맞아요. 저는 한국사를 전공했습니다. 저는 어렸을 때부터 역사에 관심이 많았습니다.
남 다양한 진로 선택권이 있었을 텐데 왜 여행 가이드가 되고 싶은지 궁금해요.
여 제가 방문한 모든 곳에는 재미있는 이야기들이 있었고, 그것들은 항상 제 호기심을 자극했어요. 하지만 어떤 사람들은 역사를 알고 싶어 하지 않아요. 그래서 자라면서 저는 항상 역사를 좀 더 이해하기 쉽게 만들고 싶었습니다.
남 흥미롭군요. 그 일이 당신이 생각하는 것만큼 재미있지 않을 수도 있어요. 정말 열정적이지 않다면 매우 어렵고 힘들 수 있어요.
여 일의 어려운 부분은 이해하지만, 이것이 제게 딱 맞는 직업이라고 생각합니다.
남 그렇군요. 덧붙이고 싶은 것이 있나요?
여 아니요. 그게 다입니다. 빠른 시일 내에 소식을 듣길 바랍니다.

① 걱정하지 마세요. 제가 도와드릴게요.
② 네. 더 부지런히 일을 했어야 했어요.
③ 여행사에 좀 더 일찍 지원했어야 했어요.
④ 아뇨. 역사를 더 공부할 수 있는 기회가 있나요?

15 | 정답 | ⑤

Susan이 집에 과제를 두고 와서 Mike에게 점심시간에 집에 가서 가져오겠다고 말하는 상황이다. 5교시에 맞춰서 돌아오도록 도와주기로 결심한 Mike가 할 말로 가장 적절한 것은 ⑤ '내가 네 집까지 자전거로 데려다주는 건 어때? 더 빠를 거야.'이다.

* assignment 과제
* due ~하기로 되어 있는[예정된]
* timetable 시간표
* period 교시, 수업 시간
* make it 시간 맞춰 가다

W Susan and Mike are high school students. They worked on a science group assignment together, which is due today. Susan is supposed to finish the last part and bring it to school today. However, when she arrives at school, **she realizes she left it at home**. She calls her mother, but she isn't answering her phone. Then she checks the timetable and finds out science class is after lunch in fifth period today. She tells Mike that she'll **go home and get it during lunchtime**. But Mike thinks that Susan won't have enough time to come back before the science class. He realizes if he **takes her to her house on his bike**, they will make it before the class. So **he decides to go with** Susan and get the assignment together. In this situation, what does Mike most likely say to Susan?

Mike How about if I take you to your house by bike? It'll be faster.

여 Susan과 Mike는 고등학생이다. 그들은 같이 과학 그룹 과제를 했고, 그건 오늘까지이다. Susan이 마지막 부분을 끝내고 오늘 학교에 가져오기로 했다. 하지만 그녀가 학교에 도착할 때, 그것을 집에 두고 온 것을 깨닫는다. 그녀는 엄마에게 전화하지만, 엄마는 전화를 받지 않으신다. 그러고 나서 Susan은 시간표를 확인하니 오늘 과학 수업은 점심 이후 5교시에 있다는 걸 알게 된다. 그녀는 Mike에게 점심시간 동안 집에 가서 과제를 가져오겠다고 말한다. 하지만 Mike는 Susan이 과학 시간 전까지 돌아올 시간이 충분하지 않다고 생각한다. 그는 자신의 자전거로 그녀를 집까지 데려다 준다면, 수업 전에 올 수 있다는 것을 깨닫는다. 그래서 그는 Susan과 같이 가서 과제를 가져오기로 결심한다. 이러한 상황에서 Mike가 Susan에게 할 말로 가장 적절한 것은?

Mike 내가 네 집까지 자전거로 데려다주는 건 어때? 더 빠를 거야.

① 정말 미안해. 보고서를 어디에서도 찾을 수가 없어.
② 오늘 수업이 끝나기 전에 보고서를 제출해도 될까?
③ 보고서를 끝낼 시간을 좀 더 줄 수 있어?
④ 너희 엄마가 집에 계시면, 도움을 요청하는 게 어때?

16 | 정답 | ⑤

아이가 집안일을 할 때마다 다양한 방법으로 격려하여 스스로 집안일에 참여하게 만드는 방법을 소개하는 내용으로 남자가 하는 말의 주제로 가장 적절한 것은 ⑤ '아이들이 집안일을 하도록 동기를 부여하는 방법'이다.

17 | 정답 | ⑤

아이를 집안일에 참여시키는 방법으로 '놀이공원 가기'는 언급되지 않았으므로 정답은 ⑤이다.

* household chores 집안일
* unwilling 꺼리는, 마지못해 하는
* willingly 자진해서, 기꺼이
* clean up 정리하다, 청소하다
* bar graph 막대그래프
* color 〜에 색칠하다
* keep a record 기록해 두다
* lawn-mowing 잔디 깎기
* gardening 정원 손질
* pocket money 용돈
* reward 보상하다
* earn (돈을) 벌다
[선택지]
* bring up 〜을 양육하다, 기르다

M Hello, ladies and gentlemen! There are many household chores to do, but sometimes your children **can be a little unwilling to help out**. How can we encourage our children to participate in the housework willingly? Here are some ideas. First, you can **start giving your child a special dessert** whenever he or she helps to clean up. Second, you can also give your child a sense of achievement. Just draw a bar graph for each child, and then every time they do chores, **color one block on their graph**. Third, keep a record on a calendar. If you think your child is doing chores very well, you should give them a small present at the end of the month. If your child is big enough to do things like lawn-mowing and gardening, **why not give some pocket money** instead of rewarding them with treats? This will also teach children about earning money.

남 안녕하세요, 신사 숙녀 여러분! 해야 할 집안일은 많은데, 때때로 아이들은 도와주기를 조금 꺼릴 수 있습니다. 어떻게 하면 아이들이 자진해서 집안일을 하게 할 수 있을까요? 여기에 몇 가지 아이디어가 있습니다. 첫째로, 여러분은 아이가 청소를 도울 때마다 특별한 디저트를 줄 수 있습니다. 두 번째로, 여러분은 아이에게 성취감을 줄 수도 있습니다. 각 아이에 대한 막대그래프를 그리고, 아이가 집안일을 할 때마다 그들의 그래프에 한 칸씩 색을 칠해 보세요. 세 번째는, 달력에 기록을 남기세요. 만약 여러분의 아이가 집안일을 아주 잘하고 있다고 생각한다면, 여러분은 그달 말에 그들에게 작은 선물을 주어야 합니다. 만약 여러분의 아이가 잔디 깎기나 정원 가꾸기와 같은 것들을 할 수 있을 만큼 충분히 크다면, 그들에게 간식으로 보상하는 대신에 용돈을 주는 것은 어떨까요? 이것은 또한 아이들에게 돈을 버는 것에 대해 가르쳐줄 것입니다.

16 ① 현명하게 아이를 양육하는 방법
② 집에서 맛있는 음식을 만드는 방법
③ 효율적으로 집안일을 하는 방법
④ 아이들이 저축하도록 장려하는 방법
⑤ 아이들이 집안일을 하도록 동기를 부여하는 방법

01 | 정답 | ⑤

신문사에서 양질의 신문을 계속 제공하기 위해 금전적인 지원이 필요하다고 하면서 기부금을 요청하고 있으므로 여자가 하는 말의 목적으로 가장 적절한 것은 ⑤이다.

- provide 제공하다
- regardless of ~와 관계없이
- budget 예산
- deliver 배달하다
- quality 양질의
- journalism 신문; 저널리즘
- contribution 기부(금)
- factual 사실을 담은, 사실의
- necessity 필수품
- deserve ~할 만하다

W Hello, I'm Ella Brown from the Globe. We feel happy and proud that more people are reading and supporting our newspaper. Recently we made the choice to provide our readers with less advertising for their convenience, **regardless of the effect it has on our budget**. For that reason, we have a small favor to ask of you. **We need support from you** to keep delivering quality journalism. Every reader contribution, however big or small, is so valuable. Support the Globe with as little as $1. It only takes a minute. At a time when factual information is a necessity, we believe that people **deserve access to accurate reporting** and useful information. Your support will allow the Globe to keep up its quality journalism. We will make a continued effort to report the most critical issues of our time for you. Thank you.

여 안녕하세요. 저는 Globe의 Ella Brown입니다. 저희 신문을 구독하고 지원해 주시는 분들이 늘어나고 있어서 행복하고 자랑스럽습니다. 최근에 저희 재정에 주는 영향과 관계없이 독자 여러분의 편의를 위해서 광고량을 줄이기로 하였습니다. 그런 이유로 저희는 여러분께 작은 부탁을 드리고자 합니다. 양질의 신문을 계속 제공하기 위해서는 여러분의 지원이 필요합니다. 많든 적든 독자 여러분의 후원 모두가 매우 소중합니다. 1달러씩만 Globe를 지원해 주세요. 1분이면 됩니다. 사실을 담은 정보가 꼭 필요한 이때에, 저희는 여러분이 정확한 보도와 유용한 정보를 접할 자격이 있다고 믿습니다. 여러분의 지원이 Globe가 양질의 언론 활동을 계속할 수 있게 해 줄 것입니다. 여러분들을 위해서 우리 시대에 가장 중요한 문제를 보도하기 위한 지속적인 노력을 다할 것입니다. 감사합니다.

02 | 정답 | ①

여름에 아르바이트를 할 것이라는 여자에게 남자는 전공과 관련지어 인턴으로 일하게 되면, 졸업 후 그 경험을 살려 직업을 구할 수 있다고 설명하고 있다. 따라서 남자의 의견으로 ①이 가장 적절하다.

- save up 모으다
- major 전공
- accounting 회계학
- stand a chance (~을 할) 가능성이 있다
- put A into practice A를 실행에 옮기다
- head to ~를 향해 가다

M Mina, do you have any plans for this summer?
W I think I'll get a part-time job at a restaurant. It'll be a great chance to save up money before graduation.
M That's true. We only have one year left until graduation. Why don't you try something **related to your major**?
W What do you mean?
M Since your major is accounting, **working as an intern in an accounting firm** is a good way to spend your summer.
W Actually, that doesn't sound too bad. I could **get some valuable experience and get paid** at the same time.
M Exactly. You may not make much but you can use that experience after you graduate to get a job.
W Do you think I stand a chance? I'm only in my third year in college.
M You've learned all the basics. Now, you need to **start putting that knowledge into practice**.
W You're right. I should head to the job center on campus.
M That's a good place to start. It has lots of useful information.

남 Mina, 이번 여름에 계획이 있니?
여 식당에서 아르바이트를 할 것 같아. 졸업하기 전에 돈을 모을 수 있는 좋은 기회가 될 거야.
남 맞아. 우리 이제 졸업이 1년밖에 안 남았어. 전공과 관련 있는 일을 해 보는 게 어때?
여 무슨 뜻이야?
남 네 전공이 회계학이니까, 회계 회사에서 인턴으로 일하는 게 네 여름을 보내는 좋은 방법이 될 것 같아.
여 사실, 그게 그렇게 나쁘게 들리진 않네. 귀중한 경험을 얻고 동시에 돈도 벌 수 있으니까.
남 바로 그거야. 돈을 많이 벌지는 못하겠지만 졸업 후에 그 경험을 살려서 직업을 구할 수도 있어.
여 나한테 가능성이 있을까? 난 이제 겨우 3학년인데.
남 기초는 다 배웠잖아. 이제 배운 것을 실행에 옮겨 보기 시작해야지.
여 네 말이 맞아. 학교의 취업 센터에 가봐야겠다.
남 시작하기 좋은 곳이지. 거기에는 많은 유용한 정보가 있어.

03 | 정답 | ④

학습 효율성을 개선하는 비법으로 공부하기 전에 책상을 깔끔하게 정리하라고 조언하고 있으므로 여자가 하는 말의 요지로 가장 적절한 것은 ④이다.

- efficiency 효율성, 능률
- neatly 깔끔하게, 단정하게
- conducive 도움이 되는, 좋은
- distraction 주의산만
- enhance 향상하다
- psychologically 심리적으로
- tidy up ~을 깔끔하게 정리하다
- stick around (어떤 곳에(서)) 가지 않고 있다[머무르다]

W Hi everyone, welcome to *Melanie's Learning Lounge*! Today, I have an effective trick **that can help improve your learning efficiency**. Before you study, try to neatly organize your desk. This will create a conducive environment for focus and concentration. **A tidy desk reduces distractions**, enhances productivity, and psychologically prepares you for a more effective and efficient study. Believe me, and tidy up your desk. **It works wonders**! I will give you an example from my experience. So stick around!

여 안녕하세요, 여러분. Melanie의 학습 라운지에 오신 것을 환영합니다! 오늘, 저는 여러분의 학습 효율성을 개선하는 데 도움이 되는 효과적인 비법을 가지고 있습니다. 공부하기 전에 여러분의 책상을 깔끔하게 정리하세요. 이것은 주목과 집중에 도움이 되는 환경을 만들어 줄 것입니다. 말끔히 정돈된 책상은 주의 산만을 줄이고 생산성을 향상시키며 여러분이 심리적으로 더 효과적이고 효율적인 공부를 할 수 있도록 준비시켜 줍니다. 저를 믿고 책상을 정리하세요. 놀라운 효과가 있습니다! 제 경험에서 나온 예를 들어보겠습니다. 그러니 지켜봐 주세요!

04 | 정답 | ④

자전거 도로 옆에 귀여운 곰 동상이 있다고 했으나, 그림에는 돌고래 동상이 있으므로 대화의 내용과 일치하지 않는 것은 ④이다.

* lamppost 가로등
* lane (좁은) 길, 도로
* entire 전체의, 전부의
* statue 동상
* mascot 마스코트

M Hello, Judy. How was your family trip?

W It was good. I went to the Namhan River. Would you like to see a picture?

M Sure. *[Pause]* Oh, there are **lampposts next to the river**.

W Yes, there are. At night, the light from the lampposts makes the river more beautiful.

M And **who are the girls sitting on the bench**?

W They're my cousins. They really enjoyed riding the two-person bike standing next to them.

M That must have been great. Oh, the bicycle lane goes along the river.

W Yes, you can see the entire river while riding.

M Wonderful. And there's **a cute bear statue next to the road**.

W Yes, it's the area's mascot.

M I'll try to visit next fall. Oh, I think I see you! Is that you under the pine tree?

W Yes, that's me. I was really tired from riding my bike.

남 안녕, Judy. 가족 여행 어땠어?

여 좋았어. 남한강에 갔었어. 사진 볼래?

남 좋아. *[잠시 후]* 아, 강 옆에 가로등이 있구나.

여 응. 가로등이 있어. 밤에는 가로등 불빛 때문에 강이 더욱 아름다워.

남 벤치에 앉아 있는 여자아이들은 누구니?

여 내 사촌들이야. 옆에 세워 둔 2인용 자전거 타는 걸 정말 좋아했어.

남 정말 재미있었겠다. 아, 강을 따라서 자전거 도로가 있구나.

여 응. 자전거 타면서 강 전체를 볼 수가 있어.

남 멋지구나. 그리고 길옆에 귀여운 곰 동상이 있네.

여 그래. 그 곰 동상이 그 지역의 마스코트야.

남 가을에 가봐야겠다. 아, 너 보이는 것 같아! 소나무 아래 있는 사람이 너지?

여 그래. 나야. 자전거 타느라 너무 지쳤었어.

---

05 | 정답 | ⑤

남자가 분실물 보관소의 위치를 자신의 전화번호로 보내달라고 요청했으며, 여자는 전화를 끊은 후에 위치를 문자로 알려주겠다고 했으므로 정답은 ⑤이다.

* Lost and Found 분실물 보관소
* briefcase 서류 가방
* by any chance 혹시
* strap 끈, 혁대
* location 위치
* text message 문자 메시지

[Telephone rings.]

W Lost and Found. What can I do for you?

M Hello, I lost my briefcase this morning. Do you have a black leather briefcase by any chance?

W We have a few black leather briefcases here. **Could you please describe yours in more detail**?

M Certainly. It has a long strap. Oh, there should be a blue tumbler inside.

W All right. Let me check first. *[Pause]* Oh, yes. It's here. May I have your name, please?

M It's Mike West.

W Okay, Mr. West. We are open until 6 p.m. today. Please come in 30 minutes before then. It could take a while to **fill out the form**.

M I don't think I can find the time to visit today. I'll come and pick it up tomorrow morning.

W That's fine. Please bring your ID with you when you visit. You know where our office is located, right?

M No, I don't. Could you **send your location** to this number?

W Okay, **I'll send you the directions** by text message after this call.

M Thank you so much. I'll see you tomorrow.

[전화벨이 울린다.]

여 분실물 보관소입니다. 무엇을 도와드릴까요?

남 안녕하세요. 제가 오늘 아침에 서류 가방을 잃어버렸어요. 혹시 검은색 가죽 서류 가방이 들어왔나요?

여 여기 검은색 가죽 서류 가방이 몇 개 있는데요. 가방을 좀 더 자세히 설명해 주실래요?

남 네. 가방에 긴 끈이 달려 있어요. 아, 그리고 안에 푸른색 텀블러가 있을 거예요.

여 알겠어요. 먼저 한 번 살펴볼게요. *[잠시 후]* 아, 네. 여기 있어요. 성함을 말씀해 주실래요?

남 Mike West입니다.

여 알겠습니다. West 씨. 저희는 오늘 오후 6시까지 열려 있습니다. 30분 전까지 오세요. 서류를 작성하는 데 시간이 좀 걸릴 겁니다.

남 오늘은 방문할 시간을 낼 수 없을 것 같습니다. 내일 아침에 찾으러 갈게요.

여 좋아요. 방문하실 때 신분증도 가지고 오세요. 우리 사무실이 어디 있는지 아시죠, 맞으시나요?

남 아니요, 모르는데요. 이 번호로 위치를 보내주실 수 있으세요?

여 알겠습니다. 전화 끊고 나서 오실 방향을 문자로 보내 드릴게요.

남 감사합니다. 내일 뵙겠습니다.

---

06 | 정답 | ④

호텔 숙박 요금은 1박에 100달러이고, 총 2박을 했으므로 200달러이다. 룸서비스와 마사지 서비스로 지불한 금액은 각각 30달러와 50달러이다. 20% 할인되는 호텔 체인 회원권이 있으나, 숙박료에만 적용되므로 숙박료 160달러를 포함한 총비용은 240달러이다. 따라서 정답은 ④이다.

* check out 퇴실하다
* proceed 진행하다
* confirm 확인하다
* rate 요금
* in addition 그 외에
* charge (요금을) 청구하다; 요금

M Hello, I'd like to check out, please. Here is my room key.

W Certainly, sir. How did you enjoy your stay at our hotel?

M It was lovely. I really loved the pool and spa here.

W I'm glad to hear that. Before we proceed with the payment, I need to confirm a few things.

M All right.

W Our record shows that you stayed for 2 nights, **and the room rate was $100 per night**. Is that correct?

M Yes, that was the price when I made the reservation.

W In addition, you ordered room service yesterday, which was $30. Is that right, sir?

M That's right. Oh, I also had a massage the day before. **I believe it was charged to the room**.

W Yes, sir. The massage was $50. Please check the screen

남 안녕하세요, 퇴실하려고 합니다. 방 열쇠 여기 있어요.

여 네, 손님. 저희 호텔에 계시는 동안 즐거우셨는지요?

남 아주 즐거웠어요. 수영장과 스파가 정말 좋았어요.

여 말씀 고맙습니다. 결제를 도와드리기 전에, 몇 가지 확인하겠습니다.

남 알겠습니다.

여 저희 기록을 보니까 이틀 밤 지내셨고, 요금은 1박에 100달러였습니다. 맞나요?

남 네, 그게 제가 예약할 때 요금이었습니다.

여 그 외에, 어제 룸서비스를 받으셨네요, 그건 30달러입니다. 맞으시나요, 손님?

남 네, 맞습니다. 아, 그 전날 마사지도 받았어요. 그것도 제 객실로 청구되었을 겁니다.

여 네, 손님. 마사지 요금은 50달러입니다. 화면에 총액을 확인해 주세요.

* **apply to** ~에 적용되다

for the total price.

M Okay. I have a membership with this hotel chain. Is there any discount available?

W Of course. We provide a 20% discount, **but it only applies to the room charge**.

M Oh, that's fine. Here's my credit card.

남 알겠습니다. 저한테 이 호텔 체인 회원권이 있습니다. 혹시 적용 가능한 할인 혜택이 있나요?

여 물론 있습니다. 저희가 20% 할인해 드리고 있습니다만, 숙박료에만 적용이 됩니다.

남 아, 괜찮네요. 신용 카드 여기 있어요.

---

07 | 정답 | ②

여자는 법학 수업이 필수가 아니라 선택 강의이며, 한 학기에 6개의 과목을 따라갈 수 있을지 확신이 없다고 했으므로 정답은 ②이다.

* **registration** 등록
* **drop** 취소하다, 그만두다
* **have no choice** 어쩔 수 없다, 달리 방법이 없다
* **keep up with** 따라가다, 뒤처지지 않다
* **optional** 선택의
* **requirement** 필수(품), 요건

M Hey, Cindy. Where are you going now?

W Hey, John. I'm going to the registration building to see **if I can drop one of my classes**.

M What class is that?

W It's a law class, LAW 321. That's the one with Professor Kelly.

M He is one of the most popular professors here on this campus. Some of my friends **couldn't get into his class** because it was already full.

W I know. But I have no choice.

M Oh, did you get a job?

W No, I really want to **focus on school for now**.

M Then why are you dropping the law class?

W I'm not sure **if I can keep up with 6 courses**. Besides, the law class is an optional class, not a requirement.

M That makes sense. Can one of my friends take your place?

W Sure.

남 안녕, Cindy. 지금 어디 가니?

여 안녕, John. 지금 내가 수강 신청한 과목을 취소할 수 있는지 알아보러 등록처 건물에 가고 있어.

남 어떤 과목인데?

여 법학이야, LAW 321 강의. 그거 Kelly 교수님 강의거든.

남 우리 대학에서 가장 인기 있는 교수님 중 한 분이잖아. 내 친구들 몇 명은 이미 강의 인원이 다 차서 등록하지 못했어.

여 그래. 하지만 어쩔 수 없어.

남 아, 취업했니?

여 아니, 나는 지금은 정말 학업에만 열중하고 싶어.

남 그럼, 왜 법학 강의를 취소하려고 그러니?

여 내가 6개 과목을 따라갈 수 있을지 모르겠어. 게다가 법학 과목은 선택이거든, 필수가 아니고.

남 무슨 말인지 알겠어. 내 친구 한 명이 너 대신 들어갈 수 있을까?

여 물론이지.

---

08 | 정답 | ⑤

SNT 콘서트는 22일 런던에서 있었고, 관객은 6만 명이었다. 콘서트의 가격은 무대와 관객석 사이의 거리에 따라 100달러에서 300달러 사이라고 했으며, 다음 공연은 8월에 파리에서 있다고 하였으나 할인 정보에 대한 언급은 없었으므로 정답은 ⑤이다.

* **perform** 공연하다
* **incredible** 믿기지 않는
* **sell out** 매진되다, 다 팔리다
* **depend on** ~에 따라 다르다
* **range from A to B** 범위가 A에서 B에 이르다
* **log on to** ~에 접속하다

M Lucy, what are you reading? Anything interesting?

W I was just reading an article about my favorite K-pop group, SNT.

M I heard they performed at London Stadium last week.

W Yes, they **had only one show on the 22nd**.

M The concert must have been so exciting.

W Yes. I **wish I were one of the 60,000 fans** who went to the concert.

M That's incredible!

W I know. And it only took 10 minutes for all 60,000 tickets for the concert to sell out.

M That's so fast. How much were the tickets?

W It depended on how close to the stage you were. I heard the prices ranged from $100 to $300.

M Wow, I didn't know SNT was that popular in the UK.

W Yes, 140,000 fans **logged on to their website to buy the concert tickets**.

M When is their next concert?

W It'll be in August in Paris. I wish I could go!

남 Lucy, 뭘 읽고 있니? 뭐 재미있는 거 있니?

여 내가 가장 좋아하는 K-pop 그룹 SNT에 관한 기사를 읽고 있었어.

남 그들이 지난주에 London Stadium에서 공연했다고 들었어.

여 맞아, 22일에 한 번만 공연했어.

남 그 공연은 분명 정말 신났을 거야.

여 그래. 내가 그 공연장에 간 6만 명의 팬들 중에 한 명이면 얼마나 좋을까.

남 정말 대단하구나!

여 맞아. 공연 입장권 6만 장이 겨우 10분 만에 매진되었대.

남 정말 빠르네. 입장권이 얼마였는데?

여 무대에서 얼마나 가까우냐에 따라 달라. 100달러에서 300달러 사이라고 들었어.

남 와, SNT가 영국에서 그렇게 인기가 있는 줄 몰랐어.

여 응. 공연 입장권을 사려고 14만 팬들이 그들의 웹사이트에 접속했어.

남 다음 공연은 언제야?

여 8월에 파리에서 한대. 나도 갈 수 있으면 참 좋겠다!

---

09 | 정답 | ②

시속 400마일로 가고 있으며, 런던에는 오후 9시에 도착인데, 기존 도착 예정 시간보다 15분 더 이르다고 했으므로 원래 런던 도착시간은 9시 15분임을 알 수 있다. 20분 후에 간단한 간식이 제공될 것이라 했으며, 기내 영화는 그 이후에 시작될 것이라 했으므로 일치하지 않는 것은 ②이다.

M Good afternoon passengers. This is your captain speaking. I'd like to welcome everyone on Blue Star Airlines. We are currently cruising at an altitude of 33,000 feet at an airspeed of 400 miles per hour. The time is 1:25 p.m. The weather looks good and we have the wind on our side. **We are expecting to land in London** at 9 p.m., approximately fifteen minutes ahead of schedule. The cabin crew will be coming around in about twenty minutes to **offer you a light snack and beverage**. The in-flight **movie will**

남 안녕하세요. 탑승객 여러분. 저는 기장입니다. Blue Star Airlines 탑승객 여러분을 환영합니다. 우리는 지금 33,000피트 고도에서 시속 400마일의 대기 속도로 순항하고 있습니다. 현재 시각은 오후 1시 25분입니다. 날씨는 쾌청하며 바람 또한 순풍입니다. 우리 비행기는 예정보다 15분 정도 일찍 오후 9시에 런던에 도착할 예정입니다. 약 20분 후에 객실 승무원들이 탑승객 여러분께 간단한 간식과 음료를 제공할 것입니다. 기내 영화는 그 직후에 시작될 겁니다. 목적지에 도착하기 전에 다시 한번 여러분께 안내해 드리겠습니다. 그

- currently 현재
- cruise 순항하다
- altitude 고도
- airspeed 대기 속도
- approximately 대략
- ahead of ~보다 앞서
- cabin crew 객실 승무원
- beverage 음료
- in-flight 기내의
- destination 목적지

begin shortly after that. I'll talk to you again before we reach our destination. Until then, sit back, relax and enjoy the rest of the flight.

때까지 편안히 앉아 쉬면서 남은 비행을 즐기시기 바랍니다.

---

10 | 정답 | ③

민감한 치아와 잇몸에 좋은 치약으로 가격은 25달러 이하이며 크기가 작고 민트향이 나는 치약이 여자가 구매할 것이므로 정답은 ③이다.

- particular 특별한
- dental 치아의
- sensitive 민감한
- gum (복수형) 잇몸
- strengthen 강화하다
- flavor 향
  [선택지]
- feature 특징, 특성
- capacity 용량

M Good morning. How may I help you?
W Hello. There are so many types of toothpaste. I don't know which one to choose.
M Okay. Let me help you with that. **Is there any particular kind** you are looking for?
W Well, I want something that can improve my dental health. **I have very sensitive teeth and gums**.
M I see. For sensitive teeth and gums, these are very popular ones. They are also highly recommended by dentists.
W Really? They sound perfect. How much are they?
M Since they repair and strengthen teeth and gums, they are more expensive than other ones.
W Well, I don't want to **spend more than $25 for one tube of toothpaste**. It seems a bit too much.
M All right, then. They also come in different sizes.
W **I'd rather go for a small one** since I might not like it.
M Okay. This brand has two different flavors.
W I'll take the fresh mint one because I'm used to it.
M Sure. Here you are.

남 안녕하세요. 무엇을 도와드릴까요?
여 안녕하세요. 치약 종류가 너무 많네요. 어느 것을 선택해야 할지 모르겠어요.
남 네. 제가 도와드릴게요. 특별히 찾고 있는 종류가 있으신가요?
여 음, 치아 건강에 도움이 되는 것을 찾고 있어요. 제 치아와 잇몸이 아주 민감하거든요.
남 그렇군요. 민감한 치아와 잇몸에는 이런 치약들이 인기가 있어요. 치과 의사들도 강력히 추천하는 것이지요.
여 그래요? 아주 좋아요. 얼마인가요?
남 치아와 잇몸 부분을 개선, 강화하는 것이라서 다른 것들보다 좀 비쌉니다.
여 저, 치약 한 통에 25달러 넘게 쓰고 싶지 않아요. 좀 너무 비싸군요.
남 알겠습니다. 크기도 다양하게 있습니다.
여 마음에 안 들 수 있으니까 작은 것으로 하는 것이 좋겠어요.
남 알겠습니다. 이 브랜드는 두 가지 향이 있습니다.
여 제게 익숙한 신선한 민트향으로 할게요.
남 좋아요. 여기 있습니다.

---

11 | 정답 | ②

토요일 미용실 예약 문의에 대해 예약 가능한 시간은 오전 11시 이전이라고 여자가 설명하였으므로, 이어질 남자의 응답으로 ② '좋아요. 그럼 10시 30분으로 할게요.'가 가장 적절하다.

- make an appointment 예약을 하다
- opening 빈자리
  [선택지]
- clinic 병원, 의원
- overdue 연체된

[Telephone rings.]
W Jun's Hair. How may I help you?
M Hello. I'd like to make an appointment for a haircut. **Is there an opening** this Saturday?
W **Let me check the books first.** [Pause] The only time we have on Saturday is before 11 in the morning.
M Great. Then I'd like to schedule it for 10:30.

[전화벨이 울린다.]
여 Jun's Hair입니다. 어떻게 도와드릴까요?
남 안녕하세요. 이발 때문에 예약을 하려고 하는데요. 이번 토요일에 자리가 있나요?
여 먼저 예약 장부를 좀 볼게요. [잠시 후] 토요일에 빈 시간은 오전 11시 이전밖에 없네요.
남 좋아요. 그럼 10시 30분으로 할게요.

① 알겠어요. 정오 전에 오셔야 합니다.
③ 아뇨, 괜찮아요. 다른 병원을 찾아볼게요.
④ 좋아요. 이 책에 대한 연체료가 있습니다.
⑤ 미안합니다. 이번 금요일 예약을 취소해야겠습니다.

---

12 | 정답 | ④

남자가 지금 가지고 있는 신분증이 운전면허증뿐이라는 말에 가장 적절한 여자의 응답은 ④ '네. 저희는 정부가 발행한 것이면 어떤 신분증도 인정합니다.'이다.

- exchange rate 환율
- license 면허증
  [선택지]
- issue 발행하다
- exchange 환전하다

M Hello. I'd like to change 500 U.S. dollars into euros, please.
W Okay. **Did you check the exchange rate?** One dollar is worth 1.2 euros today.
M That's fine. Oh, and **the only ID I have is my driver's license**. Is that all right?
W Yes. We take any form of ID issued by the government.

남 안녕하세요. 미화 500달러를 유로화로 환전하려고 하는데요.
여 알겠습니다. 환율은 확인하셨나요? 오늘은 1달러가 1.2 유로입니다.
남 괜찮습니다. 아, 그런데 제가 가진 신분증이 운전면허증밖에 없네요. 괜찮을까요?
여 네, 저희는 정부가 발행한 것이면 어떤 신분증도 인정합니다.

① 괜찮아요. 제 차에 다른 신분증이 있습니다.
② 죄송합니다. 신분증에 사진과 생년월일이 포함되어 있어야 해요.
③ 물론입니다. 이쪽으로 오시면 당신 차를 보여드릴게요.
⑤ 안 되겠는데요. 유로를 미화로 환전하는 것만 가능합니다.

13 | 정답 | ④

마라톤 경주를 완주한 남자에게 축하와 격려의 말을 하는 상황이다. 기존 목표에 이르지 못했지만 다음에 잘 해낼 거라는 여자의 말에 이어질 응답으로 가장 적절한 것은 ④ '고마워요. 엄마가 저를 지지해 주셔서 정말 기뻐요.'이다.

* make it 해내다, 성공하다
* get injured 부상당하다
* modest 겸손한
* prepare 준비하다
* close to ~에 가까이

W You made it! I am proud of you, David. How do you feel?
M I'm so excited. I can't believe I finished the race!
W You did so well. I was so worried that **you'd get injured** during the marathon.
M Mom, you didn't need to worry. It was only a 10 km race.
W Don't be so modest. You have prepared for this race for the past two months. I know **how hard you've trained for this**.
M I didn't do well enough. I didn't even get close to the goal I had in mind.
W It's good to set high goals, but you shouldn't **be too hard on yourself**.
M Right. I'll do my best to complete the half marathon next time.
W You shouldn't **put too much stress on yourself**. But I'm sure you can do it.
M Thank you. I'm so glad to have your support.

여 네가 해냈구나! 나는 네가 자랑스러워, David. 기분이 어떠니?
남 아주 좋아요! 내가 경주를 마치다니, 믿기지 않네요.
여 정말 잘했다. 마라톤 경주 중에 다치지 않을까 걱정했단다.
남 엄마, 걱정하실 필요 없었어요. 그저 10km 경주인걸요.
여 너무 겸손해하지 마라. 너는 이번 경주를 위해서 지난 두 달 동안 준비를 했어. 네가 이번 경주를 위해서 얼마나 열심히 훈련했는지 알아.
남 충분히 잘하지 못했어요. 제가 생각했던 목표에 가까이 가지도 못했거든요.
여 목표를 높게 잡는 것은 좋지만, 자신을 너무 몰아붙이면 안 돼.
남 맞아요. 다음에는 하프 마라톤을 완주할 수 있도록 최선을 다해 볼게요.
여 스스로 너무 많은 스트레스를 주지 않는 게 좋아. 하지만 너는 할 수 있다고 확신해.
남 고마워요. 엄마가 저를 지지해 주셔서 정말 기뻐요.

① 물론이죠. 더 열심히 훈련하는 것을 잊지 마세요.
② 실망시켜서 죄송해요. 모두 제 잘못입니다.
③ 알았어요. 다음에는 완주하도록 노력할게요.
⑤ 맞아요. 다음 마라톤은 다를 거예요.

14 | 정답 | ②

엄마 생신 선물로 가족 여행을 계획하는 상황이다. 먼저 여행 날짜를 아빠와 상의해 보겠다는 남자의 말에 이어질 응답으로 가장 적절한 것은 ② '좋아. 일단은 날짜가 정해지면, 호텔을 찾아볼게.'이다.

* matter 중요하다
[선택지]
* persuade 설득하다

M Jane, we decided to send Mom on a trip for her 50th birthday, correct?
W Yes, but I think we have to cancel.
M Why? She said **she wished to travel to Europe** like Tom's mom did.
W I know what she said. But Tom's mom took the trip with her entire family. I think that's what Mom really wants.
M You think so? But I don't think I can afford for all of us to go to Europe.
W I think the destination doesn't matter. **Spending time with us is more important to her**.
M Then how about taking a trip to somewhere nearby? A place within a two-hour drive should be okay.
W That's a great idea. Since Mom loves hiking, we should head to Mt. Taebaek.
M That sounds like a good plan. Besides, this time of the year is **the perfect time to enjoy nature**.
W I know. She'll enjoy the autumn leaves.
M I can't wait! First, let's discuss the dates with Dad.
W Okay. Once the dates are set, I'll look for hotels.

남 Jane, 우리가 엄마 50번째 생신에 여행 보내드리기로 했잖아, 맞지?
여 응, 그런데 취소해야 할 것 같아.
남 왜? 엄마가 Tom의 엄마처럼 유럽 여행을 하고 싶다고 말씀하셨잖아.
여 나도 엄마가 그렇게 말씀하신 거 알아. 그렇지만 Tom의 엄마는 가족이 다 같이 여행을 다녀온 거잖아. 엄마가 진짜 원하는 것은 그거인 것 같아.
남 그렇게 생각해? 그런데 우리 모두 같이 유럽에 갈 정도의 여유는 안 될 것 같아.
여 여행 목적지는 중요하지 않은 것 같아. 우리와 함께 시간을 보낸다는 것이 엄마한테는 더 중요하지.
남 그럼 가까운 곳으로 여행을 다녀오는 게 어떨까? 두 시간 정도 운전해서 다녀올 수 있는 곳이면 괜찮을 것 같아.
여 좋은 생각이야. 엄마는 등산을 좋아하시니까 태백산으로 가자.
남 괜찮은 계획 같네. 게다가 일 년 중 지금이 자연을 즐기기 가장 좋은 때이지.
여 맞아. 엄마는 단풍을 즐기실 거야.
남 너무 기대된다! 먼저 아빠와 날짜를 정해보자.
여 좋아. 일단 날짜가 정해지면, 호텔을 찾아볼게.

① 좋은 생각이야. 근데 엄마는 그것에 실망하실 거야.
③ 일리가 있지만, 엄마를 어떻게 설득하지?
④ 물론 그렇지만, 우리가 뭘 먹을지 생각해야 해.
⑤ 그래. 엄마한테 여행 목적지에 대해 말씀드리자.

15 | 정답 | ⑤

Robert는 크리스마스에 대해 신나지 않은 Carol을 위해 무엇을 해야 할지 고민하는 상황이다. 산타가 존재하지 않는다고 생각하는 Carol에게 크리스마스의 의미에 관해 설명하라는 조언을 찾은 Robert가 할 말로 가장 적절한 것은 ⑤ '크리스마스의 의미는 다른 사람을 돕고 아낌없이 주는 거야.'이다.

* closet 벽장
* exist 존재하다
* tip 조언

M Every Christmas, Robert would buy Christmas gifts for his children and hide them in the closet. On the night of Christmas Eve, Robert would tell his children a story about Santa Claus. However, this Christmas season, Robert **notices something strange about his daughter** Carol. She doesn't talk about what she wants to get from Santa. Even when she sees Santa on TV, **she doesn't seem so excited about it**. Then Robert realizes Carol may have found out Santa doesn't exist. So, he starts to look for tips on how to tell kids about Santa. He finds a comment by another parent. It says that **explaining the true meaning of Christmas is the best way**. After

남 크리스마스 때마다 Robert는 아이들 크리스마스 선물을 사서 벽장에 숨겨 놓곤 했다. 크리스마스이브날 밤에 Robert는 아이들에게 산타클로스에 관해 이야기를 해주었다. 그러나 이번 크리스마스에 Robert는 딸인 Carol이 뭔가 좀 달라진 것을 알게 된다. Carol은 산타에게서 자기가 뭘 받고 싶어 하는지 이야기를 하지 않는다. 텔레비전에서 산타를 보고도, 별로 신나 하지 않는 것 같다. 그리고 나서 Robert는 Carol이 아마 산타가 존재하지 않는다는 것을 알아 버린 것이 아닐까 하고 생각한다. 그래서 그는 아이들에게 산타에 대하여 어떻게 이야기할지에 대한 조언을 찾기 시작한다. 그는 다른 부모가 남긴 한 의견을 찾는다. 거기에서는 크리스마스의 진정한 의미를 설명하는 것이 가장 좋다고 한다. 그걸 읽고 난 후, Robert는 Carol을 데리고 점심

- comment 의견

[선택지]
- generously 아낌없이, 후하게

reading the comment, Robert takes Carol out to lunch. When they finish their meal, he decides to talk about Christmas. In this situation, what would Robert most likely say to Carol?

Robert Christmas is about helping others and giving generously.

을 먹으러 간다. 식사를 마친 후에, Robert는 크리스마스에 관해서 이야기하기로 마음을 먹는다. 이러한 상황에서 Robert가 Carol에게 할 말로 가장 적절한 것은 무엇인가?

Robert 크리스마스의 의미는 다른 사람을 돕고 아낌없이 주는 거야.

① 기운 좀 내. 산타 할아버지가 곧 오실 거야.
② 선물 포장을 시작해 볼까?
③ 치즈버거가 어떠니? 네가 가장 좋아하는 거잖아.
④ 산타 할아버지보고 크리스마스에 집에 오시라고 할까?

---

16 | 정답 | ③

로봇은 인간 교사가 가지고 있는 인성과 능력이 없으므로 교사라는 직업은 인공지능으로 대체할 수 없다고 설명하는 내용이다. 정답은 ③ '로봇이 교사를 결코 대체할 수 없는 이유'이다.

17 | 정답 | ⑤

인간 교사가 가지고 있는 능력 중에 '지식 전달력'에 대한 언급은 없었으므로 정답은 ⑤이다.

- automate 자동화하다
- replace 대체하다
- artificial intelligence 인공 지능 《약어 AI》
- empathy 공감, 감정이입
  cf. empathize 공감하다
- pursue 추구하다
- diverse 다양한
- value 《복수형》 가치관
- creativity 창의성
- improvise (연주 등을) 즉흥적으로 하다
- sacrifice 희생
- with respect to ~에 대하여
- be capable of ~할 수 있다
- superior 우수한, 우세한

W According to a recent report, about half of today's jobs could be automated by 2055. Does this mean teachers can be replaced by Artificial Intelligence? **Human teachers have something very important** that robots don't have. It's empathy. Human teachers can empathize with students and encourage them to pursue their goals. While robotic guidance would be limited because they have no feelings, teachers help **students to follow their dreams**. Also, teachers have the ability to understand young people with diverse backgrounds and values. They have the experience and understanding to support students as they grow through childhood. And, human teachers **have the power of creativity**, which robots don't have. For example, teachers improvise and add their own stories, which makes the classes more interesting. Lastly, teachers have a spirit of sacrifice with respect to their students. Only human beings can **sacrifice themselves to help others**. Because human teachers are capable of providing greater support than AIs, I believe they will always be superior. Knowledge alone is not enough to become a good teacher.

여 최근 보고에 따르면, 2055년이 되면 오늘날 직업 중 거의 절반은 자동화될 것이라고 합니다. 이 말은 교사들이 인공지능으로 대체될 수 있다는 뜻일까요? 인간 교사는 로봇이 가지고 있지 않은 아주 중요한 것을 가지고 있습니다. 그것은 공감 능력입니다. 인간 교사는 학생들과 공감하고 그들이 자신의 목표를 추구하도록 격려할 수 있습니다. 로봇은 감정이 없기 때문에 그들의 가르침은 제한적일 수 있는 반면 교사는 학생들이 자신의 꿈을 찾아가도록 도와줍니다. 또한 교사는 다양한 배경과 가치관을 가진 젊은 사람들을 이해하는 능력을 갖추고 있습니다. 교사들은 학생들이 어린 시절을 지나 성장해 갈 때 그들을 도울 수 있는 경험과 이해심을 가지고 있습니다. 그리고 인간 교사들은 로봇이 가지고 있지 않은 창의력을 가지고 있습니다. 예를 들어 교사는 이야기를 즉흥적으로 꾸며 내기도 하고 자기 이야기를 더하기도 해서 수업을 더욱 재미있게 만듭니다. 마지막으로, 교사들은 자기 학생에 대해 희생정신을 가지고 있습니다. 오직 인간만이 남을 돕기 위해 희생할 수 있습니다. 인간 교사는 인공지능보다 더 많은 것을 제공할 수 있기 때문에, 저는 그들이 항상 더 우수할 것이라고 믿습니다. 지식만으로는 훌륭한 교사가 되기에 충분하지 않습니다.

16 ① 학습할 때 로봇과 협동하는 방법
② 로봇 교사의 강점과 약점
③ 로봇이 교사를 결코 대체할 수 없는 이유
④ 인공지능을 이용한 교실 시스템 개발
⑤ 인공지능과 인간 교사의 교육 수준 차이

01 | 정답 | ②

남자는 재고 정리 세일에 대한 내용을 고객들에게 안내하고 있으므로 남자가 하는 말의 목적으로 가장 적절한 것은 ②이다.

- loyal customer 단골 고객
- inform 알리다
- upcoming 다가오는, 곧 있을
- clearance sale 재고 정리 세일
- stop by 잠시 들르다
- merchandise 상품
- household goods 가정용품

M Hello, dear customers of G-mart. Thank you for using G-mart and being a loyal customer of our store. We would like to **inform you of our upcoming clearance sale**. The sale starts on September 13th and lasts until the last day of the month, so **please stop by during this period** to enjoy our biggest sale of the year. For those who have a membership with us, there will be flyers sent out by mail. You can check the items on sale and the prices. Most of our merchandise will have up to a 70% discount, including groceries, household goods, car parts, and so on. Thank you again and we **look forward to seeing you at our clearance sale**.

남 G마트 고객 여러분, 안녕하세요. G마트를 이용해 주시고 저희 매장의 단골 고객이 되어 주셔서 감사합니다. 다가올 재고 정리 세일에 대해 안내하고자 합니다. 할인은 9월 13일에 시작해서 같은 달 말일까지니, 이 기간에 들르셔서 연중 가장 큰 할인을 즐기십시오. 멤버십이 있으신 분들께는 우편으로 전단지가 발송될 것입니다. 할인 중인 물건들과 가격을 확인하실 수 있습니다. 식료품, 가정용품, 차량용 부품 등을 포함해 대부분의 상품은 최대 70%까지 할인될 예정입니다. 다시 한 번 감사드리며 재고 정리 세일에서 뵙기를 기대합니다.

02 | 정답 | ②

여자는 박물관 투어나 문화유산 탐방을 현장 학습의 주제로 생각하고 있다고 말한다. 나아가 현장 학습도 학교 교육과정의 일부로서 교육적 목적이 있어야 한다고 말하고 있으므로 정답은 ②이다.

- field trip 현장 학습
- relieve 해소하다, 완화하다
- go on (the) rides 놀이기구를 타다
- cultural heritage 문화유산
- curriculum 교육과정
- serve (목적에) 도움이 되다

M Good morning, Ms. Schneider.
W Hello, Mr. Long. Did you think of places **where we should go for this year's field trip**?
M Well, I have a few ideas. I think a field trip should be a day to have fun.
W Sure. We should make it fun. Through a school field trip, students can relieve stress.
M Exactly. So I think an amusement park will be the perfect place to go.
W An amusement park is not the only way to relieve stress. Students will **feel better just by getting out of class**. Besides, some students might not like going on rides at all.
M Oh, I didn't think about that. Do you have any better ideas?
W I thought of a museum tour or a cultural heritage spot in our town. The field trip is part of the curriculum so **I believe it should serve an educational purpose**.
M You are right. But I'm worried that students could get bored.
W Well, **we have to think of a way to make it fun**. That's our responsibility.
M You're right. Let's discuss it with the other teachers at the meeting.

남 좋은 아침이에요, Schneider 선생님.
여 Long 선생님, 안녕하세요. 올해 현장 학습을 어디로 가야 할지 생각해 보셨나요?
남 음, 몇 가지 아이디어가 있긴 해요. 저는 현장 학습은 즐거운 시간이 되어야 한다고 생각하거든요.
여 물론이죠. 우리가 재미있게 만들어야 해요. 현장 학습을 통해 학생들은 스트레스를 해소할 수 있거든요.
남 맞아요. 그래서 저는 놀이공원이 현장 학습을 가기에 완벽한 장소라고 생각해요.
여 놀이공원이 스트레스를 해소할 유일한 곳은 아니에요. 학생들은 교실에서 나오는 것만으로도 기분이 나아질 수 있죠. 게다가 어떤 학생들은 놀이기구 타는 걸 전혀 좋아하지 않을 수도 있어요.
남 아, 그건 미처 생각하지 못했네요. 더 좋은 생각이 있으세요?
여 저는 우리 도시의 박물관 투어나 문화유산 유적지를 생각했어요. 현장 학습은 교육과정의 일부이기 때문에 교육적 목적에 도움이 되어야 한다고 생각해요.
남 선생님이 옳으세요. 하지만 학생들이 지루해할까 봐 걱정되네요.
여 글쎄요, 우리가 그걸 재미있게 만들 방법을 생각해 봐야죠. 그게 우리의 책임이니까요.
남 맞습니다. 회의 때 다른 선생님들과 논의해 봅시다.

03 | 정답 | ④

생산성을 극대화하기 위한 방법으로 아침에 일을 처리하는 것의 장점을 설명하고 있으므로 남자가 하는 말의 요지로 가장 적절한 것은 ④이다.

- maximize 극대화하다, 최대화하다
- solid 단단한, 튼튼한, 고체
- strategy 전략, 작전
- complete 완료하다, 끝마치다
- ensure 보장하다, 확실하게 하다
- efficiently 효율적으로

M Hello, I'm Ian Baldwin, your productivity advisor. One key to maximizing productivity is having a solid strategy. So, let me ask: **do you find yourself more productive in the morning or evening**? Completing important tasks in the morning is more effective. By starting your day with crucial tasks, you can ensure you have the energy and focus needed to accomplish them efficiently. The morning is the most productive time **to complete essential tasks compared to any other time**. To make things more visual, **we'll start using a productivity chart** that breaks down our productivity by time of day. Would you like to take a look at it?

남 안녕하세요, 저는 생산성 조언자인 Ian Baldwin입니다. 생산성을 극대화하기 위한 한 가지 열쇠는 탄탄한 전략을 갖는 것입니다. 그래서 제가 묻겠습니다. 여러분은 스스로가 아침이나 저녁 중 어느 쪽이 생산성이 더 높다고 생각하나요? 아침에 중요한 일을 끝내는 것이 더 효과적입니다. 하루를 중요한 업무로 시작함으로써, 여러분은 그것들을 효율적으로 완수하는 데 필요한 에너지와 집중력을 확실히 가질 수 있습니다. 아침은 다른 어떤 시간에 비해 필수적인 일들을 끝내는 데 가장 생산적인 시간입니다. 상황을 보다 더 시각적으로 만들기 위해, 우리의 생산성을 시간대별로 분석하는 생산성 차트를 사용하겠습니다. 한번 살펴보시겠어요?

04 | 정답 | ③

여자는 그림 속 남자의 그림자가 보이지 않는다고 지적했고, 이에 대해 남자는 그림자를 추가하여 고치겠다고 말하고 있으므로 대화 내용과 일치하지 않는 것은 ③이다.

- capital letter 대문자
- review 논평, 평론
- critic 평론가
- quotation mark 따옴표
- colleague 동료
- response 반응, 응답
- revise 수정하다

[Telephone rings.]

M Hello, London Publishers. How can I help you?

W Hello, this is Lisa James calling. Is this Mr. Jennings?

M Oh, hello, Ms. James. I was about to call you so we could talk about your book cover.

W Yes, you sent the design to my e-mail address. I am looking at it right now.

M Good. I am, too. **Do you see your name at the top**? I put it in capital letters to make it stand out.

W Yes. And I also like the title under my name in tall, thin letters.

M How do you like the drawing under the title?

W **The shadow of the man is missing**. I see the cat's shadow, but not the man's shadow.

M Oh, my mistake. I am terribly sorry. I will **tell the design team to add the shadow.**

W Okay. Everything else is great. I really like that you added a review from a critic in quotation marks.

M That was my colleague's idea. I'm glad you like it. Also, I **added five stars at the bottom** to show that your book got a great response in the review.

W That's a great idea. Thank you for your hard work.

M My pleasure. I will send you the revised design as soon as I have it.

[전화벨이 울린다.]

남 여보세요, 런던 출판사입니다. 무엇을 도와드릴까요?

여 안녕하세요. 저는 Lisa James인데요, Jennings 씨이신가요?

남 아, 안녕하세요. James 씨. 작가님의 책 표지에 대해 논의하려고 막 전화 드리려던 참이었어요.

여 네, 제 이메일로 디자인을 보내셨더라고요. 지금 보고 있습니다.

남 잘됐네요. 저도요. 작가님의 이름이 맨 위에 보이시나요? 눈에 잘 띄도록 대문자로 썼습니다.

여 네, 그리고 제 이름 아래에 길고 가느다란 글씨로 제목이 쓰인 게 마음에 들어요.

남 제목 아래 그림은 마음에 드시나요?

여 남자의 그림자가 빠졌어요. 고양이의 그림자는 보이는데 남자의 그림자는 보이지 않아요.

남 아, 제 실수입니다. 정말 죄송합니다. 디자인 부서에 그림자를 추가하도록 전달하겠습니다.

여 네. 나머지 다른 것들은 멋집니다. 따옴표 안에 평론가의 서평 하나를 추가한 점이 정말 마음에 들어요.

남 그건 제 동료의 생각이었어요. 마음에 드신다니 다행이네요. 맨 아래 별 다섯 개도 넣어서 작가님의 책이 서평에서 좋은 반응을 얻었다는 걸 보여 주고 싶었어요.

여 좋은 생각이네요. 고생 많으셨어요.

남 별말씀을요. 수정된 디자인은 제가 받는 대로 보내 드리겠습니다.

05 | 정답 | ④

남자는 누나가 충전기를 가져갔다는 말을 듣고 누나에게 전화를 걸어 충전기를 어디에 두었는지 물어봐 줄 수 있냐고 여자에게 부탁하고 있으므로 정답은 ④이다.

- dry cleaner's 세탁소
- damage 손상
- theft 도난
- charger 충전기

W Jerry, have you packed everything for the school trip?

M I am doing it right now, Mom. Do you know where my light jacket is?

W It's at the dry cleaner's now, but I asked your father **to pick it up on his way home**.

M Oh, good. I really need that jacket to wear at night.

W I know. It can get cold at night.

M That's right. What else do I need? Oh, I almost forgot to **take my digital camera with me**.

W Don't put your camera in your bag. Carry it with you all the time to prevent damage or theft.

M I will. Don't worry.

W And don't forget **to take the charger for the camera**. The charger is in your sister's room.

M Are you sure? I looked in her room a while ago and I didn't see it there.

W Really? She took the camera and the charger into her room yesterday to move the photos to her computer.

M Then could you call her and **ask her where she put the charger**? I have to continue packing for tomorrow.

W Of course, honey. I'll do that right now.

여 Jerry, 학교 수학여행을 위한 짐은 다 챙겼니?

남 지금 하고 있어요, 엄마. 제 얇은 재킷 어디 있는지 아세요?

여 지금은 세탁소에 있는데, 아빠한테 집에 오시는 길에 찾아와 달라고 했어.

남 다행이다. 밤에 그 재킷이 꼭 필요하거든요.

여 그래. 밤엔 추워질 수 있지.

남 맞아요. 또 뭐가 필요하죠? 아, 디지털카메라를 안 챙길 뻔했네요.

여 카메라를 가방 안에는 넣지 마. 손상이나 도난을 막으려면 항상 지니고 다녀야 한단다.

남 그럴게요. 걱정 마세요.

여 그리고 카메라 충전기 가져가는 것도 잊지 말렴. 충전기는 네 누나 방에 있어.

남 확실해요? 아까 누나 방에서 찾아봤는데 없었거든요.

여 정말이니? 어제 카메라에 있는 사진을 컴퓨터로 옮기려고 카메라와 충전기를 방으로 가져가던데.

남 그러면 누나한테 전화해서 충전기를 어디에 두었는지 물어봐 주실래요? 저는 내일을 위해 계속 짐을 챙겨야 해요.

여 물론이지, 아들. 지금 바로 할게.

06 | 정답 | ⑤

여자는 한 통에 20달러인 페인트 3통과 5달러짜리 브러시 한 개, 7달러짜리 롤러 두 개를 구입했으므로 지불할 총금액은 ⑤이다.

- eco-friendly 친환경적인
- container 통, 용기

M Welcome to Everything Eco-Friendly. How can I help you?

W Hello. I'm looking for eco-friendly paint. Could you recommend one for me?

M Sure. This type right here is **the most popular one for painting walls at home**.

W How much is it for one container?

M They are $20 each. Would you like to see some color samples, too?

남 Everything Eco-Friendly에 오신 것을 환영합니다. 무엇을 도와드릴까요?

여 안녕하세요. 친환경 페인트를 찾고 있습니다. 추천 좀 해주시겠어요?

남 물론이죠. 바로 여기 있는 이 종류가 집에서 벽을 칠하는 데 가장 인기 있는 종류예요.

여 한 통에 얼마인가요?

남 한 통에 20달러입니다. 색깔 샘플도 좀 보여드릴까요?

	W	Sure. *[Pause]* Wow, this one is great. **I'll take three containers of this color**, please.	여	물론이죠. *[잠시 후]* 우와, 이거 좋네요. 이 색깔로 세 통을 살게요.
	M	Certainly. Is there anything else you need?	남	물론입니다. 더 필요하신 것은 없으신가요?
	W	Oh, yes. **I need brushes to paint with**.	여	아, 네. 페인트칠을 할 브러시가 필요합니다.
	M	I strongly recommend using both a brush and a roller. Rollers are better for painting a large area, and brushes are better when finishing the corners.	남	브러시와 롤러를 함께 쓰실 것을 강력하게 추천합니다. 롤러는 더 넓은 부위를 칠하는 데 적합하고 브러시는 모서리를 마무리할 때 더 좋습니다.
	W	How much are they?	여	얼마인가요?
	M	Brushes are $5 each while rollers are $7 each.	남	브러시는 하나에 5달러, 롤러는 7달러입니다.
	W	**Then I'll take one brush and two rollers.**	여	그러면 브러시 하나와 롤러 두 개 주세요.
	M	Certainly. I'll have them ready for you at the counter.	남	물론입니다. 카운터에 준비해 두겠습니다.

---

07 | 정답 | ②

남자는 누나의 결혼식과 교수의 퇴임식이 같은 날이라 퇴임식에 가지 못 한다고 말하고 있으므로 정답은 ②이다.

- barbershop 이발소
- trim 다듬다, 손질하다
- retirement 퇴임, 퇴직
- enthusiastic 열정적인
- ceremony 의식, 식

	W	You need to go to a barbershop. Your hair is so long that it covers your eyes.	여	너 이발소에 가야겠다. 머리가 너무 길어서 눈을 가리고 있잖니.
	M	I know. I was going to get it trimmed a bit later today. I want to look good for my job interview next week.	남	맞아. 조금 있다가 다듬으러 갈 생각이야. 다음 주에 있을 취업 면접에서 잘 보이고 싶거든.
	W	I see. I hope you get the position you're applying for.	여	그렇구나. 네가 지원한 자리에 합격했으면 좋겠다.
	M	Thank you. Where are you going?	남	고마워. 너는 어디 가니?
	W	I am going to the store **to buy a present for** Professor Robertson's retirement.	여	Robertson 교수님의 퇴임을 위한 선물을 사러 가.
	M	Oh, right. **I can't believe he is already retiring**. He was one of my favorite professors.	남	아, 맞다. 교수님이 벌써 퇴임하신다니 믿어지지 않아. 내가 가장 좋아하는 교수님 중 한 분이셨거든.
	W	I know. He is so enthusiastic in class. So are you going to his retirement ceremony?	여	맞아. 그분은 강의에서 너무도 열정적이시지. 그래서 넌 퇴임식에는 갈 거야?
	M	I really wish I could, but unfortunately I can't.	남	정말 가고 싶은데, 유감스럽게도 못 갈 것 같아.
	W	Why not? Is it because of your job interview?	여	왜? 취업 면접 때문이니?
	M	No. My sister is getting married, and **the wedding is on the same day as the ceremony**.	남	아니. 누나가 결혼을 하는데, 결혼식이 퇴임식과 같은 날이야.
	W	That's too bad. But everyone will understand.	여	안됐다. 하지만 모두가 이해할 거야.
	M	But I am going **to drop by his office soon** and give him my congratulations.	남	하지만 교수님 연구실에 들러서 축하를 전해 드릴 거야.
	W	Good idea. He will be very pleased.	여	좋은 생각이야. 교수님께서 무척 좋아하실 거야.

---

08 | 정답 | ②

남자는 헬스클럽의 이름이 Cal-Burn이며 러닝머신과 최신식 근력 운동 기구가 있다고 한다. 또한 무료 수업을 제공하며 회원권 가격은 3개월에 100달러라고 말하고 있으므로 언급되지 않은 것은 ②이다.

- treadmill 러닝머신
- tricky 어려운
- on-site 현장에서 (바로)
- reserve (자리 등을) 따로 잡아 두다
- trial 체험, 시험

	W	I'm looking for a gym to join. Do you know any good ones?	여	난 등록할 헬스클럽을 찾고 있어. 좋은 데 알고 있니?
	M	Oh, you should join the gym I go to. **It just opened about two months ago**. It's really nice.	남	아, 내가 다니고 있는 헬스클럽에 등록해 봐. 약 두 달 전에 막 개업했어. 정말 좋아.
	W	Okay, what's its name?	여	그래. 이름이 뭐야?
	M	It's called Cal-Burn Gym. **The name comes from burning calories**. Do you get it?	남	Cal-Burn Gym이라고 해. 칼로리를 태운다는 뜻의 이름이지. 이해돼?
	W	Oh, that's a good name for a gym. What about the machines?	여	아, 헬스클럽에 어울리는 이름이네. 운동 기구는 어때?
	M	There are many treadmills. The gym also **has the latest weight machines**. The staff is always there to help you out with the tricky machines.	남	러닝머신이 많아. 그 헬스클럽에는 최신 근력 운동 기구들도 있어. 직원들이 항상 어려운 기구를 사용하는 걸 도와줘.
	W	There are people who can help on-site? That's nice. In some gyms you have to pay extra for that.	여	그 자리에서 바로 도와주는 사람들이 있단 말이야? 정말 좋다. 어떤 헬스클럽에서는 그것을 위해 추가로 돈을 내야 하잖아.
	M	I know. Cal-Burn also offers free classes. But you might have to reserve a spot since classes like yoga are really popular.	남	맞아. Cal-Burn은 무료 수업도 제공해. 하지만 요가 같은 수업은 정말 인기가 많아서 미리 자리를 잡아두어야 할 수도 있어.
	W	I see. I'll think about that. So **how much does it cost per month**?	여	그렇구나. 생각해 볼게. 그래서 한 달에 얼마야?
	M	It's $100 for a three-month membership. Before you decide on anything, get a free trial workout.	남	3개월 회원권이 100달러야. 결정하기 전에 무료 체험 운동을 해 봐.

---

09 | 정답 | ⑤

여자는 식사비용이 프로그램에서 제공되지 않는다고 말하고 있으므로 일치하

	W	How many of you have gone scuba diving before? It's not a common experience, and our swimming center is offering you **a chance to participate in a scuba diving**	여	스쿠버다이빙을 해보신 분이 얼마나 계신가요? 흔한 경험이 아닌데, 여러분께 저희 수영센터가 스쿠버다이빙 캠프에 참여할 기회를 제공할 예정입니다. 해당 캠

지 않는 것은 ⑤이다.

- **common** 일반적인, 흔한
- **expense** 비용, 경비
- **available** 이용 가능한
- **sign up** 등록하다
- **exotic** 이국적인, 외래의
- **equipment** 장비
- **aqua shoes** 아쿠아슈즈
- **oxygen tank** 산소통
- **note** 주의, 주목, 유의

camp. Even though the camp normally costs over $500, all the expenses for the camp will be covered by our center. But this camp is only available to members who have signed up for a membership of six months or more. The camp will be at an area known as "Fish Eye" and **you can see different types of exotic fish** you have never seen in person before. The camp provides all the equipment needed for scuba diving, including aqua shoes and an oxygen tank. However, **expenses for meals are not provided by the program**, so please make note of this point.

프는 원래 500달러 이상의 비용이 들지만 캠프에 드는 모든 비용은 저희 센터에서 지불할 예정입니다. 하지만 본 캠프는 6개월 이상의 회원권을 등록한 분들만 이용 가능합니다. 캠프는 'Fish Eye'로 알려진 지역에서 이루어질 것이고 실제로 한 번도 보지 못한 다양한 종류의 이국적인 물고기들을 보실 수 있습니다. 캠프는 아쿠아슈즈와 산소통을 포함해 스쿠버다이빙에 필요한 모든 장비를 제공합니다. 그러나 식사비용은 프로그램에서 제공하지 않으므로 이 부분을 유의해 주시기 바랍니다.

---

10 | 정답 | ④

여자는 세 달 이상의 프로그램 중 특별 식단을 추가하겠다고 말하고 있으며, 주말에는 올 수 없다고 말하고 있으므로 여자가 선택할 프로그램으로 가장 적절한 것은 ④이다.

- **get A used to A** ~에 적응시키다
- **intense** 집중적인, 강력한
- **personalized** 개별화된
- **likely** ~할 것 같은
- **fill out** 작성하다

M Welcome to Always Stay Fit. How may I help you?
W Hello. I'd like to sign up for a CrossFit program at your gym.
M Okay. As you can see, there are five different beginner programs offered.
W All right. How long should I take the class to see changes?
M It depends on how hard you work. I recommend to **try it out for at least 3 months**. That's how long it takes to get your body used to an intense workout.
W I see. I will follow your advice. What is this special diet?
M Many people don't know **what to eat and what to avoid** while you are working out. So, we make a personalized meal plan for each client.
W Wow, that's amazing. **I'd like to choose a program that includes** the special diet.
M Okay, the three remaining classes are every two days, three times a week. You just have to choose the time you'll be most likely to come.
W I don't think **I can make it on weekends**.
M All right. Then, this is the class for you. Please fill out this form. After you're done, I'll show you around.

남 Always Stay Fit에 오신 것을 환영합니다. 무엇을 도와드릴까요?
여 안녕하세요. 이 체육관의 CrossFit 프로그램에 등록하고 싶습니다.
남 알겠습니다. 보시다시피 다섯 개의 초보자 프로그램이 제공됩니다.
여 그렇군요. 변화를 보려면 수업을 얼마나 오래 수강해야 할까요?
남 그건 고객님이 얼마나 열심히 하시는지에 달려 있습니다. 적어도 세 달은 시도해 보시길 권장하고 있습니다. 그 기간이 신체가 집중적인 운동에 적응하는 데 걸리는 시간이거든요.
여 그렇군요. 충고를 따를게요. 이 특별 식단은 무엇인가요?
남 많은 분들이 운동하는 동안 어떤 것을 먹어야 하고 피해야 하는지를 모르세요. 그래서 각 고객님께 개별화된 식단을 만들어 드립니다.
여 우와, 정말 좋네요. 특별 식단을 포함하는 프로그램으로 할게요.
남 알겠습니다. 세 개의 남은 수업들은 이틀마다 일주일에 세 번입니다. 가장 오시기 편한 시간을 정하기만 하시면 됩니다.
여 주말에는 못 올 것 같은데요.
남 알겠습니다. 그럼 이 수업이 좋겠습니다. 이 신청서를 작성해 주세요. 다 끝나시면 실내를 좀 보여드리겠습니다.

---

11 | 정답 | ⑤

여자가 남자에게 아버지께 선물한 사진첩이 어떻게 생겼는지 물었으므로 이에 대한 남자의 응답으로 가장 적절한 것은 ⑤ '이걸 봐. 매 페이지의 사진을 휴대폰에 저장해 두었어.'이다.

- **come up** 다가오다

W My father's birthday is coming up, and I don't know what to get him.
M How about **making a special photo album**? That's what I gave my father, and he loved it.
W That's a great idea. **What did yours look like**?
M Look at these. I saved pictures of each page on my phone.

여 우리 아빠의 생신이 다가오는데 뭘 사드려야 할지 모르겠어.
남 특별한 사진첩을 만들어 드리는 건 어때? 그게 내가 우리 아빠께 드렸던 건데 아주 좋아하셨어.
여 좋은 생각이네. 네가 만든 건 어떻게 생겼어?
남 이걸 봐. 매 페이지의 사진을 휴대폰에 저장해 두었어.

① 한 주간 더 비가 올 것 같아.
② 걱정 매 네가 보이고 싶은 대로 보이니까.
③ 미안하지만 그게 어떻게 생겼는지 난 전혀 모르겠어.
④ 사진첩을 만드는 데 비용이 그렇게 많이 들지 않아.

---

12 | 정답 | ④

남자는 목 통증을 해결하기 위해 다른 병원을 찾아봐야겠다고 말하며 여자에게 추천해 주길 부탁하고 있으므로 이에 대한 여자의 응답으로 가장 적절한 것은 ④ '목 통증을 전문적으로 다루는 새로 생긴 병원이 시내에 있어.'이다.

- **treatment** 치료
- **recommendation** 추천

[선택지]
- **specialize** 전문적으로 하다

M Ouch! My neck hurts so much.
W **You don't seem to be getting better**. Haven't you been getting treatment for a while?
M Well, maybe I should go to a different clinic. **Do you have any recommendations**?
W There is a new clinic downtown that specializes in neck pain.

남 아야! 목이 너무 아파.
여 너 나아지지 않는 것 같아. 한동안 치료를 받지 않았니?
남 글쎄. 아마 다른 병원에 가야 할 것 같아. 추천해 줄 만한 데 있니?
여 목 통증을 전문적으로 다루는 새로 생긴 병원이 시내에 있어.

① 다른 의사에게 가봐야 해. 그게 도움이 될 수도 있어.
② 물론이지. 아이들을 위한 좋은 병원 목록을 줄게.
③ 더 심해지기 전에 의사에게 가보는 걸 추천해.
⑤ 미안하지만 허리 통증을 완화하는 것에 대해 난 아무것도 몰라.

13 | 정답 | ③

여자는 작동을 멈춘 전자레인지에 대해 상점에 전화를 걸어 상황을 설명하고 나서 어떻게 할지 결정하자고 말하고 있으므로 이에 대한 남자의 응답으로 가장 적절한 것은 ③ '알겠어요. 영수증을 찾고 매니저에게 전화할게요.'이다.

* exchange 교환하다; 교환
* warm up (음식을) 데우다
* defective 결함이 있는
  [선택지]
* receipt 영수증
* refund 환불(금)

W Whoa!
M What's wrong?
W The microwave suddenly stopped working.
M Really? We just bought it last week.
W I know. I think we should **take it to the store and ask to exchange it**.
M Hmm... Can I have a look? Let's see what went wrong. What did you put in it?
W I just wanted to warm up some food. It's a glass container. I didn't put in **anything that could cause a problem**.
M Well, we have used it for a week already. I don't think they will give us a new one.
W We could try. **This microwave could be defective**.
M It could be. Let's go over the manual here. *[Pause]* It doesn't say anything about what to do when it won't turn on.
W See? Let's just **call the store and explain what happened**. They will help us.
M Okay. I'll get the receipt and call the manager.

여 앗!
남 무슨 일이에요?
여 전자레인지가 갑자기 작동을 멈췄어요.
남 정말요? 바로 지난주에 구매했잖아요.
여 그러니까요. 상점에 가져가서 교환해 달라고 말해야 할 것 같아요.
남 음… 내가 살펴봐도 될까요? 뭐가 잘못됐는지 봅시다. 이 안에 무엇을 넣었나요?
여 음식을 데우고 싶었을 뿐이에요. 유리 용기예요. 문제를 일으킬 만한 무언가를 넣지 않았어요.
남 음. 우리가 이미 일주일을 사용했어요. 그들이 새것을 줄 것 같진 않아요.
여 시도해 볼 수 있잖아요. 이 전자레인지에 결함이 있을 수도 있으니까요.
남 그럴 수도 있죠. 여기 설명서를 살펴봅시다. *[잠시 후]* 켜지지 않을 때 어떻게 해야 할지에 대해서는 아무런 말이 없네요.
여 그렇죠? 상점에 전화해서 무슨 일이 있었는지 설명하자고요. 그곳에서 우리를 도와줄 거예요.
남 알겠어요. 영수증을 찾고 매니저에게 전화할게요.

① 물론이죠. 제가 직접 문제를 해결했어요.
② 고마워요. 당신이 제시한 선택지들을 고려해 볼게요.
④ 저는 전액 환불을 원합니다. 여기 제 신용카드입니다.
⑤ 유일한 선택은 전원을 끄고 다시 전원을 켜는 것이에요.

14 | 정답 | ④

남자는 여행 중에 쇼핑을 가자는 여자의 말에 대해 시간이 없지 않겠냐고 말하고 있다. 따라서 이에 대한 여자의 적절한 응답은 ④ '할 수 있을 것 같아요. 우리가 여행 계획을 잘 짜기만 하면 돼요.'이다.

* sightseeing 관광
* confirm 확인하다
* double-check 재확인하다
* suitcase 여행 가방
* nearby 근처에
  [선택지]
* store 보관[저장]하다

M Honey, I can't believe the concert is only a week away!
W I know. I've been waiting for it for so long.
M Yes. Since the concert is in the evening, why don't we do some sightseeing in the city before the concert?
W Good idea. Oh, **did you confirm the reservation with the hotel**?
M Of course. I even double-checked that we will get an ocean-facing room.
W Great. **I am so thrilled about our trip**. It will definitely be a good time for us.
M I agree. By the way, what do you plan to bring since we are spending a night there?
W I think I'll have to bring a small suitcase. Oh, I heard **there is a big shopping center nearby**. Do you want to go shopping?
M Sure. But do you think **we can find time to go shopping**? We are only staying in the city for two days.
W I think we can. We'll just have to plan our trip well.

남 여보, 콘서트가 일주일밖에 안 남지 않았다는 게 믿기지 않아요!
여 그러니까요. 너무도 오래 기다렸어요.
남 네. 콘서트가 저녁에 있으니까 콘서트 전에 도시 관광을 좀 하는 게 어때요?
여 좋은 생각이에요. 아, 호텔에 예약 확인했나요?
남 물론이죠. 바다를 향한 객실을 배정받을 수 있는지 두 번이나 확인했어요.
여 잘됐군요. 우리의 여행 때문에 정말 설레요. 확실히 좋은 시간이 될 것 같아요.
남 맞아요. 그건 그렇고, 우리가 거기서 하룻밤을 보내야 하는데 가져갈 것은 정했나요?
여 작은 여행 가방을 하나 챙겨야 할 것 같아요. 아, 근처에 큰 쇼핑몰이 있다고 들었어요. 쇼핑하러 갈래요?
남 물론이죠. 하지만 쇼핑할 시간이 있을까요? 우리가 그 도시에서 이틀만 있을 거잖아요.
여 할 수 있을 것 같아요. 우리가 여행 계획을 잘 짜기만 하면 돼요.

① 이 도시에서 2박 3일간 지낼 예정입니다.
② 호텔에 우리 짐을 보관해 달라고 요청합시다.
③ 동의하지 않아요. 그냥 콘서트를 취소합시다.
⑤ 쇼핑몰은 호텔에서 너무 멀어요. 그냥 집에서 지냅시다.

15 | 정답 | ③

Johnny는 자신이 신입생 시절에 환영 행사 공연을 하도록 강요받는 느낌을 받았기 때문에 학생회원들에게 대신 환영 공연을 준비하게 하려는 계획이므로, 학생회장인 Ben에게 할 말은 ③ '신입생을 환영하는 공연을 준비하자.'가 가장 적절하다.

* in charge of ~을 맡아서, 담당해서
* organize 기획하다, 조직하다
* freshman 신입생
* upper-classman 선배, 상급생
* cooperate 협력하다
* be forced to-v ~하도록 강요당하다

W Johnny is a member of the student body. He is in charge of organizing the welcoming event for new freshmen at the beginning of the school year. Traditionally, they have **the freshmen prepare vocal or dance performances** for the upper-classmen and the teachers. The purpose is to give freshmen a chance to get to know each other and learn how to cooperate. However, when Johnny was a freshman the year before, he felt like he was **forced to prepare for the performance**. He felt embarrassed on stage because he did not have any singing or dancing talent. So this year, as the student in charge of this event, he wants to try something new and have **the student body members prepare welcoming performances**

여 Johnny는 학생회의 일원이다. 그는 학기 초에 새로운 신입생을 위한 환영 행사를 기획하는 일을 담당하고 있다. 전통적으로 그들은 선배들과 선생님들을 위해 신입생들이 노래나 춤 공연을 준비하도록 한다. 목적은 신입생들이 서로를 알아가고 협력하는 법을 배우는 기회를 주기 위함이다. 하지만 작년 Johnny가 신입생이었을 때, 그는 공연을 준비하도록 강요받는 느낌이 들었었다. 그는 노래와 춤에 아무런 소질이 없어서 무대 위에서 부끄러웠다. 그래서 올해는 이 행사를 주관하는 학생으로서 새로운 것을 시도하고, 학생회원들에게 대신 환영 공연을 준비하게 하고 싶다. 하지만 그렇게 하기 위해선 먼저 학생회장인 Ben을 설득해야 한다는 것을 알고 있다. 이러한 상황에서 Johnny가 Ben에게 할 말로 가장 적절한 것은 무엇인가?

Johnny 신입생을 환영하는 공연을 준비하자.

- embarrassed 부끄러운, 당황한
- convince 설득하다
  [선택지]
- resign 사임[사직]하다

instead. But in order to do so, he knows he has to convince Ben first, as he is the student body president. In this situation, what would Johnny most likely say to Ben?

Johnny Let's prepare a performance to welcome the freshmen.

① 안됐지만 난 이 자리에서 사임해야 할 것 같아.
② 환영 행사에 나와 같이 갈래?
④ 난 선배들을 위한 공연을 하고 싶지 않아.
⑤ 신입생에게 어떤 공연을 기대하니?

---

16 | 정답 | ⑤
르네상스 화가들이 그린 벽화로 시작하여 미켈란젤로의 천장화가 그려진 과정에 대해 설명하고 있으므로 남자가 하는 말의 주제로 가장 적절한 것은 ⑤ '시스티나 성당의 역사와 유명한 천장화'이다.

17 | 정답 | ④
'레오나르도 다빈치'에 대한 언급은 나오지 않았으므로 정답은 ④이다.

- historical 역사적인
- residence 거처, 거주지
- pope 교황
- restore 복원하다
- fresco 프레스코화; 프레스코 화법 《회반죽 벽에 그림을 그리는 벽화 기법》
- ceiling 천장
- reign 재임 기간, 통치
- course 진행, 추세
- artistic 예술적인
- accomplishment 성취, 성과
  [선택지]
- tourism 관광업
- collapse 붕괴

M Welcome to the lesson, everyone. Today, we will continue talking about the historical places in Rome, Italy. Look at this picture. Can anyone tell me what you are looking at? Yes, that's right. It's the Sistine Chapel, which is located in the Vatican City, **the official residence of the Pope**. The chapel takes its name from Pope Sixtus IV, who restored it between 1477 and 1480. **The fame of the Chapel is due to** the fresco interior, particularly the Sistine Chapel ceiling painted by Michelangelo. During the reign of the same pope, Renaissance painters including the famous artist Botticelli created a series of frescos on the left and right walls. Between 1508 and 1512, under the order of Pope Julius II, Michelangelo **painted the chapel's ceiling**, a project which changed the course of Western art. This painting is **one of the major artistic accomplishments** of human history.

남 수업에 오신 것을 환영합니다. 여러분. 오늘은 계속해서 이탈리아 로마의 역사적인 장소들에 관해 얘기할 겁니다. 이 사진을 봐 주세요. 보고 있는 것이 무엇인지 얘기해 줄 사람 있나요? 네, 맞습니다. 교황의 공식 거처인 바티칸 시국(市國)에 위치한 시스티나 성당이죠. 성당의 이름은 교황 식스투스 4세의 이름에서 유래했는데, 그는 1477년에서 1480년 사이에 성당을 복원한 인물입니다. 성당의 명성은 주로 프레스코 내부 장식 때문인데요, 특히 미켈란젤로에 의해 그려진 시스티나 성당 천장화에 있습니다. 같은 교황의 재임 기간 동안 유명 화가인 보티첼리를 포함한 르네상스 화가들이 왼쪽과 오른쪽 벽에 일련의 프레스코화를 그렸습니다. 1508년에서 1512년 사이, 교황 율리우스 2세의 명령을 받아 미켈란젤로가 성당의 천장화를 그렸는데, 이는 서양 예술의 흐름을 바꾸는 작업이었습니다. 이 천장화는 인류 역사의 주요한 예술적 성과 중 하나입니다.

16 ① 미켈란젤로의 생애와 그의 작품
② 로마 역사상 가장 영향력 있었던 교황
③ 로마 관광 산업의 특성
④ 시스티나 성당의 건설과 붕괴
⑤ 시스티나 성당의 역사와 유명한 천장화

17 ① 교황 식스투스 4세
② 미켈란젤로
③ 보티첼리
④ 레오나르도 다빈치
⑤ 교황 율리우스 2세

본문 **p.112**

---

01 | 정답 | ②

여자는 학교 강당의 보수 공사가 무사히 끝났고, 그것이 모두 기부금을 내준 학생들과 가족들의 후원 덕분이라고 감사를 표한 후, 개관식에 부모님과 친구들을 모셔 오라고 말하고 있으므로 여자가 하는 말의 목적으로 ②가 가장 적절하다.

- **renovation** 보수, 개조
- **auditorium** 강당
- **gratitude** 감사
- **generosity** 관대함, 너그러움
- **appreciation** 감사
  - *cf.* appreciate 감사하다
- **support** 후원, 지지
- **committee** 위원회
- **host** (행사를) 주최하다
- **opening ceremony** 개관식
- **encourage** 권장하다
- **on behalf of** ~을 대표해서

W Good morning, everyone. Today, I'm very glad to say that **the renovation of the school auditorium has just been completed**. Many of you and your families have donated a lot of money for the renovation, so I'd like to express my deep gratitude for your generosity. To show our appreciation for your support, the school committee **is planning to host an opening ceremony** next Monday. The new auditorium will be open to the public for the first time. There will be great food from local restaurants and music by the school orchestra. **I encourage all of you to bring** your families and friends to celebrate this special event. Once again, on behalf of the committee, I appreciate your support.

여 안녕하세요, 여러분. 오늘 저는 우리 학교의 강당 보수 공사가 막 완료되었음을 알리게 되어 매우 기쁩니다. 여러분과 여러분들의 가족분들 중 많은 분들이 보수 공사를 위해 많은 돈을 기부해 주셔서, 여러분의 관대함에 깊은 감사를 표하고 싶습니다. 여러분의 후원에 대한 저희의 감사를 표하고자, 학교 위원회는 다음 주 월요일에 개관식을 열 계획입니다. 새로운 강당이 처음으로 대중에게 공개됩니다. 지역 레스토랑의 훌륭한 음식과 학교 오케스트라의 음악이 있을 예정입니다. 이 특별한 행사를 기념하기 위해 여러분 모두 가족들과 친구들을 모셔 오시길 권장합니다. 다시 한번 위원회를 대표해서 여러분의 후원에 감사드립니다.

---

02 | 정답 | ④

남자는 부모들이 아이들의 휴대폰 사용 시간을 제한하고 부모의 통제하에 사용하도록 해야 한다고 말하고 있으므로 정답은 ④이다.

- **mealtime** 식사 시간
- **wisely** 현명하게
- **parenting** 육아, 양육
- **parental control** 부모의 통제

M It seems like many parents let their kids watch videos on their phones during mealtimes.
W I know. I've seen my sister do it a couple of times.
M Cell phones may be helpful sometimes, **but only when used wisely**. Don't you think so?
W I agree, but at the same time I understand why parents let their kids use their phones.
M I know how hard and difficult parenting can be. But **kids are too young to use things like cell phones**.
W I'm sure most parents are trying hard and doing their best in their own ways.
M That's right. I'm just saying that **they should at least limit the time** or let their kids use them under parental control.
W I'm with you on that.

남 식사 시간 동안 아이들이 휴대폰으로 영상을 보게 두는 부모들이 많은 것 같아.
여 알아. 내 여동생도 그러는 걸 한두 번 봤어.
남 휴대폰이 가끔은 유용하지만, 현명하게 사용될 때만 그래. 그렇게 생각하지 않아?
여 맞아. 하지만 동시에 나는 왜 부모들이 아이들이 휴대폰을 사용하게 내버려두는지 이해가 가.
남 육아가 얼마나 힘들고 어려운지는 알아. 하지만 아이들이 휴대폰과 같은 것들을 사용하기에는 너무 어려.
여 분명히 대부분의 부모들이 그들 나름대로 노력하고 최선을 다하고 있을 거야.
남 맞아. 난 그저 부모들이 최소한 시간을 제한하거나 아이들이 부모의 통제하에서 휴대폰을 사용하게 해야 한다고 말하는 거야.
여 그 말에 나도 동의해.

---

03 | 정답 | ③

허리 통증을 겪는 사람들에게 의자에 등을 기대고 똑바로 앉으라고 조언하고 있으므로 여자가 하는 말의 요지로 가장 적절한 것은 ③이다.

- **posture** 자세
- **overall** 전반적인, 전체의
- **direct** 돌리다, 향하게 하다; 직접적인
- **recurrence** 재발, 반복

W Welcome to the Pain Clinic. I'm Dr. Olivia Williams, and today I'd like to share some tips on maintaining good posture for those who experience back pain. **When sitting down**, make sure to sit up straight with your back against the chair. This will help your body feel better **and improve your overall health**. Sitting makes up most of our waking hours. This means that poor sitting posture can cause back pain. So, sit straight in the chair with your back well-supported to prevent recurring back pain. **To help you understand this technique better**, I'll be using a visual aid. Please direct your attention to the screen.

여 통증 클리닉에 오신 것을 환영합니다. 저는 Olivia Williams 박사이고, 오늘은 허리 통증을 겪는 분들을 위해 좋은 자세를 유지하기 위한 몇 가지 팁을 공유하려고 합니다. 앉을 때는 반드시 의자에 등을 기대고 똑바로 앉아야 합니다. 이것은 몸의 기분이 더 나아지고 전반적인 건강을 향상시키는 데 도움을 줄 것입니다. 앉아 있는 것은 우리의 깨어있는 시간의 대부분을 차지합니다. 이것은 앉아 있는 자세가 나쁘면 허리 통증을 유발할 수 있다는 것을 의미합니다. 따라서 허리 통증이 재발하는 것을 예방하려면 등을 잘 받치고 의자에 똑바로 앉으세요. 이 기술을 더 잘 이해하도록 돕기 위해 시각 보조 자료를 사용하겠습니다. 화면으로 여러분의 관심을 돌려주세요.

---

04 | 정답 | ⑤

교실 가운데 있는 학생 책상 위에 케이크가 있고 다른 책상에는 카드가 있다고 했으므로 정답은 ⑤이다.

M Miss Kim, we just finished decorating the classroom for Hannah.
W Wow, it's amazing! Well done, Chris. I'm sure Hannah will love this. How did you do it?

남 김 선생님, Hannah를 위한 교실 장식이 막 끝났어요.
여 와, 놀랍구나! 잘했어, Chris. Hannah가 아주 좋아할 것 같다. 어떻게 했니?

---

* decorate 장식하다
* handwriting (손으로 쓴) 글씨
* stuffed bunny 토끼 인형

M First, **we put some balloons on each side of the board.**
W Okay. Who wrote "Welcome Back!" on the board?
M Joanna did it because she has such good handwriting.
W Did she also **draw the flowers around the words**?
M Yes, she did. She said Hannah loves flowers, so she added a few.
W They are so pretty. Oh, all the presents and the stuffed bunny are on my desk!
M Yes. **We didn't know where else to put them.** Is that all right?
W Of course. The cake is on the student's desk in the center of the room. What's that on the other desk?
M Oh, it's a card. We wrote a card for Hannah.
W Is there any space left on the card? I want to write something, too.
M Sure. Here is a pen.

남 먼저, 칠판 양쪽에 풍선을 몇 개 붙였어요.
여 알겠어. 칠판에 '돌아온 걸 환영해'는 누가 썼니?
남 Joanna가 글씨를 잘 써서 걔가 썼어요.
여 글자 주위에 꽃도 Joanna가 그린 거니?
남 네, 맞아요. Hannah가 꽃을 좋아한다고 말하면서 몇 개를 덧붙였어요.
여 아주 예쁘구나. 아, 모든 선물과 토끼 인형은 내 책상 위에 있네!
남 네. 따로 어디에 두어야 할지 몰랐어요. 괜찮은가요?
여 물론이지. 케이크는 교실 가운데 있는 학생 책상 위에 있고, 다른 책상 위에 있는 건 뭐지?
남 아, 카드예요. 저희가 Hannah에게 카드를 썼어요.
여 그 카드에 남는 공간이 있니? 나도 뭔가 쓰고 싶은데.
남 그럼요. 여기 펜이요.

---

05 | 정답 | ④

남자는 교장 선생님의 승인을 받자마자 포스터의 최종본을 인쇄하려고 기다리고 있다. 여자는 승인을 받기 전 남자에게 포스터 붙이는 걸 도와줄 사람을 찾아보라고 부탁하고 있으므로 정답은 ④이다.

* final version 최종본
* correct 고치다
* typo 오탈자, 오타
* mark 표시하다
* double-check 다시 확인하다
* principal 교장 선생님
* proceed 진행하다
* put up 내붙이다, 게시하다
* available 시간이 있는

M Hey, Annie. Have you checked the final version of the poster I sent you?
W Of course. It's perfect.
M Are you sure you corrected all those typos that I marked?
W Don't worry. **I corrected every single typo**, and I had Sarah double-check it, too.
M I'm glad to hear that. Then you can send it to Mr. Williams now.
W I already did and he really liked the design. He said he would talk to the principal about it, and she would make the final decision.
M Great. When the principal says yes, **I'll proceed with printing the final version**.
W All right. Oh, one more thing. **We need a couple of volunteers** who can put up posters. Can you ask some of our classmates if they will be available?
M Okay. I'll ask them and let you know.

남 안녕, Annie. 내가 보낸 포스터 최종본을 확인했니?
여 물론, 그건 완벽해.
남 내가 표시한 모든 오탈자 고친 거 맞지?
여 걱정 마. 하나씩 다 고쳤고 Sarah에게도 다시 확인하게 했어.
남 다행이야. 그럼 이제 그걸 Williams 선생님께 보내면 돼.
여 벌써 보냈는데 디자인을 정말 마음에 들어 하셨어. 선생님이 교장 선생님께 그것에 대해 말씀드리면, 교장 선생님께서 최종 결정을 하신다고 하셨어.
남 좋아. 교장 선생님께서 승인을 하시면 난 최종본을 가지고 인쇄를 진행할게.
여 좋아. 아, 한 가지 더. 포스터를 붙일 자원봉사자가 두세 명 필요해. 학급 친구들 중 몇 명에게 시간이 되는지 물어봐 줄래?
남 알았어. 애들한테 물어보고 너한테 알려줄게.

---

06 | 정답 | ④

남자가 구매한 케이크는 30달러이며, 5달러짜리 우유를 사면 케이크를 20% 할인을 받는다고 하여 우유를 2팩 구입했으므로 $24 + $10 = $34이다. 따라서 정답은 ④이다.

* a variety of 다양한
* in that case 그렇다면, 그런 경우에
* bitter 쓴
* sweetness 단맛
* well-balanced 균형 잡힌
* carton 팩, 갑
* payment 지불

W Hello. Can I help you?
M Yes, I'm looking for a cake for my daughter's birthday.
W Okay. We have a variety of cakes over here.
M She likes chocolate very much.
W Oh, in that case, we have this white chocolate cake which is popular with girls.
M It looks delicious. How much is it?
W It is $25, and **you get a 20% discount on cakes** if you buy our milk.
M Cool. Wait a minute. I think it's too small. Do you have anything a little bigger?
W Sure, this cake is made of dark chocolate. So this one is less sweet than the white chocolate one.
M **It's not too bitter for kids**, is it?
W No, it's not. It has sweet cream inside, so the sweetness is well-balanced.
M Oh, really? Is it also $25?
W No, sir. This one is $5 more expensive than the other one.
M All right. I'll take the dark chocolate one. Oh, I need to buy milk to get 20% off the cake, right?
W That's right. A carton of milk is $5. **Would you like to buy milk as well**?

여 안녕하세요. 도와드릴까요?
남 네. 딸 생일에 줄 케이크를 찾고 있어요.
여 네. 이쪽에 다양한 케이크가 있어요.
남 딸애는 초콜릿을 아주 좋아해요.
여 아, 그럼 여자아이들에게 인기 있는 화이트 초콜릿 케이크가 있어요.
남 맛있어 보이네요. 얼마예요?
여 25달러인데, 우유를 구입하시면 케이크에 대해 20% 할인을 받을 수 있어요.
남 좋네요. 잠깐만요. 너무 작은 것 같은데요. 조금 더 큰 거 있나요?
여 물론이죠. 이 케이크는 다크 초콜릿으로 만들어져 있어요. 그래서 이건 화이트 초콜릿 케이크보다 덜 달아요.
남 아이들에게 너무 쓰지는 않겠죠, 그렇지요?
여 아니에요. 안에 달콤한 크림이 들어있어서 달콤함이 균형 잡혀 있어요.
남 아, 정말요? 그것도 25달러인가요?
여 아니요, 손님. 이건 다른 것보다 5달러 더 비싸요.
남 알겠어요. 다크 초콜릿 케이크로 살게요. 아, 케이크를 20% 할인을 받으려면 우유를 사야 하죠, 맞나요?
여 맞아요. 우유 한 팩에 5달러예요. 우유도 함께 구입하시겠어요?

| | M | Yes, please. I'll take two cartons. Here is my credit card. | 남 | 네, 주세요. 2팩 살게요. 여기 신용카드요. |
| | W | Okay, I will help you with the payment over there. | 여 | 네, 저쪽에서 계산 도와드릴게요. |

07 | 정답 | ④

여자는 남자에게 쿠키를 환불하는 이유가 엄마가 드실 수 없기 때문이라고 말하며, 쿠키에 견과류가 들어있는데 엄마가 견과류 알레르기가 있다고 설명한다. 따라서 정답은 ④이다.

- head to ~로 향하다
- organic 유기농의
- ingredient 재료
- return 돌려주다
- refund 환불
- package 포장
- contain 포함하다
- nut 견과류
- allergic 알레르기가 있는
- contact 접촉
- pay attention 주의를 기울이다

M	Cindy, where are you heading to?
W	Hey, Tom. I'm going to Lee's Bakery.
M	Oh, I know that place. It's one of the few places in town that use only organic ingredients. What are you getting?
W	Actually, I'm going there **to return these cookies for a refund**.
M	Is there something wrong with them?
W	No, there is nothing wrong. I didn't even open the package.
M	Then why are you returning them?
W	I bought them for my mom but **she couldn't have any**.
M	Is it because she doesn't like cookies?
W	No, not that. It turns out **some of the cookies contain nuts**, and she is allergic to them.
M	Oh, I'm sorry to hear that. She didn't have any contact with them, did she?
W	No, she didn't. **I should've paid more attention**.

남	안녕, Cindy. 어디 가는 중이니?
여	안녕, Tom. Lee's Bakery에 가는 길이야.
남	아, 그 집 알아. 유일하게 동네에서 유기농 재료를 쓰는 몇 안 되는 곳 중 하나야. 뭐 사러 가?
여	사실, 난 이 쿠키들 환불 받으러 거기 가는 중이야.
남	뭐가 잘못됐어?
여	아니, 잘못된 것 없어. 아직 포장을 뜯지도 않았어.
남	그럼 왜 돌려주는 거야?
여	엄마를 위해서 샀는데, 하나도 드실 수가 없어서.
남	엄마가 쿠키를 안 좋아하셔서 그런 거야?
여	아니, 그게 아니야. 나중에 보니 쿠키 중 일부에 견과류가 들었는데, 엄마가 견과류 알레르기가 있으셔.
남	아, 그것참 유감이구나. 엄마가 만지지는 않으셨지, 그렇지?
여	응, 만지지 않으셨어. 내가 더 주의를 기울였어야 했어.

08 | 정답 | ①

canopy walkway는 금속이나 나무 소재로 되어 있고, 초기 목적은 나무 꼭대기의 야생동물을 연구하기 위한 것이었으며, 높이는 수백 피트에 달하고 길이는 약 400미터까지 뻗어 있다고 하였으나 중량에 대한 언급은 없었으므로 정답은 ①이다.

- whole 전체의
- treetop 나무 꼭대기
- canopy (지붕처럼 생긴) 덮개
- walkway 통로, 보도
- trail (산속의) 작은 길
- suspend 걸다, 매달다
- wildlife 야생동물
- foot 피트 (길이의 단위로 약 12인치)
- stretch 뻗어 있다

W	Eric, what are you up to this weekend?
M	I've been busy this whole week, so I might stay home and get some rest. How about you?
W	I'm thinking about going tree hiking.
M	Tree hiking? What's that?
W	It is hiking in the treetops with help from canopy walkways.
M	That sounds interesting. Tell me more about it.
W	You climb on bridgelike trails that are suspended high in the forest. They are **made of metal or wood**.
M	Isn't it dangerous?
W	The trails were **originally built for researchers** studying wildlife in the treetops. But now people hike them to get a great view of the forest.
M	How high are those trails?
W	**Some walkways are hundreds of feet above the ground**, and stretch about 400 meters long.
M	That sounds like a huge adventure. Can I join you this weekend?

여	Eric, 이번 주말에 뭐 하니?
남	이번 주 내내 바빴으니까 아마 집에 있으면서 푹 쉴 것 같아. 너는?
여	나는 나무 하이킹 갈까 생각 중이야.
남	나무 하이킹? 그게 뭔데?
여	canopy walkways의 도움을 받아서 나무 꼭대기를 하이킹 하는 거야.
남	재밌겠다. 더 얘기해 봐.
여	숲 안에 높이 걸려 있는 다리 같은 길을 오르는 거야. 길은 금속이나 나무로 만들어져 있고.
남	위험하지 않아?
여	그 길은 원래 나무 꼭대기에 사는 야생동물을 조사하는 연구자들을 위해 지어졌었어. 그런데 지금은 사람들이 숲의 멋진 광경을 보기 위해서 올라가.
남	그 길이 얼마나 높은데?
여	어떤 길은 수백 피트 높이이고 약 400미터 길이로 뻗어 있어.
남	엄청난 모험처럼 들린다. 이번 주말에 내가 같이 가도 될까?

09 | 정답 | ⑤

디자인이 미래지향적이고, 무게가 가벼워 바람의 저항을 최소화하며, 배터리가 충전식이고 태양에너지 판이 지붕에 있다고 하였다. 좌석에는 재활용 플라스틱이 사용되었다고 말했으므로 일치하지 않는 것은 ⑤이다.

- present 발표하다
- green 환경 보호의[친화적인]
- futuristic 미래지향적인, 미래적인
- flat 납작한, 평평한
- minimize 최소화하다
- resistance 저항
- glide 미끄러지다
- push against ~에 대고 밀다
- recharge 재충전하다
- panel 패널, 판
- convert A into B A를 B로 전환하다
- solar 태양열을 이용한; 태양의

| M | Thank you for your time today. My name is Chris and I am from Solar Motors. Today, I am presenting one of the coolest green inventions, the Eco-Car. This car looks like something from the future, **but actually this futuristic design is all about the environment**. First, its light weight and flat design help minimize wind resistance. This car glides through the wind rather than push against it. Second, it runs on a battery that goes about 160 kilometers before it needs to be recharged. Plus, it has panels on the roof, **which can convert solar energy into electricity**. The radio, air conditioner, and headlights get power from them. Even the plastic used in the seats, dashboard and carpet **is made from recycled soda and water bottles**. There is no doubt that this car is green inside and out. |

| 남 | 오늘 여러분의 시간을 내주셔서 감사합니다. 제 이름은 Chris이고 Solar Motors에서 왔습니다. 저는 오늘 Eco-car라고 하는 가장 멋진 환경친화적인 발명품 중 하나를 알려드리려고 합니다. 이 차는 미래에서 온 것처럼 생겼지만 사실 이 미래지향적인 디자인은 모두 환경에 관한 것입니다. 먼저, 그것의 가벼운 무게와 납작한 디자인은 바람의 저항을 최소화하는 데 도움을 줍니다. 이 차는 바람에 대고 밀고 나아가기보다는 바람을 가르며 미끄러져 갑니다. 두 번째, 이 차는 160킬로미터를 가서야 재충전이 필요한 배터리로 움직입니다. 게다가, 지붕에 패널이 있어서 태양에너지를 전기로 바꿔 줍니다. 라디오, 에어컨, 전조등이 거기서 동력을 얻습니다. 심지어 좌석, 계기판, 카펫에 사용된 플라스틱은 재활용된 음료수병과 물병으로 만든 것입니다. 이 차가 안팎으로 친환경적이라는 것은 의심할 여지가 없죠. |

- power 동력
- dashboard 계기판
- recycle 재활용하다

10 | 정답 | ②

저가 항공사로 가고, 하루를 낭비하지 않기 위해 오전 항공편을 이용하며, 바르셀로나 공항에 착륙하고, 직항편을 타서 시간을 허비하지 않겠다고 말하고 있으므로 두 사람이 예약할 항공편은 ②이다.

- take (days) off 휴가를 내다
- at least 최소한
- book 예약하다
- flight 항공편
- low-cost carrier 저가 항공사
- full-service carrier 일반 항공사
- connecting flight (비행기) 연결편
- non-stop flight (비행기) 직항편
- lose time 시간을 낭비하다

M Laura, we're going on a trip to Spain next month. Do you remember?
W Sure. I am taking three days off so that we can stay for at least five days there.
M Great. Did you book the flight?
W Not yet. Sorry, I've been busy finishing a project at work. Why don't we book it together now?
M Okay. Do you think we should take a low-cost carrier or full-service carrier?
W Actually, I don't care. Unless we fly business class, **the service would be almost the same**.
M Okay. If you don't mind low-cost carriers, let's go with that. Do you prefer morning flights or afternoon ones?
W **I prefer morning ones.** If we take afternoon flights, we will be wasting a whole day.
M I see. Which city do you want to visit first?
W I like Barcelona. I really want to visit the Gaudi Museum first.
M All right. Then we have two options left, **connecting or non-stop flight**.
W Well, five days may not be enough to enjoy the trip. So, **I don't want to lose time by changing to a different plane**.
M Me, too. I'll make the payment with my credit card now.

남 Laura, 우리는 다음 달에 스페인으로 여행을 가잖아. 기억하지?
여 물론이야. 거기서 최소 5일은 있을 수 있게 3일 휴가를 낼 거야.
남 좋아. 비행기는 예약했어?
여 아직. 미안해. 회사에서 프로젝트를 마무리하느라고 바빴어. 지금 같이 예약하는 건 어때?
남 좋아. 저가 항공사로 가야 할까 아니면 일반 항공사로 가야 할까?
여 사실, 상관없어. 비즈니스석으로 여행하는 게 아니라면 서비스는 거의 똑같을 거야.
남 알겠어. 저가 항공사가 괜찮다면 그걸로 가자. 오전 항공편이 좋아 아니면 오후 항공편이 좋아?
여 난 오전이 더 좋아. 오후 비행기를 타면 우리는 하루 전체를 낭비하게 될 거야.
남 알겠어. 어떤 도시를 먼저 방문하고 싶어?
여 난 바르셀로나가 좋아. 나는 가우디 박물관을 정말 먼저 가고 싶어.
남 좋아. 그다음은 (비행기) 연결편과 직항편 두 가지 선택이 남아.
여 글쎄. 5일은 여행을 즐기기 충분하지 않을지도 몰라. 그래서, 난 다른 비행기로 갈아타면서 시간을 허비하고 싶지 않아.
남 나도 그래. 지금 내 신용카드로 결제할게.

11 | 정답 | ③

여자가 수영이 체중을 줄이는 데 도움이 되는지 묻고 있으므로 남자의 응답으로는 ③ '물론이야. 난 수영이 칼로리 소모에 좋다고 들었어.'가 가장 적절하다.

[선택지]
- work out 운동하다
- go on a diet 다이어트를 시작하다
- calorie 칼로리

W Matt, do you have any plans after school?
M Yes, **I started taking swimming lessons** last week because I put on some weight.
W Swimming is great. Do you think **it will help you lose weight**?
M Sure. I heard swimming is good for burning calories.

여 Matt, 학교 끝나고 계획이 있니?
남 응. 살이 좀 쪄서 지난주부터 수영 레슨을 받기 시작했어.
여 수영 좋지. 그게 체중을 줄이는 데 도움이 될 거라고 생각하니?
남 물론이야. 난 수영이 칼로리 소모에 좋다고 들었어.

① 아니. 난 밤에 운동하고 싶지 않아.
② 잘했네. 넌 바로 다이어트를 해야 해.
④ 응. 내 꿈이 수영 코치가 되는 거야.
⑤ 물론이야. 난 더 이상 체중을 줄일 필요가 없어.

12 | 정답 | ④

동네에서 영화 시사회가 열리고 감독과 배우들이 홍보하기 위해 온다는 남자의 말에 대한 여자의 응답으로 ④ '놀랍다. 나도 직접 그들을 보러 갈 수 있다면 좋을 텐데.'가 가장 적절하다.

- movie premiere 영화 시사회
- take place in ~에서 열리다
- scene 장면
- film 촬영하다, 찍다
- promote 홍보하다

[선택지]
- in person 직접

M Did you hear that there is going to be a movie premiere in our town?
W Really? I thought movie premieres usually **take place in big cities**. Why our town?
M Maybe it's because **a few scenes were filmed here**. The director and actors are coming to promote the movie.
W That's amazing. I wish I could go there to see them in person.

남 우리 동네에서 영화 시사회가 있을 거라는 거 들었니?
여 정말? 나는 영화 시사회가 보통 큰 도시에서 열린다고 생각했는데. 왜 우리 동네래?
남 아마 일부 장면이 여기서 촬영되어서 그런가봐. 감독과 배우들이 영화를 홍보하러 온다.
여 놀랍다. 나도 직접 그들을 보러 갈 수 있다면 좋을 텐데.

① 좋은 생각이야. 그럼 내가 저녁을 살게.
② 아니, 괜찮아. 난 그날 이미 계획이 있어.
③ 알겠어. 한 시간 후에 영화관에서 만나.
⑤ 오, 안 돼! 폭풍우 때문에 쇼를 취소하다니 믿을 수 없어.

13 | 정답 | ①

여자는 남자에게 결혼식 사회는 처음이니 대본대로 사회를 보고 더 연습해야

W Honey, what time are you heading out for the wedding tomorrow?
M I have to be there by noon, so I was thinking about leaving

여 여보, 내일 결혼식에 몇 시에 출발할 거예요?
남 거기 정오까지 도착해야 해서 11시 반쯤 출발할까 생각하고 있었어요.

한다고 충고하고 있으므로 남자의 응답으로 가장 적절한 것은 ① '맞아요. 당신이 말한 대로 할 생각이에요.'이다.

* head out 출발하다
* take A's place A를 대신하다
* MC 사회자
* make it 시간 맞춰 가다
* on time 제시간에
* go with the flow 흐름에 맡기다
* bride 신부
* groom 신랑
* ruin 망치다
* stick to ~을 고수하다[지키다]
* tone 억양, 어조

around 11:30.

W It starts at one in the afternoon. Why are you going there so early?

M Oh, I forgot to tell you. Jason **asked me to take his place as the MC** at the wedding.

W Really? Is he not coming to the wedding?

M He is coming, but he said he wasn't sure he could make it on time.

W I see. Then did you have enough time to practice?

M Not really. Jason gave me the script today, but he told me to try to go with the flow.

W Go with the flow? But **you've never done this before**, have you?

M No, it's my first time.

W Honey, the wedding day is very special to the bride and groom. You could ruin it by making mistakes.

M I don't want to do that. Maybe **I should just stick to the script** and practice more.

W You should. That way you won't forget what to say and when to say it. Oh, make sure you practice the tone, too.

M You're right. I think I'll do exactly what you said.

여 오후 1시에 시작이잖아요. 왜 그렇게 일찍 가려고 해요?

남 아, 당신에게 말한다는 걸 잊어버렸네요. Jason이 나에게 대신 결혼식 사회를 봐달라고 부탁했어요.

여 정말요? 그 사람은 결혼식에 안 온대요?

남 오긴 오는데, 제시간에 올 수 있을지 잘 모르겠어요.

여 알겠어요. 그럼 연습할 시간은 충분했어요?

남 별로요. Jason이 오늘 대본을 줬는데 그냥 흐름에 맡기라고 했어요.

여 흐름에 맡긴다고요? 하지만 당신은 전에 이런 걸 해본 적이 없잖아요, 그렇죠?

남 네, 이번이 처음이에요.

여 여보, 결혼식 날은 신부, 신랑에게 아주 특별해요. 당신이 실수를 하면 결혼식을 망칠 수도 있어요.

남 그러고 싶지 않아요. 아마 대본을 지키면서 더 연습해야겠네요.

여 그래야 해요. 그렇게 해야 당신이 무슨 말을 할지, 언제 그 말을 해야 할지를 잊어버리지 않을 거예요. 아, 억양도 연습하는 거 잊지 말고요.

남 맞아요. 당신이 말한 대로 할 생각이에요.

② 당신은 내일까지 대본을 완성해야 해요.
③ 내게 그렇게 경력 있는 사회자를 소개해 줘서 고마워요.
④ 괜찮다면, 당신이 내 결혼식 사회를 맡아 주세요.
⑤ 다시 생각해 보니, 그게 나에게 더 많은 자신감을 줄 것 같아요.

---

14 | 정답 | ⑤

남자가 사진 앨범을 만드는 데 함께 하고 싶다고 말하며 도울 일이 없냐고 물었으므로 여자의 응답으로 가장 적절한 것은 ⑤ '물론 있지. 사진 몇 장을 확대해 줄 사람이 필요해.'이다.

* abroad 해외로
* tough 힘든
* decision 결정
[선택지]
* enlarge 확대하다

M Cindy, did you know that Jessie is going abroad to study?

W Yes, she told me yesterday. **I am going to miss her so much**.

M Same here. When is she leaving?

W She's leaving next month. The school year starts in September, so she is going there **a month earlier to get things ready**.

M I see. Do you know how long she's going away?

W I heard she is planning to stay there until she graduates from high school.

M Wow, that's longer than I thought. It must've been a tough decision for her to move.

W I know. So, I was thinking **about making a photo album for her** to remember us by.

M That sounds great. I want to be a part of it. Is there **anything I could do to help**?

W Definitely. I need someone to get a few photos enlarged.

남 Cindy, Jessie가 유학 가는 거 알고 있었어?

여 응, 어제 Jessie가 말해 줬어. 정말 많이 보고 싶을 것 같아.

남 나도 그래. 언제 떠난대?

여 다음 달에 떠나. 9월에 학기가 시작해서, 여러 가지를 준비하기 위해 한 달 일찍 거기 가는 거야.

남 그렇구나. 얼마나 가 있는지 알아?

여 고등학교 졸업할 때까지 거기 있을 계획이라고 들었어.

남 와, 생각했던 것보다 더 기네. 걔한테 이사하는 건 힘든 결정이었을 거야.

여 맞아. 그래서 Jessie가 우리를 기억하도록 사진 앨범을 만들까 생각 중이었어.

남 그거 좋은 것 같아. 나도 동참하고 싶어. 내가 도울 일이 있을까?

여 물론 있지. 사진 몇 장을 확대해 줄 사람이 필요해.

① 응, 부탁해. 우리는 일찍 출발할 계획이야.
② 걱정 마. 앨범은 이미 만들었어.
③ 물론이야. 그녀가 거기서 너를 보면 기뻐할 거야.
④ 별로. 난 더 이상 앨범을 만들고 싶지 않아.

---

15 | 정답 | ⑤

Carol은 위층의 이웃인 Lydia와 좋은 관계를 유지하기 위해 그녀의 아들이 시끄럽게 떠드는 상황을 참다가, Lydia에게 말하기로 결심했다는 내용으로 보아 Carol이 Lydia에게 할 말로 가장 적절한 것은 ⑤ '저는 아래층에서 왔는데요. 아들을 조금 조용히 시킬 수 있을까요?'이다.

* soundproof 방음의, 방음 장치의
* peaceful 평화로운
* concentrate on ~에 집중하다
* be on good terms with ~와 좋은 관계를 유지하다
* yell 소리 지르다
* take a nap 낮잠 자다

M Carol works at home as a writer. She lives in an apartment that doesn't have good soundproof walls. Her neighbor, Lydia, has a 10-year-old boy who is very active. When he is at school, **everything is quiet and peaceful**. But when he comes home, he starts making terrible noise and Carol can't concentrate on her work. She wants to be on good terms with Lydia, but **she has difficulty working every afternoon** because of her son. One day, Carol hears the boy screaming and yelling when she is taking a nap. This time, she makes up **her mind to talk to her neighbor**. In this situation, what would Carol most likely say to Lydia?

Carol I'm from downstairs. Could you please make your boy be quiet?

남 Carol은 작가로 집에서 일한다. 그녀는 벽이 방음이 잘 되지 않는 아파트에 산다. 그녀의 이웃 Lydia에게는 아주 활동적인 10살짜리 아들이 있다. 그가 학교에 있을 때는 모든 게 조용하고 평화롭다. 하지만 그가 집에 오면, 끔찍한 소음을 만들기 시작하고 Carol은 그녀의 일에 집중할 수 없다. 그녀는 Lydia와 좋은 관계를 유지하고 싶지만 그녀의 아들 때문에 매일 오후 일하는 데 어려움을 겪는다. 어느 날, Carol은 낮잠을 자다가 윗집 아이가 비명을 지르고 소리치는 걸 듣는다. 이번에는 그녀가 이웃과 얘기하기로 마음먹는다. 이러한 상황에서 Carol이 Lydia에게 할 말로 가장 적절한 것은 무엇인가?

Carol 저는 아래층에서 왔는데요. 아들을 조금 조용히 시킬 수 있을까요?

① 정말 미안해요. 그를 조용히 시킬게요.

② 피곤해 보이네요. 낮잠을 자는 건 어때요?
③ 고마워요. 들러 주시다니 매우 친절하시네요.
④ 그는 정말 다정한 아이예요. 아이를 위해 사탕을 좀 가져왔어요.

- make up A's mind 결심하다
[선택지]
- drop by 잠깐 들르다

---

16 | 정답 | ②

여자는 나방과 나비의 차이점을 설명하고 있으므로 정답은 ② '나방과 나비는 어떻게 다른가'이다.

17 | 정답 | ④

나비와 나방의 특징 중 '알 부화 시기'에 대해서는 언급하지 않았으므로 정답은 ④이다.

- moth 나방
- gather 모으다
- mostly 주로
- tend to-v ~하는 경향이 있다
- closely 자세히
- antennae (곤충의) 더듬이
- feather 깃털
- differ in ~가 다르다
- in general 일반적으로
- dull 칙칙한
[선택지]
- have A in common A를 공통점으로 가지다

W Hello, students. Today, we are going to learn about one of the most beautiful insects in nature, the butterfly, and its similar-looking relative, the moth. **Does anybody know the difference between them**? They may look alike, but they are quite different in some ways. First, **butterflies are active during the day**, while moths are active at night. Butterflies are seen to gather food in the daytime, but moths are seen mostly at nighttime. Second, though butterflies tend to rest with their wings closed, moths do so with their wings open. Third, if you look closely at their antennae, you will see they are very different. Moth antennae **tend to be shaped like short feathers**. However, butterflies have long and thin ones. Lastly, **they differ in color**. In general, moths are duller and less colorful, whereas butterflies have brightly colored wings. Now let's take a look at some photos, and then we'll meet these amazing insects in person.

여 안녕하세요, 학생 여러분. 오늘은 자연에서 가장 아름다운 곤충 중 하나인 나비와 그것과 비슷하게 생긴 친척인 나방에 대해 배울 거예요. 그것들의 차이점에 대해 아는 사람 있나요? 그것들은 비슷하게 생겼지만 몇 가지 면에서 꽤 다릅니다. 먼저, 나비는 낮에 활동적인 반면 나방은 밤에 활동적이에요. 나비는 낮에 먹이를 모으는 것이 보이지만 나방은 밤에 주로 보여요. 두 번째로, 나비는 날개를 접고 쉬는 경향이 있지만 나방은 날개를 펴고 쉬지요. 세 번째로, 그들의 더듬이를 자세히 보면 매우 다르다는 것을 알게 될 거예요. 나방의 더듬이는 짧은 깃털 같은 모양인 경향이 있어요. 하지만 나비는 길고 얇은 모양을 가지고 있지요. 마지막으로 그들은 색깔이 달라요. 일반적으로 나방은 더 칙칙하고 덜 다채로운 반면 나비는 밝은색의 날개를 가지고 있어요. 이제 사진 몇 장을 함께 본 후에 이 놀라운 곤충들을 직접 보러 갈 것입니다.

16 ① 나비를 어떻게 특징짓는가
② 나방과 나비는 어떻게 다른가
③ 나방과 나비의 공통점들
④ 나비는 왜 날개를 펴고 자는가
⑤ 나방과 나비는 어떻게 식량을 찾는가

20회 실전 듣기 모의고사

| 01 ④ | 02 ④ | 03 ① | 04 ⑤ | 05 ④ | 06 ③ | 07 ⑤ | 08 ③ | 09 ② | 10 ④ |
| 11 ① | 12 ⑤ | 13 ② | 14 ④ | 15 ④ | 16 ① | 17 ② | | | |

본문 p.118

01 | 정답 | ④

날씨의 영향으로 인한 교통 체증과 이후 일기예보에 따른 정체가 예상된다고 말하면서 여러 분기점의 교통 상황을 설명하는 내용으로 보아 남자가 말하는 목적으로 가장 적절한 것은 ④이다.

- **head** 가다, 향하다
- **commute** 통근; 통근 거리
- **delay** 지체
- **interchange** (고속도로의) 분기점, 인터체인지
- **melt away** 녹아 없어지다
- **patch** 부분, 일부; 조각
- **black ice** 살얼음판, 도로 위 빙판
- **forecaster** 일기예보관
- **predict** 예측하다, 예보하다
- **freezing** 몹시 추운, 영하의
- **extreme** 극심한, 지극한
- **caution** 주의, 신중함
- **northbound** 북쪽으로 가는

M This is Bob from Channel 11 News, reporting to you live. For those of you heading south on your commute home from work, expect some delays around the 200 Interchange. The snowfall this morning **caused traffic accidents and severe traffic jams** at that interchange. However, the snow melted away and some reports have come in on patches of black ice on roads in that area. Forecasters predict freezing rain later into the night, so **extreme caution should be taken** if you are traveling around that area. The northbound highway looks good until you reach the 17 Interchange, but from there you **should be prepared for some delays again**.

남 채널 11 뉴스의 Bob이 생방송으로 전해드립니다. 직장에서 집으로 돌아가시면서 남쪽을 향하고 계신 분들은 200번 분기점에서 정체 상황이 있다는 것을 예상하셔야 합니다. 오늘 아침 내린 눈으로 해당 분기점에 교통사고와 심각한 교통 체증이 발생했습니다. 이제 눈은 다 녹았으나 도로에 빙판이 군데군데 있다는 소식이 들어오고 있습니다. 이후 야간에는 차가운 비가 내릴 것이라는 일기예보가 있으니 이 지역에서 운전하시는 분들은 특별히 조심하셔야겠습니다. 북쪽 방향 고속도로는 17번 분기점에 이를 때까지는 별문제 없어 보입니다만, 거기서부터는 다시 어느 정도 정체에 대비하셔야 합니다.

02 | 정답 | ④

미세먼지로 심해진 대기오염에 대해 여자는 운전하는 것 대신 대중교통을 이용하거나 운전 외에 한 단계 더 나아가 조치를 취해야 한다고 말하고 있다. 따라서 여자의 의견으로 가장 적절한 것은 ④이다.

- **fine dust** 미세 먼지
- **concentration** 농도
- **limit** 제한하다
- **bother** 신경 쓰다, 애를 쓰다
- **convenience** 편의, 편리
- **hybrid** 복합의, 혼종의
- **vehicle** 차량
- **other than** ~ 이외에
- **take extra steps** 추가 조치를 취하다
- **awareness** 인식

M Judy, did you hear the news about the fine dust? The concentration level is so high that outdoor activities should be limited.
W Yes. These days, I don't see any children playing outside anymore.
M I know. I can't believe **the air quality in our country is getting worse**.
W Me neither. The surprising part is that people don't even bother to improve the air quality.
M What do you mean?
W Well, I believe if we just gave up a little convenience, **it could really make a huge difference**. For example, we can take public transportation instead of driving.
M You are right. Driving a hybrid or electric vehicle is another option.
W Exactly. But other than driving, we should **take extra steps to reduce pollution**.
M I agree with you. I can't remember the last day I went outside without a mask.
W Maybe we should **do something at school to raise awareness** about the air pollution.
M How about discussing it with the student council to get more ideas?
W That sounds great. I'll think of something, too.

남 Judy, 미세 먼지에 관한 뉴스 들었니? 농도가 너무 높아서 야외 활동을 줄여야 한대.
여 그래. 요즘은 밖에서 노는 아이들이 보이지 않아.
남 맞아. 우리나라 공기 질이 점점 나빠지고 있다는 게 믿기지 않아.
여 그러게 말이야. 놀라운 것은 사람들이 공기 질을 개선하려고 하지도 않는다는 거야.
남 무슨 의미야?
여 내 말은, 우리가 편리한 생활을 조금만 포기하면, 실제로 큰 변화를 가져올 수 있다고 생각하거든. 예를 들면, 운전하는 것 대신에 대중교통을 이용할 수 있잖아.
남 맞아. 하이브리드 차나 전기 차를 운전하는 것도 또 다른 대안이지.
여 바로 그거야. 하지만 차를 운전하는 것 이외에도 공해를 줄이기 위한 추가 조치를 취해야 해.
남 나도 같은 생각이야. 마지막으로 마스크를 쓰지 않고 밖에 나갔던 날이 언제였는지 기억도 못 하겠어.
여 우리도 학교에서 공기 오염에 대한 인식을 높이기 위해 뭔가를 하는 게 좋겠어.
남 아이디어를 더 많이 얻기 위해서 학생회에서 상의하는 게 어떨까?
여 그게 좋겠다. 나도 좀 더 생각해 볼게.

03 | 정답 | ①

운동을 너무 심하게 하면 몸에 무리가 되고 부상을 입을 수 있다고 하면서 무리하게 운동하지 말라고 조언하고 있다. 따라서 남자가 하는 말의 요지로 가장 적절한 것은 ①이다.

M Greetings, listeners! I'm Noah, your broadcasting sports coach. As we all know, exercising is an excellent way to maintain good health. However, if not done carefully, **it can have negative consequences**. It's advisable to exercise **without pushing yourself too hard**. Some

남 안녕하세요, 청취자 여러분! 저는 여러분의 방송 스포츠 코치인 Noah입니다. 우리 모두 알다시피, 운동은 건강을 유지하기 위한 훌륭한 방법입니다. 그러나 주의해서 하지 않으면, 부정적인 결과를 가져올 수 있습니다. 여러분 자신을 너무 심하게 몰아붙이지 않고 운동을 시작하는 것이 바람직합니다. 어떤 사람들은 즉

- broadcasting 방송
- negative 부정적인
- consequence 결과, 결말
- advisable 바람직한, 현명한
- excessive 과도한, 지나친
- moderation 적당, 절제

people tend to go beyond what is expected, wanting immediate results. This excessive approach can put unnecessary pressure on the body and lead to injuries. **Remember, less is more**, and moderation is key. This is especially important if you're new to exercise. Next time, we'll talk about common exercise injuries. See you then!

각적인 결과를 원하여 예상되는 것을 넘어서는 경향이 있습니다. 이러한 과도한 접근 방식은 신체에 불필요한 압력을 가하고 부상으로 이어질 수 있습니다. 덜 하는 것이 더 좋고, 적당히 하는 것이 핵심이라는 걸 기억하세요. 이는 운동을 처음 시작하는 경우 특히 중요합니다. 다음 시간에는 일반적인 운동 부상에 대해 이야기 하겠습니다. 그때 뵙겠습니다!

---

04 | 정답 | ⑤

오른쪽에 남자가 혼자 벤치에 앉아있다고 했으므로 일치하지 않는 것은 ⑤이다.

- deserve ~할 자격이 있다
- amazing 놀라운
- close to ~에 가까이
- lamppost 가로등
- intend 의도하다
- compared to ~와 비교하여
- striking 확연한
- contrast 대비, 대조

W Hey, Gary. I heard you won first prize in an art contest. Congratulations!
M Thanks. I think I got pretty lucky.
W I'm sure you deserved it. Too bad I didn't get to see your painting.
M Oh, I have a picture of it. Would you like to see it?
W Of course. *[Pause]* Wow, it's amazing. The people in the center are supposed to be a couple, right?
M Right. That's why I drew them **walking so close to each other** under an umbrella.
W The two lampposts on the left side seem to be guiding them.
M Yes, that's what I intended. I also put trees behind those lampposts.
W Nice. I guess they are heading home because it's raining.
M Yes, and that's their house in front of them.
W Oh, **who is this man on the bench**?
M You mean the guy on the right side of the painting?
W Yes, **he looks so lonely compared to the couple**.
M I wanted the couple to show a striking contrast with the lonely man.

여 안녕, Gary. 네가 미술대회에서 1등 상을 받았다는 이야기 들었어. 축하해!
남 고마워. 운이 좋았다고 생각해.
여 너는 상 받을 자격이 분명 있었다고 확신해. 네 그림을 보지 못해서 아쉽네.
남 아, 그 그림을 찍은 사진이 있는데. 그걸 보여줄까?
여 물론이지. *[잠시 후]* 와, 정말 대단하구나. 가운데 있는 사람들은 부부인 것 같아, 맞아?
남 맞아. 그래서 내가 두 사람이 우산 아래에 서로 가까이 붙어서 걸어가는 모습을 그린 거야.
여 왼쪽 가로등 두 개가 그들을 안내하고 있는 것 같이 보인다.
남 그래, 그게 내가 의도했던 거야. 그 가로등 뒤에 나무도 그려 넣었어.
여 멋있네. 내 생각에 그들은 비가 오니까 집으로 가고 있는 것 같은데.
남 그래, 그리고 바로 앞에 있는 게 그 부부의 집이야.
여 아, 벤치에 앉아 있는 이 사람은 누구야?
남 그림 오른쪽에 있는 남자 말이니?
여 그래. 그 부부에 비해서 무척 외로워 보인다.
남 나는 그 부부가 이 외로워 보이는 남자와 확실히 대비되게 하고 싶었어.

---

05 | 정답 | ④

여자가 공항은 여행자 보험을 구매할 수 있는 마지막 장소이기 때문에 사람이 많다고 남자에게 설명하고 있다. 여자의 말을 듣고, 바로 지금 온라인으로 구매하겠다고 했으므로 남자가 할 일로 가장 적절한 것은 ④이다.

- pack 짐을 싸다
- luggage (여행용) 짐, 수하물
- confirmation 확인
- just in case 만일의 경우를 대비하여
- purchase 구입하다
- insurance 보험
- depart 출발하다, 떠나다
- meanwhile 그동안에

M Honey, **do we have everything prepared for** tomorrow's trip?
W I think so. We booked all the tickets we needed, reserved a room for two, and packed our luggage.
M I just want to make sure since we are leaving for the airport really early in the morning.
W I know. Don't worry. **I printed out the reservation confirmation e-mails** just in case.
M Great. I was just checking where to park at the airport. That way we don't have to walk far to the terminal we check in at.
W I see. *[Pause]* Did you purchase traveler's insurance?
M Actually, no. I was going to do that at the airport before we check in.
W I don't know if we will have enough time at the airport. There could be a long waiting line. **The airport is the last place you can buy the insurance** before departing.
M All right. Then I will do that online right now.
W Okay. Meanwhile, **I will check our luggage for the last time**, just to make sure we didn't miss anything.
M All right, thanks.

남 여보, 내일 여행 준비 다 되었어요?
여 그런 것 같아요. 필요한 표는 모두 예매했고, 2인용 객실도 예약했고요, 짐도 다 쌌어요.
남 내일 아침에 아주 일찍 공항으로 나가야 하기 때문에 다시 확인하고 싶었어요.
여 알아요. 걱정 마세요. 혹시 몰라서 예약 확인 이메일들을 인쇄해 두었어요.
남 잘했어요. 전 차를 공항 어디에 주차해야 하는지 확인하고 있었어요. 그렇게 하면 우리가 탑승 수속을 할 터미널까지 너무 많이 걷지 않아도 되니까요.
여 알겠어요. *[잠시 후]* 여행자 보험 들었어요?
남 아니요, 수속 밟기 전에 공항에서 하려고 했어요.
여 공항에서 시간이 충분할지 모르겠어요. 기다리는 사람들이 많을 수도 있고요. 출발하기 전에 보험을 구매할 수 있는 마지막 장소가 공항이거든요.
남 알겠어요. 그럼, 지금 바로 온라인으로 구매할게요.
여 그래요. 그동안에, 우리가 가지고 갈 짐에 빠진 게 없는지 마지막으로 확인할게요.
남 알겠어요. 고마워요.

---

06 | 정답 | ③

100달러짜리 무선 이어폰을 두 개 구매하면 전체 금액에서 10% 할인되며, 마지막에 여자가 제시한 5% 쿠폰까지 포함하여, 총금액에서 15% 할인이 된다고

W I'd like to buy earphones. Where can I find them?
M They're here in the display case, ma'am. Do you have any particular design in mind?
W **I was thinking about getting wireless ones.** They seem to be very convenient.

여 이어폰을 사고 싶은데요. 어디에 있나요?
남 여기 진열장 안에 있어요. 생각해 두신 디자인이 있나요?
여 무선 이어폰을 구입할까 해요. 그게 아주 편할 것 같아서요.

마지막에 말하고 있다. 따라서 무선 이어폰 두 개의 가격 200달러에서 15% 할인되어 여자가 지불할 금액은 170달러로, 정답은 ③이다.

* display 진열; 전시하다
* particular 특별한
* wireless 무선의
* a good deal 좋은 가격

M They are very popular these days. How about this pair? There are three colors available, white, black, and pink.
W They are nice. How much are they?
M They are $100. But if you buy two pairs, **you can get 10% off the total price**.
W That seems like a good deal. I'll take two pairs, then.
M Of course. What colors would you like?
W I'll take one pair in white, and the other in black, please.
M Okay, is there anything else you need? We also sell cases.
W No, thanks. I think **I spent enough already**. Oh, can I use this 5% coupon here, too?
M Let me check. [Pause] Yes, you can use it. With this coupon, **today you get 15% off in total**.
W That sounds great. Here's my credit card.

남 그것들은 요즘 가장 인기가 있어요. 이건 어떠세요? 흰색, 검은색, 분홍색, 이렇게 세 가지 색상이 있습니다.
여 좋군요. 얼마인가요?
남 100달러입니다. 그렇지만 2개 사시면 총금액에서 10% 할인해 드립니다.
여 괜찮은 가격인 것 같네요. 그러면 2개 살게요.
남 그러시죠. 색깔은 어떤 걸 드릴까요?
여 흰색 하나, 검은색 하나로 할게요.
남 알겠습니다. 더 필요하신 것이 있으신가요? 케이스도 판매합니다.
여 괜찮아요. 이미 돈을 많이 쓴 것 같아요. 아, 이 5% 할인 쿠폰 여기서 쓸 수 있나요?
남 확인해 볼게요. [잠시 후] 네, 쓰실 수 있어요. 이 쿠폰으로 오늘 총 15% 할인받으실 수 있습니다.
여 좋네요. 여기 제 신용 카드예요.

---

07 | 정답 | ⑤

오디션을 보라고 제안하는 여자에게 남자는 같은 시간에 출장에서 돌아오는 아빠를 마중하기 위해 공항에 가야 한다고 말했으므로 정답은 ⑤이다.

* sign up for ~을 신청하다
* make it 시간 맞춰 가다
* appointment 예약, 약속
* how come 왜, 어찌하여
* be supposed to-v ~하기로 되어 있다

W Patrick, the community center will have an audition for a play. You should sign up for it.
M That's great news. I have wanted to act in another play for a while. **When is the audition being held**?
W The audition is this Saturday at 4 p.m.
M At 4 p.m.? I don't think I can make it.
W Oh, is it because of your dentist appointment?
M **The appointment is in the morning**, and it won't take long.
W Then how come you have to miss it?
M I'm going to the airport with my mom and sister. My dad is coming home from a business trip, and **his flight is supposed to arrive at 4 p.m.**
W I see. It would've been nice to see you acting again. It's been a while **since I've seen you in a play**.
M Thanks. I hope I have the chance to act again soon.

여 Patrick, 우리 지역 센터에서 연극 오디션이 있을 거야. 너도 오디션에 참가 신청하는 게 좋을 것 같아.
남 좋은 소식이네. 한동안 다른 연극에 출연하고 싶었거든. 오디션은 언제 열리니?
여 오디션은 이번 토요일 오후 4시야.
남 오후 4시? 나는 참가할 수 없을 것 같아.
여 아, 치과 예약 때문이니?
남 치과 가는 것은 오전이고 오래 걸리지 않을 거야.
여 그럼 왜 참가하지 못하니?
남 엄마, 누나랑 같이 공항에 가야 해. 아빠가 출장에서 돌아오시는데, 비행기가 오후 4시에 도착 예정이야.
여 그렇구나. 네가 다시 연기하는 걸 보면 참 좋을 텐데. 네가 연극에 나오는 걸 못 본 지가 꽤 되었잖아.
남 고마워. 나도 곧 다시 연기할 기회가 생겼으면 좋겠어.

---

08 | 정답 | ③

송별회에 관하여 이번 주 토요일에 학교에서 먼저 만나서 예약한 한식당을 갈 것이라 설명하였으며, 식사와 선물을 위한 회비는 인당 20달러라고 언급하였다. 따라서 언급되지 않은 것은 ③이다.

* farewell 송별, 작별
* debate 토론
* in advance 미리

W Jack, would you like to come to a farewell party for Jane this Saturday? She is going back to Switzerland next Monday.
M Of course I will.
W Great. This is a farewell party for our debate club members. I already made a reservation at a restaurant.
M Okay, what are we going to do at the party?
W Well, first, **we will meet at our school** at 9 a.m. to take some photos. And then we will go to **the restaurant where we had dinner** last month.
M Ah, that Korean restaurant! Great.
W You **should pay your share** in advance. It's for the meal and some special gifts for Jane.
M Okay, how much is it?
W It's $20. Would that be okay?
M Of course. I'll bring the money tomorrow.

여 Jack, 너 이번 토요일에 Jane을 위한 송별회에 올 수 있니? Jane이 다음 주 월요일에 스위스로 돌아가거든.
남 물론 갈게.
여 좋아. 이건 우리 토론 동아리 회원들을 위한 송별회야. 이미 음식점 예약을 했어.
남 알았어, 송별회 때 뭐 할 거니?
여 아, 우선 오전 9시에 학교에서 만나서 사진을 찍을 거야. 그리고 나서 우리가 지난달에 저녁 식사를 했던 식당으로 갈 거야.
남 아, 그 한식당! 좋아.
여 미리 네 몫을 내야 돼. 식사하고 Jane에게 줄 특별 선물 때문이야.
남 알았어, 얼마야?
여 20달러야. 괜찮겠니?
남 물론이지. 내일 돈 가지고 올게.

---

09 | 정답 | ②

아마존 열대 우림은 지구 전체 산소의 20%를 만들어내며 화재는 지난해보다 80% 늘었고, 이 화재는 온실가스 배출로 이어지며 아마존 열대 우림 보호 집회는 이번 주말에 열릴 것이라고 설명한다. 인공위성 데이터에 따르면 1,750건의 화재가 진행 중이라고 했다. 산불

W Hello, everyone. I'm Sandy Jones, representative of the Youth Amazon Watch. I'm here to tell you about the Amazon rainforest. **The Amazon generates 20% of the oxygen on Earth** so it is sometimes called the "lungs of the planet." However, **it has been on fire** for a few months. The satellite data shows that more than 1,750 fires have been active in the area. There has been an 80% increase

여 여러분 안녕하세요. Youth Amazon Watch 대표 Sandy Jones입니다. 저는 아마존 열대 우림에 대한 말씀을 드리려고 이 자리에 섰습니다. 아마존은 지구의 산소 중 20%를 만들어 내기 때문에 종종 '지구의 허파'로 불리기도 합니다. 그러나 이 아마존에 몇 달간 화재가 나고 있습니다. 인공위성 데이터는 그 지역에서 1,750건이 넘는 화재가 진행되고 있다는 걸 보여줍니다. 지난해보다 80%가 늘어난 수치입니다. 화재는 아마존 파괴를 촉진하고 온실가스 배출의 원인이 되지요. 이

을 진화했다는 내용은 상반되는 내용이므로 일치하지 않는 것은 ②이다.

* representative 대표
* rainforest 열대 우림
* generate 생성하다
* oxygen 산소
* lung 허파, 폐
* planet 행성
* satellite (인공)위성
* contribute to ~에 기여하다
* destruction 파괴
* emission 배출
* crisis 위기
* urgent 급박한
* rally 집회, 시위
* aware of ~을 인식하는

from last year. **Fires contribute to the destruction of the Amazon** and cause greenhouse gas emissions. **This only worsens the climate crisis**. Due to this urgent situation, we are planning to hold an Amazon Protection Rally at the City Hall Plaza this weekend. The rally is **to make people aware of the importance of protecting** the Amazon rainforest. I ask for your participation and strong support.

것은 기후 위기를 악화시키기만 합니다. 이러한 위급한 상황 때문에, 저희가 시청 광장에서 이번 주말에 아마존 보호 집회를 열 계획입니다. 그 집회는 사람들이 아마존 열대 우림을 보호하는 일의 중요성을 인식하게 하기 위함입니다. 여러분의 참여와 적극적인 지원을 부탁드립니다.

---

10 | 정답 | ④

여자가 구입하려는 믹싱 볼은 스테인리스 재질의 뚜껑이 있는 중간 크기의 믹싱 볼이며 뚜껑 때문에 30달러 넘게 쓸 수밖에 없다고 말하고 있으므로 가격이 40달러인 ④가 정답이다.

* a variety of 다양한, 여러 가지의
* preference 선호
* material 재질
* dishwasher 식기세척기
* take up (공간을) 차지하다
* lid 뚜껑
* have no choice but to-v ~할 수밖에 없다

M Welcome to Kay's Kitchen. How may I help you?
W Hello. I'm looking for mixing bowls.
M Oh, we have a large variety of mixing bowls. This way, please. **Do you have a preference for any material?** We have plastic and stainless bowls.
W **I don't want a plastic one** because they cannot be cleaned in a dishwasher.
M I see. They usually come in three different sizes. What size are you looking for?
W Well, I was thinking about a medium bowl. **Large ones take up too much space**.
M Okay, then do you prefer to have one with or without a lid?
W I prefer one with a lid.
M The one with a lid is $10 more expensive than the one without. Is that all right?
W I didn't want to spend more than $30, but I guess **I have no choice but to do that**.
M Good choice. The lid is good for keeping food fresh.

남 Kay's Kitchen에 오신 걸 환영합니다. 어떻게 도와드릴까요?
여 안녕하세요. 믹싱 볼을 찾고 있는데요.
남 아, 저희는 아주 다양한 믹싱 볼이 있어요. 이쪽으로 오세요. 선호하시는 재질이 있나요? 플라스틱과 스테인리스가 있는데요.
여 식기세척기로 세척할 수 없어서 플라스틱은 원하지 않아요.
남 그렇군요. 크기는 보통 세 가지로 나오는데요, 어떤 크기를 찾으세요?
여 음, 중간 크기를 생각하고 있었어요. 큰 것은 자리를 너무 많이 차지해서요.
남 알겠습니다. 그럼 뚜껑이 있는 것 아니면 없는 것을 선호하시나요?
여 뚜껑이 있는 게 더 좋아요.
남 뚜껑이 있는 것은 없는 것보다 10달러 더 비싸요. 괜찮으세요?
여 30달러 넘게 쓰고 싶지 않았지만, 그렇게 할 수밖에 없을 것 같네요.
남 좋은 선택이에요. 뚜껑은 음식을 신선하게 보관하는 데 좋아요.

---

11 | 정답 | ①

수학을 어려워하는 여자에게 도움을 제안하는 남자의 마지막 말에 대한 여자의 응답으로 가장 적절한 것은 ① '그래, 부탁할게. 너는 정말 친절하구나.'이다.

[선택지]
* relieved 안심한, 안도한
* You can say that again. 네 말이 맞아.
* a piece of cake 쉬운 일, 식은 죽 먹기

M What are you going to do during the winter vacation?
W I'm going to take a course in math. **Math is so hard for me**.
M Really? I thought you were quite good at it. **Do you want me to help you**?
W Yes, please. That is really kind of you.

남 겨울 방학 동안에 뭐 할 거니?
여 나는 수학 강의를 들을 거야. 나한테는 수학이 너무 어렵거든.
남 그래? 나는 네가 수학을 꽤 잘한다고 생각했어. 내가 좀 도와줄까?
여 그래, 부탁할게. 너는 정말 친절하구나.

② 그래, 그렇지만 나는 가끔 안심하게 돼.
③ 네 말이 맞아. 수학은 정말 식은 죽 먹기야.
④ 잠깐만. 너 수학 선생님 알아?
⑤ 왜? 너는 이미 똑같은 온라인 강의를 들었잖아.

---

12 | 정답 | ⑤

짝이 맞지 않는 양말을 신어서 당황했다는 여자의 마지막 말에 남자가 위로의 말을 전하는 상황이다. 따라서 남자의 응답으로 가장 적절한 것은 ⑤ '걱정하지 마. 아무도 알아채지 못했어.'이다.

* embarrassed 당황한
* mismatched 짝이 맞지 않는
[선택지]
* refund 환불(금)
* notice 알아차리다

W **I was so embarrassed** when I attended the staff meeting this morning.
M Why? What happened?
W **I was wearing mismatched socks**. I didn't realize until the end of the meeting!
M Don't worry. Nobody noticed.

여 나 오늘 아침에 직원회의 갔다가 무척 당황했어.
남 왜? 무슨 일 있었어?
여 내가 짝이 맞지 않는 양말을 신고 있었어. 나는 회의 끝날 때까지 몰랐어!
남 걱정하지 마. 아무도 알아채지 못했어.

① 음, 그 양말 어디서 샀는데?
② 정말 안됐다. 너는 의사 만나보는 게 낫겠어.
③ 네가 별문제 없이 환불받을 수 있다고 확신해.
④ 절대로 다시는 회의에 늦지 않을게.

13 | 정답 | ②

긴 여행 일정으로 호텔에서 머물겠다고 말하는 여자에게 남자가 게스트 하우스의 이점에 관해 설명하는 내용이다. 여행은 사람들을 만나면서 다른 문화를 경험하는 것이라는 남자의 의견을 듣고 여자가 게스트 하우스에 머물겠다고 결정하는 상황에서 가장 적절한 여자의 응답은 ② '좋아. 어차피 호텔은 돈이 너무 드니까.'이다.

* overseas 해외로; 해외의
* be done with ~을 마치다
* accommodation 숙소
* option 선택, 방안
* explore 탐험하다
* regret 후회하다
  [선택지]
* rush 바삐 서둘러야 하는 상황

M Mary, are you taking a trip overseas this vacation?
W Yes, I'm going to go to France.
M Wow, that sounds like fun. How long are you going for?
W I'm going away for two weeks. **I'm almost done with planning**. I haven't booked my accommodation yet, but I'm thinking about staying at a hotel.
M Why don't you stay at a guesthouse? You like to make friends with people from other countries.
W I know, but **a hotel would be a better option** than a guesthouse because it'll be a long trip.
M Sure, hotels can be really convenient and **you need a good rest during a trip**. I just think it'll be a great chance to meet people and experience different cultures.
W You're right. Traveling abroad is about **exploring and enjoying yourself as much as you can**.
M Exactly. You won't regret it.
W Okay. Hotels cost too much money, anyway.

남 Mary, 이번 방학에 해외여행 가니?
여 응, 프랑스로 갈 거야.
남 와, 재미있겠구나. 얼마나 오래 있을 거니?
여 2주 동안 갈 거야. 계획은 거의 다 세웠어. 숙소는 아직 예약하지 않았는데 호텔에 묵을까 생각하고 있어.
남 게스트 하우스에 머무는 것이 어때? 너는 다른 나라 사람들과 친구 맺는 거 좋아하잖아.
여 맞아. 그렇지만 긴 여행이라서 호텔이 게스트 하우스보단 더 나은 선택이 될 거야.
남 물론, 호텔은 아주 편리할 수 있고 너는 여행 중에 충분히 쉬어야 하지. 다만 사람들을 만나고 다른 문화를 경험하는 좋은 기회가 될 것 같아.
여 네 말이 맞아. 해외여행은 탐험하면서 최대한 많이 즐기는 것과도 같지.
남 바로 그거야. 너는 후회하지 않을 거야.
여 좋아. 어차피 호텔은 돈이 너무 드니까.

① 걱정하지 마. 내가 직접 해결할 수 있어.
③ 이해를 못 하겠어. 그게 무슨 뜻이니?
④ 왜 그렇게 서둘러? 그것에 대해 좀 더 이야기해야 해.
⑤ 그렇게 하지 마. 너는 내 말을 이해하게 될 거야.

14 | 정답 | ④

실수로 짜게 만든 불고기를 어떻게 할지 모르겠다고 말하는 여자에게 남자가 이것을 고칠 방법이 있다고 말하고 있다. 따라서 가장 적절한 남자의 응답으로는 짜게 된 음식을 해결하는 방법이 언급되는 ④ '물을 좀 넣어서 덜 짜게 하면 되지요.'이다.

* recipe 요리법
* grill 굽다
* salty 짠
* soy sauce 간장
* refrigerator 냉장고
  [선택지]
* instructor 강사
* means 수단

M I'm home, honey. What are you cooking?
W Come on in. Remember the bulgogi we ate at the Seoul Food Festival? It was really delicious, wasn't it?
M Sure, it was. So, is that what you are making?
W Yes, I wanted to make it after **I learned the recipe from an online cooking class**. Here, try some.
M All right. [Pause] Hmm...
W Well, is it all right? What do you think?
M It's not bad, but I think **it is a little salty for me**.
W Oh, no. I was afraid you'd say that.
M I think **you added too much soy sauce to it**.
W Really? There's more bulgogi in the refrigerator. What should I do with it?
M No problem, honey. We can fix it.
W How can we do that?
M You can add some water to make it less salty.

남 집에 왔어요, 여보. 무슨 요리를 하고 있어요?
여 어서 와요. 당신 우리가 서울 음식 축제에서 먹었던 불고기 기억하지요? 정말 맛있었죠, 그렇지 않아요?
남 정말 맛있었지요. 그래서 그걸 만들고 있는 건가요?
여 네, 온라인 요리 교실에서 요리법을 배워서 만들어 보고 싶었어요. 여기, 좀 먹어 보세요.
남 알았어요. [잠시 후] 음…
여 괜찮아요? 어때요?
남 나쁘지는 않은데 저한테는 조금 짠 것 같아요.
여 아, 이런. 당신이 그렇게 말하지 않을까 걱정했어요.
남 간장을 너무 많이 넣은 것 같아요.
여 정말요? 냉장고에 불고기가 아직 더 있어요. 그걸 어떻게 해야 할까요?
남 걱정하지 말아요, 여보. 고치면 되지요.
여 어떻게 하면 될까요?
남 물을 좀 넣어서 덜 짜게 하면 되지요.

① 음. 요리 강사 선생님이 그렇게 하라고 말했어요.
② 그렇게 생각해요. 우리가 그렇게 할 방법이 없어요.
③ 네, 당신이 맞아요. 그렇게 합시다.
⑤ 우리 온라인 요리 교실에 등록하는 게 좋겠어요.

15 | 정답 | ④

Jason이 그동안 같이 일했던 Lisa의 도움으로 승진하게 되어 감사의 표시로 점심을 사 주고 싶어 하는 상황이다. 따라서 Jason이 Lisa에게 할 말로 가장 적절한 것은 ④ '오늘 점심으로 뭘 드시고 싶어요? 제가 사겠습니다.'이다.

* co-worker 직장 동료
* boss 상사
* promote 승진시키다
  cf. promotion 승진, 진급
* transfer 이동하다, 옮기다
* department 부서
* congratulate 축하하다
* accomplish 완수하다, 성취하다
* treat 대접(하다), 한턱(내다)
* appreciation 감사

M Jason and Lisa are co-workers. They have worked on several projects together as a team. Today their boss calls them into his office for the first time. He tells them **they both are promoted to managers** for their hard work, but one of them has to be transferred to a different department. Jason and Lisa get excited at first, but then realize that from now on, they won't be able to work together. As they leave the meeting with their boss, they congratulate each other on their promotions. Jason feels that **he has accomplished many things** because of Lisa's support. So, to celebrate, he wants **to treat Lisa to lunch** to show his appreciation for her help. In this situation, what would Jason most likely say to Lisa?

Jason What do you want for lunch today? It's my treat.

남 Jason과 Lisa는 직장 동료이다. 그들은 한 팀으로 여러 가지 프로젝트를 함께 해 왔다. 오늘 그들의 상사가 처음으로 그들을 자기 사무실로 불렀다. 그는 그들이 둘 다 열심히 근무해서 매니저로 승진하게 되었는데, 그들 중 한 사람은 다른 부서로 이동해야 한다고 말한다. Jason과 Lisa는 처음에는 기분이 좋았지만 이제부터는 함께 일할 수 없다는 것을 깨닫는다. 그들은 상사와 회의를 끝내고 나와서, 승진한 것에 대해서 서로 축하한다. Jason은 Lisa의 도움으로 자신이 많은 것을 이루었다고 생각한다. 그래서 그는 축하하기 위해 Lisa가 자신을 도와준 것에 대한 감사 표시로 그녀에게 점심을 대접하기를 원한다. 이러한 상황에서 Jason이 Lisa에게 할 말로 가장 적절한 것은 무엇인가?

Jason 오늘 점심으로 뭘 드시고 싶어요? 제가 사겠습니다.

① 아주 배불러요. 점심 먹으러 갈 수 없을 것 같아요.
② 드디어 회의가 끝나서 기뻐요.
③ 커피 마시러 가는 길입니다. 한 잔 갖다 드릴까요?
⑤ 마감 시간이 다가오고 있어요. 다시 일합시다.

16 | 정답 | ①

외향적인 사람들이 친절하고 사교적이기만 한 것은 아니라고 하면서, 실제로는 사람들과 같이 일하는 것을 즐거워하지만 어떤 상황에서는 덜 사교적이거나 조용하고 심지어 부끄러움도 탄다고 설명하는 내용으로 보아 여자가 하는 말의 주제로 가장 적절한 것은 ① '외향적인 사람의 실제 모습'이다.

17 | 정답 | ②

외향적인 사람의 성격으로는 '신중한'은 언급되지 않았으므로 정답은 ②이다.

* extrovert 외향적인 사람
* outgoing 사교적인, 활동적인
* energize 활기를 북돋우다
* A rather than B B보다는 A
* chance 가능성
* degree 정도
* vary 다르다
* circumstance 상황, 정황
* surprisingly 놀랍게도
* immediately 즉시
* brighten up 밝아지다
* crave 열망[갈망]하다
* company 사람들의 모임, 동행
* interaction 상호작용, 교류
  [선택지]
* personality 성격, 인격
* misconception 오해
* overcome 극복하다
* trait 특질, 특성

W Would you call yourself an extrovert? Most people believe that extroverts are friendly and outgoing. While that may be true, that is not the full meaning. An extrovert is a person **who is energized by being around other people**. If you enjoy working on a team project or in a study group rather than working alone, the chances are high that you are extroverted. However, while extroverts can be very quick **to start a conversation with others and make new friends**, the degree of such behavior varies more within a person than between people. It means that extroverts are strongly social in some circumstances and less in other situations. Surprisingly, **they may be quiet**, too. Once they're around others, they may immediately brighten up. Another thing that many people don't realize is that **an extrovert can also be shy**. Though extroverts really do crave company, the shyness can make it difficult to succeed in interactions with people they don't know.

여 당신은 자신을 외향적인 사람이라고 생각합니까? 대부분의 사람들은 외향적인 사람들이 친절하고 사교적이라고 생각합니다. 그것은 사실일 수도 있지만 그게 전부는 아닙니다. 외향적인 사람은 다른 사람들과 함께 있을 때 기운이 나는 사람입니다. 만약 당신이 혼자 일할 때보다 팀 프로젝트를 하거나 스터디 그룹에서 일하기를 좋아한다면, 당신은 외향성일 가능성이 높습니다. 외향적인 사람들이 빠르게 다른 이들과 대화를 시작하고 친하게 지낼 수 있기는 하지만, 다른 사람들 사이에서보다 그 사람 내적으로 그 행동의 정도가 다릅니다. 그것은 외향적인 사람들이 어떤 상황일 때는 굉장히 사교적이다가도 또 다른 어떤 상황에서는 그 정도가 덜 하다는 걸 의미합니다. 놀랍게도 그들은 말이 없을 때도 있습니다. 일단 다른 사람들과 있게 되면 즉시 표정이 밝아질 수도 있습니다. 많은 사람들이 인식하지 못하는 또 한 가지는 외향적인 사람들도 수줍어할 수 있다는 것입니다. 외향적인 사람들은 여러 사람들과 함께 있는 것을 열망하지만, 수줍음 때문에 자신들이 알지 못하는 사람들과 어울리는 것을 어려워할 수도 있습니다.

16 ① 외향적인 사람의 실제 모습
② 성격을 바꾸는 방법
③ 내향적인 사람에 대한 오해
④ 소극적인 성격 특성을 극복하는 방법
⑤ 내향적인 사람과 외향적인 사람의 차이

17 ① 외향적인 ② 신중한 ③ 사교적인
④ 조용한 ⑤ 수줍어하는

01 | 정답 | ②

여자는 모인 사람들에게 세미나가 세 부분으로 나눠지고 어떤 내용이 진행되는지에 대해 설명하고 있으므로 여자가 하는 말의 목적으로 ②가 가장 적절하다.

- customer satisfaction 고객 만족
- hand out 나눠주다
- define 정의를 내리다
- case study 사례 연구
- lead to ~로 이어지다
- specific 특정한
- industry 업계

W Good morning and thanks for attending this one-day seminar on customer satisfaction here in San Diego. We've just handed out the program sheet. Does everyone have one? Okay. If you look at the program, you will see this seminar is divided into three main sessions. During the first session, you are going to be given a lecture. In the lecture, we are going to define "customer satisfaction." After that, we are going to share some case studies that show how customer satisfaction leads to an increase in sales. Finally, we are going to have a Q&A session where you will all be given an opportunity to ask questions related to your specific industries.

여 좋은 아침이네요, 그리고 이곳 샌디에이고의 고객 만족에 관한 일일 세미나에 참여해 주셔서 감사합니다. 우리는 방금 프로그램 안내문을 나눠드렸습니다. 모두 안내문을 가지고 계신가요? 좋아요. 프로그램을 보시면 이 세미나가 세 개의 주요 부분으로 나누어져 있는 것을 아실 겁니다. 첫 번째 시간에는 강의를 들으실 겁니다. 강의에서는 '고객 만족'에 대해 정의를 내릴 것입니다. 그다음에 우리는 고객 만족이 어떻게 매출 증가로 이어지는지를 보여주는 사례 연구들을 공유할 것입니다. 마지막으로, 여러분의 특정 업계와 관련된 질문을 할 기회가 모두에게 주어지는 질의응답 시간을 가지게 됩니다.

02 | 정답 | ④

남자와 여자는 중국어 단어 시험의 분량에 대해 말하고 있다. 남자는 교사가 긍정적인 피드백으로 학생을 격려해야 한다고 말하며 외워야 할 분량이 너무 많으면 학생들이 포기해 버린다고 말하고 있으므로 남자의 의견으로 ④가 가장 적절하다.

- vocabulary 단어, 어휘
- frustrating 절망적인
- memorize 외우다
- challenging 어려운, 도전적인
- encourage 격려하다
- feedback 피드백
- average 평균의; 평균

W How was the Chinese vocabulary quiz yesterday?
M It was frustrating. I couldn't finish half of the questions. How about you?
W I didn't do better than you.
M Don't you think Mr. Young has been very hard on us?
W I do. It is impossible to memorize 200 words just for one quiz.
M Exactly. I don't understand why.
W Maybe he thinks that we wouldn't study hard if the quiz weren't challenging.
M Well, if he wants us to work hard, he should encourage us with positive feedback. Students just give up if there are too many words to memorize.
W I know what you mean. I'm not expecting my grade to be high.
M Same here. The average score is going to be so low.

여 어제 중국어 단어 시험은 어땠니?
남 절망적이었어. 문제의 절반도 끝내지 못했거든. 넌 어때?
여 너보다 나을 것 없어.
남 Young 선생님이 우리에게 너무 심한 것 같지 않아?
여 맞아. 한 번의 시험에 단어 200개를 외우는 건 불가능해.
남 그러니까. 왜 그렇게 해야 하는지 모르겠어.
여 시험이 어렵지 않으면 우리가 공부를 열심히 하지 않을 거라고 생각하시나 봐.
남 음, 공부를 열심히 하길 원하신다면 우리에게 긍정적인 피드백으로 격려해 주시는 게 좋을 것 같아. 학생들은 외워야 하는 단어가 너무 많으면 그냥 포기해 버리거든.
여 무슨 말인지 알아. 내 점수가 높을 것이라고 기대 안 하고 있어.
남 나도 그래. 평균 점수가 엄청 낮을 거야.

03 | 정답 | ①

작가가 되기 위해 특정한 시간을 비워 매일 글을 쓰라고 조언하고 있으므로 여자가 하는 말의 요지로 가장 적절한 것은 ①이다.

- extensively 광범위하게; 대규모로
- sufficient 충분한
- set aside 챙겨두다, 남기다
- jot down 쓰다
- commitment 헌신, 전념

W Hello, future authors! My name is Anne Rooney, and I'll be your writing instructor today. We'll talk about becoming a writer this session. You may have heard tips like reading extensively. While this advice is useful, it's not sufficient. To become a writer, you must develop a habit of writing every day. Set aside a specific time each day to jot down your thoughts, feelings, and dreams. This daily commitment will help you improve your writing skills. Now, let's learn about more important tips for new writers.

여 안녕하세요, 미래의 작가님들! 저는 오늘 여러분의 글쓰기 강사가 될 Anne Rooney이라고 합니다. 이번 시간에는 작가가 되는 것에 대해 이야기 할 것입니다. 여러분은 광범위하게 읽는 것과 같은 조언을 들어보셨을 겁니다. 이 조언은 유용하지만 충분하지는 않습니다. 작가가 되려면, 여러분은 매일 글을 쓰는 습관을 길러야 합니다. 여러분의 생각, 느낌, 그리고 꿈을 적을 특정한 시간을 매일 비워두세요. 이 매일의 헌신은 여러분의 글쓰기 능력을 향상시키는 데 도움을 줄 것입니다. 이제 초보 작가들을 위한 몇 가지 더 중요한 조언들을 알아봅시다.

04 | 정답 | ①

대화에서 여자는 오래된 TV와 TV용 스탠드를 버리고 TV용 스탠드가 필요 없는 새 벽걸이 TV를 샀다고 했으므로 일치하지 않는 것은 ①이다.

- interior 인테리어, 내부
- throw away 버리다
- stand (~용) 스탠드, 세움대

M Helen, is this a picture of your new living room?
W Yes, I changed the interior.
M Great. What has changed?
W We threw away our old TV stand and TV.
M Oh, then the wall-hanging TV over there is brand-new?
W Yes, isn't it nice? It has a bigger screen.
M Wow. It looks so much better.
W I agree. And since it doesn't require a TV stand, it doesn't take up as much space.

남 Helen, 이게 너의 새 거실 사진이니?
여 맞아. 인테리어를 바꿔봤어.
남 멋지다. 뭐가 바뀌었니?
여 우리는 예전 TV용 스탠드와 TV를 버렸어.
남 오, 그러면 저쪽의 벽걸이 TV는 새것이니?
여 응. 멋지지 않니? 더 큰 화면을 가지고 있어.
남 와. 훨씬 더 좋아 보여.
여 맞아. 그리고 TV용 스탠드가 필요하지 않아서 공간을 그렇게 많이 차지하지 않아.
남 아, 내 그림을 왼쪽 벽에 걸어놓았네.

- hang 걸다
- take up 차지하다
- space 공간
- aquarium 수족관
- shaped ~의 모양[형태]의
- cost (값·비용이) 들다

M Oh, you hung my painting on the wall on the left.
W Yes, I really like your painting. It feels like we have a real aquarium.
M I'm glad that you like it. Did you change your sofa, too?
W That's right. I bought an L-shaped sofa because we have a large family.
M I see. It must've cost you a lot to change all that furniture.
W Well, it wasn't as much as you'd think it'd be. Do you see the square-shaped tea table in the middle? It came with the sofa, so it was free.

여 응. 난 너의 그림이 정말 마음에 들어. 마치 진짜 수족관을 가지고 있는 느낌이야.
남 네가 마음에 든다니 기뻐. 소파도 바꿨니?
여 맞아. 우리가 대가족이라서 L자 모양의 소파로 샀어.
남 그렇구나. 모든 가구를 바꾸는 데 돈을 많이 썼겠다.
여 음. 네가 생각하는 만큼 많이 들지는 않았어. 가운데 정사각형 모양의 티 테이블이 보이지? 그건 소파에 딸려 나온 거라서 무료였어.

---

05 | 정답 | ②

여자는 남자가 노래 경연대회에 나가보라고 격려하자 망설이다가 대회에 참여하기로 마음을 먹고 대회 참가를 위한 신청서를 출력하겠다고 말하고 있으므로 정답은 ②이다.

- participate in ~에 참가하다
- besides 게다가
- exception 예외
- get over 극복하다
- stage fright 무대공포증
- experience 경험
- give it a try 한번 시도해 보다

M Have you decided to participate in the singing contest?
W No, Mr. Hanks. I'm not sure I can sing very well.
M You have a great voice, and you are good at singing. What else do you need?
W I've never sung in a contest before. Besides, I'm nervous about being in front of many people.
M It requires practice, that's all. Anyone can be nervous on the stage. I'm not an exception.
W When is the contest?
M It's May 17th. That's more than a month away.
W Do you think I can get over the stage fright?
M As you said, this is your first time singing in a contest. Experience can be the best teacher.
W Okay. I think I'll give it a try. Could you help me choose a song?
M Of course. Don't worry. I will be with you every step of the way.
W Thanks a lot. Then I'll print out the application from the website.

남 노래 경연대회에 참가하는 것 결정했니?
여 아니요, Hanks 선생님. 제가 노래를 잘 부를 수 있는지 모르겠어요.
남 넌 훌륭한 목소리를 가졌고, 노래도 잘해. 뭐가 더 필요하니?
여 저는 대회에 나가서 노래해 본 적이 없어요. 게다가 많은 사람들 앞에 있으면 떨려요.
남 그건 연습이 필요해. 그게 다야. 누구나 무대에서 긴장해. 나도 예외는 아니란다.
여 대회가 언제예요?
남 5월 17일이야. 한 달도 더 남았어.
여 제가 무대공포증을 극복할 수 있을까요?
남 네가 말했듯이, 이번이 대회에서 노래하는 게 처음이잖아. 경험이 최고의 선생님이 될 거야.
여 알겠어요. 한번 해볼게요. 노래 선택하는 걸 좀 도와주시겠어요?
남 물론이지. 걱정 마. 네가 하는 모든 과정에 내가 함께 할 테니까.
여 감사합니다. 그럼 웹사이트에서 신청서를 출력할게요.

---

06 | 정답 | ②

남자는 60달러짜리 회색 이동 가방 하나와 20달러짜리 강아지 패드 두 개를 구매하여 총금액은 100달러이지만, 할인쿠폰을 사용한다고 했다. 따라서 10% 할인을 적용한 90달러가 남자가 지불할 금액이므로 정답은 ②이다.

- suggestion 제안
- lightweight 경량의
- waterproof 방수의
- fabric 원단, 직물
- maximum 최대
- hold (무게를) 견디다[지탱하다]
- pad (액체 흡수용) 패드
- purchase 구매품

M Excuse me, I'm looking for a small dog carrier. Where do you keep them?
W Let me show you, sir. Is there any particular design you have in mind?
M Not really, but I'm open to any suggestions.
W All right. How about this one? It's made of lightweight and waterproof fabric.
M It seems nice. What's the maximum weight it can hold?
W It can hold up to 7 kilograms. There are three colors available, black, gray, and pink.
M I'll take the gray one. How much is it?
W It's $60. Is there anything else you need?
M I also need some dog pads in the smallest size. Do you have the ones from Four Paws?
W Yes, we do. A box of 75 sheets is $20. Would you like one?
M I'll take two boxes, please.
W All right. Do you have a membership with us? You can get a 5% discount on every purchase if you are a member.
M Yes, I have a membership card here, and I also have this 10% coupon.
W I'm sorry, but you have to choose either the coupon or membership discount.
M All right. Then I'll just use the coupon this time.

남 실례합니다. 작은 강아지 이동 가방을 찾고 있는데요. 어디에 있나요?
여 제가 보여 드릴게요, 손님. 생각해 두신 특정 디자인이 있으세요?
남 딱히 없지만 어떤 제안이든 환영이에요.
여 알겠습니다. 이건 어때세요? 경량 방수 원단으로 만들어져 있어요.
남 좋은 것 같네요. 견딜 수 있는 최대 중량은 얼마인가요?
여 7킬로그램까지 견딜 수 있어요. 검정, 회색, 그리고 분홍색, 세 가지 색상이 있어요.
남 회색으로 할게요. 얼마예요?
여 60달러예요. 더 필요한 게 있으신가요?
남 가장 작은 크기로 강아지 패드도 필요해요. Four Paws에서 나온 거 있나요?
여 네, 있어요. 75매 들어있는 한 상자에 20달러예요. 하나 드릴까요?
남 두 개 주세요.
여 알겠습니다. 저희 회원이신가요? 회원이시면 모든 구매에 5% 할인을 받으실 수 있어요.
남 네, 여기 회원권 있고, 또 이 10% 쿠폰도 있어요.
여 죄송하지만 쿠폰이나 회원 할인 중 하나를 선택하셔야 해요.
남 알겠습니다. 그럼 이번에는 쿠폰을 사용할게요.

07 | 정답 | ⑤

남자가 시험이 끝났으니 스케이트를 타러 가자고 하는 말에 여자는 오늘 엄마에게 집에 일찍 가겠다고 약속했다고 한다. 남자가 그 이유를 묻자 아버지 생신 때문에 쇼핑을 간다고 하고 있으므로 정답은 ⑤가 가장 적절하다.

* midterm exam 중간고사
* relieved 다행으로 여기는, 안도하는
* handout (수업 시간에 나눠주는) 수업 자료, 인쇄물
* say no 거절하다
* promise 약속하다
* can't wait 너무 기다려지다

M Finally, midterm exams are over!
W I know. I am just relieved that I get to take a break from all the books and handouts.
M You're right. I can't wait to go out and have fun now that all the exams are over.
W What are you planning to do?
M I'm going ice skating today. Do you want to come?
W I'm afraid I have to say no.
M Why not? Is it because you don't know how? I can teach you if you want.
W That's not why. I promised my mom that I'd be home early today.
M Why do you have to be home early today?
W She asked me to go shopping with her for my dad's birthday.
M Oh, I see. How about this weekend? It'll be fun.
W Sure. I can't wait!

남 드디어 중간고사가 끝났다!
여 그래. 모든 책과 수업 자료들을 멀리하게 되어 다행이야.
남 네 말이 맞아. 이제 모든 시험이 끝났으니까 얼른 나가서 놀고 싶어.
여 무얼 할 계획이니?
남 오늘은 스케이트 타러 가려고 해. 같이 갈래?
여 미안하지만 거절해야 할 것 같아.
남 왜 안 되는데? 어떻게 타는지 몰라서 그래? 원한다면 내가 가르쳐 줄게.
여 그게 아냐. 엄마에게 오늘은 집에 일찍 오겠다고 약속했어.
남 오늘 왜 일찍 가야 하는데?
여 엄마가 아빠 생신이라고 같이 쇼핑 가자고 하셨어.
남 아, 알겠어. 그럼 이번 주말은 어때? 재미있을 거야.
여 물론이야. 너무 기다려진다!

---

08 | 정답 | ②

남자가 다녀온 온천은 Colorado에 있으며 입장료는 20달러이고, 식음료 반입은 되지 않으며 폐장 시간은 오후 6시이다. 그러나 수영복을 입고 목욕하는 곳이라 했지만 수영복 대여에 관한 언급은 없었으므로 정답은 ②이다.

* awesome 굉장한, 아주 멋진
* hot spring 온천
* bathe 목욕하다
* swimsuit 수영복
* admission 입장료
* include 포함하다
* nearby 근처의

W How was your trip to Colorado last week?
M It was awesome. I went with my parents and my older brother.
W So, what did you do there? I heard there's a great hot springs park in Colorado.
M Yes, I went to Strawberry Hot Springs Park. There are quite a lot of hot springs in Colorado.
W What are the hot springs like? I've never seen one before.
M Oh, think of it as a small pool filled with hot spring water. You usually bathe in a swimsuit.
W That sounds cool. I hope I can go there, too. How much is admission?
M It's not too expensive. It's $20 for adults, which includes towels.
W Not too bad. Can we eat or drink inside?
M No, eating or drinking is not allowed. Also, the park closes at 6 p.m., so it'd be better to go out for dinner at a nearby restaurant.

여 지난주 콜로라도 여행은 어땠니?
남 너무 좋았어. 부모님과 형이랑 같이 갔거든.
여 그럼 거기서 무엇을 했니? 콜로라도에는 큰 온천 공원이 있다고 들었는데.
남 응. 나는 Strawberry 온천 공원에 갔었어. 콜로라도에는 꽤 많은 온천이 있거든.
여 온천은 어떤 곳이야? 한 번도 본 적이 없어.
남 아, 뜨거운 온천물로 가득 찬 작은 수영장이라고 생각하면 돼. 보통 수영복을 입고 목욕을 해.
여 멋지다. 나도 갈 수 있으면 좋겠다. 입장료는 얼마야?
남 그렇게 비싸지 않아. 성인이 20달러이고 수건이 포함된 가격이야.
여 나쁘지 않네. 안에서 먹거나 마실 수 있어?
남 아니, 먹거나 마시는 건 허용되지 않아. 또, 공원이 6시에 닫으니까 근처 식당으로 저녁 먹으러 가는 게 더 좋을 거야.

---

09 | 정답 | ⑤

온라인으로 사전 등록 시 받을 수 있는 혜택은 무료 입장료이며, 할인된 현금 상품권은 웹사이트에서 구매가 가능하다고 했으므로 일치하지 않는 것은 ⑤이다.

* expo 박람회
* feature 특별히 포함하다
* beverage (물 외의) 음료
* demo 시연; 시연하다
* renowned 저명한
* nutrition 영양
* manufacturer 제조사, 제조자
* supplier 공급업체, 공급자
* mouth-watering 군침이 돌게 하는
* cash voucher 현금 상품권

M Hello, listeners. I'm pleased to tell you today about the Yummy Food Expo. This upcoming event will be held in Singapore next month. The expo will feature various kinds of food and beverages, so make sure you bring an empty stomach. This 4-day event will include cooking demos, health talks, and food recommendations by some renowned nutrition experts. Over 150 Food & Beverage manufacturers and suppliers will join the event and serve endless mouth-watering food options. If you book online in advance, the admission is free. If you want to get a discounted cash voucher, visit our website at www.yummyfood.org. Don't miss out on this great opportunity!

남 청취자분들, 안녕하세요. Yummy Food 박람회에 대해 오늘 알려드리게 되어 기쁩니다. 이 다가오는 행사는 다음 달 싱가포르에서 열릴 예정입니다. 박람회는 다양한 종류의 음식과 음료가 특별히 포함될 예정이니 꼭 빈속으로 오세요. 이번 4일간의 행사는 몇몇 저명한 영양 전문가들에 의한 요리 시연, 건강 강연, 그리고 음식 추천을 포함할 예정입니다. 150개가 넘는 식음료 제조사들과 공급업체들이 행사에 참여하여 군침 돌게 하는 무한한 음식들을 제공할 것입니다. 온라인으로 미리 예매하시면 입장료는 무료입니다. 할인된 현금 상품권을 구매하고 싶은 분은 www.yummyfood.org으로 방문해 주세요. 이 멋진 기회를 놓치지 마세요!

---

10 | 정답 | ④

두 사람이 구매할 휴대용 선풍기는 손전등 기능이 없고 USB 포트로 충전할

W There are more and more people carrying those portable fans these days.
M That's why I came here to get one. I just can't take the

여 요즘 저런 휴대용 선풍기를 가지고 다니는 사람들이 점점 더 많아지네.
남 그래서 나도 하나 사려고 여기 왔잖아. 정말 더위를 더 이상 견딜 수가 없어.

수 있지만 40달러를 넘지 않는 모델이다. 해당하는 두 선풍기 중 배터리 시간이 더 긴 것을 구매하기로 했으므로 정답은 ④이다.

* portable 휴대용의
* fan 선풍기
* flashlight 손전등
* function 기능
* definitely 반드시
* gear 기구, 장비
* last 지속되다

heat any longer.
W Maybe I should get one, too.
M Look. This one looks nice. It even has a flashlight on it.
W It could be useful in dark areas, but I don't think we need that function.
M I agree. Oh, we should definitely get one which you can recharge with a USB port.
W We can use it while it's recharging, right?
M I think so. What about the price?
W I definitely don't want to spend more than $40.
M Then we are down to these two. Should we choose the cheaper one of the two?
W Did you check the battery life? I think it is pretty important, especially for portable gear.
M [Pause] This one says its battery lasts 4 hours longer than the other one's.
W Then let's choose that one even though it's more expensive.
M Perfect! Let's go with it.

여 혹시 모르니 나도 하나 사야겠다.
남 봐. 이거 괜찮아 보인다. 심지어 손전등도 달렸어.
여 어두운 곳에서는 유용할 수도 있지만 그 기능이 필요할 것 같지는 않아.
남 맞아. 아. 반드시 USB 포트로 충전할 수 있는 걸 사야 해.
여 충전하면서도 사용할 수 있지, 그렇지?
남 그런 것 같아. 가격은?
여 40달러 넘게는 절대 쓰고 싶지 않아.
남 그러면 이 두 개가 남았네. 둘 중에 더 저렴한 것을 선택해야 할까?
여 배터리 사용 시간을 확인했니? 특히 휴대용 장비라는 점 때문에 그건 정말 중요한 것 같아.
남 [잠시 후] 이건 배터리가 다른 것보다 4시간 더 길게 지속된다고 적혀 있어.
여 그러면 더 비싸더라도 그걸 선택하자.
남 좋아! 그걸로 하자.

---

11 | 정답 | ⑤

여자가 나갔다 온 사이에 컴퓨터가 고장이 나서 남자의 컴퓨터를 사용해도 되는지 물어보고 있으므로 남자의 응답으로는 ⑤ '미안한데, 내가 12시까지 끝내야 하는 보고서가 있어.'가 가장 적절하다.

* work 작동하다
[선택지]
* for the time being 당분간

W Mark, did anyone use my computer while I was out?
M I don't think so. Is there something wrong with it?
W Well, it doesn't seem to be working. It won't turn on. Can I use yours for a minute?
M Sorry, but I have a report to finish by noon.

여 Mark, 내가 나간 사이에 누가 내 컴퓨터를 썼니?
남 그런 것 같지 않아. 뭐가 잘못됐어?
여 음. 그게 작동하지 않는 것 같아. 전원이 켜지지가 않아. 내가 잠깐 네 걸 써도 될까?
남 미안한데, 내가 12시까지 끝내야 하는 보고서가 있어.

① 응. 난 그걸 당분간 쓸 수 있어.
② 내가 네 것을 쓰게 도와줘서 고마워.
③ 아니, 난 지금 보고서를 끝낼 필요가 없어.
④ 아니, 네가 당장 로그인할 수는 없을 것 같아.

---

12 | 정답 | ②

자신이 수집한 데이터에 착오가 있어서 발표를 미뤄도 되는지 물어보는 남자의 말에 대한 여자의 응답으로 ② '괜찮아요. 이번 주 금요일로 회의 일정을 변경할게요.'가 가장 적절하다.

* postpone 미루다
* miscalculation 계산 착오
* correct 바로잡다
* error 실수, 오류
[선택지]
* competitor 경쟁자, 경쟁 상대
* reschedule 일정을 변경하다

M Ms. Smith, I was wondering if my presentation could be postponed until this Friday.
W This Friday? Is there something wrong?
M I found out there had been some miscalculations in the data I collected. I just need a couple of days to correct those errors.
W That's fine. I will reschedule the meeting for this Friday.

남 Smith 씨, 제 발표를 이번 주 금요일까지 미룰 수 있을까 해서요.
여 이번 주 금요일이요? 뭐가 잘못됐나요?
남 제가 수집한 데이터에 몇 가지 계산 착오가 있었다는 것을 발견했어요. 그 오류들을 바로잡으려면 이틀 정도 필요할 것 같아요.
여 괜찮아요. 이번 주 금요일로 회의 일정을 변경할게요.

① 문제없어요. 우리는 경쟁사들로부터 우리 데이터를 보호해야 해요.
③ 정말이요? 당신은 발표를 더 일찍 해야 했어요.
④ 그거 유감이군요. 제 발표를 미룰게요.
⑤ 좋아요, 당신이 그 말을 하길 기다렸어요.

---

13 | 정답 | ②

줄이 긴 가게로 가자고 제안하는 남자에게 여자는 기대에 비해 실망하게 된다고 설명하는 상황이다. 점심시간이 짧아서 기다리기 어렵다는 여자의 말에 대한 남자의 응답으로 가장 적절한 것은 ② '알겠어. 그럼 다른 먹을 것을 생각해 보자.'이다.

* gluten-free 글루텐이 없는
* protein 단백질
* grain 곡물
* wheat 밀
* wait in line 줄서서 기다리다
* once in a while 가끔

M It's almost lunchtime. Do you want to try that new sandwich place across the street?
W Oh, that place always has a long waiting line.
M Yes, I heard that their sandwiches are very healthy and special.
W Really? What is so special about them?
M The sandwiches are made with gluten-free bread. Gluten is a protein found in certain grains, like wheat. People started to eat gluten-free food because having too much wheat can lead to serious health problems.
W So that's why there are so many people waiting in line. But I'm not sure it is worth the wait.
M What do you mean? Don't you want to try a popular place

남 거의 점심시간이네. 길 건너편에 새로 생긴 그 샌드위치 집 가볼래?
여 아, 거긴 늘 기다리는 줄이 길잖아.
남 맞아. 거기 샌드위치가 아주 건강하고 특별하다고 들었어.
여 정말? 그게 뭐가 그렇게 특별한데?
남 샌드위치를 글루텐이 없는 빵으로 만든대. 글루텐은 밀과 같은 특정 곡물에 들어 있는 단백질이야. 너무 많은 밀을 먹으면 심각한 건강 문제로 이어질 수 있기 때문에 많은 사람들이 글루텐이 들어 있지 않은 음식을 먹기 시작했거든.
여 그래서 거기 줄을 그렇게 많이 서 있구나. 하지만 그게 기다릴만한 가치가 있는지 잘 모르겠어.
남 무슨 소리야? 가끔씩 인기 있는 곳에 가보고 싶지 않아?

- disappointed 실망한
- expectation 기대
[선택지]
- allergic (~에 대해) 알레르기가 있는
- awful 끔찍한, 지독한

once in a while?

W Well, I've done it a few times before. But most of the times, the food wasn't that great, and the service was worse because there were too many people.

M I know what you mean. Some people get disappointed after waiting for a long time because their expectations are high.

W Exactly. Just because there is a long waiting line doesn't always mean the place serves good food. Besides, we only have an hour for our lunch.

M All right. Then let's think of something else to eat.

여 글쎄. 전에 몇 번 그랬지. 하지만 대부분, 음식은 그렇게 좋지도 않았고, 사람들이 너무 많아서 서비스는 더 별로였어.

남 무슨 말인지 알아. 일부 사람들은 기대가 커서 오래 기다린 다음에 실망하기도 해.

여 바로 그거야. 기다리는 줄이 길다고 해서 그 집이 항상 좋은 음식을 제공한다는 의미는 아니잖아. 게다가. 우리 점심시간이 한 시간뿐이야.

남 알겠어. 그럼 다른 먹을 것을 생각해 보자.

① 미안해. 근데 나는 글루텐 알레르기가 있어.
③ 괜찮아. 난 이번 주말 내내 완전히 자유야.
④ 말도 안 돼. 밀가루 없는 샌드위치는 끔찍한 맛일 거야.
⑤ 당연하지. 난 먹는 데 많은 돈을 쓰고 싶지 않아.

---

14 | 정답 | ⑤

남자는 여자와 수강 신청을 어제 끝냈으나 오늘 수업이 하나 취소되어서 다른 강좌를 신청해야 한다는 여자의 말을 듣고 자신도 다른 강의를 신청해야 한다고 말하고 있으므로 여자의 응답으로 ⑤ '그 강의를 신청하러 서두르는 게 좋겠어.'가 가장 적절하다.

- head 향하다
- occupied 사용 중인
- registration 등록
- semester 학기

M Why are you in such a hurry?

W I'm going to an Internet cafe.

M Are you heading there to play games?

W No, I'm not. My computer is broken, and I need to use one.

M There are many computers available at school, you know.

W I'm sure they are all occupied because tomorrow is the last day of registration for classes.

M You are right, but we finished signing up yesterday, didn't we?

W We did, but there's a problem. Did you not hear about it?

M No, I don't have a clue what you are talking about. What's the problem?

W World History 2 was canceled because only a few students signed up.

M Oh, in that case, I have to sign up for another class, too.

W There are only two classes that still have seats available: World History 1, which we took last semester, and Art History, which looks like our only option.

M I should go with you right now.

W We'd better hurry to sign up for that class.

남 왜 그렇게 바쁘니?
여 난 PC 방에 가는 길이야.
남 게임하러 거기 가는 거야?
여 아니. 내 컴퓨터가 고장 났는데 컴퓨터를 써야 해서.
남 학교에 이용할 수 있는 컴퓨터가 많이 있는 거 알잖아.
여 내일이 수강신청 등록 마감일이라서 컴퓨터가 분명히 다 사용 중일 거야.
남 네 말이 맞지만, 우린 어제 수강신청 끝냈잖아. 그렇지 않아?
여 그랬는데 문제가 생겼어. 그 문제에 대해 못 들었어?
남 네가 무슨 말을 하고 있는지 모르겠어. 뭐가 문제인데?
여 세계사 2가 신청한 학생이 적어서 취소됐어.
남 아. 그렇다면 나도 다른 강의를 신청해야 하네.
여 아직 자리가 있는 강의는 두 개밖에 없는데, 지난 학기에 우리가 수강했던 세계사 1과. 우리의 유일한 선택지인 것 같은 미술사야.
남 지금 바로 너랑 같이 가야겠다.
여 그 강의를 신청하러 서두르는 게 좋겠어.

① 만약을 대비해서 내가 메시지를 다시 확인할게.
② 내가 그것에 대해 알려주지 않은 건 미안해.
③ 네가 수강신청할 수 있게 네 컴퓨터 고쳐줄게.
④ 오늘까지 신청해야 해.

---

15 | 정답 | ④

인스턴트식품을 자주 섭취하는 Gary의 건강을 걱정하는 Linda가 나쁜 습관을 고치자고 제안하는 상황이다. 예전에 야외에서 놀았던 것처럼 운동을 자주 하자는 내용이 오는 것이 자연스럽다. 따라서 Linda가 Gary에게 할 말로 가장 적절한 것은 ④ '나랑 같이 운동을 좀 하는 건 어때? 재미있을 거야!'이다.

- outdoor 야외의
- regular 규칙적인, 정기적인
- to make matters worse 설상가상으로
- pick up a bad habit 나쁜 습관이 들다
- junk food 인스턴트식품
- soda 탄산음료
- go around in circles 제자리를 맴돌다
- at risk 위험에 처한

W Gary and Linda have been friends since elementary school. They used to play a lot of outdoor activities together. But since Gary entered high school, he hasn't made time for regular exercise because he has too many classes to study for. To make matters worse, he is very stressed from studying. That has made him pick up a bad habit, eating junk food. Gary wants to go on a healthy diet, but always ends up eating junk food and drinking soda again. After watching Gary go around in circles, Linda has become very worried about him. She thinks if he doesn't stop eating junk food, his health will be at risk. She looks for ways to help him and then finds some to fix Gary's bad habit. One of them is to exercise and drink a lot of water. So Linda wants to suggest to him that they do more outdoor activities like they used to. In this situation, what would Linda most likely say to Gary?

Linda How about doing some exercise with me? It'll be fun!

여 Gary와 Linda는 초등학교 때부터 친구이다. 그들은 함께 많은 야외활동을 하곤 했다. 그러나 Gary가 고등학교에 들어간 이후로 공부해야 할 과목이 너무 많아서 규칙적인 운동을 할 시간이 없다. 설상가상으로 그는 공부에 너무 스트레스를 받고 있다. 그것은 오히려 그가 나쁜 습관이 들게 했는데, 바로 인스턴트식품을 먹는 것이다. Gary는 건강한 다이어트를 하길 원하지만. 결국 다시 인스턴트식품을 먹고 탄산음료를 마시게 된다. Gary가 제자리를 맴도는 것을 본 후, Linda는 그에 대해 매우 걱정하게 된다. 그녀는 그가 인스턴트식품을 먹는 것을 멈추지 않으면 그의 건강이 위험해질 것이라 생각한다. 그녀는 그를 돕기 위해 여러 방법을 찾고 나서 Gary의 나쁜 습관을 고칠 몇 가지 방법을 발견한다. 그중 하나는 운동을 하고 물을 많이 마시는 것이다. 그래서 Linda는 예전에 둘이 그랬던 것처럼 더 많은 야외활동을 하자고 제안하고 싶어 한다. 이러한 상황에서 Linda가 Gary에게 할 말로 가장 적절한 것은 무엇인가?

Linda 나랑 같이 운동을 좀 하는 건 어때? 재미있을 거야!

① 넌 학교에서 잘하고 있어. 너무 스트레스 받지 마.
② 초콜릿은 어때? 네 기분을 더 좋게 해줄 거야.
③ 넌 너무 말랐어. 몸무게를 좀 늘려야 해.
⑤ 너 치과에 가야 해. 그렇지 않으면 치통이 생길 거야.

16 | 정답 | ⑤

남자는 실제로 나는 동물과 나는 것 같이 보이는 동물들을 예시로 들며 차이점을 설명하고 있으므로 정답은 ⑤ '나는 동물과 나는 것처럼 보이는 동물들이 어떻게 다른가'이다.

17 | 정답 | ③

실제 나는 동물로 새와 벌레 그리고 박쥐를 언급했고, 나는 것 같이 보이는 동물로 다람쥐와 거미를 언급했지만, '닭'에 대한 언급은 없었으므로 정답은 ③이다.

* **flier** 나는 것
* **hollow** (속이) 빈
* **mammal** 포유류
* **unique** 독특한
* **enable** ~할 수 있게 하다
* **direction** 방향
* **squirrel** 다람쥐
* **glide** 활공하다
* **rather than** ~라기보다는
* **act like** ~의 역할을 하다, ~처럼 작용하다
* **sail** 돛
* **breeze** 산들바람
* **web** 거미줄
  [선택지]
* **mechanism** 방법, 메커니즘
* **predator** 포식자
* **seemingly** 겉보기에는

M Hello, class. Today, I'd like to introduce some interesting animals. There are actually two kinds of fliers in the animal kingdom. First, let's talk about animals that do fly. Birds are amazing fliers, as you know. Their hollow bones make them light. The shape of their wings also helps them fly far. Bugs are also strong fliers because they are small and light. Bats fly, too. What's interesting about bats is that they are actually mammals. Their unique wings enable them to change directions quickly while flying. On the other hand, there are animals that only seem to fly. Have you ever thought that some squirrels can fly? Actually, they glide rather than fly. The flying squirrel has loose skin along the sides of its body, which acts like a sail to catch the breeze. Some spiders are even more interesting. Their webs catch the wind and carry them far and high. Now, let's take a look at some of their photos on the board together.

남 안녕하세요, 여러분. 오늘은 몇몇 흥미로운 동물들을 소개하려고 합니다. 동물의 왕국에는 사실 두 종류의 나는 것들이 있습니다. 먼저 정말로 나는 동물들에 대해 말해 봅시다. 여러분도 알다시피 새들은 놀라운 날짐승이죠. 그들의 빈 뼈가 무게를 가볍게 합니다. 그들의 날개 모양도 그들이 멀리 날게 돕죠. 벌레도 작고 가벼워서 잘 납니다. 박쥐도 날고요. 박쥐의 흥미로운 점은 사실 그들이 포유류라는 점입니다. 박쥐의 독특한 날개는 그들이 날면서 방향을 빨리 바꿀 수 있게 합니다. 반면에, 단지 나는 것처럼 보이는 동물들이 있어요. 일부 다람쥐가 날 수 있다고 생각해 본 적 있나요? 사실 그들은 날기보다는 활공합니다. 날다람쥐는 몸 옆쪽을 따라 헐렁한 가죽이 있어서 이것이 바람을 잡는 돛의 역할을 하죠. 일부 거미들은 훨씬 더 흥미롭습니다. 그들의 거미줄은 바람을 잡고 그들을 멀리 또 높이 이동시킵니다. 자, 이제 칠판에서 그들의 사진 몇 장을 함께 봅시다.

16 ① 동물의 세계에서 나는 것은 무엇을 의미하는가
② 왜 어떤 포유동물은 날지만 다른 포유동물은 날지 못하는가
③ 동물들은 날기 위해 어떤 방법을 사용하는가
④ 나는 것이 동물들을 포식자로부터 어떻게 도망치게 하는가
⑤ 나는 동물과 나는 것처럼 보이는 동물들이 어떻게 다른가

17 ① 새 ② 벌레 ③ 닭 ④ 박쥐 ⑤ 다람쥐

01 | 정답 | ⑤

여자는 시의 정전 사태 때 회사가 대비하지 못해서 피해를 입었기 때문에 에너지 지침을 마련하게 되었다고 말하면서 에너지 절약 지침을 사원들에게 전달하고 있으므로, 여자가 하는 말의 목적으로 ⑤가 가장 적절하다.

- **power outage** 정전
- **delay** 지연
- **operation** 운영
- **unprepared** 대비가 안 된
- **in an effort to** ~하려는 노력으로
- **screensaver** 화면 보호기, 스크린세이버
- **consuming** 소모적인
- **hibernation mode** 절전모드
- **enforce** 시행하다
- **exception** 예외
- **cooperation** 협조, 협력

W Attention, everyone. I'd like to inform you of some of the important guidelines that you should follow from next month. The recent power outage in our town has caused some delays in our company's operations. And it was damaging to all the departments in our company because we were unprepared for it. So, our energy management team has decided to make some guidelines in an effort to save energy. Turn off your computer when not in use. The screensaver option is energy consuming, so please turn it off and switch it to hibernation mode. When you are the last person to leave a room, make sure all the lights are off. During the winter, keep the blinds open on sunny days. This will heat the room naturally. Also, it is better to close the blinds at night to prevent heat from escaping. Starting next month, this will be enforced in every department every day with no exceptions. Thank you for your understanding and cooperation.

여 주목해 주세요, 여러분. 여러분이 다음 달부터 따라야 하는 중요한 지침 몇 가지를 알려드리고자 합니다. 우리 시의 최근 정전 사태가 우리 회사 운영에 약간의 지연을 초래했습니다. 그리고 우리가 이것에 대비하지 못했기 때문에 우리 회사의 모든 부서에 손해가 있었습니다. 그래서 우리 에너지 관리팀은 에너지를 절약하기 위한 노력으로 몇 가지 지침을 만들기로 결정했습니다. 사용하지 않을 때는 컴퓨터의 전원을 꺼 주세요. 화면 보호기 옵션은 에너지를 소모하므로 그것을 끄고 절전모드로 바꿔 주세요. 사무실을 마지막으로 나가는 분은 모든 불이 다 꺼져 있는지 확인해 주세요. 겨울 동안 화창한 날에는 블라인드를 열어두세요. 이것이 자연스럽게 사무실을 따뜻하게 해줄 것입니다. 또한 밤에는 열이 빠져나가는 것을 막기 위해 블라인드를 닫는 것이 낫습니다. 다음 달부터 이것은 예외 없이 매일 모든 부서에서 시행될 예정입니다. 여러분의 이해와 협조에 감사드립니다.

02 | 정답 | ④

여자는 남자가 발표를 잘하는 것을 부러워하며 자신은 발표할 때 긴장을 많이 한다고 말한다. 거기에 대해 남자는 자신의 발표에만 집중하면 극복할 수 있다고 말하고 있으므로, 남자의 의견으로 ④가 가장 적절하다.

- **well-organized** 정리가 잘 된
- **freeze** (공포 등으로 몸이) 얼어붙다, 굳어지다
- **get over** 극복하다
- **care about** ~에 신경 쓰다
- **persuade** 설득하다
- **easier said than done** 행동보다 말이 쉬운
- **concentrate** 집중하다
- **in no time** 곧
- **keep in mind** 잊지 않고 있다, 명심하다

W Gary, your presentation was well-organized. And you didn't look nervous at all.
M Thanks. I was really focused on delivering the details. I even forgot how nervous I was.
W I wish I could be more like you. I just freeze in front of many people.
M I used to be just like you. I would get really nervous on stage.
W Then how did you get over it?
M In my case, I stopped caring about what other people would think of me.
W What do you mean?
M You just have to focus on the main goal, which is to persuade people into believing what you say.
W Well, that is easier said than done.
M Just concentrate only on your speech. Then it will be easy to forget about being nervous. You will get better in no time.
W I'll keep that in mind. I hope my presentation goes as well as yours.

여 Gary, 너의 발표는 정리가 잘 되었어. 그리고 너는 전혀 긴장하는 것처럼 보이지 않았어.
남 고마워. 난 세부 사항을 전달하는 데 정말 집중했어. 심지어 얼마나 긴장하고 있는지도 잊어버렸어.
여 나도 너처럼 됐으면 좋겠어. 난 많은 사람들 앞에서 그냥 얼어붙게 돼.
남 나도 예전에는 너와 같았어. 무대에서 정말 긴장했었지.
여 그럼 그걸 어떻게 극복했어?
남 내 경우엔, 다른 사람들이 나를 어떻게 생각하는지 신경 쓰는 것을 멈췄어.
여 무슨 뜻이야?
남 사람들이 네가 하는 말을 믿도록 설득한다는 주된 목표에 집중하면 돼.
여 글쎄, 그게 말이 쉽지.
남 네가 하는 말에만 집중해 봐. 그럼 긴장하는 것에 대해 잊기 쉬워지거든. 곧 나아질 거야.
여 잊지 않을게. 내 발표도 네 발표처럼 잘되면 좋겠어.

03 | 정답 | ②

돈을 관리하는 요령으로 매일의 지출 내역을 기록하라고 조언하고 있으므로 여자가 하는 말의 요지로 가장 적절한 것은 ②이다.

- **host** 진행자, 사회자
- **keep track of** …의 자국을 뒤밟다, 기록하다
- **trick** 비결, 요령
- **expense** 지출, 경비
- **impulsively** 충동적으로

W Welcome, everyone! This is Emily, the host of "Our Friendly Accountant". Sometimes, we spend money without even realizing it, and it can be difficult to keep track of where all our money is going. However, there's a simple trick to manage your money better: Start by keeping a record of all your daily expenses. You can use a smartphone or a notebook to write down your expenses. This will help you understand your spending patterns and make it easier to avoid spending money impulsively. In this episode, I'll explain how you can record your daily expenses effectively. So, stay tuned!

여 모두 환영합니다! "우리의 친절한 회계사"의 진행자인 Emily입니다. 때때로 우리는 자신도 모르게 돈을 쓰고, 우리의 모든 돈이 어디로 가는지 계속 추적하기가 어려울 수 있습니다. 하지만, 여러분의 돈을 더 잘 관리하는 간단한 요령이 있습니다. 여러분의 모든 매일의 지출을 기록하는 것부터 시작하세요. 스마트폰이나 노트를 사용하여 지출을 기록할 수 있습니다. 이것은 자신의 소비 패턴을 이해하고 충동적으로 돈을 쓰는 것을 방지하기 더 쉽도록 도울 것입니다. 이번 일화에서는 매일의 지출을 어떻게 효과적으로 기록할 수 있는지 설명해 드리겠습니다. 그러니, 채널을 고정하세요!

---

04 | 정답 | ⑤

여자는 램프 아래에 튤립을 놓겠다고 했으므로 일치하지 않는 것은 ⑤이다.

* **rearrange** 재배치하다
* **necklace** 목걸이
* **safe** 안전한
* **pencil holder** 연필꽂이
* **left-handed** 왼손잡이의
* **check out** 확인하다

M	Wow, Sally. You did a great job cleaning up.
W	I cleaned the desk and rearranged things a little. What do you think?
M	It's excellent. Whose necklace is this?
W	That heart-shaped necklace on the left side? It's mine. Mom bought it for me.
M	Please keep it in a safe place. I wonder why you placed the pencil holder on the left side.
W	Since I'm left-handed, it's better to keep it on the left.
M	Oh, it looks like you need a new calendar. The one in the middle is for 2022.
W	I see. I'll get a new one for this year later. Did you check out the lamp on the right?
M	I've never seen it before. Is it new?
W	Yes, I got it from my friend for my birthday. Isn't it nice?
M	It is. I brought something for your clean desk.
W	Tulips! I love them! They are my favorite flowers. I'll put them under the lamp. *[Pause]* Don't they look nice there?
M	Yes, they do.

남 와, Sally. 청소를 아주 훌륭하게 했구나.
여 책상을 치우고 몇 가지를 좀 재배치했어요. 어떤 것 같아요?
남 훌륭하구나. 이건 누구의 목걸이야?
여 왼쪽에 있는 저 하트 모양의 목걸이요? 제 거예요. 엄마가 사주셨거든요.
남 그건 안전한 곳에 보관하렴. 연필꽂이는 왜 왼쪽에 놨는지 궁금하네.
여 제가 왼손잡이라서 왼쪽에 두는 게 더 좋아요.
남 아, 네게 새로운 달력이 필요해 보이네. 가운데 있는 달력은 2022년 거야.
여 그러네요. 올해 새 달력은 나중에 구할게요. 오른쪽에 램프는 보셨어요?
남 전에 못 보던 건데. 새것이니?
여 네, 생일에 친구에게서 받은 거예요. 멋지지 않아요?
남 그렇구나. 나도 너의 깨끗한 책상에 놓을 뭔가를 가져왔어.
여 튤립이네요! 저는 튤립을 좋아해요! 제가 가장 좋아하는 꽃이에요. 램프 아래 놓을게요. *[잠시 후]* 거기에 있으니 좋아 보이지 않아요?
남 응. 좋아 보이는구나.

---

05 | 정답 | ③

남자가 관광지를 추천해 달라고 하자 여자는 이탈리아에 있는 친구가 관광 가이드로 일한다며 집에 가서 친구의 이메일 주소를 보내 주겠다고 했으므로 정답은 ③이다.

* **tourist spot** 관광지
* **Catholic church** 성당
* **you name it** ((사물을 열거한 뒤)) 무엇이든지 말해 봐
* **tour guide** 관광 가이드

M	Amy, is that you? It's good to see you again. Where have you been?
W	Kevin! Long time no see. I've been in Italy. One of my friends works there, so I visited her.
M	Really? I'm going to Italy next week. So, where in Italy does your friend work?
W	She works in Rome, so I stayed in Rome for a month. What about you? Where in Italy are you planning to visit?
M	I'm visiting Rome and Venice. Oh, since I'm staying in Rome for three days, can you recommend me tourist spots? Did you go to many tourist spots?
W	Rome is full of things to see. The Colosseum, the Vatican City, the Pantheon, Trevi Fountain, and all the wonderful Catholic churches, you name it.
M	Wow, I don't know if I will have enough time to see all that.
W	Actually, my friend works as a tour guide there. If you want, I can give you her email address.
M	Great. I was a little worried about what to do there.
W	When I get home, I'll send it to you by email. I'm sure she will be a big help.
M	Thanks a lot.

남 Amy, 너 맞니? 다시 만나서 반갑다. 어디 갔었어?
여 Kevin! 오랜만이야. 이탈리아에 다녀왔어. 내 친구 중 하나가 거기서 일해서 방문차 갔었어.
남 정말? 나 다음 주에 이탈리아 가. 친구가 이탈리아 어디에서 일하니?
여 로마에서 일해서 나는 거기서 한 달간 머물렀어. 넌 어때? 이탈리아 어느 곳을 방문할 계획이니?
남 로마와 베니스를 방문할 거야. 아, 3일 동안 로마에 머무르는데 여행지를 추천해 줄래? 관광지에 많이 갔었니?
여 로마는 볼 것들이 아주 많아. 콜로세움, 바티칸 시국, 판테온, 트레비 분수, 그리고 멋진 성당들, 뭘 볼지 말만 해.
남 와, 그거 다 볼 시간이 충분할지 모르겠다.
여 사실 친구가 거기서 관광 가이드로 일해. 네가 원한다면 내 친구 이메일 주소를 줄 수 있어.
남 잘됐다. 거기서 뭘 해야 할지 조금 걱정했었거든.
여 내가 집에 가서 이메일로 보내줄게. 그 애가 분명히 큰 도움이 될 거야.
남 정말 고마워.

---

06 | 정답 | ②

남자의 아빠에게 선물할 가죽 지갑이 150달러이고 벨트가 50달러인데 10% 할인되어서 180달러이고 선물 포장이 4달러이므로 남자가 지불할 금액은 ②이다.

* **leather** 가죽
* **budget** 예산
* **have in mind** 생각하고 있다, 염두에 두다
* **reasonable** 합리적인
* **rarely** 거의 ~않는

M	Julie, can you help me choose a birthday present for my dad?
W	Sure. Is there a particular item you are thinking of?
M	Yes. I'd like to buy a wallet. I have a brochure here.
W	Let's see. *[Pause]* This brown leather one seems okay.
M	But, it's $250. It's way out of my budget.
W	How about this one? It's $150. It even has a money clip.
M	That's the type I had in mind. The price is reasonable, too.
W	Okay, but do you think a wallet is enough? How about adding this tie? It says it's $40.
M	He rarely wears a tie. How about a belt?

남 Julie, 아빠를 위한 생일 선물을 고르는 걸 도와줄 수 있니?
여 물론이지. 특별히 생각하고 있는 물건이 있니?
남 응. 지갑을 사고 싶어. 여기 광고 책자가 있어.
여 한번 보자. *[잠시 후]* 이 갈색 가죽 지갑이 괜찮은 것 같아.
남 하지만 그건 250달러야. 내 예산을 완전히 벗어나.
여 그럼 이건 어때? 150달러야. 게다가 지폐 클립도 있어.
남 그게 내가 생각했던 종류야. 가격도 합리적이네.
여 알겠어. 그런데 지갑 하나로 충분한 것 같아? 이 넥타이를 추가하는 건 어때? 40달러라고 쓰여 있어.
남 아빠는 거의 넥타이를 매지 않으셔. 벨트가 어때?

	W That's a great idea. This leather one is $50. **M** Perfect. Should I have them gift-wrapped, too? There is an extra charge of $2 for each item. **W** That'll be good. **M** And I have this 10% coupon. **W** Well, it says it can't be applied to the gift-wrapping service. **M** That's fine. I'll order them now.	**여** 좋은 생각이야. 이 가죽 벨트는 50달러야. **남** 완벽해. 선물 포장도 해야 할까? 품목마다 추가로 2달러래. **여** 그게 좋을 거야. **남** 그리고 10% 쿠폰이 있어. **여** 음. 선물 포장 서비스에는 적용할 수 없다고 나와 있네. **남** 괜찮아. 그것들을 지금 주문할게.

---

07 | 정답 | ④

남자는 여자에게 방에 가서 사진을 출력해달라고 부탁하지만 여자는 컴퓨터가 잠겨있어서 Dan한테 도움을 요청하라고 했으므로 정답은 ④이다.

* vacuum 청소기로 청소하다
* relax 진정하다; 긴장을 풀다
* in a hurry 서두르는
* completely 완전히
* be supposed to-v ~하기로 되어 있다
* be busy -ing ~하느라 바쁘다
* lock 잠그다

M Can you vacuum the living room? We don't have much time left.
W Dad, relax. Why are you in such a hurry?
M We have some guests coming over to the house tonight. Didn't I tell you that?
W Oh, I completely forgot about it. What time are they supposed to come?
M They'll be here in an hour. Your mom is busy cooking in the kitchen, too.
W All right. After I vacuum the living room, I will help out in the kitchen.
M Instead, can you go to Dan's room and print some pictures for me?
W I can't. You have to ask him.
M He's not home until 10. Is the printer broken?
W No, it's not. I saw him use it a few days ago.
M Then how come you can't do it?
W Well, Dan locks his computer when he's not home.
M I'll talk to him when he gets home.
W Okay. Then should I vacuum and help Mom?
M Yes. Look at the time. Let's hurry!

남 거실을 청소기로 청소해 줄래? 시간이 많이 남지 않았어.
여 아빠, 진정해요. 왜 그렇게 서둘러요?
남 오늘 밤에 손님들이 오기로 되어 있잖아. 내가 말하지 않았니?
여 아, 완전히 잊어버렸어요. 몇 시에 오시기로 되어 있죠?
남 한 시간 후에 오실 거야. 엄마도 주방에서 요리하느라고 바빠.
여 알겠어요. 거실 청소한 후에 주방 일을 도울게요.
남 대신에, Dan의 방에 가서 사진 좀 출력해 줄 수 있니?
여 저는 못 해요. 오빠에게 부탁하셔야 해요.
남 걔는 10시에나 집에 온단다. 프린터가 고장 났니?
여 아니요. 오빠가 며칠 전에 사용하는 걸 봤어요.
남 그럼 왜 못 한다는 거니?
여 아, Dan 오빠가 집에 없을 때는 자기 컴퓨터를 잠가놔요.
남 집에 오면 걔한테 얘기할게.
여 알겠어요. 그럼 청소하고 엄마를 도와야겠죠?
남 그래. 시간 좀 봐라. 서두르자!

---

08 | 정답 | ③

남자는 뉴욕의 자유의 여신상에 다녀온 이야기를 하고 있다. 자유의 여신상의 높이는 93미터이고 입장료는 무료이다. 교통편으로는 여객선이 있으며, 색은 자연에 노출되어 특이한 초록색을 가지게 되었다고 말하고 있으므로 언급되지 않은 것은 ③이다.

* awesome 굉장한
* impressive 인상적인
* ferry 여객선
* approximately 대략
* fascinated 매료된, 매혹된
* originally 원래
* copper 구리, 동
* exposure 노출
* distinctive 특이한

W How was your trip to New York?
M It was awesome. I'll never forget what I saw there.
W Did you visit the Statue of Liberty?
M Yes, it was impressive. I couldn't believe my eyes. It is 93 meters tall.
W Wow! Is it free to enter?
M It is free, but you have to go there by ferry, which costs $12.
W How long is the ferry trip?
M It takes approximately 15 minutes to get to the island.
W Did you go inside?
M Of course. There is an elevator, but you have to climb the steps from the feet to the crown of the statue.
W That sounds exciting. I've always been fascinated by the color of the statue.
M Did you know that the statue was originally the color of copper?
W No, what happened?
M The exposure to rain, wind and sun gave the statue its distinctive green color.

여 뉴욕 여행은 어땠니?
남 굉장했어. 내가 거기서 본 걸 절대 잊지 못할 거야.
여 자유의 여신상에도 갔어?
남 응. 인상적이었어. 내 눈을 믿을 수가 없었어. 높이가 93미터거든.
여 왜 들어가는 건 무료야?
남 무료지만 여객선을 타고 거기 가야 하는데 그건 12달러야.
여 여객선은 얼마나 걸리는데?
남 그 섬까지 가는 데 대략 15분 걸려.
여 안에 들어갔어?
남 물론. 엘리베이터가 있지만 발부터 동상의 왕관까지는 계단을 걸어 올라가야 해.
여 재미있겠다. 나는 항상 그 동상의 색에 매료되었었어.
남 그 동상이 원래 구리색이었던 걸 알고 있었어?
여 아니. 무슨 일이 있었던 거야?
남 비, 바람 그리고 햇빛에 노출되어서 그 동상이 지금의 특이한 초록색을 가지게 된 거야.

---

09 | 정답 | ⑤

학교 연극의 오디션 결과는 다음 날 이메일 통보가 아니라 3일 후 학생위원회 사무실 옆의 게시판에 게시된다고 했으므로 정답은 ⑤이다.

M Good morning, everyone. I'm the principal of the Gold Arts School. Today, I'd like to tell you about the auditions for the school play. I know every student in our school has a talent. However, if you don't share your talent, nobody will know about it! So, if you think you are good

남 안녕하세요, 여러분. 저는 Gold 예술학교의 교장입니다. 오늘 저는 학교 연극을 위한 오디션에 대해서 여러분에게 얘기하고자 합니다. 우리 학교의 모든 학생들이 재능을 가지고 있는 것을 저는 압니다. 그러나 여러분이 재능을 공유하지 않으면 아무도 그것에 대해 알 수 없을 거예요! 그래서 만약 여러분이 노래, 춤 또는

* principal 교장
* student council 학생위원회
* cafeteria 구내식당
* bulletin board 게시판
* regarding ~에 대해서
* contact 연락하다

at singing, dancing or acting, sign up for this great opportunity and be a star on the stage. You can sign up for auditions from May 6th through 10th. There will be student council members outside the cafeteria during the lunch break. Auditions will be held on May 20th and 21st from 4 to 6 p.m. Results will be posted three days later on the bulletin board next to the student council room. If you have any questions regarding the auditions or school play, contact Mr. Jenkins. We can't wait to see a wonderful play this year.

연기를 잘한다고 생각한다면 이 멋진 기회에 신청하시고 무대에서 스타가 되어 보세요. 5월 6일부터 10일까지 오디션에 신청할 수 있습니다. 점심시간 동안 교내 식당 밖에 학생위원회 위원들이 있을 겁니다. 오디션은 5월 20일과 21일 오후 4시부터 6시까지 열릴 예정입니다. 결과는 3일 후에 학생위원회 사무실 옆에 있는 게시판에 게시될 것입니다. 오디션이나 학교 연극에 대해 질문이 있으시면 Jenkins 선생님께 연락하세요. 올해 아주 멋진 연극을 보는 것이 너무 기다려집니다.

---

10 | 정답 | ③

두 사람이 주문할 티셔츠는 최소 주문 수량이 50장 이하이고, 재질은 면이 아니며, 장당 5달러 이하에 색상은 두 가지여야 한다고 했으므로 정답은 ③이다.

* fix (날짜, 인원 등을) 정하다
* minimum 최소
* material 재질
* campsite 야영장
* require ~을 필요로 하다
* cotton 면
* available 사용 가능한

M Wow, it's already June. We'd better hurry up and get ready for the summer camp.
W I know. So far, 35 students have signed up.
M That's good. Oh, we are supposed to order T-shirts today, right?
W Right. I called T-shirt World, and got the list of what we can choose from.
M All right. Let's have a look. [Pause] Oh, the number of students is not fixed yet. How many should we order?
W I think we should order 50 T-shirts because there could be more students who sign up. I guess this one is out since the minimum is 60.
M Yes. What material should we get?
W Well, the campsite has a pool which requires swimmers not to wear anything cotton. Anything besides cotton should be okay.
M I see. What's our budget on T-shirts? It's not very high, is it?
W No, it's not. We can't spend more than $5 for one T-shirt.
M Okay then. It looks like there are two options available.
W We need to get two different colors. One for girls and the other for boys.
M Right. Then we should order this one.

남 와, 벌써 6월이야. 서둘러 여름 캠프를 준비해야겠어.
여 알아. 여태까지 35명이 신청했어.
남 좋아. 아, 오늘 티셔츠를 주문하기로 했지, 맞지?
여 맞아. T-shirt World에 전화해서 우리가 고를 수 있는 목록을 받았어.
남 좋아. 한번 보자. [잠시 후] 아, 학생들의 수가 아직 정해지지 않았어. 우리가 얼마나 주문해야 할까?
여 더 많은 학생들이 등록할 수 있기 때문에 티셔츠를 50장 주문해야 할 것 같아. 이건 최소한 60장을 주문해야 하니까 안 되겠고.
남 그래. 어떤 재질로 살까?
여 글쎄. 야영장에 면으로 된 것은 입지 못하게 하는 수영장이 있어. 면으로 된 것만 아니면 괜찮을 거야.
남 알겠어. 티셔츠에 대한 우리 예산은 얼마야? 그렇게 높지 않지, 그렇지?
여 응. 높지 않아. 티셔츠 한 장에 5달러 넘게 쓸 수 없어.
남 좋아. 그럼. 남은 게 두 가지가 있는 것 같군.
여 우리는 두 개의 다른 색을 골라야 해. 여자아이들 것과 남자아이들 것으로.
남 맞아. 그럼 이걸로 주문해야겠다.

---

11 | 정답 | ④

남자가 시험을 준비하면서 수학 공식을 잘 모르겠다고 하자 여자가 도와주겠다고 제안하고 있으므로 남자의 응답으로는 ④ '잘됐다. 여기 내가 도움이 필요한 문제 몇 개가 있어.'가 가장 적절하다.

* formula 공식
* review 복습하다

W Nick, the exams are next week. How are you getting along with your studies?
M I'm doing my best, but I'm still having trouble understanding some of the formulas.
W Really? I finished reviewing the difficult formulas yesterday. Can I help you with anything?
M Great. Here are some of the questions I need help with.

여 Nick, 시험이 다음 주야. 공부는 어떻게 되어가?
남 최선을 다하고 있는데 아직도 공식 몇 개를 이해하는 데 어려움을 겪고 있어.
여 정말? 난 어제 어려운 공식들을 복습하는 것을 끝냈어. 내가 뭐 좀 도와줄까?
남 잘됐다. 여기 내가 도움이 필요한 문제 몇 개가 있어.

① 나도 그래. 나도 수학을 좋아하지 않아.
② 걱정 마. 난 수학을 꽤 잘해.
③ 미안해. 지금은 너를 도와줄 충분한 시간이 없어.
⑤ 견뎌 봐. 너도 모르게 모든 게 끝날 거야.

---

12 | 정답 | ⑤

위급한 일이 생겨서 영화 보러 가지 못해 미안하다고 말하고 있으므로 여자의 응답으로 ⑤ '미안해하지 마. 내가 도울 게 있으면 알려줘.'가 가장 적절하다.

* urgent 위급한
* come up 생기다, 발생하다

M Bella, I have something to tell you.
W What is it? [Pause] What's wrong? Is everything all right?
M Not really. Something urgent came up, so I don't think I can go to the movies with you tonight. I'm really sorry.
W Don't be. Let me know if I can help.

남 Bella, 너에게 할 말이 있어.
여 뭔데? [잠시 후] 뭐가 잘못됐어? 다 괜찮은 거야?
남 아니. 그렇지 않아. 위급한 일이 생겨서 오늘 밤에 너와 영화 보러 못 갈 것 같아. 정말 미안해.
여 미안해하지 마. 내가 도울 게 있으면 알려줘.

① 모르겠어. 그 영화에 대해 전에 들은 적이 없어.
② 걱정 마. 이번에는 잊지 않겠다고 약속할게.
③ 신경 쓰지 마. 내가 문제를 해결할 수 있어.
④ 미안해. 나 혼자 거기 가려는 의도는 아니었어.

13 | 정답 | ③

손톱을 깨무는 습관을 고치려는 남자에게 여자는 습관의 원인은 스트레스이며, 스트레스를 줄여보라고 조언하는 상황이다. 스트레스에 관한 책들도 많으니, 확인해 보라는 여자의 말에 대한 남자의 응답으로 가장 적절한 것은 ③ '그래. 아마 그것에 대한 책을 읽는 게 유용할 수도 있겠다.'이다.

* bite 깨물다
* mental 정신적
* stress 스트레스; 스트레스를 주다
* anxious 불안해하는, 염려하는
* manage 관리하다, 다루다
[선택지]
* inspiring 고무[격려]하는
* copy (책·신문 등의) 한 부

W You are doing it again.
M What do you mean?
W You are biting your nails again. You said you wanted to stop.
M Right. I've been trying to fix my bad habit for a while. But I don't seem to be getting any better.
W What have you tried so far?
M I cut my nails really short so that I don't have any to bite. And I try to keep my hands busy with a pen. But nothing seems to work.
W Well, I heard that biting nails can be a sign of mental stress. You may be nervous or anxious and you don't know it.
M I've been under a lot of stress lately. But I haven't really talked to anyone because I'm not really used to talking about my feelings.
W How about relieving your stress? You could try something like exercising, getting more sleep or relaxing.
M You're right. I should focus more on managing my stress.
W There are also books on how to do it. You should also check them out.
M Okay. Maybe reading books about it could be helpful.

여 너 다시 그걸 하고 있네.
남 무슨 의미야?
여 네 손톱을 다시 깨물고 있어. 그만하고 싶다고 했었잖아.
남 맞아. 한동안 나쁜 습관을 고치려고 노력해 왔어. 근데 더 나아지지 않는 것 같아.
여 지금까지 어떤 걸 시도해 왔어?
남 손톱을 깨물 수 없도록 정말 짧게 자르지. 그리고 펜으로 내 손을 바쁘게 움직이기도 하고. 그런데도 아무 소용이 없는 것 같아.
여 음. 손톱을 깨무는 것은 정신적 스트레스의 징후라 들었어. 너는 긴장하거나 불안해할 수도 있고 그걸 넌 의식하지 못하는 거야.
남 최근에 스트레스를 많이 받기는 했어. 근데 내 기분에 대해 말하는 것이 익숙지 않아서 아무한테도 얘기하지 않았거든.
여 네 스트레스를 좀 해소하는 게 어때? 운동을 하거나, 더 많이 자거나, 휴식하는 것과 같은 걸 해볼 수 있잖아.
남 네 말이 맞아. 내 스트레스를 관리하는 것에 더 주력해야 할 것 같아.
여 그걸 하는 방법에 관한 책들도 있어. 그것들도 확인해 봐.
남 그래. 아마 그것에 대한 책을 읽는 게 유용할 수도 있겠다.

① 확실하지 않아. 그것에 대해 다른 사람한테 얘기하는 것이 낫겠어.
② 괜찮아질 것 같아. 지금 당장 어떤 도움도 필요 없어.
④ 좋은 생각이야. 넌 곧 네 목표를 이룰 수 있어.
⑤ 그 책들은 정말 고무적이야. 한 권을 사야겠어.

14 | 정답 | ②

여자가 옛 친구들이 잘 지내는지 물으며 빨리 친구들을 만나고 싶다고 하였고 남자는 사실 여자를 위한 환영파티가 내일 준비되어 있으니 파티에 와서 친구들을 보라고 말하고 있으므로 여자의 응답으로 가장 적절한 것은 ② '걱정 마. 이제부터 하나도 놓치지 않을게.'이다.

* rewarding 보람찬
* definitely 분명히
* get together 모이다
* room 공간
* for oneself 스스로
[선택지]
* miss 놓치다
* from now on 지금부터

M How was the volunteering work in Africa?
W It was pretty hard but rewarding. At first, I had no time to think about what I was doing or thinking. There were so many things to do.
M Working abroad must've been such a great learning experience.
W It definitely was. I wanted to stay longer, but I had to come back earlier than I expected.
M Well, we are just glad to have you back home.
W Thanks a lot. Why don't we get together with some of our old friends sometime soon?
M Actually, we have a party prepared for you tomorrow.
W Oh, really? Where?
M It will be at Kelly's cafe. She said she would always have room for you.
W She is such a good friend. I am so happy to have friends like you guys.
M It's been two years. Everybody wants to know what you've been doing.
W Me, too. How's everyone doing?
M You should come and see for yourself. Your welcome back party is at 5 p.m. tomorrow.
W Don't worry. I won't miss a thing from now on.

남 아프리카의 자원봉사 일은 어땠어?
여 꽤 힘들었지만 보람 있었어. 처음엔 내가 뭘 하고 있는지 무슨 생각을 하는지 생각할 겨를이 없었어. 할 일이 너무 많았거든.
남 해외에서 일한다는 건 분명히 아주 대단한 학습 경험이었을 거야.
여 분명히 그랬어. 더 머무르고 싶었지만 내가 예상했던 것보다 더 일찍 돌아와야 했어.
남 그래. 우리는 네가 집에 돌아와서 기쁘기만 해.
여 정말 고마워. 빠른 시일에 우리 옛 친구들과 함께 모이는 건 어때?
남 사실, 내일 너를 위해 파티를 준비했거든.
여 아, 정말? 어디서?
남 Kelly네 카페에서 있을 거야. 그 애가 너를 위한 공간은 항상 있을 거라고 말했거든.
여 걘 정말 좋은 친구야. 너희들 같은 친구들이 있어서 너무 행복해.
남 벌써 2년 됐어. 모두 네가 뭐 하고 지냈는지 알고 싶어 해.
여 나도 그래. 모두 잘 지내지?
남 네가 직접 와서 봐야 해. 너의 환영 파티는 내일 오후 5시야.
여 걱정 마. 이제부터 하나도 놓치지 않을게.

① 물론. 난 곧 다시 아프리카로 떠나.
③ 알겠어. 분명히 아무도 파티에 나타나지 않을 거야.
④ 몰라. 내가 아직 준비가 되어 있는지 모르겠어.
⑤ 당연하지. 난 항상 훌륭한 레스토랑에서 외식하는 걸 즐겨.

15 | 정답 | ④

새로운 요리법을 두고 Tom과 June의 의견이 달라 다른 요리사에게 의견을 요청해야 하는 상황이다. 보다 공정하게

W Tom and June are cooks working at the same restaurant. This year, they have to develop a new recipe for diners at the restaurant. Tom wants to develop a simple healthy dish that requires little time to prepare but attracts many

여 Tom과 June은 같은 레스토랑에서 일하는 요리사이다. 올해, 그들은 레스토랑 손님들을 위한 새 요리법을 개발해야 한다. Tom은 준비하는 데는 시간이 오래 걸리지 않지만 건강에 관심 있는 많은 고객들을 유치할 간

의견을 구하기 위해, 모든 요리사가 두 가지 다른 의견 중 하나만 선택하도록 Tom이 June에게 제안할 말로 가장 적절한 것은 ④ '우리 공정하게 이걸 투표에 부치는 게 어때?'이다.

* develop 개발하다
* recipe 요리법
* diner 식사 손님
* attract 끌어들이다
* concerns 관심, 걱정
* sophisticated 정교한
* differentiate 차별화하다
* opposite 반대의
  [선택지]
* voting booth (투표장 안의) 기표소
* put A to a vote A를 투표에 부치다
* acceptable 받아들여지는

clients who have health concerns. However, June thinks something more sophisticated should be developed to differentiate their restaurant from others nearby. Since they have opposite opinions, they decide to ask other chefs whose opinion is better. To find out the other chefs' opinions, Tom wants to suggest to June that all the chefs choose between Tom's and June's opinion. In this situation, what would Tom most likely say to June?

Tom Why don't we put this to a vote to be fair?

단하고 건강한 요리를 개발하고 싶어 한다. 그러나 June은 근처의 다른 레스토랑과 그들의 레스토랑을 차별화하기 위한 뭔가 더 정교한 것이 개발되어야 한다고 생각한다. 그들이 정반대의 의견을 가지고 있어서 다른 요리사들에게 누구의 의견이 더 나은지 물어보기로 결정한다. 다른 요리사들의 의견을 알아보기 위해서 Tom은 June에게 모든 요리사가 Tom과 June의 의견 중 하나를 선택하도록 제안하고 싶다. 이러한 상황에서 Tom이 June에게 할 말로 가장 적절한 것은 무엇인가?

Tom 우리 공정하게 이걸 투표에 부치는 게 어때?

① 난 네가 내 의견을 따라주면 좋겠어.
② 두 요리 다 개발하는 건 어때?
③ 나 대신 기표소를 만들어 줄 수 있니?
⑤ 네 아이디어는 그리 받아들여질 것 같지 않아.

---

16 | 정답 | ④

남자는 프랑스에 관한 기본 정보에 대해 설명하고 있으므로 정답은 ④ '프랑스에 관한 기본 정보'이다.

17 | 정답 | ②

프랑스는 서유럽에 있으며, 360개 종류의 치즈와 품질 좋은 와인을 생산한다고 설명하고, 프랑스 출신의 유명 작가에 대해서도 언급하고 있다. 하지만 '인구'에 대한 언급은 없었으므로 정답은 ②이다.

* Arc de Triomphe 개선문
* officially 공식적으로
* tourism 관광업
* tourist attraction 관광명소
* outstanding 뛰어난
* contribute to ~에 기여하다
* literature 문학
  [선택지]
* historical 역사적, 역사상의

M Hello, students. How much do you know about France? The Eiffel Tower? The Arc de Triomphe? France, officially known as the French Republic, is the largest country in Western Europe. It is also the third-largest country in Europe. As most of you know, France is one of the most visited countries for tourism. Each year, nearly 80 million people visit to see famous tourist attractions with their own eyes. Did you know that there are 360 different types of cheese made in France? Can you imagine how much French people enjoy cheese? Along with cheese, France is a well-known wine producer. It is the second largest producer of outstanding quality wines in the world. Also, as you know, there are many famous French authors who have contributed to literature. Well-known books such as *The Hunchback of Notre Dames*, *The Phantom of the Opera*, *Sleeping Beauty*, and even *Cinderella* were written by writers from France.

남 여러분, 안녕하세요. 프랑스에 대해 얼마나 알고 있나요? 에펠탑? 개선문? 공식적으로는 프랑스 공화국이라고 알려진 프랑스는 서유럽에 있는 가장 큰 나라입니다. 유럽에서는 또한 세 번째로 큰 국가이죠. 여러분 대부분이 알다시피, 프랑스는 관광으로 가장 많이 방문하는 나라 중 하나예요. 매년, 거의 8천만 관광객들이 직접 보려고 유명한 관광지들을 방문합니다. 여러분은 프랑스에서 만들어진 치즈의 종류가 360가지나 있다는 걸 알고 있었나요? 여러분은 프랑스 사람들이 치즈를 얼마나 즐기는지 상상이 되시나요? 치즈와 더불어 프랑스는 잘 알려진 와인 생산국입니다. 세계에서 뛰어난 품질의 와인을 생산하는 두 번째로 큰 생산국이죠. 또한 알다시피 문학에 기여한 유명한 프랑스 작가들이 있습니다. 〈노트르담의 꼽추〉, 〈오페라의 유령〉, 〈잠자는 숲속의 공주〉, 그리고 심지어 〈신데렐라〉와 같은 잘 알려진 책들이 프랑스 작가들에 의해 쓰였지요.

16 ① 프랑스의 유명한 문학 작품들
② 프랑스가 매우 잘 알려진 이유
③ 프랑스의 역사적 배경
④ 프랑스에 관한 기본 정보
⑤ 프랑스에서 갈 만한 최고의 장소

01 | 정답 | ⑤

남자는 그림 그리기가 어느 나이에나 배울 수 있는 기술이라고 말하면서 온라인 미술 수업에 대해 설명하고 있으므로 정답은 ⑤이다.

- intermediate 중급의
- advanced 고급의
- tutorial 개별 지도 (시간)
- promising 유망한
- last 지속되다
- progress 발전

M Hello, everyone. I'd like to invite all of you to join our online art classes. It's not too late to learn drawing because it is a skill you can master at any age. There are three classes offered based on level of difficulty: beginner, intermediate, and advanced. Each class contains 24 tutorials designed by 20 promising local artists, and some of them are available to try for free. So, if you are not sure, try one of our free trial tutorials of your choice. And when you first sign up for a class this month, you will be offered a 10% discount. This event lasts only this month. Please visit our website and make instant progress in your drawing skills now!

남 여러분, 안녕하세요. 저는 여러분 모두를 온라인 미술 수업에 함께하도록 초대하고 싶습니다. 그림 그리기는 나이에 상관없이 숙달할 수 있는 기술이기에 지금도 배우기에 늦지 않았습니다. 난이도에 기초하여 제공되는 초급, 중급, 그리고 고급의 세 개의 수업이 있습니다. 각 수업은 20명의 유망한 지역 예술가들에 의해 설계된 24개의 개별 지도를 포함하며, 일부는 무료로 수강이 가능합니다. 그러니, 확신이 들지 않으시는 분들은 저희 무료 수강 과정 중 하나를 선택해서 들어보세요. 그리고 이번 달에 수업을 처음 신청하시면 10%의 할인을 제공받습니다. 이 행사는 이번 달만 진행합니다. 저희 웹사이트에 방문하셔서 여러분의 그리기 실력의 즉각적인 발전을 지금 이루어 보세요!

02 | 정답 | ⑤

남자가 여행사에서 패키지여행을 알아본다고 하자 여자는 여행사보다는 여러 다른 자원을 이용해서 직접 알아보고 원하는 곳을 가고 원하는 것을 하는 여행을 추천하고 있으므로 정답은 ⑤이다.

- travel agency 여행사
- convenient 편리한
- go along with ~을 따르다
- itinerary 일정
- save (수고를) 덜어주다
- resource 자원
- broaden 넓히다
- a wide selection of 다양한

W Peter, you are going on a trip to Hawaii this summer, aren't you?
M Yes, I'm planning to. I visited several travel agencies, but I couldn't find any good package tours.
W Why do you need a guide?
M I just thought it'd be more convenient to go along with an itinerary.
W Well, sure, it saves you the trouble of making plans and reservations. But what's the fun in going to places you don't want to go?
M Then what are you suggesting I should do?
W Do research on your own. Find what's available and what you truly want to do in Hawaii. There are many resources you can use to get information other than travel agencies.
M You're right. I should broaden my options.
W You should visit the library near the city hall. It has a wide selection of travel books. You could also check out more information on the Internet.
M It looks like this trip is going to be quite an adventure!

여 Peter, 너 이번 여름에 하와이로 여행 가지, 그렇지 않니?
남 응. 그럴 계획이야. 여러 여행사를 방문했는데, 좋은 패키지여행을 하나도 못 찾았어.
여 왜 가이드가 필요하니?
남 난 그저 일정을 따르는 게 더 편리할 거라고 생각했어.
여 글쎄, 물론 계획하고 예약하는 수고를 덜어주긴 해. 하지만 네가 원하지 않는 곳에 간다면 무슨 재미가 있겠니?
남 그럼 내가 뭘 해야 한다고 제안하는 거야?
여 네가 직접 조사해 봐. 하와이에서 무엇이 가능하고 네가 정말로 무엇을 하고 싶은지를 찾아봐. 여행사 외에도 정보를 얻기 위해 활용할 수 있는 자원이 많이 있어.
남 맞아. 선택의 폭을 넓혀야겠어.
여 시청 근처에 있는 도서관에 가봐. 여행 서적들이 다양하게 있거든. 또 인터넷에서 더 많은 정보를 알아볼 수 있어.
남 이 여행은 굉장한 모험이 될 것 같아!

03 | 정답 | ④

바쁜 직장인들에게 자전거를 타고 출퇴근을 해서 운동 시간을 확보하라고 조언하고 있으므로 남자가 하는 말의 요지로 가장 적절한 것은 ④이다.

- commute 통근하다
- suggestion 제안, 제의
- cycle 자전거를 타다
  cf. cyclist 자전거를 타는 사람, 사이클리스트
- workout (건강을 위한) 운동
- make the most of ~을 최대한 활용하다
- additional 추가의

M Hello everyone, I'm Adam Paterson, your "Life Tips" guide. How do you commute to work every day? Have you ever considered adding exercise to your routine? For those of you who lead busy lives, here's a valuable suggestion: try cycling to and from work. By biking for an hour instead of driving for 30 minutes, you not only get a good workout but also make the most of your commute time. In this scenario, the cyclist invests an additional hour in commuting but gains two hours of meaningful exercise. I'll be back with more life tips next time. Take care!

남 안녕하세요, 여러분, 저는 여러분의 "생활 팁" 가이드인 Adam Paterson입니다. 여러분께서는 매일 어떻게 통근하시나요? 여러분의 일과에 운동을 추가하는 것을 생각해 본 적이 있으신가요? 분주한 삶을 사는 여러분을 위해, 여기 가치 있는 제안 하나를 드립니다. 자전거를 타고 출퇴근을 해보세요. 30분 동안 자동차를 운전하는 대신 한 시간 동안 자전거를 타면, 여러분은 좋은 운동을 할 수 있을 뿐만 아니라 통근 시간을 최대한 활용할 수 있습니다. 이 시나리오에서, 자전거를 타는 사람은 통근에 한 시간을 더 투자하지만, 두 시간 동안 의미 있는 운동을 합니다. 다음에는 더 많은 생활 팁을 가지고 올게요. 안녕히 계세요!

04 | 정답 | ④

체스판 위에는 체스 말이 2개가 있다고 하였으므로 대화의 내용과 일치하지 않

M Have you decided on the design of our T-shirt?
W I'm still working on it, but I'm almost done. Do you want to see it?

남 우리 티셔츠 디자인 정했니?
여 아직 작업 중이지만 거의 다 하긴 했어. 볼래?

는 것은 ④이다.

* spot (특정한) 곳, 자리
* point at ~을 가리키다
* chessboard 체스판
* piece (체스 등의) 말
* in the air 공중에
* distracting 산만하게 하는, 집중이 안 되게 하는
* phrase 글귀, 문구
* font 서체, 폰트

M Sure. [Pause] I love it. I don't think there is much to change.
W Thanks. Anyways, I put "Chessmate," the name of our club, at the top.
M I think that's the perfect spot for the name. And you added a girl wearing a crown under the name.
W Yes, I made the girl point at the chessboard. I wanted chess to look like a fun and interesting game.
M That was a great idea. Is there any reason why you only used a few chess pieces on the t-shirt?
W I didn't want to put too many pieces on the T-shirt. So, there are three pieces in the air and two on the board.
M It's much better like this. A t-shirt with too many pieces on it would have been too distracting.
W Exactly. Oh, do you see the phrase under the chessboard?
M Under the chessboard? Do you mean the phrase "I Love Chess" in a small font?
W Yes, I wasn't sure if I should add something under the board.
M I think it looks good there. Let's go with this design.

남 그럼. [잠시 후] 마음에 쏙 든다. 바꿀 곳이 많지 않은 것 같아.
여 고마워. 어쨌든, 난 우리 동아리 이름 'Chessmate'를 제일 위에 넣었어.
남 거기가 이름을 넣기에 완벽한 곳인 것 같아. 그리고 그 이름 아래에 왕관을 쓰고 있는 여자애를 추가했네.
여 응, 그 여자애가 체스판을 가리키게 했어. 체스가 아주 재밌고 흥미로운 게임이라는 것을 보여주고 싶었거든.
남 좋은 생각이야. 티셔츠에 체스 말을 몇 개만 사용한 이유가 있니?
여 티셔츠 위에 체스 말을 너무 많이 두고 싶지 않았어. 그래서 공중에 3개가 떠 있고, 판 위에는 2개만 있는 거야.
남 이렇게 한 게 훨씬 좋은 것 같아. 체스 말이 많이 나온 티셔츠는 너무 산만해 보였을 거야.
여 맞아. 아, 그 체스판 아래 글귀 보여?
남 체스판 아래에? 작은 서체로 쓰인 'I Love Chess'를 말하는 거야?
여 그래. 체스판 아래에 뭔가를 추가해야 할지 확신이 서지 않았거든.
남 보기 좋은 것 같아. 이 디자인으로 하자.

05 | 정답 | ②

여자가 자신의 생물학 수업 복습을 도와주기로 한 남자의 연락처가 없어졌다고 하자 남자가 여자에게 전화를 걸었고 여자는 번호를 저장하겠다고 말하고 있으므로 정답은 ②이다.

* semester 학기
* biology 생물학
* definitely 당연하지, 물론
* remind 상기시키다
* contact 연락처

W Tommy, can I talk to you for a minute?
M Sure. What's up?
W This semester I'm taking Biology. Since it's my first time taking a biology class, I'm having trouble understanding.
M I know how you feel. I've been there. The course is really tough without any basic knowledge.
W Well, that's why I wanted to talk to you. I have a favor to ask.
M Okay. What is it?
W If you are not busy, could you help me review for the course after school?
M Definitely. I can help you with that. Luckily, I still have my old notes from the course.
W Great. I have that class on Wednesdays. Can you help me every Wednesday?
M If I don't have anything special to do, I'd be happy to do that.
W Thank you so much. You don't know how much this means to me.
M No problem. Just give me a call to remind me the day before, okay?
W Of course. Oh, I recently got a new phone and lost all of my contacts. Do you have mine?
M I'm not sure. Let me check first. [Pause] Here it is. And I'm calling you now.
W I see your number. I'll save it now.

여 Tommy, 잠깐 얘기할 수 있니?
남 물론이야. 무슨 일이야?
여 이번 학기에 나는 생물학을 들어. 생물학 수업을 듣는 건 처음이라서 이해하는 데 어려움이 있어.
남 어떤 기분인지 알아. 나도 그랬었거든. 그 과정은 기본 지식이 전혀 없으면 정말 어려워.
여 음, 그래서 너한테 얘기하고 싶었어. 부탁 하나 할 게 있는데.
남 그래. 그게 뭔데?
여 바쁘지 않으면 방과 후에 그 수업을 복습하는 걸 도와줄 수 있니?
남 당연하지. 도와줄 수 있어. 다행히 나는 그 수업의 예전 노트를 지금도 가지고 있거든.
여 잘됐다. 그 수업이 수요일마다 있어. 매주 수요일에 도와줄 수 있니?
남 특별한 일 없으면, 기꺼이 도와줄게.
여 정말 고마워. 이게 나한테 얼마나 많은 걸 의미하는지 넌 모를 거야.
남 괜찮아. 그 전날 내가 잊지 않게 전화나 해줘, 알겠지?
여 물론이야. 아, 최근에 내가 새 휴대폰을 사서 연락처가 다 없어졌어. 내 번호 갖고 있니?
남 모르겠어. 우선 확인해 볼게. [잠시 후] 여기 있네. 지금 전화 걸게.
여 네 번호 뜬다. 지금 저장할게.

06 | 정답 | ③

남자는 5일간 차를 빌리려고 하므로 렌트비는 100달러이고, 보험은 50달러에서 10% 할인을 받아 45달러이므로 정답은 ③이다.

* economy car 경차
* luxury 고급의, 호화로운
* sedan 세단형 자동차
* have in mind 생각하고 있다, 염두에 두다

W Hello. Can I help you?
M Yes, please. I'd like to rent a car for five days.
W Okay. We have all kinds of cars from small economy cars to luxury sedans. What type of car do you have in mind?
M I just need a midsize car for two people.
W Sure. We have several midsize cars right here. They are $20 per day.
M Okay. I think I'll go with this blue one. Does it run on gasoline or LPG?

여 안녕하세요. 도와드릴까요?
남 네. 5일간 차를 빌리고 싶은데요.
여 알겠습니다. 저희는 경차부터 고급 대형 승용차까지 모든 종류의 차가 있어요. 어떤 종류의 차를 생각하고 계신가요?
남 두 사람이 탈 중형차면 됩니다.
여 네. 바로 이쪽에 중형차가 몇 대 있어요. 하루에 20달러입니다.
남 좋아요. 이 파란 차로 할게요. 휘발유로 달리나요, 아니면 LPG로 달리나요?

- midsize 중형의
- purchase 구매하다
- insurance 보험
- paperwork 서류 작업
- payment 결제

W This model only comes with a gasoline engine. Is that all right with you?

M That's fine. And I'd also like to purchase insurance. How much does it cost?

W For this model, car insurance is $10 a day, so you need to pay $50 for five days. But if the driver is over the age of 40, we offer a 10% discount.

M That sounds perfect. I just turned 41 this year.

W Great. There is some paperwork that needs to be done. After that, I'll help you with the payment.

여 이 모델은 휘발유 엔진으로만 나옵니다. 괜찮으신가요?

남 괜찮아요. 그리고 보험도 구매하고 싶은데요. 비용이 얼마나 드나요?

여 이 모델의 경우 자동차 보험은 하루에 10달러이므로, 고객님은 5일에 50달러를 지불하시면 됩니다. 하지만 운전자가 40세가 넘으면 10% 할인을 제공해 드려요.

남 완벽하네요. 올해 막 41세가 되었거든요.

여 잘됐네요. 필요한 서류 작업이 좀 있습니다. 그 후에 결제를 도와드릴게요.

---

07 | 정답 | ②

남자가 여름에 중국에 갈 계획을 얘기하면서 여자에게 같이 가자고 하지만 여자는 여름에 중요한 출장이 두 개가 있다고 말하고 있으므로 정답은 ②이다.

- capital 수도
- Great Wall of China 만리장성
- merry 즐거운
- business trip 출장
- scheduled 일정이 잡힌

W You have so many travel books here. Are you planning a trip yourself?

M Oh, yes. I'm thinking about visiting China this summer.

W Wow, you're going to China? Where in China do you want to go?

M I'm thinking of going to Beijing first. It's the capital of China, so I think it's a good place to start.

W I've really wanted to go there to see the Great Wall of China.

M Then why don't we go together? Sam and Helen will join me, and maybe others. I'm asking people to join the trip because the more the merrier.

W Thanks for asking, but I'm afraid I have to say no.

M Oh, do you already have plans for your summer vacation?

W Well, there are two important business trips scheduled for this summer.

M Really? I wish you could come with us. Maybe we can travel together another time.

W Of course. I do hope you guys have fun.

M Thanks.

여 너 여기에 여행 책들이 엄청 많이 있네. 여행을 직접 계획하고 있니?

남 아, 응. 이번 여름에 중국을 방문할까 생각 중이야.

여 와, 중국에 가? 중국 어디에 가고 싶은데?

남 먼저 베이징에 갈 생각이야. 중국의 수도이니까 출발지로 좋은 곳 같아서.

여 나도 거기에 만리장성을 보러 정말 가고 싶었어.

남 그럼 같이 가는 게 어때? Sam과 Helen도 나랑 갈 예정이고 아마 다른 사람들도 갈지도 몰라. 더 많을수록 더 재미있으니까 사람들에게 합류하라고 권하고 있어.

여 물어봐 줘서 고맙지만 나는 안 될 것 같아.

남 아, 이미 여름휴가 계획이 있니?

여 음, 이번 여름에 일정이 잡힌 중요한 출장이 두 개 있어.

남 정말? 너도 우리랑 같이 가면 좋을 텐데. 다음에 다 같이 여행 갈 수 있을 거야.

여 물론이야. 너희들이 즐겁게 보냈으면 정말 좋겠다.

남 고마워.

---

08 | 정답 | ④

약사협회 회원만이 참가할 수 있고 날짜는 6월 28일, 29일이며, 장소는 Grand National 호텔이고 소요 시간은 8시간 걸린다고 했으므로 언급되지 않은 것은 ④이다.

- pharmaceutical association 약사협회
- employee 직원
- be held 열리다, 개최되다
- tight 빡빡한
- describe 설명하다
- in detail 자세히

W Our department is attending the Medicine Seminar next month. Did you hear about that?

M Really? No, I didn't. But can anybody attend the seminar?

W Well, only the members of the Pharmaceutical Association are invited. But this year, the CEO of our company is attending as a guest speaker, so all the employees get a free pass to the event.

M That sounds good. When will it be held?

W It'll be on June 28th and 29th, which fall on Thursday and Friday.

M Oh, okay. Where will the seminar take place?

W It will be held at the Grand National Hotel. I think the company will provide us with buses to get there.

M That's great. That'll save us the trouble of getting there. Do you know how long the seminar is?

W It's a total of 8 hours long with a one-hour lunch break.

M The schedule seems a bit too tight.

W That's because there will be many guest speakers and discussions. Don't worry. There will be an e-mail sent out describing it in detail.

여 우리 부서가 다음 달에 의학 세미나에 참석해. 그 소식 들었어?

남 정말? 못 들었어. 하지만 그 세미나에 아무나 참석할 수 있어?

여 글쎄, 약사협회 회원들만 초대받는데. 하지만 올해는 우리 회사 대표님이 초청 연사로 참석해서 모든 직원이 행사에 무료입장권을 받는대.

남 그거 좋네. 언제 열리는데?

여 6월 28일과 29일에 열리는데, 목요일과 금요일이야.

남 아, 그렇구나. 세미나는 어디서 열려?

여 Grand National 호텔에서 열릴 거야. 회사가 그곳으로 가는 버스를 제공할 것 같아.

남 잘됐다. 거기로 가는 수고를 덜어 주겠네. 세미나가 얼마나 오래 하는지 아니?

여 점심시간 1시간 포함해서 총 8시간짜리야.

남 일정이 좀 너무 빡빡한 것 같은데.

여 초청 연사가 많고 토론이 있을 예정이어서 그래. 걱정 마. 일정을 자세히 설명하는 이메일을 보내줄 거야.

---

09 | 정답 | ②

학교 기부 행사는 지역 학생들을 돕기 위한 것으로 현금을 제외한 모든 물품을 기부할 수 있다고 말하고 있으므로

W Good morning, students. I'd like to tell you about the upcoming school event, Veritas High School Charity Collection Week. As you all know, we will be holding our school charity collection next week to help local students.

여 안녕하세요, 학생 여러분. 저는 여러분에게 다가오는 학교 행사인 Veritas 고등학교 자선모금 주간에 대해 이야기하려고 합니다. 여러분 모두 알다시피, 우리는 다음 주에 지역 학생들을 돕기 위한 학교 자선모금을

일치하지 않는 것은 ②이다.

- **upcoming** 다가오는
- **charity** 자선
- **collection** 모금
- **cooperation** 협조
- **meaningful** 의미 있는
- **electronics** 가전제품
- **auditorium** 강당
- **donation** 기부, 기증

Last year we helped a lot of students thanks to your cooperation. I hope all of you join this meaningful event again. Except for cash, all items are welcome, including clothes, bags, books and small electronics. The way you donate is the same as last year. Put the items you want to donate into a box and write your name on it. Then leave your box at the collection point in the school auditorium. Charity Collection Week will be held for 11 days from September 10th to 20th. After the 20th, we won't take any donations, so make sure you bring your box by the 20th. I hope all of you have a great day.

열 예정입니다. 작년에 여러분의 협조로 많은 학생들에게 도움을 주었습니다. 여러분 모두 이 뜻깊은 행사에 다시 한번 동참해 주기를 바랍니다. 현금을 제외한 옷, 가방, 책, 소형 가전제품을 포함한 모든 물품을 환영합니다. 기부하는 방식은 작년과 동일합니다. 기부하고자 하는 품목을 상자에 넣고 그 위에 여러분의 이름을 쓰세요. 그다음 학교 강당에 있는 모금 장소에 상자를 놓아두세요. 자선모금 주간은 9월 10일부터 20일까지 11일간 계속됩니다. 20일 이후에는 어떤 기부도 받지 않으니 20일까지 상자를 꼭 가져오세요. 여러분 모두 멋진 하루를 보내기를 바랍니다.

---

10 | 정답 | ③

남자는 가격대가 1,000달러 이내인 은색의 냉장고로 저장량이 350리터이고 별 5개 등급의 에너지 효율이 좋은 모델을 구매하기로 하였으므로 정답은 ③이다.

- **refrigerator** 냉장고
- **top-selling** 가장 잘 팔리는
- **banner** (광고용) 플래카드, 현수막
- **seasonal sale** 계절 할인
- **price range** 가격대
- **storage volume** 저장량
- **sufficient** 충분한
- **energy rating** 에너지 등급
- **energy efficient** 에너지 효율이 좋은

W Hello. What can I do for you?
M I'm looking for a refrigerator.
W Let me show you our top-selling models.
M I saw the banner that says you are having a seasonal sale. Is that right?
W Of course. What price range do you have in mind?
M No more than $1,000, I guess.
W Some of our refrigerators with two doors are within your budget range. Would you take a look?
M Sure. I don't need anything too big or too small.
W Okay. Look at these. They are all 350-liter ones.
M The storage volume is sufficient. And, what colors do you have?
W We have them in black, and silver.
M Oh, I would prefer a silver one.
W I see. In that case, these two models are what you can choose from.
M What is the difference between those two?
W They have different energy ratings. I recommend this five-star model which is more energy efficient.
M Okay. I'll take the five-star one, then.

여 안녕하세요. 무얼 도와드릴까요?
남 냉장고를 찾고 있는데요.
여 가장 잘 팔리는 모델로 보여드릴게요.
남 계절 할인 중이라고 하는 현수막을 봤는데요. 맞나요?
여 물론이죠. 생각하시는 가격대가 얼마인가요?
남 1,000달러보다 많으면 안 될 것 같아요.
여 양문형 냉장고 중 일부가 손님의 가격대에 맞네요. 구경하시겠어요?
남 좋아요. 너무 크거나 너무 작은 건 필요하지 않아요.
여 알겠어요. 이것들을 보세요. 모두 350리터 모델이에요.
남 저장량은 충분하네요. 그리고 색은 어떤 게 있나요?
여 검은색과 은색으로 있습니다.
남 아, 저는 은색이 좋아요.
여 알겠습니다. 그렇다면 이 두 모델 중에 고르실 수 있어요.
남 그 둘의 차이점이 뭔가요?
여 에너지 등급이 달라요. 저는 에너지 효율이 더 좋은 이쪽의 별 다섯 개 모델을 추천합니다.
남 좋아요. 그럼 별 다섯 개인 것으로 할게요.

---

11 | 정답 | ②

여자가 보고서 작업을 늦게까지 하고 있어서 남자가 제시간에 끝낼 수 있는지 묻고 있으므로 정답은 ② '네, 할 수 있어요. 마지막 페이지예요.'이다.

- **hand in** 제출하다 (= turn in)
- **on time** 제시간에

M Lucy, are you still working on the computer? It's almost midnight.
W I know, Dad. I haven't finished my history report yet. I have to hand it in tomorrow.
M You should've started it earlier. Do you think you can finish it on time?
W **Yes, I can. I'm on the last page.**

남 Lucy, 아직도 컴퓨터로 작업 중이니? 거의 자정이야.
여 알아요, 아빠. 제 역사 보고서를 아직 끝내지 못했어요. 내일 제출해야 하거든요.
남 더 일찍 시작했어야지. 제시간에 끝낼 수는 있겠니?
여 **네, 할 수 있어요. 마지막 페이지예요.**

① 물론이에요. 지금 막 시작했어요.
③ 아마도요. 지금 포기할 것 같아요.
④ 물론이죠. 벌써 제출했어요.
⑤ 모르겠어요. 끝낼 필요는 없어요.

---

12 | 정답 | ①

남자가 대중교통으로 하는 관광을 추천하자 대중교통 체계를 잘 모른다는 여자의 말에 대한 남자의 응답으로 가장 적절한 것은 ① '걱정 마. 1일 이용권이 네가 가고 싶은 곳이면 어디든 데려다 줄 거야.'이다.

- **public transit** 대중교통
  [선택지]
- **pass** 이용권, 패스
- **tourist attraction** 관광 명소

W Since you live in this city, can you recommend the best way to see some nice spots?
M The city bus tour is an option, but I recommend that you use public transit to experience the culture.
W Good idea. But I have no idea about the public transit system around here.
M **Don't worry. A one-day pass will take you anywhere you want to go.**

여 네가 이 도시에 사니까 멋진 곳들을 볼 수 있는 가장 좋은 방법을 추천해 줄 수 있니?
남 도시 버스 투어를 이용할 수 있지만, 문화를 체험하려면 대중교통을 이용하는 것을 추천해.
여 좋은 생각이야. 하지만 난 여기 대중교통 체계를 잘 몰라.
남 **걱정 마. 1일 이용권이 네가 가고 싶은 곳이면 어디든 데려다 줄 거야.**

② 안됐다. 도시의 그 지역에 가려면 티켓을 사야 할 거야.
③ 알겠어. 그럼 거기서 대중교통을 타는 것이 또 다른 선택지야.
④ 그 말을 들으니 아쉽다. 나는 도시 버스 투어를 추천하려고 했는데.
⑤ 잘됐다. 지역 관광 명소에 대한 정보를 얻어 보자.

13 | 정답 | ③

남자는 여자의 슬라이드가 내용은 훌륭
하지만 청중의 관심을 계속 끌 만한 게
필요하다면서 동영상 효과를 사용해 보
라고 제안하고 있으므로 여자의 마지막
응답으로 가장 적절한 것은 ③ '맞아. 네
가 제안한 대로 바꿀게.'이다.

- nutritionist 영양사
- presentation 발표
- balanced 균형 잡힌
- vegetarian diet 채식
- audience 청중, 관객
- hardly 거의 ~ 않는
- animated (사진 등이) 동영상으로 된
- delivery 전달

W Rob, can I talk to you for a minute?
M Hi, Monica. Sure, go ahead.
W I'm working on my lecture for next week. Since you are a nutritionist, can I have your opinion about something?
M I'm not sure if I could be of any help. I haven't worked as a nutritionist in over two years.
W Don't worry. I just need your general opinion about my slides. I know you were good at presentations.
M Well, I'll see what I can do. What is it about?
W It's about balanced vegetarian diets.
M All right. [Pause] I guess you need something to keep the audience's attention.
W Yes, I thought about that, too, but vegetarian diets are so simple that I can hardly add fun facts.
M I understand, but why don't you use some animated effects on your slides?
W If I use them, would it be more interesting?
M Definitely. Even if the content is great, the delivery is more important.
W I agree. I'll make the change that you suggested.

여 Rob, 잠깐 얘기 좀 할 수 있을까?
남 안녕, Monica. 물론이야, 얘기해 봐.
여 다음 주에 할 강의를 작업 중인데. 네가 영양사니까 너의 자문을 구해도 될까?
남 내가 도움이 될 수 있을지 모르겠네. 2년 넘게 영양사 일을 쉬었거든.
여 걱정 마. 내 슬라이드에 대한 너의 일반적인 견해만 필요해. 네가 발표를 잘했다는 걸 알거든.
남 글쎄, 내가 뭘 할 수 있는지 볼게. 뭐에 관한 거야?
여 균형 잡힌 채식에 관한 거야.
남 좋아. [잠시 후] 청중의 관심을 계속 끌 만한 게 필요한 것 같아.
여 응, 나도 그 생각을 했는데, 채식은 너무 간단해서 흥미로운 사실을 거의 넣을 수가 없어.
남 알아. 하지만 슬라이드에 동영상 효과를 좀 사용하는 건 어때?
여 그걸 사용하면, 좀 더 흥미로워질까?
남 물론이지. 내용이 훌륭해도 전달이 더 중요해.
여 맞아. 네가 제안한 대로 바꿀게.

① 신경 쓰지 마. 네게 어떤 충고도 구하지 않을게.
② 미안해. 내 강의의 대상은 아이들이 아냐.
④ 훌륭해. 난 강의 끝에 질의 응답시간을 가져.
⑤ 고마워. 난 네 발표가 내 것보다 더 좋았다고 생각해.

14 | 정답 | ⑤

여자는 학교 댄스 팀에 합격했지만 그
전에 친구의 개인지도 일을 돕기로 해
서 남자에게 조언을 구하는 상황이다.
댄스 팀 연습은 매일이지만, 개인지도는
매주 화요일이므로 댄스 팀이 자신의
경우를 예외로 해줄 수 있는지 물어보
는 여자의 말에 대한 남자의 응답으로
가장 적절한 것은 ⑤ '네가 매주 화요일
에 빠져도 되는지 내가 팀원들한테 물
어볼게.'이다.

- get accepted 합격하다
- awesome 굉장한
- tutoring 개인지도
- session (특정한 활동을 위한) 시간[기간]
- besides 게다가; ~말고는
- make an exception 예외로 하다
- case (특정 상황의) 경우
[선택지]
- let A off (처벌하지 않거나 가벼운 처벌로)
  A를 봐주다

W Kevin, you remember I applied for the school dance team last week, don't you?
M Sure. I was there when you auditioned for the team. Did you hear anything from them?
W Yes. I got a call from one of the members last night. I got accepted.
M That's awesome! Now we will dance together on the same team.
W But I promised to help Andy with the tutoring program for the rest of the semester.
M Oh, really? But there is a dance practice session every day. You can't miss more than 3 in a semester.
W I know, but I only have to go to the tutoring program every Tuesday. Besides, the program needs a lot of helping hands.
M I heard about that, too. Did you talk to anyone about this besides me?
W Not yet. I came to you first. Do you think the dance team can make an exception in my case?
M I'll ask the team members if they can let you off every Tuesday.

여 Kevin, 내가 지난주에 학교 댄스 팀에 지원한 거 기억하지, 그렇지?
남 물론이야. 네가 팀 오디션 볼 때 내가 거기 있었잖아. 무슨 소식 들었니?
여 응. 어젯밤에 회원 중 한 명에게서 전화를 받았어. 합격했다고.
남 정말 잘됐다! 이제 우리 같은 팀에서 함께 춤추게 되었어.
여 하지만 Andy에게 남은 학기 동안 개인지도 프로그램을 돕기로 약속했거든.
남 아, 정말? 근데 댄스 연습 시간이 매일 있잖아. 한 학기에 3번 넘게 빠지면 안 돼.
여 그래, 근데 개인지도 프로그램을 매주 화요일에는 가야 하거든. 게다가 그 프로그램은 도움이 많이 필요해.
남 나도 그건 들었어. 나 말고 다른 사람들한테도 얘기해 봤어?
여 아직 안 했어. 너한테 제일 먼저 왔어. 댄스 팀에서 내 경우를 예외로 해줄 것 같아?
남 네가 매주 화요일에 빠져도 되는지 내가 팀원들한테 물어볼게.

① 동의해. 너는 그렇게 자주 약속을 어기면 안 돼.
② 잘 모르겠어. 아마 둘 다 포기하는 것이 제일 좋을 것 같아.
③ 절대 안 돼. 난 네가 다른 학생들을 지도하는 걸 그만두지 않았으면 좋겠어.
④ 네가 댄스 경연대회를 포기하지 않는 게 좋을 것 같아.

15 | 정답 | ③

Nick은 현재 대학생이고 학교에 다니면
서 일할 수 있도록 시간제 일을 구하려
고 한 것이므로, 학교가 현재는 최우선
이라고 하면서 거절하는 게 가장 적절
하다. 따라서 정답은 ③ '정말 죄송해요.
지금은 학교가 최우선이에요.'이다.

- help-wanted 구인의
- convenience store 편의점
- impressed 좋은 인상을 받은
- candidate 후보

M Nick is a college student. This year he decides to get a part-time job to earn money. One day, he finds a help-wanted poster at a convenience store near his house. He thinks it will be convenient for him to work there and go to school. So he calls and makes an appointment to have an interview with the store manager, Jenny. On the day of the interview, he arrives 10 minutes early, and Jenny is impressed. After the job interview, Jenny realizes that Nick is the most suitable candidate for the job and she wants him to work full-time instead of part-time. So

남 Nick은 대학생이다. 올해 그는 돈을 벌기 위해 시간제 일을 구하기로 결심한다. 어느 날, 그는 집 근처의 편의점에서 구인 포스터를 발견한다. 그는 자신이 거기에서 일을 하고 학교에 다니는 게 편리할 것이라고 생각한다. 그래서 점장인 Jenny에게 전화를 걸어 면접을 볼 약속을 잡는다. 면접 날, 그는 10분 일찍 도착하고 Jenny는 좋은 인상을 받는다. 면접 후에 Jenny는 Nick이 그 일에 가장 적합한 후보라는 걸 깨닫고 그가 시간제 대신에 전일 근무로 일해주기를 원한다. 그래서 그녀는 전화를 해서 Nick에게 전일 근무를 제안한다. 하지만 Nick은 학교에도 가야 되고, 그것이 그에게는 더 중요하기 때문에 그저 시간제로만 일하고 싶다. 그

* **work full-time** 전일 근무하다
* **decline** 거절하다

she calls Nick and offers him a full-time job. However, Nick only wants to work part-time since he has to go to school too, which is much more important to him. So he decides to decline the job offer. In this situation, what would Nick most likely say to Jenny?

Nick I'm so sorry. School is my top priority right now.

래서 그는 그 제안을 거절하기로 결심한다. 이러한 상황에서 Nick이 Jenny에게 할 말로 가장 적절한 것은 무엇인가?

Nick 정말 죄송해요. 지금은 학교가 최우선이에요.

① 안 될 것 같아요. 저는 전일 근무를 하고 싶어요.
② 괜찮아요. 저는 지금의 일에 만족해요.
④ 왜! 여기서 일할 수 있어서 너무 감사해요!
⑤ 정말 친절하시네요. 하지만 저는 다른 일자리 제안을 받았어요.

---

16 | 정답 | ③

여자는 saguaro 선인장의 독특한 특징들에 대해 설명하고 있으므로 정답은 ③ 'saguaro 선인장의 독특한 특징'이다.

17 | 정답 | ②

가운데 큰 줄기에서 팔과 같은 작은 줄기가 나와서 똑바로 자란다고 했으며 최대 200년의 수명. 봄에 피는 꽃과 6월에 맺는 열매에 대해 언급했지만 '뿌리'에 대한 내용은 없었으므로 정답은 ②이다.

* **cactus** 선인장
* **feature** 특징
* **harsh** 척박한
* **primarily** 주로
* **noted for** ~로 유명한
* **appearance** 외형, 외모
* **stem** 줄기
* **straight up** 곧장 위로
* **up to** ~까지
* **bear** (열매를) 맺다
* **wood pecker** 딱따구리
  [선택지]
* **survival of the fittest** 적자생존

W Hello, students. Today, we will learn about a unique cactus called the saguaro cactus. This cactus is a common feature in some parts of the American Southwest and Mexico. It grows in harsh desert conditions. Do you know what it is primarily noted for? It has a unique appearance. It has one large stem in the middle, which can grow to be more than 15 meters high. Other small stems grow on the large stem like arms. And the arms also grow straight up toward the sky. Do you know how many years it lives for? This cactus has a relatively long lifespan, living for up to 200 years. You can't even see the small arms until it is about 75 years old. In spring, white and yellow flowers bloom on the cactus. In June, the cactus bears a red fruit. The saguaro cactus is home to many birds, including owls and wood peckers. They make nests in holes in the cactus. Let me show you some pictures of the saguaro cactus flowers.

여 안녕하세요, 학생 여러분. 오늘은 saguaro 선인장이라는 한 독특한 선인장에 대해 배워 봅시다. 이 선인장은 미국 남서부와 멕시코 일부의 공통된 특징입니다. 그것은 척박한 사막 환경에서 자랍니다. 그것이 주로 무엇으로 유명한지 아시나요? 그것은 독특한 외형을 가지고 있습니다. 하나의 큰 줄기가 가운데에 있는데, 그것은 15미터가 넘게 자랄 수 있습니다. 다른 작은 줄기들은 그 큰 줄기에서 팔처럼 자라납니다. 그리고 이 팔들은 또한 하늘을 향해 똑바로 자랍니다. 그것이 몇 년을 사는지 아시나요? 이 선인장은 상대적으로 긴 수명을 가지고 있는데, 200살까지 살 수 있습니다. 심지어 작은 팔들은 약 75살 정도가 될 때까지 보이지 않습니다. 봄에는 선인장에 하얀 꽃과 노란 꽃이 핍니다. 6월에는 빨간 열매를 맺고요. saguaro 선인장은 올빼미와 딱따구리를 포함한 많은 새들에게 집이 되어 줍니다. 그들은 선인장에 난 구멍 안에 둥지를 짓습니다. saguaro 선인장의 꽃 사진을 몇 장을 보겠습니다.

16 ① 사막의 식물들이 가져올 수 있는 이점
② 선인장이 왜 오랫동안 생존하는가
③ saguaro 선인장의 독특한 특징
④ 선인장을 어떻게 섭취하는가
⑤ 적자생존

17 ① 줄기 ② 뿌리 ③ 수명
④ 꽃 ⑤ 열매

4회 고난도 듣기 모의고사

| 01 ⑤ | 02 ⑤ | 03 ⑤ | 04 ② | 05 ② | 06 ④ | 07 ④ | 08 ② | 09 ② | 10 ① |
| 11 ④ | 12 ④ | 13 ④ | 14 ② | 15 ⑤ | 16 ④ | 17 ③ | | | |

01 | 정답 | ⑤

여자는 지금 상황에 대해 불평할 것을 찾는 것보다 감사할 것을 찾고 그것을 즐김으로써 행복할 수 있다고 말하고 있으므로 정답은 ⑤이다.

- **down** 우울한
- **dreary** (풍경·날씨 등이) 음울한, 쓸쓸한
- **look back** (과거를) 돌이켜보다
- **take A for granted** A를 당연한 일로 여기다
- **fade into the background** 존재가 희미해지다
- **savor** 만끽하다; 음미하다
- **gratitude** 감사
- **circumstance** 상황

W Hello, students. This is your school counselor speaking, and I'd like to say a few words about happiness. Some of you seem a little down as the weather is getting dreary. Some students may be upset about grades that won't improve. Others might complain they have nothing fun to do. However, if you look back, there must have been events in your life that made you happy. The problem is, happiness doesn't usually last. What's my solution there? Give thanks for everything around you. Don't take it for granted or let it fade into the background. Try to savor what you are enjoying now. When you have a sense of gratitude, you will realize how fortunate you are in your current circumstances compared to the less fortunate.

여 안녕하세요, 학생 여러분. 저는 학교의 상담교사이고, 행복에 대해 몇 가지 말하고자 합니다. 여러분 중에 일부는 날씨가 음울해져서 기분이 조금 우울해 보이네요. 어떤 학생들은 오르지 않는 성적에 화가 난 것 같고요. 다른 학생들은 재미있는 게 아무것도 없다고 불평을 하기도 합니다. 하지만 돌이켜 보면, 여러분을 행복하게 만든 사건들이 살면서 분명히 있었을 거예요. 문제는 보통 행복은 오래가지 않는다는 거죠. 저의 해결책은 무엇이냐고요? 여러분 주위에 있는 모든 것에 감사하세요. 그걸 당연하게 받아들이거나 존재가 희미해지게 두지 마세요. 지금 누리고 있는 것을 마음껏 즐기세요. 감사의 마음을 가지면 여러분이 현재 상황에서 운이 덜 좋은 사람에 비해 얼마나 운이 좋은지 깨닫게 될 거예요.

02 | 정답 | ⑤

여자가 잠을 잘 못 잔다는 말에 남자는 잘 먹어야 잘 잘 수 있다고 말하고 있으므로 정답은 ⑤이다.

- **keep A up** A가 잠을 못 자게 하다
- **skip** 건너뛰다
- **caffeine** 카페인
- **decaffeinated** 디카페인의
- **contain** 함유하다

W Hi, Robert. Did you sleep well last night?
M Sure. I get a good night's sleep every night. Why?
W I don't seem to get much sleep these days.
M Really? What keeps you up at night?
W I don't know. I don't have anything to worry about or too much stress.
M What did you eat last night?
W I usually skip dinner or just drink coffee not to gain any more weight.
M Oh, that explains why. Caffeine keeps you up, you know.
W I drink decaffeinated coffee. So it is not the coffee that keeps me up.
M No, you've got it wrong. Decaffeinated coffee also has caffeine, though it contains less than regular coffee does. Besides, you have to eat well to sleep well.
W Really? I didn't know eating and sleeping are related.
M You should avoid alcohol, caffeine, and heavy meals. By changing your eating habits, you will be able to sleep way better than before.

여 안녕, Robert. 어젯밤에 잘 잤어?
남 그럼. 매일 밤 잘 자는 편이야. 왜?
여 요즘 나는 잠을 충분히 못 자는 것 같아.
남 정말? 왜 밤에 잠이 안 오는데?
여 모르겠어. 걱정거리도 없고 스트레스도 그렇게 많지 않은데.
남 어젯밤에 뭘 먹었니?
여 체중이 더 늘지 않도록 보통 저녁을 먹지 않거나 커피만 마셔.
남 아, 그래서 그렇네. 알잖아, 카페인이 너를 못 자게 해.
여 디카페인 커피를 마시거든. 그래서 날 못 자게 하는 게 커피가 아니야.
남 아니, 잘못 알고 있어. 보통 커피보다는 적은 양을 함유하고 있긴 하지만 디카페인 커피도 카페인을 가지고 있어. 게다가, 잘 자기 위해서는 잘 먹어야 해.
여 정말? 먹는 것과 수면이 관련이 있는 줄 몰랐어.
남 술, 카페인, 과식을 피해야 해. 식습관을 바꿈으로써 전보다 더 숙면할 수 있게 될 거야.

03 | 정답 | ⑤

직업은 단순히 돈을 버는 것 이상이며 자기 성취와 만족의 원천이 될 수 있도록 자신의 재능을 발휘할 수 있는 직업을 구하라고 조언하고 있다. 따라서 여자가 하는 말의 요지로 가장 적절한 것은 ⑤이다.

- **consultant** 상담가; 컨설턴트
- **way** 수단, 방법; 길
- **self-fulfillment** 자기 성취
- **content** 만족하는; 내용물; 목차

W Hello, everyone! I'm Sophia, your job consultant. When you're looking for a job, you may think about how much money you want to make. Money is important because it can impact your quality of life. However, the most important thing is to choose a job that allows you to fully use your talents. A job is more than just a way to earn money. It can also be a source of self-fulfillment and satisfaction. When you're doing something you're good at, it can make you feel fulfilled and content. Now, let's talk about how to find a job like that. Pay attention, okay?

여 안녕하세요, 여러분! 저는 여러분의 직업 상담가인 Sophia입니다. 일자리를 구할 때, 여러분은 얼마나 많은 돈을 벌고 싶은지에 대해 생각할 수 있습니다. 돈은 여러분의 삶의 질에 영향을 미칠 수 있기 때문에 중요합니다. 하지만 가장 중요한 것은 여러분의 재능을 충분히 사용할 수 있게 해주는 직업을 선택하는 것입니다. 직업은 단순히 돈을 버는 수단 그 이상입니다. 그것은 또한 자기 성취와 만족의 원천이 될 수 있습니다. 자신이 잘하는 일을 할 때, 그것은 여러분에게 성취감과 만족감을 느끼게 할 수 있습니다. 이제 그런 직업을 찾는 방법에 대해 이야기 해봅시다. 집중해 주세요, 알겠죠?

04 | 정답 | ②

남자는 무대 뒤의 벽에는 산타클로스가 뛰어다니는 크리스마스 풍경 그림이 있

W What do you have in your hand? Is that a picture?
M Yes, it is a picture of last year's Christmas party. Do you want to see it?

여 손에 든 게 뭐야? 사진이야?
남 응. 작년 크리스마스 파티 때 사진이야. 너도 볼래?

- **dress up as** ~의 복장을 하다, ~으로 분장하다
- **landscape** 풍경
- **flower pot** 화분
- **audience** 관객

W Sure. *[Pause]* Is this you dressed up as an angel?
M Yes, that's me. I was in a musical and sang two songs in it.
W I've never heard you sing before. Are you good at it?
M I think I'm okay. But I practiced hard to be on the stage.
W Who is the other angel on the stage standing next to you?
M That's Jason, my closest friend in school. You see the big picture on the wall behind the stage?
W You mean the Christmas landscape painting where Santa Claus is jumping between the houses?
M Yes, He painted that.
W Really? I can't believe it. *[Pause]* Did he paint the small tree on the left, too?
M No, that's a real tree. Those seven flower pots on the right are real plants, too.
W Wow, they are my favorite flowers.
M Oh, do you see the Christmas presents under the tree? We gave them away to the audience after the musical.

여 좋아. *[잠시 후]* 천사 복장을 한 사람이 너야?
남 응. 그게 나야. 뮤지컬에 출연해서 노래를 두 곡 불렀어.
여 난 네가 노래하는 걸 전에 들어본 적이 없어. 노래 잘해?
남 그냥 웬만큼 하는 것 같아. 하지만 무대에 오르기 위해 열심히 연습했어.
여 무대에서 네 옆에 서 있는 다른 천사는 누구야?
남 학교에서 가장 친한 친구인 Jason이야. 무대 뒤 벽에 큰 그림 보이지?
여 산타클로스가 집들 사이로 뛰어다니는 크리스마스 풍경 그림 말하는 거야?
남 응. 걔가 그린 거야.
여 정말? 믿을 수가 없다. *[잠시 후]* 왼쪽에 있는 작은 나무도 그 애가 그린 거니?
남 아니, 저건 진짜 나무야. 오른쪽에 있는 7개의 화분도 진짜 식물이야.
여 와, 내가 가장 좋아하는 꽃들이네.
남 아, 나무 아래 크리스마스 선물들 보여? 뮤지컬이 끝나고 관객들에게 나누어 줬어.

---

05 | 정답 | ②

여자가 자신이 시력 교정 수술을 받은 얘기를 해주자 남자는 자신도 수술하는 것을 생각해 봐야겠다고 말하고, 여자가 그에 대해 오늘 안과 의사와 상담해 보라고 권유하고 있으므로 정답은 ②이다.

- **appointment** (업무 관련) 약속
- **corrective** 교정의
- **surgery** 수술
- **scared** 무서운
- **sensitive** 민감한
- **consider** 고려하다
- **bother** 귀찮게 하다

M Lisa, I forgot to tell you. I got this afternoon off.
W Okay. Is everything all right?
M It's fine. I need to get a new pair of glasses, so I made an appointment with an eye doctor later today.
W I see. How long have you been wearing glasses?
M For as long as I can remember. I thought about getting corrective eye surgery, but I got too scared.
W I got the surgery when I was in college. It didn't hurt much.
M Really? I heard some people have to stay home wearing sunglasses for a week.
W That's right. After the surgery, I had to do that because my eyes were sensitive to light. But a few days later, it was like a new world.
M Maybe I should consider doing it. Changing glasses every two years bothers me.
W You really should. Why don't you ask your eye doctor today?
M I will. Thanks.

남 Lisa, 너한테 말하는 걸 깜빡했어. 나 오늘 오후에 휴가 냈어.
여 알겠어. 다 괜찮은 거지?
남 괜찮아. 새 안경이 필요해서, 오늘 이따 안과에 예약을 했어.
여 그렇구나. 안경을 얼마나 오래 썼니?
남 내가 기억하는 한 오래 써왔어. 시력 교정 수술을 할까 생각했었는데 너무 무서웠거든.
여 나는 대학 다닐 때 수술했어. 많이 아프지 않았어.
남 정말? 일주일 동안은 집에서 선글라스를 끼고 있어야 한다고 들었어.
여 맞아. 수술 후에는 눈이 빛에 민감해져서 그렇게 해야만 했지. 하지만 며칠 지난 후엔 마치 새로운 세상 같았어.
남 어쩌면 나도 수술하는 걸 생각해 봐야겠네. 안경을 2년마다 바꾸는 것도 귀찮아.
여 정말 생각해 봐. 오늘 안과 의사에게 물어보는 건 어때?
남 그럴게. 고마워.

---

06 | 정답 | ④

여자가 구매하려는 운동화는 200달러인데 회원 할인 10%를 받아 180달러이다. 추가로 1달러인 운동화 끈 한 쌍도 구매하였으므로 여자가 지불할 금액은 ④이다.

- **running shoes** 운동화
- **sole** (구두 등의) 바닥, 밑창
- **fill out** 작성하다
- **form** 서식, 양식
- **purchase** 구입하다
- **shoelace** 운동화 끈
- **include** 포함하다

W I would like to buy a pair of running shoes.
M Okay. Do you have any special design or color in mind?
W Not really. I want to check if there are any new arrivals this season.
M Sure. Here are some of the latest ones. This year, bright colors will be popular.
W I like this orange pair. Can I try them on?
M Of course. What size do you wear?
W Usually, size 6.
M Oh, these ones are just perfect for you. Please take a seat here and try them on. *[Pause]* How are they?
W Let me walk a little. The air cushion soles make me feel comfortable while walking. I'll take them.
M All right. They are $200. Do you have our membership? We can give a 10% discount.
W No, I don't. Can I get a membership and get 10% off now?
M Of course. Please fill out this form. And because you are purchasing one of the latest models, you can get a pair of shoelaces for only $1. By the way, they are not

---

여 운동화를 한 켤레 사려고 하는데요.
남 네. 생각하시는 특별한 디자인이나 색이 있나요?
여 아니요. 이번 시즌에 새로 나온 게 있는지 확인하고 싶어요.
남 물론이죠. 여기 최신 모델이 몇 개 있어요. 올해는 밝은색이 유행할 거예요.
여 이 오렌지색이 마음에 드네요. 신어 봐도 될까요?
남 그럼요. 몇 사이즈 신으세요?
여 보통 6 사이즈요.
남 아, 이게 딱 맞겠는데요. 여기 앉아서 신어보세요. *[잠시 후]* 어떠세요?
여 조금 걸어 볼게요. 에어쿠션 바닥이 걸을 때 편안하네요. 이걸로 할게요.
남 알겠습니다. 200달러입니다. 저희 회원이신가요? 10% 할인됩니다.
여 아니요. 지금 회원 가입하고 10% 할인받을 수 있나요?
남 물론이죠. 이걸 작성해 주세요. 그리고 최신 모델 중 하나를 구입하시기 때문에 운동화 끈 한 쌍을 1달러에 구입할 수 있어요. 그런데 그건 회원 할인에 포함되지 않아요.

included in the membership discount.

W That's okay. Then I'll take a pair of white shoelaces, too.

여 괜찮아요. 그럼 하얀 운동화 끈도 한 쌍 살게요.

---

07 | 정답 | ④

남자는 여동생이 교통사고로 병원에 입원하게 되어 병원비를 보태느라고 수업을 도중에 그만두고 돈을 벌어야 했다고 말하고 있으므로 정답은 ④이다.

- **graduation ceremony** 졸업식
- **drop out** 도중에 그만두다
- **semester** 학기
- **retake** 재수강하다
- **24/7** 언제나, 하루 24시간 1주 7일 동안
- **hire** 고용하다
- **professional** 전문적인
- **caregiver** 간병인

M I hear you are graduating this year at the top of your class. Congratulations!

W Thanks, are you coming to the graduation ceremony?

M Of course. Most of my friends are graduating this year.

W You are graduating too, aren't you?

M Oh, I'm not graduating this time. I had to drop out of all my classes this semester. I'm planning to retake them again this summer.

W I didn't know that. Did something happen?

M Well, last semester my sister got into a serious car accident. So somebody had to be with her 24/7.

W Oh, I'm sorry to hear that. So you had to be with her to take care of her.

M No, my family had to hire a professional caregiver.

W So why did you drop out?

M I had to get a job and make some money to help out with hospital bills.

W I see. How is your sister doing now?

M She is much better now. She has started walking again.

W That's great to hear!

남 네가 올해 과 수석으로 졸업한다고 들었어. 축하해!
여 고마워. 졸업식에 오는 거지?
남 물론이야. 내 친구 대부분이 올해 졸업해.
여 너도 졸업하잖아, 그렇지 않아?
남 아, 나는 이번에 졸업 못 해. 이번 학기에 수업을 도중에 다 그만둬야 했어. 올여름에 모두 재수강할 계획이야.
여 그런 줄 몰랐어. 무슨 일이 있었니?
남 음, 지난 학기에 내 여동생이 심각한 교통사고를 당했어. 그래서 항상 누군가가 곁에 있어야 했거든.
여 아, 그거 참 유감이네. 그래서 동생을 돌보려고 옆에 있어야 했구나.
남 아냐. 우리 가족은 전문 간병인을 고용해야 했어.
여 그럼 너는 왜 수업을 그만뒀니?
남 일자리를 구해서 병원비에 보탤 돈을 벌어야 했어.
여 그렇구나. 여동생은 지금 어때?
남 지금은 많이 나아졌어. 다시 걷기 시작했거든.
여 그거 좋은 소식이다!

---

08 | 정답 | ②

남자가 다녀온 수족관은 애틀랜타에 있고 입장료는 24.99달러이며 돌고래, 상어, 거북 등을 보유하고 있고 내년에 더 많은 상어를 들여놓을 계획이 있다고 했으므로 언급되지 않은 것은 ②이다.

- **marine biology** 해양생물학
- **modest** 겸손한
- **aquarium** 수족관
- **admission fee** 입장료
- **and so on** 등등
- **species** 종(種)

W Hey, Sam. I heard you got a perfect score on the quiz. You must've studied hard for it.

M Oh, you mean in marine biology? I think I got pretty lucky this time.

W Don't be so modest. How did you prepare yourself for the quiz?

M Actually, I visited the Georgia Aquarium the week before, which helped me a lot.

W You mean the one in Atlanta? How was it?

M It was really fun and I learned a lot, too. Did you know the Georgia Aquarium is the biggest in the world?

W Really? Then the admission fee must be quite high.

M General admission tickets cost $24.99 for teens and adults.

W That's not too expensive at all. So, what did you see there?

M I saw dolphins, sharks, turtles, and so on. Oh, and you can see whale sharks there.

W What is so special about whale sharks?

M They are the largest known fish species. And the aquarium has plans to get more sharks sometime next year.

여 안녕, Sam. 네가 시험에서 만점을 받았다고 들었어. 공부 열심히 했나 봐.
남 아. 해양생물학 말이니? 이번에 내가 운이 좋았던 것 같아.
여 너무 겸손해하지 마. 시험 어떻게 준비했니?
남 사실, 그 전주에 Georgia 수족관을 방문했었는데, 그게 도움이 많이 됐어.
여 애틀랜타에 있는 거 말이야? 어땠어?
남 정말 재미있었고 많은 것을 배우기도 했어. Georgia 수족관이 세계에서 가장 큰 거 알고 있었어?
여 정말? 그럼 입장료가 꽤 비싸겠는데.
남 일반 입장권은 청소년과 성인과 24.99달러야.
여 그렇게 비싸지 않네. 그래서 거기서 뭘 봤어?
남 돌고래, 상어, 거북 등등을 봤어. 아, 거기서 고래상어도 볼 수 있어.
여 고래상어가 뭐가 그렇게 특별해?
남 가장 큰 어종으로 알려져 있어. 그리고 수족관은 내년 중에 상어를 더 많이 들여놓을 계획이래.

---

09 | 정답 | ②

Limestone 배드민턴 프로그램은 월, 수, 금 오후 5시부터 10시까지 진행된다고 했으므로 일치하지 않는 것은 ②이다.

- **effective** 효과적인
- **course session** 수업 시간
- **tuition fee** 수업료
- **available** 사용 가능한
- **for free** 무료로
- **register** 등록하다
- **community center** 주민 센터

M Good afternoon, everyone. I'm the president of the Pick the Shuttlecock Club. Today, I'd like to introduce one of the best sports programs to you. Many of you are interested in living a healthy lifestyle, but don't know how to start. If you are looking for a simple and effective sports program, this is it, the Limestone Badminton Program. Course sessions will be held three days a week for 8 weeks from May 18th to July 14th. Courses will be given on Mondays, Wednesdays and Fridays from 5 p.m. to 10 p.m. The tuition fee is $100 per person. The fee does not include a racket or shuttlecocks. Make sure

남 안녕하세요, 여러분. 저는 Pick the Shuttlecock 동아리 회장입니다. 오늘 저는 여러분에게 최고의 스포츠 프로그램 중 하나를 소개하려고 합니다. 여러분 중 많은 사람들이 건강한 삶을 사는 데 관심이 있지만 어떻게 시작해야 할지 모릅니다. 만약 여러분이 간단하고 효과적인 스포츠 프로그램을 찾고 계신다면 바로 Limestone 배드민턴 프로그램이 정답입니다. 수업은 5월 18일부터 7월 14일까지 8주 동안 일주일에 3일 진행될 것입니다. 수업은 월, 수, 금요일 오후 5시부터 10시까지 있을 예정입니다. 수업료는 일 인당 100달러입니다. 수업료에는 라켓이나 셔틀콕이 포함되지 않습니다. 본인의 배드민턴 라켓과 셔틀콕을 꼭 가져오세요. 무료로 사용할 수 있는 개인 사물함의 수가 제한되어

you bring your own badminton racket and shuttlecocks. There are a limited number of personal lockers available for free, so you should sign up quickly. You can register for this course via email or call the Limestone Community Center. Thank you.

있으니, 빨리 등록하셔야 합니다. 이 수업은 이메일이나 Limestone 주민 센터에 전화하셔서 등록할 수 있습니다. 감사합니다.

---

10 | 정답 | ①

여자는 가벼운 재질인 스테인리스와 플라스틱으로 만들어진 것을 선호하고 가격은 200달러 미만, 용량은 1.5리터를 원하며 필터는 필요 없다고 했으므로 정답은 ①이다.

* electric kettle 전기 주전자
* stainless steel 스테인리스 (강철)
* mind 신경 쓰다
* filter 필터
* gift-wrap 선물용으로 포장하다
* right away 곧바로

M Good afternoon. How may I help you?
W Hi. Do you have electric kettles?
M Sure. We have many different designs and brands. This way. This one is made of glass.
W I'd prefer a lighter one.
M Okay. Then, we have plastic ones and stainless steel ones over here.
W Which one would you recommend?
M I always recommend the stainless steel. It's better for your health, I think. It's higher in price, though.
W I don't mind what it is made of as long as it is light and costs less than $200.
M Don't worry. It's well within your budget.
W Does it come in many sizes?
M We have 1.5-liter and 1.8-liter ones.
W I'd like a 1.5-liter one.
M Would you like the one with a filter for making tea?
W No, I don't think it's necessary.
M Would you like me to gift-wrap it for you?
W No, thanks. I'm going to use it right away.

남 안녕하세요. 어떻게 도와드릴까요?
여 안녕하세요. 전기 주전자가 있나요?
남 물론이죠. 여러 다양한 디자인과 브랜드가 있어요. 이쪽이에요. 이건 유리로 만들어져 있어요.
여 저는 가벼운 게 더 좋아요.
남 좋아요. 그럼 이쪽에 플라스틱과 스테인리스로 된 것들이 있어요.
여 어떤 걸 추천하시겠어요?
남 저는 늘 스테인리스를 추천해요. 건강에 더 좋은 것 같아서요. 가격은 조금 더 비싸지만요.
여 가볍고 200달러 미만이기만 하면 무엇으로 만들어져도 상관없어요.
남 걱정 마세요. 손님 예산보다 한참 아래예요.
여 다양한 크기로 나오나요?
남 1.5리터와 1.8리터가 있어요.
여 1.5리터가 좋아요.
남 차를 만들 때 사용하는 필터가 있는 것을 원하시나요?
여 아니요, 필요 없을 것 같아요.
남 선물용으로 포장해 드릴까요?
여 아니에요. 바로 사용할 거예요.

---

11 | 정답 | ④

여자는 요리하는 걸 싫어하지만 남자처럼 활력을 얻기 위해서라면 요리할 수 있다고 말하고 있으므로, 남자의 응답으로 가장 적절한 것은 ④ '네가 원한다면 간단한 요리법 몇 가지 보내줄게.'이다.

* energetic 활기 있는
* recently 최근에
  [선택지]
* recipe 요리법

W Brian, you look very energetic these days. What's going on?
M I started eating healthy recently. I am cooking healthy meals at home.
W Wow! I hate cooking, but if I could be energetic like you, why not?
M If you want, I'll send you some simple recipes.

여 Brian, 너 요즘 아주 활기차 보인다. 무슨 일 있니?
남 최근에 건강하게 먹기 시작했거든. 집에서 건강한 식사를 요리하고 있어.
여 왜! 난 요리하는 건 싫어하지만, 너처럼 활력이 생길 수 있다면 왜 안 하겠어?
남 네가 원한다면 간단한 요리법 몇 가지 보내줄게.

① 네가 원할 때는 언제든지 외식할 수 있어.
② 나는 요리가 많은 시간과 에너지가 든다는 것을 알고 있어.
③ 매일 30분씩 운동하기를 추천해.
⑤ 난 네가 요리하는 데 시간을 낭비하지 않기를 바라.

---

12 | 정답 | ④

남자는 앉아서 영화만 보는 여자에게 오래 앉아 있는 것은 허리에 좋지 않다고 말하고 있으므로, 여자의 응답으로 가장 적절한 것은 ④ '그래. 잠시 산책 좀 하러 갈게.'이다.

* obsessed with ～에 사로잡힌, ～에 빠진
* lose track of time 시간 가는 줄 모르다

M You look busy, but did you know you've been sitting around for 3 hours now?
W Have I? I was so obsessed with this superhero movie series that I lost track of time.
M Watching movies is not bad, but sitting for a long time is bad for your back.
W I know. I'll go take a walk for a while.

남 바빠 보이네. 근데 너 지금 3시간째 앉아 있는 거 알고 있었니?
여 내가? 이 슈퍼 영웅 영화 시리즈에 푹 빠져서 시간 가는 줄 몰랐어.
남 영화 보는 건 나쁘진 않지만 오랫동안 앉아 있는 건 허리에 안 좋아.
여 그래. 잠시 산책 좀 하러 갈게.

① 안 돼. 퇴근 후에는 운동할 시간을 낼 수가 없어.
② 신경 쓰지 마. 내가 너를 깨우려고 했어.
③ 아주 좋아. 영화 보러 나갈래?
⑤ 미안해. 너를 해칠 의도는 전혀 없었어.

---

13 | 정답 | ④

여자가 트레이닝 앱을 사용하고 2주마다 자신에게 작은 보상을 한다고 말하는 것에 대해 남자는 좋은 생각이라며 자신도 그렇게 해봐야겠다고 말하는 것이 가장 적절하므로 정답은 ④ '좋은 생각이다. 나도 그렇게 하는 것에 대해 생각해 봐야겠어.'이다.

W Wow. You look pretty fit these days. Have you been working out lately?
M I have. I've worked very hard to stay in shape. I gain weight easily because I love deep-fried food.
W Same here.
M But you look great yourself, too. Do you work out?
W Sure. In my case, I prefer home training.

여 와. 너 요즘 꽤 건강해 보인다. 최근에 운동하고 있니?
남 맞아. 건강을 유지하려고 아주 열심히 노력해 왔지. 나는 튀긴 음식을 좋아해서 쉽게 살이 찌거든.
여 나도 그래.
남 하지만 너도 좋아 보여. 운동하니?
여 그럼. 내 경우에는 홈 트레이닝을 선호해.

- fit 건강한
- work out 운동하다
- stay in shape 건강을 유지하다
- hardly 거의 ~ 않는
- motivate 동기를 부여하다
- willpower 의지력
  [선택지]
- special occasion 특별한 경우

M Really? I never work out at home. I don't even walk around much at home.	남 정말? 나는 집에서는 절대 운동하지 않아. 집에서는 많이 돌아다니지도 않아.
W I know what you mean, but I hardly have time to go to the gym.	여 무슨 말인지 알지만 난 헬스장에 갈 시간이 거의 없거든.
M But how do you do it? I mean, there are machines and trainers at the gym to guide you.	남 하지만 어떻게 그렇게 해? 내 말은, 헬스장에는 너를 이끌어 줄 기계와 트레이너가 있잖아.
W I can work out without machines. Besides, there are many home training apps available.	여 기계 없이도 운동할 수 있어. 게다가 사용할 수 있는 홈 트레이닝 앱도 많아.
M It must be difficult to motivate yourself. The important thing must be that you have the willpower to keep doing that.	남 스스로에게 동기부여를 하는 게 어려울 것 같아. 중요한 건 네가 계속하려는 의지력을 갖는 걸 거야.
W You've got a point. I use those training apps to control my weight, and every two weeks or so, I give myself a small treat.	여 바로 그거야. 나는 체중을 유지하기 위해 그런 트레이닝 앱을 사용하고 2주 정도마다 작은 선물을 나 자신에게 줘.
M That's a good idea. I will think about trying that myself.	남 좋은 생각이다. 나도 그렇게 하는 것에 대해 생각해 봐야겠어.

① 안됐다. 내가 어떻게 살을 빼는지 알려줄 수 있어.
② 신경 쓰지 마. 그 기계를 어떻게 사용하는지 알아.
③ 정말? 나는 수년간 개인 트레이너로 일해 왔어.
⑤ 그럼 고맙겠어. 특별한 경우에 나는 그 앱을 사용할 수 있어.

---

14 | 정답 | ②

영화를 보기 전에 원작 소설을 읽어야 영화의 이야기를 더 잘 이해할 수 있다는 남자의 말에 대한 여자의 응답으로 가장 적절한 것은 ② '네 말을 믿어 볼게. 한 권 사는 게 좋겠어.'이다.

- critic 평론가
- worth ~할 가치가 있는
- performance (개인의) 연기, 연주
- leading actor 주연 배우
- fantastic 환상적인
- be based on ~에 토대를 두다
- keep up with ~을 따라잡다
- storyline 줄거리
  [선택지]
- take A's word for it A의 말을 그대로 믿다

W Hi, Zach. What are you reading?	여 안녕, Zach. 뭘 읽고 있니?
M Hey, Lily. I'm reading a review of the movie *Absolute Heaven*.	남 안녕, Lily. 난 영화 〈Absolute Heaven〉의 후기를 읽고 있어.
W Oh, *Absolute Heaven*? I'm planning to see that this weekend. Are the reviews good or bad?	여 아, 〈Absolute Heaven〉? 이번 주말에 볼 계획인데. 후기가 좋아 아니면 나빠?
M Movie critics have a different taste in movies from regular viewers. So what they say doesn't really matter.	남 영화 평론가들은 영화에 관해서 일반 관객들과 다른 취향을 가지고 있잖아. 그래서 그들이 말하는 건 별로 중요하지 않아.
W Well, the movie attracted 3 million viewers within just two weeks, so I'm sure it's worth seeing.	여 음. 그 영화는 겨우 2주 안에 3백만 관객을 끌어들였으니 볼 가치가 있다고 확신해.
M Yes, most of the critics say the performance by the leading actor is fantastic.	남 그래. 평론가들 대부분이 주연 배우의 연기가 환상적이래.
W Wow, I can't wait to see it. I heard the movie was based on a novel. Should I read the novel first?	여 와, 빨리 보고 싶어. 그 영화가 소설을 바탕으로 만들어졌다고 들었어. 소설을 먼저 읽어야 할까?
M In my case, I read the novel first and then saw the movie. I'd say you should do the same.	남 내 경우에는 소설을 먼저 읽고 나서 영화를 봤어. 너도 그렇게 하는 게 더 좋을 것 같아.
W Why do you say that?	여 왜 그런데?
M You will enjoy the movie more if you read the novel first. The movie skipped a few chapters of the book, so it may be hard to keep up with the storyline without reading the book.	남 소설을 먼저 읽으면 영화를 더 즐기게 될 거야. 영화는 몇몇 챕터를 건너뛰기 때문에 책을 읽지 않고는 줄거리를 따라잡기가 어려울 거야.
W I'll take your word for it. I'd better get a copy.	여 네 말을 믿어 볼게. 한 권 사는 게 좋겠어.

① 놀랍다! 나도 어젯밤에 같은 책을 읽었어.
③ 동의해. 그 이야기 흐름이 이해하기 힘들었어.
④ 알겠어. 이야기는 그만하고 영화관에 들어가자.
⑤ 정말? 그 영화를 보느니 차라리 TV를 보겠어.

---

15 | 정답 | ⑤

Greg과 Daisy가 인공지능에 관해 토론하고 있는 상황이다. 자신과 반대의 의견을 가진 Daisy의 주장을 듣고 그것에 더 많은 증거가 필요하다고 생각하는 Greg이 할 말로 가장 적절한 것은 ⑤ '당신은 당신의 의견을 뒷받침할 더 많은 증거가 필요한 것 같아요.'이다.

- debate 토론
- point of view 견해
- take away 빼앗다
- fierce 격렬한
- competition 경쟁
- possibility 가능성
- take advantage of ~을 이용하다
- wage 임금

M Greg and Daisy are in the same debate club. Today's issue is AI and Greg and Daisy have different points of view. Greg wants to invent a robot someday in the future so that he can have a more convenient life. He thinks that the more robots we have, the better our lives will be. However, Daisy has the opposite opinion. She is worried that too many robots will take away human jobs. As more and more people lose jobs, there will be more fierce competition between them. She argues that there is a possibility that some business owners could take advantage of this opportunity to lower wages. However, Greg thinks Daisy's theory is groundless and needs more evidence to be supported. In this situation, what would Greg most likely say to Daisy?	남 Greg과 Daisy는 같은 토론 동아리에 있다. 오늘의 주제는 인공지능이며 Greg과 Daisy는 다른 견해를 가지고 있다. Greg은 더 편리한 삶을 살 수 있도록 미래에 언젠가 로봇을 발명하고 싶어 한다. 그는 우리가 더 많은 로봇을 가질수록 삶이 더 나아질 것이라고 생각한다. 하지만, Daisy는 반대 의견을 가지고 있다. 그녀는 너무 많은 로봇이 인간의 직장을 빼앗아 갈 것이라고 염려한다. 점점 더 많은 사람들이 직장을 잃게 됨에 따라 그들 사이에 더 격렬한 경쟁이 생기게 될 것이다. 그녀는 일부 사업주들이 임금을 낮추기 위해 이 기회를 악용할 수 있는 가능성이 있다고 주장한다. 그러나 Greg은 Daisy의 의견이 근거가 없고 뒷받침할 더 많은 증거가 필요하다고 생각한다. 이러한 상황에서 Greg이 Daisy에게 할 말로 가장 적절한 것은 무엇인가?

- **theory** 이론; 의견, 생각
- **groundless** 근거 없는
- **evidence** 증거
  [선택지]
- **assumption** 가정
- **back up** ~을 뒷받침하다

Greg I think you need more evidence to back up your theory.

Greg 당신은 당신의 의견을 뒷받침할 더 많은 증거가 필요한 것 같아요

① 우리는 어떻게 토론하는지에 대해 더 많이 배워야 해요.
② 나는 내 이론을 증명할 어떤 증거도 찾을 수 없어요.
③ 당신의 이론은 완전히 잘못된 가정에 근거하고 있어요.
④ 당신은 해결책을 마련하기 위해서 최선을 다해야 해요.

---

16 | 정답 | ④
포유류와 파충류의 특징을 두 부류의 차이점을 예시로 들며 설명하고 있으므로 여자가 하는 말의 주제는 ④ '포유류는 파충류와 어떻게 다른가'이다.

17 | 정답 | ③
포유류와 파충류의 특징 중 '먹이'에 대한 언급은 없었으므로 정답은 ③이다.

- **mammal** 포유류
- **reptile** 파충류
- **biological** 생물학적
- **trait** 특성
- **warm-blooded animal** 온혈 동물
- **constant** 끊임없는
- **supply** 공급
- **rely on** ~에 의지하다
- **give birth to** ~을 낳다
- **offspring** 자식
- **in contrast** 반면에, 대조적으로
- **replace** 대체하다; 교체하다

W Good morning, everyone. Today, let's talk about the differences between mammals and reptiles. Actually, you will find them very different as soon as you see them. But we are going to study the differences in their biological traits. The major difference is that mammals are warm-blooded animals. That means that they can control their body temperatures. So, they need a constant supply of energy to keep themselves warm. However, reptiles don't have to eat like mammals do because they can rely on the sun to heat their bodies. While reptiles lay eggs, mammals generally give birth to babies. Females take care of their offspring. Another interesting difference is that mammals have hair or fur on their bodies. Even those that live in the water have hair. In contrast, reptiles have no hair at all. Instead, reptiles have teeth that are continually replaced. Okay, now let's talk about more differences between them after watching this interesting video clip.

여 좋은 아침이에요, 여러분. 오늘은 포유류와 파충류 사이의 차이점에 대해서 말해 봅시다. 사실, 여러분은 보자마자 그들이 매우 다르다는 것을 알 수 있습니다. 하지만 우리는 그들의 생물학적 특성의 차이를 공부할 것입니다. 주요 차이점은 포유류가 온혈 동물이라는 겁니다. 그것은 그들이 체온을 조절할 수 있다는 의미합니다. 그래서 그들은 자신을 따뜻하게 유지하기 위해 끊임없는 에너지 공급이 필요합니다. 그러나 파충류는 몸을 따뜻하게 하기 위해 태양에 의존할 수 있기 때문에 포유류처럼 먹을 필요는 없습니다. 파충류가 알을 낳는 반면 포유류는 보통 새끼를 낳습니다. 암컷이 자식을 돌보죠. 또 한 가지 흥미로운 차이점은 포유류가 몸에 털을 가지고 있다는 겁니다. 심지어 물에 사는 것들도 털이 있지요. 반면에 파충류는 털이 전혀 없습니다. 대신에 파충류는 계속 교체되는 이빨을 가지고 있죠. 자, 이제 이 흥미로운 비디오 클립을 보고 나서 그들 사이의 더 많은 차이점에 대해 얘기해 봅시다.

16 ① 포유류는 어떻게 새끼를 낳는가
② 포유류와 파충류는 어떻게 생존하는가
③ 포유류는 파충류보다 왜 우월한가
④ 포유류는 파충류와 어떻게 다른가
⑤ 포유류는 어떤 특별한 특징들이 있는가

ANSWER

01회

01 ②	02 ⑤	03 ⑤	04 ③	05 ⑤
06 ③	07 ①	08 ⑤	09 ⑤	10 ②
11 ④	12 ③	13 ③	14 ①	15 ①
16 ①	17 ④			

02회

01 ②	02 ②	03 ③	04 ⑤	05 ②
06 ③	07 ②	08 ④	09 ③	10 ③
11 ⑤	12 ①	13 ①	14 ⑤	15 ⑤
16 ③	17 ②			

03회

01 ②	02 ④	03 ②	04 ⑤	05 ①
06 ②	07 ③	08 ⑤	09 ②	10 ②
11 ①	12 ⑤	13 ①	14 ①	15 ④
16 ④	17 ②			

04회

01 ③	02 ③	03 ②	04 ⑤	05 ⑤
06 ④	07 ⑤	08 ①	09 ④	10 ④
11 ⑤	12 ⑤	13 ②	14 ⑤	15 ④
16 ⑤	17 ④			

05회

01 ①	02 ③	03 ④	04 ③	05 ④
06 ④	07 ⑤	08 ③	09 ③	10 ④
11 ③	12 ④	13 ④	14 ②	15 ③
16 ①	17 ④			

06회

01 ④	02 ⑤	03 ②	04 ⑤	05 ⑤
06 ②	07 ②	08 ②	09 ⑤	10 ①
11 ②	12 ⑤	13 ⑤	14 ⑤	15 ②
16 ⑤	17 ③			

07회

01 ⑤	02 ⑤	03 ②	04 ⑤	05 ①
06 ④	07 ⑤	08 ②	09 ④	10 ⑤
11 ⑤	12 ⑤	13 ④	14 ⑤	15 ①
16 ①	17 ③			

08회

01 ⑤	02 ⑤	03 ⑤	04 ④	05 ⑤
06 ④	07 ③	08 ⑤	09 ④	10 ⑤
11 ⑤	12 ⑤	13 ④	14 ②	15 ②
16 ①	17 ④			

09회

01 ③	02 ⑤	03 ②	04 ②	05 ③
06 ②	07 ④	08 ④	09 ⑤	10 ③
11 ③	12 ③	13 ③	14 ⑤	15 ⑤
16 ④	17 ④			

10회

01 ⑤	02 ①	03 ⑤	04 ⑤	05 ③
06 ②	07 ⑤	08 ②	09 ⑤	10 ④
11 ④	12 ④	13 ①	14 ①	15 ①
16 ②	17 ⑤			

11회

01 ⑤	02 ②	03 ⑤	04 ⑤	05 ④
06 ③	07 ②	08 ②	09 ⑤	10 ④
11 ⑤	12 ③	13 ⑤	14 ⑤	15 ④
16 ②	17 ⑤			

12회

01 ⑤	02 ④	03 ③	04 ⑤	05 ④
06 ④	07 ③	08 ④	09 ⑤	10 ④
11 ③	12 ④	13 ②	14 ⑤	15 ③
16 ④	17 ①			

13회

01 ②	02 ⑤	03 ⑤	04 ④	05 ⑤
06 ③	07 ①	08 ②	09 ①	10 ④
11 ④	12 ③	13 ③	14 ⑤	15 ④
16 ③	17 ⑤			

14회

01 ②	02 ④	03 ⑤	04 ⑤	05 ⑤
06 ③	07 ④	08 ③	09 ②	10 ⑤
11 ③	12 ⑤	13 ④	14 ①	15 ④
16 ②	17 ⑤			

15회

01 ⑤	02 ①	03 ④	04 ⑤	05 ⑤
06 ④	07 ③	08 ④	09 ③	10 ②
11 ③	12 ⑤	13 ⑤	14 ⑤	15 ④
16 ③	17 ③			

16회

01 ②	02 ③	03 ⑤	04 ⑤	05 ①
06 ⑤	07 ⑤	08 ④	09 ⑤	10 ②
11 ③	12 ⑤	13 ①	14 ⑤	15 ⑤
16 ⑤	17 ⑤			

17회

01 ⑤	02 ①	03 ④	04 ④	05 ⑤
06 ④	07 ②	08 ⑤	09 ②	10 ③
11 ②	12 ③	13 ④	14 ④	15 ⑤
16 ③	17 ⑤			

18회

01 ②	02 ②	03 ④	04 ③	05 ④
06 ⑤	07 ②	08 ②	09 ⑤	10 ④
11 ⑤	12 ④	13 ③	14 ④	15 ③
16 ⑤	17 ④			

19회

01 ②	02 ②	03 ③	04 ⑤	05 ④
06 ④	07 ④	08 ①	09 ⑤	10 ②
11 ③	12 ④	13 ①	14 ④	15 ⑤
16 ②	17 ④			

20회

01 ④	02 ④	03 ①	04 ④	05 ④
06 ③	07 ⑤	08 ③	09 ②	10 ④
11 ①	12 ⑤	13 ②	14 ④	15 ④
16 ①	17 ②			

고난도 1회

01 ②	02 ④	03 ①	04 ①	05 ②
06 ②	07 ⑤	08 ②	09 ⑤	10 ④
11 ⑤	12 ②	13 ④	14 ⑤	15 ④
16 ⑤	17 ③			

고난도 2회

01 ⑤	02 ④	03 ②	04 ⑤	05 ③
06 ②	07 ④	08 ③	09 ⑤	10 ②
11 ④	12 ⑤	13 ③	14 ②	15 ④
16 ④	17 ②			

고난도 3회

01 ⑤	02 ⑤	03 ④	04 ④	05 ②
06 ③	07 ②	08 ④	09 ②	10 ③
11 ②	12 ①	13 ④	14 ⑤	15 ③
16 ③	17 ②			

고난도 4회

01 ⑤	02 ⑤	03 ⑤	04 ②	05 ②
06 ④	07 ④	08 ②	09 ②	10 ①
11 ④	12 ④	13 ④	14 ②	15 ④
16 ④	17 ③			

MEMO